GREAT LIVES
FROM
HISTORY

GREAT LIVES FROM HISTORY

American Series

Volume 1
A-Cod

Edited by

FRANK N. MAGILL

SALEM PRESS

Pasadena, California   Englewood Cliffs, New Jersey

Library of Congress Cataloging-in-Publication Data
Great lives from history.
    Bibliography: v. 1, p.
    Includes index.
    Summary: A five-volume set of biographical
sketches of some 400 Americans, presenting their
contributions and impact on United States history
and development and including individual bibliog-
raphies.
    1. United States—Biography. [1. United States
—Biography] I. Magill, Frank Northen, 1907-
CT214.G74   1987   920'.073 [B] [920]   86-31561
ISBN 0-89356-529-6 (set)
ISBN 0-89356-530-x (volume 1)

PUBLISHER'S NOTE

Great Lives from History, American Series, is the first set in a series which, when complete, will provide readily accessible accounts of the lives and achievements of outstanding individuals from antiquity to the present. The second set in the series, devoted to significant figures from British history, is scheduled for publication in 1987; subsequent sets will extend this perspective worldwide.

This initial five-volume set, covering 2,592 pages of text, includes articles on 456 individuals whose lives have had a distinct impact on American society and culture. The articles range from approximately 2,000 to 3,000 words in length and follow a standard format. Each article begins with ready reference listings, including a brief statement summarizing the individual's contribution to American life. The body of the article is divided into three parts. Early Life, the first section, provides facts about the individual's upbringing and family life and sets the stage for the heart of the article, the section entitled Life's Work. This section consists of a straightforward chronological account of that period during which the individual's most significant achievements were made. The concluding section, the Summary, is not a recapitulation of what has been discussed but rather an analysis of the individual's life and achievements in the larger context of American culture. Each essay is supplemented by an annotated, evaluative bibliography, a starting point for further research; the works listed are generally available in a large number of libraries. Each essay has been written expressly for publication in this work by an academician who specializes in the area of discussion; a full list of contributors appears in volume 1.

Several features distinguish this set from other biographical reference works. This is the only source which provides current bibliographies. The articles combine breadth of coverage (in contrast to the brief entries typical of many biographical dictionaries) with a format that offers the user quick access to the information needed (in contrast to longer encyclopedic-type entries which do not follow a standard format). The individuals represented here are drawn not only from politics and public life, invention and technology, and other traditional areas of achievement but also from the worlds of sports and entertainment. The range is wide in time as well, from early explorers such as Francisco Vásquez de Coronado and Samuel de Champlain to contemporary figures such as Neil Armstrong, James Baldwin, and Sandra Day O'Connor.

Perhaps the most distinctive feature of this set, however, is its emphasis on the larger context of American history and culture: Each individual subject is seen in the light of his or her contribution to the mosaic of American life. This concept played a significant part in determining who should be included in the set. The editors sought to provide both a basic and a well-rounded assemblage of figures who, together, wrought the foundations of American society in all its manifestations. Hence, to the aforementioned broad historical and professional criteria was added a third: Will this individual be judged historically to have gone beyond his or her own immediate field of endeavor to affect the everyday lives of most, if not all, Americans? By applying this final, selective, criterion, we have been able to cover in greater depth athletes as well as artists, social reformers as well as industrialists, builders as well as planners, religious as well as political leaders whose part in creating this society will remain unquestionable. This definition, in the final consideration of the contents, was selected rather than using percentages or quotas in order to reflect an interpretative view of American life.

For convenience of reference, the set is indexed by area of achievement as well as by name; subsequent sets in the series will follow the same format.

PREFACE

THE BIOGRAPHICAL STUDIES in *Great Lives from History*, American Series, offer a running account of the development of one of the world's greatest nations, sparked by a series of events occurring in the shortest time ever required for such advanced growth. In less than four normal life spans an unplanned mixture of various adventurers, among them many losers, built a mature nation devoted to freedom and democratic principles unique in the Western world. Such an achievement is a lesson in civil development worthy of serious note and deserving of emulation in underdeveloped areas of the world.

Throughout the course of events, the word "vision" is called for time and time again as representative of the thinking of those responsible for acts of leadership. For example, the vision of liberty from British rule—freedom to develop the new nation as they wished, without any dictation from abroad—seldom left the minds of the leaders attempting to influence the social structure slowly taking shape in the new land. Again, the vision of a cohesive, coast-to-coast nation was the thing that fired the continual westward movement of the hardy pioneers. They were anxious to test the mettle of the Spanish conquerors and eventually found Spain too weak, or at least unwilling, to hold California. At last the coast-to-coast goal was won.

Among the visions in the Northern states was that of "freeing the slaves" in the South (which some critics claim was an effort to assuage the Northerners' guilt over their own earlier inhuman treatment of the Indians in their path) an act which was at last officially accomplished with the close of the Civil War.

The new nation continued to grow and mature, but it did not lose its vision of and dedication to freedom for all men, and in 1917 it acted upon its native impulse in following President Woodrow Wilson's dictum to make the world "safe for democracy" by entering World War I when the independence of Great Britain, France, and most of Europe was seriously threatened by Imperial Germany. After all, as Wilson had also pointed out persuasively, ". . . the right is more precious than peace." The fact that this act was a mere prelude to a much greater threat less than a generation later did not cloud the vision of American leadership in 1941, and the nation again joined in the Western effort to preserve Franklin D. Roosevelt's "Four Freedoms" by following the president into World War II. The vision of democracy for all men has continued to be tested since World War II. Each time, the leadership has attempted to respond in accordance with the traditional vision, not always, however, with the success sought.

In addition to that of freedom, the nation has seen other goals arise. One has been especially important since the late 1890's, that of scientific development in the areas of electronics, nuclear power, astronomy, and advanced medical technologies, as well as numerous new fields requiring basic research. Many of these developments have been greatly augmented by Europeans and others, fleeing the oppression of their native lands and seeking the uninhibited shores of the United States.

The tenor of the set under discussion is expressed in the format of the presentation of individual achievements. The background of each individual is given including parentage, often back to the second generation, then the early preparation for life, stressing formal education or work experience. The reason for the selection of the individual is then explained, along with details of the contribution to society as it affects life at the time as well as in the future. Such contributions are not necessarily of grave importance, though most are beneficial to the community in general. Scientists are included, as are authors and artists. Political leaders join space explorers, entertainers appear alongside professors, warriors, inventors, and psychologists. Contributions to the culture and development of the society have been considered the most important element in the editorial decision concerning selection for inclusion. Limited to 456 individuals for study, the staff has been forced into some difficult decisions, but every effort has been made to generalize the selections without undue personal involvement. The reader is referred to the Publisher's Note on pages v-vi for a further explanation of the purpose of this work and the format of the articles.

If one seeks a developmental factor responsible for the unique growth of the United States from a primitive community of social experimenters to one of the world's leading nations in a relatively short period of time, the identifying theme would probably be the fact that diversity could thrive because there were few impediments based on class distinction or social taboos, and thus the new could be accepted or rejected on its merits. This factor has had a substantial influence on the development of the list of individuals selected for inclusion in this work.

Some of the entries would seem to be automatic: explorers, for example. There is Hernando de Soto (c. 1496-1542), who led the first expedition to explore intensively the area that now comprises several American Southern states. He is also credited with being the "discoverer" of the Mississippi River. Another important early explorer was Daniel Boone, who did much to open up the territory west of the Appalachian Mountains, particularly in the Kentucky area. The eyes of young America were turned ever westward and it was the Lewis and Clark expedition that crossed to the Pacific's eastern shore in November, 1805, and became a legend for schoolchildren thereafter.

An explorer who turned to conservation was John Muir, whose enthusiasm and foresight were largely responsible for creation of the nation's national park system. Another American who must be included in any list of explorers is Neil Armstrong, the first Earth-man to walk on the surface of the Moon. Without the rocketry vision of Wernher von Braun, however, Armstrong might never have made the trip.

Law, politics, and government began to evolve slowly under the leadership of Alexander Hamilton, Patrick Henry, Thomas Jefferson, John Hancock, and numerous other patriotic figures who seem to have had a sixth sense for what the new nation needed. Later public figures who carried forward the idea of public service for its own sake include Edwin M. Stanton, Abraham Lincoln's masterful secretary of war, whose advice and administrative genius contributed greatly to the Union victory in the Civil War, and Charles Evans Hughes (1862-1948), a great secretary of state under President Warren G. Harding, and later perhaps the greatest Chief Justice of the United States. Equally noteworthy are Eleanor Roosevelt, who often acted as unofficial assistant president in support of her permanently disabled husband, four-term-president Franklin D. Roosevelt; and Adlai E. Stevenson (1900-1965), whose service and party loyalty for years were unquestionable but never led to the presidency for which he secretly yearned.

As a nation born out of war, it was natural for the new United States to develop a military orientation. Not surprisingly, the new nation's foremost general, George Washington, became the first president. Washington did not live to participate in the new nation's second war, the War of 1812; otherwise, he would doubtless have been involved in some way. This war, however, catapulted another military man, Andrew Jackson, into national renown, gaining for him a reputation that later contributed greatly to his election as the seventh president of the United States. Among other important military leaders represented in these volumes are Ulysses S. Grant (who became the eighteenth president of the United States), Douglas Mac-Arthur, and George C. Marshall—all men with outstanding military achievements.

Each president of the United States, good or mediocre, has been important if only because of the awesome power the office holds under the Constitution—which, fortunately, does place some limitations on the office. If voters were asked to select, say, the "best" ten presidents (one-fourth of the total), there would be great variety in the selections, but here is one example that might be acceptable to many unbiased readers:

1. George Washington (1789-1797)
2. Thomas Jefferson (1801-1809)
3. James Madison (1809-1817)
4. James Monroe (1817-1825)
5. Andrew Jackson (1829-1837)
6. Abraham Lincoln (1861-1865)
7. William McKinley (1897-1901)
8. Theodore Roosevelt (1901-1909)
9. Woodrow Wilson (1913-1921)
10. Franklin D. Roosevelt (1933-1945)

It may be noted that half of these presidents were involved in serious wars during their administrations, perhaps not unique for a nation "born out of war." It may also be noted that four of the ten administrations cover less than forty years of the nation's history. Yet these first formative years were vital in establishing the goals of the new nation and the ideals under which these goals must be obtained.

Science and invention, engineering and industry, are among the strongest forces that made America stand out among the world's leading nations. Samuel F. B. Morse with his telegraph; Alexander Graham Bell, with his perfection of the telephone; and Lee de Forest, "the father of radio," brought instant communication into being and altered forever the way ideas may be rapidly exchanged both for business and for social purposes.

Many times, improvements in method are as valuable as inventions, as was the case when Henry Ford adopted the "assembly-line method" for building automobiles and thus sharply lowered the cost of producing his product; this technique became standarized in industry. In like manner, new products can spark entirely new industries, as when Charles Goodyear discovered how to vulcanize rubber and thus created the new tire industry, which made the automobile cheaper to own and operate. Other important inventions that made life better for nineteenth and twentieth century Americans were Elias Howe's sewing machine and the reaper invented by Cyrus Hall McCormick, the latter changing forever certain American agricultural methods.

The freedom to experiment and the rewards for success in America make the efforts intriguing and sometimes result in total victory, as in the case of Wilbur and Orville Wright's first airplane, or Nikola Tesla's revolutionary alternating current motor and his Tesla coil for television sets, or even the exotic cyclotron invented by Ernest Orlando Lawrence. Society in general and the individual as well benefit from this open environment dedicated to improving the status quo.

The same sort of philosophy applies to science, where new experimental knowledge always has the chance to improve the state of the art. Such a potential is the force that impels the researcher to seek new answers to new questions. One example is that of Enrico Fermi, who helped developed the controlled chain reaction so that atomic energy could be used safely in nuclear power plants. Another such example is the work of Edwin Mattison McMillan, discoverer of neptunium, element 93, and codiscoverer of plutonium, element 94, so vital in the development of nuclear energy.

Other prominent scientists discussed in these volumes are Theobald Smith, whose work in microbiology is fundamental; Edward Teller, one of the leading scientists in the development of the hydrogen bomb; and Robert Burns Woodward, a specialist in the development of synthetic antibiotics such as penicillin, a material often rare in nature yet strategic in wartime when needed to combat infections.

The space in this preface is limited, and many subjects covered in the

PREFACE

five-volume set are not discussed here—areas such as medicine, psychology, religion, education, art, literature, entertainment, and the plight of American Indians and other minorities. The subject of civil rights in general, however, is well covered in the set, for the struggle has been long and continuous. Fortunately, the 1960's saw changes begin and the mid-1980's find notable improvement in various areas, including many openings for women in important areas of politics, law, and commerce. Additionally, articles discussing the achievements of A. Philip Randolph, Harriet Tubman, Booker T. Washington, Frederick Douglass, W. E. B. Du Bois, Martin Luther King, Jr., and Thurgood Marshall are especially recommended.

I wish to acknowledge with thanks those who have contributed to the research, development, and execution of these five volumes. A list of contributing reviewers appears on pages xi-xv.

FRANK N. MAGILL

CONTRIBUTING REVIEWERS

Michael Adams
Independent Scholar

John Aiken
*State University of New York
College at Buffalo*

John M. Allswang
California State University, Los Angeles

J. Stewart Alverson
University of Tennessee at Chattanooga

Richard J. Amundson
Columbus College

Stanley Archer
Texas A&M University

James R. Arnold
University of California at San Diego

Bryan Aubrey
Maharishi International University

John W. Bailey
Carthage College

William J. Baker
University of Maine at Orono

Betty Balanoff
Roosevelt University

Dan Barnett
Butte College

Robert A. Becker
Louisiana State University, Baton Rouge

Ronald M. Benson
Millersville University of Pennsylvania

Gordon Bergquist
Creighton University

Robert L. Berner
University of Wisconsin at Oshkosh

Robert E. Bieder
Indiana University, Bloomington

Terry D. Bilhartz
Sam Houston State University

David Warren Bowen
Livingston University

John Braeman
University of Nebraska at Lincoln

Harold Branam
University of Pennsylvania

Gerhard Brand
California State University, Los Angeles

Francis J. Bremer
Millersville University of Pennsylvania

Jeanie R. Brink
Arizona State University

J. R. Broadus
Independent Scholar

Terrill Brooks
Baker College

Kendall W. Brown
Hillsdale College

Norman D. Brown
University of Texas at Austin

William H. Burnside
John Brown University

Donald Burrill
California State University, Los Angeles

Larry W. Burt
University of Utah

Stephen Burwood
State University of New York at Binghamton

Charles J. Bussey
Western Kentucky University

Jack J. Cardoso
*State University of New York
College at Buffalo*

Elof Axel Carlson
State University of New York at Stony Brook

W. Bernard Carlson
University of Virginia at Charlottesville

John Carpenter
University of Michigan at Ann Arbor

John M. Carroll
Lamar University

Ellen Clark
Independent Scholar

Michael J. Clark
California State University, Hayward

Albert B. Costa
Duquesne University

Lesley Hoyt Croft
Arizona State University

Carol I. Croxton
University of Southern Colorado

Light Townsend Cummins
Austin College

Annette Daniel
Arkansas College

Robert R. Davis, Jr.
Ohio Northern University

Frank Day
Clemson University

James I. Deutsch
George Washington University

John E. DiMeglio
Mankato State University

Charles A. Dranguet, Jr.
Southeastern Louisiana University

Charles Duncan
Atlanta University

Harry J. Eisenman
University of Missouri at Rolla

Thomas J. Elliott
California State Polytechnic University

Robert P. Ellis
Worcester State College

Thomas L. Erskine
Salisbury State College

Paul F. Erwin
University of Cincinnati

Norman B. Ferris
Middle Tennessee State University

James E. Fickle
Memphis State University

Donald M. Fiene
University of Tennessee at Knoxville

Paul Finkelman
State University of New York at Binghamton

Roy E. Finkenbine
Florida State University

Edward Fiorelli
Saint John's University, New York

Kirk Ford, Jr.
Mississippi College, Clinton

Robert J. Forman
Saint John's University, New York

Douglas A. Foster
David Lipscomb College

C. E. Frazier
Sam Houston State University

Richard G. Frederick
University of Pittsburgh at Bradford

Dana Gerhardt
Independent Scholar

Joseph A. Goldenberg
Virginia State University

Robert M. Goldman
Virginia Union University

Marvin Goldwert
New York Institute of Technology, New York

Clinton A. Gould
University of Pennsylvania

Lewis L. Gould
University of Texas at Austin

Larry Gragg
University of Missouri at Rolla

C. L. Grant
Georgia State University

Lloyd J. Graybar
Eastern Kentucky University

Christopher E. Guthrie
Tarleton State University

D. Harland Hagler
North Texas State University

William I. Hair
Georgia College

Maureen A. Harp
Regis High School, New York

Lowell H. Harrison
Western Kentucky University

Fred R. van Hartesveldt
Fort Valley State College

John Harty
University of Florida

Joseph M. Hawes
Memphis State University

David S. Heidler
Salisbury State College

Carlanna L. Hendrick
Francis Marion College

Richard L. Hillard
University of Arkansas at Pine Bluff

Hal Holladay
Simon's Rock of Bard College

CONTRIBUTING REVIEWERS

Ari Hoogenboom
City University of New York,
  Brooklyn College

Ronald Howard
Mississippi College

Carlton Jackson
Western Kentucky University

Reese V. Jenkins
Rutgers, New Brunswick

D. Barton Johnson
University of California at Santa Barbara

J. A. Jungerman
University of California at Davis

Cynthia Lee Katona
Ohlone College

Jacquelyn Kegley
California State College, Bakersfield

Jeanette Keith
Vanderbilt University

Steven G. Kellman
University of Texas at San Antonio

Kenneth F. Kiple
Bowling Green State University

Wm. Laird Kleine-Ahlbrandt
Purdue University, West Lafayette

Carl E. Kramer
Indiana University Southeast

Paul E. Kuhl
Winston-Salem State University

Karl G. Larew
Towson State University

Bruce L. Larson
Mankato State University

Leon Lewis
Appalachian State University

Monroe H. Little, Jr.
Indiana University–Purdue University
  at Indianapolis

James D. Lockett
Stillman College

John L. Loos
Louisiana State University, Baton Rouge

Rita E. Loos
Framingham State College

Adele Lubell
Independent Scholar

Al Ludwick
Augusta Chronicle-Herald

Maxine N. Lurie
Rutgers, New Brunswick

Arthur F. McClure
Central Missouri State University

Robert McColley
University of Illinois at Urbana-Champaign

George McJimsey
Iowa State University of Science
  and Technology

Kerrie L. MacPherson
University of Hong Kong

James B. McSwain
Memphis State University

Paul D. Mageli
Independent Scholar

Henry S. Marks
Independent Scholar

Marsha Kass Marks
Alabama Agricultural and Mechanical
  University

John F. Marszalek
Mississippi State University

Elaine Mathiasen
Independent Scholar

Anne Laura Mattrella
Southeastern University

Charles E. May
California State University, Long Beach

Laurence W. Mazzeno
United States Naval Academy

Bernard Mergen
George Washington University

Norton Mezvinsky
Central Connecticut State University

Richard D. Miles
Wayne State University

Randall M. Miller
Saint Joseph's University

Clarence Mondale
George Washington University

William Howard Moore
University of Wyoming

Gordon R. Mork
Purdue University, West Lafayette

Robert E. Morsberger
California State Polytechnic University

Raymond Lee Muncy
Harding University

Roger L. Nichols
University of Arizona

Frank Nickell
Southeast Missouri State University

Richard L. Niswonger
John Brown University

Parker Bradley Nutting
Framingham State College

James W. Oberly
University of Wisconsin — Eau Claire

James H. O'Donnell III
Marietta College

Keith W. Olson
University of Maryland at College Park

Gary B. Ostrower
Alfred University

Robert J. Paradowski
Rochester Institute of Technology

Harold M. Parker, Jr.
Western State College of Colorado

Judith A. Parsons
Sul Ross State University

Thomas R. Peake
King College

Karen Resnick Pellón
Independent Scholar

William Pemberton
University of Wisconsin — La Crosse

Robert C. Petersen
Middle Tennessee State University

Donald K. Pickens
North Texas State University

Evelyne L. Pickett
University of Nevada at Reno

Marilyn Plotkins
Suffolk University

Robert Pollie
Independent Scholar

Richard Gid Powers
*City University of New York
  College of Staten Island*

William S. Pretzer
Henry Ford Museum and Greenfield Village

Charles H. Pullen
Queen's University at Kingston

Sanford Radner
Montclair State College

Thomas Rankin
Independent Scholar

James A. Rawley
University of Nebraska at Lincoln

Peter P. Remaley
Eastern Kentucky University

Clark G. Reynolds
Independent Scholar

Leo P. Ribuffo
George Washington University

John S. Rigden
University of Missouri at St. Louis

Joseph F. Rishel
Duquesne University

S. Fred Roach
Kennesaw College

Craig H. Roell
University of Texas at Austin

James P. Ronda
Youngstown State University

Joseph Rosenblum
University of North Carolina at Greensboro

Marc Rothenberg
Smithsonian Institution

Bruce A. Rubenstein
University of Michigan at Flint

Victor Anthony Rudowski
Clemson University

Allen Safianow
Indiana University at Kokomo

Stephen P. Sayles
University of La Verne

J. Christopher Schnell
Southeast Missouri State University

Robert W. Seidel
*Bradbury Science Museum, Los Alamos
  National Laboratory*

Robert W. Sellen
Georgia State University

CONTRIBUTING REVIEWERS

Patricia Sharpe
Simon's Rock of Bard College

J. Lee Shneidman
Adelphi University

R. Baird Shuman
University of Illinois at Urbana-Champaign

L. Moody Simms, Jr.
Illinois State University

David Curtis Skaggs
Bowling Green State University

C. Edward Skeen
Memphis State University

Harold L. Smith
University of Houston–Victoria

Katherine Snipes
Eastern Washington University

Katherine R. Sopka
Four Corners Analytic Sciences

C. Fitzhugh Spragins
Arkansas College

David L. Sterling
University of Cincinnati

James Brewer Stewart
Macalester College

Marian E. Strobel
Furman University

Roger H. Stuewer
University of Minnesota at Minneapolis

James Sullivan
California State University, Los Angeles

Joseph E. Suppiger
Limestone College

Patricia E. Sweeney
Independent Scholar

Alice Taylor
Shorter College

James H. Toner
Norwich University

Judith Ann Trolander
University of Minnesota at Duluth

Vernon L. Volpe
Texas A&M University

LeRoy J. Votto
The Urban School of San Francisco

Harry M. Ward
University of Richmond

Brent Waters
University of Redlands

Donald V. Weatherman
Arkansas College

Orren P. Whiddon
Independent Scholar

Sherrill Whyte
University of California at Berkeley

William C. Widenor
University of Illinois at Urbana-Champaign

Barbara Wiedemann
University of Alabama at Huntsville

John D. Wild
Independent Scholar

Sue Williams
Yavapai College

David L. Wilson
Southern Illinois University at Carbondale

John Wilson
Independent Scholar

Major L. Wilson
Memphis State University

George Wise
Independent Scholar

Michael Witkoski
*Office of Research, South Carolina House
of Representatives*

Donald Yacovone
Florida State University

Lamont H. Yeakey
California State University, Los Angeles

Clifton K. Yearley
State University of New York at Buffalo

Irwin Yellowitz
*City University of New York
City College*

Robert F. Zeidel
University of Nebraska at Lincoln

LIST OF BIOGRAPHIES IN VOLUME ONE

LIST OF BIOGRAPHIES IN VOLUME ONE

DEAN ACHESON

Born: April 11, 1893; Middletown, Connecticut
Died: October 12, 1971; Sandy Spring, Maryland
Area of Achievement: Diplomacy
Contribution: As secretary of state from 1949 to 1953, Acheson conducted
  negotiations leading to the establishment of the North Atlantic Treaty
  Organization and dealt with crises involving the victory of Communism in
  China and American participation in the Korean War; his policies deter-
  mined the basic framework of the United States' security commitments in
  Europe and Asia during the Cold War.

Early Life
  The son of a Canadian couple who had moved to the United States only
the year before, Dean Gooderham Acheson was born on April 11, 1893, in
Middletown, Connecticut. His father, Edward Acheson, had served with a
Canadian militia regiment before settling upon a career as an Episcopalian
minister. Eleanor Gooderham Acheson, the boy's mother, was from a prosperous and socially prominent family in Toronto. Margot and Edward, Jr., a
sister and a younger brother, were born during the next ten years. Acheson
recalled that his childhood was unusually happy, a golden age of games, pony
riding, and Fourth of July celebrations. He never quarreled with his father
until he was in college; he had a particularly fond and close relationship with
his mother. During his adolescent years, Acheson was educated at the
Groton School in southeastern Connecticut. After six languid years there, he
spent the summer of 1911 in Canada, working on the Temiscaming and
Northern Ontario Railroad; the experience of unrelenting physical labor
among rough-hewn railway men left enduring memories of life in the wild
that Acheson cherished in later life. That autumn, he enrolled at Yale
University, and with only a modicum of effort he received passing grades and
was graduated in 1915.
  Acheson then entered the law school of Harvard University; he found academic demands there far more rigorous but also more challenging and stimulating. Particularly rewarding was his relationship with Professor Felix Frankfurter, who encouraged him in the study of constitutional law. For some time
Acheson had seen his sister's roommate at Wellesley College, Alice Stanley,
the daughter of a Michigan lawyer; in 1917 he married her. The following
year, after he had earned his law degree, Acheson enlisted in the Naval
Auxiliary Reserve, and for several months, until World War I ended, he
served as an ensign at the Brooklyn Navy Yard. He then intended to pursue
graduate studies in law, but after six months at Harvard, Professor Frankfurter obtained a position for him as secretary to Supreme Court Justice
Louis D. Brandeis. In 1919, Acheson moved to Washington, D.C.; as he

attended to the myriad details of cases brought before the high court, he received lasting impressions of Brandeis' unstinting standards of excellence. Devoted to the justice's work, Acheson provided needed assistance and support when Brandeis' wife suffered a nervous breakdown. In appreciation, Brandeis made an unusual offer, extending Acheson's appointment as his secretary for a second year.

Life's Work

At about this time, Acheson's life became more settled. A daughter, Jane Acheson, was born in 1919, followed by a son, David, and a younger daughter, Mary. In 1920, the family moved into a small house in Washington; later they acquired a quaint old farmhouse in Sandy Spring, Maryland, which Acheson regarded as a welcome refuge from legal and political cares. By his own account, Acheson was a liberal in politics, and the Republican ascendancy of the 1920's evidently deepened these convictions. In 1921, he joined Covington and Burling, a promising new law firm in the nation's capital. Although often aroused by political issues, he spent the next twelve years handling cases at law, some of which had international implications. In 1922, he represented Norway in proceedings arising from wartime shipping contracts; with others in the firm, Acheson argued this case before the Court of International Justice in the Hague. Other legal work concerned corporations or involved claims of water rights in the United States.

Dean Acheson was six foot three, with a spare but powerful build. His oval features were set off by a large protruding nose; he had brown hair, which he combed back in spite of its tendency to recede in later years. He had thick, bushy eyebrows which seemingly were underscored by the mustache he had cultivated since early manhood; to the delight of cartoonists, he often combed the ends upward, producing a curiously flamboyant effect. His manner perplexed many of those around him. He could be supercilious to the point of overt arrogance, but he could also act with a distinct stoicism, which possibly arose from his father's religious calling. He was able to endure direct affronts with quiet dignity. His style of speaking and writing, which was urbane and refined, bore the hallmarks of careful and discriminating reading; at times he would invoke great American or British thinkers or quote aphorisms in Latin.

In 1933, Franklin D. Roosevelt's Democratic administration assumed power, and Felix Frankfurter's intercession with the new president secured for Acheson an appointment as under secretary of the treasury. Major disagreements ensued, however, over the government's policy of manipulating the price of gold in an effort to stimulate economic growth. Acheson had misgivings about the legal basis for such action and believed that it was improper in view of existing gold contracts. After six months in office, he resigned and returned to his law practice. In 1939, Felix Frankfurter was nominated as a Supreme Court justice; Acheson served as adviser and representative to his old mentor during the Senate confirmation hearings. Acheson then became chairman of a committee advising the attorney general. During the next year, President Roosevelt considered means by which American destroyers might be sent to Britain, to aid in its war with Nazi Germany; Acheson assisted in legal work facilitating this transfer of military vessels. In 1941, Acheson was appointed assistant secretary of state for economic affairs. He played an important part in financial planning during World War II and aided in the establishment of such organizations as the World Bank and the International Monetary Fund. As under secretary of state from 1945 to 1947, he participated in deliberations leading to the European Recovery Program, or Marshall Plan. He was also the chairman of a special committee which considered problems surrounding proposals for the international control of atomic energy.

Although he had often expressed his wishes for a return to private life, and indeed left the State Department in 1947, President Harry S Truman appreciated his experience and his skill in coordinating administrative work. Accordingly, Acheson accepted his appointment to the nation's highest diplomatic post, in January, 1949. He had first to deal with proposals for mutual security arrangements, which had been considered among Western nations as a means to deal with Soviet expansionism. Enlarging upon projects that had already been advanced, involving Great Britain and several European states, Acheson carried out negotiations for a formal defense alliance. By reassuring hesitant states, such as Norway and Denmark, and encouraging those eager to join, such as Italy, the particular concerns of various governments were reconciled. In all, twelve original members joined the Atlantic alliance, which, while committed to maintaining peace, affirmed that an armed attack upon any signatory would be regarded as an attack upon all. Acheson also appeared before the United States Senate and adroitly dispelled the doubts of those who were wary of overseas commitments. In July, 1949, the Senate ratified the North Atlantic Treaty, and thus the nation embarked upon a military alliance in peacetime.

More intractable were problems in China, where for several years Communist insurgents steadily had won control of major provinces; in October, 1949, they entered the capital, whereupon their Nationalist opponents fled to the island of Formosa. The State Department and the Administration at large had come under criticism for their seeming inaction. Acheson, called upon to answer for the United States' China policy, firmly insisted that no reasonable measures could have prevented a Communist victory; he held to this position both in the State Department's official publications and in his testimony before the Senate.

Anxiety also had arisen about Communist influence in the United States. An alleged Communist, Alger Hiss, was a former State Department officer who at one time had worked under Acheson. When he was convicted of perjury, Acheson expressed his personal compassion for the man. The secretary of state's critics charged that he was doing little to oppose Communist inroads. Senator Joseph R. McCarthy later insinuated that Acheson was somehow subservient to international Communism.

In Korea, Communist forces launched a direct attack from across the demarcation line dividing the peninsula, in June, 1950; President Truman, upon consultation with Acheson and other members of his cabinet, authorized the use of American troops to drive back the invaders. During the crisis, Acheson coordinated efforts to obtain support from America's allies and the United Nations. By November, North Korean troops had been compelled to retreat, but Chinese Communist armies then entered the war and threatened the wholesale rout of United Nations forces. While insisting upon the stalwart defense of positions in Korea, Acheson resisted demands for direct action against China itself. Nevertheless, General Douglas MacArthur, the American and United Nations commander in Korea, called for expanded action and, in defiance of a standing directive from Washington, issued his own version of possible peace terms in a virtual ultimatum to the other side. President Truman consulted with other military leaders and members of his cabinet; they concluded that MacArthur had exceeded his authority and, in April, 1951, he was removed from his command. Acheson supported this measure; in June, 1951, he testified before the Senate for eight days in justification of Truman's decision. Throughout the Korean War, Acheson maintained that the peninsula had to be defended, but in a limited war that would avoid the risk of major confrontations elsewhere. Thus he supported the defense of Formosa but rejected proposals for involving Nationalist China in action against the Communists.

Diplomatic activity affecting other parts of the world was guided by Acheson's concerns for European security and the defense of Asia. He authorized American aid to support French forces fighting Communist guerrillas in Indochina; Middle Eastern concerns, such as a major government crisis in Iran in March, 1951, and the Egyptian revolution of July, 1952, he handled guardedly. In September, 1951, the United States concluded negotiations for a peace treaty with Japan, which Acheson endorsed as a means of strengthening the United States' security arrangements in the Far East.

When Republican Dwight D. Eisenhower became president in January, 1953, Acheson left the State Department. During the last eighteen years of his life he took on the role of elder statesman. He published seven books; two collections of essays and an anthology of his letters appeared posthumously. He did perform some legal work, and once again he was involved in international litigation at the Hague. Widely respected for his deftly conjoined views of politics and diplomacy, he was in some demand as a public speaker. Although he did not seek any permanent appointments, he was called back to Washington as an adviser during the Cuban missile crisis of 1962; Presidents Lyndon B. Johnson and Richard M. Nixon also consulted with him on means by which a resolution might be found for the Vietnam War. Late in life he was increasingly affected by physical ailments, which he bore with some fortitude; finally, on October 12, 1971, Dean Acheson died of a heart attack and was found slumped over his desk at his home in Sandy Spring, Maryland.

Summary

Having witnessed political upheaval on the international stage during the first half of the twentieth century, Dean Acheson became secretary of state during a critical period, when the United States' role in world politics awaited clear definition. After World War II, various responses were considered to meet challenges from the Soviet Union and its allies. Profoundly distrustful of the counsels of isolationism, which still appeared in certain guises, Acheson also was skeptical that international organizations such as the United Nations in and of themselves would ensure peace and security. His approach was to underscore the United States' commitment to international order, first and foremost by organizing the Atlantic alliance and involving the United States directly in the defense of Europe. Communist advances in Asia he took to be manifestations of Soviet ambitions in the Far East; nevertheless, he recognized the limitations of the United States' ability to act. It could not reverse the course of events in China, where massive political turmoil had engulfed the world's most populous nation; even while at war in Korea, the United States could not court wider and more dangerous confrontations. The course Acheson charted established commitments for the defense of Korea and Japan but left the United States with somewhat broader concerns about Communist penetration in other regions of the world as well.

Acheson's views of foreign policy were distinctively shaped by the temper of his times; he had seen the rise of dictators preceding World War II, and his dealings with the Soviet Union came during the most intransigent period of Stalinist diplomacy, when most other Communist parties monotonously echoed the Soviet line. Thus the measures Acheson took reflected certain assumptions about the postwar world; during his later years, he steadfastly maintained that the Soviet Union benefited from the efforts of Chinese and Vietnamese Communism. For a time he defended American involvement in Vietnam; only after several years of war did he conclude that victory there was not possible. Much in the world changed after he left the State Department, and many new concerns arose, but the basic structure of American foreign policy continued to rest on security alliances Acheson negotiated for the common defense of Western Europe and of major Asian nations in the Pacific region.

Bibliography

Acheson, Dean. *Among Friends*. Edited by David S. McLellan and David C. Acheson. New York: Dodd, Mead and Co., 1980. A group of letters selected from among those written between 1918 and the last month of his life, this collection often shows Acheson in various offhand moods, commenting on issues of the day to his family, friends, and public officials. Useful as a guide to his way of thinking over the years.

_____. *Morning and Noon*. Boston: Houghton Mifflin Co., 1965. Whimsical sketches of Acheson's first forty-eight years, which recapture childhood joys, assess his education, and point to the influence of great jurists, such as Felix Frankfurter and Louis D. Brandeis, in the development of his legal career. The formation of his political outlook and his brief but stormy period of service in the Treasury Department are also discussed.

_____. *Present at the Creation: My Years in the State Department*. New York: W. W. Norton and Co., 1969. Sweeping panoramic memoirs that trace the entire ambit of Acheson's formal diplomatic career, written with some regrets but no apologies. Acheson was forthright in his judgments of men and events, and his dry, mordant wit is often in evidence; particularly vivid and illuminating are his reflections on the Atlantic alliance, the Korean War, and Senator Joseph McCarthy's anti-Communist campaign. For this work, Acheson was awarded the Pulitzer Prize.

_____. *This Vast External Realm*. New York: W. W. Norton and Co., 1973. Acheson's unsentimental views of international power politics, and his unshaken conviction that Soviet influence must be kept in check, are set forth in this collection of articles and speeches. Also noteworthy are his piquant suggestions for instilling a greater sense of realism in American diplomacy.

McLellan, David S. *Dean Acheson: The State Department Years*. New York: Dodd, Mead and Co., 1976. A careful scholarly examination of Acheson's diplomatic practice, this work delineates his approach to foreign policy from among the divergent standpoints that existed at the time in the State Department and in other branches of government. Due balance is assigned to the demands of Cold War crises abroad and domestic political pressures that affected Acheson's positions on issues that shaped the postwar world.

Smith, Gaddis. *Dean Acheson*. New York: Cooper Square Publishers, 1972. This thoroughgoing and thoughtful exposition of Acheson's work as secretary of state, volume 16 of the series "The American Secretaries of State and Their Diplomacy," sets forth the particular means by which his handling of European and Asian crises defined America's foreign policy objectives. Sympathetic though not uncritical, the author is incisive in conveying the historical context against which American diplomacy under Acheson was carried out.

Stupak, Ronald J. *The Shaping of Foreign Policy: The Role of the Secretary of State as Seen by Dean Acheson*. New York: Odyssey Press, 1969. A brief study of problems of organization and bureaucracy in the State Department, this work is studded with the terminology of political science and reaches no larger conclusions about the direction of American foreign policy under Acheson's stewardship.

J. R. Broadus

HENRY ADAMS

Born: February 16, 1838; Boston, Massachusetts
Died: March 27, 1918; Washington, D.C.
Area of Achievement: History and literature
Contribution: Adams was a first-rate historian who wrote several biographies
and the monumental nine-volume *History of the United States of America*
(1889-1891), covering the administrations of Thomas Jefferson and James
Madison. His two most famous works are interconnected and autobio-
graphical: *Mont-Saint-Michel and Chartres* (1904) and *The Education of
Henry Adams* (1907).

Early Life

Henry Brooks Adams was born February 16, 1838, the fourth of five children of Charles Francis Adams and Abigail Brown Brooks. His father was a
cold and distant figure, and it was to his mother that he looked for affection.
It is not surprising that Henry would always feel out of place. His elite Brahmin heritage both paved the way for his future and controlled it. A kinsman,
Samuel Adams, had become involved in the American Revolution as a
manipulator of mobs. His great-grandfather John Adams helped draft the
Declaration of Independence, was the first vice president, and the second
president. Henry's grandfather John Quincy Adams served as secretary of
state and then as president. Henry's father served as ambassador to England
during the crucial diplomatic period of the Civil War and was later elected to
Congress.

In addition to his distinguished heritage, Henry's immediate family was
one of the wealthiest in Boston, based on the mercantile fortune of his
mother, Abigail Brooks. Adams' full name appears to sum up his life—
"Henry" betokening the scholar rather than the man of action; "Brooks," the
moneyed inheritance that was his by birth; and "Adams," the line of blue-
blooded forefathers who had taken such an active part in the creation of the
United States. Henry's dilemma was to live a successful life in the shadow of
such eminence.

Adams attended Harvard from 1854 through 1858. In *The Education of
Henry Adams*, he later stated that he had learned nothing while there. Upon
graduation, in typical patrician fashion, he set out on a tour of Europe. He
studied law and learned to speak German while at the University of Berlin,
from 1858 to 1860. While in Europe, he also began his efforts in journalism,
which he would continue throughout his life.

In 1861, as the Civil War broke out in the United States, President Abraham Lincoln appointed Adams' father minister to England, a critical position, since the South was attempting to gain recognition from England. At
age twenty-three, Adams accompanied his father and acted as his private sec-

retary. While there, Adams continued his journalism, working anonymously for *The New York Times*, and he also began his historical work by writing articles for the *North American Review*.

Life's Work

In 1868, Adams returned to Washington. He and his brothers decided that politics had done nothing but bring sorrow to the family. Adams' worldview might be broken into two segments: his philosophical speculations about the world, especially the United States, and what he was going to do with the remainder of his life. As it turned out, Adams spent the remainder of his life looking for answers to both questions through an interaction of the two. In a way, Adams became an intellectual dilettante, one of the best America has ever produced.

Adams did not spend his whole life behind a desk. He enjoyed parties, people, and friendships immensely, and his family fame brought him into contact with the celebrities of the time. Although short in stature, he was handsome, and he became known as one of the three best dancers in Washington.

From 1868 until 1870, Adams was a free-lance journalist, serving as a correspondent for *The Nation* and other leading journals as he plunged into both the social and the political worlds of Washington. His primary interest was the reconstruction of a war-shattered nation. He fought for civil service reform and the retention of the gold standard. He wrote articles exposing political corruption and warning against economic monopolies, especially within the railroads.

In 1870, Charles W. Eliot, the famous Harvard president, asked Adams to become assistant professor of medieval history. Out of tune with the world for which he was destined, Adams accepted. Despite having one of the best minds in the country, Adams was ill-trained to be a teacher. He threw himself furiously into his new task, often staying only one lecture ahead of his class. Without planning it, Adams was preparing the groundwork for what would become one of his masterpieces, *Mont-Saint-Michel and Chartres*. Adams also became the first American to employ the seminar method in his classes.

Adams' work at Harvard became his first step toward studying the American past. In 1877, he resigned from Harvard to complete two biographies, *The Life of Albert Gallatin* (1879) and *John Randolph* (1882). This research increased his interest in the early American period, and hoping to understand the nature of an evolving American democracy, he began what was to become his nine-volume *History of the United States of America*.

In 1872, Adams married Marian "Clover" Hooper, a woman with impeccable family connections, great intelligence, and a solid income. The two took a yearlong wedding trip which included a tour of Europe and boating up the Nile. Henry and Clover made a complementary couple, and Adams would later speak of their years together as years of happiness. Their union produced no children.

Adams published two novels anonymously, *Democracy: An American Novel* (1880) and *Esther: A Novel* (1884). Neither novel was a success, since Adams did not possess the artistic talents necessary to produce fiction. Of the two, *Democracy* was the more popular and the superior. *Democracy* was a *roman à clef*, which accounted for its initial demand. Mrs. Lightfoot Lee is the heroine through the eyes of whom Washington is revealed. She becomes a confidante of a Midwestern senator, and she is introduced to the processes of democracy. She meets the president and other high-ranking figures, only to find them all to be vacuous. She represents Adams' alter ego; indeed, both came up with much the same summation of Washington: After an initial attraction for the cause, they both reject it in the end because of the emptiness and moral ambiguity they find there. *Democracy* served Adams as a trial run for *The Education of Henry Adams*.

Adams' second novel, *Esther*, is less interesting. It is similar in that it also has a woman as its main character, this one based on Adams' wife. As a novel of ideas, *Esther* investigates the relationship between religion and modern science, a theme that Adams pursued throughout his life. As the novel ends, the heroine, in her quest for meaning, stares at and listens to Niagara Falls, Adams' overpowering symbol for the life force. The roar symbolizes a natural representation of the dynamo Adams was to make so much of and of the eternal law of history.

In 1885, Adams was stunned when his wife of thirteen years took potassium cyanide and killed herself. There was no discernible motive for her suicide except that she feared madness, which existed in her family. Strangely, Adams had a sculpture of a mysterious, cloaked woman placed on her grave. At the time of her death, Adams had been working on his *History of the United States of America*. He set the manuscript aside and began a period of restless traveling that included Japan.

As time passed, Adams narrowed his travel to winters in Washington and summers in Paris. He eventually returned to his *History of the United States of America* and completed it in September, 1888. The work was published in nine volumes between 1889 and 1891. Initially, it was met by apathy, but eventually it would be considered of the highest order, second only to the work of Francis Parkman.

Adams' best-known works, *Mont-Saint-Michel and Chartres* and *The Education of Henry Adams*, were privately printed and distributed to friends and only later were published for general use. The two works are interconnected and are based on thoughts that Adams spent a lifetime trying to untangle.

Mont-Saint-Michel and Chartres is a work of history, aesthetics, philosophy, and theology. The book is like a Symbolist poem, with one event flowing into another and all rules of chronology and reason being defied.

Adams' starting point for *Mont-Saint-Michel and Chartres* can be found in his travels to France and his visits to the thirteenth century cathedrals. Adams was in search of a fixed point from which to measure motion down to his own time, and that point became the medieval worldview as expressed especially in the cathedrals. Adams believed that their monumental structures expressed the deepest emotions that man ever felt. For Adams, an entire age could be said to have unity, purpose, mission, and fullness of experience toward an ideological unity represented by the Blessed Virgin Mary.

The Education of Henry Adams was not finished until Adams was sixty-eight years old. It remains his single best-known work and one of the most distinguished autobiographies of all time, compared by some to St. Augustine's *Confessions* (c. 1397). Whereas the Virgin had been the center for *Mont-Saint-Michel and Chartres*, the symbol for the twentieth century became the dynamo, one of which Adams had seen at the Chicago World's Fair. Adams found the twentieth century to be incomprehensible. Under the impact of the alarming growth of science and technology, historical forces had accelerated, leading to what Adams called the "multiverse" of the modern world.

Adams died on March 27, 1918, in Washington, D.C., the city from which he could not separate himself. World War I was still raging, and the breakup of the modern, civilized world, which Adams had predicted, had become reality. Adams was buried next to his wife in the Rock Creek Cemetery. At his direction, the grave was unmarked.

Summary

Henry Adams' life situation allowed him the freedom to be rebellious. He scornfully accepted the mantle of responsibility that destiny had given him. He became America's first modern historian. He briefly shared his enormous intellect with students and then resigned permanently from teaching, undertaking full-time the completion of his research and compiling his *magnum opus*, the nine-volume *History of the United States of America*.

Adams also made his mark on the historical and literary world with his *Mont-Saint-Michel and Chartres* and his *The Education of Henry Adams*. These two works, especially *The Education of Henry Adams*, are still widely read by students and the general public. One central connection between the two is the juxtaposition Adams proposed between the Virgin of the thirteenth century and the dynamo of the twentieth. Adams was interested in power—religious power, political power, and scientific power.

Adams was almost as good a prophet as he was a historian. He believed that the twentieth century was heading toward chaos; mankind was being swept away by seemingly uncontrollable technology, represented by the dynamo. Ahead of his time and unable to comprehend modern man, Adams foresaw the ultimate possibility of man's self-destruction.

Bibliography

Adams, Henry Brooks. *The Education of Henry Adams*. Edited with an introduction by Ernest Samuels. Washington, D.C.: Privately printed, 1907. Reprint. Boston: Houghton Mifflin Co., 1974. One of the most distinguished autobiographies of the twentieth century. Adams' best-known work.

_____. *The Letters of Henry Adams*. 3 vols. Edited by J.C. Levenson et al. Cambridge, Mass.: The Belknap Press of Harvard University Press, 1982. Includes bibliographical references and index. Adams' letters are valuable in that they reveal his thoughts and reflect the times in which he lived.

_____. *Mont-Saint-Michel and Chartres*. With an introduction by Ernest Samuels. Washington, D.C.: Privately printed, 1904. Reprint. New York: New American Library, 1961. The best starting point for a study of Adams would be the above works, especially *The Education of Henry Adams*, one of the great autobiographies of all time.

Byrnes, Joseph F. *The Virgin of Chartres: An Intellectual and Psychological History of the Work of Henry Adams*. Rutherford, N.J.: Fairleigh Dickinson University Press, 1981. Discusses Adams' relationships with women. Concentrates mainly on *Mont-Saint-Michel and Chartres* and Adams' thoughts concerning the Virgin Mary.

Harbert, Earl N., ed. *Critical Essays on Henry Adams*. Boston: G.K. Hall, 1981. The editor has compiled essays on Adams by R.P. Blackmur, H.S. Commager, Ernest Samuels, Charles Anderson, Howard Mumford, J.C. Levenson, and others. The essays cover various matters, including Adams' fiction and his two autobiographical works. Other matters covered include Gene Koretz's essay, which concludes that *The Education of Henry Adams* is very nearly the equivalent of Augustine's *Confessions*. Levenson compares Adams with William Shakespeare's famous character Prince Hamlet. Earl Harbert has two essays, one of which examines the autobiographical aspects of *The Education of Henry Adams* and another which contains details concerning Adams' trip to Asia.

_____, ed. *Henry Adams: A Reference Guide*. Boston: G.K. Hall, 1978. This ninety-six-page annotated bibliography contains Adams' major writings and critical work about him from 1879 to 1975. The introduction contains a compact discussion of Adams' reputation and major works, a brief survey of important critical articles and books, and a short discussion about the methods used to compile the bibliography and its major contents.

Levenson, J.C. *The Mind and Art of Henry Adams*. Boston: Houghton Mifflin Co., 1957. This critical work concentrates on Adams' life and on his enormous distinction as a writer. Levenson examines Adams' monumental achievement as an interpretive scholar and connects the historical research with the artistic talent. Major concepts associated with Adams, such as modern man existing within a "multiverse" and Adams' thesis concerning the Unity found in *Mont-Saint-Michel and Chartres*, are developed and discussed in detail.

Samuels, Ernest. *The Young Henry Adams*. Cambridge, Mass.: The Belknap Press of Harvard University Press, 1948.

_____. *Henry Adams: The Middle Years*. Cambridge, Mass.: The Belknap Press of Harvard University Press, 1958.

_____. *Henry Adams: The Major Phase*. Cambridge, Mass.: The Belknap Press of Harvard University Press, 1964. The above three works constitute the standard biography of Henry Adams. Samuels examines the pattern of failure and futility which Adams experienced during his attempts at education, his observations of others' efforts, and his perplexities with language itself. The works are comprehensive and distinguished.

John Harty

JOHN ADAMS

Born: October 30, 1735; Braintree, Massachusetts
Died: July 4, 1826; Quincy, Massachusetts
Areas of Achievement: Political science, government, and diplomacy
Contribution: As a member of the Continental Congress, Adams helped
bring the American Colonies to the point of independence in 1776. As one
of the new nation's first diplomats, he helped negotiate the treaty that
ended the American War of Independence. He was the second president
of the United States.

Early Life

John Adams was born on October 30, 1735, in Braintree, Massachusetts,
where his family had lived for nearly a century. His father was a farmer and a
town constable who expected his eldest son, John, to become a Congregational minister. The young Adams attended the Free Latin School in Braintree and then enrolled at Harvard College in 1751. On graduation in 1755, he
taught school for a while at Worcester before deciding to abandon the ministry to take up law instead. In 1758, the intelligent, studious Adams returned
to Braintree to practice law in what was still a country town only ten miles
from Boston.

Six years later, he married Abigail Smith of Quincy, Massachusetts, a
woman who matched him in intelligence and ambition and perhaps exceeded
him in practicality. Short and already stocky (colleagues later called him ro-
tund), Adams seemed to be settling into the life of a successful country
courthouse lawyer who might, in time, aspire to a seat in the legislature
when, in 1765, Parliament altered American Colonial politics forever by
passing the Stamp Act. The ensuing Stamp Act crisis offered to the ambitious
Adams a quick route to popularity, influence, and public office. He did not
miss his chance.

Life's Work

In 1765, Adams denounced the Stamp Tax in resolutions written for the
Braintree Town Meeting. When they were reprinted around the colony, his
reputation as an opponent of British arrogance began to grow. Those in Boston who led the opposition to English taxes (including John's distant relative,
Samuel Adams) began to bring him more actively into their campaigns. He
moved to Boston and won a seat in the Massachusetts General Court. He
became, in effect, the local antigovernment party's lawyer, writing some of its
more important public papers for the Boston Town Meeting and defending
its members in court against charges brought by the Crown.

When Parliament answered the Boston Tea Party with the Intolerable Acts
in 1774, the General Court chose Adams as a delegate to the intercolonial

congress scheduled to meet in Philadelphia that fall, to discuss what the Colonies should do. He wrote a "Declaration of Rights," which the First Continental Congress adopted, that based Colonial rights to self-government not only on their charters and on the inherent rights of Englishmen but also on "the immutable laws of nature." Those were the grounds on which many colonists would soon challenge not merely England's right to tax them, but England's right to govern them at all. In good part, those were the grounds that underlay the Declaration of Independence.

Before the Congress met again, war began at Lexington in April, 1775. When Adams arrived at the Second Continental Congress in the spring of 1775, he already believed that the only true constitutional connection between the Colonies and England was through the king—a position he set out in newspaper essays signed "Novanglus." He had not yet, however, openly called for a severing of all ties to the mother country. He had seen the colonists' rage run out of bounds in the Stamp Act riots of 1765. He had been disturbed and angered by the joy with which some colonists greeted the closing of civil and criminal courts in Massachusetts when British authority collapsed in the colony. He was worried that a revolution might get out of hand and establish not liberty, but mob rule. Although such worries stayed very much in his mind, by the time the Second Continental Congress met, Adams realized that there were no practical alternatives left but armed resistance or submission to Parliament. At the Congress, therefore, he worked both openly and by guile to bring reluctant and sometimes timid delegates to accept the inevitability of independence. When the Congress finally agreed to act, after more than a year of war, it was Adams who wrestled Thomas Jefferson's declaration through to adoption on July 4, 1776.

Adams had applauded Thomas Paine's *Common Sense* when it appeared in January, 1776, but he disliked the very democratic plan of government advocated by Paine. The kind of government Adams favored can be seen most clearly in the plan he drew up for Massachusetts' revolutionary constitution. Adams thought the purpose of the Revolution was to preserve old liberties, not to establish new ones, and that the new Constitution ought to conserve as much of England's admirable constitutional heritage as possible. The constitution he drafted included relatively high property qualifications for voting and holding office (to ensure stability); it left the structure of Massachusetts' government much as it had been before independence, except for replacing English officials with elected American ones.

For more than a year after independence, Adams served on a variety of committees in Congress and in Massachusetts, doing work that was as exhausting as it was important. In October, 1777, he withdrew from Congress and returned to Massachusetts, but in November, Congress named him one of its emissaries to France, charged with raising loans for the Republic across Europe and with negotiating treaties of friendship, trade, and alliance, especially with the French nation.

That alliance was concluded before Adams arrived at Paris, but he stayed on and was immediately caught up in the roiling jealousies that were endemic at the American mission there. Adams especially disliked and distrusted Benjamin Franklin, whose demeanor, integrity, honesty, and morals he judged inferior to his own. Adams returned to Massachusetts in August, 1779, but by December, he was back in France to help negotiate a peace treaty with England. He feuded with Franklin almost constantly over which of them was responsible for what in conducting the Republic's diplomacy, but ultimately, all three peace commissioners (Adams, Franklin, and John Jay) agreed to negotiate a separate treaty between the United States and England, a treaty that did not directly involve France.

Though Franklin was responsible for the broad outlines of the agreement, Adams worked out some crucial compromises, without which the treaty may well have failed. Adams persuaded the English, for example, to concede to American fishing rights off the Newfoundland and Nova Scotia coasts in return for the new nation agreeing to open its courts to Loyalists. Adams stayed on for a year in France after the war ended in 1783, and then moved to London as the United States' first minister to the Court of St. James in 1785. He spent three years there, trying with little success to iron out problems between the United States and England (mostly involving noncompliance with the peace treaty).

While in London, he wrote a three-volume *A Defense of the Constitutions of Government of the United States of America* (1787), in which he explained his conservative and primarily English approach to the proper constitution of civil governments. The work was frank in its praise of the basic principles of the British constitution and earnest in its cautions about the risks of letting government rely too heavily on popular majorities to determine policy and law. Indeed, some Americans began to consider Adams soft on aristocracy and even monarchy. The first volume of *The Defense of the Constitutions of Government of the United States of America* appeared in time to influence the thinking of delegates at the Constitutional Convention.

Adams returned home in 1788, and he was chosen as George Washington's vice president under the new Constitution of 1787. He did not like the job. "My country," he wrote to his wife, "has in its wisdom contrived for me the most insignificant office that ever the invention of man contrived or his imagination conceived." For the next eight years, nevertheless, he served Washington loyally, presiding over the Senate and breaking tie votes in favor of Federalist policies. His reward came in 1797, when, as Washington's chosen successor, Adams defeated Jefferson and became the second president of the United States.

Adams' presidency was at best only a partial success. He had hoped, as Washington had in 1789, to become president of a united people. By the time he took office, however, the people had already divided themselves into two rival political parties: the Federalists (ostensibly led by Adams) and the National (or Jeffersonian) Republicans, led by Adams' vice president and old friend, Thomas Jefferson. Further, world affairs all but guaranteed that his presidency would be troubled. As Adams took office, for example, the United States was already dangerously close to war with France. The French, who had already fought their own revolution and created a republic of sorts, were at war with England and were angry that the United States had refused to aid France. By 1797, the French were beginning to seize American ships on the high seas. When American peace commissioners, whom Adams had sent to France to try to work things out short of war, reported that the French had demanded bribes to begin serious negotiations, Americans reacted angrily. Adams asked Congress to prepare for a war that seemed inevitable, but, at the same time, he refused to abandon his efforts to avoid it if possible. For the remainder of his presidency, Adams stuck to the same policy—prepare for war, but work for peace—until (just as he left office) it yielded a new treaty of amity between the United States and France.

In the meanwhile, the Federalist Party, influenced by Alexander Hamilton more than by Adams, forced through Congress very high (and very unpopular) taxes to pay for the war which they confidently expected to begin at any moment. Moreover, Federalist congressmen passed, and Adams signed, the unpopular Alien and Sedition acts in 1798. The first act raised the number of years an immigrant had to live in the country before becoming a citizen to fourteen and was evidently designed to prevent recent Irish immigrants from voting against Federalists, whom they rightly believed to be pro-English. The second, the Sedition Act, made the publication of virtually all criticism of federal officials a crime. Both laws lost whatever legitimacy they may have had in the eyes of the public when the supposedly imminent war, which might have justified them as national defense measures, failed to come. Federalist judges and prosecutors enforced the laws anyway, jailing, for example, several prominent Republican newspaper editors for violating the Sedition Act by criticizing Adams (though no Federalist editor ever went to jail for vilifying Jefferson). The partisan application of the law left Adams and the Federalists saddled with a reputation as opponents of free speech as the election of 1800 approached. Adams was further crippled by growing divisions in his own party (Hamilton actually campaigned against him) and by the slow pace at which his diplomacy worked. Most voters did not know, for example, until after they had voted, that Adams' policy had succeeded and that a lasting peace with France had been arranged.

In the election of 1800, Adams lost to Jefferson by eight electoral votes. Exhausted, bitterly disappointed, and tired as well of the constant bickering and criticism, public and private, of the last four years, Adams retired from public life on the day Jefferson was inaugurated. He returned to his home in

Quincy to spend his time farming, reading, and writing an occasional essay on law or history. He died on July 4, 1826, a few hours after his great antagonist and greater friend, Jefferson, died in Virginia.

Summary

Throughout his life, Adams never got the praise he thought was his due. He was an important writer in the years preceding independence, but none of his writings had the broad impact of John Dickinson's *Letters from a Farmer in Pennsylvania, to the Inhabitants of the British Colonies* (1767-1768) or the great popular appeal of Thomas Paine's *Common Sense* (although in the long run, through his writings on government and constitutions, Adams contributed as much or more to the development of republican constitutional thought than all but two or three of the founders). His work in Europe negotiating the peace treaty of 1783 was at times brilliant, but it was the colorful and cunningly rustic Benjamin Franklin who caught the public's eye. Adams was president of the United States, but he immediately followed Washington in that office and inevitably Americans compared the two and found Adams the lesser president. Adams claimed that he did not seek the people's praises, but all of his life he watched men who were no more intelligent than he, no more dedicated to the Republic, and no more successful in serving it, win the kind of warm public applause that seemed beyond his grasp. He was respected but not revered, and he knew it.

Broadly speaking, Adams made three major contributions to the Revolution and the new Republic. First, he worked in Massachusetts and in Congress to keep the Revolution from running amok and destroying what was good in the British political tradition. He demonstrated to skeptical Tories and doubtful rebels, by both his words and his work, that independence need not be an invitation to anarchy, despotism, or mob rule, and so he helped make independence an acceptable alternative to submission. Second, he (with Jay and Franklin) protected American interests in the double-dealing diplomatic atmosphere of Paris and London during the war, and won for the Republic a treaty that secured its independence as well as the vast undeveloped territories and other economic resources it needed to survive and develop. Third, as president, he kept the new Republic out of what would have been a bitter, divisive war fought under a new, untested Constitution; thanks to Adams' skillful foreign policy, the Republic did not have to face its first war under the Constitution for another twelve years. Yet Adams never completely accepted the more democratic implications of the Revolution, and so, by the end of his career, he was both one of the most important of the Republic's founders and one of the least appreciated.

Bibliography
Bowen, Catherine Drinker. *John Adams and the American Revolution.* Bos-

ton: Little, Brown and Co., 1950. As much novel as history: Much of the book's dialogue was created by Bowen. Nevertheless, the book is generally historically accurate and is beautifully written. Conveys a more rounded picture of Adams than most strictly historical biographies do.

Butterfield, H. L., et al., eds. *The Book of Abigail and John: Selected Letters of the Adams Family, 1762-1784*. Cambridge, Mass.: Harvard University Press, 1975. An excellent way to discover John and Abigail through their own words. Their letters to each other illustrate their remarkable relationship and the private and public worlds in which they lived.

Cappon, Lester J., ed. *The Adams-Jefferson Letters: The Complete Correspondence Between Thomas Jefferson and Abigail and John Adams*. 2 vols. Chapel Hill: University of North Carolina Press, 1959. Covers the years 1777 to 1826. Excellent in conveying the revolutionary and early national periods through Adams' eyes. The letters following 1812 are remarkable. In them, the two aging rebels reminisce about the Revolution and their presidencies and speculate about the nation's future.

Jensen, Merrill. *The Founding of a Nation: A History of the American Revolution, 1763-1776*. New York: Oxford University Press, 1968. One of the best accounts of the origins and events of the Revolution from the Grenville Program of 1763 to the Declaration of Independence. Narrative in form, scholarly, and nicely written.

Kurtz, Stephen G. *The Presidency of John Adams: The Collapse of Federalism, 1795-1800*. Philadelphia: University of Pennsylvania Press, 1957. Good basic account of Adams' term in office and its impact on the Federalist Party. More recent studies are less well written and add little except detail to Kurtz's account.

Morris, Richard B. *The Peacemakers: The Great Powers and American Independence*. New York: Harper and Row, Publishers, 1965. The best available account of the negotiations leading to peace in 1783. Highly detailed, but Morris writes well. Not all of his judgments about the motives of the men and governments involved are convincing, but most are.

Shaw, Peter. *The Character of John Adams*. Chapel Hill: University of North Carolina Press, 1976. Examines Adams' ideas in the light of his background (especially his Puritan background) and his personal experiences at each stage of his life and career. Controversial but interesting and insightful.

Smith, Page. *John Adams*. 2 vols. Garden City, N.Y.: Doubleday and Co., 1962. The most complete and detailed life of Adams available. At times, oppressively detailed. Especially helpful as a source for a good, thorough chapter or two on particular incidents or periods of Adams' life.

Robert A. Becker

JOHN QUINCY ADAMS

Born: July 11, 1767; Braintree, Massachusetts
Died: February 23, 1848; Washington, D.C.
Areas of Achievement: Government and politics
Contribution: As diplomat, secretary of state, president, and member of the
House of Representatives, in a career spanning the early national period to
nearly the time of the Civil War, John Quincy Adams helped to shape
America's major foreign and domestic policies, always in the direction of
strengthening the nation as a unified whole.

Early Life

John Quincy Adams was born in Braintree (later Quincy), Massachusetts,
on July 11, 1767, the second child and first son of John and Abigail (Smith)
Adams. At such a time and in such a family, he was a child of both the Revolution and the Enlightenment, nurtured as well with a strong Puritan sense of
duty and destiny, directed throughout his life toward politics (and its atten-
dant sacrifices), always striving to fulfill the expectations and retain the ap-
probation of his parents, especially the redoubtable Abigail. His unorthodox
and irregular education was to produce both a scholar and a nationalist,
unswerving in his principles and forever unsatisfied with his performance,
always striving to increase his learning and improve his habits, and never able
to mingle easily with others or develop satisfying personal relationships.

As a boy, John Quincy imbibed patriotism in the midst of the Revolution
and then spent a number of years in Europe while his father was engaged in
the nation's diplomatic business; in France, Holland, and Russia he learned
languages, associated with important men of the time, studied sporadically,
and began what was to be a lifelong diary. Returning to America in 1785
(while his father remained as minister to England), he became again a
schoolboy and was graduated from Harvard in 1787. In his commencement
address, he referred to this time as a "critical period." He then studied law in
Newburyport with Theophilus Parsons until his admission to the bar in 1790.
Uninterested in the legal profession yet reluctant to be drawn into the hardships of public service, John Quincy entered the newspaper battles with
essays on the French Revolution (against Thomas Paine's *Rights of Man*,
1791) and the Genêt affair. His arguments in favor of American neutrality
won for him the attention of President George Washington and the post of
minister resident at The Hague, in 1794. He took up his position at this
excellent listening post during the Napoleonic expansion over Europe,
reporting in detail to Washington and to the secretary of state on its course,
his ideas influencing Washington's foreign policy statements in the Farewell
Address.

John Quincy Adams' appointment as minister to Portugal was changed before he took it up, and he and his wife, Louisa, whom he had married in 1797, traveled to Berlin, where the new minister plenipotentiary to Prussia negotiated a treaty, saw his wife successfully enter court society, and began a volume of descriptive letters about a visit to Silesia. Recalled by his father, John Adams, who had lost reelection to the presidency, Adams brought his wife and son (George Washington Adams, born April 12, 1801) to an America they had never seen in order to renew an interrupted law practice. Drawn inevitably to public service, Adams was elected to the Massachusetts Senate in April, 1802, and to the United States Senate in February, 1803. He immediately demonstrated the qualities that were to characterize and frustrate his political career: commitment to the nation rather than to any party, consistency of principle and attention to detail, and the inability to deal effectively with varied personalities and the social demands of the Washington political scene.

The young senator was five feet, seven inches tall, balding, with rather sharp and expressive features; he had always been careless in his dress, and despite his lifelong habit of exercise frequently suffered from dizziness, insomnia, stomach trouble, and attacks of anxiety and depression. Always introspective and self-critical, he was reserved and humorless; formally a Unitarian, he was well versed in the Bible, classical literature, science, and the humanities.

Although Adams opposed the Republican administration's acquisition of Louisiana for constitutional reasons, he soon demonstrated his differences from the Federalists on the important issues of the Aaron Burr intrigue, Judge John Pickering's impeachment, and the *Chesapeake* incident and embargo policy. His nationalism and independence in supporting Republican policies provoked Federalist hostility in both political and personal relations; he resigned his Senate seat before his Federalist replacement took over, and he experienced problems even in his lectures as Boylston Professor of Oratory and Rhetoric at Harvard. Without consulting Louisa, he accepted President James Madison's appointment as minister plenipotentiary to Russia; the two older boys remained with their grandparents in Quincy, and Adams, Louisa, and Charles Francis (born August 18, 1807) arrived in St. Petersburg late in 1809.

Despite inadequate funds, both Adamses established themselves with the diplomatic community and at the extravagant court of Czar Alexander I. John Quincy was able to achieve some diplomatic successes with the Russian government, attend to his youngest son, and maintain a correspondence with his older sons filled with stern expectations for their education and achievements—expectations which neither was ever able to fulfill.

As Alexander and Napoleon Bonaparte fell out over the Continental System and the War of 1812 opened, Adams was an obvious choice for the commission to negotiate peace with Great Britain. When its five members met finally in Ghent in 1814, they achieved a satisfactory treaty based on the prewar status quo. Adams then journeyed to Paris to meet Louisa, who had, by herself, wound up their affairs in Russia and traversed Europe with young Charles in the aftermath of war and during the Hundred Days. The Adamses then spent the next two years happily in London, as John Quincy had been appointed by President James Monroe as minister plenipotentiary to Great Britain. It became apparent that Great Britain was willing to negotiate and arbitrate the points still at issue after the Treaty of Ghent.

Adams' appointment as Monroe's secretary of state brought the family back to the United States late in 1817 and renewed the pattern of separation (the parents in Washington, the boys educated elsewhere) and family problems. Adams, at fifty, reentered domestic politics by becoming embroiled with the new generation of politicians. He was still and always a nationalist and an independent in a time of growing partisanship and sectional controversy and reserved and scholarly during the development of popular sovereignty and anti-intellectualism. For the rest of his long life, despite personal tragedy and bitter political disappointments, he was to shape much of America's domestic and foreign policy.

Life's Work

Adams became secretary of state as the Era of Good Feelings began to dissolve in personal and partisan contention for the presidency, and at a time when the State Department conducted both foreign and domestic affairs with one chief clerk and seven assistant clerks. Adams organized the department and its papers, did much of the office work himself during long days and nights (even cutting down on his reading), and attended to the census, congressional printing, extraditions, and commissions. He had, early in his career as a Federalist, demonstrated his political independence; he had received his appointments from Republican administrations; as secretary of state and son of John Adams, he was inevitably a presidential candidate. His foreign policy positions therefore developed as much in response to domestic political concerns as to the international situation. Yet his early principles dominated: He was a nationalist and an expansionist, cautious but determined to develop a hemispheric role for the United States.

Attempting to defend and expand American trade interests, Adams concentrated on the problem of discriminatory British customs duties in the West Indies trade. British interests and disturbed world conditions, however, meant the retention of those duties. Boundary problems with Great Britain and Russia in the Northwest presented less difficulty than those with Spain in Florida. The Treaty of 1818 settled United States–Canadian boundary and fisheries problems and provided for joint United States–British occupation of Oregon for ten years (the northern boundary fixed with Russia at 54°40' in the Convention of 1824). When General Andrew Jackson's sensational raid into Florida threatened an international incident, Adams alone in the Cabinet supported the general and used the uncontrolled Florida situation as an effective point in the negotiations that led to the 1819 Adams-Onís (Transcontinental) Treaty. Acquisition of Florida and the demarcation of a clear southwestern boundary to the Pacific represented major gains for the United States, even though Adams' opponents then and later attacked him on certain details (in which he had been uncharacteristically careless) and charged him with deliberately giving up Texas. Although he was not directly involved in the Missouri Compromise, Adams was against slavery and fearful that the sectional controversy had the potential to dissolve the Union. Even more immediately threatening was the possibility of European powers acting in the Western Hemisphere to regain newly independent colonies. Adams urged a unilateral American statement and greatly influenced the formulation of the basic policies of nonintervention and noncolonization, and American non-involvement in Europe, points which President Monroe incorporated into his December, 1823, message, later known as the Monroe Doctrine.

A presidential nominating system still in flux made social events crucial for politics: Protocol for formal calls was subject matter for Senate resolutions and cabinet papers; Louisa Adams' entertaining was vital for the cold, unsocial, and ambitious John Quincy, who furthermore refused to pursue the nomination actively, preferring it unsought as recognition of his ability and service. Throughout his political career he was to spurn the idea of active campaigning directed at the mass of voters, seeing public service as properly in the hands of the dedicated and qualified rather than the "popular" politicians.

In the election of 1824, Adams received eighty-four electoral votes to Jackson's ninety-nine, but as there was no majority, the House was to decide between Jackson, Adams, and Henry Clay, the third runner-up. While Adams actively swayed some Federalists, it was Clay's influence that turned the tide; "Harry of the West" feared the rash general more than a fellow nationalist, and the two rivals realized their basic agreement on major issues. With Clay's influence added, the House chose Adams to be president; Adams' appointment of Clay as secretary of state (and therefore a potential next president) led the Jacksonians to open their presidential campaign almost immediately, based on the charge of "bargain and corruption." The accusation of an Adams-Clay collusion continued to affect American politics for many years.

President like his father, and like his father a single-term executive facing the more popular candidate, Adams was a minority president in a period of great partisan pressures, a nationalist in an era of deepening sectionalism, and an executive with a program at a time of legislative dominance. He never really controlled the National Republicans, nor could he prevent the development of the Democratic Republican Party. Determined to avoid party considerations in appointments, he kept many in his cabinet and other offices (such as Postmaster General John McLean) who worked actively against him. He proposed large-scale national government action for general improvement in both learning and scientific activity (a national university, national observatories) and in the specifics of the "American System," usually identified as Clay's program, but which Adams claimed as his own. Not surprisingly, Adams considered foreign affairs very important; he had a Jeffersonian view of developing American world trade, with an emphasis on reciprocity and neutral rights. The Administration's diplomatic failures, particularly Great Britain's closure of West Indies trade, were often a result of domestic politics and sectional interests. The same was true of Adams' concept of the United States' democratic mission vis-à-vis Latin America: Any possibility of United States leadership in the Western Hemisphere was broken on the reefs of partisan opposition. The Panama Congress and the sensitive status of Cuba overshadowed negotiations and consultations which often laid the foundations for later administrations' successes.

Adams delegated much domestic policy to his cabinet and was therefore not deeply involved in the sectional maneuvering which produced the Tariff of Abominations. He strongly supported internal improvements, regarded the public lands as a long-term national resource, and backed off from a confrontation with Georgia over states' rights stemming from the Indian removal policy. Despite his concept of interdependent sectional interests producing national unity, Adams was usually identified with the economic interests of the Northeast.

A large antiadministration majority in Congress after the 1826 midterm elections left Adams a lame-duck president, depressed, ill, and socially isolated in the White House, mourning his father (who had died on July 4, 1826) and attempting to come to terms with his wife's depression and illness and the total disappointment of his hopes for his two elder sons, George, a debt-ridden depressive, and John, something of a rake. A developing interest in botany was a diverting hobby, although the live-oak plantation he established in Florida (to benefit naval construction) was abandoned by the next administration. All of Adams' personal difficulties, combined with his political ineptitude, helped ensure his isolation in the campaign of 1828, one of the bitterest and most vicious ever waged.

Adams was politically inept for a variety of reasons. The Adams family considered its members to be different from the general public, more principled and determined and therefore doomed to popular misunderstanding and lack of support. Adams preferred not to respond to public criticism or to explain and justify his actions; he refused to "electioneer," and his public speeches were scholarly, elaborate, and open to ridicule. His handling of the patronage (a difficult field complicated by factions within the parties) alienated his supporters and gave aid and comfort to his political enemies. He had not been able to rally support for a nonpartisan federal government program of wide-ranging improvements for the national benefit; he could not develop an effective party organization or even meld Federalists and nationalistic Republicans into a politically supportive bloc. His administration ignored the developing labor movement and the broadening popular base of voters and played into Jacksonian egalitarian propaganda. The well-organized Jacksonians easily set the cold Yankee aristocrat against the man of the people, concentrating on Jackson's personal popularity rather than his positions on issues (such as the tariff and internal improvements), which would alienate his disparate supporters.

John Quincy Adams, like his father before him, felt his defeat deeply, taking it as his country's repudiation, refusing (also like his father) to attend his successor's inauguration and moving into regular routines, exercise, and writing in order to make the transition to private life. On April 30, 1829, George Washington Adams jumped or fell from a steamboat and drowned in Long Island Sound, leaving a mass of debts and an illegitimate child. Adams at sixty-two was a failed president with his eldest son dead; nevertheless, mutual guilt brought him and Louisa closer (they had left George with others to rear; they had pushed him too hard) and helped them to concentrate on their two grandchildren and their youngest and favorite son. The latter soon married a wealthy and passive wife and began to produce a large family (Louisa Catherine II, John Quincy II, Charles Francis, Jr., Henry, Arthur, Mary, and Brooks). Political ambition (which Adams regarded as his chief character flaw) led him to agree (as usual, without consulting his wife) to represent his district in the House of Representatives. In 1831, he was elected by a large popular majority, a victory he regarded as the most satisfying of his entire political career. He missed politics and needed the salary, and for seventeen years and eight elections he carved out another and even more effective position in the service of the nation.

Still short, stout, and bald except for a fringe, Adams, as he had done all of his life, rose early, read his Bible and classical works regularly, swam, and walked; he developed into a connoisseur of wine and mellowed socially. He accepted Anti-Masonic support for a presidential nomination in 1832 (which did not eventuate) and lost the election for governor of Massachusetts in 1833 and Massachusetts (Whig) senator in 1835; none of this lessened his commitment to his House career. The House chamber had bad acoustics, as a result of which Adams at his desk could hear whispers from everywhere; his own high-pitched voice was to become a feared instrument in the coming House debates. After he spoke against Daniel Webster in connection with the "French Question" (of treaty payments) in 1836, he began to be called "Old Man Eloquent."

In the Nullification controversy, Adams recognized again the divisive potential of sectionalism, but in the next few years he focused more on the slavery issue as the greatest threat to the Union. He was neither an egalitarian nor an abolitionist per se; while Louisa began to acquaint herself with the problem, associating with the Grimkés and other abolitionists and coming to see the parallels between black slavery and the oppression of women, Adams viewed slavery in terms of principle: as morally reprehensible and politically dangerous to the continued existence of the nation. It was fitting, therefore, that he reacted first to the House's vote, in May of 1836, to table without reading all petitions dealing with slavery. The long battle against the "gag rule" invigorated Adams; the issue of the rights of petition and free speech gave him a broad ground on which to stand and aided him in debate when he dealt with slavery as a threat to the Union, a possible provocation of war with Mexico, a politically divisive question, and the source of the denial of basic rights of citizens. In this period also he began to examine the question of slavery in a broader context. Reading his mother's papers (Abigail Adams had died on October 28, 1818) and reacting to his wife's growing involvement with feminism, Adams came to support the concept of women's political rights, although without endorsing specific issues or deflecting his emphasis on the slavery question.

Always a political independent, Adams supported many of the Jackson Administration's policies, disagreeing, however, on bank policy. As an independent and a skilled parliamentarian, he was able in 1839 to effect the necessary organization of the House committees despite paralyzing partisan divisions. Southern members frequently opposed his actions and called for resolutions of censure. Although his early ponderous and erudite *Report on Weights and Measures* (1821) had never had any direct influence, Adams was able, from 1838 to 1846, to direct the use of the fund that established the Smithsonian Institution.

Despite bitter opposition, Adams maintained his battle in the House on all issues connected with slavery, although he believed that he could only begin what must be a long struggle. He opposed the 1838 attempt to annex Texas for constitutional reasons and because he believed that it would lead to a free-land policy to gain Western political support, thus dissipating a national resource. In 1841, he argued for the defense in the *Amistad* case before the Supreme Court, never submitting a bill for his legal services. In 1842, demonstrating great intellectual resources and physical stamina, he conducted a six-day, successful defense against a House resolution to censure him. He now received and enjoyed public adulation, and in December of 1844, on his resolution, the House rescinded the gag rule.

Feebler and somewhat absentminded, Adams continued to oppose the Mexican War, being reelected as a Conscience Whig in November of 1846. Nearing eighty, he had had to discontinue his daily early morning swims in the Potomac, and on November 20, 1846, he suffered a stroke but was able to resume his seat in early February, 1847. He spoke only once, in opposition to indemnifying the *Amistad* owners, and on February 21, 1848, had another stroke in the House. Carried to the Speaker's room in the Capitol, he died two days later without having regained consciousness. The national mourning ceremonies were like none since Washington's death. John Quincy Adams was buried in the family plot in Quincy. Louisa remained in Washington, keeping in touch with politics, buying and freeing a woman slave, and for much of the time suffering from ill health; she died on May 15, 1852.

Summary

President of a disintegrating party, politically impotent halfway into his only term, his personal life marred by an unsatisfying relationship with his wife and bitter disappointments with his two elder sons, Adams left—almost fled—the nation's highest political office, the lifelong goal of his great ambition and dynastic sense of duty and destiny. He seemed to be facing a lifetime in the ebb tide of politics and the treacherous shoals of financial insecurity and family disappointment. Even as his personal tragedy deepened with the death of his eldest son, he entered into a new phase, a time nearly as long as his life until then. He experienced a growing satisfaction, a greater harmony in relationships and decision-making within his own family: his remaining son, his growing brood of grandchildren, and his wife, finding her way to her own identity and a political role which could afford her a long-delayed satisfaction in contributing to and participating in the real life of the nation, rather than the confined, ornamental, subservient place expected by contemporary society.

During the course of his "two careers," John Quincy Adams contributed mightily to the basic elements of American foreign policy, influenced domestic issues, and stood as a beacon in the sectional controversy which, as he foresaw, was to lead the Union into civil war.

Bibliography
Bemis, Samuel Flagg. *John Quincy Adams and the Foundations of American Foreign Policy*. New York: Alfred A. Knopf, 1949. A detailed, scholarly, analytical work by a major authority on diplomatic history. Focuses on Adams' "first career" as diplomat and continentalist.
——————. *John Quincy Adams and the Union*. New York: Alfred A. Knopf, 1956. A companion volume, completing the biography, dealing with Adams' "second career." As effective as the preceding work; lacks details of Adams' personal life.
Clark, Bennett Champ. *John Quincy Adams: "Old Man Eloquent."* Boston: Little, Brown and Co., 1932. A rather popularized biography, not a panegyric but somewhat filiopietistic. Accurate and adequate; reads well.
East, Robert A. *John Quincy Adams: The Critical Years, 1785-1794*. New York: Bookman Associates, 1962. Deals with the early period of Adams'

life, vital for shaping his basic concepts. Fulsome in spots; may read too much importance into the early years.

Falkner, Leonard. *The President Who Wouldn't Retire*. New York: Coward-McCann, 1967. Based on Bemis and various primary documents but chiefly on secondary works. Popularized; emphasizes Adams' congressional career.

Hargreaves, Mary W. M. *The Presidency of John Quincy Adams*. Lawrence: University Press of Kansas, 1985. Detailed and scholarly examination of Adams' presidency, including the political and economic background. Concludes that Adams' term was more positive in goals and action than many historians have judged it. Dense but readable.

Hecht, Marie B. *John Quincy Adams: A Personal History of an Independent Man*. New York: Macmillan Publishing Co., 1972. Provides political background, with good attention to various personalities. Admires John Quincy, but is rather critical of Louisa. Lengthy but not dull.

Lipsky, George A. *John Quincy Adams: His Theory and Ideas*. New York: Thomas Y. Crowell, 1950. A good biographical chapter, but mainly concerned with Adams' intellectual system. Good analysis but a rather convoluted style. Unbounded admiration for a cold intellect. Adams seems a sanctimonious prig in some of the author's admiring references, somewhat more than he probably was.

Morse, John T., Jr. *John Quincy Adams*. Boston: Houghton Mifflin Co., 1882. Written in 1882 for and by the editor of the "American Statesmen" series. Brief (three hundred small pages), basic narrative.

Oliver, Andrew. *Portraits of John Quincy Adams and His Wife*. Cambridge, Mass.: The Belknap Press of Harvard University Press, 1970. Portraits, busts, silhouettes, including the later daguerreotypes. Accompanying text informative.

Shepherd, Jack. *Cannibals of the Heart: A Personal Biography of Louisa Catherine and John Quincy Adams*. New York: McGraw-Hill Book Co., 1980. Extensive research in the primary sources. An insightful view of the private life of a very public man, with equal attention to the lives of his wife and children. Well written; the psychological analysis is not intrusive. Good blend also of political and social background.

Marsha Kass Marks

SAMUEL ADAMS

Born: September 27, 1722; Boston, Massachusetts
Died: October 2, 1803; Boston, Massachusetts
Area of Achievement: Politics
Contribution: Strategically placed in Boston, the center of resistance to British colonial policies, Adams was one of the most significant organizers of the American Revolution.

Early Life

Samuel Adams' American ancestry began with Henry Adams, who emigrated from Devonshire, England, to Quincy, Massachusetts, in the early seventeenth century. One branch of the family included John Adams, who became second president of the United States. Samuel Adams' grandfather was a sailor, Captain John Adams. His father, Samuel Adams, Sr., lived his entire life in Boston, operating a malt house, or brewery, and was an active member of the old South Church in Boston. He was also active in local politics, establishing the first of the Boston "Caucus Clubs," which played a vital role in the early upheavals of the Revolutionary period.

Samuel Adams, then, was born into an active and influential civic-minded Boston family. He grew up with a familiarity with and keen interest in local politics and knew most Boston political leaders through their friendship with his father. Many of those leaders were prominent in Massachusetts colonial politics as well. Samuel absorbed the traditional independent-mindedness of Boston and thought of Massachusetts as autonomous and largely self-governing within the broader parameters of the British Empire.

Educated in the small wooden schoolhouse in the rear of King's Chapel, Samuel received a traditional grounding in Latin and Greek grammar, preparatory to entering Harvard College. When he received the A.B. degree in 1740 and the master of arts in 1743, his interest in politics was already clear. He titled his thesis, "Whether It Be Lawful to Resist the Supreme Magistrate, if the Commonwealth Cannot Otherwise Be Preserved."

Life's Work

Samuel Adams thus embarked upon his life's work in colonial politics, but he also had to make a living for his family. To that end, his father gave him one thousand pounds to help him get started in business. He promptly lent five hundred pounds to a friend (who never repaid the loan) and lost the other five hundred through poor management. His father then took him into partnership in his malt house, from which the family made a modest living.

Adams lived an austere, simple life and throughout his life had little interest in making money. At a time of crisis just before the war, General Thomas Gage governed Massachusetts under martial law and offered Adams an annuity of two thousand pounds for life. Adams promptly rejected the offer; "a guinea never glistened in my eyes," he said. A man of integrity, he would not be bribed to refrain from doing what he believed to be right. His threadbare clothing was his trademark, reflecting his austerity and lack of interest in material things.

In 1748 his father died, leaving him one-third of his modest estate. Adams gradually sold most of it during the busy years of his life and was rescued from abject poverty in his retirement years only by a small inheritance from his son. (During most of his life, his only income was a small salary as a clerk of the Massachusetts General Assembly.)

Adams married Elizabeth Checkley, the daughter of the minister of New South Congregational Church, in 1749. She died eight years later, survived by only two of their five children, a boy and a girl. Adams reared the children and managed alone for seven years but remarried—in 1764, to Elizabeth Wells. He was then forty-two; she, twenty-four.

Adams was of average height and muscular build. He carried himself straight in spite of an involuntary palsied movement of his hands and had light blue eyes and a serious, dignified manner. He was very fond of sacred music and sang in the choir of New South Church. Personable, he maintained a close relationship with his neighbors and was constantly chatting with those he met along the street. He had a gift for smoothing over disputes among his friends and acquaintances and was often asked to mediate a disagreement. Adams was a hard worker, and through the years his candle burned late at night as he kept up his extensive correspondence, much of which does not survive today. He second cousin, John Adams, likened him to John Calvin, partly because of his deep piety but also because of his personality: He was "cool . . . polished, and refined," somewhat inflexible, but consistent, a man of "steadfast integrity, exquisite humanity, genteel erudition, obliging, engaging manners, real as well as professed piety, and a universal good character. . . ."

Samuel Adams was very interested in political philosophy and believed strongly in liberty and Christian virtue and frugality. He helped organize discussion clubs and the *Public Advertiser*, a newspaper to promote understanding of political philosophy. He served in political offices large and small, as fire ward, as moderator, and as tax collector. An orthodox Christian, he warned of the political implications of the "fallen" nature of man, susceptible as most men were to self-aggrandizement, if not corruption. Colonial Americans believed that power had the tendency to corrupt, and Adams was no exception. Speaking for the Boston Town Meeting, Adams said;

[Such is] the depravity of mankind that ambition and lust of power above the law are . . . predominant passions in the breasts of most men. [Power] converts a good man in private life to a tyrant in office.

Despite mythology to the contrary, Adams was not a mob leader, though he was popular with the common workers of Boston. He was opposed to violence and sought to achieve his aims by political means. No evidence has ever been found placing Adams at any of the scenes in Boston involving mob violence such as the Boston Massacre, the wrecking of Lieutenant Governor Thomas Hutchinson's house, or the physical harassment of merchants. He has often been charged with "masterminding" these events, but only by conjecture, not on the basis of historical evidence.

In his early forties, Adams was well-known in Boston politics when the Stamp Act crisis occurred in 1764-1765—the beginning of the revolutionary period. Along with his friend James Otis, Adams spoke out strongly and wrote much against the dangers of the Stamp Act. Before the Boston Town Meeting, Adams denied the right of the British Parliament to tax the colonists. The Massachusetts Charter gave Americans the right "to govern and tax ourselves." If Parliament could tax the Colonies, then the Englishmen living in America would become "tributary slaves" without representation. Adams called for a unified resistance to this "tyranny" throughout the Colonies. The Boston Town Meeting then elected Adams to a seat in the Massachusetts General Assembly, where he was soon elected to the position of clerk, a position he held for ten years.

This principle of opposing taxation without representation became one of the most significant rallying points for resisting British control of the Colonies. Adams nevertheless stressed that he had no desire for colonial representation in the British Parliament. Since the colonists would be considerably outnumbered and since travel to England was so slow, it would be "impracticable for the subjects in America" to have a tiny voice in Parliament. Instead, Adams and most of his fellow American strategists wanted to be able to make their own laws in their own American "parliaments." "All acts," wrote Adams, "made by any power whatever other than the General Assembly of this province, imposing taxes on the inhabitants, are infringements of our inherent and unalienable rights as men and British subjects. . . ."

On November 1, 1765, the day the Stamp Act was to go into effect, Boston buildings were draped in mourning black and the church bells tolled slowly. Governor Francis Bernard ordered the Boston militia to muster as a precautionary peacekeeping measure. Yet the men would not respond; one drummer sounded the call only to have his drum promptly broken. The rest of the drummers preserved their instruments by not using them. In direct violation of the Stamp Act, the Massachusetts General Assembly voted 81 to 5 to open the law courts of the province without using stamped papers, as required by the act.

In 1772, Adams sought and received the authorization of the Boston Town Meeting to create a committee of correspondence to inform and consult with other towns in the province, with a view to concerted and coordinated action. This was not a new idea. It had been customary for many years in Europe and in America for legislative bodies to use committees to handle official correspondence with other such governing authorities. As early as 1768, Richard Henry Lee had suggested to the Virginia House of Burgesses the formation of an intercolonial system of correspondence among the provincial assemblies. It was in Boston, however, that the idea was finally implemented.

As clerk of the Massachusetts General Assembly, Adams expanded the circular-letter type of correspondence to include all the Colonies. In time, those letters contributed significantly to the unified action of the Colonies. Realizing the potential strength in such an arrangement, the British secretary of state for the Colonies, Lord Hillsborough, instructed the governor of Massachusetts to order the General Assembly to rescind a circular letter sent to other colonies. Instead, the General Assembly, in a heated debate, voted 92 to 17 to refuse to rescind the letter. The governor dissolved the legislature, but Adams—a pioneer in realizing the enormous importance of communication and information in sustaining any cause—published the names of the seventeen who had voted against the measure, impairing their political future. Britain now sought to obtain evidence to arrest and deport to England for prosecution those who resisted British law. Adams also published that letter, and the effect was electrifying, because it showed the clear intention of the British government to bypass the cherished English right of trial by jury of one's peers.

The political year of 1773 began with now-governor Thomas Hutchinson's opening speech to the Massachusetts General Assembly on the issue of parliamentary supremacy; did the British Parliament have authority over the elected assembly of Massachusetts, and, if so, to what extent? Adams headed the committee of the assembly designated to reply to the governor. He simply and cleverly took Hutchinson's own famous book, *History of Massachusetts Bay* (1760), and compared what he had written earlier with the current message. Adams found many inconsistencies and contradictions. The governor's book, for example, acknowledged that the founders of Massachusetts Bay Colony had been assured by the Crown that "they were to be governed by laws made by themselves" and not by Parliament.

Adams also had a hand in the Boston Tea Party later that same year. The British East India Company was partially owned by the British government but, because of mismanagement, had stockpiled a great quantity of tea that needed to be sold before it spoiled. The Tea Act of spring, 1773, gave the company a monopoly on tea sales in America but sharply cut the price of tea. The controversial tea tax (set by the Townshend Acts of 1767) would continue to be levied, but the actual price, including the tax, paid in America for tea would only be about one-half that paid by a Londoner for his tea.

This monopoly on the tea trade could be seriously damaging to American free enterprise. Without competition, merchant trade could not prosper, and the Americans would eventually pay unnecessarily high prices for imports. Moreover, a precedent would be set regulating trade excessively instead of following more of a free market system. Adams, however, chose to focus on the taxation issue rather than the monopoly issue, because the former could be defended more emotionally and symbolically. When American patriots refused to allow the tea to be landed, the governor refused to allow the merchant ships to return with their cargoes of tea. The standoff ended when colonists destroyed thousands of pounds of tea by dumping it into the bay.

The response of the British government inflamed the angry Americans. The Boston Port Act closed the port of Boston and threatened to ruin Boston as a commercial center. Salem and Marblehead merchants responded by inviting the merchants of Boston to use their docks and warehouses free of charge. Contributions of food and supplies came from many colonies. Adams asked the people of Massachusetts to support a "Solemn League and Covenant" not to buy British goods. (The wording of the boycott was significant, reminiscent to American colonists of the English Civil War and of the heroism of the later Scottish Covenanters.)

General Gage in effect established martial law in Boston and even dissolved the General Assembly. The assembly, however, was in the process of selecting delegates to the First Continental Congress in Philadelphia. When General Gage's messenger arrived to order the assembly to disband, Adams, the clerk, locked the doors to keep the messenger out until the delegation process was completed. The elected delegates included both Samuel Adams and John Adams. General Gage considered arresting Samuel Adams but did not want to provoke a violent reaction, which such a measure would assuredly incite.

The three-hundred mile trip to Philadelphia was the longest of Adams' life. Even there, however, he found himself influential politically, becoming the key member of the newly organized Committee of Safety, a coordinating group. Adams was also the chairman of the Donation Committee, which distributed gifts of food and supplies collected all along the Atlantic seaboard for the aid of the unfortunate people of the Boston area. The Committee of Safety began collecting weapons and supplies—and even stored cannon at Concord.

An active member of the Continental Congress, Adams played a significant political role throughout the Revolutionary War. After the war, he approved of the new Constitution of the United States—but only after assurances were given him that a bill of rights was to be added. Adams became lieutenant governor of Massachusetts in 1789 and governor in 1793, retiring from that office in 1797. On October 2, 1803, at the age of eighty-one, he died, having devoted his life to the cause of liberty and independence in a new nation, the United States of America.

Summary
It would be difficult to overestimate the importance of Samuel Adams to the American Revolution. Along with Virginia, New York, and Pennsylvania, Massachusetts led the way to independence. There was no center of power quite so volatile, however, as Massachusetts; it was there that the events which sparked the revolution occurred: resistance to the Stamp Act, the Boston Massacre, the *Liberty* incident, organized boycotts, letters of protest, and so on.

Samuel Adams was involved in all of these events. His importance, moreover, was recognized in the very highest echelons of the British government. When King George III ordered Governor Hutchinson to London for consultation, one of the questions he asked him was what accounted for the importance of Samuel Adams in the Colonies. Hutchinson's reply reflected his frustration with Adams: "A great pretended zeal for liberty and a most inflexible natural temper. He was the first that publicly asserted the independency of the colonies upon the kingdom."

It is true that Samuel Adams was a principal advocate of complete independence from Great Britain, but not until 1775. All that he had advocated for years following the Stamp Act crisis was self-government within the British system. He did not push for independence until it became obvious to him that the king was a "tyrant [with] an unalterable determination to compel the colonies to absolute obedience."

Bibliography
Adams, Samuel. *The Writings of Samuel Adams*. Edited by H. A. Cushing. 4 vols. New York: G. P. Putnam's Sons, 1904-1908. Indispensable primary material: Adams' ideas in his own words—in letters, newspaper articles, and official correspondence of the Massachusetts General Assembly.

Bailyn, Bernard. *The Ideological Origins of the American Revolution*. Cambridge, Mass.: The Belknap Press of Harvard University Press, 1967. Not much on Adams directly, but essential for understanding his ideological milieu. Bailyn finds, as did Adams, that the war was fought over constitutional issues.

Chidsey, Donald Barr. *The Great Separation: The Story of the Boston Tea Party and the Beginning of the American Revolution*. New York: Crown Publishers, 1965. Written in a popular novelist's style, this book brings to life the issues and actions surrounding the Boston Tea Party, including Adams' role.

Galvin, John R. *Three Men of Boston*. New York: Thomas Y. Crowell, 1976. A retelling of the events leading up to the Revolution in Boston through the significant parts played by Thomas Hutchinson, James Otis, and Samuel Adams. Galvin captures the complexity of the period and demonstrates how the issues and events were interrelated.

Hosmer, James K. *Samuel Adams*. Boston: Houghton Mifflin Co., 1885. This is the standard nineteenth century biography of Adams.

Maier, Pauline. *The Old Revolutionaries: Political Lives in the Age of Samuel Adams*. New York: Alfred A. Knopf, 1980. Chapter 1, "A New Englander as Revolutionary: Samuel Adams," is a brilliant analysis of Adams' importance in history. Maier analyzes the interpretive data on Adams and introduces many fresh insights. Her subtitle indicates the absolutely dominant role that Adams played in the Revolutionary era.

Miller, John C. *Sam Adams: Pioneer in Propaganda*. Stanford, Calif.: Stanford University Press, 1936. A pioneer work analyzing Adams' propaganda warfare against the British. Adams' techniques in communications are described in detail.

Montross, Lynn. *The Reluctant Rebels: The Story of the Continental Congress, 1774-1789*. New York: Harper and Brothers, Publishers, 1950. The important role of the Continental Congress in the conduct and winning of the American Revolution, as well as Adams' contribution during that phase of his career.

Umbreit, Kenneth. *Founding Fathers: Men Who Shaped Our Tradition*. Port Washington, N.Y.: Kennikat Press, 1941. One useful chapter on Adams. He is ranked along with Thomas Jefferson, John Adams, John Hancock, Patrick Henry, and George Washington as a "founding father."

William H. Burnside

JANE ADDAMS

Born: September 6, 1860; Cedarville, Illinois
Died: May 21, 1935; Chicago, Illinois
Area of Achievement: Social reform
Contribution: In hundreds of books and articles and as cofounder and direc-
tor of the Hull House settlement in Chicago, Addams promoted a variety
of social reforms designed to facilitate the adjustment to urban, industrial
America from 1890 to 1935.

Early Life

Jane Addams was born on September 6, 1860, in the village of Cedarville
in northern Illinois. Her father, John Huy Addams, owned a local mill and
had investments in land and other enterprises in several states; his belief in
civic responsibility led him to represent his district in the Illinois senate from
1854 to 1870. Her mother, Sarah, died when Jane was barely two years old,
and an older sister supervised the Addams household until John Addams
remarried in 1868. Anna Haldeman Addams, the widow of a Freeport merchant, was a self-educated woman with a high regard for social position,
travel, dress—in general, the cultural aspects of life. Jane received tutelage
from her stepmother in these areas, which supplemented the information she
gleaned from books in the local subscription library, conveniently located in
John Addams' house. Her formal education began in the village school in
Cedarville; in 1877, she entered nearby Rockford Female Seminary (of
which her father was a trustee), an institution dedicated to instilling in young
women religious piety, cultural awareness, and domesticity. That Jane
became president of her class, valedictorian, and editor of the class magazine
attests her popularity and intellectual qualities.

Shortly after her graduation from the seminary, in 1881, John Addams
died. This shock combined with her indecision about a career to produce several years of irresolution and depression. She began medical study at the
Woman's Medical College in Philadelphia, but poor health forced her to
leave after a few months. She was then bedridden for six months following
an operation on her spine to correct the slight curvature caused by childhood
spinal tuberculosis. At the urging of her stepmother, she toured Europe for
twenty-seven months from 1883 to 1885, absorbing Old World culture with
Anna and a few college classmates. Her purposelessness persisted after her
return. She accompanied her stepmother to Baltimore for two winters and
engaged in some charity work there, but her nervous depression continued.
It was not until her second trip to Europe, in 1887-1888, in the company of
her former teacher, Sarah Anderson, and college friend, Ellen Gates Starr,
that she perceived a means to reconcile her intellectual and cultural interests
with a useful career. In London she visited Toynbee Hall, a social settlement

in the city's East End, and discussed the institution's social and cultural activities with its founder, Canon Samuel A. Barnett. She also toured the People's Palace, an institute for the working class. These experiences acquainted her with the attempts of other educated men and women to deal with the problems of modern society by living and working in a poor neighborhood. Before leaving Europe she discussed her plan for founding a Chicago settlement with Starr; a few months after arriving home, the two women opened Hull House, on September 18, 1889.

Life's Work

While the model of Toynee Hall initially influenced Addams' establishment of Hull House, the ethnically mixed population around the Halsted Street settlement had a greater impact on its development in the 1890's. When the two women residents moved into the old Hull mansion, they had no formal program of activities and sought to establish contact with their neighbors by sharing their literary enthusiasms in a series of "reading parties." Soon, however, the needs of area residents dictated programs. A wide variety of activities evolved in the first decade, including classes, clubs, social and cultural events, and a day nursery. Many of these activities drew on the cultural backgrounds of immigrants; Greeks staged classical Greek dramas at the Hull House Theater, and Italian and German immigrants discussed Dante and Johann Wolfgang von Goethe. As the functions of the settlement multiplied and Hull House added new buildings, Addams stood as the central figure—still a young woman, her brown hair drawn back into a bun, her pleasant face distinguished by pensive dark eyes—radiating goodwill and competence.

Her changed awareness of the nature of urban problems began to emerge in the 1890's. While her original impulse in establishing Hull House had reflected the religious and humanitarian principles of her early years, a combination of circumstances now led her to consider the causes of poverty and maladjustment to industrial society. Florence Kelley, who came to Hull House as a resident in the early 1890's, contributed her infectious interest in scientific investigations of the neighborhood as a basis for reform proposals. Her work culminated in the 1895 publication of *Hull-House Maps and Papers: A Presentation of Nationalities and Wages in a Congested District of Chicago, Together with Comments and Essays on Problems Growing Out of the Social Conditions*, a series of essays by Hull House residents, including "The Settlement as a Factor in the Labor Movement," by Addams. Addams was critical of current labor practices, an outgrowth of her involvement in the unsuccessful mediation of the Pullman strike in 1894. She also criticized the response to the depression of 1893-1894 by existing charitable organizations, which too often stressed laziness and other individual vices as the determinants of poverty. Her developing view was to consider the underlying causes of labor problems and social ills: the dislocation caused by modern industrial organization. Her promotion of scientific inquiry was abetted by members of the new department of sociology at the University of Chicago, particularly Dr. Albion Small, who encouraged her to publish in the *American Journal of Sociology*, which he began editing in 1896.

Addams' far-flung activities of the early 1900's aimed at achieving harmony between industrialism, on the one hand, and traditional ideas of morality and culture, on the other. She was particularly interested in children and their development through educational and social activities. She promoted public parks and playgrounds in Chicago, established a kindergarten at Hull House, and set up a Hull House camp for neighborhood children outside the city. She promoted reform in education, believing that traditional educational methods and subjects insufficiently prepared children for modern life. She served on the Chicago Board of Education from 1905 to 1908 and was a founder of the National Society for the Promotion of Industrial Education. (Founded in 1906, the Society's efforts culminated in the 1917 Smith-Hughes Act, which provided federal support for vocational education in high schools.) She was also a founding member of the National Child Labor Committee, which supported compulsory education laws as well as restrictive legislation for child labor in factories.

By the time she published her autobiographical masterpiece, *Twenty Years at Hull House* (1910), Addams was widely recognized as an expert in social problems and a spokesperson for major programs for progressive reform. A leading suffragist (and officer of the National American Woman Suffrage Association from 1911 to 1914), she was attracted by the woman's suffrage and industrial justice planks of the Progressive Party in 1912. She delivered a stirring speech seconding Theodore Roosevelt's nomination at the party's convention in Chicago and subsequently traveled more than seven thousand miles campaigning for the party. When Woodrow Wilson won the election, she opined that he would pursue a program of Progressive democracy. The war in Europe in 1914 impaired Progressive aspirations for reform, however, and directed Addams' attention to the cause she would pursue for the rest of her life: world peace.

During the period of American neutrality, until April, 1917, she worked for international arbitration, believing that neutral nations could resolve the war's causes and mediate with the belligerents. With Carrie Chapman Catt, she issued a call to women to attend a conference in Washington in January, 1915, resulting in the formation of the Woman's Peace Party, with Addams as its chair. Later in the year, she was elected president of the International Conference of Women at The Hague. (When the group reorganized after the war as the Women's International League for Peace and Freedom, she was elected president and retained the post until 1929.) When mediation did not materialize and the United States entered the war, she did not support the war effort, although in 1918 she worked for Herbert Hoover's Department of Food Administration, which she viewed as a humanitarian response to the upheaval of war. Her patriotism came under attack, and the Daughters of the American Revolution withdrew her lifetime honorary membership. In the years following the war, she continued to search for ways to ensure lasting peace; her efforts were recognized by the award of the Nobel Peace Prize in 1931, which she shared with Nicholas Murray Butler.

Her final years were marked by tributes and honors from organizations throughout the world. Her activities were hampered, however, by failing health. She underwent major surgical operations and suffered a heart attack in the early 1930's; she died on May 21, 1935. Following services at Hull House, she was buried in the cemetery at Cedarville.

Summary

Jane Addams was in the vanguard of Progressive reformers. Rather than exhibiting a populist-type aversion to modern industrial conditions, she shared with other urban reformers a belief that social, political, and economic relationships could be modified in a democratic fashion to deal with changed conditions. The belief in evolutionary change toward a new "social morality" was the theme of her first book, *Democracy and Social Ethics* (1902), a collection of essays on such diverse topics as charity organizations, family relationships, women in domestic employment, labor-management relations in industry, education, and the roles of bosses and reformers in politics.

Her experiences at Hull House provided her with a vantage point which few other reformers enjoyed. Observations of the ordinary led her to formulate social theories. For example, her reflections on the activities of neighborhood children led to a remarkable book, *The Spirit of Youth and the City Streets* (1909), in which she discussed the importance of the natural instinct toward play among children and the "urban democracy" exhibited on the playground.

The neighborhood was also a place where social experimentation could occur, where ideas could be translated to practice, for Addams was a rare combination of social theorist and pragmatic reformer. As such, she attracted other educated and talented people to join the settlement, many of whom were young women who faced the same career quandary with which she had dealt in the 1880's. She was willing to draw upon the observations and ideas of this group in formulating her own programs. This open-minded deference to ideas, including those of William James and John Dewey, may have been her greatest strength in attempting to apply democratic idealism to an urban industrial setting in new ways which represented a profound break from the genteel tradition in which she was reared and educated.

Her attitude toward war rested on the same ideal of Progressive democracy as her social theories. Like other Progressives, she believed that war destroyed social progress and moral civilization. Unlike most other Progressives, however, she could not support the United States' involvement in the war, citing as her reasons the sanctity of human life and the irrationality of war as an instrument of change. As a practical idealist, she supported such postwar initiatives as the League of Nations, the World Court, and the Kellogg-Briand Pact, hoping that they would serve as instruments to direct world public opinion against war. In international affairs, as well as in industrial relations, Jane Addams was always willing to pursue numerous programs, never losing her faith in achieving human progress through social change.

Bibliography

Addams, Jane. *Democracy and Social Ethics*. Edited by Anne Firor Scott. New York: Macmillan, 1902. Reprint Cambridge, Mass.: The Belknap Press of Harvard University Press, 1964. Originally published in 1902, the book was a compilation of earlier magazine articles (revised for the book), which addressed the problem of applying ethics to an evolving democratic system. This edition includes an excellent introduction to the life and thought of Addams by the editor.

_____. *The Social Thought of Jane Addams*. Edited by Christopher Lasch. Indianapolis: Bobbs-Merrill Co., 1965. An excellent introduction to Addams through her published and unpublished writings. Following a biographical introduction by Lasch, the material is organized under five subject headings, which reflect Addams' diverse interests.

_____. *Twenty Years at Hull House with Autobiographical Notes*. New York: Macmillan, 1910. A good source for understanding Addams and the Progressive reform movement, as the book is at once autobiography, publicity for Hull House, and a consideration of reform ideas in the twenty years preceding its publication.

Davis, Allen F. *American Heroine: The Life and Legend of Jane Addams*. New York: Oxford University Press, 1973. A balanced biography that establishes Addams' writing and other activities in a broader cultural context. The most realistic appraisal of her accomplishments.

Farrell, John C. *Beloved Lady: A History of Jane Addams' Ideas on Reform and Peace*. Baltimore: Johns Hopkins University Press, 1967. The first study to analyze the thought of Addams, rather than concentrate on her humanitarian sentiments or involvement in settlement activity. Particularly good in demonstrating that her ideas often conflicted with later historical accounts of the "average" Progressive reformer.

Lasch, Christopher. *The New Radicalism in America, 1889-1963: The Intellectual as a Social Type*. New York: Alfred A. Knopf, 1965. In a perceptive essay on Addams, Lasch examines her early life and motivation for reform;

he finds that her gradual emergence as an adherent to the "new radical-ism" (marked by interest in educational, cultural, and sexual reform) was based on the conflict between the genteel values of her parents' generation and her own perceptions of life and society.

Levine, Daniel. *Jane Addams and the Liberal Tradition*. Madison: State Historical Society of Wisconsin, 1971. An intellectual biography of Ad-dams, which asserts that she was a radical in urging rapid change. The book deals with three facets of her life: Hull House, her publicizing of social problems, and activism in national affairs.

Linn, James Weber. *Jane Addams: A Biography*. New York: D. Appleton-Century Co., 1935. An admiring but thorough biography by Addams' nephew. Not interpretive, but valuable for detail, as the author had access to all of Addams' manuscripts and files prior to her death, and discussed the biography with her.

Richard G. Frederick

LOUIS AGASSIZ

Born: May 28, 1807; Motier-en-Vuly, Switzerland
Died: December 14, 1873; Cambridge, Massachusetts
Areas of Achievement: Natural history and education
Contribution: Agassiz created an awareness of the importance of the study of natural history in the United States with his founding of the Museum of Comparative Zoology at Harvard University. He was an early pioneer in making scientific studies an integral part of the curriculum at American colleges and universities.

Early Life

Jean Louis Rodolphe Agassiz was born May 28, 1807, in Motier-en-Vuly, Canton Fribourg, Switzerland. The son of a Protestant clergyman, Agassiz was one of four children. At the age of ten, Agassiz was sent to school at Bienne, where he spent much of his time observing freshwater fish, which fascinated him. In 1822, he entered the Academy of Lausanne. Upon graduation, out of deference to his parents, he enrolled in the school of medicine at the University of Zurich. After two years of studies in medicine, he enrolled in the University of Heidelberg, where he developed a special interest in natural history. The following year, he transferred to the University of Munich to study under Ignaz von Döllinger, a pioneer embryologist whom Agassiz credited as the source of his scientific training.

In 1829, he received a doctorate in philosophy at Erlanger and returned to Munich to complete his studies in medicine. The following year, he received a doctorate in medicine and thereafter never examined a patient; his mind was set on pursuing studies in ichthyology, paleontology, and glacial geology.

While Agassiz was enrolled in Munich, Lorenz Oken, one of his professors, presented a paper on Agassiz's discovery of a new species of carp. In 1829, Agassiz published his first book on this species of Brazilian fish based on his study of a collection of specimens from the Amazon brought to Munich in 1821 by J. B. Spix and K. F. Philip von Martius. The book was written with such beauty and clarity that it was soon evident that Agassiz would become not only a man of science but also a man of letters.

Agassiz married Cecile Braun, sister of the eminent botanist Alexander Braun. There were three children born to the union, a son and two daughters. Cecile was a natural history artist whose drawings of fossil and freshwater fish forms appeared in several of Agassiz's books. She died of tuberculosis in 1848.

Agassiz was a large, robust man, slightly above medium height, who had keen brown eyes which could light up with enthusiasm. He had chestnut brown hair that gradually thinned with age but retained its color into his declining years.

Life's Work

The professional life of Agassiz is clearly divided into two chapters: his work as a research scientist in Europe, in the course of which he made significant advances in the fields of ichthyology and glacial geology, and his teaching career in the United States, during which he dedicated himself to making science an integral and respected part of the curriculum of higher education in his adopted country.

Upon completion of his formal schooling, Agassiz went to Paris to continue his studies in medicine. While there, he spent much of his time at the museum of natural history at the Jardin des Plantes, where he met Georges Cuvier, the master of comparative anatomy. The aging Cuvier willingly turned over much of his unfinished work to the young naturalist to complete. Agassiz also met the naturalist Friedrich Humbolt, who in 1832 secured for him an appointment as professor in natural history at the University of Neuchâtel.

While at Neuchâtel, Agassiz formed a natural history society and took scientists on excursions into the Alps to study and observe flora and fauna. Agassiz turned Neuchâtel into a research center, and over the course of fifteen years he published more than two hundred works, including twenty substantial volumes illustrated with more than two thousand plates. Before Agassiz began his research, only eight generic types of fossil fish had been named in formal publications. Agassiz identified 340 new genera, many of them in his books *History of the Fresh Water Fishes of Central Europe* (1839-1842) and *Monograph on the Fossil Fishes of the Old Red or Devonian of the British Isles and Russia* (1844-1845).

While at Neuchâtel, Agassiz's attention was drawn to the nearby glacier of the great median moraine of the lower Aar valley, and this sent his scientific investigations in a new direction, that of glacial geology. He concluded from his observations that gravity controls glacial movements and that glaciers travel faster in the middle and at the surface, disproving the commonly held theory that glaciers are pushed along by water freezing underneath. He published his findings in *Études sur les glaciers* (1840; studies on glaciers) and *Systèmes glaciaires* (1846; glacial systems). Agassiz came to accept Karl Schimper's "ice age" thesis and added that Europe had been subjected once to a period of extreme cold from the North Pole to the Mediterranean and Caspian seas in a widespread Pleistocene ice age. He studied earth surfaces all over Europe and concluded that drift material and polished and striated boulders gave evidence of earlier glacial movements.

A gift from the King of Prussia in 1846 enabled Agassiz to pursue his work in the United States. Sir Charles Lyell had arranged for him to participate in a course of lectures at the Lowell Institute in Boston. Agassiz's life took another turn. His intense research gave way to teaching and campaigning on behalf of natural history as a legitimate academic endeavor.

Agassiz continued to write of his discoveries with verbal precision and lucid description. He could devote fifty pages of unmatched prose describing the interior of an egg. He set about to produce a twelve-volume series entitled *Contributions to the Natural History of the United States*. More than twenty-five hundred advance subscriptions were taken, but only four volumes were ever produced (1857-1862). These four volumes represented a triumph of thought and scholarship and contributed to the nature-consciousness of the American public.

In 1848, Agassiz accepted the chair of natural history of the new Lawrence Scientific School at Harvard University, and the same year he published his popular *Principles of Zoology*. When he visited Washington, D.C., he was disappointed to find so little scientific activity in the nation's capital. At the time, the Smithsonian Institution had not begun to function. Agassiz was later made a member of the Smithsonian Board of Regents, and the institution's natural history division was developed.

In 1850, Agassiz married Elizabeth Cary, and the following year he accepted a teaching appointment at the Medical College of Charleston, South Carolina. After two years, he resigned because he found the climate unsuitable and returned to Harvard. He and his wife opened a school for young women in Cambridge which became the precursor of Radcliffe College.

Agassiz was quite disappointed with Harvard's science department and claimed that the chemistry laboratory at Cambridge High School was better equipped; he often did his work there. In 1859, Agassiz founded the Museum of Comparative Zoology at Harvard and helped to create a new era in American higher education. He emphasized advanced and original works as factors in mental training and stressed the direct, hands-on study of nature. Ralph Waldo Emerson complained that something ought to be done to check this rush toward natural history at Harvard. Agassiz countered that the rest of the curriculum should be brought up to the standards he had set for the zoology laboratories. Agassiz found a kindred soul in Henry David Thoreau and often visited Walden Pond. At a dinner hosted by Emerson, Thoreau and Agassiz once talked of mating turtles, to the disgust of Emerson. From Walden, Thoreau sent Agassiz varieties of fish, turtles, and snakes, and was paid handsomely for them.

The same year that Agassiz opened the museum at Harvard, Charles Darwin published his *On the Origin of Species by Means of Natural Selection* (1859). The theory of evolution did not begin with Darwin, and Agassiz was thoroughly acquainted with the works of Georges-Louis Leclerc Buffon, Jean Baptiste de Monet de Lamarck, Charles Darwin's own grandfather, Erasmus Darwin, and their ideas of the gradual, continuous progress of species which contributed to the theory of evolution. Also, much of the knowledge of embryology which is integral to Darwin's theory was originally discovered by Agassiz. Agassiz once admitted that he had been on the verge of anticipating Darwinism when he found that the highest fishes were those that came first, and therefore he rejected the theory. Sharks, one of the most primitive species, had the largest brains and the most specialized teeth and muscular systems. Two years before Darwin's theory was published, Agassiz wrote "An Essay on Classification," in which he asserted that the plan of creation was the "free conception" of an all-powerful intelligence in accordance with a predetermined pattern for each of the species, which, he argued, were destined to remain changeless.

Agassiz became Darwin's most formidable opponent in the United States. His studies of fossils led him to conclude that the changes which animals undergo during their embryonic growth coincide with the order of succession of the fossils of the same type in past geological ages. He believed that all species had been immutable since their creation. From time to time, the Creator may have annihilated old species and created new ones. His exhibits at the Harvard museum were intended to reflect the permanence of the species.

Agassiz regarded himself as the "librarian of the works of God," but he was not a theologian and gave no support to those ministers who parroted his responses to Darwin. He claimed that in Europe he was accused of deriving his scientific ideas from the Church and in the United States he was regarded as an infidel because he would not let churchmen pat him on the head. Agassiz believed that there was a creator and even went so far as to posit a multiple creation theory. He claimed that blacks were created separately and were a different species from whites, an argument which gave great comfort to the defenders of slavery in the South.

Only a few American scientists, such as his Harvard colleague Asa Gray, dared to take open issue with the erudite and popular Agassiz before his death. Gray argued that the species had originated in a single creative act and that their variations were the result of causes such as climate, geographical isolation, and the phenomena described by the same glacial theory that Agassiz had done so much to establish.

Agassiz became an American citizen in 1861 and continued his opposition to Darwinism. He fought a losing battle for fifteen years with the Darwinists and went to his grave denying the reality of evolution. His last article, published posthumously in the *Atlantic Monthly* (1874), was entitled "Evolution and the Permanence of Type."

Agassiz was appointed a visiting professor at Cornell in 1868, but the following year he suffered a stroke. Although this slowed him considerably, he continued his strenuous schedule of speaking and writing. In 1872, he sailed on board a coastal survey ship from Boston around the horn to San Francisco. The trip was disappointing, since Agassiz was unable to make the scientific progress he had hoped on the voyage. In 1873, John Anderson of New York deeded the island of Penikese in Buzzards Bay off the coast of Massachusetts and gave fifty thousand dollars to help Agassiz create a summer school for science teachers. The Anderson School of Natural History became the forerunner of the Woods Hole Biological Institute.

Summary

Louis Agassiz was the man who made America nature-conscious. He was a major figure in American nineteenth century culture, in the fields of both literature and science. He assumed that the organization of nature was everyone's concern and that each community should collect and identify the elements of its own zoology and botany.

Agassiz would appear to have been the most likely to champion the theory of evolution, particularly with his vast knowledge of paleontology and embryology. Instead, he chose to do battle with the evolutionists and to maintain stoutly his belief in the unchanging forms of created species. In his *Methods of Study in Natural History* (1863), Agassiz wrote: "I have devoted my whole life to the study of Nature, and yet a single sentence may express all that I have done. I have shown that there is a correspondence between the succession of Fishes in geological times and the different stages of their growth in the egg,—this is all."

Agassiz had done much more than he modestly claimed. In the age of Chautauqua speakers, he was a spellbinder. Above all, he was a teacher who was not only a dedicated scholar but also a friend to his students. With all of his talents as lecturer and author, he might have been a wealthy man, but he remained in debt all of his life and even mortgaged his house to support the museum at Harvard.

Agassiz wished above all to be remembered as a teacher. When he died in 1873, an unshaped boulder brought from the glacier of the Aar marked his grave at Boston's Mount Auburn Cemetery. On it were carved the words he had requested: "Agassiz the Teacher."

Bibliography

Agassiz, Louis. *Studies on Glaciers: Preceded by the Discourses of Neuchatel*. Translated and edited by Albert V. Carozzi. New York: Hafner Press, 1967. Carozzi's introduction is excellent. Included is a reprint of the atlas which Agassiz used.

Baird, Spencer Fullerton. *Correspondence Between Spencer Fullerton Baird and Louis Agassiz—Two Pioneer American Naturalists*. Edited by Elmer Charles Herber. Washington, D.C.: Smithsonian, 1964. Baird was the editor of the papers of the Smithsonian Institution and carried on extensive correspondence with Agassiz. The letters contained the latest news on discoveries in natural history.

Cooper, Lane. *Louis Agassiz as a Teacher*. Ithaca, N.Y.: Comstock, 1917. An excellent account of Agassiz's expertise as a teacher. Included are many anecdotes of classroom experiences, told by students.

Davenport, Guy, ed. *The Intelligence of Agassiz: A Specimen Book of Scientific Writings*. Boston: Beacon Press, 1963. The foreword by Alfred Romer is an excellent overview of the work of Agassiz. Davenport has selected Agassiz's most incisive works and introduces each with a skill which makes this slim volume invaluable.

Lurie, Edward. *Louis Agassiz: A Life in Science*. Chicago: University of Chicago Press, 1960. A persuasive interpretation of Agassiz and an exhaustive study of his papers. Lurie acknowledges Agassiz's weaknesses and pictures a genius with faults.

Marcou, Jules. *Life, Letters, and Works of Louis Agassiz*. 2 vols. New York: Macmillan, 1896. Valuable for range and accuracy of details, including an annotated list of American and European publications concerning Agassiz. Also included is a complete catalog of his 425 scientific papers.

Tharp, Louise Hall. *Adventurous Alliance: The Story of the Agassiz Family of Boston*. Boston: Little, Brown and Co., 1960. An account of the personal lives of Agassiz and his second wife, Elizabeth. An interesting story which relates something of the background of late nineteenth century Boston society. Also a treatise on education.

Raymond Lee Muncy

MUHAMMAD ALI
Cassius Marcellus Clay, Jr.

Born: January 17, 1942; Louisville, Kentucky

Area of Achievement: Boxing

Contribution: Ali is probably the greatest as well as the best-recognized sports personality of the twentieth century. He brought heavyweight boxing matches to areas of the world never before regarded as important in boxing circles.

Early Life

Cassius Marcellus Clay, Jr., was born in Louisville, Kentucky, on January 17, 1942, the son of Cassius Marcellus Clay, Sr., and Odetta Lee Grady Clay. His father was a commercial artist specializing in sign painting; he also painted murals for churches and taverns. His mother sometimes worked as a domestic for four dollars a day to help support the family. Some of the Clays trace their name to Ali's great-great-grandfather, who was a slave of Cassius Marcellus Clay, a relative of Henry Clay and ambassador to Russia in the 1860's.

Ali became involved in boxing at an early age. Unlike most boxers, however, he was reared in a lower-middle-class environment. His father often remarked that eating and sleeping were Ali's two most strenuous activities. Ali's bicycle was stolen when he was twelve. The boy reported the theft to a Louisville policeman who gave boxing lessons in a gymnasium operated in Ali's neighborhood. This white policeman, Joe Elsby Martin, was to guide Ali through most of his outstanding amateur boxing career. After six weeks of boxing lessons, Ali had his first fight, weighing in at eighty-nine pounds. He won a split decision and was regarded as an average boxer at that time. Yet two characteristics had already manifested themselves in Ali, his dedication to his newfound interest, a dedication to make himself into "the greatest" (a slogan he adopted relatively early in his career), and his propensity toward talking back to people, particularly his detractors. He was known as a smart aleck, a sassy person.

Ali attended Du Valle Junior High School and was graduated from Central High School in Louisville, 376 in his class of 391. He was known more for his marble-shooting and rock-throwing prowess than for any interest in academics. Ali's first exposure came in Louisville, when he was booked for fights on "Tomorrow's Champions," a local weekly television boxing show. By this time, he was also training four hours a day under Fred Stoner, a black trainer at the Grace Community Center, a gymnasium in the all-black section of Louisville. Ali later said that Stoner molded his style, his stamina, and his system.

During his illustrious amateur career, Ali won one hundred of 108 fights, six Kentucky Golden Gloves championships, and two national Amateur Athletic Union championships. During his last two years as an amateur, he lost only once, to Amos Johnson in the 1959 Pan-American Games trials. By this time, he wanted to box professionally, but Martin convinced him to remain an amateur and enter the 1960 Olympics, as this would give him national recognition and ensure his professional success. Ali, who was already advertising himself as the next heavyweight champion of the world, stopped off in New York City on the way to the Olympic Games in Rome and visited Madison Square Garden, then the mecca of professional boxing. He won the light-heavyweight title at the Olympics and returned to the United States in triumph. Soon afterward, however, he was refused service in a restaurant in his hometown and had to fight a white motorcycle gang leader to escape from the restaurant. This incident so embittered him that he threw his Olympic Gold Medal into the Ohio River.

When Ali turned to professional boxing in 1960, he was already six feet, three inches tall. In his heyday, he weighed more than two hundred pounds, usually weighing in at around 220 pounds. Ali did not look like a boxer. His rather large, round face was unmarked, and he was not muscle-bound. Body-building has long been anathema to boxers; heavy surface muscles restrict the movement of hands and arms, and Ali's forte already was speed and defense in the ring. Indeed, one of his most celebrated slogans was "Float like a butterfly, sting like a bee."

Three days before his first professional fight, on October 29, 1960, Ali signed a contract with eleven white businessmen from Louisville and New York City. These men were willing to invest in a potential heavyweight champion. Known as the Louisville Sponsoring Group, it was headed by William Faversham, Jr., vice president of the Brown-Forman Distillers Corporation. Ali received a ten-thousand-dollar bonus for signing, a salary of four thousand dollars annually for the first two years and six thousand dollars annually for the following four years, as well as having all of his expenses paid. He was also to receive fifty percent of all of his earnings.

Ali began his professional training under former light-heavyweight champion Archie Moore. Angelo Dundee soon supplanted Moore, also becoming Ali's *de facto* manager during Ali's early professional career. Angelo was calm under fire and saved Ali's championship at least twice. He was an excellent cornerman who had come up through the ranks. His brother, Chris Dundee, was at the time promoting a weekly fight card on Miami Beach. Angelo joined Chris, and they established their training headquarters on the second floor of a two-story building on the corner of Fifth Street and Washington Avenue, in Miami Beach. This gymnasium later became known as the Fifth Street Gym and was probably the best-known and most respected training center in the United States.

Ali won his first seven fights as a professional, beginning with the defeating of Tunney Hunsaker. Some of his early fights were held in Louisville, and his first national television exposure was against Alonzo Johnson. Johnson was then twenty-seven years old and an experienced boxer. The bout, televised by the National Broadcasting Company (NBC) on the Gillette Cavalcade of Sports, was a difficult one for Ali, but he won and was on his way.

Ali was soon showing all the braggadocio for which he became noted: talking constantly to confuse his opponents, writing short ditties deriding them, and predicting the round in which he would stop them. There was, however, a method to his madness. His behavior increased the spectators' enthusiasm for his fights and brought him fame and fortune, along with derision. It is said that Ali had watched the antics of Gorgeous George, one of the first truly flamboyant wrestlers to appear on television, noting his ability to enrage most of the spectators at his matches. Yet these same spectators paid as much money for tickets to see George lose as did his fans to see him win. Fifty percent of all revenue from fights was still coming to Ali. More than twelve thousand people came to see him knock out Alejandro Lavorante, in California, in five rounds, and his fight with Archie Moore in California in November, 1962, drew more than sixteen thousand people. In March, 1963, he fought Doug Jones in Madison Square Garden, filling it for the first time in more than a decade; more than eighteen thousand people came to see him win or lose, paying $105,000 for this privilege. Ali then went to England to box British heavyweight champion Henry Cooper. Ali predicted a fifth-round knockout of Cooper, but late in the third round, Cooper knocked Ali down and stunned him. Dundee, however, noticed that one of Ali's gloves was split, and the extra minutes needed to fix it enabled Ali to clear his head. Cooper's propensity to be cut easily allowed Ali to win by a technical knockout in the fifth round, as he had predicted.

Life's Work

Ali finally had the opportunity to fight for the heavyweight championship of the world. Sonny Liston was then regarded as the quintessential champion and was a prohibitive favorite to retain his crown. Yet at the weigh-in before the fight in Miami Beach on February 25, 1964, Ali distracted Liston with a carefully rehearsed display of hysteria and paranoia. During the fight, he taunted Liston and, using his superior speed and longer reach, peppered Liston with long-range jabs and right-hand punches. He so wore down his opponent that Liston was unable to answer the bell for the seventh round. Ali was declared the heavyweight champion of the world. In a return match with Liston, held in Lewiston, Maine, on May 25, 1965, Ali knocked him out with a very quick right-hand punch in the first round. He next defeated the former champion, Floyd Patterson, winning a technical knockout in the twelfth round, in Las Vegas, Nevada. Many believed that Ali could have ended the fight earlier, but that he chose instead to bait and mock Patterson unmercifully. In 1966, he stopped all five of his challengers. Only one, George Chavallo, went the distance. Early in 1967, he defeated Ernie Terrell and was recognized as the undisputed heavyweight champion. Only one month later, he knocked out Zora Folley.

By this time, Ali's activities beyond the ring were receiving more notoriety than were his successful title defenses. Immediately after he won the championship from Liston, he announced that he had joined the black nationalist Nation of Islam and changed his name from Cassius Clay to Muhammad Ali. Popularly known as the Black Muslims, the sect was regarded then by white America as a dangerous and subversive antiwhite group. Also, Ali had been married twice by this time. His first marriage to Sonje Roi, was dissolved in 1966. His second marriage was to Belinda Boyd (Khalilah Toloria), who bore him four children. He wooed Belinda when she was seventeen years old and was working in a Chicago Nation of Islam bakery. They were divorced in 1977. He was married a third time, to Veronica Porche, in 1977. This third marriage produced two children.

Many whites began to compare Ali to the former champion Jack Johnson, a black boxer who had defied the stereotypes of his time by living a fast and integrated life. This comparison was ironic, for Ali was probably the best-trained heavyweight champion of all time, and he neither smoked nor drank. In 1966, the Selective Service Board reclassified him as 1-A, thus removing his deferred status of 1-Y. Ali then appealed, citing conscientious-objector status on religious grounds. He formally refused induction into the army on April 18, 1967. The World Boxing Association then stripped him of his championship, as did the New York Athletic Commission. Thus, for three years, during what was the prime of his athletic life, Ali was unable to fight. In 1970, however, a federal court ruled that the revocation of his license was arbitrary and unreasonable, and Ali was able to resume his career.

Against all odds, Ali again won the heavyweight championship. After two losses and fifteen wins, he faced George Foreman for the title in Kinshasa, Zaire, Africa, on October 30, 1974, in what became known as the "Rumble in the Jungle." Here he used his "rope-a-dope" tactics, lying back on the ring ropes and letting Foreman tire himself out. Only his superior hand speed and movement enabled him to do this. Foreman was knocked out in the eighth round. During this period, Ali lived very well, with Belinda, his second wife, on what was described as a baronial, four-and-a-half-acre estate, with a three-car garage containing his-and-hers Rolls Royces. During this period, Ali successfully defended his title against Joe Frazier, in what became known as the "Thrilla in Manila." Yet Ali's skills were waning; after barely defeating two mediocre boxers, he lost his crown to Leon Spinks in Las Vegas, Nevada, on February 15, 1978. Summoning all of his strength, Ali trained hard for a rematch, winning the title for an unprecedented third time on

September 15, 1978. His last fight he lost to Larry Holmes in October, 1980.

Ali's record includes fifty-six victories and five defeats. During his career, he earned more than fifty million dollars. Much of this money went for taxes, an expensive life-style, and divorces; a third of it went to Herbert Muhammad, who became Ali's manager of record in 1966. By the 1980's Ali was showing signs of mental and physical decay, the result of a disease that caused symptoms similar to Parkinson's disease, not as some conjectured, from brain damage resulting from his fights.

Summary

Muhammad Ali is America's premier heavyweight champion of all time. He is credited with reviving interest in boxing and helping to promote international acceptance for the sport. His fights in Zaire and Manila made him history's most recognized boxer. Nevertheless, his stand for the principles in which he believed cost him dearly. Most Americans came to admire him for his courage, if not for his beliefs.

Bibliography

Brenner, Teddy, and Barney Nagler. *Only the Ring Was Square*. Englewood Cliffs, N.J.: Prentice-Hall, 1981. Typical breezy sports biography, but with interesting sidelights into Ali's career.

Frazier, Joe. "Cassius Who?" *Ebony* 27 (May, 1972): 68-72. By one of Ali's greatest opponents, in the famous "Thrilla in Manila." An anti-Ali diatribe, claiming that Frazier was responsible for Ali's success.

"The Greatest Is Gone." *Time* 111 (February 27, 1978): 72-75. Good synopsis of Ali's boxing life, written just after he had lost his title to Leon Spinks. Imparts a good understanding of the boxer's milieu.

Greene, Bob. "Muhammad Ali Is the Most Famous Man in The World." *Esquire* 100 (December, 1983): 134-136. Tidbits of Ali's later life and a synopsis of Ali's career in an appendix labeled "Dossier."

Massaquoi, Hans J. "The Private World of Muhammad Ali." *Ebony* 27 (September, 1972): 144-148. Depicts the opulent life-style of Ali when he was still fighting. Provides many examples of Ali's beliefs on various aspects of life, especially on women's rights.

Pacheco, Freddy. *Fight Doctor*. New York: Simon and Schuster, 1983. Pacheco was Ali's physician, who split with him shortly before Ali's first fight with Leon Spinks. He was the first to notice deterioration in Ali's physical and mental well-being and the first to advise Ali to quit the ring.

Smith, Gary. "After the Fall." *Sports Illustrated* 61 (October 8, 1984): 62-80. Ten years after the Foreman-Ali fight in Zaire in 1974, Smith discusses Ali's religious beliefs and his problems with his health.

Henry S. Marks

JOHN PETER ALTGELD

Born: December 30, 1847; Niederselters, Prussia
Died: March 12, 1902; Joliet, Illinois
Area of Achievement: Statesmanship
Contribution: Altgeld furnished American political life with a high standard of moral courage and, during a crucial historical period, helped to establish the principle that maintenance of the welfare of society is an obligation of government.

Early Life

John Peter Altgeld was born December 30, 1847, in Niederselters, in the Prussian province of Nassau, the eldest son of a wagon-maker, also named John Peter Altgeld, and his wife, Mary Lanehart. The family came to the United States in the spring of the following year, and Altgeld grew up on farms near Mansfield, Ohio. Because his father was against the idea of education for his children, Altgeld attended country schools for only three terms. When he was sixteen, he enlisted in an Ohio militia regiment and was sent to Virginia. There, he contracted a fever which permanently damaged his health, but he refused to be sent home and finished out the hundred days for which the regiment had been mustered.

When he returned to Ohio, Altgeld, much against his father's wishes, attended high school in Mansfield and a teacher-training school in Lexington, Ohio, and taught school for a time. Until he was twenty-one, he turned over all of his wages to his father, but in the spring of 1869, perhaps because the parents of Emma Ford would not permit her to marry him, he headed west on foot, working on farms as he went. He arrived finally in St. Louis with only fifteen cents, worked there for a time in a chemical plant, and later worked on a railroad that was being built in southern Kansas. When a recurrence of his fever forced him to quit, he went to northwestern Missouri, most of the way on foot. Dressed in rags, he collapsed at a farm near Savannah, Missouri, and was taken in by a farmer who restored him to health and gave him work. Later, he taught school and read law, and in April, 1871, was admitted to the bar and began legal practice in Savannah. He had not revealed any interest in politics until this time, beyond a devotion to the ideals of Thomas Jefferson, but he served as city attorney for Savannah for a year and ran successfully as the Populist candidate for prosecuting attorney of Andrew County in 1874.

For reasons which remain obscure, Altgeld resigned this office after a year and, with only one hundred dollars, moved to Chicago. There he established a law practice, and in 1877, on a visit to his parents in Ohio, he married Emma Ford. During the next years, Altgeld achieved great success investing in Chicago real estate and in 1890 held property valued at a million dollars.

Life's Work

In 1884, Altgeld was the unsuccessful Democratic candidate for Congress in the traditionally Republican Fourth District. At this time, he was an apparent conservative in politics and part of the Chicago economic establishment. In the same year, however, he published *Our Penal Machinery and Its Victims*, which revealed many of the ideas for reform that he sought to implement later in his political career. The book pleaded for the elimination of the causes of crime and the rehabilitation of criminals, and it condemned police brutality against vagrants. In 1886, in the immediate wake of the Haymarket Riot, he wrote a newspaper article in which he argued for the compulsory arbitration of strikes.

That year, he ran successfully for judge of the Cook County Superior Court, serving for five years. Apparently Altgeld regarded the judgeship as the first step toward his ultimate goal—a seat in the United States Senate, the highest office possible for him because of his foreign birth. When he resigned his judgeship and failed to win election to the Senate, he embarked on his greatest project in real estate—the construction of the sixteen-story Unity Block, at that time one of Chicago's greatest buildings.

In 1892, he was nominated by the Democrats for the Illinois governorship, probably more for his success as a businessman than for any stand he had taken on social issues. In this campaign, he revealed the strict ethics and liberal instincts for which his followers admired him, mixed with a real hunger for power and an occasional tendency to political chicanery. As the first Democratic governor of Illinois in forty years, Altgeld cleared out all the Republicans in state government, and though many of his replacements were brilliant, he fired some able Republicans and appointed some incompetent Democrats.

In the aftermath of the Haymarket Riot, when a bomb killed several policemen, eight anarchists had been sentenced to death; one of them committed suicide in prison, and four others were hanged. The sentences of the other three—Samuel Fielden, Michael Schwab, and Oscar Neebe—had been commuted to life imprisonment. Altgeld's supporters expected him to pardon these three men and assumed that he would be motivated only by feelings of mercy. Yet when the pardons were issued on June 26, 1893, it was clear that though he detested anarchism, he was convinced that the eight men had been convicted not for their deeds but for their opinions, that the jury had been impaneled improperly, that the judge was prejudiced, and that five of the accused were, in effect, the victims of judicial murder. Altgeld issued a pamphlet of eighteen thousand words in which he presented his arguments with great clarity and logic, but this explanation could not allay the storm of abuse which fell upon him for his act. Those who had favored the sentences now raged at him in virtually every newspaper in the country, and those who had favored a pardon were angered that he had issued an absolute pardon and that the pamphlet exposed the errors of the judicial system itself. Altgeld was accused of being an anarchist; this was said by many editorialists to be the result of his foreign birth.

The charge that he was an anarchist seems absurd when one considers his use of the Illinois militia during the labor troubles of his term as governor. Only two weeks before he issued the pardons, he sent the militia to Lemont in response to a plea from local authorities that they could not maintain order in a labor dispute. In June, 1894, he sent the militia to Mount Olive, where striking miners were interfering with mail trains. These affirmations of the power of the state did not satisfy his enemies, because, unlike his pre-decessors, Altgeld used the militia only to maintain order, not to break the strikes.

This was one of several issues that led to Altgeld's break with President Grover Cleveland. In July, 1894, when the Pullman Company had locked out its employees and federal troops had been dispatched by Cleveland to break the "strike," Altgeld, in a letter to the president, condemned his action on the grounds that sufficient Illinois militia were available on the scene to pre-serve order. The Chicago newspapers, still harping on Altgeld's supposed anarchism, wildly denounced him for this protest, but in fact violence did not occur until the federal troops arrived, and then Chicago police and the state militia put it down. In fact, the disorder actually ended when a company of Altgeld's militia killed seven men by firing point-blank into a mob.

This dispute was only one of Altgeld's quarrels with the president. Altgeld saw Cleveland as an unquestioning supporter of "government by injunction," the use of the courts to rule strikes illegal, and he condemned the Supreme Court when it struck down the federal income tax in 1894, in an opinion writ-ten by Cleveland's appointee, Chief Justice Melville Fuller. Altgeld saw little difference between Republicans and Cleveland Democrats on the tariff ques-tion or on the silver issue. By thorough study, he made himself the outstand-ing authority on the latter question in American public life, and he embraced the silver issue in 1895, calling for the coinage of silver to increase the money supply. By this time, in spite of the campaign of vilification against him in the press for the Haymarket pardons and his stand on the Pullman dispute, Altgeld was the most influential Democrat in the country. With the laboring class throughout the country, he enjoyed an affection which verged on idola-try, and his stand on silver gave him a large following in the West and South. As a result, there is little reason to doubt that, had it not been for his foreign birth, he would have been the Democratic nominee for president in 1896.

As it was, he was clearly the master of the Democratic convention of that year. The platform reflected his views—free coinage of silver and gold at a ratio of sixteen to one, opposition to government by injunction, arbitration of labor disputes involving interstate commerce, protection of the rights of labor, and an income tax. While he did not favor the nomination of William

Jennings Bryan, Altgeld worked mightily for his election, even at the expense of his own reelection campaign. He did not want another term as governor—his finances had suffered from the economic depression of the time, and his health was bad—but he bowed to the party's wishes. The Republican strategy, in the face of a national trend away from the gold standard, was to depict Bryan as the tool of the "anarchist" and communist Altgeld. Not for the last time in the nation's history, political profit was made from calling an opponent a communist. On October 17, 1896, in a great speech at Cooper Union, Altgeld took the fight to the enemy, arguing against government by injunction and against federal interference in the rights of states to maintain order within their own borders. Throughout the campaign, he literally rose from a sickbed to speak, sometimes seven or eight times a day.

In the Bryan debacle, Altgeld's defeat for reelection was probably inevitable, and he was defeated in the legislature as a candidate for the United States Senate. He returned to Chicago to attempt to rebuild his shattered finances, but he lost control of the Unity Building and returned to the practice of law. As governor, he had rejected a bribe of a half-million dollars from the Chicago traction magnate Charles Yerkes, and he had always favored public ownership of monopolies. On this platform, he ran unsuccessfully as an independent for mayor in 1899.

In the 1900 presidential campaign, Altgeld was still a powerful influence, as was evident in the Democratic Party's repetition of its 1896 stand on the silver issue, and he campaigned with great energy for Bryan. At this time, he was also condemning American policy in the Philippines. He died suddenly on March 12, 1902, a few hours after making a speech which condemned the treatment of Boer women and children in British concentration camps in South Africa.

Summary

During his governorship, John Peter Altgeld achieved much for Illinois in the improvement of existing state institutions and the building of others, and his use of the state's police power to preserve order reflected a deep conservative respect for the rights of property, contrary to the charge of anarchism leveled against him by journalistic hacks and by politicians who must have known better. His pardoning of Samuel Fielden, Michael Schwab, and Oscar Neebe, an act of courage with few parallels in American political life, was consistent with his stands on social and economic issues—stands which have been vindicated by history. In 1896, he forced the Democratic Party to commit itself for the first time to social reform, and the achievements of the Progressive era and the New Deal were the fruits of the seeds he planted. Indeed, it is an irony of history that Altgeld is forgotten by most Americans, while Theodore Roosevelt, who once in a foolish speech called him an apologist for wholesale murder, is a hero of American Progressivism because he enacted much of Altgeld's program. Altgeld remains what Vachel Lindsay called the "wise man, that kindled the flame."

Bibliography

Barnard, Harry. *Eagle Forgotten: The Life of John Peter Altgeld*. Indianapolis: Bobbs-Merrill, 1938. The definitive biography of Altgeld, not likely to be superseded, and the basic source for information on his early years.

Browne, Waldo R. *Altgeld of Illinois*. New York: B. W. Huebsch, 1924. The first biography of Altgeld, written out of profound respect for its subject and informed by a deep sense of social justice. Lacks a thorough account of Altgeld's pre-Chicago years. Valuable, though superseded by Barnard's biography.

Christman, Henry M., ed. *The Mind and Spirit of John Peter Altgeld*. Urbana: University of Illinois Press, 1960. Includes a useful though brief biographical account and a representative selection of Altgeld's writings, including the Cooper Union speech of 1896 and "Reasons for Pardoning Fielden, Neebe, and Schwab."

Ginger, Ray. *Altgeld's America*. New York: Funk and Wagnall's Co., 1958. A thorough study of Altgeld's achievements in developing a progressivism which would adapt American political idealism to modern industrial conditions.

Whitlock, Brand. *Forty Years of It*. New York: D. Appleton and Co., 1925. Whitlock served in the Illinois government during Altgeld's governorship and was his close associate. This autobiography provides a firsthand account of events surrounding the Haymarket pardons and the Pullman dispute.

Wish, Harvey. "Altgeld and the Progressive Tradition." *American Historical Review* 46 (July, 1941): 813-831. Emphasizes the progressivism of Altgeld's social and economic beliefs. Puts his career in a perspective which is frequently lacking in those accounts which concentrate on his role in the Haymarket case.

Robert L. Berner

MARIAN ANDERSON

Born: February 27, 1902; Philadelphia, Pennsylvania

Area of Achievement: Music
Contribution: Anderson was a world-renowned contralto. Her career has come to have symbolic meaning in the battle against racial prejudice.

Early Life
Marian Anderson was born February 27, 1902, in a black residential section of Philadelphia, Pennsylvania. Her father, John, sold ice and coal, and her mother, Anna, supplemented the modest family income by doing laundry. The family was active in the Union Baptist Church in Philadelphia, and Marian, at age six, was enrolled in its junior choir. She later joined the senior choir, demonstrating the range of her voice by singing all vocal parts. The church afforded many singing opportunities for Anderson, including travel with its choir.

While a student at South Philadelphia High School, she began to accompany herself on piano and appeared at various black college and church functions. Anderson's first voice lessons were with Mary S. Patterson. Through Patterson she was introduced to the music of Franz Schubert and began work with her first accompanist. Monies raised by the Philadelphia Choral Society enabled Anderson to continue study with contralto Agnes Reifsnyder. Prior to her high school graduation, she was accepted as a pupil with Giuseppe Boghetti. She began a wide range of music studies, including French and Italian arias.

Anderson and her accompanist expanded their touring after she was graduated. Practice was difficult on these early tours, as she was obliged to stay in private homes. She was very sensitive about disturbing her hosts; much of her time was spent with the host's neighbors and friends. At this early age, she was developing the regal, commanding physical presence that later reviewers would note.

At age twenty, Anderson considered giving up her career after a debut at New York Town Hall. The reviews were unfavorable and she did not yet have sufficient command of German to sing lieder. With her mother's encouragement, she overcame her despair, resuming the touring and lessons.

Two triumphs came in 1923 and 1925. The first was winning a contest sponsored by the Philharmonic Society; the second was winning first prize in a contest held at Lewisohn Stadium. She was chosen, out of three hundred competitors, to appear with the New York Philharmonic.

Anderson had a new tutor, Frank LaForge, and was under the management of Arthur Judson. She now had many engagements and received higher fees; she also, however, had to compete with well-established singers.

Acknowledging that she was accepting the same engagements each year and that her command of German needed improvement, she decided to go abroad. She won a scholarship from the National Association of Negro Musicians and in 1926 sailed to England aboard the *Île de France*.

Life's Work

Anderson made many trips abroad, interspersed with American concert commitments, during her career. In 1929, she returned to New York for an engagement at Carnegie Hall. In 1930, she appeared at London's Wigmore Hall. She won a Julius Rosenwald scholarship, which enabled her to study abroad through 1933. She toured the Continent, spending considerable time in the Scandinavian countries, giving more than one hundred concerts in those countries. These tours were a great success; the Finnish composer Jean Sibelius dedicated his song "Solitude" to her. She gathered further esteem at the 1935 Mozarteum in Salzburg, Austria, when Arturo Toscanini described her voice as one that came along only once in a hundred years.

The year 1935 also marked the beginning of Anderson's association with impresario Solomon Hurok and her second debut at New York Town Hall. Hurok, on the spur of the moment, had attended her Paris recital at the Salle Gaveau. He signed her to an exclusive contract and was her manager for the remainder of her career. The second Town Hall appearance, December 31, 1935, revealed the progress Anderson had made. In this concert, the full range of her voice was presented, and the reviews were superb. The drama of the recital was heightened because Anderson sang with a cast around her ankle, which she had broken on the journey back to the United States. Later concerts at Carnegie Hall were equally successful. Anderson's perseverance as a student and public performer in Europe had proved its worth.

Her reputation assured, Anderson began, in 1936, touring Europe, Africa, South America, Russia, and the United States. In that year, she also made an appearance before President and Mrs. Franklin D. Roosevelt. She began an intensive concert tour in the 1937-1938 season, giving seventy concerts in the United States, including the Southern states. The following season, she gave seventy-five concerts in sixty cities.

Anderson was catapulted to national attention in 1939. The Daughters of the American Revolution refused to allow her to sing in its headquarters, Constitution Hall in Washington, D.C. Protests came from many leading figures, including Eleanor Roosevelt, who resigned from the organization. The United States government offered the Lincoln Memorial as an alternate site. There, on Easter Sunday, April 9, 1939, Marian Anderson sang before a crowd of seventy-five thousand people. The concert, an emotional and significant event, included Schubert's *Ave Maria* (1825) and a selection of black spirituals.

Anderson was awarded the Spingarn Medal in 1939; the Bok Award followed in 1940, allowing her to establish the Marian Anderson Award for talented singers. In 1943, she married Orpheus K. Fisher, an architect. In 1955, at the age of fifty-three, she became the first black soloist at New York's Metropolitan Opera. The 1955 debut cast her in the role of Ulrica from Giuseppe Verdi's *A Masked Ball* (1857-1858). When she appeared on stage, she received a standing ovation.

Anderson became an emissary of the State Department in 1957 and made a concert tour of India and the Far East. In 1958, she was a delegate to the Thirteenth General Assembly of the United Nations. She sang at President John F. Kennedy's inaugural ball in 1963 and was awarded the Presidential Medal of Freedom by Lyndon B. Johnson. She made farewell tours in the United States and abroad in 1964-1965, retiring in 1965.

Anderson was awarded numerous honorary degrees and decorations from foreign governments. A tribute to her seventy-fifth birthday was held at Carnegie Hall; singers included Leontyne Price, who ended the program with Anderson's favorite, "He's Got the Whole World in His Hands." She said that the happiest day of her life was August 22, 1979, Marian Anderson Day in Philadelphia. In 1982, black singers Grace Bumbry and Shirley Verrett gave a joint recital at Carnegie Hall to honor her. She was chosen in 1986 by President Ronald Reagan to receive the National Medal of Arts.

Millions of listeners heard the voice of Marian Anderson; it was estimated in 1950 that she had performed before four million people. Her voice, compared to velvet, had a range of more than three octaves. Her repertoire included the song literature of Johann Sebastian Bach, Johannes Brahms, Ludwig van Beethoven, George Frideric Handel, Schubert, Gustav Mahler, and always, black spirituals.

Summary

Despite the success of black concert singer Roland Hayes, America of the 1920's and 1930's did not readily embrace black classical musicians. Marian Anderson dealt with formidable racial barriers: She was turned away by a music school, had to travel in the Jim Crow train car, and faced the reluctance of concert managers to book her on tours. Yet her church supported her career with funds and opportunities to sing. Her mother had instilled in her a deep faith that she could succeed. This she did in an era in America when vigorous protest against racism was unknown. The seriousness of her desire to sing, to achieve impeccable linguistic skills in her songs, and to broaden her repertoire strengthened her resolve to succeed. Anderson's long struggle to perfect her voice revealed her fortitude and inner strength.

Marian Anderson gave the world her singing and America a challenge to its racist attitudes. Her later role as an American goodwill ambassador was a fitting tribute to her endurance and grace.

Bibliography

Anderson, Marian. *My Lord, What a Morning*. New York: Viking Press, 1956. An endearing autobiography; reveals the determination of the author to become a serious classical singer. Balances the personal toll taken by her career with frank self-criticism and acknowledgment of support received from family, church, and coworkers. The author's even-tempered, philosophical personality in dealing with racism and balancing her career and home life shines through.

Hurok, Solomon, with Ruth Goode. *Impresario: A Memoir*. New York: Random House, 1946. Hurok, manager of opera, ballet, and theater stars, recounts his thirty-year career with clients such as Anna Pavlova, Isadora Duncan, and Marian Anderson. More than a manager, he shows himself a friend and champion of Anderson, smoothing her path in the era of segregation and plotting her career to her best advantage.

Klan, Barbara. "An Interview with Marian Anderson." *American Heritage* 27 (February, 1977): 51-57. Anderson's responses in this interview reflect little change in her overall philosophy since the 1956 autobiography. Answering standard questions about her career, she reveals that racist encounters, especially being turned away by a Philadelphia music school, made a permanent impression on her. Her relationship with Solomon Hurok is further explored here as well.

Lovell, John, Jr. *Black Song: The Forge and the Flame.* New York: Macmillan Publishing Co., 1972. This comprehensive study of the evolution of spirituals discusses their meaning and social impact and presents hundreds of examples of this distinctively American art form. Anderson is cited among artists who exposed audiences to spirituals on a national and international level. Includes the author's evaluation of Anderson's approach to this musical tradition.

Pleasants, Henry. *The Great Singers from the Dawn of Opera to Caruso*. New York: Simon and Schuster, 1966. Asserts that Anderson's slowness in achieving artistic maturity was the result of an inferior education. Comparing her early career to that of the sophisticated black tenor Roland Hayes, Pleasants shows the tremendous influence of the European tours. Offers a critical evaluation of Anderson's voice and its appeal in the course of this opinionated account of opera over three centuries.

Schonberg, Harold C. "A Bravo for Opera's Black Voices." *New York Times Magazine* (January 17, 1982): 24-27. A review of the 1982 joint concert of black stars Grace Bumbry and Shirley Verrett in honor of Marian Anderson. (It was Bumbry's 1961 role as Venus in *Tannhäuser* that again stirred racial prejudices in the opera world.) Interviewees say that while black classical singers are not shown overt prejudice, prejudice still exists.

Truman, Margaret. *Women of Courage*. New York: William Morrow and Co., 1976. Anderson is given as an example of one possessing fortitude in her career despite the hurdles of racial prejudice. A behind-the-scenes account of the rebuff by the Daughters of the American Revolution and Solomon Hurok's role in staging the appearance at Lincoln Memorial. A study of the evolution of women of courage in America, from frontier days to the twentieth century.

Vehanen, Kosti. *Marian Anderson: A Portrait.* New York: McGraw-Hill Book Co., 1941. Written by Anderson's accompanist from the start of her second Scandinavian tour until 1939. He urged her study of Scandinavian songs and arranged the meeting with Sibelius in Finland. Although disjointed, provides both a serious and whimsical account of their touring life and his contributions in perfecting her repertoire. A book by an unabashed admirer.

Sue Williams

SUSAN B. ANTHONY

Born: February 15, 1820; Adams, Massachusetts
Died: March 13, 1906; Rochester, New York
Area of Achievement: Women's rights
Contribution: A gifted and relentless worker for feminist causes, Anthony was for five decades the preeminent voice and inspiration of the women's suffrage movement.

Early Life

Susan Brownwell Anthony was born on February 15, 1820, in Adams, Massachusetts, the second child of Daniel and Lucy Read Anthony. Her mother, a sullen, withdrawn woman, grudgingly accepted her domestic role as housewife and mother of six. The girl loved but pitied her mother, and learned from her more what to avoid than emulate. Her father, in contrast, always loomed large in his daughter's eyes. A radical Quaker, Daniel Anthony was liberal in creed and illiberal toward those who tolerated the social evils that he so adamantly despised. Strong-willed and independent of mind, Daniel Anthony taught his children to be firm in their convictions and to demonstrate their love for God by working for human betterment.

As an owner of a small cotton mill, Daniel Anthony had the means to provide for his daughter's education. A precocious child, Anthony took full advantage of her opportunities, first attending the village school and later receiving private instruction from a tutor hired by her father. At age seventeen, Anthony left with her older sister Guelma for a Quaker boarding school in Philadelphia. Anthony's seminary training, however, was cut short by the Panic of 1837. With mounting business debts, Daniel Anthony was forced to auction his cotton mill, homestead, furniture, and even his personal belongings, and to relocate as a dirt farmer on a small tract of land outside Rochester, New York.

In response to the family crisis, Susan Anthony left boarding school, secured a teaching position, and began sending half of her two-dollar weekly salary home to the family. For the next decade, Anthony remained in the classroom, instructing her pupils in the three R's, even as she augmented her own education with extensive reading and study. Intelligent yet unpretentious, Anthony matured into an athletic, tall, and slender woman with thick brown hair and warm blue eyes. Hardly the ugly, unsexed "battle-axe" her future enemies portrayed her to be, Anthony was courted by several suitors and remained single largely because none of her admirers, in her opinion, equaled her father in character or conviction.

Like her father, Anthony was a reformer who yearned for a society free from the evils of slavery and alcoholism. An idealist but not a dreamer, Anthony worked actively in these reform efforts, serving during her twenties as president of the Canajoharie Daughters of Temperance. In 1849, at her father's request, Anthony resigned from teaching to take over management of the family farm near Rochester. This relocation enabled Daniel Anthony to devote his full attention to a new business venture (an insurance agency that eventually made him prosperous again). The move also allowed Anthony to commit herself more fully to reform activity.

Life's Work

While still a teacher in Canajoharie, Anthony read a newspaper account of a meeting in nearby Seneca Falls, where a group of sixty-eight women and thirty-two men issued a Declaration of Women's Rights. This declaration demanded free education, equality of economic opportunity, free speech, the right to participate in public affairs, and the right to vote. As a schoolteacher making only one-third the salary of her male colleagues, Anthony sympathized with many of these demands for equal rights. Her Quaker upbringing, however, had convinced her that no person should participate in a government that waged war or condoned slavery, and she was thus not yet ready to take up the cause of women's suffrage.

In 1851, while attending an antislavery lecture in Seneca Falls, Anthony met the renowned Elizabeth Cady Stanton. The two women developed an instant friendship which led to a strong partnership in reform work. Together they organized the Woman's State Temperance Society of New York and petitioned the state legislature for a prohibition law. On numerous occasions during the 1850's, Anthony left Rochester for Seneca Falls to care for Stanton's children while their mother was away on speaking tours.

While agreeing with Stanton on most issues, Anthony for several years refrained from embracing Stanton's call for women's suffrage. Gradually, however, the arrogance and disregard of many male reformers for the rights of women altered Anthony's view. Finally, in 1853, after the male delegates of the New York Woman's Temperance Society monopolized the annual convention and rudely ousted Stanton as president, Anthony declared her full allegiance to the women's crusade for equal rights and political equality.

Anthony's political conversion brought new life to the fledgling women's movement. An experienced worker willing to assume the time-consuming chores that no one else wanted, Anthony labored around the clock for feminist causes, organizing women into local associations, scheduling conventions and arranging speakers, seeking contributions, and paying administrative expenses. During the winter of 1854-1855, Anthony personally visited fifty-four of the sixty New York counties, collecting signatures in support of legal rights for married women. When the legislature failed to act, Anthony promised to return with petitions every year until the inequities were rectified. For five years the tireless Anthony kept her promise, and in 1860, following a stirring address by coworker Stanton, the New York legislature granted property and guardian rights to married women. Much to Anthony's and Stanton's dismay, however, two years later the same body repealed portions of the marriage reform bill. This setback confirmed what Anthony had been saying for a decade: Benevolent legislation alone was insufficient; women would be fully protected only when they enjoyed full political powers.

For Anthony and her associates, the decade of the 1860's was eventful but largely disappointing. Before the Civil War, Anthony campaigned hard for the American Anti-Slavery Society, and during the war she helped establish the Women's Loyalty League to lobby for a constitutional amendment that would abolish slavery and guarantee civil and political rights for all Americans. Yet, despite her lifelong commitment to black rights, after the war Anthony opposed both the wording of the Fourteenth Amendment, because it inserted the word "male" in reference to citizen's rights, and the Fifteenth Amendment, for its failure to include the word "sex" in protecting voting rights for all citizens. Berated by her former allies, who insisted that women must not endanger the long-awaited liberation of blacks with additional demands for women's rights, Anthony countered the accusations by asserting that if reformers linked these two great causes, then the moment in history called by some "the Negro's hour" could be the woman's hour as well. This controversy ultimately split the women's movement. Following an explosive Equal Rights Association convention in 1869, Anthony and Stanton organized the National Woman Suffrage Association (a "for women only" organization committed to the passage of a national woman's suffrage amendment), while the more conservative reformers established the American Woman Suffrage Association (a rival body that focused its efforts at the state rather than the national level).

At this time, Anthony's commitment to feminist goals did not deter her from other reform activities. In 1868, Anthony organized the Working Woman's Association in a futile attempt to unionize woman workers and build female solidarity across class lines. In the same year, Anthony and Stanton allied themselves with the eccentric millionaire George Francis Train and began publishing a radical newspaper entitled *The Revolution*. On its masthead was the motto: "Principle, not policy; justice, not favors. Men, their rights, and nothing more: Women, their rights and nothing less." This paper, which opened its columns to editorials on greenback currency, divorce laws, prostitution, and a variety of other controversial issues, survived only two years, and left Anthony with a debt of ten thousand dollars. It took six years, but Anthony ultimately repaid the entire debt from income she gained delivering suffrage lectures on the Lyceum circuit. Following this experience, Anthony determined to disassociate herself from other controversial reforms and focus all of her energy on the crusade for woman's suffrage.

In 1872, Anthony gained national media attention when she registered and voted in the presidential election. Several weeks later, a federal marshall issued her an arrest warrant for illegal voting. While awaiting trial, Anthony went on a whirlwind tour delivering the lecture, "Is It a Crime for a U.S. Citizen to Vote?" Her defense was that the Fourteenth Amendment made her a citizen, and citizenship carried with it the right to vote. During her trial, the judge refused to allow her to testify on her own behalf, demanded the jury to render a guilty verdict, and fined her one hundred dollars. Outraged by this travesty of justice, thousands sent contributions to the NWSA treasury. Although she lost the trial, Anthony (who never paid the fine) won added respect for herself and her cause.

Anthony spent the last three decades of her life recruiting and training a new generation of suffragist leaders, including, among many others, Anna Howard Shaw and Carrie Chapman Catt. In 1889, at age sixty-nine, Anthony worked to secure a merger of the rival NWSA and AWSA. Three years later, she accepted the presidency of the unified National American Woman Suffrage Association, and served in this capacity until 1900, when she passed her mantle of leadership onto her hand-picked successors. As honorary president emeritus, Anthony remained the dominant figure in the movement until the time of her death in 1906.

Summary

When Anthony joined the women's rights movement at age thirty-three, women held little social, professional, or educational standing. They were denied the right to vote, to hold office, or to be tried by their peers. As wives, they lost their legal individuality, having no rights to inherit property, keep earnings, sign contracts, or claim more than one-third of their husbands' estates. As mothers, they lacked legal custody or control over their own children. By the time of Anthony's death, however, eighty percent of American colleges, universities, and professional schools admitted women. In many states women had legal control over their own earnings and property and, in case of divorce, generally were awarded custody of their children. Although much discrimination remained, reform legislation along with advances in the medical treatment of women had increased the life expectancy of women from forty to fifty-one years. In four states, women enjoyed full suffrage rights, and in the majority of the remaining states, women voted in school or municipal elections.

Many of these changes were in part a consequence of the Industrial Revolution, which freed many women from a portion of their domestic chores, created new opportunities for employment, and provided increasing numbers with the wealth and leisure to sponsor reform work. The improved status of American women, however, was also a result of the heroic efforts of individuals who endured decades of hardship and ridicule in their quest for equal rights. For more than half a century, Anthony campaigned tirelessly for feminist goals. A radical visionary, the "Napoleon of Feminism" was also a shrewd, practical politician who did more than any other reformer to change the minds of men toward women, and of women toward themselves. Although vilified throughout much of her career, by the time of her death Anthony was the heroine of a second generation of suffragists, who in 1920 would win the victory she had fought so hard to achieve.

Bibliography

Anthony, Katherine S. *Susan B. Anthony: Her Personal History and Her Era*. Garden City, N.Y.: Doubleday and Co., 1954. A detailed, although somewhat tedious, account of Anthony's career, with lengthy descriptions of her family ancestry in England, her parentage, and her many friends in the battle for women's rights.

Bryan, Florence H. *Susan B. Anthony: Champion of Women's Rights*. New York: Julian Messner, 1947. The best of the many biographies of Anthony geared for younger readers. Not overly fictionized.

Buhle, Mary Jo, and Paul Bulhe. *A Concise History of Woman Suffrage: Selections from the Classic Works of Stanton, Anthony, Gage and Harper*. Urbana: University of Illinois Press, 1978. An abridged volume of the basic sources of the women's suffrage movement. Provides useful selections from the writings of Anthony and other eminent suffrage leaders.

Dorr, Rheta L. *Susan B. Anthony: The Woman Who Changed the Mind of a Nation*. New York: Frederick A. Stokes Co., 1928. A dated, warmly partisan, and undocumented biography that portrays Anthony as a radical heroine. Weak coverage of Anthony's latter years. Despite its shortcomings, its lively prose makes this entertaining book worth reading.

Flexner, Eleanor. *Century of Struggle: The Woman's Rights Movement in the United States*. Cambridge, Mass.: Harvard University Press, 1959. An overview of the women's rights movement that offers insights into the intellectual origins of American feminism. It remains the standard history of the suffrage crusade.

Harper, Ida H. *The Life and Work of Susan B. Anthony*. 3 vols. Indianapolis: Bowen-Merrill Co., 1898-1908. The authoritative biography, written with Anthony's assistance. The only source for numerous Anthony papers that were destroyed after its publication.

Kugler, Israel. "The Trade Union Career of Susan B. Anthony." *Labor History* 6 (Winter, 1961): 90-100. An interesting and informative account of a little-known aspect of Anthony's career as a reformer.

Lutz, Alma. *Susan B. Anthony: Rebel, Crusader, Humanitarian*. Boston: Beacon Press, 1959. A well-documented, straightforward biography. Informative, but like the other dated biographies, it makes no attempt to penetrate beyond the surface record of events.

Riegel, Robert. *American Feminists*, Lawrence: University of Kansas Press, 1963. This collection of biographical essays on pioneer feminists attempts to analyze the factors that contributed to the rise of American feminism. The sketch on Anthony accentuates her shortcomings, portraying her as physically, mentally, and historically inferior to Elizabeth Cady Stanton.

Truman, Margaret. *Women of Courage*. New York: William Morrow and Co., 1976. A popular collection of biographical sketches of noted American women. The Anthony essay concentrates on her arrest, trial, and conviction for illegal voting in the 1872 presidential election.

Terry D. Bilhartz

EDWIN H. ARMSTRONG

Born: December 18, 1890; New York, New York
Died: January 31, 1954; New York, New York
Area of Achievement: Radio electronics
Contribution: From the infancy of radio, Armstrong was the leading edge of
its technical development, inventing the basic circuitry of modern AM-FM
broadcasting.

Early Life

Edwin Howard Armstrong was born on December 18, 1890, to a middle-
class New York City family. His youth was a reflection of America's fascination with the revolutionary technical innovations then transforming the
nation's society. As a boy, Armstrong displayed a markedly precocious ability
with things mechanical and developed a strong interest in trains and
locomotives. He read voraciously of the then-popular Horatio Alger "Rags
to Riches" adventure books for boys as well as the new science-fiction stories. He declared in later life that his career in science began at fourteen,
when, after reading about the exploits of inventor Guglielmo Marconi, he
decided to become an inventor himself. Fabricating his own coherers, detec-
tors, and hand-wound coils, he had, by his mid-teens, built his own spark-
based station for listening to wireless broadcasts. Radio had become his
consuming interest by the time he entered Columbia University to study
electrical engineering. While working there in the graduate radio laboratory,
he was exposed to Lee de Forest's then-recent invention of the Audion, or
three-element vacuum tube. Although de Forest had at that time used the
tube only for the amplification of audio signals, Armstrong immediately saw
the possibility of using the tube to generate radio frequency signals, and in a
short time he developed the regenerative or feedback amplification circuit.
Because he was unable to persuade his father to fund a prompt patent application, his claim for the invention was delayed until January, 1913, when a
drawing of the regenerative circuit was notarized. By this time, de Forest had
realized this important application of the Audion tube and filed his own patent, followed by Alexander Meissner in Germany and C. S. Franklin in
England.

Thus, when Armstrong was graduated from Columbia University in May,
1913, he found himself embroiled in an international dispute over patent
rights to a major invention, defending his position against some of the greatest names in radio. This legal dispute over patent rights was the beginning of
a pattern that would follow him for the remainder of his life.

Life's Work

Armstrong's time during his twenties was spent in bitter litigation with de

Forest, and although de Forest eventually won the patent, de Forest continued the deep animosity between the men by maintaining interference proceedings for the next ten years.

During World War I, Armstrong served in Paris as a United States Signal Corps officer attached to the radio laboratory of the École Militaire. By his later account, he was there struck by the difficulty of building triode amplifiers capable of intercepting the extremely weak, shortwave signals then used by the Germans in their field communications. The amplifiers in use could not sustain the power levels required without breaking into self-driven oscillation from unwanted feedback.

Armstrong's solution was to convert the incoming signal to a fixed frequency by heterodyning them to a local oscillator in the receiver and obtaining the needed sensitivity by processing the signal at the lower imposed frequency, where stability was more readily secured. It was an elegant design and has proved basic to all later receiver circuitry. In the summer of 1920, after additional research at Columbia University, he was awarded the United States patent for the superheterodyne receiver circuit.

Although he possessed the most fundamental receiver and transmitter patents, Armstrong's position was by no means secure. His patent for the regenerative circuit was under attack by de Forest in the U.S. Patent Office, incurring heavy legal expenses. In the fall of 1920, he sold the superheterodyne receiver patent to Westinghouse for $335,000 in cash, with an additional $200,000 to be paid if he won the interference proceedings against de Forest.

While setting up a courtroom demonstration in 1921, he noticed an unusual mode of radio detection and, following experimental development, filed patent application for the superregenerative detector, which was awarded in 1922.

In 1924, his patent for the superheterodyne circuit was challenged by the American Telephone and Telegraph Company (AT&T), which possessed the American rights to the patent of Lucien Levy, a French radio engineer. Levy claimed to have invented the superheterodyne receiver during the war while stationed at the École Militaire and that Armstrong had stolen the invention while serving there in the signal corps.

Armstrong spent his energy and personal financial resources defending the patent position in the courts against bitter professional and sometimes personal attacks. Although he retained rights to the regenerative circuits, he ultimately lost all the claims for the superheterodyne circuit to Levy, backed by AT&T.

During these legal battles, from 1928 to 1933, he developed, with little assistance, his finest invention, the wideband frequency modulation (FM) system of broadcasting, proving a static and distortion-free technique, far superior to AM. In the winter of 1933, he was awarded four patents which completely covered the FM system and which established him as its sole inventor. As the newly appointed professor of electrical engineering at Columbia University, he announced his invention to the world by reading a paper before the Institute of Radio Engineers and surprising his audience with a demonstration broadcast from an experimental station he operated with the help of a friend. His system was obviously superior to any AM system in use, yet its introduction was met with the skepticism of industry, which had invested heavily in AM broadcasting. Much of the remainder of his life was spent in trying to have FM adopted as the prime radio broadcasting system. He refined the techniques, set up stations, and traveled extensively, but with little result.

During World War II, he developed FM units for military communications, demonstrated long-range FM signaling, and worked on continuous-wave FM radar.

Harassed by seemingly never-ending patent litigation and frustrated by the slow adoption of his FM broadcasting system, Armstrong committed suicide in New York on January 31, 1954.

Summary

Edwin Armstrong's career spanned the golden age of radio development and broadcasting and reflected the spirit of the individual scientific pioneer that was typical of the early twentieth century. His work, from his undergraduate days, was always on the very basic phenomena of radio operations, his early contributions making possible the dream of voice radio transmission.

Much of his energy in the later years of his life was spent fighting challenges to his patents. If this time could have been devoted to invention and research, his scientific output could have been much higher. Despite this drain on him, he invented some of the most important circuits of modern radio, his creative output spanning the whole of his career.

Although he died feeling frustrated and unrecognized, the world has since seen the adoption of his systems as the standard of broadcasting and his ranking as one of the great scientists of modern electronics. His awards include the First Medal of Honor from the Society of Radio Engineers, the Franklin Medal, and the United States Medal of Merit. He is one of twenty world scientists honored in the Pantheon of the Union Internationale des Télécommunications in Geneva.

Bibliography

Aitken, Hugh G. *The Continous Wave: Technology and American Radio, 1900-1932*. Princeton, N.J.: Princeton University Press, 1985. The best history of the development of radio available. Covers Armstrong's patent and business dealings in depth as well as his impact on the development of the Radio Corporation of America (RCA), and Westinghouse as the dominant companies of early radio. Very well researched and documented, both historically and technically.

_____. *Syntony and Spark: The Origins of Radio*. New York: John Wiley and Sons, 1976. An excellent chronological history of the technical evolution of radio. Gives a broad picture of Armstrong's technical innovations and how they affected the rapid pace of radio's development at the time.

Lessing, Lawrence. *Man of High Fidelity: Edwin Howard Armstrong*. Philadelphia: J. B. Lippincott Co., 1956. The only biography yet written on the life of Armstrong, and the only source for information on his private life. Well written but sympathetic toward Armstrong's difficulties. Provides a more personable view of the legal charges and accusations against Armstrong.

Lewis, Thomas S. W. "Radio Revolutionary." *American Heritage of Invention and Technology* 1 (Fall, 1985): 34-41. A sympathetic but accurate brief account contrasting his tragic life with his triumphant inventions, especially FM.

Orren P. Whiddon

LOUIS ARMSTRONG

Born: 1898?; New Orleans, Louisiana
Died: July 6, 1971; New York, New York
Area of Achievement: Music
Contribution: Armstrong's importance to the development of jazz is inestimable. Whether played or sung, almost all aspects of jazz style and technique were influenced directly by his innovations of the 1920's. His concepts of range, tone, phrasing, and rhythm, along with his sophisticated choice of pitch, were widely imitated.

Early Life

The son of Willie Armstrong, a turpentine worker, and Mary Ann (or Mayann) Armstrong, the granddaughter of slaves, Louis Armstrong was born most likely in the year 1898—the exact date is not known—in a district of New Orleans, Louisiana, called, according to Armstrong, "The Battlefield." Armstrong himself said that "Daniel" (given in many sources) was never part of his name, and that he was not even sure how he acquired it. Whoring, shootings, knifings, drunkenness, and gambling were common in the area where Armstrong spent the first years of his life. His parents separated when he was five. He and his sister lived in poverty with his mother and grandmother near the dance halls and saloons, whose music, along with what he sang and heard in church, was his initial influence. As a boy, Armstrong worked at odd jobs, sang for pennies, and formed part of a strolling vocal quartet. After firing a pistol into the air on New Year's Eve of 1913, he was arrested, taken to jail, and then sent to the Colored Waifs' Home, generally known as the Jones Home, in New Orleans. There he received his first formal musical training from Peter Davis, the home's band master and drill instructor. Within the year, Armstrong was playing the cornet and leading the home's brass band.

When he was finally released to his mother, who was ill, in 1914, Armstrong supported both of them by working at various day-jobs, including delivering coal and selling newspapers. He also began taking cornet lessons from his lifelong idol, jazz cornetist Joe "King" Oliver. Armstrong quickly undertook the development of those jazz skills which he had, until then, been able to admire only at a distance. Slowly, he became one of the most sought-after musicians in New Orleans, one of the few who was good enough to earn his living by playing. In 1918, he married Daisy Parker; they would be divorced in 1923.

After King Oliver left for an engagement in Chicago in 1919, Armstrong replaced him in Kid Ory's Brownskin Band. Given his improvising abilities, clarity of tone, formidable technique, and rhythmic freedom, Armstrong soon became a drawing card in his own right. Joining Fate Marable's band on various Mississippi excursion boats, he played up and down the river in the summers of 1920 and 1921. Around this time, Armstrong wrote one of his first songs, "Get Off Katie's Head" (published as "I Wish I Could Shimmy Like My Sister Kate"); he received from the publishers neither the fifty dollars they had promised for the song nor credit as the composer. In New Orleans, he continued to play at various clubs and also did street parade work, appearing regularly with Pap Celestin's Tuxedo Band.

Life's Work

As Armstrong's reputation spread, Fletcher Henderson, a rising bandleader in New York, offered him a job. Armstrong was timid and agreed to the move only if his friend, drummer Zutty Singleton, was hired too. Since Henderson already had a drummer, Armstrong remained in New Orleans until King Oliver summoned him to Chicago in the summer of 1922. Oliver's Original Creole Jazz Band was unusually disciplined, and the demands of his second cornetist's role further improved Armstrong's musicianship. The sensitivity and discipline of his second cornet parts to Oliver's lead are especially apparent on a recording of "Mabel's Dream." While his first recorded solo with the band, "Chimes Blues," is undistinguished, it was toward individual, not collective, playing that Armstrong moved—steadily and surely. Nevertheless, it took Lillian (Lil) Hardin, the band's pianist, whom he married in 1924, to persuade him to leave an environment which had begun to restrict him. Armstrong's sense of obligation ran deep.

In 1924, Armstrong reluctantly accepted Fletcher Henderson's invitation to join his big band in New York. As a section player, Armstrong conformed in his ensemble playing to the stiff rhythms then favored by Henderson, but his sophisticated solos brought a novel style to the city's dance and jazz music. He exerted a broad influence on New York musicians, among them Henderson's arranger, Don Redman, who soon developed orchestral counterparts to Armstrong's devices. While in New York, Armstrong made a memorable series of recordings with Perry Bradford's Jazz Phools, with Clarence Williams' groups, and as an accompanist to Bessie Smith and other blues singers.

Generally known as "Satchmo" (an abbreviation for "Satchel-mouth"), Armstrong acquired early a basic strength and beauty of sound which is apparent in his work with Oliver and Henderson. To the melodic richness, emotional depth, and rhythmic variety of the blues, he added an already exceptional technique allowing every note to be full and every phrase to be perfectly shaped. No matter what the tempo, his playing sounded unhurried: such relaxation led to a deep and consistent swing. All these abilities combined with a vein of melodic invention so rich that it did not falter for many years.

An essential part of his style once he left Oliver's band, Armstrong's singing was inimitable. He sang like he played, or vice versa, which is not surprising given the important connection in the African heritage between speech and music. His scat singing (using nonsense syllables) was clearly a vocalization of his instrumental inflection and phrasing. Armstrong once made the unlikely claim that he invented scat singing, but he was the first to use it on records. His voice had a buoyancy and roughness which quickly became legendary.

A more accomplished musician for his big-band schooling and brimming with energy and inventiveness, Armstrong returned to Chicago in 1925. There, he played with his wife's group and with bands headed by Erskine Tate and Carroll Dickerson. For most of 1927, he led his own group. Armstrong had also begun making a series of recordings under his own name in 1925. He established an international reputation with these records, revealing the power of his musical ideas and his range and originality as an improviser. These recordings also show Armstrong looking for an appropriate accompaniment for his increasingly virtuosic solo style.

The earliest of these accompanying groups—those of the Hot Five and Hot Seven recordings with Hardin, the Dodds brothers, Kid Ory, and Johnny St. Cyr—were modeled on New Orleans ensembles. Masterpieces of the later New Orleans style such as "Butter and Egg Man," "Struttin' with Some Barbeque," and "Potato Head Blues" come from this 1926-1927 period. Then in 1928, Armstrong turned to a more modern small band, collaborating with Earl Hines and Zutty Singleton. Trumpet, piano, and drums dominated, there being no further pretense of New Orleans equality. Armstrong now appeared at his most modernistic; the music is characterized by virtuosity, double-time spurts, complex ensembles, rhythmic juggling, and unpredictable harmonic alterations. From this period come "West End Blues," "Beau Koo Jack," and "Weatherbird Rag," the latter a remarkable duet with Hines.

It is difficult to see how Armstrong's intense musical conversation with Hines could have been maintained longer than it was. Consequently, in mid-1929, Armstrong adopted the format he was to use until 1947, a big band providing a neutral accompaniment to his now large-scale, virtuoso conceptions of his playing and singing. Perhaps his further development was possible only against a purely subsidiary background. Initial results were excellent, with 1933 marking the peak of this period. Having done everything then possible with traditional jazz material, he began to concentrate on a popular repertory. While his technical innovations ceased, he still performed with great artistic merit, demonstrating his power and maturity on such classics as "Body and Soul," "Star Dust," "Sweethearts on Parade," and "I Gotta Right to Sing the Blues."

After 1933, Armstrong embarked increasingly upon an all-too-thorough commercialization of his talent under the guidance of his longtime manager,

Joe Glaser. His popular hits began with Fats Waller's "Ain't Misbehavin'," which he debuted in the *Hot Chocolates* revue of 1930, and culminated in the hit song from the Broadway show *Hello, Dolly!* in the 1960's. There was a strong streak of ham in Armstrong, and his comic posing and patter, which endeared him to many, embarrassed others, such as Benny Goodman, who thought his music excellent and his vaudevillian antics corny and unworthy of him.

Over the years, Armstrong seemed to become more and more indifferent to what he played and with whom he played. A meaningful context was lacking, given the gap between his own majestic playing and his often abysmal accompaniment. Even his magic was unable to transform the increasing amount of novelty material he recorded. Nevertheless, Armstrong also used his craft and experience to distill and simplify his playing. In place of virtuoso performance, every note was made to count.

During the 1930's, Armstrong toured and recorded with large groups, both in the United States and in Europe. He worked off and on with such band leaders and musical directors as Luis Russell, Chick Webb, and Les Hite. Throughout the late 1930's, he played residencies and toured with his own orchestra. Armstrong also began to make film appearances, the first in *Pennies from Heaven* with Bing Crosby in 1936. Hundreds of records of his own and other groups made him influential as a player and singer of popular music and brought him an ever wider audience. His best recordings of the 1930's are nearly all remakes of old successes, including "Save It, Pretty Mama," "Mahogany Hall Stomp," and "Monday Date." Obtaining a divorce from Lil, Armstrong married Alpha Smith in 1938. The marriage was not built on a very sound foundation, and no one was surprised when it did not last. In 1942, Armstrong married Lucille Wilson, the woman who was to be his wife for the rest of his life.

Eventually, Armstrong returned to playing with small groups; there were still some great records to come, as well as many pleasant ones. Following successful appearances with small groups in 1947, including one in the film *New Orleans*, he formed his All-Stars, with which he worked until his death. A sextet based on the New Orleans model, its instrumentation remained the same, though the personnel varied. Among those associated with the All-Stars over the years were pianist Earl Hines, trombonists Trummy Young and Jack Teagarden, clarinetists Ed Hall and Barney Bigard, and drummers Cozy Cole and Sid Catlett. Armstrong was frequently able to demonstrate with the All-Stars his superb quality as a jazz musician.

During the 1950's, besides working in the United States and Canada, the All-Stars toured in Europe, South America, Africa, Australia, and the Far East. Exasperated by the Eisenhower Administration's do-nothing policy toward black civil rights in the South, Armstrong, in protest, once canceled his Department of State–backed tour of the Soviet Union. This was not the

Armstrong of records or stage; regardless of such social activism, Armstrong always seemed the wellspring of goodness, which was very advantageous to the image of jazz, both at home and abroad.

Throughout the 1960's, the All-Stars did even more international touring, earning for Armstrong the nickname "Ambassador Satch." He had come to symbolize jazz to the world. During the late 1960's, illness incapacitated Armstrong several times, taking its toll on his playing. For more than a year, in 1969 and 1970, he was only able to sing in public appearances. He resumed playing but suffered a heart attack in March of 1971. Armstrong died in New York City on July 6 of that year.

Summary

Louis Armstrong's contribution to the development of jazz was partly that of innovator and stylist, partly one of pure virtuosity, both imaginatively and technically, and partly one of showmanship. He was responsible, more than anyone else, for the fact that jazz became not so much a collective ensemble style as a soloist's art. Moreover, he was the bridge between Dixieland and swing, the next important development in jazz. By the time of his death, he had exerted a profound influence upon his fellow jazz musicians—such as trumpeters Roy Eldridge, Dizzy Gillespie, and Miles Davis—to whom Armstrong is "Pops," the patriarch of their own stylistic development.

The influence of Armstrong on the history of jazz—dubbed by some as "America's classical music"—is so pervasive that it has on occasion been blithely dismissed by those who fault him for not having kept up with the changes in the music. It is clear, however, that Armstrong's continued success as player and singer helped make jazz a vital force in the general culture of the United States and, to some degree, of the rest of the world. His radiant optimism, his virtuosity, and his indefatigable sense of fun played an important role in promoting jazz everywhere.

Bibliography

Armstrong, Louis. *Swing That Music*. New York: Longmans, Green and Co., 1936.

_____. *Satchmo: My Life in New Orleans*. Englewood Cliffs, N.J.: Prentice-Hall, 1955.

_____. *A Self-Portrait: The Interview with Richard Merryman*. New York: Eakins Press, 1971. The three works under Armstrong's name must be used with care. They are not always reliable and should be used in conjunction with a well-researched biographical treatment such as that of Collier.

Chilton, John, and Max Jones. *Louis: The Louis Armstrong Story, 1900-1971*. Boston: Little, Brown and Co., 1971. A reasonably good biography of Armstrong.

Collier, James Lincoln. *Louis Armstrong: An American Genius*. New York: Oxford University Press, 1983. The definitive biography. Factually reliable. Good in dealing with the myths and sheer fiction which have become part of the Armstrong story. (Collier points up, for example, the inaccuracy behind the commonly listed birth date for Armstrong, July 4, 1900.) Contains a brief discography.

_____.*The Making of Jazz: A Comprehensive History*. Boston: Houghton Mifflin Co., 1978. An excellent history of jazz, including a chapter devoted to Armstrong, "The First Genius."

Schuller, Gunther. *Early Jazz: Its Roots and Musical Development*. Vol. 1, *The History of Jazz*. New York: Oxford University Press, 1968. The definitive study of the development of jazz prior to the early 1930's. Armstrong's significance is emphasized. Uses an ethnomusicological approach to the African elements in jazz.

Tirro, Frank. *Jazz: A History*. New York: W. W. Norton and Co., 1977. A solid jazz history, good on detail.

Westerberg, Hans. *Boy from New Orleans: Louis "Satchmo" Armstrong*. Copenhagen, Denmark: Jazzmedia Aps, 1981. Far and away the most complete discography of Armstrong's work.

Williams, Martin. *Jazz Makers of New Orleans*. New York: Macmillan Publishing Co., 1967. A collection of essays on New Orleans jazzmen, including Armstrong.

L. Moody Simms, Jr.

NEIL ARMSTRONG

Born: August 5, 1930; Wapakoneta, Ohio

Area of Achievement: Space exploration
Contribution: The first man to walk on the surface of the Moon, on July 20, 1969, Armstrong was commander of *Apollo 11*, the first spacecraft to carry men to the Moon and back to Earth.

Early Life
Neil Alden Armstrong, the first man to set foot on the Moon, was born August 5, 1930, on a farm in Auglaize County near Wapakoneta, Ohio. He was the eldest son of Stephen and Viola Armstrong; his younger brother, Dean Alan, was born in Jefferson, Ohio, and had a long career with the Delco Division of General Motors Corporation at Anderson, Indiana; Neil also had a sister, June Louise. Stephen Armstrong was an auditor for the State of Ohio, and his work took the family across the state to many towns The Armstrongs moved from Warren to Jefferson, to Ravenna, to St. Mary's, Upper Sandusky, and finally to a more permanent home in Wapakoneta. The Armstrongs were descendants of Scotch-Irish immigrants, while the mother's ancestors were of German background. Neil's father eventually was made the assistant director of mental hygiene and corrections of the state of Ohio.

Armstrong begun his formal education in the public schools of Warren, Ohio, where he attended Champion Heights Elementary School. His advanced reading ability (he had read ninety books in the first grade) permitted him to skip the second grade. Known as a shy and modest boy, he played baseball and football with friends and enjoyed school activities.

Influenced by his father, Armstrong had an early interest in aviation. His family attended the National Air Races at the Cleveland airport, and as a six-year-old boy, he accompanied his father in a plane called a "Tin Goose" that provided air rides near their home in Warren. During the Great Depression, Armstrong developed a deep interest in building model airplanes, a hobby that soon filled his room with the smell of glue and balsa wood. He quickly advanced from hobby kits to creating bigger and more powerful models of his own, which he tested at the town park. During his high school years, to improve his homemade planes, Armstrong built a small wind tunnel in the basement of his family's house.

One neighbor, Jacob Zint, owned a powerful telescope and often invited youngsters to look at the Moon, stars, and planets. Armstrong remembered these stargazing experiences as awe-inspiring and began more study of the universe. He loved to learn; his schoolbooks, which his parents saved, reflect his thorough study and wide reading in the fields of science and mathematics.

With his collection of the popular *Air Trails* magazine, he kept pace with aviation advancements. As a high school student, at fifteen, he worked in stores to earn enough money to take flying lessons. On his sixteenth birthday, he was granted a student pilot's license even before he had a driver's license.

Armstrong pedaled on his bike day after day in 1946 to the Auglaize Flying Field at Wapakoneta, where flight instructor Aubrey Knudegard trained him to fly in an Aeronca 7AC Champion, built in Middletown, Ohio. The Aeronca Airplane Company had been a pioneer in the production of light, single-wing aircraft for private flying, and Armstrong learned to fly it with skill. Since the initial flights in 1903 of the Wright brothers in Dayton, Ohio, the growth of aerospace research had been concentrated at the Wright-Patterson Air Force Base there, and the Miami Valley had become a center of postwar aviation development and testing. Armstrong was flying from a local airfield not far from this national air base.

In the fall of 1947, following his graduation from Wapakoneta High School, Armstrong entered Purdue University at Lafayette, Indiana, on a United States Navy scholarship. Enrolled in the College of Engineering, he had completed about two years of study when the navy ordered him to report to Pensacola, Florida, for special flight training. After the outbreak of the Korean War in July, 1950, Armstrong was the youngest member of his unit when it was sent overseas for active duty. He flew seventy-eight combat missions from the flight deck of the aircraft carrier the USS *Essex*. One mission nearly cost him his life: His Panther jet knicked a cable stretched across a North Korean valley, and, with grim determination and skill, he guided the plane back into South Korea before parachuting to safety. Armstrong won three Air Medals for his combat duty.

Upon completion of his navy service in 1952, Armstrong returned to Purdue to finish his bachelor of science degree in aeronautical engineering and was graduated in 1955. On campus, he met Janet Shearon of Evanston, Illinois, who shared his love for flying; their college courtship led to marriage on January 28, 1956. Three children were born to the Armstrongs: Eric, born in 1957, Karen, born in 1959 (she died near the age of three), and Mark, born in 1963.

Armstrong had by then matured into a handsome aviator with a strong physical stature, standing nearly six feet tall. Reserved in speech but quite able to express himself, Armstrong had keen blue eyes which reflected the intensity of concentration and the good judgment of his mind. Always a good listener, he had absorbed a remarkable amount of information about airborne flight and from that reservoir often drew vital information.

Life's Work

Armstrong went to work at the Lewis Flight Propulsion Laboratory in Cleveland, Ohio, serving as a research pilot. After six months at Lewis, he transferred to the High Speed Flight Station at Edwards Air Force Base in California, where he served as an aeronautical research pilot testing many pioneering aircraft, including the X-15 rocket airplane (he took it to more than 200,000 feet above the earth's surface and flew at speeds of nearly four thousand miles per hour), the X-1, F-100, F-101, F-102, F-104, F5D, B-47, and the paraglider. In all, he flew more than two hundred different kinds of aircraft. While in California, he began his master of science degree in aerospace engineering at the University of Southern California, completing it in 1969.

Spurred by the Soviet Union's successful launching of the first earth-orbiting satellite, *Sputnik I*, on October 4, 1957, the United States in 1958 established the National Aeronautics and Space Administration (NASA) to coordinate all space research projects sponsored by the federal government. Soon the United States was sending its satellites skyward and NASA began training spacecraft pilots called astronauts for manned orbital flights. *Explorer 1* became the first successful American data-gathering space satellite, launched in January, 1958. It was Soviet cosmonaut Yuri Gagarin, however, who became the first man in space orbit, in April, 1961, aboard the *Vostok I*; the United States sent its first manned capsule into suborbital flight in May, 1961, with Alan B. Shepard, Jr., flying in *Freedom 7*. That month, President John F. Kennedy, in an address to Congress, called for the nation to land the first man on the Moon by the end of the decade, a goal that was achieved.

While still working at NASA's facility at Edwards Air Force Base (consolidated into NASA), Armstrong applied to be one of the United States' astronauts. The requirements favored men from military units, but Armstrong was accepted in 1962; he was the first civilian admitted to the astronaut program by NASA. The Armstrongs moved to El Lago, Texas, and Armstrong joined the nation's second recruit class of astronauts in training at the new NASA Manned Spacecraft Center in Houston for a two-year intensive program of classroom study and training for space travel.

NASA developed three space programs while Armstrong worked as an astronaut. The first, designated Project Mercury, was to develop the technology and experience to send a man into earth orbit; on February 20, 1962, the first manned orbital flight launched by the United States carried John H. Glenn, Jr., as pilot of a three-orbit space trip. The Gemini program, created in 1962, launched a series of two-man spacecraft in earth orbit during 1965 and 1966, including two unmanned and ten manned ventures. Project Apollo, created in 1960, was redirected in 1962 to land a man on the Moon by 1970, utilizing a three-man crew. Eventually, seventeen Apollo flights of lunar orbit and landings were made by the end of that program in 1972.

Armstrong was assigned as a command pilot for the *Gemini 8* mission launched on March 16, 1966. He successfully performed the first docking of two vehicles (one manned, the other unmanned) in space. He and David R.

Scott found the two crafts pitching and spinning out of control; Armstrong detached their Gemini capsule and then, as it began to roll even faster, brought it back under control and made an emergency landing in the Pacific Ocean.

It was as spacecraft commander of *Apollo 11*, the first manned lunar landing mission in history, that Armstrong gained the distinction of being the first man to land a craft on the Moon and the first man to step on its surface, an event that was achieved on July 20, 1969, four days after the craft's launch. Michael Collins served as command module pilot of the *Columbia*, which orbited the Moon while Armstrong and Colonel Edwin E. Aldrin, Jr., aboard the four-legged lunar module called the *Eagle*, landed near the so-called Sea of Tranquillity (at about 4:18 P.M., eastern daylight time) and explored the surface before the rendezvous with the *Columbia* for the return trip.

The next day, *The New York Times* ran the headline, "Men Walk on Moon: Astronauts Land on Plain; Collect Rocks, Plant Flag." Relating one of humanity's most historic moments, a journalist recounted,

> About six and a half hours [following the lunar landing], Mr. Armstrong opened the landing craft's hatch, stepped slowly down the ladder and declared as he planted the first human footprint on the lunar crust:
> "That's one small step for man, one giant leap for mankind."
> His first step on the moon came at 10:56:20 P.M., as a television camera outside the craft transmitted his every move to an awed and excited audience of hundreds of millions of people on earth.

Colonel Aldrin soon joined Armstrong and, in a two-and-a-half-hour stay outside the *Eagle*, the two set up a camera for live television transmission, conducted seismographic and laser experiments, planted a United States flag, and collected samples of Moon soil and rocks. After twenty-two hours, they blasted off to rejoin the *Columbia*, climbed back into the command module, jettisoned the lunar *Eagle*, and returned to earth to splash down southeast of Hawaii to be personally welcomed by President Richard M. Nixon aboard the USS *Hornet*. Nixon said: "You have taught man how to reach for the stars."

For eighteen days after the splashdown, the three lunar astronauts were kept in isolation to avoid any contamination from the Moon's environment. New York City welcomed them with the greatest ticker-tape parade since Charles A. Lindbergh's solo flight to Paris in 1927. At the White House, they received the nation's highest civilian honor: The Medal of Freedom was given to each of them. In the next months, they visited twenty-two nations and were awarded medals and citations from governments and scientific organizations around the world.

Armstrong was reassigned to the position of deputy associate administrator for aeronautics, Office of Advanced Research and Technology, NASA Headquarters, Washington, D.C. He was responsible for the coordination and management of NASA research and technology work related to aeronautics.

In the fall of 1971, at the urging of his friend, Dr. Paul Herget, astronomer and professor of space science, whose work in the field of minor planets and in satellite orbits had won world recognition, Armstrong accepted an appointment as professor of engineering at the University of Cincinnati, an interdisciplinary post he retained until 1980. After their return to Ohio, the Armstrongs lived on a farm near Lebanon, Warren County, where their sons were graduated from high school.

Between 1979 and 1981, Armstrong worked part-time for the Chrysler Corporation and appeared in a national advertising campaign for the Detroit car manufacturer. For a short time, he and his brother Dean owned and operated the Cardwell International Corporation, a producer and exporter of oil field equipment. He later headed CTA, Inc., an aviation company based in Charlottesville, Virginia. Sought by many major corporations, Armstrong accepted positions on the board of directors of several companies, including Gates Learjet and United Airlines. In the 1980's, although carefully guarding his schedule, he became a popular speaker at national conventions and trade associations as well as a commencement speaker for many universities, some of which awarded him honorary degrees.

Following the explosion of the *Challenger* space shuttle on January 28, 1986, in which seven astronauts lost their lives, President Ronald Reagan named William Rogers chairman and Neil Armstrong vice chairman of a presidential commission to investigate the causes of the *Challenger*'s failure. For the next six months, Armstrong served as an active member of that commission, appearing on television and before Congress with the chairman to report on the findings of the body.

Summary

When the three astronauts of *Apollo 11* addressed a joint session of the United States Congress on September 16, 1969, Neil Armstrong recalled how they had left a bronze plaque on the *Eagle*'s remnants. It declared: "Here men from the planet Earth first set foot upon the Moon. July 1969, A.D. We came in peace for all mankind." Such sentiments reflect the noble convictions of Armstrong: He saw his individual role in the gigantic space exploration mission as that of only one member of the nation's great team; his accomplishment as a victory for the whole of human endeavor: "a giant leap for mankind," "in peace for all mankind." Hence, he was able to return quietly to university and business activities after becoming the world's greatest explorer of all time.

Governor James A. Rhodes led a drive for the erection of a globelike museum honoring Armstrong on the edge of his hometown at Wapakoneta, Ohio, which houses a vast collection of the awards, citations, gifts, and honors given the Ohio native. As a new American hero, a skillful and courageous commander in the tradition of Christopher Columbus, Ferdinand Magellan, and others, Armstrong confidently walked on the Moon first and confidently returned to work among his fellowmen.

Bibliography
Westman, Paul. *Neil Armstrong: Space Pioneer*. Minneapolis: Lerner Publications Co., 1980. A preliminary biography of Armstrong in conversational style packed into sixty-four pages with fine black-and-white photographs largely supplied by NASA. Contains an appendix of all United States manned space flights from *Mercury 3* through Project Apollo.
Mission Moon '69. Satellite Beach, Fla.: Scarboro Publications, 1969. A documentary prepared in advance of the first lunar landing describing the men and machines that were involved in the various stages of the projected *Apollo 11* program.
"Man on the Moon": A Picture Chronology of Man in Space Exploration. Dallas, Tex.: Galina, 1969. An extensive collection of color plates of Project Apollo provided by NASA, with more scientific text explaining the purposes and goals of the Moon project and describing how technology and men mastered them by 1969.
Crouch, Tom D. *The Giant Leap: A Chronology of Ohio Aerospace Events and Personalities, 1815-1969*. Columbus: Ohio Historical Society, 1971. A graphic story of man in flight from the time of early balloons, aircraft, and dirigibles through to *Apollo 11*'s splashdown in 1969.

Paul F. Erwin

BENEDICT ARNOLD

Born: January 14, 1741; Norwich, Connecticut
Died: June 14, 1801; London, England
Area of Achievement: The military
Contribution: Despite his skillful leadership of the Colonial forces in the American Revolution, Arnold's betrayal of his country has made his name a synonym for treason.

Early Life

Benedict Arnold was born January 14, 1741, in Norwich, Connecticut. His mother had been a wealthy widow and a member of one of the first families to settle in Norwich. Her maiden name was Hannah Waterman, but she became Hannah King and inherited her husband's estate before marrying Benedict Arnold III, the father of the famous general and traitor. The first Benedict Arnold had served three times as governor of Rhode Island. Benedict Arnold III had been a cooper of limited means but later became involved in the West Indies trade.

Benedict Arnold IV attended local schools, including one directed by the Reverend James Cogswell, a relative of his mother, at Canterbury, Connecticut. He was only a fair student, and he earned a reputation for being boisterous, a daredevil, and a prankster. Shortly after he entered his teens, he was apprenticed to an apothecary, but the humdrum routine bored him, and he soon enlisted as a young recruit in the French and Indian War. Almost as quickly as he arrived in New York for training, he deserted the cause and returned home to Norwich. One description of his appearance at the time portrayed him as having dark hair, a dark complexion, and light gray eyes. As he matured, he developed a strong, stocky frame. He was energetic and possessed unusual endurance.

Hannah Arnold died when Benedict was eighteen years old. Without the restraining influence of his mother, his father became a drunkard. After his father's death in 1761, the young Benedict left Norwich for the larger town of New Haven, where he became a druggist and a bookseller. He later became a successful merchant and expanded his trade connections with the West Indies and Canada. On Febuary 22, 1767, he married Margaret Mansfield, the daughter of a prominent New Haven government offical. "Peggy," as he preferred to call her, gave him three children: Benedict, Richard, and Henry. Arnold labored to provide his family with the luxuries that wealthy families then enjoyed. In pursuing this goal, he traveled often to the West Indies and Quebec. On trips to the West Indies, his ships carried lumber and horses. On the return voyages, he brought to New England molasses, sugar, and rum. He probably owed his wealth, in part at least, to smuggling. One incident in Honduras during one of his voyages revealed his hot temper as well as his early affinity for use of weapons. When a drunken British sea captain cursed him, Arnold challenged him to a duel. At the first shot, Arnold wounded his opponent, who then decided to apologize rather than face a second round.

The aggressive Arnold became a captain in the Connecticut Militia in December, 1774. When the conservative New Haven town fathers faced the issue of war, upon news of the battles at Lexington and Concord, they decided to remain neutral. Arnold, however, favored war and led his patriots into the streets of New Haven. He demanded and received the keys to the powder house. Arnold was ready and eager for action.

Life's Work

Taking his militia company to Cambridge, he asked the Massachusetts Committee of Safety to sponsor him in an expedition against Ticonderoga. The committee gave him a colonel's commission and authorized him to recruit troops and to seize the eighty cannons at the fort. Unfortunately for Arnold, Ethan Allen, of Vermont, set out on the same mission. Arnold, without his own troops, joined with Allen's forces, but the two disagreed on who should have command. They issued joint orders but continued to disagree on who was the rightful superior. They took Fort Ticonderoga in May, 1775, and the cannons were later carried across New England to Boston, where they would be the major factor in forcing the British to evacuate that city. Meanwhile, Arnold's own troops arrived, and he sailed north on Lake Champlain and conquered the fort at St. John's in Quebec. When the Massachusetts government began to question his conduct in the Lake Champlain area, Arnold resigned his commission and returned to New Haven. The Massachusetts congress refused to pay Arnold for supplies he had purchased for his troops in the Lake Champlain struggle. To add to his woes, his wife had died on June 19, 1775, before his return home.

Despite discouragements, Arnold went to Cambridge and discussed with George Washington a plan to lead a force against Quebec City by way of Maine. The typical approach for armies had been by way of Lake Champlain and the St. Lawrence River. A force led by Philip Schuyler would indeed follow this traditional route, but Arnold's men would set out across the Maine woods to meet Schuyler's force before reaching Quebec. Arnold eagerly accepted leadership of the Maine expedition and set out in September, 1775. The journey was an arduous and heroic adventure. Many of the seven hundred men he took with him turned back rather than face the hardships of ice, snow, and short provisions. When Schuyler became ill, General Richard Montgomery assumed command and met with Arnold before the assault on Quebec. During a blinding snowstorm on New Year's Eve, 1775, the two armies attacked Quebec City. Despite their heroism, the venture failed, leaving Montgomery dead and Arnold wounded. Arnold now laid siege to the city until spring, when British reinforcements arrived. He then began a skillful retreat that inflicted heavy losses on the British. After his retreat, charges of misconduct in Canada were brought against him, but after much delay the American Congress finally cleared his name in May, 1777.

Arnold began to get the clear impression that his heroic efforts for the revolutionary cause were going unappreciated. After a brilliant campaign on Lake Champlain, in which he defeated a large fleet of British vessels in October, 1776, Congress created five new major generals, all of whom had been of lesser seniority than Brigadier General Arnold. Washington scarcely restrained Arnold from resigning his commission. Arnold returned to Connecticut and while there held off a British attack on Danbury. In recognition of this service, the Congress now gave him the major generalship he had coveted.

During 1777, Arnold had a major role in preventing the British from severing New England from the rest of the Colonies. The British plan—which, if successful, would have been a fatal blow to the Colonial cause—called for an assault from Canada, in the north, by way of the Lake Champlain route, to be led by John Burgoyne. At the same time, William Howe was to lead his army from New York up the Hudson River to join with Burgoyne. A third force would come in from the west, via the Mohawk Valley. In August, 1777, Arnold foiled the movement from the west by capturing Fort Stanwix in the Mohawk Valley, barely firing a shot. By this time, General Horatio Gates commanded the American forces along the Hudson River. After Arnold returned from Fort Stanwix to link his forces with those of Gates, he quarreled with General Gates and was relieved of his leadership position. Although he was technically not in command, he led his forces into battle at the Second Battle of Saratoga and helped win one of the most strategic victories of the American Revolution. In the battle he suffered a wound to the same leg that had been injured at Quebec. Congress now restored to him the seniority that he had lost when the five major generals were moved ahead of him.

In June of 1778, he took command of the city of Philadelphia and began living there a life-style that demanded more than his trifling salary as an officer could support. In April of 1779, he married a Philadelphia socialite, Margaret Shippen. Her associations with leading loyalists may have been a factor in Arnold's treason. Arnold was again distressed by renewed charges against him by enemies in the Congress. He demanded a court-martial, which vindicated him of all the significant charges. He was infuriated, however, by George Washington's gentle rebuke of him for minor offenses. Meanwhile, he began corresponding with the British commander in chief Henry Clinton and offered to provide military secrets in exchange for money.

In July, 1780, Arnold became commander of West Point. He arranged to betray that vital fort to Clinton for twenty thousand British pounds. Clinton sent Major John André to discuss plans for seizure of the fort. After the meeting with Arnold, André was returning to the British ship the *Vulture*, on the Hudson River. André was captured by American soldiers, however, and his papers were found in a stocking. Because he had donned civilian clothes for his mission he was executed as a spy. News of the capture led Arnold to flee to the waiting British vessel. He then entered the British army as a brigadier general and led forces in both Virginia and his native Connecticut. He spent his remaining ten years in England and Canada. He died an embittered and maligned man on June 14, 1801.

Summary

Arnold's life is a study in contrast. Through two-thirds of his life he received adoration and admiration from American patriots. He was one of the bravest and most skilled of American military leaders. His military genius may have surpassed that of George Washington. His character lacked, however, one of the most important virtues of his commander in chief: the patience and the willingness to endure in a noble cause even when appreciation and respect are at low ebb. Although Arnold's name has become a byword for treachery, one should not forget his years of valiant service in the struggle for independence. At the same time, none of his heroic acts can erase the memory of his treachery in the West Point conspiracy. Even the British people refused him the respect he sought in his later years.

Arnold hoped that the British would give him a proper command for a general of his abilities, but they used him in only two minor ventures in the American Revolution. He led a force in Virginia that burned Richmond, and he later made a foray into Connecticut, dismaying his former neighbors by an assault on New London. Back in England, he hoped to be given a position in the struggle on the Continent against the French Revolution. The British were suspicious of the former traitor, however, and the Earl of Louderdale warned the House of Lords, in a speech, that Arnold was the very symbol of treachery. Arnold thereby had one last opportunity for battle. He challenged the earl to a duel. In the contest, Arnold missed and the earl refused to fire. Arnold's business ventures followed the same unfortunate pattern as his military career, and in death he left an impoverished wife and family behind.

Bibliography
Arnold, Isaac N. *The Life of Benedict Arnold: His Patriotism and His Treason*. Chicago: A. C. McClurg and Co., 1880. The author was a distant relative of Arnold. He requests at least "one drop of pity" for the man whose name would have been canonized in American history if he had fallen on the battlefield at Saratoga. Although this is one of the older biographies and seems to be anxious to refurbish Arnold's reputation, it is still one of the better ones.
Codman, John, II. *Arnold's Expedition to Quebec*. New York: Macmillan,

1902. This book is based on numerous journals and diaries of those involved in the ill-fated Quebec expedition. It covers the planning of the invasion of Canada as well as the trek through the Maine Woods and the assault on the city of Quebec. In order to understand better the terrible sufferings of the soldiers on their journey, the author traversed either on foot or in canoe most of Arnold's course along the Kennebec, the Dead River, and the Chaudierre.

Decker, Malcolm. *Son of the Havens.* New York: Antiquarian Press, 1961. In Decker's view, Arnold would today be called a "status seeker." He sought to be a part of Philadelphia's social set. The move to Philadelphia was his downfall because it placed in his hands the food supply of the city and gave him the opportunity to deal with traders and to put his hand in the till.

Flexner, James Thomas. *The Traitor and The Spy: Benedict Arnold and John André.* Boston: Little, Brown and Co., 1975. Literary style and scholarly research are both present in this exciting account of both Arnold and his comrade in the West Point plot, Major André. The book contains illustrations, footnotes, and a useful bibliography.

Tillotson, Harry Stanton. *The Exquisite Exile: The Life and Fortunes of Mrs. Benedict Arnold.* Boston: Lothrop, Lee and Shepard Co., 1932. This is an attempt to exonerate Margaret Shippen from guilt in the treachery of her husband. Although she grew up in luxury and high society, she accepted the failing fortunes of her husband with patience and understanding. The book does not seem to be successful in removing the suspicion that Shippen's Tory connections and her desire to live well might have been factors in moving her husband to treason.

Van Doren, Carl. *Secret History of the American Revolution.* New York: Viking Press, 1941. One of the most valuable contributions of this work is the reproduction, in an appendix, of sixty-eight letters dealing with the affairs of Arnold and André. The Arnold-André correspondence was reproduced from the Clinton Papers at the University of Michigan. The work is a general history of treason during the revolution, and it attempts to place Arnold in that context. Van Doren does not see Arnold as a disillusioned hero who was sincerely converted to the loyalist cause, but as an unscrupulous traitor. Flexner's book provides better documentation and a more useful bibliography.

Wallace, Willard M. *Traitorous Hero: The Life and Fortunes of Benedict Arnold.* New York: Harper and Brothers, Publishers, 1954. A student of the American Revolution provides in this work an objective and readable account of Arnold. He concludes that Arnold was the most talented battlefield commander to fight in the Revolution.

Richard L. Niswonger

CHESTER A. ARTHUR

Born: October 5, 1829; Fairfield, Vermont
Died: November 18, 1886; New York, New York
Areas of Achievement: Education, law, politics, and government
Contribution: Arthur's presidency, virtually free of corruption, comforted a
nation grieving over the death of President James A. Garfield, maintained
peace and order, promoted economic growth, and demonstrated the stability and adaptability of the American political system, particularly during
emergencies.

Early Life
Chester Alan Arthur was born October 5, 1829, in Fairfield, Franklin
County, Vermont, the oldest of seven children. His mother, Malvina Stone,
was a Canadian whose ancestors immigrated from England, and were Baptist; his father, William Arthur, was an Irish immigrant turned Baptist minister as well as a respectable scholar. Under the tutorship of his father, Arthur showed an intense interest in learning and a high aptitude in the
subjects he studied, matriculating at Union College in Schenectady, New
York (at that time, one of the best known colleges in the East), on September 5, 1845, at the age of fifteen. He became a member of the Psi Upsilon
Society, taught in the local schools to help defray the cost of his education,
and in July, 1848, at the age of eighteen, was graduated with high honors,
including membership in the Phi Beta Kappa honor society.
After his graduation from college, Arthur pursued his ambition to become
a lawyer by enrolling in the law school at Ballston Springs, New York, where
he studied for a few months, continuing his studies at home and teaching. In
1851, he became principal and teacher at the North Pownal Academy in
Bennington County, Vermont, ten miles from his family across the border in
Hoosick, New York. During Arthur's tenure as principal there, James A.
Garfield served for a time as a faculty member, teaching business and penmanship—a circumstance that was to be fully exploited in the presidential
campaign of 1880. In 1852, Arthur became principal of an academy at
Cohoes, New York; in 1853, he continued his legal studies in the office of the
prestigious firm of Erastus D. Culver.
On May 4, 1854, after having been certified to the Supreme Court of New
York by the Culver firm that he had satisfactorily completed his studies, Arthur was admitted to the bar. He joined Culver's firm and began practicing
law. In 1856, upon becoming a judge of the Civil Court of Brooklyn, Arthur
formed a partnership with an old friend, Henry D. Gardiner. For three
months, Arthur and his friend tried to establish a practice out West but returned to New York City after becoming disillusioned by widespread lawlessness. Two of Arthur's first and most celebrated cases involved the Fu-

gitive Slave Law and discrimination against black people on New York City streetcars. As a staunch abolitionist, Arthur found in these two cases an opportunity to make a significant contribution to the antislavery movement.

As a Whig delegate from Brooklyn, dedicated to the abolitionist movement, Arthur participated in the convention that met at Saratoga in August of 1854, for the purpose of developing methods for combating the Kansas-Nebraska Act, which repealed the Missouri Compromise of 1820. The action of the convention led to the birth of the Republican Party. In the party's first campaign for the presidency, Arthur wholeheartedly supported and campaigned for the first presidential nominee of the Republican Party, John C. Frémont. During the campaign, Arthur served on an executive committee that worked for the election of Frémont. On election day, Arthur served as an inspector of elections at the polls.

In October, 1859, Arthur married Ellen Lewis Herndon, a member of a distinguished Virginia family and sister of a good friend, Dabney Herndon. Their union produced two sons (one son died at the age of four) and one daughter. Arthur's wife died in January, 1881.

Life's Work

After joining the state's militia, Arthur gained extensive knowledge of military science especially concerning strategy and logistics. His highly rated performance led to his appointment as Judge Advocate-General of the Second Brigade of the New York Militia. Having fully assisted him in his bid for reelection, the governor of New York appointed Arthur as engineer-in-chief and charged him with the responsibility of drawing plans to protect the state. After the Civil War began, the governor promoted Arthur to the position of inspector general of New York troops in the field. Later, he was appointed assistant quartermaster general, then quartermaster general of New York, responsible for raising regiments to fight on the battlefields and maintaining the troops. While serving in the post of quartermaster general, Arthur got his long-awaited chance to participate in direct combat on the battlefields; on two occasions, he was elected first by the Ninth Regiment of the New York Militia and, second, by the Metropolitan Brigade of New York City to lead them in battle. Both times, the governor successfully dissuaded Arthur, convincing him to remain in his post as quartermaster general, wherein he ably carried out his responsibilities for the cause of the Union.

After he resigned his position following the election of a Democrat as governor of the Empire State, Arthur spent much time in Albany and Washington working on war claims and drafting important bills that required quick action, soon becoming one of the best lawyers in New York. In 1866, Arthur helped Roscoe Conkling get elected to the United States Senate, then became his chief henchman until he became president.

In 1867, Arthur was elected to the Century Club, a prestigious intellectual and social organization, and was elected chairman of the executive committee of the New York Republican Party. In 1871, Arthur established one of the most outstanding law firms in New York; in the same year, President Ulysses S. Grant appointed him collector of the Port of New York—the most important political position outside Washington, D.C. Impressed with Arthur's management of the Port of New York, Grant reappointed him to the collectorship, and the Senate confirmed the reappointment unanimously.

In 1878, however, President Rutherford B. Hayes dismissed Arthur from the collectorship on the grounds that his positions in the government and the Republican Party were incompatible with respect to civil service reforms. The outrageous scandals of Grant's two administrations had convinced Hayes of the dire need for an appreciable reform program in government designed to take politics out of the bureaucracy. The removal of Arthur was therefore not based on his competence but on the fact that, as a consummate politician, he had manipulated his position in a way that made him the undisputed "boss" of the Republican Party of New York City as well as chairman of the Central Committee of the Republican Party of the state. Upon his removal, a petition signed by some of the most reputable persons of the time, asking that Arthur be retained, was suppressed by Arthur. Like Garfield, Arthur never sought a position; he wished to retain the collectorship on his own merit, but as a result of a bitter struggle between the Hayes Administration and the Conkling machine, he chose to return to practicing law.

In 1879, as chairman of the Republican Central Committee, Arthur worked hard to strengthen the Republican Party of his state—particularly the Stalwarts (1869-1880), the "regular" or machine wing of his party, who were opposed to the reform program of Hayes's administration—and, disregarding the two-term tradition honored by all the presidents since George Washington, strongly advocated and worked to secure a third term for Grant. In Chicago in June, 1880, at the Republican National Nominating Convention, destiny brought Garfield and Arthur together again as it had twenty-six years earlier at the North Pownal Academy in Vermont. This time their relationship was reversed: Arthur worked under Garfield. The nomination of Garfield and Arthur as candidates for president and vice president of the Republican Party startled the nation, including the candidates themselves.

Both men went to Chicago to do everything within their power to help get the leader of their wing nominated. A bitter struggle was expected between the Stalwarts and the Half-breeds (a wing of the Republican Party, 1876-1884, which supported Hayes's conciliatory policy toward the South, opposed a third term for Grant, and supported the nomination of Garfield), but there were those who believed that the leaders would find a way to resolve the struggle with some kind of compromise. Finally, in order to end the deadlocked convention, the Half-breeds turned to Garfield on the thirty-sixth ballot and nominated him to lead the Republican Party to victory in 1880.

Because they knew that they had no chance of winning the presidency without the support of the Stalwarts, they offered the nomination for vice president to the second most powerful boss of the New York political machine, Chester A. Arthur.

Arthur's nomination was based on political strategy designed to produce some semblance of unity within the Republican Party. On the basis of his experiences of all the candidates available in 1880, Arthur was one of the least qualified to serve as vice president and had no qualifications that would have justified his nomination for the office of the president. Arthur was chosen because he was Conkling's right-hand man. Without the support of the New York political machine, the Republican Party could not win the election. At the outset, Conkling squawked at Arthur's decision to join the Garfield forces, but before the campaign ended, he gave some support.

As the campaign got under way in 1880, the jockeying by the various factions for control left the Republican Party in a state of disarray, and consequently, the opposing forces expediently closed ranks. One of the most thrilling national political conventions in American history produced one of the most unusual tickets in the history of presidential nominating conventions: The presidential candidate thoroughly qualified, with seventeen years of yeoman's service in the House of Representatives on behalf of the people of his district and the nation; the vice presidential candidate was a skilled politician deeply tied to a powerful political machine, with all of his work experience limited to his home state, and with no experience that equipped him to serve as president. The ticket that had surprised the party, the nation, and the candidates themselves succeeded in achieving a narrow victory at the polls in November.

Only a few months after his inauguration, however—on July 2, 1881— Garfield was shot by a deranged office-seeker, Charles J. Guiteau, in a Washington railroad station. Eighty days later, Garfield died, and the agonizing wait of the people who had prayed so hard for his recovery came to an end. Arthur remained extremely apprehensive throughout the lingering death struggle, hoping that somehow Garfield would survive, recover, and resume his duties as president. When Arthur accepted the invitation to run on the ticket with Garfield, he did so on the basis that it would give him the opportunity to escape the continual and perplexing problems associated with his management of the political machine. After his removal from his position as collector of the New York Customhouse by the outgoing President Hayes, Arthur regarded his selection as vice presidential candidate as a vindication of his integrity.

Garfield's tragic death cast the nation into a state of shock that for a while quelled the political discord that to an appreciable degree remained constant in the wake of the presidential campaign of the previous year. As the shock gradually subsided, however, consternation gripped the nation, for the office and power of the president had devolved on the second most powerful political boss in the country, who himself was the chief lieutenant of the most powerful boss in America. To allay such fears, Arthur gradually dissolved his relationship with Conkling and his machine.

During his term as president, Arthur fought hard for a canal in Nicaragua, owned and operated by the United States; advocated a program of reciprocal trade agreements; developed America's first modern steel navy; prosecuted those who defrauded the Post Office Department; and vetoed the Chinese Exclusion Act, changing the suspension of Chinese immigration from twenty to ten years. Possibly Arthur's greatest achievement was his strong support of the act that became the foundation of civil service reform—the Pendleton Act of 1883.

In addition, Arthur recognized the significance of issues which, while not resolved during his presidency, were later to confirm the soundness of his judgment. Among the recommendations Arthur proposed were statehood for Alaska, a building for the Library of Congress, a law determining who should count the electoral votes in order to avoid the type of dispute that occurred in 1876, and the regulation of interstate commerce. In order to avoid another presidential succession crisis, Arthur strongly recommended a constitutional amendment that would provide for the expedient resolution of questions pertaining to presidential succession. Arthur's proposal concerning presidential succession was ultimately realized with the ratification of the Twenty-fifth Amendment to the Constitution on February 10, 1967.

Arthur's long bout with Bright's disease (he had it at the time he assumed the presidency) failed to affect his administration significantly; it did, however, to a large extent prevent him from succeeding himself, which was a goal he very much desired. After his unsuccessful efforts to obtain the nomination of his party in 1884, his supporters in the Republican Party of New York tried to urge him for a seat in the United States Senate in their efforts to repair their badly damaged "machine." Because of his infirmity and lack of interest (after having been president, he considered campaigning for the Senate to be improper), he rejected the idea. He attended ceremonies opening the Brooklyn Bridge in May, 1883. Just before his term expired, Arthur dedicated the Washington monument, on February 22, 1885.

After Arthur left office, he was elected president of his fraternity, Psi Upsilon, and elected the forerunner of the subway system of New York City, the New York Arcade Railway. Arthur died on November 18, 1886, at his home in New York City.

Summary

Arthur showed that the aura of the office and power of the presidency can transform a politician wedded to a political machine into a president who dissociates himself from the machine and bases his policies and programs on what he deems best for the people and the nation. Under the leadership of President Arthur, the intense perturbation of the American people caused by the assassination of Garfield was greatly alleviated. Arthur demonstrated that a man of limited experience could be inspired by prestige, office, and authority of the presidency to exploit his talents and experience to the fullest extent possible, to become an effective president.

When the leading historians in the United States were polled to rate the presidents, they evaluated their subjects as great, near great, above average, average, or below average, with a final slot reserved for outright failures. The historians assigned Arthur to the average class, along with seven other presidents: William McKinley, William Howard Taft, Martin Van Buren, Rutherford B. Hayes, Benjamin Harrison, Zachary Taylor, and Jimmy Carter. Arthur's rating indicates that he overcame his political handicaps and commendably performed his responsibilities as president.

Bibliography
Brisbin, James S. *From the Tow-path to the White House: The Early Life and Public Career of James A. Garfield, Including Also a Sketch of the Life of Honorable Chester A. Arthur.* Philadelphia: Hubbard Brothers, 1880. A classic work containing a readable story of the life of Arthur.
Doenecke, Justus D. *The Presidencies of James A. Garfield and Chester A. Arthur.* Lawrence: University Press of Kansas, 1981. This is a revisionist work inspired by the renewed examination occurring during the centennial of the Guilded Age (1870-1896). Includes brilliant notes and bibliographical essays.
Howe, George Frederick. *Chester A. Arthur: A Quarter-Century of Machine Politics.* New York: Dodd, Mead and Co., 1934. One of the most significant biographical studies of Arthur. This was the only major scholarly biography of Arthur until the publication of Thomas C. Reeves's study in 1975 (see below). Howe's major thesis is that Arthur filled a place of power and responsibility far above his aspirations, bravely and adequately, if not with greatness.
Levin, Peter R. *Seven by Chance: Accidental Presidents.* New York: Farrar, Straus and Co., 1948. This work is a study of the seven men who became president because of the death of the president. The most valuable section of Levin's work is that in which the author assesses the method of choosing a vice-presidential candidate. The author mentions a number of ways to improve the vice presidency. An erudite work that provides an excellent source for studying the vice presidency.
Reeves, Thomas C. *Gentleman Boss: The Life of Chester Alan Arthur.* New York: Alfred A. Knopf, 1975. The author covers Arthur's career in New York politics before he became president, showing that Arthur was a more skillful political organizer and manager than previous accounts indicate.

Reeves's work provides a fresh view of Arthur and has become the standard biography.

Sievers, Harry J., ed. *Six Presidents from the Empire State*. Tarrytown, N.Y.: Sleepy Hollow Restorations, 1974. This volume is a scholarly study of the impact on the presidency of the six presidents from New York. They are divided into three pairs whose terms in office correspond broadly to three major eras in the history of the presidency: Martin Van Buren and Millard Fillmore, pre–Civil War; Chester A. Arthur and Grover Cleveland, the Gilded Age; and Theodore Roosevelt and Franklin Delano Roosevelt, the modern presidency. Includes the Schlesinger polls on presidential greatness, a selected bibliography of the Empire state presidents and their contemporaries, splendid illustrations of the six presidents, and sketches of the thirteen outstanding contributors and the editor.

James D. Lockett

JOHN J. ASTOR

Born: July, 17, 1763; Waldorf, near Heidelberg, Germany
Died: March, 29, 1848; New York, New York
Area of Achievement: Business
Contribution: Combining a shrewd eye for profits with relentless determination, Astor became in turn America's first monopolist, its leading fur trader, its leading trader to China, and "landlord of New York." When he died, he was by far the richest man in the United States.

Early Life

John Jacob Astor was born July 17, 1763, in the village of Waldorf near the ancient city of Heidelberg, Germany. Information concerning the origins of his family is not completely clear, but it seems certain that the Astors (or Ashdoers) were not originally German. The first Astor in Germany arrived in either the sixteenth or the eighteenth century, was either Italian or Spanish, a religious refugee or a soldier, depending on which story is preferred. In any case, the Astor family was not a wealthy one. Astor's father was a butcher who had very little aptitude for business. His mother, fortunately, was methodical and frugal, qualities she passed on to her four sons. John Jacob was the youngest.

With the death of his mother and the arrival of a stepmother, John Jacob became very unhappy and discontented. He left home at the age of sixteen or seventeen and worked his passage down the River Rhine to join an older brother in London. For two or three years, John Jacob worked in his brother's piano manufacturing company, learning English and saving money to travel to America, where a second brother was established as a butcher in New York.

In November, 1783, Astor set sail bound for Baltimore with money enough to tide him over, a stock of German flutes to trade, and a berth in steerage for the trip. The ship arrived in the Chesapeake in January but remained icebound for two months, unable to reach its destination. During that time, Astor became acquainted with a young German returning to America, where he had previously been a fur trapper and trader. Once aroused to the potential for fabulous profits, Astor inquired into the minutest details of the trade and determined to enter the fur business himself. In March, 1784, Astor arrived in New York and soon obtained a job with an old Quaker fur trader. His marriage to Sarah Todd in 1785 brought him a handsome dowry of three hundred dollars, connections with the upper classes of New York City and with various sea captains, and a wife with great business ability of her own. The following year, Astor was able to set up business on his own account as a fur trader and agent for the sale of imported musical instruments.

Life's Work

John Jacob Astor quickly became affluent. To be truly successful as a fur trader, Astor had to compete with the giant Hudson's Bay Company and the Northwest Company, both based in Montreal, and which, between them, dominated much of the trade. With a secure financial base from the music shop run by his wife Sarah, he was able to spend the time to gain the confidence of trappers and Indians in upstate New York through personal contact and by offering a better price than his enormous rivals.

In 1789, Astor was invited to attend the annual meeting of the Northwest Company at Fort William on Lake Superior. What he saw convinced him that if he was ever to compete seriously, he had to develop trade in volume. Consequently, Astor began to develop a regular trade in furs between Montreal and London, and between London and New York (direct trade between Canada and the newly independent United States was illegal until 1796). At the same time, he continued to develop his contacts and agents in the woods in anticipation of the day when he could replace the two great Canadian fur companies.

As his income soared, Astor took his brother's advice and began to invest in real estate. To further his financial interests, John Jacob began to frequent the meeting places of powerful city merchants and became a member of the Masons. By the time of Jay's Treaty in 1796, by which Great Britain agreed to leave the rich hunting grounds south of the Great Lakes and to end the trade ban on goods from Canada to the United States, Astor was in a good position to attempt to rival the great fur companies. He was, by then, one of the leading merchants of New York, estimated to be worth fifty thousand dollars.

In 1800, Astor invested in a cargo of furs bound for China. His share of the profit from this one voyage was estimated at fifty-five thousand dollars and was reinvested in the China trade. By 1803, he had ships of his own built and was becoming America's leading merchant in the China trade. All the while, Astor continued to invest several thousand dollars per year in Manhattan real estate, trading in anything that would bring a good profit from the return journeys of his fur ships, and extending his contacts among fur trappers in the woods.

In 1808, Astor was ready to exploit the possibilities opened up by the Louisiana Purchase. He founded the American Fur Company to monopolize the fur trade west of the Mississippi. The company was capitalized at one million dollars, all of it supplied by Astor himself, and was blessed by the American government, which was full of Astor's business acquaintances and clients. The key to Astor's scheme was to establish a settlement at the mouth of the Columbia River on the Pacific coast—to be called Astoria—as a clearinghouse for furs caught in the region; they could then be sent directly to China, the world's best market. Never before had the merchant taken such a big gamble. The venture was accompanied by great suspicion between Americans hired to run the settlement and the Scots-Canadians hired for their expertise. It was a suspicion shared by Astor himself and was compounded by his assignment of responsibilities. The result was the complete failure of an overland expedition sent to set up trading posts on its way to Astoria and the subsequent loss of the ship that Astor sent out to build the settlement. Worse yet, the War of 1812 allowed the Northwest Company to send an armed ship to Astoria to claim it for Great Britain. Astor's Scots-Canadians sold the settlement to their former employers, the Northwest Company, for a fraction of its real value. It was Astor's greatest setback, one of remarkably few. The nearly one-million-dollar loss sustained by Astor was subsequently made up from profits derived from his investment in American war bonds.

After the war, Astor was in a strong position. He had been able to buy several ships at cheap rates and had invested in real estate and mortgages, both at low prices as a result of wartime depression and a British blockade. Also, despite the Astoria catastrophe, the American Fur Company after 1815 was able to drive out or take over all rivals in the rich Missouri country and around the Great Lakes. It achieved a complete monopoly by 1822.

During the decade of the 1820's, Astor wound down his interests in the China trade as commodities such as tea glutted the market. He shifted his investments to transportation, insurance companies, banks, federal and state securities, and, most heavily, to real estate. In the 1830's, returns from land and property in Manhattan were so great that Astor decided to liquidate all of his interests in commerce and concentrate instead on his investments, particularly real estate. By this time, the fur trade was in decline and so was Astor, now in his seventies.

To perpetuate his name, Astor built the finest hotel in New York, Astor House, and commissioned the writing of a novel defending his actions in the Pacific Northwest. Both Astor House and *Astoria*, by Washington Irving, were completed in 1836. Both were immediate and conspicuous successes.

The Panic of 1837 drove many businessmen to ruin, but not Astor. His great wealth cushioned him and, indeed, he took advantage of the economic depression to extend his investments in Manhattan real estate. With recovery came a huge influx of immigrants, all desperately in need of housing. The value of Astor's investments soared as New York expanded as never before.

John Jacob Astor died on March 29, 1848, having suffered for several years from palsy, extremely poor circulation, and painful stomach disorders. To his son, William Backhouse Astor, he left the bulk of his fortune.

Summary

John Jacob Astor's career spanned the period from the infancy of the young American republic to the early years of its industrial revolution. It was a time of great commercial opportunity. No other single individual was able to capitalize on the possibilities with such singular success. His drive and determination to make money dominated all those with whom he did business. It mattered little to Astor in what branch of commerce or finance he made money; profit margins were all that counted. Astor is principally remembered, however, for his achievement in building the first private monopoly in United States history. It was his American Fur Company which, over the course of fifteen years, attained almost total control over the fur trade in the United States. His purchase of large tracts of Manhattan and the dispersal of investments in banking, insurance, and government stocks secured Astor's fortune for his family and ensured that it would thrive.

Bibliography

Chittenden, Hiram M. *The American Fur Trade of the Far West*. New York: Press of the Pioneers, 1935. Reprint. Stanford, Calif.: Academic Reprints, 1985. A comprehensive examination of the complex structure and pattern which existed before and during the establishment of the American Fur Company. It follows the policies and actions by which independent trappers and companies were driven out of business or incorporated into Astor's company, the ways in which the Indians were dealt with, the employees kept in line, and the trade rationalized.

Gebhard, Elizabeth L. *The Life and Ventures of the Original John Jacob Astor*. Hudson, N.Y.: Bryan Printing Co., 1915. A highly colored and favorable account of the great man, written by a descendant of Astor's friend and fellow German immigrant, John Gabriel Gebhard. Full of detail.

Irving, Pierre M. *The Life and Letters of Washington Irving*. 4 vols. New York: Putnam, 1863. An account of the great literary figure by his nephew. Washington Irving was a longtime friend of Astor, which was why he was commissioned to write *Astoria*. Pierre and his uncle lived in Astor's house for two years preparing materials for the novel. There are a number of revealing letters and episodes concerning Astor.

Irving, Washington. *Astoria*. Philadelphia: Carey, Lea, and Blanchard, 1836. Reprint. Edited by Richard Dilworth Rust. Boston: Twayne Publishers, 1976. This is the authorized version of Astor's astounding career, written by a longtime friend and literary client. It is the most detailed version of Astor's early career and serves as the main reference point for all later accounts, though some of its facts have been questioned, since Irving seems to have accepted many of the myths propagated about, and by, Astor. The book was a best-seller when it appeared.

Minnigerode, Meade. *Certain Rich Men*. New York: G. P. Putnam's Sons, 1927. Of the seven men studied, Astor merits the second chapter, following his friend Stephen Girard the banker. This is a balanced account that stresses Astor's ruthless business practice and his love of family.

Porter, Kenneth Wiggins. *John Jacob Astor: Business Man*. 2 vols. Cambridge, Mass.: Harvard University Press, 1931. Easily the most detailed and informative account of Astor's career. Porter questions some of Irving's assumptions. The author was a research assistant in the Graduate School of Business Administration at Harvard at the time and concentrates largely on Astor's financial interests. He does not, however, neglect the personal aspects in interesting asides and in the first two and last two chapters of the work.

Sinclair, David. *Dynasty: The Astors and Their Times*. London: J. M. Dent and Sons, 1983. A book primarily about the fortune bequeathed by John Jacob Astor. The elder Astor fills the first part of a four-part work. It is an iconoclastic view which subjects Astor in places to biting criticism and which, throughout, is informed by a skepticism about business practices and "great men." A good corrective to some of the other, favorable, accounts cited above.

Stephen Burwood

JOHN JAMES AUDUBON

Born: April 26, 1785; Les Cayes, Haiti
Died: January 27, 1851; New York, New York
Areas of Achievement: Ornithology and art
Contribution: A gifted artist with a love of nature and a passion for discovery,
Audubon became the greatest painter of birds of his time, an important
natural scientist, and an inspiration to conservationists.

Early Life

John James Audubon, American naturalist, was born in Haiti on April 26,
1785, the illegitimate son of Jean Audubon, a French naval officer, and
Jeanne Rabin, a French servant girl from Brittany. After his mother's death,
Audubon's father took him and a younger half sister to France, where he legally adopted his children in 1794. In school, Audubon early revealed his talents for drawing and music. He learned to play the violin and flute and by
age fifteen had begun drawing birds and collecting birds' eggs. After he
proved unfit for a naval career, the elder Audubon sent him to Mill Grove,
his farm near Valley Forge, Pennsylvania. In 1808, following a four-year
engagement, Audubon married Lucy Bakewell, a girl of English descent who
lived on a neighboring estate. Of their four children, two sons—Victor
Gifford and John Woodhouse—survived to adulthood and provided significant help to their father in his painting and publishing projects.

In the United States, Audubon formed a partnership with Ferdinand
Rozier, an older Frenchman whom his father had sent to look after him.
They became frontier merchants, with stores in Kentucky, first in Louisville,
then in Henderson, and finally in Ste. Genevieve, Missouri. Yet Audubon
preferred to trek the forests, observing and painting birds and other wildlife.
Finding business irksome, he dissolved the partnership and entered into an
ill-fated trade arrangement with his brother-in-law, Thomas Bakewell. In
1813, Audubon and a group of associates built a combination sawmill and
gristmill in Henderson, Kentucky. It proved far too ambitious a project to be
sustained by the local economy, and its failure left him bankrupt. After being
imprisoned for debt, he worked as a taxidermist for the Western Museum in
Cincinnati, receiving additional income from portrait painting. In 1820, he
set out for New Orleans to continue work as an artist, but, more important,
to add to his portfolio of bird paintings. His wife worked as a tutor to support the family, and the two endured many months apart before she joined
him in Louisiana.

Life's Work

For Audubon, an avocation developed into a vocation, though it is not
known precisely when the change occurred. In 1810, while he and Rozier

were in their Louisville store, Alexander Wilson, the pioneer American ornithologist, showed them his bird paintings and sought a subscription to support publication of his nine-volume *American Ornithology* (1808-1814). After seeing Wilson's work, Rozier remarked that his partner's paintings were better. By allowing Audubon to realize that his amateur work surpassed the work of a professional, this incident probably served as a catalyst to his fertile imagination.

He gradually developed the idea for *The Birds of America* (1827-1838), an ambitious portfolio of all American species, life-size, in their natural habitats. In its scope, scale, and fidelity to nature, Audubon's work would eclipse that of his predecessors. In order to include all the known species, he would rely upon the discoveries and observations of others for some of his paintings, not limiting the work to his own observations as Wilson had done. By the time he left for New Orleans in late 1820, the outlines of the work, which would require almost two decades to complete, were formed.

An experienced hunter and skilled woodsman, Audubon combined an intense interest in nature with a sharp eye and essential survival skills. He was equally comfortable alone or in company, and equally ingratiating to Indians or European noblemen. At five feet ten and a half inches tall, he was a man of almost regal appearance, with smooth facial lines, long brown hair, somewhat receding, and blue eyes. A contemporary, Mrs. Nathaniel Wells Pope, described him as "one of the handsomest men I ever saw . . . tall and slender. . . . His bearing was courteous and refined, simple and unassuming."

In Audubon's time, a naturalist needed to collect specimens (usually by shooting), to record his observations in a journal, and to sketch or paint all that he found interesting. To collect specimens, he shot thousands of birds on his expeditions. The collecting, however, did not stop there: He obtained insects, reptiles, and mammals for many other scientists throughout the world. In his lengthy journals, often romantic and even grandiloquent in tone, he made detailed notes about bird sightings and behavior. An almost compulsive painter, he sometimes began sketching a bird by placing its body on a sheet of paper and drawing an outline. Although Audubon occasionally painted live birds, his normal mode was to paint dead ones, which he wired into positions that suited him.

After his efforts to interest New York and Philadelphia publishers in his work failed, Audubon embarked in 1826 for England, where he attempted to attract wealthy patrons for his project by exhibiting his paintings. There, where he was regarded as a natural untaught genius, he became something of a celebrity, being named a fellow of the Royal Society. For *The Birds of America* he sought two hundred subscribers willing to pay one thousand dollars each; he eventually obtained 161, about half of them from the United States. Subscribers paid for a set of five prints at a time, with eighty sets, or four hundred prints, projected.

The publication, requiring eleven years, began in 1827, in Edinburgh, under the engraver William Lizars. Audubon quickly changed to Robert Havell and Company in London, after Havell impressed the painter with his ability to reproduce color tones. The images were etched on copper plates using aquatint, producing shades of gray and black on a light background. They were engraved on sheets measuring thirty-nine and a half by twenty-six and a half inches, forming the Double Elephant Folio, one of the largest books ever printed. After the engraving, artists colored the prints professionally by hand to match Audubon's original paintings.

When completed, the work included life-size color prints of 489 species on 435 pages. The total number of bird paintings was 1,065, for Audubon attempted to illustrate different color phases of each species, and for birds of varied coloration he often produced several poses to reveal the colors more effectively. One of his own favorite paintings, that of the wood duck, includes four birds so positioned as to reveal the rich coloration of the species. His painting of the little blue heron shows a full-size adult in the foreground and, at a distance, standing in a marsh, the white immature representative of the species.

During the production of his major work, Audubon returned to the United States three times to collect more specimens and to complete his paintings, leaving publication in the hands of his son Victor and Havell. In the United States, he mounted extended expeditions into the interior of the country, along the Gulf of Mexico, and to Labrador. Meanwhile, with the assistance of the gifted Scottish ornithologist William MacGillivray, he prepared and issued five volumes of commentaries as companion volumes to the paintings, *Ornithological Biography* (1831-1839). The work names and describes each species, provides an account of its behavior and habitats, and often includes vivid narration of Audubon's experience with the species, the primary source being his unpublished journals.

After completing *The Birds of America*, Audubon issued the work in a smaller and less expensive edition. He then turned to a new project, this time concerning North American mammals, *Viviparous Quadrupeds of North America* (1846-1854; plates, 1842-1845), in collaboration with his friend John Bachman. Seeking specimens to paint, he organized his last great expedition in 1843, traveling up the Missouri River to the mouth of the Yellowstone in North Dakota. After age sixty, he suffered a rapid decline in health, marked by a loss of mental powers. He died quietly at his New York home, Minnie's Land, on January 27, 1851, leaving completion of his work on the mammals to his sons and to Bachman.

Summary

In ornithology, art, and conservation, Audubon's fame and influence have endured. During his time, taxonomy was in its early stages, and science developed largely through observation and compilation. Vast areas of the world lay unexplored and unstudied. To discover new species of flora or fauna was an obvious route to achievement, possibly even to fame. Never a theorist and little inclined toward experimentation, Audubon possessed intense curiosity about nature, keen eyes, and a questing, somewhat romantic nature. He discovered a dozen subspecies, more than twenty species, and one genus of American birds. The list, though impressive, is shorter than he believed, because he mistook several variant color phases for new species and unwittingly claimed some prior discoveries of others.

The artistic quality of *The Birds of America* surpassed that of its predecessors, and the work has not been equaled since in its scale, scope, and aesthetic appeal. Although he occasionally painted with oils, Audubon achieved his best effects using watercolors with an overlay of pastels to enhance color and sharpen detail. Critics, however, have called attention to his limitations as an artist. He sometimes posed his subjects in unnatural positions and uncharacteristic settings, gave some birds human expressions, and could not sustain a uniformly high aesthetic level throughout the long project. Yet he succeeded in arousing widespread interest in ornithology and made the birds of the New World familiar to the Old.

In the twentieth century, his name has become synonymous with conservation of wildlife, a legacy not without irony considering the number of birds he felled with his gun. Still, toward the end of his life, he spoke out against egg collecting as a threat to bird populations. During his final Western expedition, he was troubled by the indiscriminate slaughter of bison. He genuinely loved the primitive frontier and feared that it might disappear under the pressure of civilization. In 1886, his protégé and admirer, George Bird Grinnell, organized the first Audubon Society to preserve some of the natural beauty and living creatures of the land Audubon loved.

Bibliography
Audubon, John J. *The 1826 Journal of John James Audubon*. Edited by Alice Ford. Norman: University of Oklahoma Press, 1967. Careful editing and extensive commentary supplement this important surviving Audubon journal. It reveals Audubon as a careful observer of birds from shipboard during his journey to England.
Chancellor, John. *Audubon: A Biography*. London: Weidenfeld and Nicholson, 1978. A readable brief biography of Audubon, with a judicious assessment of his achievement. Rich in illustrations.
Ford, Alice. *John James Audubon*. Norman: University of Oklahoma Press, 1964. Now the standard biography, it gives a carefully researched account of Audubon's origins and early life, adding extensive details about his early life in France.
Fries, Waldemar H. *The Double Elephant Folio: The Story of Audubon's*

Birds of America. Chicago: American Library Association, 1973. A scholarly historical and bibliographic account of the production and distribution of Audubon's greatest work. Traces the location and provides description of all extant copies.

Harwood, Michael. "Mr. Audubon's Last Hurrah." *Audubon* 87 (November, 1985): 80-117. A lengthy account of Audubon's journey to North Dakota in 1843, the article provides numerous excerpts from his journals and those of contemporaries.

Harwood, Michael, and Mary Durant. "In Search of the Real Mr. Audubon." *Audubon* 87 (May, 1985): 58-119. This article traces Audubon's career in detail, assesses the many myths that surround him, and provides a critique of his biographers. Generously and judiciously illustrated, with numerous reproductions.

Herrick, Francis Hobart. *Audubon the Naturalist: A History of His Life and Time*. 2 vols. New York: D. Appleton and Co., 1917, 1938. Although somewhat dated in its research, the biography remains a valuable resource for its comprehensive treatment and its inclusion of many original letters, papers, official records, and documents.

Lindsey, Alton A. *The Bicentennial of John James Audubon*. Bloomington: Indiana University Press, 1985. A collection of essays by various hands, the book assesses Audubon's character, his contributions to science and art, and his influence on conservation.

Stanley Archer

STEPHEN FULLER AUSTIN

Born: November 3, 1793; Wythe County, Virginia
Died: December 27, 1836; Columbia, Texas
Areas of Achievement: Colonization and statesmanship
Contribution: Austin established the first Anglo-American colony in Texas and played a significant role in the Texas Revolution, which resulted in that province securing independence from Mexico.

Early Life

Stephen Fuller Austin was born on November 3, 1793, in Wythe County, Virginia. His father, Moses Austin, was a mine owner who came from a family of Connecticut merchants. His mother, née Maria Brown, had a New Jersey Quaker heritage. The Austin family moved to the province of Spanish Louisiana in 1798 to seek better lead deposits for mining. Moses established and operated a lead mine south of St. Louis. There young Stephen passed his childhood until the age of eleven years. In 1804, his family sent him to Connecticut to begin his formal education. He spent several years as a pupil at Bacon Academy and then entered Transylvania University in Kentucky. In 1810, the youth returned to Missouri, which had become part of the United States because of the Louisiana Purchase. The young man worked at a bank in St. Louis and, for a time, engaged in storekeeping. In 1814, his neighbors elected him as a delegate to the Missouri Territorial Legislature, a post he held until 1820.

In 1817, Austin took charge of the financially troubled family mining operating at Potosi. He was, however, unable to make it a profitable business. In 1820, he therefore followed his brother-in-law James Perry to the Arkansas Territory. There he established a farm near Long Prairie on the Red River. The governor of Arkansas appointed him a district judge in July of 1820.

By early adulthood, it had become obvious that Austin had natural leadership ability. He had a pleasing personality along with a mature outlook. He was a physically small person of slight build, only five feet, six inches in height. Dark haired and fine featured, Stephen was no doubt a handsome youth who inspired confidence in all whom he met. His greatest strengths, however, were his moderate personal habits. A well-educated man, he was charitable, tolerant, and loyal in his relationships with others. Also, although he never married, he seldom lacked companionship from the many friends he made throughout his life. It is not surprising, therefore, that Austin decided upon the practice of law as his career. In 1821, he went to New Orleans to study for the bar.

Events set in motion about this time by his father, however, changed forever the course of Austin's life. Moses Austin decided to found a colony in the Spanish province of Texas. The fertile and unsettled land there had rich agricultural potential. Many Anglo-Americans from the United States, especially cotton farmers from the South, would probably be glad to immigrate to Texas. They would exploit the land, something the Spanish had never done. Moses went to San Antonio, where he secured a colonization career from the Spanish governor in 1821. This grant permitted him to settle three hundred families in the province. These immigrants would agree to become Spanish subjects in return for grants of land. Moses Austin, however, died in 1821, before he could begin his colonization venture. With his dying breath, he asked that Austin carry through this enterprise and bring it to successful conclusion. This his son agreed to do.

Life's Work

The summer of 1821 found Austin in San Antonio. There he secured a reconfirmation of his father's colonization grant from the Spanish authorities. Unfortunately, however, Mexico became independent from Spain in early 1822, and, consequently, the grant was no longer valid. Austin, who could not secure a renewal from the incoming Mexican authorities in Texas, decided to travel to Mexico City to speak about his grant directly with the newly independent government. He arrived there on April 29, 1822, in the hope that meeting with the Mexican leaders would restore his concession. In the meantime, various Anglo-American farmers began moving to Texas in anticipation of Austin's success in Mexico City.

Austin remained in Mexico for a year while he witnessed the turmoils and instabilities of the new Mexican government. Because of problems related to establishing a workable form of government, Austin could not immediately secure a confirmation of his Texas concession. He did use this time in Mexico City to personal advantage, however, learning to speak and write Spanish with marked fluency. He also made many friends among the Mexican leaders, including Miguel Ramos Arispe, who authored the Mexican Constitution of 1824. Austin furnished Arispe with a translated copy of the United States Constitution and made recommendations concerning the contents of the Mexican document.

The Mexican government confirmed the Austin grant in early 1823. Austin returned to Texas and assumed direction of the colony, which grew rapidly. By the end of 1824, almost all three hundred colonists permitted by the colonization charter had received grants. The Austin colony centered along the rich land of the Brazos River. Most colonists settled in a region called "the bottom," several leagues inland from the Gulf coast. The small town of San Felipe became its chief settlement. A formal census of the colony taken in 1825 showed eighteen hundred residents, of whom 443 were slaves.

During the summer of 1824, the Mexican government approved the establishment of additional Anglo colonies in Texas. Any prospective colonizer could apply for an *empresario* contract, the Spanish term used to describe these concessions. In all, Mexico issued several dozen such contracts to various individuals during the following decade. Most of them did not enjoy success, although Austin continued to do so. His original contract fulfilled, he applied for additional colonial grants under the *empresario* provisions. The additional settlements which he sponsored brought hundreds of families into Texas. By 1830, Austin had attracted some five thousand people into Texas. This influx, added to the families who came under the leadership of the other *empresarios*, resulted in a considerable Anglo population in the province by the end of the 1820's.

Austin became involved in Mexican politics which, during this period, was chaotic and complicated by factions. The Anglo-Texans increasingly came to identify with the Federalists, a Mexican political group whose beliefs seemed similar to their own. The Centralists, the opposing faction, thus began to identify Austin and the Anglo-Texans as members of the Federalists by the early 1830's. Therein lay one of the causes of the Texas Revolution.

In addition, the Mexican government was concerned that too many Anglo-Americans had immigrated to Texas. As a result, it passed the law of April 6, 1830, which (among other restrictions) ended all future immigration into Texas from the United States. Austin worked hard to secure a repeal of this law. He once again went to Mexico City to lobby for measures favorable to Texas. Although he failed to secure all the concessions he wanted, he did convince the government to repeal some of the most objectionable aspects of the law. By the time he returned to Texas in late 1831, events during his absence had made it increasingly difficult for Anglo-Texans to reconcile themselves to continued Mexican rule.

The actions of the post commander at Anahuac on the Texas coast had caused great dissatisfaction among Anglo residents. During the summer of 1832, the colonists took to arms to force his removal. The military commander in Texas eventually removed the offensive garrison commander at Anahuac. For a time, this forestalled additional armed confrontations with the increasingly unhappy Anglo population. By then, however, the crisis had begun. The town council of San Felipe issued a call for a convention of Anglo colonists to discussion common problems and desires. The fifty-eight delegates who composed this group assembled in October, 1832, and elected Austin the presiding officer.

This Convention of 1832, as it subsequently came to be called, drafted a long list of concessions which the Anglo-Texans wanted from the Mexican government. It also created a standing committee of correspondence in each area of Texas for the purpose of monitoring additional problems with Mexico. The delegates also agreed that another convention would be held the following year. This second convention met in 1833 and drafted a provincial constitution for Texas as a separate state within the Mexican government. The Convention of 1833 delegated Austin to deliver this document to the central government. Austin left Texas in May, 1833, on a journey which would result in a two-year absence from Texas. He spent much of this time in a Mexican prison.

Austin arrived in Mexico City, where he presented the proposed constitution to government officials. He also wrote a letter to the town council in San Antonio which complained about the political situation in Mexico. A government official intercepted this letter en route to Texas and believed that it contained treason. Austin, arrested for this in early January of 1834, remained in prison until December of that year. He did not return to Texas until July 11, 1835. Austin's confinement in Mexico City, much of it in the harsh Prison of the Inquisition, permanently ruined his health. During his absence from Texas, dissatisfaction there with Mexico continued. By late 1835, many Anglo-Texans, including Austin, had come to favor a break with Mexico.

The Texas Revolution began on October 2, 1835, with a skirmish between Anglo and Mexican troops near Gonzales, Texas. A committee of colonists issued a call for a provincial convention which appointed Austin commander of the revolutionary army. He held this position for only a few months. The Texas government then appointed him as an agent to the United States, charged with finding materials and supplies for the revolt. Austin spent much of the Texas Revolution in the United States, visiting Washington, D.C., Richmond, Philadelphia, and other cities. He returned to Texas during the summer of 1836 after the Texas Revolution had ended in an Anglo-American victory. Austin permitted his supporters to place his name in candidacy as president of the Republic of Texas. When Sam Houston won election to this office, Austin looked forward to retiring to private life. Houston, however, prevailed upon him to become secretary of state in the new government, which Austin reluctantly agreed to do. He served only a few months. His health broken by the imprisonment in Mexico, Austin died on December 27, 1836.

Summary

Stephen Fuller Austin played a significant role in the westward expansion of the United States. Although credit for the Anglo colonization of Hispanic Texas belongs to his father, Austin carried out the dream, and its success belongs to him. He approached the colonization of Texas with a single-minded determination which consumed all of his efforts. In fact, he had time for little else from 1821 until the events of the Texas Revolution. Although he initially believed that Texas should remain a part of Mexico, Austin had become a vocal advocate of independence by 1835. His activities during the revolt materially assisted the Texan victory. It had been his intention to retire from public life after the success of the revolt. He had earlier selected a picturesque, unsettled location—on the lower Colorado River in Texas—as the site for his home. It is fitting that the modern city of Austin, the state capital, occupies that location. It is there Stephen Fuller Austin rests, in the State Cemetery.

Bibliography

Barker, Eugene C. *The Life of Stephen F. Austin, Founder of Texas, 1793-1836: A Chapter in the Westward Movement of the Anglo-American People.* Nashville: Cokesbury Press, 1925. Standard scholarly biography from original sources, mainly the Austin family papers. This is the most detailed and complete study of Austin and his impact on American history. It is the only full-length biography and provides a solid history of the entire Austin colony.

_____. "Stephen F. Austin." In *Handbook of Texas*, vol. 1, edited by Walter P. Webb. Austin: University of Texas Press, 1952. Provides highlights of Austin's career in a short biography. It offers a concise, short treatment of Austin's life in a factual manner.

_____, ed. *The Austin Papers.* 3 vols. Washington, D.C.: American Historical Association, 1919-1926. Collection of personal papers and letters of Moses and Stephen F. Austin. Covers the early years of the Austin family in Missouri, with the major part of the collection dealing with the period from 1822 to 1836.

Glascock, Sallie. *Dreams of Empire: The Story of Stephen Fuller Austin and His Colony in Texas.* San Antonio, Tex.: Naylor, 1951. Well-written biography designed for the general reader or for young readers. Good starting place for those unfamiliar with Austin's life.

Holley, Mary Austin. *Texas: Observations, Historical, Geographical, and Descriptive.* Baltimore: Armstrong and Plaskett, 1833. Holley was Austin's cousin. Provides a firsthand account of life and events in the colony and useful insights into the Austin settlement.

Tracy, Milton, and Richard Havelock-Bailie. *The Colonizer: A Saga of Stephen F. Austin.* El Paso, Tex.: Guynes Printing Co., 1941. Concentrates on the *empresario* career. Makes few improvements on the Barker biography of Austin but is a solid, general assessment of Austin's life, placing him in historical perspective.

Light Townsend Cummins

GEORGE BALANCHINE
Georgi Melitonovitch Balanchivadze

Born: January 22, 1904; St. Petersburg, Russia
Died: April 30, 1983; New York, New York
Area of Achievement: Dance
Contribution: Balanchine transformed ballet into a diverse, vibrantly contemporary, American medium. He established a training tradition and brought ballet to the forefront of the performing arts in the United States.

Early Life

George Balanchine was born on January 22, 1904, in St. Petersburg, Russia, a city more European than Russian in its culture. His father, Meliton Balanchivadze, was a composer of modest means best known for his arrangements of folk songs from his native Georgia in the Caucasus. As a child, Balanchine studied the piano and considered careers in the military or the church. These early plans foretold his future work, which was to combine extraordinary physical discipline with spiritual expression inspired by music.

Balanchine entered the world of ballet by accident. Unable to enroll in the Imperial Naval Academy in August, 1914, he accompanied his sister to an audition at the Imperial School of Ballet and was invited to audition as well. He passed (she failed), and, because of the family's financial difficulties, he was enrolled and left there the same day. A reluctant student (he immediately ran away from school), Balanchine nevertheless passed the probationary first year. The turnaround in his attitude toward the profession chosen for him occurred during his second year, when he appeared in a performance of Peter Ilich Tchaikovsky's ballet *The Sleeping Beauty* (1890), performed by the Imperial Ballet Company at the Maryinsky Theatre. The experience dazzled him, and performing became the motivation for undergoing the rigorous training at the school.

Meanwhile, political events were affecting the cloistered, tradition-bound existence of his world. Balanchine entered the Imperial School of Ballet the month in which World War I was declared, and in 1917, the Bolshevik Revolution closed the school until the following year, during which time Balanchine scrounged the city for food and took menial jobs in order to survive. The commissar for education, Anatole Lunarcharsky, convinced Vladimir Ilyich Lenin, chairman of the Soviet government, that the performing arts should be considered a valuable heritage of the working class rather than a decadent practice of the aristocracy. While the argument saved the school, this same viewpoint would eventually threaten Balanchine's early choreographic career.

Reminiscences of fellow students from this period refer to Balanchine's modest, untemperamental, yet authoritative manner and his great capacity for gaiety and wit. He was a slender, dark-haired man with brooding eyes reflecting an intense concentration.

The groundwork for Balanchine's unique contributions to choreography was laid as he explored his varied artistic interests. While still a student, he distinguished himself by his unusual musical ability and by choreographing small works for student concerts. Upon graduation in 1921, he entered the Imperial Ballet Company as a member of the corps de ballet and at the same time became a student at the Petrograd (Leningrad) Conservatory of Music for three years to study piano and composition. At the end of his studies, deciding that he could not become a significant composer, he directed his life totally to the world of ballet.

In the early days of the Revolution, there were no consistent policies to inhibit a young choreographer such as Balanchine in his experimentation. Influenced by aspects of the choreography of Marius Petipa (1822-1910), the established Michel Fokine, and his contemporary Kasyan Goleizovsky, Balanchine was drawn to develop a new dance vocabulary that would interpret music and evoke moods, unfettered by the constraints of presenting an actual story and undistracted by complicated costumes and scenery.

In 1923, after the second of his controversial special performances, "Evenings of the Young Ballet," the directors of the Maryinsky Theatre announced that any dancers taking part in such programs without special permission would be fired. This decree effectively ended Balanchine's endeavors in the Soviet Union. The following year, he joined a small performing group that had received permission to tour in Germany, and with the first of his four dancer wives, Tamara Gevergeyeva (later Geva), Balanchine left the Soviet Union for the West.

Balanchine saw his education as having two phases: his training in Russia and his five years as choreographer with Sergei Diaghilev's Ballets Russes in Monte Carlo, a post he obtained shortly after he left the Soviet Union in 1924. Diaghilev was an impresario of remarkable vision and taste, who employed the most notable artists of the early twentieth century, including painters Pablo Picasso and Henri Matisse, composers Igor Stravinsky and Erik Satie, and dancers Anna Pavlova and Vaslav Nijinsky, to create and perform ballets throughout Europe. Both the intellectual elite and the fashionable society of Europe were fascinated by Diaghilev's experimentation and achievements. Balanchine's lifelong collaboration and friendship with Stravinsky date from these years.

Life's Work

Two of Balanchine's highly acclaimed works of the 1920's were considered to be turning points in choreographic development: *Apollo* (1928), for its contemporary interpretation of classical ballet style, which closely reflected Stravinsky's score; and *The Prodigal Son* (1929), a biblical theme to music by

Sergey Prokofiev, danced expressionistically with a vocabulary inspired by circus movements. After Diaghilev's death in 1929, Balanchine choreographed for several companies including the newly formed Ballets Russes de Monte Carlo and his own struggling group Les Ballets 1933, in Paris.

At this point, Lincoln Kirstein, a wealthy, cultivated young American, who sought to establish ballet as a permanent art form in the United States, approached Balanchine and convinced him to embark on this endeavor, assisted by several benefactors, notably Nelson Rockefeller and Edward Warburg. The School of American Ballet opened in New York City in January, 1934, followed a year later by the American Ballet company. Its first performance included *Serenade* (1935; music by Tchaikovsky), considered by many to be Balanchine's signature work. During this early period, Balanchine was considered by some critics to be too international and decadent in flavor and therefore not "American" enough to develop an American style and a school of ballet. His experiences in the following dozen years gave him the broadest possible scope of American theatrical enterprises and at the same time enriched them with his own innovations.

The precarious financial position of his company caused Balanchine to affiliate it with the Metropolitan Opera Company. He presented his first Stravinsky Festival in 1937 with *Apollo*, *The Card Game*, and *The Fairy's Kiss*. He then worked for the Ringling Brothers Circus (he and Stravinsky created a ballet for elephants), Broadway (eighteen musicals and revues), and Hollywood (four films). In the cinema and musical comedy he introduced diversified choreography integrated into the plot, a dream ballet sequence that was a favorite of Broadway choreographers for thirty years, and innovations in filming dance utilizing the advantages of camera effects.

Balanchine's American Ballet company was summoned back into temporary existence by the State Department in 1941, for a goodwill tour of Latin America. This tour marked the first performing arts sponsorship by the United States government and the beginning of cultural exchange programs. The School of American Ballet became a permanent institution, producing young American dancers of the highest caliber under Balanchine's exacting standards.

Balanchine and Kirstein founded the Ballet Society in 1946. The premiere included one of his most unusual works, *The Four Temperaments*, to music by Paul Hindemith, a forceful yet impersonal and technically difficult ballet. In 1948 came *Orpheus* (with music by Stravinsky), in which the choreography interpreted the Greek legend with great poignancy and dramatic style.

In 1948, the Ballet Society became the New York City Ballet, the resident company of the New York City Center for Music and Drama (owned by the City of New York), the first American ballet company to become a public institution. By this time, Balanchine had choreographed more than fifty ballets and was nurturing a nucleus of dancers, trained at his school, who would develop into the ideal Balanchine dancer: slim, elongated, with impeccable technique and a highly developed sense of musical phrasing that would combine to respond to Balanchine's complex interpretation of music.

Frequent European tours beginning in 1950 established the company as one of the most important in the world, with a unique repertory and style which would nevertheless continue to be controversial. Important ballets followed, including *La Valse* (music by Maurice Ravel), *Metamorphoses* (Hindemith), *Opus 34* (Arnold Schönberg), *Ivesiana* (Charles Ives), and *Western Symphony* (Hershy Kay), the last of which reflected Balanchine's enthusiasm for the Wild West. He was also a guest choreographer for leading European ballet and opera companies.

Balanchine was fascinated by female dancers and often said that "ballet is woman." His second marriage was to Vera Zorina, his third to Maria Tallchief. His fourth wife, the brilliant young dancer Tanaquil LeClercq, contracted polio in 1956. Although it was feared that Balanchine would retire after this tragedy, he returned to the company the following year and continued to develop his repertory for the next twenty-five years. *Agon* (1937; music by Stravinsky) completed his Greek mythology trilogy. A contest of technique between dancers, it presented seventeenth century dance forms updated by contemporary rhythms. *The Nutcracker* (1954; music by Tchaikovsky) his first evening-length ballet, became an annual, sold-out Christmas season presentation.

In 1962, the New York City Ballet made a State Department–sponsored tour of the Soviet Union. While acclaimed for the quality of the dancers and for his choreographic abilities, Balanchine was sharply criticized in the Moscow press for his plotless ballets. Yet the Moscow audience, reticent at first, became highly enthusiastic. Leningrad, more cultivated and Europeanized, was captivated by the performances, which coincided with the beginning of a reaction against Soviet realism in the arts. Throughout the tour, the Soviets attempted to point out Balanchine's ties to Russian culture. Diplomatically, Balanchine would accept the honors bestowed upon him on behalf of the United States and the New York City Ballet and then assert that he was an American.

Tangible successes followed in the 1960's. The Ford Foundation made an unprecedented grant in 1963 of more than $7.75 million, almost all of which was awarded to Balanchine's organizations. In 1964, the New York City Ballet became the resident company of the New York State Theatre at Lincoln Center, which was probably the first theater to be designed according to the specifications of a choreographer. In 1967, the company established a yearly summer residency at the Saratoga Performing Arts Center in New York. Balanchine choreographed four full-length ballets during this decade: William Shakespeare's *A Midsummer Night's Dream* (music by Felix Mendelssohn), *Harlequinade* (Ricardo Drigo), *Don Quixote* (Nicholas Nabokov), and *Jewels*, the first full-length plotless ballet, with music by Gabriel-Urbain Fauré, Stravinsky, and Tchaikovsky.

Notable achievements in the 1970's were festivals for Stravinsky and Ravel (the latter included *Le Tombeau de Couperin*, choreographed entirely for sixteen members of the corps de ballet, with no soloists), a full-length *Coppelia* (music by Leo Delibes), the highly popular *Vienna Waltzes*, and the first of a series of ballet telecasts for *Dance in America* on National Educational Television. In the 1980's, despite failing health, Balanchine presented a Tchaikovsky Festival and a retrospective Stravinsky Festival. He died in 1983 in New York City.

Summary

Balanchine brought the Old World art of ballet to the United States, blended its traditions into a contemporary, diversified language, and established his version of it around the country and the world as a uniquely American product. His school became the first institution in the United States to establish permanent, high-quality standards of dance training. He choreographed children's roles into many of his ballets to give children the same opportunity he had had to experience the joys and wonder of the theater. He organized lecture-demonstration tours for schools, free ballet performances for underprivileged children, free annual seminars for dance teachers, and gave free advice and use of his ballets to other ballet companies. The landmark grant from the Ford Foundation was the signal for other philanthropic foundations to contribute to performing arts organizations in the United States.

In evolving a contemporary choreography, Balanchine was influenced primarily by music, and as such exposed his audience to a vast range of modern as well as earlier composers, including the Americans George Gershwin, John Philip Sousa, and Richard Rodgers. He brought a tradition-bound art form into the twentieth century, freeing it from the excesses of stylization that had obscured the beauty and expressiveness of dance. When presenting a story, a subtly portrayed emotion or outlook, he produced mime and nonballetic aspects that were easily recognizable from everyday gestures. Balanchine's ballets explored different cultures, human relationships, and theatrical forms, and integrated them into his unique interpretation of the music. He emphasized what has been called an American energy in his dancers. He developed their technical range at all levels and for both sexes, achieving more harmonious dance compositions by greater participation of all the dancers on the stage.

Balanchine's fifty years of work in the United States brought to millions a highly developed art form which was respectful of its traditions yet forged ahead in innovations and integrated various cultures and fields.

Bibliography

Ashley, Merrill. *Dancing for Balanchine*. New York: E. P. Dutton, 1984. Autobiography of a Balanchine dancer with Balanchine as special focus. Gives a fascinating account of Balanchine's methods as teacher, choreographer, and mentor.

Balanchine, George, and Francis Mason. *Balanchine's Complete Stories of the Great Ballets*. Garden City, N.Y.: Doubleday and Co., 1977. Plot summaries and historical data on four hundred important ballets. Includes valuable articles by Balanchine on his life and views of ballet.

Katz, Leslie George, and Harvey Simmonds, comp. *Choreography by George Balanchine: A Catalogue of Works*. New York: Eakins Press Foundation, 1983. Complete chronological list of Balanchine's 425 works with opening-night casts and notes, and extensive bibliography. Indispensable catalog of Balanchine's work.

Kirstein, Lincoln. *Thirty Years: The New York City Ballet*. New York: Alfred A. Knopf, 1978. Interesting, though chatty and somewhat rambling, selective memoirs. Worthwhile secondary text by Balanchine's patron and adviser.

McDonagh, Don. *George Balanchine*. Boston: Twayne Publishers, 1983. Concise, well-rounded biography combined with analytical discussion of selected ballets and Balanchine's development. Invaluable study.

Reynolds, Nancy. *Repertory in Review: Forty Years of the New York City Ballet*. New York: Dial Press, 1977. Excellent historical perspective on the company's repertory and periods, including informative articles on the school and Balanchine.

Taper, Bernard. *Balanchine: A Biography*. New York: Macmillan, 1974. Thorough, well-rounded chronicle of Balanchine's life and work, with illustrative anecdotes.

Karen Resnick Pellón

EMILY GREENE BALCH

Born: January 8, 1867; Jamaica Plain, Massachusetts
Died: January 9, 1961; Cambridge, Massachusetts
Areas of Achievement: Social reform and education
Contribution: Among the first generation of women to graduate from college in large numbers, Balch authored the frequently cited *Our Slavic Fellow Citizens* (1910) and, as a reward for her peace activities, received the Nobel Peace Prize.

Early Life
Emily Greene Balch was born January 8, 1867, in Jamaica Plain, Massachusetts. Her parents were Unitarians of English descent who could trace their ancestors back to the early seventeenth century Colonies. Her father, Francis Vergnies Balch, was a lawyer. Her mother, Ellen Maria (Noyes) Balch, was a housewife who produced six children and died at the age of forty-seven, when Emily was seventeen.

Balch received an unusually good education for her time. While attending private schools, she lived with her family in suburban Boston. At a time when women college graduates were regarded as social oddities and were less likely to marry, her father encouraged her to go to college. She chose the new school of Bryn Mawr because that was where her best friend was going. Bryn Mawr was founded by members of the Quaker religion, a religion which Balch eventually adopted. She was graduated in three years with a major in classics and won Bryn Mawr's European fellowship as the outstanding senior. After privately studying sociology with Franklin H. Giddings, she used the fellowship to spend a year in Paris researching the public relief system there. The result was her book, *Public Assistance of the Poor in France*, published by the American Economic Association in 1893.

Life's Work
Balch's career can be divided into several phases, the first of which centered on social work. She became an expert on agencies and laws dealing with juvenile delinquency, and, in 1895, published the seventy-two-page *Manual for Use in Cases of Juvenile Offenders and Other Minors in Massachusetts*. Four years later, concerned women in Chicago brought about the first juvenile court. Subsequently, Balch revised her manual twice, in 1903 and 1908. Meanwhile, she met Jane Addams and others involved in the settlement house movement. In 1892, Balch joined a grouped of female college graduates in founding Denison House in Boston and headed that settlement during its first year. Through her continued involvement in Denison House, Balch came into direct contact with the poor, learning at first hand about working conditions and obstacles to labor organizing. After several years of

charitable volunteering, however, she decided that she would have more impact as a teacher of social and economic subjects, inspiring her students to work for reform and guiding them in the best ways to achieve it.

To prepare for teaching, the second phase of Balch's career, she studied briefly at Radcliffe (then called Harvard Annex), the University of Chicago, and the University of Berlin. At the last institution, she became especially familiar with socialism. Attending with her was another woman from Boston, Mary Kingsbury, who was later married to a student from Russia, Vladimir Simkhovitch, and who founded Greenwich House, a settlement in New York City. Balch and Kingsbury became lifelong friends and were also part of a national network of settlement leaders and reformers, many of them women, that provided support for one another's goals and causes. On Balch's return to Boston in 1896, she accepted a half-time position teaching economics at Wellesley College. The following year, she became a full-time instructor, in 1903, an associate professor, and in 1913, a professor.

At Wellesley, she taught courses on socialism with Karl Marx's *Das Kapital* (1867) as the text, as well as courses on the labor movement, urban problems, economic history, and immigration. Balch was the kind of teacher who was actively involved in what she taught and who sought to stimulate a similar involvement on the part of her students. After 1913, Balch headed Wellesley's Department of Economics and Sociology. She also continued her social activism. At one point, the president of Wellesley told Balch that she was not given the normal promotion because she had loaned two hundred dollars to a union whose bitter strike she had supported. If such a warning had any effect on Balch, it was to deepen her commitment to social activism. Balch was among the founders, in 1903, of the Women's Trade Union League, serving for a time as its president. She also served on a variety of boards and commissions, including Boston's City Planning Board (1914-1917), two state commissions—one on industrial education (1908-1909) and another on immigration (1913-1914)—and the committee on immigration of the Progressive Party (1912).

Balch's landmark accomplishment as a professor was her definitive study of Slavic immigration, published as *Our Slavic Fellow Citizens* in 1910. When Balch began this project on a sabbatical leave in 1904, the systematic study of a particular immigrant group was largely untried. Balch did her research on both sides of the Atlantic—traveling to Austria-Hungary to investigate the conditions that caused immigrants to leave their homeland and then traveling around the United States to visit Slavic communities. To facilitate her research, she acquired a rudimentary knowledge of the Czech language. In addition to her sabbatical year, she took a second year off without pay and met all of her own research expenses. She described how the Slavs, by migrating, had gained in both self-respect and freedom, and she predicted that they would add richness and vitality to American culture. *Our Slavic Fellow*

Citizens dispelled many misconceptions and prejudices directed against immigrants and provided ammunition for those fighting against a restrictive immigrant policy. The work is still frequently cited and excerpted in books about immigration.

When World War I broke out, Balch began her involvement in peace activities, which constituted the third and best-known phase of her career. A number of women connected with the settlement-house movement, Balch among them, followed Jane Addams' lead and, in 1915, went to The Hague for the International Congress of Women. Congress moved to send representatives to meet with heads of state to urge them to back a plan for neutral mediation of the war. Out of more than eleven hundred voting members, Balch was chosen as one of the seven official representatives. She visited with top officials in half a dozen countries, including President Woodrow Wilson. The scheme came to nothing, but Balch helped edit the proceedings of the congress and also joined Alice Hamilton and Jane Addams in writing *Women at the Hague* (1915). The congress was significant in that it was the initial gathering of women from many countries to work for peace. As such, it laid the foundation for the Women's International League for Peace and Freedom.

Balch thought that Henry Ford's ideas on how peace could be obtained were crude, but with no overtly positive government response to the mediation efforts of the Women's Congress, Balch, in 1916, participated in the Ford-sponsored Neutral Conference for continuous mediation in Stockholm. Again, she met with President Wilson to push for a plan for mediation. During this period, the United States was moving toward war.

As peace work continued to occupy Balch, her ties to Wellesley loosened. She took a sabbatical leave during 1916-1917 in order to take courses at Columbia University and to work for various peace organizations. She was active in the Women's Peace Party, the Fellowship of Reconciliation, the Collegiate Anti-Militarism League, and the Committee Against Militarism. Once the United States declared war, pacifism became decidedly unpatriotic. Balch, however, did not swerve from her beliefs. At a time when faculty were not protected by tenure, she thought it prudent to extend her leave from Wellesley. In 1918, she published her thoughts on the impending peace settlement, *Approaches to the Great Settlement*. Also, about that time, her Wellesley appointment expired, and the college declined to reappoint her, the final decision coming in 1919. That decision ended Balch's academic career of more than twenty years and left her professionally stranded without a pension at the age of fifty-two. Faculty protests were ineffective. While Balch's pacifist activities were the main reason for Wellesley's action, her liberal social views on other issues played a role. Balch refused to press her case further. As time passed, Wellesley's position softened. The college invited her back to speak in 1935, and, in 1946, Wellesley's president helped Balch secure the Nobel Peace Prize.

During this time, Balch found a job on the editorial staff of *The Nation*. Then, with the establishment of the League of Nations, the Women's International League for Peace and Freedom decided to open an office in Geneva. Balch was the group's secretary-treasurer and had the task of finding suitable quarters and developing the organization's work with the League of Nations. She oversaw publication of a newsletter, entertained visitors from around the world, made the headquarters a quiet retreat from the bustle going on in the League of Nations, and organized the group's Third International Congress in 1921. In 1922, she went to Varese, Italy, to organize a summer school, but at the last minute switched the location of the school to Lugano, Switzerland, because Fascist bands had invaded Varese. Exhausted, she resigned from her official duties with the Women's International League in the fall of 1922 but continued her involvement with that organization. A special league project in 1927 was an investigation of social, economic, and political conditions in Haiti, which the United States Marines had occupied since 1915. Balch accompanied five others to Haiti, then edited and wrote most of their report, which was published as *Occupied Haiti* (1927). Subsequently, Balch met with President Coolidge. Several years later, Herbert Hoover's policy of restoring self-government was reminiscent of the recommendations made by the Women's International League.

During the early 1930's, Balch was president of the American section of the Women's International League for Peace and Freedom. She continued to maintain a lively interest in a variety of international issues, ranging from disarmament to the Spanish Civil War. In the mid-1930's, she was once again elected secretary-treasurer of the Women's International League, and then, later, honorary president.

Balch believed that pacifists needed to confront the moral issues that arose as a result of World War II. Two of Balch's concerns were the treatment of Japanese-Americans and refuge for Jews from Nazi Germany. Her international outlook was vindicated: In 1946, she was a corecipient of the Nobel Peace Prize with John R. Mott, the international Young Men's Christian Association leader. She gave the seventeen-thousand-dollar award to the Women's League.

Balch never married and refused the offers of women friends to live with them permanently, preferring to live her life in her own way. She eschewed fashionable dress, but she enjoyed sketching with pastels and, in 1941, published a book of poetry, *The Miracle of Living*. Her disciplined intelligence, varied interests, and public experiences were the expressions of a rich inner life. Active in League affairs into her nineties, she died in a nursing home in Cambridge, Massachusetts, at ninety-four.

Summary

Emily Greene Balch represents the best of the first generation of women to be graduated from college in significant numbers. These women believed themselves to be special, and they felt an obligation to do something useful with their college education. Initially, Balch was attracted to social work, a profession unique in that women not only dominated it numerically but also in terms of leadership. Balch became part of a lifelong network of women reformers, even though she soon left social work for college teaching. As a professor, her greatest accomplishment was the highly regarded *Our Slavic Fellow Citizens*. A woman of firm convictions, she persisted in pacifist activities even though they cost her her college career. Much of her peace efforts went into the Women's International League for Peace and Freedom, an organization that is also part of her legacy. Idealistic, determined, and with high intellectual standards, she was an outstanding example of what an educated woman could do.

Bibliography

Balch, Emily Greene. "Women for Peace and Freedom." *Survey Graphic* 35 (October, 1946): 358-360. Balch's World War II observations on Europe and on the Women's International League for Peace and Freedom.

Bussey, Gertrude, and Margaret Tims. *Women's International League for Peace and Freedom, 1915-1965: A Record of Fifty Years' Work*. London: George Allen and Unwin, 1965. Balch is frequently mentioned in this historical account of the organization which absorbed so much of her peace efforts.

Davis, Allen F. *American Heroine: The Life and Legend of Jane Addams*. New York: Oxford University Press, 1973. A biographical account of Jane Addams that is also a good source for her relationship to Balch.

"Plain People: 'A' for Effort." *Time* 48 (November, 1946): 33. Brief account of the circumstances surrounding Balch's receipt of the Nobel Peace Prize.

Randall, John Herman, Jr. "Emily Greene Balch." *The Nation* 164 (January, 1947): 14-15. Recalls Balch's work on the editorial staff of *The Nation*.

_____. *Emily Greene Balch of New England: Citizen of the World*. Washington, D.C.: Women's International League for Peace and Freedom, 1946. A twelve-page summary of Balch's career.

Randall, Mercedes M. *Improper Bostonian: Emily Greene Balch*. New York: Twayne Publishers, 1964. The only book-length biography of Balch. Charming, insightful, and carefully crafted. The author was an associate of Balch in the Women's International League for Peace and Freedom.

Judith Ann Trolander

JAMES BALDWIN

Born: August 2, 1924; New York, New York

Area of Achievement: Literature

Contribution: During the racial unrest in the United States in the 1960's, Baldwin was the most visible and respected literary figure in the Civil Rights movement. His best work has focused on racial concerns and on homosexuality.

Early Life

James Baldwin, the son of Berdis Jones Baldwin and the stepson of David Baldwin, a Baptist preacher, was born and grew up in New York City's black ghetto, Harlem; he was the oldest of nine children. By the time he was fourteen years old, Baldwin, then a student in New York's De Witt Clinton High School, was preaching in Harlem's Fireside Pentecostal Church. His earliest writing appeared in *The Magpie*, his high school's student newspaper, to which he contributed three stories before becoming coeditor in chief, a job he shared with fellow student Richard Avedon.

Upon graduation from high school in 1942, Baldwin, rejected for military service, took a job working for a railroad in New Jersey. He had just renounced the church and, although he has never gone back to it and has scorned Christianity for what he perceives as its racism, much of the rhythm of black preaching and much of the drama of evangelical church services are found in most of his work. Baldwin sought refuge in the church during an uncertain period in his adolescence, but as he analyzed seriously his position as both a member of a racial minority and a homosexual, he found in literature more helpful solutions to the problems that plagued him than he had found in religion.

Between 1942 and 1944, Baldwin held menial jobs, some of them in the thriving wartime defense industries. A turning point came for him in 1944, when, having moved to New York City's Greenwich Village, he met Richard Wright, one of the leading black writers in the United States. Baldwin was working on his first novel, "In My Father's House," at that time. Although the novel remained unpublished, Wright arranged for Baldwin to receive the Eugene F. Saxton Memorial Trust so that he could concentrate on his writing. Baldwin first appeared in print in 1946 in *The Nation*, where he published a book review. He also wrote book reviews for *The New Leader* during the same year.

In 1948, Baldwin, slight of stature and with a countenance that reflected both intensity and anguish, received the Rosenwald Fellowship. This award enabled him to move to Paris. That year, he also published an essay, "The Harlem Ghetto," and a short story, "Previous Condition," in *Commentary*.

Baldwin was to live abroad for the next decade, in the middle of which his first novel, *Go Tell It on the Mountain* (1953), was published.

Life's Work

Baldwin's first two novels, *Go Tell It on the Mountain* and *Giovanni's Room* (1956), are autobiographical. The former concentrates on the problems of growing up black in a predominantly white United States. The book explores the impact that religion has had on the black experience in the United States and accurately depicts the economic and social struggles with which black families cope on a regular basis. The book is also concerned with the sexual tensions that exist for the black who is coming of age and who is beset by deep-seated interracial conflicts.

Giovanni's Room, set in France, was one of a rash of novels on homosexuality to appear between 1948 and 1956. The protagonist's lover, Giovanni, kills an older man who forces him into a sexual encounter and is duly tried, found guilty, and executed for this crime. David, the protagonist, has to cope not only with the guilt of his homosexuality but also with feelings of not having been the loyal friend that Giovanni needed.

When *Go Tell It on the Mountain* appeared, Baldwin was working on a play, *The Amen Corner*, that was performed at Howard University in 1954 but that took nearly a decade to reach Broadway, where it was produced in 1964 largely because of the New York success of Baldwin's *Blues for Mister Charlie*, which the American National Theater Association (ANTA) brought to Broadway in the spring of 1964.

The publication of *Go Tell It on the Mountain* led to Baldwin's being awarded a Guggenheim Fellowship in 1954, which afforded him the opportunity to do extensive revisions on *The Amen Corner* and to complete his much-acclaimed *Notes of a Native Son* (1955), a fierce, well-written book that articulates the outrage which Baldwin, as a sensitive black American, felt because of the social inequities that face blacks. Perhaps this book makes its greatest impact with its contention that racial hatred destroys not only the objects of that hatred but also the people who are possessed by it. *Notes of a Native Son* was to become one of the most influential statements about racial inequality during the Civil Rights movement that was beginning to gain momentum in the late 1950's and that emerged full-blown in the 1960's.

Giovanni's Room brought Baldwin increased recognition in the form of a Partisan Review Fellowship and an award from the National Institute of Arts and Letters. He returned to the United States from France in 1957 and made his first visit to the South. He wrote about this trip in both *Harper's Magazine* and *Partisan Review*. A Ford Foundation grant-in-aid enabled him in November, 1959, to return to Paris, where he spent the winter. On returning to the United States in the spring of 1960, Baldwin wrote articles for *Esquire* and *Mademoiselle*. In the late summer, he went to Tallahassee, Florida, as a participant in strategy sessions held by the newly formed Congress of Racial Equality (CORE), and in so doing he cast his lot with the activists in the Civil Rights movement.

In 1961, Baldwin published another collection of essays, *Nobody Knows My Name: More Notes of a Native Son*. This collection, vivid and subtle, emphasizes that blacks are simultaneously like and unlike other people. Baldwin depicts the black quest as a quest for love and for acceptance at the personal and interpersonal levels as well as at the broader social level.

Baldwin holds that humankind's only possible salvation is love, although as time has passed, Baldwin has become increasingly pessimistic about the possibility of the human race approaching the idyllic state that, he cautions in his two earliest collections of essays, must be achieved if the race is to survive. Baldwin accuses Americans of not judging individuals by their work but rather of leaping to conclusions about them based on preexisting stereotypes.

In his next novel, *Another Country* (1962), Baldwin deals with love between a black woman and a white man who have defied the conventions of their society and whose quest is to discover their own and each other's real identities. Again, Baldwin emphasizes that people are individuals. It does not matter with whom or how they pursue love. Society and its mores should have nothing to do with such matters because it is the individuals and their love that are all-important. In the year in which *Another Country* was published, Baldwin traveled to Africa in an attempt to find a closer identity with his heritage.

Baldwin's collection of essays issued under the title *The Fire Next Time* (1963) focuses on the mental and spiritual turmoil of American blacks. Enthusiastically received by Civil Rights activists of the time, the book won for Baldwin the George Polk Memorial Award. Though he lived largely outside the United States, Baldwin had become the undisputed literary leader of the Civil Rights movement.

Going to Meet the Man (1965) appeared shortly after *Blues for Mister Charlie* and *The Amen Corner* were presented on Broadway. Interest in Baldwin was high. His next novel, however, *Tell Me How Long the Train's Been Gone* (1968), was badly misfocused and did not have the impact of much of his earlier work. Some critics thought that Baldwin was on a downhill course after the publication of this book. *No Name in the Street* (1972), *One Day, When I Was Lost* (1972), and *If Beale Street Could Talk* (1974) did little to recapture his fading reputation. His collaborations, *Nothing Personal* (1964) with Richard Avedon, *A Rap on Race* (1971) with Margaret Mead, and *A Dialogue* (1975) with Nikki Giovanni, were not taken as seriously as his earlier works had been. He redeemed himself, however, in the eyes of many readers with *Just Above My Head* (1979), a novel about a child evangelist which reiterates much that Baldwin had previously written about the need for love and for judging people as individuals.

The Devil Finds Work (1976) was received with some critical indifference, but *The Evidence of Things Not Seen* (1985), on the Atlanta child murders and the trail of the alleged killer, has had a significant impact and was considered of sufficient importance to be reprinted by the American Bar Association. Baldwin's nonfiction writing has been collected in *The Price of the Ticket: Collected Nonfiction, 1948-1985* (1985).

Summary

James Baldwin has served as the conscience of the Civil Rights movement and as the conscience of liberal whites, to whom he has pointed out that the destructive force of racial intolerance and bigotry is felt not only by those at whom it is aimed but also by those within the dominant society. Baldwin's voice is anguished, but he is a well-informed spokesperson for the cause of racial equality, having been brought up in a society from which he continually felt alienated. Not only has Baldwin been able to identify the problems caused by racial strife, but, more importantly, he has been able to propose an overall solution based upon love and acceptance.

Baldwin usually communicates more persuasively in his essays than he does in his novels, where he has sometimes fallen victim to the problem that he has warned others against, that of dealing with stereotypes rather than with well-defined individuals.

Bibliography

Clark, Kenneth B. *The Negro Protest: James Baldwin, Malcolm X, Martin Luther King Talk with Kenneth B. Clark.* Boston: Beacon Press, 1963. Clark's interview with Baldwin focuses more on the writer's political stance than on him as a literary figure. The portion of the book devoted to Baldwin provides strong insights into his moral philosophy and into his hopes for the human race, which he was later to moderate.

Eckman, Fern Marja. *The Furious Passage of James Baldwin.* New York: M. Evans, 1966. Eckman's critical biography depicts the inner tumult that was the driving force behind Baldwin's most forceful writing. Shows the effect that Baldwin's religious upbringing and that his own early religious involvement had in shaping his thinking.

Kinnamon, Keneth, ed. *James Baldwin: A Collection of Critical Essays.* Englewood Cliffs, N.J.: Prentice-Hall, 1973. These thirteen well-chosen and representative essays deal with Baldwin from a variety of critical standpoints. They range from critical biography to essays on Baldwin's ontology. The editor provides a penetrating, short introduction.

Macebuh, Stanley. *James Baldwin: A Critical Study.* New York: Third Press, 1973. This study focuses on Baldwin's inner torment and relates it directly to the religious influences of his early youth. Claims that much of his best writing is an attempt to exorcise his personal dread of Hell.

O'Daniel, Therman B., ed. *James Baldwin: A Critical Evaluation*. Washington, D.C.: Howard University Press, 1977. Contains one of the best considerations of Baldwin's prose style as well as insights into his Americanness and his ability to focus on his alienation particularly when he was living abroad. The twenty-two essays in the book are enhanced by a comprehensive bibliography, which, although dated, provides a good starting point for researchers.

Pratt, Louis H. *James Baldwin*. New York: Twayne Publishers, 1978. An excellent overview with a well-selected bibliography and a succinct but useful chronological table. The book is sometimes more event-oriented than idea-oriented. It will, however, be serviceable to readers lacking familiarity with Baldwin and his work.

Sylvander, Carolyn Wedin. *James Baldwin*. New York: Frederick Ungar Publishing Co., 1980. A brief but valuable study, balancing Baldwin, the political activist, and Baldwin, the writer. The book is carefully thought out and objective. The bibliography is also useful.

R. Baird Shuman

GEORGE BANCROFT

Born: October 3, 1800; Worcester, Massachusetts
Died: January 17, 1891; Washington, D.C.
Areas of Achievement: Historical scholarship, politics, and diplomacy
Contribution: Contributing greatly to both scholarly and popular thought in the nineteenth century United States, George Bancroft explained the transformation of the British Colonies into the United States in terms of the growth and development of liberty, democracy, and nationalism.

Early Life

George Bancroft was born on October 3, 1800, in Worcester, Massachusetts. He was the eighth of thirteen children produced by the union of Aaron Bancroft and Lucretia Chandler, both of whom came from old-stock New England families. Lucretia Chandler, the daughter of Judge John Chandler, known as "Tory John" because he had opposed independence, was a good-natured and spirited woman, unlettered, but devoted to her husband and children. Aaron Bancroft was a struggling Congregational minister who played a leading role in the early Unitarian movement. Devoted to education as the basis for personal and social reform, he introduced young George to the classics, emphasized the virtues of self-discipline and obedience, and passed on to his offspring the conviction that mankind is essentially good, but not without sin, and flawed by ignorance and misunderstanding. George attended Phillips Exeter Academy, entered Harvard College at thirteen, and became a favorite of President John Thornton Kirkland. Moral philosophy dominated the Harvard curriculum at that time, and like his father before him, Bancroft found that particular mixture of Lockean rationalism and Scottish common sense captivating. It clearly categorized knowledge, stressed the importance of faith as well as reason, and acknowledged divine law as the driving force of the universe. In fact, moral philosophy provided the intellectual and theological perspective that would stay with Bancroft all of his life.

Taking his A.B. degree in 1817, Bancroft continued at Harvard for another year as a graduate student in divinity before continuing his education at the University of Gottingen in Germany. He was encouraged to go to Gottingen by Edward Everett, Joseph Green Cogswell, and George Ticknor, three young Harvard teachers who had done graduate work there and confirmed its reputation as the leading university in Europe. Thanks to President Kirkland, Bancroft got financial support from Harvard and began his studies at Gottingen in the fall of 1818. For the next two years, he rose early and studied late, immersed himself in German literature, and took courses in philosophy, biblical criticism, and history from some of the leading scholars in Europe. His hard work allowed him to take the grueling doctoral examinations early. In September, 1820, he successfully defended his thesis and was awarded the degree of Doctor of Philosophy and Master of Arts. After six more months of study at the University of Berlin, Bancroft traveled Europe and the British Isles for the next year. He met and talked with Johann Wolfgang von Goethe, George Gordon, Lord Byron, the Marquis de Lafayette, and Alexander von Humboldt, to mention the most prominent personages whom he sought out. Bancroft grew up, both intellectually and psychologically, during his four years in Europe.

When he returned to America in 1822, Bancroft was still thinking in terms of either teaching or preaching. He was an engaging young man, known for his social grace and dignified bearing. He was shorter than average and slight in build, rather handsome, and distinguished by clear-cut facial features which included a prominent nose, strikingly alert eyes, and carefully trimmed hair and beard. Some of his former Harvard teachers were put off by his foreign manners, his suggested reforms for the college, and his pompous request that he be given a professorship. President Kirkland remained a faithful ally, however, and secured for him an appointment as tutor in Greek. Though the opportunity hardly offered him the status he had had in mind, Bancroft decided to make the most of it. He added new rigor to his Greek courses and drove his students to the brink of rebellion, though they reportedly were far ahead of other Greek students. During the year of his rather unsuccessful tutorship, he also tried his hand at preaching in various churches on several occasions. He seems to have pleased few people with his sermons, not even his father, and certainly not himself. In early 1823, disheartened by his failure to reform Harvard and by the resistance of the students, Bancroft joined with Joseph Cogswell to set up the Round Hill School for Boys at Northampton. For the next eight years, he labored to adapt the educational methods of the German gymnasium to the United States. Round Hill was ahead of its time and widely praised, but it had financial problems, and Bancroft, the primary teacher, contributed to them with his demanding academic standards and less than cordial relations with students. In 1831, he sold his interest of Round Hill to Cogswell and put classroom teaching behind him.

Bancroft married Sarah Dwight in 1827. Her family was involved in various business enterprises in Springfield, Massachusetts, and Bancroft became an agent for the Dwight banking interests. To the chagrin of his young wife, who stayed home and often felt neglected, he traveled much of the time on business. He also embarked upon a literary career. His first published work had been a pedestrian volume of poetry (*Poems*, 1823), whose existence he later found embarrassing. While teaching at Round Hill, he translated several German works on Latin and Greek grammar and three volumes of history by Arnold H. L. Heeren, one of the distinguished professors who had taught him at Gottingen. Under the encouragement of editor Jared Sparks, he became a regular contributor of book reviews and essays on finance, politics, and scholarly topics to the *North American Review*. Sparks was much involved in collecting documents and writing history and may well have influenced Bancroft to embark upon his own work in American history. Bancroft was ambitious—so much so that Lillian Handlin, one of his biographers, maintains that he was rather insensitive toward his first wife and never very sympathetic toward his children. Sickly and morose, Sarah Bancroft died in 1837, shortly after the death of an infant daughter. Thereafter, relations between Bancroft and his three surviving children—Louise, John, and George—were seldom harmonious and often very strained.

Life's Work

While achieving a measure of success in business, Bancroft became even more committed to the notion that a man of letters could and should play an important part in improving society. That conviction increasingly shaped his political involvement and scholarly ambitions. In an oration that he delivered on July 4, 1826, at Northampton, Bancroft had made it clear that he was a Jeffersonian Democrat, favoring the dispersion of property and the removal of voting restrictions. His views were in sympathy with the emerging Jacksonian Party. Writing in the *North American Review* in 1831, he analyzed the National Bank in terms that pleased Jacksonians and shocked his Whig associates. His Harvard friends as well as the Dwights were almost solidly against Andrew Jackson, and Massachusetts itself was completely dominated by the Whigs. The Jacksonians in the state were badly divided, as Bancroft himself found out when the Northampton Workingmen nominated him for the General Court but failed to line up the other elements of the fragmented Democratic coalition in the election of 1834. Viciously attacked by the Whigs in the press and distrusted by many Jacksonians, Bancroft got few votes. Nevertheless, he was attracted to politics, and Jacksonian leaders recognized his talents and cultivated him.

Rebuffed politically, Bancroft experienced considerable scholarly acclaim in 1834 with the publication of the first volume of his history of the United States. He may have acquired an interest in history from his father, who had written a modestly successful popular biography of George Washington years before. At Gottingen, he studied history under Hereen. While at Round Hill, he had worked up an outline of American history for a proposed world history course at Round Hill. By the early 1830's, he had decided that there was a real need for a "critical history" of the United States and believed himself superbly equipped to write it. The first volume, which carried development of the American Colonies to 1650, was popular with both the literary critics and the general public. "You have written a work which will last while the memory of America lasts," wrote Edward Everett, still a good friend despite diverging politics. It was a classic, Everett continued, "full of learn-

ing, information, common sense, and philosophy; full of taste and eloquence; full of life and power." Ralph Waldo Emerson was equally complimentary, writing that the grandeur of the work made him weep. Emerson
proclaimed it "the most valuable and splendid piece of historical composition, not only in English, but in any tongue."

Heady praise indeed, calculated to encourage the masterful young scholar,
and it did. Two other volumes, the second published in 1837 and the third in
1840, followed the development of the Colonies to 1748. The central theme
was clear enough. From the beginning of English settlement, America had
progressively expanded the twin realms of economic and political liberty.
Indeed, political and economic monopoly gave way to the rise of representative politics and free enterprise economics in Colonial America. According to
Bancroft, this burgeoning freedom nurtured an emerging American nationality. It was a grand and inspiring story, and Bancroft told it with an eloquence
and appreciation for drama that appealed not only to Emerson but also to
thousands of his countrymen disturbed by growing sectional tensions which
threatened national unity in the 1830's. By 1841, his annual income from
sales of the three volumes reached $4,350. Bancroft was almost unique
among scholars; he made scholarship pay, and pay handsomely.

Political success came upon the heels of scholarly recognition. In 1837, as a
reward for Bancroft's efforts on behalf of the Democratic Party in Massachusetts, President Martin Van Buren appointed the budding historian collector
of the Port of Boston, a most important patronage position. Over the next
few years, Bancroft emerged as the leader of the Democratic Party in Massachusetts and edited its leading newspaper. He was the Democratic nominee for governor in 1844, and though he lost that election, his efforts on behalf of James K. Polk secured for him a place in the new president's cabinet
as secretary of the navy (1845-1846). While serving in that position, Bancroft
endorsed Polk's expansionist plans and the Mexican War, tied promotion in
the navy more to merit than to seniority, and founded the Naval Academy at
Annapolis. What he wanted most, however, was a diplomatic assignment,
and Polk obligingly appointed him ambassador to England in 1846, where he
served for the next two years and relished every minute. He moved in the
highest political and literary circles, gained access to collections of documents in both England and France, and made friends with the English
historians Thomas Macaulay, Henry Milman, and Henry Hallam and the
French historians François Guizot and Louis Adolphe Thiers. He hired
clerks to copy significant documents and undoubtedly had more information
available to him than any previous American historian. His tenure as minister to the Court of St. James certainly enriched subsequent volumes of his
history of the United States.

Returning to the United States in 1849, Bancroft decided to make his
home in cosmopolitan New York. His first wife having died in 1837, he had

remarried in 1838, taking as his second wife Mrs. Elizabeth (Davis) Bliss, a Boston widow with two sons of her own. Her first husband had been a law partner of Daniel Webster. She was bright, witty, and urbane; Bancroft found her the perfect mate and reveled in their marriage. He and his three children, however, remained on less than cordial terms, despite the efforts of Elizabeth to heal the breach. From 1849 to 1867, Bancroft devoted himself to writing his history and participating in the intellectual and social life of New York City and Newport, Rhode Island, where he maintained a summer home. He wrote six more volumes that brought his *History of the United States* to the year 1782. These volumes recounted American nationalism being forged by the fires of protest and revolution. They were quite popular and sold well, though the critics were less laudatory than before. Bancroft provoked a minor storm when he dared to question the military decisions of certain American generals in the Revolution; the descendants of the generals responded with vehemence in what became known as the War of the Grandfathers.

Much more troubling to him was the talk of nullification and secession that increasingly threatened the nation by the late 1840's. Bancroft took refuge in his work as the nation drifted toward civil war. As a politician and as a historian, he showed little concern regarding slavery, though he privately deplored the peculiar institution and the threat it posed to the Union. Once the war began, though still a states' rights Democrat, Bancroft came to appreciate Abraham Lincoln's leadership, subsequently advised President Johnson during Reconstruction, and was rewarded by appointment as ambassador to Prussia, where he served from 1867 to 1874. Once again, he took advantage of diplomatic service to search for American materials in European archives. He became an ardent supporter of Prince Otto von Bismarck and German unification and made friends with Leopold von Ranke and other German scholars. His public statement praising the Germans during the Franco-Prussian War enraged the French, but President Grant retained him as ambassador to Germany because of his intimacy with Bismarck and the Prussian elite.

Returning to the United States in 1874, Bancroft lived the remainder of his life in Washington, D.C., usually spending the summers in Newport. That same year, he finished the tenth volume of his history, focusing on the closing years of the American Revolution. Two years later, he published the "Centenary Edition" of his *History of the United States* in six volumes. In 1882, he brought out two volumes entitled *History of the Formation of the Constitution of the United States of America*, apparently inspired by recent Supreme Court decisions which, in his opinion, violated the principles of the Founding Fathers. Interestingly, he portrayed the Constitution as enshrining democratic ideas which ought not to be tampered with either by the Supreme Court or by legislative majorities. His last published work was a biography,

Martin Van Buren to the End of His Political Career (1889), which he had begun in the early 1840's but put aside when Van Buren did not run in 1844. During his last years, Bancroft, still as charming and urbane as ever and wearing a flowing white beard, was the acknowledged patriarch of Washington literary and social circles. After his wife died in 1886, a daughter of his eldest son, George, stayed with him for a few years, and he then lived with his youngest son, John Chandler Bancroft. He died in Washington in 1891.

Summary

Upon his death, George Bancroft was eulogized as the Father of American History. His contribution was truly profound. It is sometimes forgotten that Bancroft pioneered the collection of American documents from foreign archives. He joined Jared Sparks and Peter Force in collecting and encouraging others to preserve early American documents scattered throughout the United States. In 1869, Bancroft estimated that he had spent between fifty and seventy-five thousand dollars in paying copyists, collecting, and researching. By the time of his death, that figure was well over $100,000. As a diplomat in England and later Germany, he had unparalleled access to both public and private archives in Europe and exploited his privileges to the fullest; his several hundred volumes of collected documents, located now in the New York Public Library, bear eloquent testimony to his industry. Whatever his shortcomings as a historian, Bancroft recognized that the sources were all important, and he must be credited with doing much to make sure that subsequent generations would have access to them.

Bancroft believed that his writing of American history accurately reflected the sources. He was not a little offended when the great von Ranke told him that "his history" was the best ever written from the democratic point of view. The fact is, though, that Bancroft projected his own patriotism and politics into his interpretation of American history. As J. Franklin Jameson put it, Bancroft voted for Jackson throughout his historical writing. He also had a tendency to quote material rather loosely, leaving himself open to the charge of manipulating the sources. By the time of his death, academic historians were dismissing his work as simply not adequate in terms of the canons of critical scholarship. Yet Bancroft was zealous, not dishonest, and his shortcomings were no worse than those of most other gentlemanly scholars of his day. Like his peers, he slighted economics and social factors, emphasizing instead politics, military affairs, and religion. Despite his knowledge of the English sources, he virtually neglected the British point of view of the American Revolution and constantly equated Catholicism with corruption and tyranny.

In the late twentieth century, Bancroft's writings have not been widely read because of his unabashed nationalism. Much of his basic interpretation has been retained, however, by scholars of the so-called Consensus School of

American history, and that interpretation, though considerably more complex than Bancroft's limited point of view, still dominates American historiography. Yet Bancroft did more than simply write history. He explained American nationalism in terms of heroic deeds, economic and political freedom, and the inevitable triumph of goodness and justice over abusive tyranny. His popular history reinforced a national mythology that brought comfort to nineteenth century Americans stunned by civil war, the Industrial Revolution, and political turmoil. He found a unity of purpose and experience in early American history that continues to appeal to the pluralistic America of the late twentieth century. George Bancroft's legacy has proven to be a lasting one. He shaped the past in terms of the dreams and aspirations of his generation. If any historian deserves to be called the Herodotus of the American people, Bancroft is surely the one.

Bibliography
Bassett, John Spencer. *The Middle Group of American Historians*. New York: Macmillan Publishing Co., 1917. Reprint. Freeport, N.Y.: Books for Library Press, 1966. A fine study of those nineteenth century historians known loosely as the Patriotic School, with special emphasis on leading figures such as Jeremy Belknap, George Bancroft, Jared Sparks, William Hickling Prescott, John Lothrop Motley, and Peter Force. Critical of Bancroft's methods and political bias, it is excellent for placing his life and work in its cultural context. Credits Bancroft for his literary style and ability to reflect the nationalistic aspirations of his generation of Americans.
Fisher, Sidney George. "Legendary and Mythmaking Process in Histories of the American Revolution." *Proceedings of the American Philosophical Society* 51 (April, 1912): 53-75. An incisive critique of the Patriotic School, Fisher's attack reflects the reaction of the rising generations of academic historians who thought of themselves as "scientific" scholars. Especially harsh judgment of Bancroft's methods and style.
Handlin, Lilian. *George Bancroft: The Intellectual as Democrat*. New York: Harper and Row, Publishers, 1984. The most recent and perhaps best biography of Bancroft in terms of integrating the personality of the man himself, his scholarship, and his politics. Emphasis is given to the influence of moral philosophy in his thinking and writing. Challenges the notion that either German Romanticism or egalitarian politics primarily influenced his work.
Howe, M. A. DeWolf. *The Life and Letters of George Bancroft*. 2 vols. New York: Charles Scribner's Sons, 1908. The authorized biography of Bancroft, this work is exceptionally detailed, filled with extensive quotations from his correspondence. Bancroft literally speaks for himself here. Not analytical, but tells much about the man and his time.
Kraus, Michael. *The Writing of American History*. Norman: University of

Oklahoma Press, 1953. Dated for historical trends after the 1950's, this is one of the best historiographical works ever written. It places Bancroft in relationship to minor and other major historians of the nineteenth century. Very good for the broad perspective. Contains a most judicious evaluation of him as a historian.

Nye, Russel B. *George Bancroft: Brahmin Rebel.* New York: Alfred A. Knopf, 1945. Beautifully written biography that focuses on the intellectual forces which shaped Bancroft as a historian. It portrays him as a political rebel but part of the mainstream of New England thought, very much in the Emerson tradition and significantly influenced by German Romanticism. Although modified by Handlin's researches, this is in many ways the most insightful biography of Bancroft.

Sloane, William M. "George Bancroft—in Society, in Politics, in Letters." *The Century Magazine* 33 (January, 1887): 473-487. Written by Bancroft's friend and former assistant, this small essay is filled with intimate details about the aging scholar. It captures Bancroft as he was seen by his friends, the sage historian who succeeded in politics, diplomacy, and scholarship.

Vitzthum, Richard C. *The American Compromise: Theme and Method in the Histories of Bancroft, Parkman, and Adams.* Norman: University of Oklahoma Press, 1974. A fascinating study that relates Bancroft and his work to the effort of two other popular nineteenth century historians. Vitzthum claims that all three were guided by the belief that Americans were driven by the struggle between separatist forces on the one hand and unifying forces on the other. Very nationalistic, they saw progress in terms of union and a strong central government.

Wood, Kirk. "George Bancroft." In *Dictionary of Literary Biography: American Historians, 1607-1865,* vol. 30, edited by Clyde Wilson. Detroit: Gale Research Co., 1984. A concise but analytical study of Bancroft as a historian and the differing views scholars have taken of him. Wood summarizes Bancroft's history and explains it in terms of the quest for American nationality and union before the Civil War.

Ronald Howard

BENJAMIN BANNEKER

Born: November 9, 1731; Baltimore County, Maryland
Died: October 9, 1806; Baltimore, Maryland
Areas of Achievement: Mathematics and astronomy
Contribution: Banneker's calculations provided the essential data for almanacs published from 1792 through 1797. A free black in a slave state, Banneker overcame obstacles of rural isolation, little formal education, racial prejudice, and alcoholism to establish himself as a respected scientist, earn a place on the crew that surveyed the District of Columbia, and become a symbol of racial equality in the abolitionist movement.

Early Life

Benjamin Banneker's American antecedents came in bonds to colonial Maryland. His grandmother, Molly Welsh, was a convict transported from England to Maryland in about 1683. After completing a period of servitude, she became a free landowner in the western part of Baltimore County near the Patapsco River. In 1692, Molly bought two Africans and in a few years restored freedom to both. One of the men, named Bannka, claimed to be the kidnaped son of an African king. In defiance of laws that forbade miscegenation, Molly married the prince and took Banneky as her surname.

The Bannekys had four daughters. The oldest, Mary, born in about 1700, married an African who recently had been given freedom as a baptismal gift. He had chosen Robert as his Christian name and, when married, took Banneky as his surname. The name's spelling varied until the mid-eighteenth century, when it settled at Banneker. Three of the four children born to Robert and Mary grew to maturity. The oldest, and the only son, was Benjamin, born on November 9, 1731.

In about 1729, Robert bought twenty-five acres of land close to Molly's farm. On March 10, 1737, when Benjamin was five years old, Robert purchased one hundred acres from the nearby Stout plantation. The title was in Robert and Benjamin's names to assure that the family could protect its freedom should Robert die suddenly. Maryland laws were not sympathetic to free blacks and authorized reenslavement of those who did not own property.

Banneker's education was rudimentary. His grandmother taught him to read from the Bible. For a few months, he attended a country school where the schoolteacher—probably a Quaker—taught black and white children. Benjamin learned to write a very clear, even beautiful, script and mastered the fundamentals of mathematics through basic algebra. At some point, he also learned to play the flute and the violin.

Though meager, this education powerfully shaped the course of Banneker's life. He purchased his own Bible in 1763, read it diligently, and sprinkled his writings with scriptural quotations. He never formally joined a

Christian denomination, but he often attended Quaker, and sometimes Methodist, services. His reading interests went beyond the Bible to literature in general. He painstakingly compiled a small library, composed essays in his own commonplace book, and wrote poetry.

Mathematics, though, was the subject that stimulated his intellectual curiosity the most. He had unusual abilities with numbers. While a young man, he became locally famous for being able to solve fairly complex computations in his head. He had a special fondness for mathematical puzzles and liked to trade tricky problems with his neighbors.

It was probably during such an exchange with a neighbor that Banneker first saw and then borrowed a watch. The timepiece fascinated him, and he dismantled it to observe its moving parts. Using the watch as a model, Banneker produced a clock made entirely of hand-carved hardwoods. The clock kept accurate time, struck the hours, and was the wonder of the Patapsco valley.

Banneker completed the clock in 1753, when he was twenty-two. His father died six years later, leaving Benjamin the sole owner of the Stout acreage. The rest of the property was divided among Benjamin and his two married sisters. Banneker lived with his mother until she died in 1775. He never married and lived the rest of his life on his well-kept, productive farm. He might have died in obscurity had not the Ellicott brothers bought land adjoining the Banneker farm.

Life's Work

Joseph, Andrew, and John Ellicott brought their large families and the families of several workers to the Patapsco valley in 1771, when Banneker was forty. Before they were fully settled, the Ellicotts and their workers bought food from the existing farms. Andrew Ellicott's young son George and Banneker developed a special friendship. At age fifteen in 1775, George was recognized as a mathematical prodigy, an accomplished surveyor, and a gifted astronomer. With George's encouragement and assistance, Banneker rapidly mastered advanced mathematics and became fascinated with astronomy. In the fall of 1788, George loaned Banneker books on mathematics and astronomy, a telescope, a set of drafting instruments, a lamp, and a large, oval drop-leaf table.

Banneker now spent clear nights in open fields observing the heavens. In cold weather he dressed heavily and wrapped himself in blankets to record his observations. At dawn he returned to his cabin and slept for a few hours. He spent most of the rest of the day at the oval table studying the borrowed books and plotting the movements of the stars. The calculation of a star's location for a particular date could involve as many as ten different algebraic and logarithmic operations.

As he gained a sure grasp of astronomy, Banneker began the ambitious project of calculating an ephemeris—a table showing the positions of the earth, moon, planets, and stars throughout the year. The ephemeris was the basis for projecting eclipses and predicting weather conditions. It was, therefore, the major component of an almanac. He was encouraged in this project by his mentor George and George's cousin Major Andrew Ellicott. Major Ellicott had prepared ephemerides for publication from 1781 through 1786, but the demands of his work as surveyor forced him to abandon the time-consuming calculations. In the summer of 1790, Banneker submitted completed ephemerides for 1791 to three publishers, but none of the editors bought his work. Although discouraged, Banneker began an ephemeris for 1792.

In January of 1791, President George Washington instructed Secretary of State Thomas Jefferson to have the District of Columbia surveyed. On February 2, 1791, Jefferson named Major Ellicott the chief surveyor. Ellicott was to find the true meridian and longitude of the future capital and to prepare a topographical map of the ten-mile square tract of land. Because he was shorthanded, Ellicott turned to Banneker for help. Banneker had no practical experience as a surveyor, but he had mastered the mathematics involved and knew how to work with most of the astronomical instruments.

On February 7, 1791, Banneker—at age fifty-nine—made his first trip outside Baltimore County. During his three-month stay at the site of the future capital, he gained valuable experience as assistant to Major Ellicott. He learned to use the astronomical clock and other instruments new to him. He also kept a resolution to abstain from drinking wine and hard liquor while working with the surveying crew.

Upon his return home, he finished the ephemeris for 1792. Meanwhile, Joseph and George Ellicott had interested the Society of Friends meetings and the antislavery societies in Baltimore and Philadelphia in Banneker. Through their assistance, Banneker's 1792 ephemeris was published by the Baltimore firm of Goddard and Angell. The almanac appeared for sale in stores in Baltimore, Philadelphia, and Alexandria in December, 1791, bearing the title: *Benjamin Banneker's Pennsylvania, Delaware, Maryland and Virginia Almanack and Ephemeris for the Year of Our Lord, 1792*. On the reverse side of the title page the editors called the work "an extraordinary Effort of Genius—a COMPLETE and ACCURATE EPHEMERIS . . . calculated by a sable Descendant of Africa. . . ." The editors argued that the almanac was proof that skin color had no relationship to mental capacity, that all people were alike, and that slavery should be ended. The first four thousand copies quickly sold out, as did a second printing by Goddard and Angell and a condensed edition printed by William Young in Philadelphia.

Banneker prepared an ephemeris that was published in an almanac each year through 1797. The almanacs were extremely popular and sold well. At least twenty-eight editions of these almanacs appeared in those six years.

Starting in 1794, Banneker computed tide tables for Chesapeake Bay, a feature that competing almanacs did not contain.

The elderly astronomer was a dark-skinned man of average height and a full head of thick, white hair. Though portly, he stood erect and carried a long staff. His posture, gentlemanly behavior, and staff gave him a dignified, patriarchal air. Banneker continued to calculate ephemerides through the year 1802. In that year, he turned seventy-one; his capacity for work had diminished, and he was unable to complete the rigorous computations. He died quietly in his home four years later on October 9, 1806.

Summary

Banneker's abilities as a mathematician and astronomer made him famous in his lifetime. There was, however, much more to his fame than his accomplishments themselves. Benjamin Banneker was the son and grandson of Africans. He was a free black in a predominantly white society that almost universally regarded black people as being mentally inferior to whites. Banneker's best-known act—in his lifetime and since—was his correspondence with Thomas Jefferson.

On August 19, 1791, Banneker sent the author of the Declaration of Independence a handwritten copy of his ephemeris and a long letter. Banneker introduced himself as a black man and then eloquently pleaded with Jefferson to use his influence to end the slavery that still kept some of the children of mankind's one Father from enjoying their "inalienable rights." Jefferson responded by expressing the hope that people would soon recognize that circumstances, not natural endowments, kept blacks in a condition that suggested inferiority, but he made no pledge to do anything more than to send Banneker's almanac to abolitionists in France.

Those two letters were printed in the 1793 alamanc and reprinted frequently in abolitionist literature in the nineteenth century. Benjamin Banneker had become a symbol of racial equality because he was an example of black achievement. His name has been invoked over the years in black educational efforts, such as Benjamin Banneker College of Prairie View A & M University at Prairie View, Texas.

Bibliography

Allen, Will W., comp. *Banneker: The Afro-American Astronomer*. Washington, D.C.: Black Heritage Library, 1921. Reprint. Freeport, N.Y.: Books for Libraries Press, 1971. First published in 1921 by the Black Heritage Library Collection, the work is based largely on primary sources but contains a paper by Daniel Murray which advances the undocumented claim that Banneker worked with Major Pierre Charles L'Enfant and had a copy of the city's plans for use after L'Enfant left the capital site in a rage. That myth has been repeated often.

Allen, William G. *Wheatley, Banneker, and Horton.* Boston: D. Laing, 1849. Reprint. Freeport, N.Y.: Books for Libraries Press, 1970. A condensation of an earlier paper based on records held by the Ellicott family.

Armistead, Wilson. *A Tribute for the Negro: Being a Vindication of the Moral, Intellectual, and Religious Capabilities of the Colored Portion of Mankind; with Particular Reference to the African Race.* Manchester: W. Irwin, 1848. Reprint. Miami, Fl.: Mnemosyne, 1969. Abolitionist literature. The material on Banneker consists of a brief biographical sketch and a reprint of the Jefferson correspondence.

Baker, Henry E. "Benjamin Banneker, the Negro Mathematician and Astronomer." *The Journal of Negro History* 3 (April, 1918): 99-118. A fine sketch based upon a rare work prepared by George Ellicott's daughter Martha Ellicott Tyson.

Bedini, Silvio A. *The Life of Benjamin Banneker.* New York: Charles Scribner's Sons, 1971. The best study of Banneker produced yet. Based on careful review of secondary materials, previously unused material from private archives, and Banneker's commonplace book and journal.

Graham, Shirley. *Your Most Humble Servant.* New York: Julian Messner, 1949. Although shelved in the biography section of libraries, this work contains many fictitious characters and events.

Miller, John Chester. *The Wolf by the Ears: Thomas Jefferson and Slavery.* New York: Free Press, 1977. Treats the correspondence between Banneker and Jefferson in the context of Jefferson's life and the slavery problem in the United States.

Paul E. Kuhl

SAMUEL BARBER

Born: March 9, 1910; West Chester, Pennsylvania
Died: January 23, 1981; New York, New York
Area of Achievement: Music
Contribution: Barber developed a style of musical composition which bridged the gap between nineteenth century Romanticism and twentieth century modernism.

Early Life
Samuel Barber was born March 9, 1910, in West Chester, Pennsylvania. His father was a physician, his mother a pianist, his aunt on his mother's side of the family the famed contralto Louise Homer. Barber's family did not, however, particularly encourage his natural inclination toward music studies. They wanted him to be "an average American boy," and for them this meant active participation in athletics, particularly football. Barber, however, was in no way average. In a letter he wrote as a schoolboy, Barber expressed to his mother his determination to become a composer, and begged, "PLEASE" (the underlining and capitalization are his own), to be allowed to pursue music studies.

Clearly, Barber's family always recognized his talent, even though they did not want their son to subject himself to the uncertainties inherent in a career in music. Still, there was no way to hold back a prodigy, and the six-year-old Barber began piano studies with William Hatton Green, himself a former student of the Polish pianist and composer Theodor Leschetizky. These early studies firmly linked Barber to European Romanticism and would leave an indelible influence on his own distinctive style. By age ten, Barber had written the first act of an opera entitled "The Rose Tree." No doubt it would have been completed had the family cook, who was also the librettist, not left the Barber household for another position. Several songs dating from the early 1920's still survive, however, in the archives of the Chester County Historical Society, West Chester, Pennsylvania.

Obviously, there was potential even in his youthful works, for with the sponsorship of Harold Randolph, then Director of the Peabody Conservatory in Baltimore, Maryland, Barber was accepted as a charter student at the then recently founded Curtis Institute of Music in Philadelphia, Pennsylvania, in 1924. He attended Curtis for eight years, during the first two of which he remained as well in his local high school to complete graduation requirements in 1926. His diversified studies at Curtis were in themselves remarkable and included composition with Rosario Scalero, piano with Isabella Vengerova, and voice with Emilio deGogorza. (A recording of his early song based on Matthew Arnold's poem "Dover Beach" was made with the Curtis String Quartet, Barber singing the tenor solo, on May 13, 1935. It was issued as a Victor 78 R.P.M., and is a collector's item since it represents the only example of Barber as vocalist.)

Photographs of Barber, most taken from the mid-1930's once his career had begun, show a young man who is at once patrician, elegant, and conservative, more like a prosperous businessman than a bohemian artist. His intelligent, piercing eyes and slightly aquiline nose remained his best features throughout his life and make the adjective "distinguished" entirely appropriate to describe Barber's appearance, even as a very young man. Except for white hair, slightly receding in his later years, Barber kept this youthful appearance to the last years of his life. His diction was similarly impeccable, perhaps in part from his vocal training, with only a trace of English accent behind otherwise uninflected speech. Unlike many composers, Barber had the ability to discuss his own compositions with great critical insight. Several radio interviews survive as transcriptions from the original broadcasts, the majority from the mid-1960's, the period following composition of his opera *Antony and Cleopatra* (1966).

Life's Work

Major recognition of Barber's talent came in 1928 when his Sonata for Violin and Piano won the Bearns Prize. This twelve-hundred-dollar award, substantial for the 1920's, encouraged the young composer. Barber would win the Bearns Prize a second time in 1935, for his overture and incidental music for Richard Brinsley Sheridan's play *The School for Scandal* (1777), by far a better-known composition, which has been recorded several times.

Barber's friendship with fellow composer Gian Carlo Menotti (1911-   ) began during their years as fellow students at Curtis. Though an unlikely musical association given the style of Menotti, which follows in the wake of Italian *verismo*, the two collaborated on several important projects. Menotti, for example, staged the revised version of *Antony and Cleopatra* in 1975, for the Juilliard Opera in New York, and again in 1983, at his Spoleto Festival in Italy and his Festival of Two Worlds in Charleston, South Carolina. These productions were a critical success and largely responsible for the opera's increased acceptance. Barber and Menotti also shared a warm personal friendship as well as a home, Capricorn, at Mount Kisco, New York.

A European tour Barber took in 1932 was important for shaping his style as a composer. It was in the summer of that year that he completed the first movement and part of the scherzo of his Sonata for Violoncello and Piano, which won for him the American Academy's Prix de Rome in 1935, as well as a Pulitzer Traveling Scholarship, also in 1935. These grants allowed Barber an academic year in residence at the American Academy in Rome (1935-1936) and provided a setting for the world premiere of his Symphony No. 1 (In One Movement), which was given by the Augusteo Orchestra, Bernardino Molinari conducting. Famed conductor Artur Rodzinski, leading the

Cleveland Orchestra, gave the American premiere later in 1936 (it was re-vised in 1942).

Barber's career was well under way by the mid-1930's, fostered as well by Arturo Toscanini's sponsorship. Barber had met Toscanini during the American Academy year. The maestro recalled his having conducted Barber's aunt, Louise Homer, in Christoph Gluck's *Orfeo ed Eurydice* (1762), and asked to see the young composer's work. What Toscanini saw were drafts of his Essay No. 1, the first of his Essays for Orchestra, and the Adagio for Strings. He would conduct these celebrated pieces with the National Broadcasting Company (NBC) Symphony Orchestra on November 5, 1938. Both works have since become standards of the symphonic literature. Though the Essays for Orchestra received mixed critical response at the time of its premiere, the Adagio for Strings gained immediate public acceptance. Its affecting lyricism makes it appreciable on first hearing. This was the music which the NBC radio network chose to play immediately after its announcement of President Franklin Roosevelt's death on April 12, 1945, and more recently it was adapted as part of the score for the motion picture *The Elephant Man* (1980). Barber would increasingly employ what he considered "literary" techniques in his compositions, and in his last years he would write other "essays," so called because they developed architechtonically from an orchestral thesis.

Barber's career continued to gain momentum in early 1941, when Eugene Ormandy and the Philadelphia Orchestra gave the premiere of his Violin Concerto, Opus 14, with Albert Spalding as soloist. Though when first composed Iso Briselli, for whom it was intended, called its final movement "unplayable" and refused to accept the piece, it has come to be highly regarded by musicians as a virtuoso work; indeed, the Philadelphia Orchestra singled it out for a cash award during its 1957-1958 season.

As was the case for many artists, World War II imposed severe limitations on Barber's composing activities. He entered the army in 1943, and served in a clerical position, though he did write his Commando March at this time. Though his name never publicly appeared as part of the controversy, it is generally known that the army refused him permission to write a piece in honor of the Russian people. Protests on his behalf by his fellow artists, the best known of whom was the Metropolitan Opera's Lawrence Tibbett, probably were responsible for Barber's quiet transfer to the Air Force. It was at this time that Barber composed his first version of Symphony No. 2, a programmatic work which contained attempts to reproduce electronically the sounds and machinery of flight. Barber was never pleased with the work, and after several attempts to revise it by eliminating all programmatic material, he saw to the destruction of all remaining undistributed published copies and withdrew the title from his catalog of works.

Barber, unlike many composers, rarely conducted or taught. He had studied conducting in the 1930's under Fritz Reiner, but Reiner considered Barber mediocre, and this opinion seems to have discouraged the young composer. Barber did conduct in later life, but only when his reputation was needed to publicize one of his compositions. For example, his Cello Concerto (1945), though critically acclaimed, was recorded in 1950 only because Barber himself agreed to conduct the orchestra. Barber's teaching was limited to a brief period at Curtis immediately after graduation from that institution. He never gave master classes.

The years following the war were especially productive. On a commission from the American soprano Eleanor Steber, Barber wrote his immensely popular *Knoxville: Summer of 1915*, Opus 24, based on the autobiographical memoir by James Agee. This work premiered April 9, 1948, with Serge Koussevitzky conducting Steber and the Boston Symphony. Here again, as he had in the Adagio for Strings and the first Essays for Orchestra, Barber showed his gift for lyricism and his affinity for literature. Indeed, the works of Barber which have these qualities are inevitably those which have remained audience favorites. *The Hermit Songs* (1952-1953), based on medieval Irish texts, are similarly popular. They premiered on October 30, 1953, at the Library of Congress, sung by Leontyne Price, who was just beginning her career, with Barber playing the piano accompaniment.

His success in vocal writing led to the opera *Vanessa*. This work, with libretto by Menotti, was given to popular acclaim but mixed critical reaction at the Metropolitan Opera Company with Steber in the title role on January 15, 1958. It did, however, win a Pulitzer Prize, and its audience popularity in several revivals led the Metropolitan Opera Company to commission *Antony and Cleopatra* for the September 16, 1966, inauguration of its new house at Lincoln Center. One problem with this work in its original form is that it was written as much to illustrate the new theater's performance capabilities as to present the composer's music. The Franco Zeffirelli production was especially lavish, and the difficult music, combined with what Barber himself believed was an inappropriate production, resulted in what is generally considered a failure, though Price, the Cleopatra of the premiere, always defended the music and kept Cleopatra's death music in her concert programs. It remains a bitter irony that the costumes for *Vanessa*, *Antony and Cleopatra*, and thirty-nine other Metropolitan Opera Company productions were destroyed in a warehouse fire on November 7, 1974. Depression set in after the failure of *Antony and Cleopatra*. Barber sold his Mount Kisco home and set about revising the opera. Its revised version runs almost a full hour less than the original, and it was given with some success by Julliard in 1975, with still more subsequently by Menotti at Charleston and Spoleto.

Barber's last years were plagued by hospitalization and treatment for cancer, and this affected his work. An eight-minute piece for oboe and string orchestra, written in 1978, is his last known composition. Though originally designed as part of an oboe concerto, it was given in late 1981 as *Canzonetta* by the New York Philharmonic, Zubin Mehta conducting, with Harold Gomberg as soloist.

Summary
It is difficult to say exactly what legacy Barber has left American music. What is clear is that he was an immensely gifted composer whose gentle, lyrical style and precision allowed many members of the general audience an introduction to modern music which they would not otherwise have had. Barber could have used his gifts to pander to audience tastes. Though this would have assured him at least short-term popularity, he refused to do so.

His greatest accomplishment was his ability to use familiar nineteenth century Romantic musical forms in undeniably modern ways. To his last days, he rejected both extreme dissonance and stripped-down minimalism. His music was almost never "American-sounding" in the manner of George Gershwin or Aaron Copland, yet he ranks with them as one of the most often performed and recorded American composers of the twentieth century.

Bibliography
Ardoin, John. "Samuel Barber at Capricorn." *Musical America* 80 (March, 1960): 4-5. An interesting, intimate portrait of the composer's private life at the house in Mount Kisco, New York, which he shared with Menotti until 1974. Barber found inspiration in the landscape and through his association with his fellow composer and longtime friend.
Broder, Nathan. "The Music of Samuel Barber." *Musical Quarterly* 34 (July, 1948): 325-335. Remains interesting for what it says about Barber's attention to form. Though Barber based many orchestral compositions on the classical sonata form, he managed to do so without slavish adherence to the past. This article illustrates Barber's ability to introduce new techniques within more traditional structures.
Demuth, Norman. *Musical Trends in the Twentieth Century*. London: Rockliff, 1952. Compares Barber's virtuosity to that of Richard Strauss; even so, Barber's music is not neoclassical but represents a Romanticism appropriate to the twentieth century.
Dexter, Harry. "Samuel Barber and His Music." Parts 1, 2. *Musical Opinion* 72 (March, April, 1949): 285-286, 343-344. A two-part article which provides good criticism of Barber's style: his emotional control and the depth of feeling which he produces in spite of this control.
Friedewald, Russell Edward. *A Formal and Stylistic Analysis of the Published Music of Samuel Barber*. Ames: Iowa State University Press, 1957. A dissertation which distinguishes between Barber's music composed before and after 1939, noting the technical enrichment of the later work and Barber's adaptations of the classical sonata form.
Hennessee, Don A. *Samuel Barber: A Bio-Bibliography*. Westport, Conn.:

Greenwood Press, 1985. Contains a brief biographical essay as well as a catalog of Barber's works and critical works available on them.

"Obituary: Mr. Samuel Barber." *The Times* (London), January 26, 1981: 14. A long article which discusses Barber's career and sees him in the tradition of Romanticism as lyrical rather than neoclassical or experimental, generally rejecting many of the trends of modern music.

Robert J. Forman

HENRY BARNARD

Born: January 24, 1811; Hartford, Connecticut
Died: July 5, 1900; Hartford, Connecticut
Area of Achievement: Education
Contribution: Combining a high regard for learning and a strong sense of
civic responsibility, Barnard stimulated and directed the development of
public education during its formative years.

Early Life

Henry Barnard was born January 24, 1811, in Hartford, Connecticut.
Barnard's mother, Elizabeth Andrus, died when Henry was four years old;
his father, Chauncey Barnard, was a former sailor and prosperous farmer-
businessman. Hartford was little more than a small country town during Barnard's childhood, but its status as one of Connecticut's capitals meant that he
grew up in an atmosphere of politics and public service.

Ironically, the man who would later be hailed as a father of the public
school so hated his first encounter with that institution that he conspired with
a classmate to run away to sea. His father overheard them and the following
day offered Henry a choice of leaving the district school and going to either
sea or boarding school. Barnard chose the latter alternative and enrolled in
Monson Academy, Monson, Massachusetts. Barnard was no bookworm, but
he enjoyed his studies at Monson and developed an interest in literature and
debating. Returning to Hartford, he received private tutoring and attended
the Hopkins Grammar School in preparation for college. In 1826, Barnard
entered Yale University, where he not only enhanced his writing and speaking skills, but also was suspended briefly for participating in a student food
protest.

Having been graduated with distinction from Yale in 1830, Barnard resolved to devote his life to public service. He taught for a year, but appears at
first to have given little thought of devoting himself exclusively to the field of
education. Instead, he became involved in Whig politics and studied law.
Barnard was admitted to the bar in 1835, but before beginning his legal practice he spent a year in Europe, where he met and talked with prominent
European intellectuals and educators.

A year after Barnard's return to the United States, Hartford voters elected
him to the Connecticut legislature, where he served from 1837 to 1840. He
was active in promoting a broad range of social reform legislation, his most
notable legislative achievement occurring in 1838, when he wrote and
secured passage of a bill creating a state board of school commissioners and a
secretary to supervise public education. This event proved to have a decisive
influence on his life.

Life's Work

In 1838, Barnard was appointed one of the board's eight commissioners. He campaigned for his friend Thomas Gallaudet, a pioneering advocate of education for the deaf, to become secretary of the board. Gallaudet declined the position, however, and Barnard himself was urged to take it. At first he hesitated, partly because the office had been created through his efforts, and partly because he had been offered a partnership in a prestigious law firm. Yet in the end, he accepted the position.

As Connecticut's first secretary of education, Barnard attempted to develop widespread support for school and library reform. He wrote a letter to the people outlining the plans of the new board, distributed questionnaires, and personally visited hundreds of school districts. He presented data on schools to the legislature and the public, founded and edited the *Connecticut Common School Journal*, and lobbied for changes in school laws. Barnard also emphasized the need for trained teachers and established teachers' institutes which were among the first, if not the first, in the nation.

Yet events in Connecticut did not go well for Barnard. His campaign to improve public education awakened public opposition in the state to school reform and disturbed local politicians. In 1842, the Democrats came to power in the state and, in a move aimed at gaining support among voters, called for an end to direct state supervision of schools. Furthermore, Barnard's past affiliation with the opposition Whig Party did not help matters. After only four years of operation, the State Board of School Commissioners was abolished.

Barnard's Connecticut experience soured him on politics, but it did not dampen his enthusiasm for school reform. In 1843, he was appointed state school commissioner in Rhode Island. Predictably, Barnard engaged in a whirlwind of activity and in a relatively short time had developed popular support for public education in that state. At his urging, the Rhode Island Institute of Instruction was established in 1845. In that same year, he also secured passage of legislation to support a public education system in the state; when he resigned in 1849 for health reasons, he had already put it into successful operation. Barnard arranged for educational supplements to appear in state almanacs and caused the proceedings of school meetings to be reported in the press. In addition, he edited the state's school journal, published a book on teachers' colleges, and completed a volume on school architecture.

By the time of his marriage in 1847, Barnard was widely known and in great demand as a speaker. He was offered at least two professorships and four city school superintendencies, all of which he declined. When his home state of Connecticut again sought his leadership, however, he could not refuse. During his term of service as Connecticut's superintendent of common schools, Barnard drew up a revised code of school legislation, prepared a history of public school legislation in the state, and served as delegate to the International Exposition of Educational Methods in London, England. Still plagued by ill health, Barnard resigned as superintendent in 1855 to edit and publish the *American Journal of Education*, a monumental work that eventually comprised thirty-two volumes of more than eight hundred pages each.

Although the journal received most of Barnard's attention during the remainder of his life, he briefly held three additional administrative posts. From 1858 to 1860, he was chancellor of the University of Wisconsin and agent of the board of regents of the normal school fund. In 1866, Barnard was named president of St. John's College, resigning the following year to become the first commissioner of the newly created United States Department of Education. From the outset, Barnard's tenure as commissioner was plagued with problems. In 1868, growing criticism of the Department of Education and Barnard led Congress to downgrade it to a bureau (later, office) within the Department of the Interior. Two years later, he was unceremoniously removed from office by President Ulysses S. Grant.

Photographs of Barnard in the latter years of his life reveal a man perfectly suited for the role of reformer. His long white beard, white hair, and benign facial features gave him a patriarchal appearance. Deeply humiliated at his dismissal by Grant, he left Washington and returned to Hartford, where he continued to edit the *American Journal of Education* until 1881. Barnard lectured frequently, continued a voluminous correspondence and in countless other ways attempted to keep busy until his death in the same house where he was born on July 5, 1900. Such activities, however, belied his true feelings. Despite the accolades he received from citizens and friends for his contribution to school reform, Barnard died doubting that his labors were sufficiently appreciated.

Summary

Barnard's contribution to the development of American education was manifold. The changes he introduced to public education in Connecticut and Rhode Island were of lasting importance and, in some degree, served as models for school reform in other states. He was always willing to offer advice and encouragement to fellow school reformers. His chief service, however, was rendered as a publicist and propagandist for education. As editor and publisher of the *American Journal of Education*, he not only furthered educational scholarship, but also helped create the necessary preconditions for the emergence of the modern teaching profession.

Undeniably, Barnard exemplified the best and the worst in nineteenth century American reform. A genuine idealist, he believed in the ability of people properly informed to make the right decision. At the same time, however, confidence in his own moral excellence could deteriorate into a brass-bolted certitude that denied any sense of rightness in other men. Indeed, at times Barnard's methods suggest that he thought the average citizen deserved little voice in school reform, except to rubber-stamp his own ideas.

The transformation which Barnard helped bring to American education is evident everywhere. It is most visible in older school-building architecture, public school systems, and schools of education throughout the United States. Less obvious, but equally important, is his role in supplying a professional literature and raising professional standards for the whole field of education.

Bibliography

Barnard, Henry. *Henry Barnard: American Educator*. Edited and introduced by Vincent P. Lannie. New York: Teacher's College Press, 1974. This collection of Barnard's writings contains excerpts from his personal correspondence from an annual report of 1841 on public education in Connecticut, and from the *American Journal of Education*. Of particular note is the introduction by Lannie, which provides a concise biographical sketch of Barnard.

_____. *Henry Barnard on Education*. Edited by John S. Brubacher. New York: McGraw-Hill Book Co., 1931. Comprising some of Barnard's most important writings, this book presents his thoughts on a variety of educational issues ranging from public interest in education to educational administration. It includes an introductory chapter which discusses Barnard's life and work.

Brickman, William W. "Early Development of Research and Writing of Educational History in the United States." *Paedagogica Historica* 19 (June, 1979): 41-76. Traces early nineteenth century developments in educational historiography and discusses the work of Barnard and others in this area. Includes an examination of European influences and the impact of teachers' college curricula on writing about the history of American education.

Rothfork, John. "Transcendentalism and Henry Barnard's School Architecture." *Journal of General Education* 29 (Fall, 1977): 173-187. Discusses the intellectual and social climate that led Barnard to advocate Greek Revival architecture for school buildings. Examines the reasons for which this style and its implicit values were popular in the nineteenth century.

Thursfield, Richard Emmons. *Henry Barnard's American Journal of Education*. Baltimore, Md.: The Johns Hopkins University Press, 1945. Somewhat dated, this book nevertheless remains indispensable. It not only presents information on the journal's founding and financing, but also attempts to assess the significance of its content and its influence on readers.

Tyack, David B. *The One Best System: A History of American Urban Education*. Cambridge, Mass.: Harvard University Press, 1974. This well-documented study mentions Barnard only in passing but provides a detailed account of the social milieu in which he worked and the ideology which guided him and other educational reformers.

Warren, Donald R. *To Enforce Education: A History of the Founding Years of the United States Office of Education.* Detroit, Mich: Wayne State University Press, 1974. Examines issues surrounding the founding of the Department of Education. Discusses the attempt by Barnard and other reformers to establish a federal bureau of education.

Monroe H. Little, Jr.

P. T. BARNUM

Born: July 5, 1810; Bethel, Connecticut
Died: April 7, 1891; Bridgeport, Connecticut
Areas of Achievement: Showmanship, politics, and writing
Contribution: With a strong business sense and the ability to take huge risks, P. T. Barnum created the modern museum and the musical concert, converted the tent carnival into the three-ring circus, and ran for a variety of political offices, serving for two terms on the Connecticut legislature and for one as a mayor of Bridgeport.

Early Life

Phineas Taylor Barnum was born on July 5, 1810, in Bethel, Connecticut. Throughout his life, Barnum always regretted that he had not been born on the Fourth of July, the perfect birth date for the man who would become one of America's first showmen. He was the sixth child of Philo and Irene Barnum, Philo's second wife. Barnum was named for his maternal grandfather, Phineas (a biblical name meaning "brazen mouth") Taylor. As Barnum's life progressed, it turned out that the name fit him and that the ancestor he was named for would influence Barnum unlike anyone else in his life.

As a boy, Barnum looked to his grandfather Phineas for amusement. Phineas Taylor, a great practical joker whose antics helped liven up the harsh New England winters, would go further than most to create his little jokes and hoaxes that he concocted to weather the stern Calvinism of his day. When Barnum was christened, grandfather Phineas deeded to him five acres of land called Ivy Island. Phineas liked to brag to others in Barnum's presence that, because of that land, Barnum would one day be wealthy, and Barnum believed this throughout his childhood. At the age of four, he began begging his father to see his inheritance; finally, when Barnum was ten, his father acquiesced. The boy was led to an ivy-infested swamp, and even at that young age he knew that he had been the butt of a long-running hoax and that his inheritance was worthless. (Ironically, later in life Barnum put Ivy Island up for collateral.) P. T. Barnum, who loved his grandfather Phineas, ended up getting the last laugh by naming his illegitimate son Phineas Taylor.

The young P. T. Barnum, who would one day prudently know when to cut his losses, excelled in mathematics. While in grammar school (high school), Barnum helped his father out on the family farm; like thinkers down through the ages, however, he detested menial work and began planning for a different life. Philo's farm was a disappointment, and so, with a partner, he bought a general store and put Barnum in charge. In that position Barnum learned much about people, about bartering, and about business. By chance, he was being trained and goaded toward his future.

Barnum's father died when Barnum was only fifteen. In charge of the family, Barnum liquidated the store only to discover that the family was bankrupt. Quickly he obtained a similar job in another store. Tiring of that, he moved to Brooklyn to clerk at a better store.

Barnum's influential grandfather, Phineas, wanted Barnum to return to Bethel and offered to set him up in business if he would come home. That was all the encouragement Barnum needed, and he returned to set up a profitable business in half of his grandfather's carriage house.

On November 8, 1829, at the age of nineteen, Barnum eloped with Charity Hallett, a twenty-one-year-old Bethel woman. One of Barnum's daughters, Frances, died before her second birthday; his surviving daughters were Caroline, Helen, and Pauline. Like King Lear, Barnum suffered much from the actions of his daughters, who let their father down innumerable times, disappointing him by their various divorce scandals and their eagerness to divide up their father's estates while he was still alive.

Barnum, disappointed that his wife never had sons, left twenty-five thousand dollars and a yearly three percent of his enterprises to his eldest grandson, Clinton H. Seeley. To receive the inheritance, Seeley was required to change his middle name to Barnum in order to perpetuate Barnum's name. Clinton Barnum Seeley accepted the bequest but dishonored Barnum by conducting licentious parties, one of which included a nude Little Egypt in the center ring.

Life's Work

P. T. Barnum's life is almost inseparable from the freaks, the oddities, the hoaxes, the hokum, the sheer entertainment that he presented to the world, from the "sucker" on the street to Queen Victoria and the president. This six-foot-two man with curly, receding hair, blue eyes, a cleft chin, a bulbous nose, and a high voice was a pitchman *par excellence* and might almost be said to have invented the art of mass publicity.

After an apprenticeship spent selling hats, working in grocery stores, running lotteries, and maintaining a boardinghouse, Barnum found his métier. The catalyst was his discovery and purchase of Joice Heth, a black woman with legal documents that proved she was 161 years old and had served as George Washington's nurse. Barnum quit his grocery job and gambled both borrowed money and his life savings to make his break from convention.

In 1835, a Mr. Lindsay showed Barnum documents on the old woman and sold her to him for one thousand dollars. Barnum hired a hall by promising the owner half the gross, and he employed several people to help him launch a publicity campaign. At her shows, Joice Heth sang hymns and told her story of rearing Washington. The newspaper helped to spread the story, and eventually the show was a success, with Barnum splitting the weekly gross of fifteen hundred dollars with his partner.

Finally the dreaded event occurred: Joice Heth died. Barnum had given

Dr. David Rogers permission to perform an autopsy, which in the end proved that Joice Heth was not more than eighty years old. Thus, the hoax was exposed and the newspapers made Barnum even more famous.

Barnum continued to collect and display oddities, both human and otherwise. He needed a central stage for his show and in 1841 acquired a dilapidated museum at Broadway and Ann Street in New York City which became known as Barnum's American Museum. For the admission fee, one could see the Feejee Mermaid (which was nothing more than a female monkey torso joined to a large stuffed fish tail), midgets, beauty contests, a bearded lady (she went to court to prove she was not a man), a tattooed man, the world's tallest woman, the Woolly Horse, the authentic Siamese twins Chang and Eng, and countless other abnormalities.

Barnum was always in search of another main attraction, and one materialized for him in 1842 when he discovered a five-year-old midget named Charles Stratton. Barnum taught him to sing and dance, to tell jokes, and to perform other stunts, all while wearing several different military uniforms. Stratton was thus converted into General Tom Thumb, one of Barnum's biggest entertainment successes.

To gain greater fame, Barnum took Tom Thumb on tour in Europe. There he was a hugh success before five million people (according to Barnum's own count), and Barnum connived to make headlines when the General performed for Queen Victoria, who presented Tom with a court uniform. When Barnum and Tom Thumb returned to the United States, the clamor was great, and even President Polk requested and got a private show at the White House.

Barnum's next big success was the signing of the famous Swedish singer Jenny Lind, whom he had neither seen nor heard, to perform on a concert tour. To finance the tour, he was forced to mortgage both his $150,000 home and his museum, as well as borrow heavily from friends. The risk paid off; Jenny Lind's tour was both a critical and a financial success. The Swedish Nightingale opened in New York City on September 11, 1850, and after ninety-five concerts in nineteen cities, Barnum had cleared profits in excess of $500,000.

In 1855, however, Barnum's time for high-risk profits had run out. As he had in the past, he became obsessed with an investment, this one with the Jerome Clock Company. Through his own bad management, Barnum carelessly invested more than $500,000 in the company, only to watch it go bankrupt. Barnum contemplated suicide, but instead, this religious man concluded that the Almighty Himself wished to teach him that there was something higher in life than money. Except for Charity's nineteen thousand dollars a year from the museum lease, all was lost. "Without Charity," he quipped, "I am nothing." This may have simply been a clever pun, however, since his financial recovery had begun immediately after the losses.

At forty-six, Barnum began his long climb toward repaying his debts. He turned to his standby, General Tom Thumb; he also realized that he himself was a viable commodity and began lecturing to packed houses. Capitalizing, as always, on a good thing, he turned his lecture notes into a best-selling pamphlet, *The Art of Money Getting*, and reused the notes a second time in his autobiography.

Fire seemed to follow Barnum around like a demon. His home, Iranistan, was lost in a fire. The Barnum American Museum burned to the ground (miraculously, the freaks with their immobile bodies all escaped). The museum loss was calculated at $400,000, with insurance covering only forty thousand dollars. Many precious objects, including irreplaceable relics of the Revolutionary War, were lost. Barnum, with his typical verve, rebuilt the museum.

One of Barnum's greatest claims to fame began when he was sixty. He joined forces with James Anthony Bailey to created "The Greatest Show on Earth." Barnum's London Zoo purchase of Jumbo the Elephant (who had given rides to some five million British children, including Winston Churchill) became one of his most famous and most disputed purchases. Queen Victoria and others in England wanted the famous elephant back. By the time Jumbo reached the American shores, the elephant was an international *cause célèbre* and had generated much free publicity. The elephant act was an instant success: The purchase price of thirty thousand dollars was recouped in six weeks, with a box-office of $336,000.

In 1873, Charity died, and in the following year Barnum married Nancy Fish, an English woman forty years his junior. Barnum and his second wife had no children.

In 1891, Barnum was eighty-one and in poor health. After a lifetime of financial reversals, he was surrounded by wealth. He remarked to a friend that he wondered how his obituary would read. Word of this got back to the New York *Evening Sun*, and the newspaper asked for and got permission to print Barnum's obituary before he died. On April 7, 1891, this American folk hero died at his home in Bridgeport.

Summary

According to Bartlett's *Familiar Quotations*, the expression "There's a sucker born every minute" is attributed to P. T. Barnum. Researchers have stated repeatedly that Barnum never said this. Indeed, in his own life he was often a "sucker." He assumed as a child that Ivy Island would make him wealthy, and as an adult he thought that he could get rich quick through his Jerome Clock investment.

Barnum knew many secrets about human nature, one of which was that although no one enjoys being duped, if the game is all in good fun, people do enjoy becoming "suckers" to an extent—so much so that they are willing to pay for the honor. Another secret Barnum learned was that of the publicist: In his pre–"global village" age, Barnum might be said to have invented the high-pressure sales campaign, creating the "hype" that sold his wares.

Barnum himself became a household name and an original American folk hero. His life was filled with contradictions. He was a good family man, yet he fathered an illegitimate son, the only son he was ever to have. He was reared in an anti-entertainment age yet believed devoutly that each person deserved to be entertained. He made a great amount of money; he lost all of his money; he made more money. He sustained spectacular triumphs unmatched by rivals. Living a long life, he experienced many personal tragedies, including the death of a daughter, the death of his wife Charity, the loss of property and money, and the divisiveness and greed of his surviving three daughters.

Barnum became an archetype of American Dream merchants such as Walt Disney, Samuel Goldwyn, Oscar Hammerstein I, John Ringling, Mike Todd, Cecil B. DeMille, Billy Rose, the brothers Shubert, Florenz Ziegfeld, Steven Spielberg, George Lucas, and hundreds of others. A lively musical, *Barnum*, and the circus that bears his name reintroduces Barnum to thousands each year.

"To the Egress," a sign in the Barnum's American Museum once read. Expecting to find another oddity, people entered and found themselves outside the museum, on the street.

Bibliography
Barnum, Phineas T. *Barnum's Own Story: Autobiography*. Edited by Waldo R. Browne. Magnolia, Mass.: Peter Smith, Publishers, 1962. As of August, 1986, this is the only autobiography in print. Browne's editing makes it less clumsy.
_____. *Selected Letters of P. T. Barnum*. Edited by A. H. Saxon. New York: Columbia University Press, 1983. The only published collection of Barnum's letters.
_____. *Struggles and Triumphs: Or, Forty Years' Recollections of P. T. Barnum*. Edited by Carl Bode. New York: Penguin Books, 1981. Good starting point for research. Barnum wrote three versions of this book, which Bode condenses into one readable volume. Bode has written an excellent introduction and has included a short, annotated bibliography.
Benton, Joel. *Life of Honorable Phineas T. Barnum*. Philadelphia: Edgewood Publishing Co., 1891. This book largely paraphrases (in the third person) Barnum's own autobiography. Benton knew Barnum, and he includes some of his own recollections.
Bryan, Joe, III. *The World's Greatest Showman: The Life of P. T. Barnum*. New York: Random House, 1956. A good juvenile book on Barnum.
Desmond, Alice Curtis. *Barnum Presents: General Tom Thumb*. New York:

Macmillan Publishing Co., 1954. The story of one of the most famous midgets in the world and how he became a gigantic drawing card for Barnum.

Harris, Neil. *Humbug: The Art of P. T. Barnum*. Boston: Little, Brown and Co., 1973. The most reliable biography. Sound scholarship is used to place Barnum in his own cultural setting.

Root, Harvey W. *The Unknown Barnum*. New York: Harper and Brothers, 1927. Provides source material on Barnum's publishing and political careers.

Sutton, Felix. *Master of Ballyhoo: The Story of P. T. Barnum*. New York: G. P. Putnam's Sons, 1968. A Literary Guild edition with large print for juveniles.

Wallace, Irving. *The Fabulous Showman: The Life and Times of P. T. Barnum*. New York: Alfred A. Knopf, 1959. One of the best introductions available on Barnum, covering all the major events. Well researched with an excellent bibliography and sixteen pages of photographs.

Werner, Morris Robert. *Barnum*. Garden City, N.Y.: Garden City Publishing Co., 1923. This was the first biography to offer a researched, objective view of Barnum's life.

John Harty

CLARA BARTON

Born: December 25, 1821; North Oxford, Massachusetts
Died: April 12, 1912; Glen Echo, Maryland
Areas of Achievement: Education, nursing, social services, and politics
Contribution: Barton tended the wounded on the battlefields of the Civil
War, founded and served as first president of the American Red Cross,
and personally led relief services in the field for many natural disasters in
the United States and abroad.

Early Life

Clarissa Harlowe Barton, or Clara, as she was always called, once wrote
that she was born into a family of teachers. Born on Christmas Day in North
Oxford, Massachusetts, she was the youngest of the five children of Stephen
and Sarah Stone Barton, and the whole family undertook her education.

Clara's father, Captain Stephen Barton, was a farmer and a soldier. He had
spent three hard years on the frontier fighting Indians and the English under
the command of Mad Anthony Wayne. One of his comrades was William
Henry Harrison, "Old Tippecanoe," who later became president of the
United States. Stephen Barton used to tell Clara stories of those days and
often discussed military strategy and military protocol with her. This instruction, along with his insistence that she know the names and functions of persons in political office, was useful to her in later life, when she was often
dealing with military personnel and politicians.

With the help of her brothers and sisters, Clara learned to read by age
three and had mastered the rudiments of spelling, arithmetic, and geography
as well. Her brother David taught her to ride, throwing her on the back of a
colt when she was barely five and telling her to hang on to the mane. He
would then leap onto another colt and they would go off on wild rides. This
early facility with horses also proved to be a blessing later, on the battlefield,
when she occasionally had to flee before advancing Confederate forces.

When Clara was eleven years old, an event happened which had a profound effect upon her and was strangely indicative of her later role as "Angel
of the Battlefield," a title given her by Brigade Surgeon James Dunn. David
was seriously injured in a fall from the top of a barn, and he lingered
between life and death for two years. Clara nursed him, hardly leaving his
side, and eventually he recovered, but Clara's own health was seriously impaired and it took some time to recover her strength. She gained only one
pound in those two years and not an inch in height—nor was she ever taller
than the five feet, three inches of that period. Moreover, the seclusion had
made her a hermit, even more timid and tongue-tied than she was before.

Barton may have been exaggerating in 1907 when she said that she remembered nothing of her early years but fear, yet timidity and bashfulness made

much of her early schooling painful. When school was out, however, idleness was torture to her. She could always live with work and self-sacrifice, but when there was nothing to do she seemed to sink into hypersensitivity and listlessness. This curious pattern persisted through much of her life, so that prolonged periods of incredible energy and tireless service alternated with complete withdrawal, physical and emotional exhaustion, and feelings of depression and inadequacy.

When Sarah Barton asked a visiting phrenologist, L. W. Fowler, what her daughter Clara should do, he gave a wise answer: "The sensitive nature will always remain. She will never assert herself for herself; she will suffer wrong first. But for others she will be perfectly fearless. Throw responsibility upon her, give her a school to teach."

Life's Work

Although Barton is best known for her service on the battlefields of the Civil War and for organizing and heading the American Red Cross, that part of her life did not begin until she was forty years old. Her earlier work also gives ample evidence of her remarkable initiative and energy. As her parents' friend had foreseen, her shyness and sensitivity were balanced by a stubborn aggressiveness when laboring for other people. Whatever she did, she proved to be a natural founder and organizer.

In 1836, at the age of fifteen, she became a teacher, and she remained in that profession for eighteen years. She chose to teach in New Jersey, which had public school laws but no public schools: The well-to-do sent their children to private schools, but twice as many children roamed the streets uneducated. When she tried to promote a public school, she was told that no one, especially a small woman such as she, could tame those undisciplined street children. Barton offered to organize and teach a school without pay to show that it could be done. She started out with six renegade boys whom she gathered off the streets; in twelve months, she had a new schoolhouse, and the six had become six hundred.

In 1854, Barton went to Washington, D.C., and was soon braving public prejudice again as the first woman appointed independently to a clerkship in the Department of the Interior. Serving in the Patent Office, she faced considerable criticism because her salary (fourteen hundred dollars a year) was the same as that of male clerks. She endured because of her skill in copying but suffered cruel harassment and slander from many of the men. After 1857, when James Buchanan became president, she was finally dismissed for political reasons.

When the Civil War began, Barton immediately began to circulate among the new recruits, many of them homesick and ill-equipped, who gathered in Washington. She appealed for supplies through the *Worcester Spy* and delivered food and comforts to the soldiers, wrote letters for them, supplied suitable clothing, and notified mothers of their sons' condition. She rented a warehouse to hold supplies and established a distributing agency.

When her father died, Barton determined to go to the battlefront. Despite resistance almost everywhere she went to get permits and help transporting her supplies, she obtained the necessary passes from the reluctant Surgeon General, from the Assistant Quartermaster General in charge of transportation, and from the Military Governor of the District of Columbia. Two days after the battle of Cedar Mountain, Brigade Surgeon James Dunn, whose supply of dressings was about exhausted, was amazed when a slight, vigorous woman of forty arrived at his hospital at midnight in a four-mule-team wagon loaded with supplies.

Barton soon collected a cadre of other women dedicated to caring for the wounded wherever they might be. They went from one battlefield to another, binding the wounds of the fallen, heating soup and coffee and feeding the men, and covering them with blankets until they could be evacuated for further medical attention. Barton was not a registered nurse. Most war fatalities at that time, however, were not from wounds alone but from exposure, dehydration, and neglect suffered in the twenty-four to forty-eight hours during which the wounded might lie on the ground without food, water, or shelter from the cold or rain. Barton wrote later of the harrowing dark nights after the Second Battle of Bull Run, when wounded men were packed side by side on the ground, which had been strewn with hay. The slightest misstep would bring groans of pain, but the greatest fear of those who tended the men was that a candle dropped in the hay might spread fire throughout the whole field of the wounded. Recalling that time, Barton wrote that she went five days and nights with only three hours' sleep and narrowly escaped capture.

In 1862, Barton rode eighty miles with four men in an army supply wagon: Their destination was Harper's Ferry, and Barton pushed on to the very edge of the battle of Antietam, where more than 100,000 men were surging back and forth. Again she arrived in the nick of time: Four surgeons were struggling with nothing but their instruments and the little chloroform they had brought in their pockets. The battle was so close that one wounded man was shot in Barton's arms as she tried to give him a drink. The next time Barton asked for transportation, she was given six army wagons with good drivers and an ambulance.

Even after the war was over, Barton could not stop. Abraham Lincoln appealed to her to determine the fates of more than eighty thousand men listed as missing in action. With the help of surviving comrades, she managed to account for nearly half that number. She was stationed at Annapolis, the receiving depot where prisoners of war were exchanged from Andersonville and other Southern prisons.

When this chore was over, Barton started lecturing throughout the country, promoting her efforts to remedy the lingering wounds of war; she was particularly concerned for the many widows and fatherless children struggling to survive. At last, the unremitting strain took its toll: She lost her voice and was ordered by her physician to go to Europe.

Barton was approached in Geneva by the International Committee for the Relief of the Wounded in War and asked why the United States had refused to sign the treaty of Geneva, providing for the relief of sick and wounded soldiers. Barton had never heard of the treaty; after studying the document, she was ashamed that her country would refuse to participate, having twice denied the request to join.

This treaty, the brainchild of Swiss banker and philanthropist Jean-Henri Dunant, had grown out of an International Congress early in 1864, attended by sixteen governments. It provided for the neutralization of wounded soldiers, the hospitals that treated them, and all persons employed in the care of the wounded. All personnel, equipment, and places where wounded soldiers received treatment were to be marked by a red cross on a white ground, a reversal of the colors of the Swiss flag.

Barton not only promised to plead with the United States government to join the Red Cross, but also became involved in distributing relief supplies in the Franco-Prussian War. After her second war service, she was so exhausted and broken in spirit that she had to wait some time before sailing for home.

In the United States, a new battle awaited her—with politicians. Finally, however, in 1882, after four years of work behind the scenes by Barton, President Arthur signed the Geneva Accords, and legislative approval soon followed. Clara Barton became the first director of the American Red Cross and personally led relief operations for natural disasters in the United States and even in Russia and Turkey. At age seventy-six, during the Spanish-American War, she was in Cuba, caring for Theodore Roosevelt's Rough Riders. She did not resign until 1904. She died seven years later, April 12, 1912, at ninety-one years of age.

Summary

The character and achievements of Clara Barton constitute one of the most fascinating and well-documented studies in the gallery of remarkable women of the nineteenth century. She epitomized independent-thinking, idealistic individualism, yet modern feminists might suggest that her compulsive nurturing was a distinctly neurotic exaggeration of a cultural stereotype, leaving little room for more ordinary manifestations of motherly or sexual impulses. Even when she had become the most honored woman in America, she suffered from feelings of self-abnegation and uselessness in those necessary intervals of recuperation from her herculean labors. It could be argued that, precisely because of this peculiar combination of selfless nurturing and the aggressive, pioneer leadership more expected of men, she was the perfect American heroine.

While Barton did not invent the idea of the Red Cross, she was instrumental in making significant changes in its policy. In America, where warfare was not ordinarily a way of life, she expanded Red Cross services to those suffering from natural disasters. Most of her Red Cross years were spent in the field, dispensing aid to sufferers of floods, hurricanes, tornadoes, earthquakes, epidemics of typhoid or yellow fever, and drought and famine. In 1884, at the Third International Conference of the Red Cross in Geneva, Barton and Judge Joseph Sheldon pushed hard for the extension of Red Cross work to cover disaster relief as well as war wounded—the so-called American amendment that was of the utmost importance to the future of the Red Cross.

By 1909, several years after Barton had resigned with some bitterness because of criticism of her autocratic style of administration, the American Red Cross was completely reorganized, with government supervision, annual reports to Congress, and audits to the War Department. An era was ended.

Bibliography
Barton, Clara. *The Red Cross in Peace and War*. Washington, D.C.: American Historical Press, 1899. In formal exposition, Barton's prose can be somewhat ponderous and rhetorical, as in the first part of this volume. When she moves into personal narrative, however, she becomes vivid and lively. Contains some of Barton's inspirational (but undistinguished) poetry.

_____. *A Story of the Red Cross: Glimpses of Field Work*. New York: D. Appleton and Co., 1904. An informative chronological account of what the Red Cross did during Barton's leadership. Barton's accounts of fieldwork are moving documents about human suffering among people whom history soon forgets: the common soldier bleeding to death in the mud, the homeless family on the flooded bayou, the bloated corpses piled high on funeral pyres on the beach at Galveston after a tidal wave, the ragged survivors in war-gutted cities.

Barton, William E. *The Life of Clara Barton*. Boston: Houghton Mifflin Co., 1922. A detailed official biography, done by Clara Barton's cousin, who, working closely with Stephen E. Barton, her authorized executor, had access to all material then known. Glosses over the difficulties of her late years.

Boardman, Mabel T. *Under the Red Cross Flag at Home and Abroad*. Philadelphia: J. B. Lippincott Co., 1915. Mabel Boardman was a leading personality in the American Red Cross from 1905 until the American entry into World War I. She was one of Barton's adversaries in administrative policies, and this account tends to underestimate Barton's contributions.

Epler, Percy H. *The Life of Clara Barton*. New York: Macmillan, 1915. Perhaps the most complete biography for the general reader and scholar.

Epler includes considerable discussion of Barton's personality and style of operation and the unfortunate conflicts that marked her last years, when her leadership was brought into question. He is even-handed and just in this, and appropriately ironic in pointing to the fact that when Clara Barton died, the White House and the Red Cross were silent.

Fishwick, Marshall W., and the editors of Silver Burdett. *Illustrious Americans: Clara Barton*. Morristown, N.J.: Silver Burdett Co., 1966. A handsomely illustrated volume that amply fulfills its promise to the reader: "Miss Barton is here studied in three significant ways: a candid new biography, a full pictorial documentation, and a long, revealing selection of her own writings." The last section, containing excerpts from her diaries and other writings, with explanatory notes by the editors, is especially fascinating.

Joyce, James Avery. *Red Cross International and the Strategy of Peace*. Dobbs Ferry, N.Y.: Oceana Publications, 1959. Joyce affirms Barton's importance as the one who virtually dragged America into the Red Cross when all others had failed. Makes interesting comparisons between Florence Nightingale's mode of operation and Barton's rugged, pioneer approach.

Ross, Ishbel. *Angel of the Battlefield*. New York: Harper and Brothers, 1956. An engaging biography of Clara Barton for the general reader. An appendix includes a few of the more important documents and letters and Barton's personal list of public figures with whom she had dealings, including seven presidents of the United States and four European sovereigns. Provides a useful bibliography.

Katherine Snipes

CHARLES A. BEARD

Born: November 27, 1874; near Knightstown, Indiana
Died: September 1, 1948; New Haven, Connecticut
Areas of Achievement: Political science and history
Contribution: More than any other twentieth century scholar, Beard shaped
   how Americans viewed their past.

Early Life

Charles Austin Beard was born November 27, 1874, on a farm near
Knightstown, Indiana, the younger of two sons of William Henry Harrison
and Mary J. (Payne) Beard. His Beard forebears were Quakers who had settled in Guilford County, North Carolina. His father, at the start of the Civil
War, had moved to Indiana, where he became a successful farmer, building
contractor, and land speculator. Although his father was a self-proclaimed
religious skeptic, Charles attended Quaker services as a boy and began his
formal education in a local Quaker-run school. After he was graduated from
Knightstown High School in 1891, his father bought for him and his older
brother a local newspaper. In 1895, however, Charles gave up journalism to
attend DePauw University. Majoring in history, he finished his undergraduate studies in three years with an impressive academic record, culminating
in his election to Phi Beta Kappa. He then went to Oxford University for further study in history. While at DePauw, he had begun to shift from his father's loyalty to the Republican Party to a sympathy for reform. His awakening
sense of social consciousness was reinforced by his experiences in England.
In response, Beard played a leading role in establishing at Oxford, in early
1899, a workingmen's college—named Ruskin Hall after the English artist-
reformer John Ruskin—for the training of future working-class leaders.

Except for a brief return trip to the United States to marry his college
sweetheart, Mary Ritter, Beard stayed in England until the spring of 1902.
From his base in Manchester, he traveled over the country, promoting the
Ruskin Hall movement in talks before workingmen's and cooperative society
groups. The major thrust of those talks—and the theme of his first book,
The Industrial Revolution (1901)—was how advancing technology, if properly
utilized for public benefit rather than private profit, had the potential for
improving the human lot. In 1902, after returning to the United States, he
began graduate work at Columbia University. For his Ph.D. dissertation, he
completed a study begun while he was at Oxford, on the evolution of the office of justice of the peace in England. He received his degree in 1904 and
was kept on as a lecturer in the history department to teach the Western
European survey and English history. Three years later, he was appointed an
adjunct professor in the department of public law, with the responsibility of
inaugurating a new undergraduate program in politics. In 1910, he was pro-

moted to associate professor; five years later, he was awarded a full professorship. A man of prodigious energy, he taught a broad range of different courses, trained a group of Ph.D. students who would go on to make reputations of their own in political science and history, and turned out almost a book a year along with an imposing roster of articles and reviews.

Life's Work

Beard first attracted attention in academic circles when he collaborated with his older colleague James Harvey Robinson in writing a two-volume text, *The Development of Modern Europe: An Introduction to the Study of Current History* (1907-1908). The attention paid to social, economic, and intellectual developments contrasted strikingly with the narrowly political, dynastic, and military focus of most competing texts; so did the authors' consciously present-minded approach, aimed at using the past to illuminate contemporary problems. Beard's 1910 *American Government and Politics* made a similarly innovative contribution to the teaching of political science by looking beyond the formal institutional structure of the American system to how things actually worked. Repeatedly updated and revised, the work remained for years the standard text for college-level introductory American government courses. Beard's dual concern with making government more responsive to the popular will and more efficient in its operations led him into involvement with the New York Bureau of Municipal Research, the United States' first research organization for the improvement of public administration. He served as supervisor of the bureau's Training School for Public Service (1915-1919) and as bureau director (1919-1920); he was instrumental in the expansion of its activities beyond the municipal level and its resulting reorganization into the National Institute of Public Administration; and he was the primary author of a set of recommendations for a far-reaching reorganization of New York state government that was carried out during the 1920's.

The debate during the Progressive Era over the legitimacy of judicial review led Beard to undertake a reexamination of the intentions of the framers of the Constitution. In his 1912 book *The Supreme Court and the Constitution*, he concluded that the framers had intended to give the Supreme Court power to declare acts of Congress unconstitutional because of their anxiety "to safeguard the rights of private property against any levelling tendencies on the part of the propertyless masses." He amplified upon this theme in his highly controversial *An Economic Interpretation of the Constitution of the United States*, published the following year. The crux of his argument was that the Constitution was "an economic document" aimed at protecting the interests of the monied class in the face of threats from the largely debt-ridden small farmers that constituted local popular majorities. He went on to conclude that the Constitution was pushed through by undemocratic, even "irregular," means. For supporting evidence, Beard relied heavily upon long-forgotten Treasury Department records for the public securities holdings of those involved in the adoption of the Constitution. The prominence given this data fostered the impression that the framers were primarily motivated by the quest for personal financial gain. There is no question that Beard's purpose in emphasizing the economic motivation of the framers was to demythologize the Constitution as a bulwark for the defense of the political status quo against reform.

An Economic Interpretation of the Constitution of the United States has been sharply attacked by many later historians as simplistic or even simply wrong. Yet the work remains a landmark in the development of American historical scholarship. The volume was the first attempt to apply the prosopographical—or collective biography—approach to a major historical problem. Beard envisaged the book as the first in a series of studies that would apply the economic interpretation to the full span of American history. His 1914 survey *Contemporary American History, 1877-1913* traced the political, legal, social, and intellectual changes resulting from the triumph of industrial capitalism in the years after the Civil War. In the following year's *Economic Origins of Jeffersonian Democracy*, he pictured the party battles of the 1790's between the Federalists and their Republican opponents as a continuation of the struggle over the Constitution between "capitalistic and agrarian interests." The climax of his attempt to apply an overarching economic interpretation to the study of the American past was the two-volume *The Rise of American Civilization* (1927), which he coauthored with his wife, Mary. The aspect of this work that most impressed professional historians was his treatment of the Civil War as a "second American Revolution," responsible for the triumph of Northern capitalism over its agrarian rival. Its portrayal of the clash of rival economic interests as the real root of historical change would exercise a pervasive influence upon the generation that came to intellectual maturity in the 1930's. At the same time, its wide popular appeal owed much to the breadth of the canvas upon which the Beards sketched their story. Going beyond politics, the work aspired to treat the full range and variety of the American national experience: political, social, and economic thought, religion, literature, education, science, art and architecture, and even music.

Although Beard was personally a supporter of American involvement in World War I, he resigned his Columbia professorship in October, 1917, in protest at the firing of antiwar faculty members. He was one of the founders of the New School for Social Research in 1919, but he soon dropped out of active involvement to devote himself to free-lance writing. His 1922 book *Cross Currents in Europe To-day* was a pioneering challenge to the widely held notion that World War I was caused solely by German aggression. That same year, he visited Japan, at the invitation of the Tokyo Institute for Municipal Research, to study and report upon Japanese municipal government; he so impressed his hosts that he was brought back after the devastating Tokyo earthquake of 1923 to advise on rebuilding the city. In 1926, he was elected president of the American Political Science Association. An investigatory trip to Yugoslavia resulted in his writing, in collaboration with George Radin, *The Balkan Pivot: Yugoslavia, a Study in Government and Administration* (1929). Despite his lack of sympathy for the complacent politics of normalcy that dominated the United States in the 1920's, Beard remained optimistic about the possibilities of a future of "unlimited progress." He continued to see in the advance of technology the potential for bringing about "an ever wider distribution of the blessings of civilization—health, security, material goods, knowledge, leisure, and aesthetic appreciation."

Beard put forth this gospel of technological utopianism in magazine articles, in symposia that he edited such as *Whither Mankind: A Panorama of Modern Civilization* (1928), *Toward Civilization* (1930), and, most fully, in a 1930 book coauthored with his son William, *The American Leviathan: The Republic in the Machine Age*. Yet his confident assumption of inevitable, even automatic, progress was dealt shattering blows by the Great Depression, the emergence of totalitarian regimes in Europe, and, as the 1930's went on, the darkening threat of another major war. Beard still retained his hope for a better world; the difference was that he now emphasized that its achievement would require purposeful and intelligent direction. To provide a guide for what policies should be adopted was the purpose of two works—written with the research assistance of George H. E. Smith—that appeared in 1934: *The Idea of National Interest: An Analytical Study in American Foreign Policy* and *The Open Door at Home: A Trial Philosophy of National Interest*. On the one hand, he called for national economic planning—or what he termed "applied engineering rationality"—to restore prosperity. On the other, he pleaded for insulation of the United States from international-trade conflicts and power rivalries through policies aimed at achieving national economic self-sufficiency.

At a more philosophical level, Beard centered his attack on any deterministic system—including by implication his own earlier economic determinism—that denied the role of men's "ethical and esthetic values" in shaping history. This new approach was inextricably intertwined with his championship of historical relativism. Starting with his December, 1933, presidential address to the American Historical Association, "Written History as an Act of Faith," Beard sharply attacked the assumption of so-called scientific history in which the historian could "describe the past as it actually was." While acknowledging the existence of verifiable facts, he argued that the historian's selection and arrangement of those facts was a matter of choice that reflected his frame of reference: his values and interests; his political, social, and economic beliefs; his conception of "things deemed necessary, things deemed possible, and things deemed desirable." Beard's major platform for pushing the message of historical relativism was the Committee on Historiography of the Social Science Research Council. The committee's influential 1946 report, *Theory and Practice in Historical Study*, affirmed that all written history "is ordered or organized under the influence of some scheme of reference, interest, or emphasis—avowed or unavowed—in the thought of the author."

At the level of practical politics, Beard started out as an enthusiastic supporter of President Franklin D. Roosevelt's New Deal as marking a break with the rudderless *laissez-faire* of the past. As the dominating member of the American Historical Association's Commission on the Social Studies, he was the moving spirit behind its call for a major revision of the curriculum and teaching methods in the public schools to prepare students for the coming new age of democratic "collectivism." By the late 1930's, however, he had grown disillusioned with Roosevelt's failure to adopt meaningful national economic planning. More upsetting still, he had come to suspect that FDR's foreign policies were leading the United States into war. He was convinced that whatever happened in Europe and Asia could not endanger United States security given this country's high degree of economic self-sufficiency and its geographical position behind the buffer of two oceans. He even accused Roosevelt of looking for foreign adventures to divert public attention from the Administration's failure to restore domestic prosperity. He accordingly became a vocal spokesman for maintaining American isolationism—or, to use his preferred term, for pursuing a "continental" policy.

The outcome of the war confirmed Beard's worst forebodings. American involvement had disrupted further reform at home, accelerated the centralization of power in the presidency and bureaucracy, and dangerously increased the influence of the military. Nor was the country's physical security safeguarded. On the contrary, the United States now faced a more dangerous enemy, the Soviet Union. The result was to strengthen Beard in his hostility toward more overseas commitments. Once again, he turned to history to supply a guide to the path his fellow countrymen should take. In a series of works—most notably *The American Spirit: A Study of the Idea of Civilization in the United States* (1942), *The Republic: Conversations on Fundamentals* (1943), and *A Basic History of the United States* (1944)—he set forth what he saw as the essential elements that had combined to create in the United States a unique civilization. His theme was an exaltation of the American system of "constitutional government"—with its balance between majority rule and the protection of "fundamental rights," between centralization of power and local autonomy—as "an eternal contradiction to the principle of authoritarian, totalitarian, dictatorial government."

The reverse side of his praise for the realism, practical wisdom, and farsighted genius of the Founding Fathers was his obsession with demolishing what he saw as the Roosevelt myth. In the first two volumes of a planned trilogy on Roosevelt's foreign policies—*American Foreign Policy in the Making, 1932-1940: A Study in Responsibilities* (1946) and *President Roosevelt and the Coming of the War 1941: A Study in Appearances and Realities* (1948)—he accused FDR of deceiving and misleading the American people by talking peace while secretly plotting war. He went so far as to suggest that FDR "was not surprised by the Japanese attack [on Pearl Harbor] when it came on December 7." The volumes sparked angry, often personally vitriolic, attacks from Roosevelt's admirers—including many of Beard's former friends—that deeply pained him. He had suffered a serious illness in 1945, and his labors upon the Roosevelt volumes further sapped his formerly robust constitution. He died September 1, 1948, before finishing the research for the planned third volume on wartime diplomacy—"a victim," a former student eulogized, "of hard work induced by a passionate drive to tell the truth as he saw it."

Summary

Charles A. Beard was a major figure in the development of political science in the United States: He played a leading role in reorienting the study of American government from the description of formal institutional structures to a realistic analysis of how things actually operated; he was one of the Progressive Era's foremost experts on municipal government; and he was a pioneer in placing the study of public administration upon a scientific, empirical basis. He looms even larger in the development of American historical scholarship. His application of the economic interpretation to American history was at the time an immensely liberating intellectual force; he was the leading spokesman for—and outstanding practitioner of—a "new history" that would broaden the scope of study of the past beyond politics to include the full range of human experience; and he did much to sensitize historians to the role played by their personal values and biases in shaping their interpretations.

Nor was Beard's influence limited to the academy. He reached, through his books and articles, a larger popular audience than probably any other American scholar of his time. As an activist in support of a wide range of causes, he achieved major status. A 1938 survey taken by *The New Republic* of liberal-left-wing intellectuals ranked Beard second only to the economist and social philosopher Thorstein Veblen among those whose work had most influenced their own thinking. Shortly after Beard's death, a poll of educators, editors, and public figures gave first place to *The Rise of American Civilization* as the book that best explained American democracy. Even hostile critics acknowledged that Beard had been the twentieth century's "most powerful single figure in the teaching of American history."

Bibliography
Beale, Howard K. *Charles A. Beard: An Appraisal*. Lexington: University

Press of Kentucky, 1954. A collection of sympathetic—and at times overly eulogistic—appraisals of Beard as teacher, scholar, and public affairs activist by friends and admirers.

Benson, Lee. *Turner and Beard: American Historical Writing Reconsidered.* Glencoe, Ill.: Free Press, 1960. A sympathetic but not uncritical examination of Beard's application of the economic interpretation to the study of American history.

Berg, Elias. *The Historical Thinking of Charles A. Beard.* Stockholm: Almqvist and Wicksell, 1957. A European scholar's abstract, and all-too-often murky, analysis of the changing philosophical assumptions underlying Beard's approach to the study of history.

Borning, Bernard C. *The Political and Social Thought of Charles A. Beard.* Seattle: University of Washington Press, 1962. A workmanlike, detailed survey of Beard's views on political and social issues traced over time.

Dahlberg, Jane S. *The New York Bureau of Municipal Research: Pioneer in Government Administration.* New York: New York University Press, 1966. The fullest available account of Beard's work in the area of public administration.

Higham, John, Leonard Krieger, and Felix Gilbert. *History.* Englewood Cliffs, N.J.: Prentice-Hall, 1965. An excellent and insightful survey of changing fashions in American historiography that illuminates Beard's place in that larger context.

Hofstadter, Richard. *The Progressive Historians: Turner, Beard, Parrington.* New York: Alfred A. Knopf, 1968. A lucidly written and penetrating analysis of the forces shaping the so-called Progressive school of American historiography and its influence by a distinguished historian who had himself been strongly influenced by Beard's work.

Kennedy, Thomas C. *Charles A. Beard and American Foreign Policy.* Gainesville: University of Florida Press, 1975. A detailed tracing of Beard's view on foreign policy issues, with major focus upon his 1930's isolationism.

Marcell, David W. *Progress and Pragmatism: James, Dewey, Beard, and the American Idea of Progress.* Westport, Conn.: Greenwood Press, 1974. Shows how Beard fitted into the larger American tradition of pragmatic philosophy.

Nore, Ellen. *Charles A. Beard: An Intellectual Biography.* Carbondale: Southern Illinois University Press, 1983. The most thoroughly researched and detailed available account of Beard's intellectual development, but somewhat lifeless on the personal side.

Strout, Cushing. *The Pragmatic Revolt in American History: Carl Becker and Charles Beard.* New Haven, Conn.: Yale University Press, 1958. A still-useful introduction to the thought of two leading American exponents of historical relativism.

White, Morton G. *Social Thought in America: The Revolt Against Formalism*. New York: Viking Press, 1949. An influential, if too abstrusely written, account of the role played by Beard, along with such other figures as John Dewey and Thorstein Veblen, in reorienting American scholarship from formalistic description to realistic analysis.

John Braeman

HENRY WARD BEECHER

Born: June 24, 1813; Litchfield, Connecticut
Died: March 8, 1887; Brooklyn, New York
Area of Achievement: The ministry
Contribution: As pastor of Plymouth Church, in Brooklyn, New York, for
forty years, Beecher rapidly became one of the most articulate ministers in
the United States, breaking with traditional methods of preaching in both
style and content. He ushered in a new age of homiletic expertise which
went far beyond his podium.

Early Life

Henry Ward Beecher was born June 24, 1813, in Litchfield, Connecticut,
one of thirteen children. His father, the Reverend Lyman Beecher, was
descended from Colonial settlers dating back to the 1630's. The elder Beecher was one of the leading lights in the American pulpit, as well as an outstanding theologian and educator. His mother, Roxana Foote, whose lineage
could be traced back to seventeenth century England, died of consumption
when Henry was three years old. Many of the elder Beecher's children later
became preachers, and one of his daughters, Harriet Beecher Stowe, became
a writer, philanthropist, and abolitionist.

Because there were so many children, there was little time for each one to
receive personal attention. Henry's stepmother, Harriett Porter, however,
engendered in them at least a sense of awe, if not affection. Yet, for the most
part, Henry was a loner, growing up somewhat aloof in disposition and self-
centered in outlook.

At the age of ten, he was sent away to school but had little success in his
studies. Later, he went to a school conducted by his sister Catharine in Hartford—the only boy among some forty girls. He then enrolled in Mount
Pleasant Classical Institute in Amherst, Massachusetts, where, for the first
time, he had contact with boys his own age. There, Beecher attained some
measure of popularity and encountered teachers who taught him to study
and to express himself.

In 1830, Beecher entered Amherst College, where he read English classics
and began writing for one of the college publications. Yet his spiritual life
languished. Since his father expected all of his sons to follow him into the
ministry, Beecher, following his graduation from Amherst, matriculated at
Lane Theological Seminary, Cincinnati, where his father was president.
Beecher's time was about equally divided between his studies and extracurri-
cular activities, particularly writing. Theology held no charm for him, and his
father's Calvinism repelled him. One May morning, alone in the Ohio
woods, however, Beecher underwent a religious experience which shaped his
ideas about God and provided the structure for his spiritual life, providing a

broad area for preaching which conformed to his own temperament and life-style.

Life's Work

After his graduation from Lane Seminary in 1837, Beecher became minister at the Presbyterian Church at Lawrenceburg, Indiana. There, he married Eunice White Bullard, with whom he would have ten children. On November 9, 1838, Beecher was ordained by the New School Presbytery of Cincinnati. The following July, he moved to the Second Presbyterian Church in Indianapolis, where he remained until October, 1948, when he went to Plymouth Church, Brooklyn, a Congregational church.

In appearance, Beecher was imposing. It has been said that he was one of the most striking figures in Brooklyn. A man of medium height and large girth, his broad shoulders accorded a resting place for his hair and a foundation for his lionesque head. His voice was responsive to every shade of emotion.

During the decade of his first two pastorates, Beecher had gradually developed his principles and his style of preaching, which was intended to bring about a moral change in his listeners. His sermons began to be published—sermons that dealt with moral renewal. Certain of these were gathered into a book, *Seven Lectures to Young Men*, published in 1844.

Like all the Beechers, he was opposed to slavery, but his thoughts on the subject were complicated and perhaps contradictory. In 1860, he announced a six-point creed on slavery: First a man may hold a slave and do no wrong; second, immediate emancipation is impossible; third, a slaveholder may still be considered a good Christian; fourth, the influence of slavery is not always evil; fifth, some slaveholders are doing more for the cause of freedom than some violent reformers; finally, antislavery bigotry is worse than the Papacy. His position on this issue probably evolved from his desire to present the Gospel to as many and as varied a group of people as possible.

Plymouth Church had only recently been organized and built when Beecher arrived. Soon afterward, the edifice burned. A new structure was then built, a large auditorium that could accommodate more than three thousand people. From his platform—he did not desire a pulpit—he gained fame as a man of eloquence and high ideals and was widely considered to be the best preacher of the age. Even after 1874, when he was accused of committing adultery with one of his parishioners, he continued to be seen almost as a national saint. This veneration was a measure of the degree to which his message had captured the spirit of popular Protestantism of the time.

Beecher's messages were frequently directed at relieving the anxieties of his affluent Brooklyn suburban audience, who sensed a conflict between their new wealth and the stern Puritan morality in which they had been reared. He preached a gospel of "virtuous wealth" as a commendable moral example to the poor, providing relief from traditional Calvinistic theological anxieties with a general liberalism that gradually unfolded as his sensibilities developed along with those of his national audience.

Beecher urged that American preaching strive for unassailable goals which would "inspire men with an idea of manhood" and kindle the "nobility of a heart opened when God has touched it." The Brooklyn preacher had discovered a formula that would, for many years, allay the apprehensions of the respectable, evangelical Americans concerning the new science and learning. He commented, "While we are taught by the scientists in truths that belong to sensual nature, while we are taught by the economists of things that belong to the social nature, we need the Christian ministry to teach us those things which are invisible." He was among the first American preachers to accept Charles Darwin's theory of evolution, by which he sought to reinterpret essential Christian convictions "in terms congenial with the assured convictions of the latest scientific theories." Beecher's acceptance of evolution had a tremendous impact on the American Protestant community. The theory of evolution, coupled with biblical criticism coming out of Germany, produced the dominant Protestant theology of the late nineteenth century, a position which was in ascendance until the rise of neoorthodoxy in the 1930's.

In 1861, Beecher became editor of the *Independent*, a Congregational journal; from 1870 to 1881, he was editor of the nondenominational *Christian Union*, which he founded. In this latter position he wrote what were considered some of the strongest editorials in the American press. His sermons were reproduced in weekly columns; others were published as pamphlets.

Beecher launched attacks against slavery, but he was not an abolitionist. He opposed the Fugitive Slave Law and the Compromise of 1850. He urged Northerners to emigrate to Kansas, using force to make it free soil. At the same time, he decried bitterness toward the South. When the Civil War erupted, he pushed for a strong prosecution by the North. In his orations, Beecher skillfully equated Christian redemptive meaning with the spirit of the Union. In 1863, he visited England, where he boldly presented the position of the North. It is questionable whether his speeches accomplished much, but they did no harm to his popularity. When hostilities ceased, Beecher went to Fort Sumter to give the oration celebrating the fourth anniversary of that fort's fall. Beecher favored Andrew Johnson's position regarding Reconstruction; he longed to see the Union reunited and the military government in the South brought to a speedy end. Indeed, he was so sympathetic to Reconstruction that he brought down upon himself the wrath of his congregation and was forced to recant.

Neither a scholar nor an original thinker, Beecher was often very impetuous in enunciating his position on various topics before thoroughly considering the logical ramifications of such pronouncements. Uninterested in theory so much as in practical application, he abhorred theological controversy, probably because his father had so delighted in it.

Summary

Beecher possessed the ability to present the most advanced thought of his generation in easily understood language and to stamp it indelibly, by means of word pictures, upon the minds of his listeners. Those who heard him were mesmerized by his delivery; those who read him were tantalized by his clarity. Many twentieth century Protestant preachers employ the same approach in their preaching, unaware that, a century earlier, Beecher was in the vanguard of those who employed such a method. Similarly, his *Yale Lectures on Preaching* (1872-1874) still rank as the apogee of instruction in the entire field of the ministry.

Henry Ward Beecher continued to be, as long as he lived, the most prominent preacher in the United States. Through a continuous stream of published sermons, in pamphlets as well as collected volumes, he preached to a whole country as completely as had any man before the coming of the radio. Beecher strongly influenced the style of delivery, worship, music, and content that has become the standard in the modern pulpit. Further, his social conscience and oratorical skill made him a spiritual and moral force in his time.

Bibliography

Abbott, Lyman. *Henry Ward Beecher*. Boston: Houghton Mifflin Co., 1903. A sympathetic biography of Beecher, written by one who was converted by his preaching and who succeeded him at Plymouth Church. Contains Beecher's 1882 theological statement, which resulted in his leaving the Congregational Church.

Beecher, Henry Ward. *Yale Lectures on Preaching*. New York: J. B. Ford and Co., 1872-1874. Probably the best material on Beecher's art of preaching and pastoral work.

Clark, Clifford E., Jr. *Henry Ward Beecher: Spokesman for Middle-Class America*. Urbana: University of Illinois Press, 1978. Interprets Beecher as one who defended the middle-class ethics and ethos of Plymouth Church, particularly during the Panic of 1873.

Garrison, Winfred Ernest. *The March of Faith: The Story of Religion in America Since 1865*. New York: Harper and Brothers, 1933. This survey includes a sympathetic account of Beecher, placing him in the context of his times.

Hibben, Paxton. *Henry Ward Beecher: An American Portrait*. New York: George H. Doran, 1927. This essentially negative biographical study asserts that Beecher was not a pioneer in the great work of liberalizing American theology and religion, but rather was able to present modern ideas in a form which the masses could grasp. Hibben argues that Beecher's personal development, moving from a rejection of his father's Calvinism to embrace religious liberalism, mirrored a transformation in American society.

McLoughlin, William G. *The Meaning of Henry Ward Beecher: An Essay on the Shifting Values of Mid-Victorian America, 1840-1870.* New York: Alfred A. Knopf, 1970. Claims that the meaning of Beecher's life lies in the story of the great shift between the Age of Jackson and the Gilded Age. Like Hibben, it points out how the development of Beecher's theological views corresponded to the major social, economic, political, and religious shifts in American society between 1840 and 1875.

Marsden, George M. *Fundamentalism and American Culture: The Shaping of Twentieth-Century Evangelicalism, 1870-1925.* New York: Oxford University Press, 1980. Places Beecher in the forefront of those who viewed progress in science and morality as the coming of the Kingdom of God.

Rugoff, Milton. *The Beechers: An American Family in the Nineteenth Century.* New York: Harper and Row, Publishers, 1981. Places Henry Ward Beecher in the family context of the Beechers, beginning with Lyman, and extending to Henry's brothers and sisters. Four chapters give a fairly objective biography of Beecher, including a succinct presentation and appraisal of Beecher's trial for adultery. Based on extensive documents.

Harold M. Parker, Jr.

ALEXANDER GRAHAM BELL

Born: March 3, 1847; Edinburgh, Scotland
Died: August 2, 1922; Baddeck, Nova Scotia
Areas of Achievement: Invention, science, and education
Contribution: One of the major inventive geniuses of modern times, Bell cre-
ated and perfected the telephone and greatly advanced the teaching of the
deaf.

Early Life

The second of three boys, Alexander Graham Bell was born into a Scottish
family prominent in the field of elocution. Both his grandfather Alexander
Bell and his father, Alexander Melville Bell, taught the subject. The former
invented a technique to check stammering, while the latter became a major
innovator and author in corrective speech. His mother, Eliza Grace Symonds
Bell, a portrait painter and musician, educated her son until his tenth year.
After three years of formal schooling, he spent a year in London with his
grandfather, who inspired the young Bell with his deep commitment to the
study of the science of sound. Bell then taught music and elocution as a student teacher in Elgin, in the midst of which he spent a year at the University
of Edinburgh. During 1866-1867, he taught at a college in Bath, England.
Thus, he was largely family-taught and self-taught; his black, penetrating
eyes and intense, though modest, manner attested his inquiring mind.

Life's Work

Bell's genius had begun to reveal itself in 1864, when, at the age of seventeen, he undertook his first experiments in the science of sound, followed the
next year by initial work in the application of electricity to transmitting
speech via sound waves. Upon the death of his grandfather, Bell's father
replaced the former in London and published his major tract *Visible Speech:
The Science of Universal Alphabetics* in 1867, the year that young Alexander
became his assistant. From his father, Bell had inherited the notion of visible
speech—that is, a visual-symbolic alphabet for use in producing spoken
sounds—and therefore also his father's dedication to improving methods for
teaching the deaf to talk. During 1868-1870, father and son established an
equal partnership, even as Bell studied anatomy and physiology at University
College, London, and applied his father's techniques of visible speech at a
school for the deaf at Kensington.

Such a heavy work load began to undermine Bell's health, alarming his
parents, inasmuch as they had recently lost both their other sons to tuberculosis. In 1870, they emigrated to Canada, settling in the countryside near
Brantford, Ontario. There, Bell's health was quickly restored, and he
resumed his work in Boston, tutoring and teaching at schools for the deaf,

opening his own school for other teachers, continuing his experiments in sound, and making an improvement in the system of visible speech that has remained a standard technique ever since. He also invented an audiometer. Formal recognition came early in 1873 when Boston University made him professor of vocal physiology and the mechanics of speech, a post he held for four years.

During 1873-1876, Bell brought together his disparate studies of the science of sound and its electrical telegraphic transmission. Ever since his first experiments with the latter in 1865, Bell spent whatever spare time he had in attempting to invent a device by which oral sounds could be transmitted via electrical wires: the telephone. Concurrently, he studied the human ear to discover the importance of the membrane for such a device, and he learned to transmit multiple electrical messages over a single wire. In applying the key element of acoustics to telegraphy, Bell sought and received the counsel and encouragement of the venerable experimental physicist Joseph Henry, who had worked along similar lines. Basically a scientist, Bell was fortunate to hire as his technical assistant Thomas A. Watson, an adept mechanic who shared his long nights of experiments on electrical sound transmission. Unable to fund this work himself, Bell found two patrons in the fathers of deaf children he was teaching. These men were Thomas Sanders and Gardiner G. Hubbard. Only rest, however, could restore Bell's physical strength from occasional fatigue resulting from these considerable labors, and Bell obtained it at his parent's home in Canada.

The first, though unintelligible, human sounds, Bell's to Watson, came through their wire in June, 1875, but it was not until the following March 10 that a twenty-foot-long wire carried the monumental, though unanticipated, first message: "Mr. Watson, come here; I want to see you." The two men rapidly improved their invention, and Bell astounded the scientific world with his first public demonstration of the telephone at the International Centennial Exposition at Philadelphia in June, 1876. The following spring, he demonstrated the first long-distance telephone conversation, between Boston and New York. In July, 1877, Bell, Hubbard, and Sanders created the Bell Telephone Company. Having patented all the related inventions, Bell finally began to enjoy the resulting financial rewards, although some six hundred lawsuits ensued, with rivals claiming credit—until 1888, when the Supreme Court ruled in Bell's favor as sole inventor of the telephone.

Though his fame was assured through his epic creation, Bell remained equally dedicated to the education of the deaf, especially after he married Hubbard's daughter Mabel, one of his deaf students, in July, 1877. She became an important source of encouragement and inspiration for the rest of his life and gave him two daughters. During their subsequent trip to Europe, where he introduced the telephone, Bell lectured on the teaching of the deaf at Oxford University. After settling in Washington in 1878, Bell enlarged his study of the physical nature of deafness and in 1880 founded the Volta Laboratory upon receiving the French Volta Prize of fifty thousands francs (about ten thousand dollars). He used the Volta Laboratory in the spirit of scientific philanthropy; instead of patenting new discoveries made there, he allowed their general use for the public good. Most important were the photophone to send words by light ray and an induction balance or electric probe to locate metal objects in the human body, the latter first used to find the assassin's bullet that mortally wounded President James A. Garfield.

Bell became an American citizen in 1882 and soon thereafter built a summer home and research laboratory at Baddeck, Cape Breton Island, Nova Scotia. Among many honors he received from European countries was a Ph.D., awarded by the University of Würzburg in Bavaria.

Bell's restless, inquisitive mind seemed to accelerate as he grew older, and his black hair, beard, and sideburns turned a striking, billowy white. At the Volta Laboratory, he improved upon Thomas Alva Edison's phonograph in the mid-1880's; proceeds from the sale of some of the patents were used to transform the Laboratory into the Volta Bureau for the Increase and Diffusion of Knowledge relating to the Deaf. His prize pupil the next decade became Helen Keller. In 1890, he founded and became first president of the American Association to Promote Teaching of Speech to the Deaf (renamed the Alexander Graham Bell Association for the Deaf in 1956). An early study of marriage among the deaf led into eugenics and the problems of longevity, research which emerged as a major book in 1918. He also supported Albert A. Michelson's first measurements of the speed of light. Bell continued to improve upon the telephone, and he and Watson inaugurated the first transcontinental phone call when, in 1915, they conversed between San Francisco and New York.

The possibilities of manned powered flight held the greatest fascination for Bell from before 1891, when he supported the pioneering work of Samuel P. Langley, until the end of his life. Bell believed that tetrahedron-shaped cells could be joined for lift, and experimented with them in immense kites. During 1907-1909, he teamed up with aviation pioneer Glenn H. Curtiss and three other young men in the Aerial Experiment Association (AEA), the brainstorm of his wife, who also funded its work. Among the aircraft the five men created at Bell's Nova Scotia laboratory and Curtiss' facility at Hammondsport, New York, was Bell's own tetrahedral plane. Though it finally flew in 1912, it proved too unwieldy, but where the tetrahedron failed as an aeronautical device, it eventually proved highly successful in architecture (as, for example, in R. Buckminster Fuller's geodesic dome). In 1916, Bell advocated American preparedness in military air power, and inasmuch as the AEA operated their craft from the water and the ice, Bell during and after World War I developed a high-speed hydrofoil motorboat for riding above the water at speeds of up to seventy miles per hour.

At his Nova Scotia laboratory and in Washington, Bell carried on his manifold experiments, which also included a home air-cooling unit, an artificial respirator, the breeding of sheep, improved methods of lithography and sonar detection, and a vertical-propelled, aircraft-type engine which anticipated the helicopter and jet propulsion. His extensive notebooks were filled with other ideas which he never had time to develop; he was working on a means to distill saltwater when he died. His chief fame, however, rests on the invention of the telephone, of which thirteen million existed worldwide at the time of his death. On the day of his funeral, August 4, 1922, all telephones in the United States and Canada fell silent for one minute in tribute to him.

Summary

Alexander Graham Bell typified the remarkable generation of American inventor-scientists of the late nineteenth century whose ability to apply scientific discoveries to everyday practical technological uses played a major part in the rise of contemporary urban civilization. Driven by an insatiable curiosity and endowed with sheer experimental (though not theoretical) genius—and perfect pitch—Bell was able to focus his many interests on two or three projects simultaneously, often complementing one another. Thus, his humanitarian work on helping the deaf to learn to speak was wedded early to his efforts to invent the practical telephone. He never lost interest in either project, although aviation commanded equal attention the second half of his life. This was a fascination shared by many prominent peers in the scientific and technological worlds, among them, for example, explorer Robert Edwin Peary, yacht designer W. Starling Burgess, and naval inventor Bradley A. Fiske.

An immensely generous person, Bell was completely selfless in his devotion to the deaf, to whose improvement he committed many of the profits from the telephone. Because he championed the diffusion of scientific knowledge, he became a major catalyst in the cause of popular science. With Hubbard, in 1883, he founded and operated for eleven years *Science* magazine, subsequently taken over by the American Association for the Advancement of Science. In 1888, Bell was a founder of the National Geographic Society, ten years later succeeding Hubbard as its president, until 1904. Under his presidency, in 1899, the *National Geographic* magazine began publication. One of his daughters married the editor Gilbert H. Grosvenor; Bell's grandson, Melville Bell Grosvenor, succeeded to the editorship half a century later. In 1891, Bell funded the creation of the Astrophysical Observatory of the Smithsonian Institution and seven years after that became a regent of the Smithsonian, a post he held the rest of his life. Largely through Bell's efforts, the remains of James Smithson were returned from Genoa, Italy, to Washington, D.C., in 1904.

Like other major inventors of his day, Bell had to protect his patents from challengers, and did so by keeping copious notes and having numerous photographs taken. His love of nature was embodied in his summer home and laboratory, named Beinn Bhreagh, the commanding view of the Bras d'Or Lakes in this "New Scotland" (Nova Scotia) reminding him of his native land. Such an idyllic environment proved especially conducive to his experiments over the last thirty-five years of his life. There he died, and there—in a mountainside—he was buried. He had shared the wonders of nature with the world at large through the pages of the *National Geographic*. The full legacy of Alexander Graham Bell is beyond measure.

Bibliography
Bruce, Robert V. *Bell: Alexander Graham Bell and the Conquest of Solitude*. Boston: Little, Brown and Co., 1973. The standard biography, this heavily annotated work focuses on the development of the telephone but gives good general treatments of Bell's life before and after its invention.
Casey, Louis S. *Curtiss: The Hammondsport Era, 1907-1915*. New York: Crown Publishers, 1981. Though a biography of pioneer aviator and manufacturer Glenn H. Curtiss in his early years of aviation, the book discusses Bell's role in the AEA, utilizing among its sources the AEA *Bulletin*.
Costain, Thomas B. *Chord of Steel*. Garden City, N.Y.: Doubleday and Co., 1960. A popular account of the invention of the telephone.
Mackenzie, Catherine Dunlap. *Alexander Graham Bell: The Man Who Contracted Space*. Boston: Houghton Mifflin Co., 1928. This early biography is a sound though dated work.
Parkin, J. H. *Bell and Baldwin*. Toronto: University of Toronto Press, 1964. Centers on the association of Bell with the Canadian F. W. "Casey" Baldwin during the AEA period with Glenn Curtiss.
Waite, Helen E. *Make a Joyful Sound: The Romance of Mabel Hubbard and Alexander Graham Bell*. Philadelphia: MacRae Smith, 1961. A moving account of the relationship between Bell and his wife, who, though twelve years his junior, emerges as a key figure in her own right and proof positive of Bell's success in overcoming the handicap of deafness. She died in 1923.
Watson, Thomas A. *Exploring Life*. New York: D. Appleton and Co., 1926. This autobiography by Bell's main assistant (1854-1934) sheds light on the great inventor's character and methods.

Clark G. Reynolds

SAUL BELLOW

Born: June 10, 1915; Lachine, Canada

Area of Achievement: Literature
Contribution: In writing nine novels and numerous short stories and articles over several decades, Bellow, as an American writer, has achieved international recognition signified only in part by his receiving the Nobel Prize for Literature in 1976.

Early Life
Saul Bellow was born in 1915, in Lachine, Canada, the fourth child of religious Jewish parents who had emigrated two years earlier from Russia. He grew up speaking English, French, Yiddish, and Hebrew. At the age of nine, he moved with his family to Chicago, where he spent all of his spare hours in the public libraries. By the time he entered Tuley High School, he had already made his first efforts at writing fiction. After graduation in 1933, he enrolled in the University of Chicago, transferring two years later to Northwestern University, where he founded a Socialist club and received, in 1937, a bachelor's degree with honors in anthropology and sociology.

He entered graduate school at the University of Wisconsin but soon dropped out. On December 31, 1937, he married Anita Goshkin, a social worker; they would have one child, Gregory, born some years later. Bellow had continued to write since high school, publishing his first story in 1941. He also wrote biographies of American authors for the Works Progress Administration Writers Project and participated in Mortimer Adler's "Great Books" program for the *Encyclopædia Britannica*. He also did some teaching. In 1944, his first novel, *Dangling Man*, and in 1947, his second, *The Victim*, were published. The novels had a mixed critical reception but were highly regarded by antiestablishment intellectuals, especially for their existentialist themes and apparent European influences, notably that of Fyodor Dostoevski.

A Guggenheim Fellowship in 1948, allowing him to begin work on his next novel, launched young Bellow on his brilliant career—a career more successful, perhaps, than that of any other contemporary American writer. Yet as often happens with successful people, Bellow's private life was turbulent: Soon his marriage to Anita failed, and, following an unfriendly divorce, he remarried—a pattern he would repeat twice more in twenty years. His dark and beautiful wives, with all of their faults and virtues, would find their way into his novels, as would Bellow himself. The characters representing the author were often larger and stronger than Bellow, but not necessarily more handsome. Bellow has deep-set brown eyes, a "theatrically chiseled" nose, and hair that turned to silver somewhat prematurely. He has been described as physically slight and boyish, about five feet nine inches tall—weighing perhaps 150 pounds in his younger years—but others have noted a certain athletic quality in his build, with a very sturdy chest. Altogether, these physical and psychological aspects of Bellow's life offer an unexpected parallel to those of Ernest Hemingway, a writer whose influence on Bellow was not great.

Life's Work

Bellow's first important success was *The Adventures of Augie March*, published in 1953—a partly autobiographical *Bildungsroman*, modeled in part on its picaresque predecessor, Mark Twain's *The Adventures of Huckleberry Finn* (1884). This exuberant, stylistically innovative novel was both a bestseller and a critical success, and after thirty-five years remains a favorite among Bellow's extremely broad and varied readership. For this work, he won the National Book Award for Fiction, the first of three such awards he would receive. In 1955, he received a second Guggenheim Fellowship, and the following year he married Alexandra Tschacbasov; they had one child, Adam.

Bellow's novella, *Seize the Day*, was published in 1956, together with three stories and a one-act play. The style of *Seize the Day* is beautifully sparse and tight (in marked contrast to the sprawling energy of *The Adventures of Augie March*); Bellow delineates the defeat of middle-aged Tommy Wilhelm, jobless, penniless, his marriage a failure. The concluding paragraphs are as famous as any in contemporary literature. Tommy chances into a funeral parlor, stands by the coffin of a stranger, and begins to weep. "Soon he was past words, past reason, coherence. He could not stop. The source of all tears had suddenly sprung open within him....." The controlled emotional power of this novella places it in contrast to most of Bellow's other works, which tend to be dominated by intellectual argument.

Bellow himself has said his own favorite among his writings is *Henderson the Rain King*, published in 1959. It is a deliberately composed "quest romance" that takes the protagonist (Bellow's first who was not Jewish) to Africa, a place that Bellow had not yet visited. The gigantic, blustering, crazed, and comic Henderson was not universally popular among reviewers and critics, but the novel nevertheless testifies to Bellow's remarkable creative diversity.

After a stay of ten years in the New York City area, Bellow returned permanently to Chicago. Having divorced Alexandra, he married Susan Glassman (in December of 1961); their son, Daniel, was born in 1963. In 1962, Bellow joined the Committee on Social Thought at the University of Chicago. His novel *Herzog*, a best-seller like all of his books from *The Adventures of Augie March* onward, was published in 1964; for it, he won four major prizes, including the National Book Award for Fiction for the second time. More than one critic found this novel "brilliant"—its almost pure realism is the mode in which Bellow works best.

In 1968 appeared *Mosby's Memoirs and Others Stories*, the title work proving that Bellow is a master of the realistic short story as well. In that year, Bellow was awarded in France the Croix de Chevalier des Arts et Lettres. By this time, Bellow had been separated from Susan; great bitterness would remain between them, as alimony payments would be contested following divorce, culminating in an open fight in court in 1977. During this same period (from the mid-1960's), Bellow lost the favor of most leftist American intellectuals following his attendance at the same White House dinner in 1965 that Robert Lowell had refused to attend in political protest against United States policy in Vietnam. Bellow's conservatism consisted chiefly in not accepting the ideas and manners of the radicals, but since that time, he has nevertheless come to be identified by many as an establishment figure.

Although *Mr. Sammler's Planet* (1970) was not enthusiastically received by reviewers, it won for its author a third National Book Award for Fiction. The protagonist, an old Polish Jew who is trying to cope with life in a huge metropolis, effectively criticizes the insanity of American culture from the point of view of rational conservatism. What is of most interest here, perhaps, is the dissimilarity of this novel to Bellow's other works.

In *Humboldt's Gift* (1975), Charles Citrine, the protagonist, reminisces about his friend Humboldt, who is based on the poets John Berryman and Delmore Schwartz, whom Bellow had known in his younger years. In this novel, the plot is casual, the style uneven, sometimes careless, but the attention to detail, one of Bellow's strongest points, is superb. The same criticism applies to *The Dean's December* (1982), though now the protagonist, Albert Corde, dramatizes through his own experience the contrast between Eastern (Romanian) Communism and Western (American) capitalism. The focus is chiefly on their faults, with those of Communism seeming to be most intractable. Bellow's conclusion here is similar to certain implications in his nonfiction work *To Jerusalem and Back: A Personal Account* (1976), where he suggests that the struggle between Jew and Arab could somehow be dealt with in an orderly way if only each side did not continually act irrationally, against its own interests.

Bellow won the Pulitzer Prize for *Humboldt's Gift* in 1975; in 1976, he received the Nobel Prize for Literature. In 1974, he had married Alexandra Bagdasar Tulcea, a professor of mathematics at Northwestern University. It seems very likely that Albert Corde's wife, Minna, a professor of astronomy, born in Romania, was based on this new woman in Bellow's life. The last scene in *The Dean's December* places man and wife together so as to show their mutual love, respect, and concern; perhaps this scene reflects a certain happiness in marriage that Saul Bellow, now in the fullness of his career, had not earlier known.

Summary

Saul Bellow's impact on American culture has been made through his novels, which reflect his own sense of himself and his relationship to his society. Bellow partly represents that older sense of America as a haven for European émigrés—first as the son of Russian-Jewish émigrés to Canada, then as a French-Canadian himself, newly arrived in Chicago. He tells of the pain of adjustment in *The Adventures of Augie March*. The pain of being Jewish in a nation that does not really love Jews is a frequent theme in his work, although, ultimately, Bellow accepts casual assimilation as a suitable choice for himself. In this respect, he could be said to symbolize the diversity of the United States without testifying to a false harmony.

Bellow sees himself as an American writer who happens to be Jewish, not as a Jewish writer—though he identifies profoundly with Jews, including Israeli Jews. Yet Bellow is not a practicing, or religious Jew. He seeks religious experience primarily within the realm of ideas. His first loyalty is that of the intellectual to the world of ideas, and it is this special world that is chiefly dramatized in his novels. In so doing, Bellow has had an important impact on Americans. In a nation where intellectual novels are uncommon, Bellow has made a career writing such works, almost all of them best-sellers. He has helped Americans examine their role as individuals in relation to society—often in opposition to it—and as individuals in conflict with themselves.

Bellow seldom speaks of patriotism, but rather tends to relegate "society" to a sort of naturalistic background. Bellow's vision is clear and honest; his characters are sensitive, aware, and vital. His perceptions are sufficiently compelling so that even many of those who have ideologically "rejected" him will still read his next book. He always opens up new worlds. Thus he has compelled citizens of the whole world, not only Americans, to read his works. His international recognition, in turn, makes his impact on Americans all the greater, offering them some hope of attaining greater sophistication, which they need.

Bibliography

Braham, Jeanne. *A Sort of Columbus: The American Voyages of Saul Bellow's Fiction*. Athens: University of Georgia Press, 1984. Although biography appears only incidentally, this monograph is of interest for its emphasis on the strictly American themes in Bellow's work.

Dutton, Robert R. *Saul Bellow*. Rev. ed. Boston: Twayne Publishers, 1982. The first chapter includes a succinct, readable biography. Also provided are a useful chronology of life and work and a selected bibliography.

Fuchs, Daniel. *Saul Bellow: Vision and Revision*. Durham, N.C.: Duke University Press, 1984. Biographical references occur only incidentally in the text, but two chapters are of special interest: "Bellow and the Modern Tradition" and "Bellow and the Example of Dostoevsky." There is also a good final chapter on *The Dean's December*.

Harris, Mark. *Saul Bellow: Drumlin Woodchuck*. Athens: University of Georgia Press, 1980. Anecdotal yet well-documented account of Mark Harris' dealings with Bellow in the 1960's. Shows how certain characters in the novels are based on Bellow and certain women in Bellow's life. Harris admires the writer, but not the man very much.

Newman, Judie. *Saul Bellow and History*. New York: St. Martin's Press, 1984. Interesting for its concentration on a subject that is central to Bellow's preoccupations. Excellent bibliography.

Wilson, Jonathan. *On Bellow's Planet: Readings from the Dark Side*. London: Associated University Presses, 1985. Original, perceptive discussion of all nine of Bellow's novels. Biographical details are given only casually. Good selected bibliography.

Donald M. Fiene

JAMES GORDON BENNETT

Born: September 1, 1795; Newmill, Keith, Banffshire, Scotland
Died: June 1, 1872; New York, New York
Areas of Achievement: Journalism and publishing
Contribution: Bennett made the American newspaper an independent enterprise and established the foundations of the profession of journalism.

Early Life

James Gordon Bennett was born on September 1, 1795, in Scotland, the first son of landholding Roman Catholic parents who abided by the teachings of the Church. At the time of Bennett's birth, there were perhaps fewer than forty thousand Catholics in all of Scotland, but his parents were steadfast in the faith and in their determination to have a son join the priesthood. Two sisters and a close younger brother named Cosmo completed the Bennett family. James Gordon in later life became embittered by the Church, blaming it for mistreatment of his brother, who died in seminary.

In the strict, Presbyterian-dominated public school system of the time, the Bible was regarded as central to education and to the development of good manners and industry. Latin, Greek, some English, mathematics, history, and a large dosage of the doctrines of John Knox constituted the curriculum, which continued until the child reached the early teens. Bennett's formal education was reinforced at home by his parents, who read the Scriptures regularly and discussed the colloquial history of the family, the region, and Scotland. Bennett attributed his later success as a newspaperman to this early training. At fifteen, he was taken to the Catholic Seminary at Aberdeen, which was some sixty miles from his home. He attended Blair's College, the smallest of three schools which would eventually combine to form the University of Aberdeen. There, he was steeped in the study of classical literature and philosophy and the criticism of the great journal the *Edinburgh Review*.

Rejecting the priesthood, training for which was to follow college, Bennett spent the years from 1814 to 1819 traveling extensively in Scotland and living for a time in Glasgow, which had replaced Edinburgh in size and economic importance. Glasgow was also the embarkation port for emigrants to the West, and literature about America was in great demand. Bennett read Benjamin Franklin's autobiography (recently reprinted in Glasgow), with which he was much impressed; twenty-five years old and at a crossroads in his life, Bennett set his sights on America.

In 1819, Bennett set sail for Halifax, Nova Scotia, with only twenty-five dollars and a classical education to his name. Halifax was little more than an English loyalist outpost, and Bennett—having inherited a Scot's hatred and fear of the English—taught bookkeeping for a time in that town and then moved on to Portland, Maine. Looking for the America he had read about in Scotland, Bennett found more of it in Maine, where he was impressed with the self-confidence of the people and saw in them something of the children of equality and liberty. He took a teaching job in the village of Addison and then continued on to Boston, where he discovered the reasons for which the people of Maine had expressed dislike of that city: Boston was a snob's town, and Bennett was quickly reminded of Edinburgh, with its arrogance and presumption as a center of learning and culture. In Boston, he did, however, find a position as a clerk with a well-known bookseller and printer. He was made a proofreader in the print shop, where he learned something more of the rudiments of the trade that was to make him famous. He took what he could from Boston before moving farther south to New York.

In New York, he was once again a new arrival with little money and even smaller prospects. The city excited him, however, as it seemed to be a microcosm of America: It was more representative of the nation about which he had read. He did some bookkeeping and proofreading, and fortune smiled on him in the person of Aaron Willington, the owner of the *Charleston Courier*, who eventually hired him to translate Spanish and French news and dispatches for his paper. In Charlestón, South Carolina, Bennett enjoyed the experience of working with well-educated and intelligent associates, men who enjoyed all that Charleston and its culture offered. The shy and withdrawn Bennett mixed only on the job, however, and then sparingly. He was aware early that appearances rather than ideas and wit counted the most in social gatherings, and in the former he was always lacking. After ten months in Charleston, he returned to New York. Bennett set about determining which were the best newspapers in New York, but he found that none of them was interested in a still-uncouth immigrant. He finally gained a job with the *National Advocate*, a moribund publication underwritten by the New York General Republican Committee, which was connected to the Tammany Hall political machine. The original editor was Mordecai Noah, who had large political aspirations for himself and even larger aspirations for creation of a Jewish colony on Grant (modern Grand) Island in the Niagara River, some fifteen miles west of Niagara Falls. The agitation provoked by this scheme led to Noah's dismissal, but he was soon brought back. Bennett, meanwhile, became known in the newspaper world as a bright and industrious young man with a flair for writing. He was soon getting free-lance work with other papers, and in 1825 he took over ownership of a struggling weekly called the *New York Courier*, the first Sunday paper in the United States. It was a doomed project, and Bennett soon found himself working for Noah, who had changed his paper's name to the *New York Enquirer*.

When Bennett offered to write some light and humorous sketches for the *New York Enquirer*, Noah accepted, and on April 27, 1827, an article entitled "Shaking Hands" appeared. It dealt with alternatives to shaking hands as a form of greeting, with examples ranging from the Philippines to Africa. Noah was amazed at the increase in the paper's circulation following the publication of this article. Bennett followed up the piece with one called "Intemperance," which was a portent of his later tactic of using a subject to take a competing newspaper to task by making fun of it. In this case, it was *The New York Times* and its claim that New York was a very moral city that came in for a spoofing. As a result, a new excitement took hold over journalism in New York, despite the fact that disgruntled competing editors were already complaining that Bennett's work was degrading the profession.

Bennett was promoted to the position of assistant editor on the death of the incumbent in a duel. Bennett asked to go to Washington to report on Congress and the Adams Administration. In a short time, he became the first full-fledged Washington correspondent in American journalism. For four years, he was everywhere politicians traveled, submitting comment on legislation, on speeches and idiosyncrasies, on merchants, bankers, and stock hustlers. He listened for tips and rumors and followed up leads to confirm information and otherwise mastered the techniques of journalism, techniques which seemed to be lost on his contemporaries. In the meantime, his paper combined with James Watson Webb's *Morning Courier* under Webb's control as publisher of the new *Morning Courier and New York Enquirer*. Bennett contributed greatly to the success of the paper, but Webb never granted him recognition by name. Like Noah, Webb took credit for Bennett's pieces or attributed them to the rewriting of others. This experience later encouraged Bennett to allow reporters their own bylines when writing for his papers. During his stay with the *Morning Courier and New York Enquirer*, the paper became perhaps the most influential in New York, though it printed only thirty-five hundred copies daily and took in an average of less than fifty dollars per issue. In 1832, the paper joined the side of the National Bank and Nicholas Biddle in its fight against the Jacksonians (though the paper had been an organ of the Democratic Party), and Bennett resigned rather than work for the opposition. The compromising of the paper's independence grated on Bennett, who now turned again to starting his own daily.

Bennett started the *Globe*, which failed to gain political support. He then went to Philadelphia, where he published the *Pennsylvanian*, which also failed. Needing capital, he appealed to Martin Van Buren and the Democrats for financing, only to be rejected. Returning to New York, he visited Horace Greeley with the hope of starting a partnership. Greeley referred Bennett to two printers with whom he had worked. The penny daily was enjoying marked success via Benjamin Day's New York *Sun*, from which spun the Philadelphia *Public Ledger* and the Baltimore *Sun*, both of which were begun by former associates of Day. With the barest of capital and a promise to print, Bennett grabbed the opportunity to create an independent newspaper.

Life's Work

Bennett started his newspaper in a basement room at 20 Wall Street with only planks and barrels for furniture. He called it the *New York Herald*. It was the traditional size for such papers—four pages with four columns to the page—and sold for one penny. The first issue appeared on May 6, 1835. Bennett worked sixteen-hour days, carefully structuring his time for each facet of publication. He spent three hours writing editorials before arriving at his office at eight o'clock and continued until he retired to his single room on Nassau Street at 10:00 P.M. Originality was his byword. Unlike his competition, he used few reprints. Fresh news flowed constantly. He sought to provide a view of the city and its people by creating scenarios, conversations, relating anecdotes with a social point of view, and delivering humorous accounts of manners, fashion, and the foibles of people generally. He brought to public view the *demi-monde*; often he relegated politicians to this realm, all to the delight of his supporters and to the rage of his growing list of enemies and competitors. Women, religion, abolitionists, bankers, speculators, and merchant hustlers all came in for a fair share of Bennett's gibes. Reformers were left to rail against his ridiculing columns. He cultivated rumor and gossip, and his coy exposition of events often of his own invention but attributable to unnamed sources foreshadowed the use of the "informed source."

Bennett took to the street to gain information firsthand and then to exploit it to its fullest. He covered an infamous murder case involving a fashionable house of prostitution to the point of questioning the guilt of the prime suspect, thereby influencing the jury's decision to acquit. He viewed the body of the dead woman, describing her in intimate detail. He also interviewed the keeper of the house in the first use of the didactic question-answer interview by a newspaper. The financial panic of 1836 and the huge fire of the same period encouraged Bennett to print the first financial news, which became an instant hit among a new business readership. He visited the fire area as well, talked to owners of properties that were burned, and interviewed displaced tenants. He printed a sketch of the burned-over area and again outdistanced his rivals.

Since the public generally bought one paper only, the one with the latest news was the one in demand, and the *New York Herald* was the paper of choice. Bennett, encouraged, hired a police reporter and expanded the size of his publication, moving the paper's offices to Broadway and Ann streets. He found more time for leisure, though he was still irascible in print. Threatened with lawsuits for libel and slander, pummeled and horsewhipped for his writings, he never wavered in his attacks. His pen was his sword. Over six feet in height and sturdy in build, he was uncoordinated in his movement and hopelessly cross-eyed; although he was always courteous and polite, he was reserved and shy.

In 1838, his wealth allowed him time to go to Europe, where he was crushed to learn of his brother Cosmo's death. Two years later, he announced his marriage to Henrietta Agnes Crean in St. Peter's Roman Catholic Church, after which they went on to Niagara Falls on their honeymoon. His declaration of his love and the description of his bride in the *New York Herald* enraged his competitors, who attacked him unmercifully. When their son, James Gordon, Jr., was born on May 10, 1841, whispers abounded as to the true father. His former associate Mordecai Noah printed the rumors, which caused Bennett to bring suit; it was successful and cost Noah a $250 fine. The Bennetts had three other children: a girl who died at eight months; a boy, Cosmo Gordon, who died within a year; and Jeanette, who married Isaac Bell and lived a long life.

Bennett enjoyed all the luxuries money could buy, but because of the harassment by his enemies, his wife spent much of her time traveling abroad or sailing. The children were taught by private tutor, and the son was especially pampered. Bennett even traded a family sailing sloop complete with cannon in return for a lieutenancy for his son in the Union navy in 1862. When the ship was put out of service in 1864, the youth promptly resigned his commission. In 1866, he was installed as managing editor of the *New York Herald* and, within two years, his father gave him ownership of the enterprise, which had grown to five hundred employees.

Bennett always put profits back into the paper by keeping a battery of reporters in Washington and as many as sixty-five in the field during the Civil War. His people were in all parts of the world. His paper was the only one Abraham Lincoln read daily because of its influence. Lincoln tried to coopt Bennett by offering him an ambassadorship to France, but to no avail. Independence had come too hard for Bennett for him to give it up so easily. Even after his retirement in 1867, he continued to visit the offices and make suggestions. His wife visited briefly in May, 1872, and he promised to join her in Europe, but he was overcome by a stroke which paralyzed his lower body and caused his death on June 1, 1872. No family members were present, though he had asked the Catholic archbishop John McCloskey to take his confession and administer the Sacraments. His son attended his funeral, accompanied by Bennett's lifelong friends and adversaries.

The *New York Herald* did not print a lengthy obituary of its own, choosing instead to reprint those of other New York papers. Every significant editor in the city had served as a pallbearer. The service was held at Bennett's home on Fifth Avenue, and he was buried in the nonsectarian Greenwood Cemetery in Brooklyn. His will left the paper to his son and his properties to his wife. His daughter's wherewithal was guaranteed in the estate. His wife did not live long after. Dying of cancer, she prevented her children from seeing her. She died in the company of strangers in Sachsen, Germany, on March 28, 1873. The *New York Tribune* was first to carry news of her death.

Summary

   James Gordon Bennett was one of the three giants of journalism and pub-lishing in America in the nineteenth century. Of the three, Horace Greeley and Charles Dana being the others, Bennett alone mastered every facet of journalism, from getting the story to editing to proofreading to printing to total management of advertising, distribution, and marketing. His public was his power. His ideas—for example, that advertisers and distributors pay cash for copy and papers—flourished and multiplied as sound practice. The byline and feature articles on styles, theater, books, business, and so on all became part of the *New York Herald* style. Bennett's organization was a model of efficiency, with meetings of the key staff held each day to plan the day's production and assign future stories and leads.

   Bennett had to survive a vicious, competitive struggle for success, and he was not above using his paper to pull down his competition. Neither money nor institutional power frightened him when he believed in a principle. His sardonic wit and sophisticated interplay of scenes and anecdotes sorely tried his enemies, and he was not reluctant to exploit the frailties inherent in the pompous and the fatuous. He instinctively knew the power he could wield with his readers, who were legion.

Bibliography
Carlson, Oliver. *The Man Who Made the News: James Gordon Bennett.* New York: Duell, Sloan and Pearce, 1942. This is the only complete biography of James Gordon Bennett. Though impressionistic and containing no illustrations, it is nevertheless very useful.

Croffut, William A. *An American Procession: A Personal Chronicle of Famous Men.* Boston: Little, Brown and Co., 1931. Reprint. Freeport, N.Y.: Books for Libraries, 1968. This is a collection of personal views and portraits of famous Americans and puts the work of Isaac Pray (see below) in perspective, showing that Pray actually tried to get Bennett to authorize his biography, which came out the same year as James Parton's biography of Horace Greeley.

Herd, Harold. *Seven Editors.* Westport, Conn.: Greenwood Press, 1977. Reprint. London: George Allen and Unwin, 1955. This work recognizes Bennett's journalistic achievements and puts them in context.

Hudson, Frederic. *History of Journalism in the United States from 1690 to 1872.* New York: Harper and Brothers, 1873. This is a very useful book by Bennett's confidant and last managing editor of the *New York Herald* during his tenure, which ended in 1867. It contains great amounts of detail about newspaper development and the personalities surrounding it.

Mott, Frank Luther. *American Journalism: 1690-1960.* 3d ed. New York: Macmillan Publishing Co., 1962. Any overview of the growth of journalism in the United States owes something to this work.

Pray, Isaac Clark. *Memoirs of James Gordon Bennett and His Times*. New York: Stringer and Townsend, 1855. Reprint. New York: Arno Press, 1970. This work was written without the cooperation of Bennett and is taken largely from the columns of the *New York Herald* and from hearsay gathered by a man who had once worked for the Bennett paper as a theater critic. Pray was also a successful playwright and managed several theaters.

Seitz, Don C. *The James Gordon Bennetts: Father and Son, Proprietors of the "New York Herald."* Indianapolis: Bobbs-Merrill Co., 1928. This is a useful introduction to Bennett in a breezy, journalistic style. It shows a heavy relationship to Pray above but contains some useful illustrations and photographic material.

Starr, Louis M. "James Gordon Bennett: Beneficent Rascal." *American Heritage* 6 (February, 1955): 32-37. A brief account of the personality of Bennett and something of his style.

Stewart, Kenneth, and John Tebbell. *Makers of Modern Journalism*. Englewood Cliffs, N.J.: Prentice-Hall, 1952. This book contains some useful material on the importance of Bennett on the shaping of modern newspapers.

Tebbell, John, and Sarah Miles Watts. *The Press and the Presidency*. New York: Oxford University Press, 1985. This has some interesting material relating to Bennett's considerable influence, most notably Abraham Lincoln, who was always a reader of the *New York Herald* and ever-concerned with that paper's editorial thrust, which was never more than lukewarm toward the Republican Party.

Jack J. Cardoso

THOMAS HART BENTON

Born: March 14, 1782; near Hillsboro, North Carolina
Died: April 10, 1858; Washington, D.C.
Area of Achievement: Politics
Contribution: A prominent United States senator from 1821 to 1851, Benton was a great champion of Western expansion, public land distribution, and "hard money." He was a leading supporter of President Andrew Jackson and his policies.

Early Life

Thomas Hart Benton, the son of Jesse and Ann Gooch Benton, was born near Hillsboro, North Carolina, on March 14, 1782. His father was a lawyer who had been a secretary to the British governor of Colonial North Carolina, a member of that state's legislature, and a speculator in Western lands. His mother was reared by her uncle, Thomas Hart, a prominent Virginia political and military leader with extensive wealth in land. Another uncle of Ann Gooch had been a British governor of Virginia.

Although his father died when he was eight, Benton's mother was able to keep the large family together. He attended local grammar schools and in 1798 enrolled at the recently established University of North Carolina, but was forced to leave in disgrace after one year when he was expelled for having stolen money from his three roommates. When he was nineteen, his mother moved the family of eight children and several slaves to a large tract of land south of Nashville, Tennessee, which had been claimed by Jesse Benton prior to his death. After three years on the family farm, young Thomas Benton left to teach school and study law. In 1806, he was admitted to the Tennessee bar and rather quickly became a successful attorney whose philosophy and practice reflected the rural frontier environment. Benton specialized in land cases, and he began to pursue the reform of the Tennessee judicial system, an issue that helped him to a seat in the state senate and wide recognition.

During the War of 1812, Benton joined Andrew Jackson in raising volunteers for the military effort against England. For this work he received an appointment as a colonel of a regiment, but Jackson apparently did not trust him enough to place him in a field command, and Benton therefore saw no action in the war. In 1813, Benton's relationship with Jackson was interrupted by a wild tavern fight in which his brother, Jesse Benton, was severely stabbed, Jackson was shot, and Thomas Benton was cut with a knife and either pushed or thrown down a flight of stairs.

In the fall of 1815, when Benton was thirty-three years of age, he moved to Missouri Territory, settling in the small riverfront village of St. Louis. He rapidly involved himself in the affairs of the city. Between 1815 and 1820, he established an active law practice, ran for local political offices, bought a house and property to which he relocated his mother and family, killed another St. Louis attorney in a duel, and for two years served as the editor of the *St. Louis Enquirer*. At this point in his life, he was clearly an imposing figure who seldom backed away from a quarrel or a fight. He was a large and physically powerful person with a wide and muscular upper body, a large head, a short, thick neck, and wide shoulders. He possessed a long nose, high forehead, and dark, wavy hair which was often worn long in the back and at the temples.

Benton used the pages of the *St. Louis Enquirer* to address current political issues. He concentrated upon the development of the West, banking and currency, and national land distribution policies, and he vigorously advanced Missouri statehood. By 1820, he was clearly established as a leader in Missouri politics. When Missouri entered the Union as a result of the great compromise of 1820, David Barton and Thomas Hart Benton were selected to represent the new state in the United States Senate.

Life's Work

After a four-week horseback ride from St. Louis, Benton reached Washington, D.C., in mid-November of 1820 to begin a celebrated thirty-year career in the Senate. En route to the capital, he stopped at the Cherry Grove Plantation, near Lexington, Virginia, and proposed marriage to Elizabeth McDowell, whom he had met in 1815. She accepted the offer and the marriage took place in March of 1821.

Once in the Senate, Benton moved quickly to an active involvement in national issues. He first pressed forward those items with a Missouri base and about which he had written in the *St. Louis Enquirer*: the opening of government mineral lands, the development of the Oregon country, federal support of the Western fur trade, and the revision of the national land distribution policy. In the early months of 1824, he introduced two proposals which became closely identified with him and which he would continue to promote throughout his senatorial career: the elimination of the electoral college and the graduated land distribution system. In the former, his goal was to amend the Constitution so that the president and vice president could be directly elected by the people; in the latter, he pursued legislation to reduce the price of public lands by twenty-five cents per acre per year until the land was available at no cost. This practice, he argued, not only would broaden the base of the new democratic system but also would effectively serve to increase the prosperity of the entire nation.

As a result of the controversies surrounding the presidential election of 1824, Benton and Jackson established a close personal and political relationship as a result of which the Missouri senator was elevated to a leadership position in the Democratic Party. When Jacksonian Democracy carried Jackson into the presidency in 1828, Benton became the leading Jacksonian in the Senate and one of the most powerful men in American government in the first half of the nineteenth century. He was often mentioned as a possible candidate for the presidency himself, but he quickly rejected such promotion. As a member of Jackson's famous Kitchen Cabinet, he led the fight to oppose the rechartering of the Bank of the United States and successfully expunged from the record the Senate resolution censuring Jackson for his role in the famous bank struggle. Benton also became the most ardent champion of hard-money policies—that is, those favoring a money system based upon the circulation of gold and silver only. It was his view that such a policy would best serve the common people, as paper currency was too easily manipulated by people of privilege. To this end, he prepared Jackson's famous 1836 Specie Circular, which required that public land purchases be made only with gold or silver coin. Because of his dedication to this issue, he received the nickname "Old Bullion."

Benton also played a key role in the Texas and Oregon annexation controversies. Although he was an ardent expansionist and Westerner, he opposed the acquisition of Texas in 1845 out of concern that it was unfair to Mexico and would lead to war between the two new nations. He was successful in his efforts to establish the northern boundary of Oregon at the forty-ninth latitude rather than the 54-40 line favored by many Americans in 1844 and 1845. His position on these two issues lost him much support in his home state, and he only narrowly won reelection to the Senate in 1844. In spite of his opposition to the Texas annexation and resulting war with Mexico, Benton supported the American war effort and served as chairman of the Senate Military Affairs Committee and as an important military adviser to President James K. Polk. In fact, Polk, who was suspicious of the leading field generals who were members of the Whig Party, extended to Benton the unprecedented position of joint military-diplomatic leader of the American war effort with a rank of major general. Benton considered the offer but rejected it when he could not receive from Polk the pledge of authority that he believed should cohere to such a position.

The American victory in the Mexican War and the subsequent annexation of vast new territories raised the issue of slavery to the forefront of the national political scene in 1848-1850. Although Benton was a slaveholder all of his adult life, he opposed slavery's expansion and expressed contempt for both secessionists and abolitionists. He reacted vigorously to John C. Calhoun's resolutions for noninterference with slavery in the new territories and was angered by the Missouri legislature's 1849 endorsement of the action. The Missouri resolutions assumed a strong proslavery position and directed the two Missouri senators to act accordingly. Benton spent most of 1849 in Missouri campaigning against this legislative policy and directive, and conducted a statewide speaking tour in an effort to reverse the action. This was a turbulent affair marked by name-calling, charges, countercharges, and threats of violence.

The 1850 session of the United States Senate was one of the most famous in its history. For Thomas Hart Benton, it was one of the most crucial. He was a vigorous opponent of the slavery sections of the great compromise of that year as he believed there was too much sympathy for proslavery interests and secessionist threats. His rhetoric of opposition to Henry Clay's resolutions was direct and critical and elicited a strong response from Southern senators. On one occasion, Senator Henry S. Foote of Mississippi drew and aimed a loaded revolver at the Missouri senator on the Senate floor. Benton's strong and highly publicized opposition to sections of the 1850 compromise left him with a severely weakened political base at home, and when the Missouri legislature in January of 1851 moved to the senatorial election, Benton lost to the Whig and anti-Benton candidate Henry S. Geyer, bringing his thirty-year Senate career to a close.

Frustrated by his defeat in the Missouri legislature for reelection to the Senate, the sixty-nine-year-old Benton launched a campaign for election to the House of Representatives. Few people have ever pursued a House of Representatives seat with as much to prove as Benton did in 1852—and, for the moment, victory was his. From 1853 to 1854, he returned to Congress as a member of the House of Representatives, where he took the lead in opposing the Kansas-Nebraska Act as well as all other attempts to extend slavery into the territories. Because of his determined position on this issue, he lost further support in his home state, and his effort to win reelection to the House seat failed in 1854. Undaunted by this reversal, he developed an unsuccessful campaign for the governorship of Missouri in 1856 and worked nationally for the election of James Buchanan and the Democratic Party, refusing to vote for John C. Frémont, who headed the newly formed and sectional Republican Party, even though Frémont was his son-in-law, having married his daughter, Jessie.

With his political defeats in 1854 and 1856 and the death of his wife in 1854, Benton retired to his Washington, D.C., home to work on a number of writing projects. He continued an active schedule of appearances at political rallies and public speeches. He published a large two-volume summary of his thirty-year Senate career in 1854-1856, a sixteen-volume *Abridgement of the Debates of Congress from 1789 to 1856* (1857-1861), and a historical and legal examination of the Dred Scott decision, *Examination of the Dred Scott Case* (1857). His work in this direction was hampered by the increasing pain and complications of cancer and a fire that destroyed his home and personal records. The final page of his collection of the debates in Congress was completed on April 9, 1858. He died early the next morning, April 10, 1858, at the age of seventy-six. His wife and two sons had preceded him in death; four daughters survived.

Summary

Thomas Hart Benton reflects, in many ways, the character and nature of America in the first half of the nineteenth century. An Easterner who became a Westerner, he was tough, bold, aggressive, egotistical, talkative, shrewd, self-educated, and fiercely independent. He found his career and gained a reputation on the frontier. He moved easily into law, banking, land investment, newspapers, the military, and politics. He extolled the strength and virtues of the common man in a society struggling with the issue of whether the elite or the common man should govern. As a leading proponent of Jacksonian democracy, Benton became the voice of union, a supporter of nationalism in an age of nationalism, and a builder of the nation in an era of change.

Benton believed that the great American West held the promise of the American future. He pressed for the development of the area from Missouri to Oregon and California and believed this region would provide unparalleled opportunity for the common man and unparalleled prosperity for the nation. To this end, more than any one in American history, Benton stands as the champion of cheap land, developing policies and procedures that anticipated the great homestead movement later in the century.

To remove the benefits of privilege in a democratic society, he fought vigorously against the use of paper currency. It was his view that a financial system based upon the use of specie would protect "the people" from exploitation by people of influence. He was, thus, the leader of Jackson's war against the Bank of the United States and was the author of Jackson's famous and controversial Specie Circular.

In order to advance the cause of Union and American nationalism, Benton sought to suppress the issue of slavery on the national political scene. He believed that this could best be accomplished by preventing the extension of slavery into the territories. His great emphasis upon this may have had much to do with keeping Missouri in the Union when the great crisis of nationalism came in 1861.

Bibliography

Benton, Thomas Hart. *Thirty Years' View: Or, A History of the Working of the American Government for Thirty Years, from 1820 to 1850.* 2 vols. New York: D. Appleton and Co., 1854-1856. An autobiographical summary of Benton's senatorial career. A valuable political commentary for insight into Benton and all American politics in the first half of the nineteenth century.

Chambers, William Nisbet. *Old Bullion Benton: Senator from the New West.* Boston: Little, Brown and Co., 1956. A well-researched biography of Benton based upon extensive manuscript material. Follows Benton's life in chronological order and provides numerous quotations from his speeches and writings. This is the most widely used biography of Benton.

Kennedy, John F. *Profiles in Courage*. New York: Harper and Brothers, 1955. This well-known book contains a laudatory chapter on Benton, clearly emphasizing his great individualism and political independence. Kennedy finds Benton's opposition to the extension of slavery in the face of Missouri's perspective to be a courageous act of principle.

Meigs, William M. *The Life of Thomas Hart Benton*. Philadelphia: J. B. Lippincott Co., 1904. An early biography of Benton that depends much upon Benton's autobiography and the memoirs of his brilliant daughter Jessie and her husband John C. Frémont. Now outdated by the research of Chambers and Smith.

Oliver, Robert T. *History of Public Speaking in America*. Boston: Allyn and Bacon, 1965. A good analysis of Benton's oratorical skills with several examples of his most striking comments and most famous speeches. Incorporates the observations from several doctoral and master's analyses of Benton's speaking methods.

Roosevelt, Theodore. *Thomas Hart Benton*. Boston: Houghton Mifflin Co., 1900. A biography in the American Statesmen series by President Theodore Roosevelt. Badly dated but reflects the interpretation of Benton held at the end of the nineteenth century. Roosevelt viewed Benton not as a great intellect but as a person unique for his hard work, determination, and speaking abilities.

Smith, Elbert B. *Francis Preston Blair*. New York: Macmillan Publishing Co., 1980. An excellent biography of Francis Blair, who was a Jacksonian editor and close personal friend of Benton. Provides good insight into Benton from the perspective of his closest friend and friendly biographer.

_____. *Magnificent Missourian: The Life of Thomas Hart Benton*. Philadelphia: J. B. Lippincott Co., 1958. A very well written biography of Benton based exclusively upon manuscript and original sources. Provides excellent coverage of Benton's senatorial career and his role on the national political scene. Especially good coverage of Benton's role in the bank war.

Frank Nickell

IRVING BERLIN
Israel Baline

Born: May 11, 1888; Temun, Russia

Area of Achievement: Music

Contribution: Berlin, one of the most prolific and recognized American song-
writers, has had the exceptional ability to make his tunes and rhythms con-
form to the style and mood of the times in which he has lived.

Early Life

In Siberia, at the time when Irving Berlin was born (as Israel Baline), Jew-
baiting was a popular local entertainment. Hordes of Russians, often from
other villages, would surge through Jewish communities, looting homes and
businesses, raping Jewish women, burning synagogues, beating and murder-
ing while the police stood idly by. Such atrocities fed the anger of some of the
czarist system's bitterest foes, who were determined to destroy it and all it
represented; others, such as Berlin's father, chose to forsake their homeland
for the uncertain future of life in the Lower East Side slums of New York.
Moses Baline's decision was particularly understandable: As a cantor in the
local synagogue, he was especially targeted for persecution. Therefore, in
1892, a year of increased legal restrictions against the Jews, he took his wife
and most of his eight children and headed westward.

The Baline family set up housekeeping in a three-room, windowless apartment on Monroe Street. The father, unable to find work as a cantor, worked
in a kosher slaughterhouse and earned extra money by giving Hebrew lessons. After three years, at the time when young Israel entered public school,
the family was able to move to slightly better quarters on Cherry Street. In
1896, the elder Baline died, and, shortly afterward, Israel left school to help
support the family. His first job was selling newspapers, a task he tried to
make less onerous by singing songs on the street corners, songs that he heard
played in the local saloons. Sometimes passersby, liking what they heard,
would toss him a few pennies.

When he was fourteen, he left home, supporting himself by casual employment as a singing waiter in a beer hall or by making the rounds of various
Bowery haunts, belting out songs on his own. He also worked for a time publicizing songs for a sheet-music seller. His first regular job came in 1908,
when he was hired as a singing waiter by Pelham's café. At Pelham's, he
earned seven dollars a week singing the favorites of George M. Cohan and
other popular tunes which he frequently parodied with his own words. While
at Pelham's, he wrote the lyrics to a song, composed by the café's piano
player, Nick Nicholson, called "Marie from Sunny Italy," earning seventy-five

cents in royalties. His name was listed on the title page as I. Berlin, a result, no doubt of a mistranslation of an incorrect pronunciation, but he liked the change so much that he decided to keep it, changing his first name as well. Irving sounded more impressive, and less biblical, than Israel.

Berlin continued to work as a singing waiter, now at a bar in Times Square, and continued to write lyrics for other people's songs, but he also started to write his own tunes. None of these early efforts, such as "Queenie, My Own" and "She Was a Dear Little Girl," was particularly memorable. Nor did his background seem to prepare him for his future success in musical comedy. He had only two years of formal schooling, none at all in music, which he could not read. He played the piano a bit, but his skill, such as it was, was restricted to using only the black keys in F sharp. Yet, by 1909, his compositions, which others transcribed, were becoming well-known, and he obtained a job as a staff composer at the Seminary Music Company, where he earned twenty-five dollars a week.

His chief assignment there was as lyricist with Ted Snyder, the firm's director, who usually provided the music. Berlin's desire to compose his own music led him, in 1911, to write the song that would establish him as one of the most famous popular composers of his day. When "Alexander's Ragtime Band" first appeared as an instrumental, its success was limited, but then Berlin added words, which he took from another of his unsuccessful songs, and it became a sensation, establishing ragtime as the popular musical idiom of the time. It was one of the first songs of Tin Pan Alley to have its verse and refrain in different keys. Berlin now became a full partner of the firm in which he worked, Waterson, Berlin and Synder Company. The firm's logo was a target with an arrow pinpointing the center, Berlin's name appearing over the bull's-eye.

Life's Work

In 1912, at the age of twenty-four, Berlin had achieved a degree of success that few musicians attain in a lifetime. His output was enormous. He could write a song a day (although his average was closer to one a week); he had made his stage debut on Broadway in a revue entitled *Up and Down Broadway* (1910), in which he sang many of his own songs; he had written the score for the *Ziegfeld Follies of 1911*; and he was making about $100,000 a year. Berlin's life was marred by a personal tragedy, however, when his bride of five months died of typhoid fever, contracted while on their honeymoon to Cuba; Berlin's first ballad, "When I Lost You," which became a national hit, was a product of this period. Berlin also began working on a revue in which he composed, for the first time, both the words and the music. *Watch Your Step* (1914) contained the famous contrapuntal song "Play a Simple Melody." The show featured the darlings of the Broadway stage, the dancing Castles, Vernon and Irene, and was featured in London the following year. Berlin was at that time involved with two other stage productions in New York City.

Berlin's theatrical career seemed to come to a temporary halt when he was inducted into the army during World War I and sent to Camp Yaphank on Long Island for training. "The U.S. Army Takes Berlin" was how one newspaper headline read. Yet Berlin's commanding officer considered the recruit's talents to be too special for combat. General Franklin Bell wanted to build a base community house for the visiting relatives of the soldiers, and he needed to raise thirty-five thousand dollars. He offered, and Berlin accepted, the proposal to put on an all-soldiers' show as a fund-raiser. Berlin demanded and received an ensemble of three hundred, half in the cast, the remainder comprising the orchestra, the production, and backstage personnel; he conducted the auditions, directed the publicity, and booked the theater. *Yip, Yip, Yaphank* opened in August, 1918, at the Century Theatre in New York City, scheduled for eight performances; it ran for thirty-two. Berlin sang two numbers, "Poor Little Me—I'm on K.P." and the showstopping "Oh, How I Hate to Get Up in the Morning." The show earned eighty-three thousand dollars for the Camp Yaphank building fund.

When the war ended, Berlin returned to civilian life and Broadway. In 1919, he did the score for the *Ziegfeld Follies* which contained "A Pretty Girl Is Like a Melody," a song which Berlin dashed off one night because Florenz Ziegfeld needed a number that would make use of the dozens of extra costumes he still had. Impresarios and music publishers were accustomed to ordering songs as one would order a drink in a saloon, and Berlin was very obliging. (Harry Waterston once needed a tune for a musical, and he called Berlin; Berlin sang him one over the telephone.) Berlin was now able to fulfill his two great ambitions: to have his own publishing house, Irving Berlin, Incorporated, and to build his own theater, the Music Box Theatre, which, beginning in 1921, staged Berlin's own revues.

Berlin wisely resisted the temptation to publish every song he wrote; if he had there would have been as many as three thousand in print instead of about a third that number. Nor did all those tunes which were released become hits. Berlin sometimes recycled those that failed, some of them becoming popular in another form, such as, for example, the song "Easter Parade," which began life as a World War I ditty. At times, Berlin might compose a song, think it inappropriate for the occasion, and release it much later. "God Bless America" was not used in *Yip, Yip, Yaphank* because Berlin thought it too much like gilding the patriotic lily; it came out in 1938 instead (Berlin donated the royalties to the Boy Scouts and Girl Scouts of America). Many of Berlin's songs, however, were successes the first time they appeared and continued in popularity, songs such as "Always," "Blue Skies," "Shaking the Blues Away," and "Puttin' on the Ritz," which became a hit for the second time in 1985.

During the 1920's and the 1930's, Berlin did four Music Box revues (1921, 1922, 1923, and 1924); he did the first musical comedy, *The Cocoanuts* (1925), starring the Marx Brothers; he wrote the film scores for such films as *Top Hat* (1935), *Follow the Fleet* (1936), *On the Avenue* (1937), *Alexander's Ragtime Band* (1938), and *Second Fiddle* (1939). On the stage, with *Face the Music* (1932) and *As Thousands Cheer* (1933), he took the musical reviews into a new, socially conscious direction. *Face the Music* was about political corruption and bossism; *As Thousands Cheer* depicted scenes from the daily newspaper. It contained the sentimental but ingratiating "Easter Parade," but it also had a sketch about a lynching, in which a black woman wonders how to tell her children that their father "ain't comin' home no more." "Supper Time" was sung by Ethel Waters, who called it a song that could tell the whole tragic story of a race.

When the United States entered World War II, Berlin returned to more conventional music fare with another all-soldiers' show, *This Is the Army*, written in response to a specific request by the Department of the Army. The revue opened on Broadway on July 4, 1942, and featured Berlin himself dressed in a World War I sergeant's uniform, again singing "Oh, How I Hate to Get Up in the Morning." The musical also contained the popular "I Left My Heart at the Stage Door Canteen" and "This Is the Army, Mr. Jones." The show lasted more than three years. After its Broadway run, it went on the road, playing in all the major American cities, as well as in American bases in Europe, Africa, Australia, and the South Pacific. It was filmed in Hollywood in 1943. Berlin appeared in the film version, which starred Kate Smith, who sang "God Bless America," as well as an assortment of Hollywood stars, including Ronald Reagan. The production earned a total of ten million dollars in royalties for the Army Emergency Relief Fund. Also during the war, Hollywood released *Holiday Inn* (1942), starring Bing Crosby and Fred Astaire, containing one of Berlin's most famous songs: "White Christmas." Few besides Berlin suspected the song's tremendous potential.

After the war, Berlin proved that he was still at the height of his powers with his best musical, *Annie Get Your Gun* (1946), in which the songs, unlike those of the revues of the past, were perfectly integrated with the story, depicting the characters for which they were written and helping to advance the plot. The production, staring Ethel Merman, opened on May 16, 1946, and ran for 1,147 performances. It spawned many road shows and was made into a film in 1950. The story, based loosely on the life of Annie Oakley, contains some of Berlin's finest songs, stunning in their variety: "The Girl That I Marry," "Doin' What Comes Natur'lly," "I Got the Sun in the Morning," "You Can't Get a Man with a Gun," "They Say It's Wonderful," and "There's No Business Like Show Business," the last written as a filler to cover a change of scenery (and almost left out of the final production because Berlin did not believe that his lyricist Oscar Hammerstein really liked it). Probably no other show had as many hits as *Annie Get Your Gun*.

After *Annie Get Your Gun*, Berlin wrote two musicals in rapid succession, both of which enjoyed success. *Miss Liberty* (1949) contained "Let's Take an Old-Fashioned Walk" and a musical version of the poem, by Emma Lazarus, which is on the base of the Statue of Liberty, the lovely "Give Me Your Tired, Your Poor." *Call Me Madam* (1953) was another vehicle for the irrepressible Merman as a fictitious Perle Mesta, the Washington party giver that President Harry S Truman appointed ambassador to Luxembourg. It contained another of Berlin's famous songs in counterpoint, "You're Just in Love." Berlin's next Broadway production appeared twelve years later. *Mr. President* (1962) lacked the memorable tunes of past productions but did not deserve the panning it received from some critics. In a sense, however, the disappointment felt by the critics serves as a measure of their admiration.

Summary

The lives of composers are often measured by what is remembered of their music, whether it be opera, symphony, or popular song. If greatness alone were based on this criterion, Irving Berlin would be considered one of the world's best, for he has certainly written more popular music than anyone that comes to mind. Moreover, it is remarkable how many of his tunes have become such a permanent fixture of his own culture and his country's history. It is impossible to remember the words of his songs without thinking of the tunes that went with them: words and music in a perfect marriage. Berlin's sense of timing and of what the public wanted, or craved, was uncanny, as was his versatility: songs for all occasions. His images, like a picture by Norman Rockwell, reflected what the American people believed themselves, or hoped themselves, to be.

Berlin's music is basic and often mundane; it has sometimes been called corny. Berlin did not care about pleasing everyone. When somebody called *Annie Get Your Gun* "old-fashioned," his retort was, "Yes, an old-fashioned smash." Yet despite his overwhelming success, he continued to be realistic about his talents, realizing that his ability to simplify was in keeping with his lack of musical training. When once told that he should study music seriously, he replied that if he were to do so, he might end up despising his own work. Many would disagree.

Bibliography
Ewen, David. *Composers for the American Musical Theater*. New York: Dodd, Mead and Co., 1968. A history of musical theater in the United States from Victor Herbert to Leonard Bernstein. The featured biography of Berlin is thus seen in context with those of the composer's peers.
Freedland, Michael. *Irving Berlin*. New York: Stein and Day, 1974. A very engaging life of the composer, revealed in a succession of anecdotes which

have been culled from interviews with his friends and associates. Directed toward the show-business aspect of Berlin's life rather than toward his music per se.

Gottfried, Martin. *Broadway Musicals*. New York: Harry N. Abrams, 1979. A lavish picture book with perceptive and knowledgeable commentary regarding this unique American art form and Berlin's contribution to its development.

Jablonski, Edward. "Through History with Irving Berlin." *The Reporter* 27 (October, 1962): 48-50. An incisive commentary on the special contribution that Berlin made to American music in the development of the popular song, a form that he purged of its European harmonic sweetness.

Logan, Joshua. "Irving Berlin." *High Fidelity and Musical America* 28 (May, 1978): 76-81. Logan, a director for three of Berlin's musicals, including *Annie Get Your Gun*, relates how he first met the great man and what it was like to work with him. "There has always been in him a passionate, unquenchable enthusiasm, a powerhouse quality that set every one near him on fire."

Stoddard, Maynard Good. "God Bless America ... and Irving Berlin." *The Saturday Evening Post* 25 (September, 1983): 58-59. Reflections on the occasion of the composer's ninety-fifth birthday, about his place in American music. The conclusion is that Berlin's melodies will last long after rock and roll music "has rolled over and died."

Wollcott, Alexander. *Story of Irving Berlin*. New York: G. P. Putnam's Sons, 1925. An impressionistic attempt to understand the composer's gift for melody by conjuring up the atmosphere, themes, and harmonies of the Bowery from whence his inspiration sprang. The book reveals almost as much about the author's own sentimentalities and values as it does about its subject's, but it is written with much style, affection, and romance.

Wm. Laird Kleine-Ahlbrandt

LEONARD BERNSTEIN

Born: August 25, 1918; Lawrence, Massachusetts

Area of Achievement: Music

Contribution: Combining unusual talent with his appealing stage presence and teaching ability, Bernstein, through his conducting and composing, has introduced classical music to a vast general audience.

Early Life

Leonard Bernstein was born August 25, 1918, in Lawrence, Massachusetts, the son of Samuel Joseph and Jennie Resnick Bernstein, both Russian immigrants. In many ways his early life contains elements often found in the lives of American child prodigies, for his was not a wealthy family, and his natural talent for music came to light almost by accident. The Bernsteins had agreed to store an old upright piano for a relative, and when it arrived, their ten-year-old son would not be parted from it. He composed simple pieces on it almost immediately and begged for lessons. He decided upon a professional career even at that early age, but though young Bernstein got his lessons, his practical father knew only too well the vicissitudes inherent in a career in music and steadfastly opposed it.

To ensure that their son received a solid and well-rounded early education, the Bernsteins sent Leonard to the prestigious Boston Latin School. While there, he participated and excelled in athletics as well as traditional academic studies. He was still determined to study music when it came time to graduate and, still against his father's wishes, registered at Harvard University as a music major. Harvard's music faculty was particularly distinguished in the 1930's, and though Bernstein intended a career as a concert pianist, he studied not only piano (with Heinrich Gebhard) but also composition (with Walter Piston and Edward Burlinghame Hill).

Bernstein was graduated from Harvard in 1939, and attended the relatively new Curtis Institute of Music in Philadelphia. Curtis had, at that time, attracted several famous German émigrés to its faculty, among them Fritz Reiner, with whom Bernstein studied conducting. He continued his studies in piano with Isabella Vengerova and orchestration with Randall Thompson while at Curtis, thus laying the foundation for the three avenues his musical career would simultaneously travel. Just as important in his early development, young Bernstein spent summers studying and working with Serge Koussevitzky, conductor of the Boston Symphony, at the Berkshire Music Center, in Tanglewood, Massachusetts.

Life's Work

Bernstein's career was just beginning as the United States entered World

War II. The war added to the uncertainties of a young musician trying to establish himself, though uncertainty did not diminish his energies. Indeed, 1941 and 1942 were spent teaching and composing the *Clarinet Sonata*, his first published work. He also produced operas for the Boston Institute of Modern Art during these years, but his first major opportunity came in September, 1942, when Koussevitzky, his former mentor, appointed him assistant conductor at Tanglewood. This position gave Bernstein the base he needed and paved the way for appearances in the 1942-1943 season at New York's Town Hall music forums and the "Serenade Concerts" at New York's Museum of Modern Art.

The New York music world began to take notice of Bernstein's unusual style and verve, and in 1943, he accepted an appointment as assistant conductor of the New York Philharmonic from Arthur Rodzinski, then its conductor. It was, indeed, a combination of talent and good fortune that advanced Bernstein's career to international status late that year. On November 12, 1943, the famous mezzo-soprano Jennie Tourel performed his song cycle *I Hate Music* at Town Hall. The very next day, he received a call from the New York Philharmonic, asking that he substitute as conductor for the suddenly indisposed Bruno Walter. Bernstein conducted the scheduled program with such skill and enthusiasm that he received not only the acclaim of the audience and his colleagues Rodzinski and Koussevitzky but also a front-page encomium in the next day's *The New York Times*. (This concert has been preserved on a long-playing record distributed by the Philharmonic.) Thus, barely two years out of Curtis, Bernstein found himself at the beginning of an international career with seemingly limitless horizons.

Late in 1943, Bernstein's *Jeremiah* Symphony premiered in Pittsburgh and Boston. It was performed again in New York on February 18, 1944. Though it received a mixed reception, enough of the critics thought it had sufficient merit to award Bernstein the New York City Music Critics Circle Award for the most distinguished new American orchestral work of the 1943-1944 season. The *Jeremiah* Symphony has since become a regularly played work among American orchestras and has won audience acceptance.

Still, broad audience popularity also distinguished Bernstein's career from its earliest years. April 18, 1944, saw the world premiere of *Fancy Free*, a ballet given by Ballet Theatre (now called American Ballet Theatre) at the Metropolitan Opera House in New York. Composer Bernstein also conducted, and his score became the basis for the musical *On the Town* (1944), with choreography by Jerome Robbins and lyrics by Betty Comden and Adolph Green. The musical was a critical success and illustrated the affinity Bernstein always enjoyed with the American musical theater.

In the years after World War II, Bernstein served as guest conductor with numerous orchestras, especially with the newly founded Israel Philharmonic, where he served as musical adviser from 1945 to 1948. He toured in the

United States with the Israel Philharmonic in 1951, sharing conducting responsibilities with Koussevitzky. In the summer of that year, he succeeded his mentor as head of the conducting department at Tanglewood and taught music at Brandeis University from 1951 to 1956. He continued his success in the musical theater with a series of perennially popular scores during these years: *Wonderful Town* (1953), *Candide* (1956), and *West Side Story* (1957). The New York City Opera later placed *Candide* in its regular repertory, and Bernstein himself has recorded *West Side Story* with operatic voices, illustrating again the affinity between what are often called "popular" music and "serious" music, a distinction which Bernstein clearly rejects. Earlier Bernstein works are still offered and remain in the record catalogs: *The Age of Anxiety* (1949), a second symphony for piano and orchestra, a short opera, *Trouble in Tahiti* (1952), incidental music for the Broadway production of *Peter Pan* (1950) and the film *On the Waterfront* (1954), for which he received an Academy Award nomination.

For the 1957-1958 season, just as the New York Philharmonic was about to leave Carnegie Hall for its new house at Lincoln Center, Bernstein was appointed coconductor of the orchestra with Dimitri Mitropoulos. He was also given directorship of the orchestra's Young People's Concerts. He invigorated the latter with his enthusiasm and energy, even bringing them to national television. Many adult concertgoers owe at least part of their musical knowledge to Bernstein's discussions of the sonata and symphonic forms, the meaning of counterpoint, and Bernstein's musical biographies, one of the most entertaining of which was dedicated to his mentor, teacher, and friend Koussevitzky.

Bernstein introduced similar innovations one year later, when he assumed full directorship of the New York Philharmonic upon Mitropoulos' retirement, introducing Thursday "Preview Concerts," in which the conductor spoke to the audience about the music to be performed as well as thematically linked concerts, which established patterns of influence among seemingly unrelated composers. Bernstein thus transformed what might otherwise have been merely evenings of entertainment into instructive, though never patronizing, educational experiences for his adult audiences.

Not content to have taken the New York audiences by storm, Bernstein toured with the New York Philharmonic in Latin America at the close of the 1957-1958 season, and in Europe and Asia the following year, taking the orchestra to twenty-nine cities in seventeen countries, including the Soviet Union, all to great popular acclaim. While in the Soviet Union, Bernstein introduced Russian audiences to a wide variety of composers rarely presented by Soviet orchestras, including his own compositions as well as those by the Russian-born émigré Igor Stravinsky.

Bernstein's great popularity with New York audiences continued throughout his active tenure with the New York Philharmonic, though after the death of his wife, Chilean-born actress Felicia Montealegre Cohn, as well as with the passing of time, he wanted to direct more of his energies to composing and guest conducting with various orchestras. It was for this reason that Bernstein resigned full-time directorship of the New York Philharmonic after the 1968-1969 season, ceding the baton to Pierre Boulez, the French-born maestro who became music director in the 1971-1972 season. The grateful New York Philharmonic awarded Bernstein the title Conductor Laureate, and he has continued to conduct the orchestra for several concerts each season.

From his youth, Bernstein has exuded charm. He looks taller than his five feet eight and one half inches, and his longish, tousled hair has turned from gray to silver. His involvement with the music he conducts is genuine, not melodramatic. He is, in truth, a showman, but a showman with real substance, and the enthusiasm that New York audiences display whenever he conducts proceeds directly from his unusual rapport with his orchestra and his clear love of music. In the years since he ended active involvement with the Philharmonic, Bernstein has conducted all over the world and has turned even more to operatic conducting (at Bayreuth and the Metropolitan). His theater piece *Mass* premiered at the Kennedy Center for the Performing Arts in Washington, D.C., in 1971, combining Roman Catholic liturgy with secular and popular tunes. Though it has received mixed criticism, it has, like so many Bernstein works, been widely acclaimed by audiences.

Summary

Bernstein, despite his undoubted success, has always been a man given to moodiness and, paradoxically, to self-doubt. He is troubled by the world's cruelty and injustice, and this sensitivity has led him not only to the themes of many of his works (the *Jeremiah* Symphony, *The Age of Anxiety*, the 1963 work *Kaddish*, *Candide*, *Mass*) and to some of his most expressive conducting (Ludwig van Beethoven, Gustav Mahler), but also to champion such unpopular causes as that of the Black Panthers at their trial in the 1960's and to oppose American involvement in the Vietnam War before it became fashionable to do so.

Regardless of Bernstein's moments of doubt and disillusionment, it remains clear that many owe much of the musical insight they possess to this gifted man. His compositions are often distinctively American, with rhythms and counterpoint which verge on popular styles, but his love of music is international and universal.

Bibliography

Bernstein, Leonard. *Findings*. New York: Simon and Schuster, 1982. Contains a short autobiography, a classified list of compositions by Bernstein, and miscellaneous essays, addresses, and lectures on musical subjects.

_____. *The Joy of Music*. New York: Simon and Schuster, 1959. Bernstein's own introduction to music, designed for adults and incorporating the teaching techniques he used so successfully in both the Thursday evening "Preview Concerts" and the "Young People's Concerts." It is filled with musical illustrations and suggestions for listening.

_____. *The Unanswered Question: Six Talks at Harvard*. Cambridge, Mass.: Harvard University Press, 1976. A technical but interesting work drawn from the undergraduate lectures Bernstein delivered at Harvard as a visiting professor there in 1973.

_____. *Young People's Concerts*. New York: Simon and Schuster, 1970. A companion volume to *The Joy of Music*, based on Bernstein's Emmy Award–winning television series. Discusses what is meant by music, classical music, and melody in terms understandable to both young adults and older listeners.

Briggs, John. *Leonard Bernstein: The Man, His Work, and His World*. Cleveland, Ohio: World Publishing Co., 1961. A biography, particularly good in assessing the reasons for Bernstein's far-ranging popularity and filled with the comments of Bernstein's colleagues and fellow composers, including remarks of the latter on Bernstein's interpretations of their works. Contains a discography to 1960.

Gruen, J., and Ken Heyman. *The Private World of Leonard Bernstein*. New York: Viking Press, 1968. A photo-text study which catches Bernstein in all of his moods. There are also candid photographs of his family and discussions of the philosophy which underlies his complex personality.

Howard, John Tasker. *Our American Music: A Comprehensive History from 1620 to the Present*. 4th ed. New York: Thomas Y. Crowell, 1965. Sets Bernstein in the tradition of American composers, considering the qualities which make his work "American" in character. Contains a capsule biography and partial list of compositions.

Robert J. Forman

HANS ALBRECHT BETHE

Born: July 2, 1906; Strasbourg, Alsace-Lorraine

Areas of Achievement: Theoretical physics and public policy
Contribution: Bethe's work in theoretical nuclear physics explained how stars
converted mass to energy and broadened the scientific understanding of
subatomic events. Long an influential advocate for restraint in the proliferation of nuclear weapons, he laid the theoretical groundwork for the
explosion of the first atom bomb.

Early Life

Hans Albrecht Bethe was the only child of Albrecht Theodore Julius
Bethe, an eminent German physiologist, and Anna (Kuhn) Bethe, a musician and playwright. Hans came from a long line of university professors;
his oldest uncle was a professor of Greek at the University of Leipzig, and
his grandmother and mother both had fathers who were professors. The
elder Bethe's family was Protestant; his wife's was Jewish. As a child, Hans
was frail, lonely, and perhaps overprotected by his mother. Numbers dominated his life. At age five, Hans made a remark to his mother about the
properties of zero, and at age seven, he filled a notebook with the powers of
two and three. His father was concerned that Hans not progress too far
beyond the mathematics appropriate to his grade in school.

The family moved to Frankfurt, Germany, in 1915, in response to an invitation to Albrecht Bethe to start a department of physiology at the University of Frankfurt. Though Hans had earlier received instruction from a private tutor, in Frankfurt, he attended the gymnasium, a nine-year school.
Hans felt estranged from the other students there since most of his life had
been spent in the company of adults. He found some solace in mathematics,
especially algebra. In his last few years at the school, the elective physics
courses he took convinced him to pursue that field at the University of
Frankfurt, which he did beginning in 1924. He discovered that he had little
facility for experimental physics, but Bethe's interest in mathematics drove
him to take up theoretical physics. One of his teachers, a spectroscopist
named Karl Meissner, persuaded Bethe to leave Frankfurt to study under
Arnold Sommerfeld, professor of theoretical physics at the University of Munich. The year 1926 was Bethe's first in Munich, and under the influential
Sommerfeld, Bethe found himself at the center of a great ferment in theoretical physics. Quantum mechanics was replacing the classical model of the
atom. The old model pictured tiny particles called electrons orbiting around
a hard central core, or nucleus. The quantum theory, however, said that if
electrons were represented as if they were waves, heretofore unexplained
subatomic phenomena could be understood. In 1926, Sommerfeld shared

with his students a new paper by Austrian physicist Erwin Schrödinger, which developed equations for quantum wave mechanics; subsequently, Sommerfeld encouraged Bethe to apply these insights to the effect of electron scattering, which took place when a beam of electrons was directed against a crystal. This study formed the basis of Bethe's doctoral degree in physics, granted in 1928. The next decade would be one of the most productive for Bethe in theoretical physics.

Life's Work

Bethe spent a short time as an instructor in physics at Frankfurt and at Stuttgart but in 1929 returned to the University of Munich at the request of Sommerfeld to work as a *Privatdozent*, a university lecturer whose fees are paid directly by students. During this time, Bethe wrote a seminal paper which gave mathematical expression to the passage of charged particles through matter. He considered the paper, which appeared in a physics journal in 1930, to be among his best work.

Concurrent with the rise of the Nazi movement in Germany in the early 1930's, Bethe, the recipient of a fellowship from the Rockefeller Foundation International Education Board, studied for a time at Cambridge University in England and at the University of Rome. In Rome, Bethe was profoundly influenced by the personality and theoretical approach of Enrico Fermi, then only thirty years old but already a physicist of international repute. From Fermi, Bethe learned a kind of experimental insight into theoretical problems, and he coauthored a paper with Fermi on electron-electron interaction which was published in 1932.

Working again with Sommerfeld in Munich in the years 1931 and 1932 brought Bethe in contact with English and American postdoctoral students. One of the Americans, Lloyd Smith from Cornell University in Ithaca, New York, would eventually ask his department chairman to offer Bethe a position. (In 1935, Bethe became an assistant professor at Cornell and a full professor there in 1937, retiring in 1975 to become the John Wendell Anderson Professor of Physics at Cornell.)

Bethe would come to Cornell highly recommended. In 1932, he collaborated with Sommerfeld on an article, "Elektronen-theorie der Metalle," published the next year in the *Handbuch der Physik*, which provided the basis for theoretical work on the solid-state basis of metals. On a more personal level, Sommerfeld was a shelter of sorts for Bethe when Adolf Hitler came to power in 1933. Since two of Bethe's grandparents were Jewish, Hans was forced to resign as assistant professor at the University of Tübingen (a job he had taken the previous year). The Nazis seemed less concerned with the activities of older researchers such as Sommerfeld but demanded doctrinal adherence from younger scientists.

The shelter was only temporary: Increasing tension politically and the threat of demonstrations against Bethe if he spoke at a physics colloquium made him eager to accept a lectureship position at the University of Manchester in England and later, in 1934, to become a fellow at the University of Bristol. The next year brought an offer of a permanent position at Cornell. Knowing little about the university, Bethe joined the physics department there in February, 1935. The department was being reorganized to involve graduate students in basic theoretical research, and Bethe found the students, as well as the professors, eager to learn about nuclear physics but lacking sufficient background. Eventually, Bethe wrote three long articles for *Reviews of Modern Physics* (the first, in collaboration with Robert F. Bacher, was published in 1936, and the remaining two, with M. Stanley Livingston, appeared in 1937). The articles virtually re-created the entire field of nuclear physics; Bethe's Bible, as they came to be known, provided the basic textbook on the subject for a generation of scientists. (Through the years, most of Bethe's major theoretical findings appeared not in books but in hundreds of research articles in a variety of journals.)

At an astrophysics conference in 1938 in Washington, D.C., Bethe met George Gamow and Edward Teller of George Washington University; he was challenged to take up the theoretical problem of how the sun produced the energy it did through thermonuclear reactions. Bethe's answer was first published in 1939; "Energy Production in Stars" won for him a prize of five hundred dollars from the New York Academy of Sciences. (In 1967, Bethe was awarded the Nobel Prize for Physics on the basis of his work in this area.) This and subsequent papers introduced the six-step carbon cycle (in which carbon acts as a catalyst in the production of energy in stars hotter and more massive than the sun), and the P-P reaction (in which protons fuse in a chain reaction that transforms hydrogen into helium, releasing large amounts of energy). The P-P reaction is central to the sun's energy production and may take a million years or more to complete.

In September, 1939, Bethe married Rose Ewald, the daughter of Paul Ewald, one of his Stuttgart professors. Rose had emigrated to the United States in 1936. Their union produced two children, Henry and Monica.

With the advent of World War II, Bethe's life entered a new era. Fearful of the progress of the Nazi regime, he sought to make a contribution to the war effort. From an article in the *Encyclopædia Britannica* on armor penetration, Bethe developed a theory that aided in the production of stronger shields for Allied ships. Ironically, Bethe's article was classified secret, and Bethe himself was not permitted to read it. Yet after becoming a naturalized citizen of the United States in 1941, Bethe received a security clearance and soon afterward began work on radar for the Massachusetts Institute of Technology Radiation Laboratory. In 1943, he received a call from J. Robert Oppenheimer to assist in the production of an atom (fission) bomb. From 1943 to 1946, Bethe was chief of the Theoretical Physics Division at Los Alamos Laboratory in New Mexico, charged with developing the theoretical base for a fission explosion. In such a reaction, the nucleus of an atom is split, releasing energy. Edward Teller, working under Bethe in the Theoretical Physics Division, insisted on the development of what he called the superbomb, one which would use the power of a fission explosion to trigger a hydrogen-fusion reaction with the subsequent release of vast destructive power. Teller seemed to find little acceptance of the idea, and his friendship with Bethe began to crumble. (It was severed, at least for a time, when in 1954, during loyalty hearings for Oppenheimer, Teller recommended against renewed security clearance for Oppenheimer.) Far from embracing the idea of a superbomb, Bethe became a kind of reluctant midwife to the atom bomb. After the successful test of the first plutonium bomb at Alamogordo, New Mexico, in July of 1945, Bethe began to consider the possibility of some kind of international control of atomic weapons and civilian control of atomic energy in the United States itself.

Nevertheless, in 1952, Bethe returned to Los Alamos for several months of design work on Teller's hydrogen bomb, apparently convinced that revised calculations made such a superbomb a real possibility; if that were true, could the Soviet Union be far behind? The pragmatic Bethe reasoned that since there was no global mechanism of arms control, the United States, in its own defense, ought to develop the hydrogen bomb, if only to maintain the balance of terror when the Soviets developed their own superbomb. Bethe did allow that the American bomb program might well spur the Soviets to mount their own program; in fact, the Soviets tested a hydrogen bomb only three years after the American test in 1952.

Bethe's scientific accomplishments ranged from theoretical physics to quantum electrodynamics to nose-cone reentry, but in the 1950's, he became increasingly concerned with public policy regarding nuclear energy. In 1955, Bethe served as a technical adviser to the United States delegation to the International Conference on the Peaceful Uses of Atomic Energy held in Geneva, Switzerland. He was a member of the President's Science Advisory Committee in the late 1950's and played a large part in the negotiations that led to the atmospheric nuclear Test Ban Treaty in 1963. After the Arab oil embargo in 1974, Bethe concentrated his efforts on advocating the development of a range of energy resources from coal to nuclear power, emphasizing the need for strong nuclear-reactor safety standards.

When, in 1983, President Ronald Reagan called for a Strategic Defense Initiative (dubbed the "space shield" or Star Wars program), Bethe was swift to call the proposal unworkable and destabilizing. The development of weapons that could destroy the very satellites used to monitor atomic testing around the world would defeat a system of checks and balances that Bethe claimed had been effective for decades.

Bethe has been described as logical and methodical in his approach to problems, whether in physics or in everyday life. A tall, heavyset man with thinning hair, craggy features, and a legendary appetite, Bethe has enjoyed some mountain climbing and skiing, but perhaps the most profound plea-sures came from his intellectual work on the stuff of matter and his insights into the very working of the stars.

Summary
   Hans Bethe's grasp of the range of theoretical physics was perhaps as great as that of anyone in history. His ability to select a problem and work out a solution, coolly and pragmatically, resonated with the American tradition of innovation and practical success. Bethe acknowledged the necessity of mili-tary weapons development, but he called on scientists to educate the public on the consequences of certain programs (though without breaking security). Reflecting the spirit of a realist, Bethe believed that the boycotting of weap-ons research was futile; rather, he advocated scientific involvement in such research. The scientific community might aid in designing wise policies, though there must be cooperation with national decisions. Bethe cham-pioned the prudent use of atomic energy, though he deplored nuclear arms proliferation. As an influential arms-control advocate, he believed that the mutual superpower reduction of nuclear warheads from tens of thousands down to around two thousand would serve to maintain nuclear deterrence but at a safer level. In sum, the United States should strive for arms control through negotiated agreements rather than the promulgation of newer, more dangerous "protective" technologies.
   For Bethe, the sheer joy of scientific discovery was tempered with the harsh realities of a world teeming with nuclear weapons. His contributions to the understanding of how stars produce their energy and his more controver-sial advocacy of atomic energy enriched and challenged the world.

Bibliography
Bergman, Elihu, Hans A. Bethe, and Robert E. Marshak, eds. *American Energy Choices Before the Year 2000*. Lexington, Mass.: Lexington Books, 1978. Contains a series of essays, two by Bethe, originally presented at an energy conference at the City University of New York Graduate Center in New York City January 13-14, 1978. Joint chairmen were Robert Marshak, president of the City College of New York, and Bethe. Bethe's first essay presents a brief overview of alternative energy sources, including nuclear; the second is a somewhat technical discussion of fusion energy and its economies.
Bernstein, Jeremy. *Hans Bethe: Prophet of Energy*. New York: Basic Books, 1980. Originally a series of articles for *The New Yorker*, this popular biog-raphy is based on a series of interviews with Bethe; a large section is given over to Bethe's views on energy resources for the twenty-first century.

Bernstein attempts a semipopular explanation of the carbon cycle and quantum mechanics. Useful but was not meant as a definitive biography.

Bethe, Hans A. "Countermeasures to ABM Systems." In *ABM: An Evaluation of the Decision to Deploy an Antiballistic Missile System*, edited by Abram Chayes and Jerome B. Wiesner, 130-143. New York: Harper and Row, 1969. A critique of the proposed antiballistic-missile system under presidents Lyndon B. Johnson and Richard M. Nixon; Bethe's contribution is an expanded reprint of his article on ABM's (coauthored with Richard Garwin) that appeared in the March, 1968, issue of *Scientific American*. In a somewhat technical discussion, Bethe concludes that the ABM is a destabilizing factor and would serve only to increase the race to produce a penetration device for any ABM shield. Though dated, it shows Bethe's logical and systematic thinking.

_____ . "Face-Off on Nuclear Defense." *Technology Review* 87 (April, 1984): 38-39. Excerpts from a debate between Bethe and Teller on President Reagan's Star Wars proposal, held at the Kennedy School of Government at Harvard in November of 1983. Bethe calls for small-scale research rather than a vastly expensive weapons program. Useful for the interplay between rival schools of thought represented by Bethe and Teller.

_____ . "The Technological Imperative." *Bulletin of the Atomic Scientists* 41 (August, 1985): 34-36. Bethe, chairman of the magazine's board of sponsors for several years, evaluates modern technological developments in weapons research and concludes that, on balance, they have produced greater world instability. The temptation of ever-new technology need not be what drives American strategic policy.

Marshak, Robert E., ed. *Perspectives in Modern Physics: Essays in Honor of Hans A. Bethe on the Occasion of His Sixtieth Birthday, July 1966*. New York: Interscience Publishers, 1966. The forty-one essays in this volume contain highly technical articles on quantum mechanics, astrophysics, and nuclear science, but there are also a number of valuable reminiscences (from Oppenheimer and others), as well as a six-page bibliography of Bethe's works.

Dan Barnett

NICHOLAS BIDDLE

Born: January 8, 1786; Philadelphia, Pennsylvania
Died: February 27, 1844; Philadelphia, Pennsylvania
Areas of Achievement: Finance and banking
Contribution: Combining superb managerial skills and a keen understanding
of finance and banking, Biddle developed the Bank of the United States
into a prototype of the modern central banking system.

Early Life
Nicholas Biddle, born January 8, 1786, in Philadelphia, Pennsylvania, was
descended from one of the most distinguished families in Pennsylvania. His
father, Charles Biddle, was a successful merchant and had become vice president of the Supreme Executive Council of Pennsylvania. His mother, Hannah Shepard Biddle, was the daughter of a North Carolina merchant.
Nicholas was extremely precocious and was admitted at the age of ten to the
University of Pennsylvania. His parents transferred him before he was graduated, and he was entered in Princeton as a sophomore at the age of thirteen.
Nicholas was graduated in September, 1801, at the age of fifteen, as the
valedictorian.

Biddle began the study of law, but his personal interests seemed to mark
him for a literary career. He contributed two pieces to Joseph Dennie's literary magazine, *The Port Folio*, which showed considerable talent. Then, in
the fall of 1804, Biddle went with General John Armstrong, Jr., who had
been appointed minister to France, as his secretary. He assisted ably in the
duties of handling claims authorized in the Louisiana Purchase, gaining valuable insights into the problems and techniques of international finance. After
a year, he departed on a grand tour of Europe, including a visit to Greece.
He served briefly as secretary for James Monroe in London, and he finally
returned to the United States in September, 1807.

Biddle had reached his adult height of five feet, seven inches. He had a
handsome oval face, a high forehead, and chestnut eyes and hair. He had a
serious and dignified demeanor and an aristocratic bearing. He decided to
practice law, but he also found time to make contributions to Dennie's *The
Port Folio*. In 1810, he was persuaded by William Clark to edit the journals
of the Lewis and Clark Expedition. Biddle did most of the work, but the
journals were eventually published under another editor's name.

In October, 1810, he was elected to the Pennsylvania legislature. The high-
light of this service was an eloquent defense of the first Bank of the United
States. He displayed a knowledge of finance that impressed all listeners.
Biddle declined renomination. One reason was that he had met and later mar-
ried Jane Craig, whose father's estate was one of the largest in Philadelphia.
During the War of 1812, he returned to the Pennsylvania legislature and

vigorously supported the war effort, parting company with his fellow Federalists.

Secure financially, Biddle spent the next few years managing his country estate, "Andalusia," and engaging in civic and philanthropic activities. In 1818, he was defeated in a race for Congress, in part because his republicanism was still suspect and because of internal splits in Pennsylvania. President Monroe, although a good friend, hesitated to appoint Biddle to office. When mismanagement occurred in the operation of the second Bank of the United States, however, and the president of the bank, William Jones, was removed early in 1819, Biddle was one of the directors chosen by the government. For the next twenty years, his life revolved around the bank.

Life's Work

Langdon Cheves of South Carolina, who replaced Jones as president of the bank, followed a policy of retrenchment. "The bank was saved," as they said in the Southwestern part of the United States, "but the people were ruined." When Cheves resigned in 1822, Biddle was chosen as the bank's third president. The position he assumed was one of the most important in the United States. The bank was in sound financial condition, but Cheves's policies had alienated many. Biddle gradually dropped many of the restrictions imposed upon the operations of the branch banks. Enlargement of the credit operations stimulated the economy, which was still suffering from the effects of the Panic of 1819. He also increased the profits of the bank and gradually gained complete control over its operations.

From his splendid Greek Revival building on Chestnut Street in Philadelphia, Biddle controlled the operations of eventually twenty-nine branches, from New Hampshire to New Orleans. He used the power of the bank to expand and contract the credit and money supply according to the fluctuations in business activity. He was a superb administrator: The result was a sound banking system and a stable currency that greatly benefited the country.

Biddle's success won for him many friends and growing support for the bank. He sought to avoid involving the bank in politics and tried to remain neutral in the presidential race between President John Quincy Adams and Andrew Jackson in 1828. Biddle was well aware that there were still many powerful people who were hostile toward the bank, and that one was Jackson himself.

After Jackson's election, some members of his party attempted to gain control of the bank. Allegations were made that some branches had exercised an improper influence in the past election by refusing loans to Jacksonians. Biddle was overly sensitive about bank operations. He tended to be defensive rather than to investigate fully charges of mismanagement. Nor did Biddle at first appreciate the depth of President Jackson's hostility to the

Bank of the United States. Jackson had a prejudice against all banks based on little more than economic ignorance and some bad personal experiences with bank notes. A large number of voters also believed that the bank, with one-fifth of the country's loans and bank notes in circulation, and one-third of the total bank deposits and specie (gold and silver), had too much money and power for the safety of the Republic. The bank was further opposed by a group who believed that it unfairly restricted loans and denied them economic opportunities, and by yet another group of state bankers and their stockholders who resented the size, wealth, and controlling influence of the bank. Despite this opposition, a substantial majority of the American people supported the bank and favored its recharter.

Jackson's attitude and the hostility of many of the advisers around him toward the bank made Biddle uncertain about the prospect of rechartering the bank. Despite conflicting advice, he chose to ask for the rechartering in 1832, four years early, basically because it was an election year and Biddle believed that Jackson would not oppose the bank for fear of losing popularity.

The recharter bill passed both houses in the summer of 1832 by comfortable margins. Biddle had miscalculated: Jackson was not easily intimidated. He responded with a veto and denounced the Bank of the United States as a monopoly, under too much foreign influence, and unconstitutional, and he asserted that it was an institution of the rich and powerful. The message was blatantly misleading, but it was undeniably a powerful and cleverly written polemic, well calculated to appeal to the prejudices of the mass of American people. Despite the goodwill that Biddle had built up for the bank, Jackson successfully changed the debate from the utility of the bank to whether it was a bastion of aristocratic privilege. He portrayed himself as saving the Republic from the "monster."

Although his victory was more a personal triumph than approval of his stand against the bank, Jackson resolved to destroy the bank. He directed the removal of government deposits, which would be placed in state banks, dubbed "pet banks" by opponents. Biddle responded by curtailing loans. While this action may have been necessary to protect the bank from a reduction of funds (and almost ten million dollars in government deposits were withdrawn), the effect of this restriction on credit staggered commercial and manufacturing interests. Business failures and bankruptcies multiplied, and wages and prices declined. Biddle was not entirely to blame; in fact, he thought that it would ultimately force Jackson to restore the deposits. Neither man was willing to budge. Public opinion, initially anti-Jackson, slowly turned against Biddle. Jackson was unrelenting. He administered a final blow to the Bank of the United States, declaring that the government would no longer accept branch drafts for the payment of taxes.

With the death of the bank imminent, in 1836 Biddle secured a charter from the Pennsylvania legislature to operate as a state bank. There was no longer a central bank to keep the state banks in order by calling upon them for specie or refusing to receive their bills. Moreover, the American economy was overheating as a result of speculation in large measure stimulated by government deposits in pet banks, which then numbered approximately ninety. The country was inundated with paper money. The frenzy of speculation was brought to an abrupt end by the Panic of 1837. The United States Bank (as it had become known) was forced in May, 1837, to suspend payment of specie for the redemption of notes, as did all other banks in the country. Biddle was still the most prominent banker in the country, and he played an important role in trying to shore up the nation's banking system and restore specie payments. Biddle also intervened massively in the cotton market exchange, thus preventing the collapse of that important part of the American economy. He also turned a profit for his bank.

Resumption of specie payments began again in August, 1838. The economy seemed to be recovering, and Biddle, in March, 1839, intending to devoted his remaining years to leisure, resigned. In the summer of 1839, however, largely because of the operations of the Bank of England, the United States and the remainder of the world was plunged again into depression. Biddle may have had the grim satisfaction of knowing that the lack of a national bank only made the situation worse, but it was small consolation, since it was also the source of the bank's and Biddle's ruin. Falling cotton prices and mismanagement by the bank's directors led to a second suspension of specie payments in October, 1839. The bank continued to operate, but its situation grew steadily worse, and the bank closed its doors forever in February, 1841.

Biddle's personal fortune, as well as the bank's, collapsed. In his last years, he was harassed by law suits, and at one point in 1842, he was arrested on charges of criminal conspiracy, but he was exonerated. Other litigations followed and were only brought to an end by his death on February 27, 1844, from complications arising from bronchitis accompanied by dropsy.

Summary

Despite his failures, Biddle was an imposing figure in American history. He had the qualities of a statesman who saw the potential of the American economy and formulated the means for realizing it. He wanted to establish American prosperity and to make the country stronger and more secure. His views were guided by a considerable intelligence, but by inclination he displayed more the traits of the idealist and the romantic than the hardheaded, pragmatic businessman. He showed a preference more for what ought to be than the situation as it was. His naïveté, even arrogance, that reason and truth would prevail in his battle with Jackson proved disastrous for the bank.

Biddle was a brilliant administrator who maintained complete control over the Bank of the United States; yet he also gave an aristocratic tone to the bank and lent credibility to the charge of its having excessive power. Because he saw the value of the bank to the nation's economy, he believed that all men of reason must see it as well. Jackson, he assumed, could not possibly destroy an institution that was in the best interest of the country. Even at the end, his actions were still guided by a larger view of the good of the country rather than the practicalities of sound business.

Perhaps, in retrospect, the country needed the *laissez-faire* economics that dominated the United States for the next three quarters of a century. The exuberant economic growth, however, was characterized by wild speculation and the persistence of monetary evils. The Bank of the United States offered a more "managed" economic growth and a more stable currency, but it might have dampened the enterprising spirit of American business. When the abuses of the "robber barons" brought on a reform movement in the early twentieth century, one reform was to reestablish a central banking system very similar to Biddle's bank.

Bibliography

Catterall, Ralph C. H. *The Second Bank of the United States*. Chicago: University of Chicago Press, 1903. Although dated both in content and interpretation, this classic work is still the most comprehensive study of the bank.

Govan, Thomas Payne. *Nicholas Biddle: Nationalist and Public Banker, 1786-1844.* Chicago: University of Chicago Press, 1959. The only satisfactory biography of Biddle. The author is partial to his subject and presents a sensitive portrayal of Biddle's role in running the bank. The book is well researched and well written.

Hammond, Bray. *Banks and Politics in America from the Revolution to the Civil War*. Princeton, N.J.: Princeton University Press, 1957. A Pulitzer Prize–winning book that is not simply about banking. Hammond pays particular attention to Biddle and gives a fair appraisal of him. Hammond's interpretation of the Bank War, while controversial, broke new ground.

McFaul, John M. *The Politics of Jacksonian Finance*. Ithaca, N.Y.: Cornell University Press, 1972. A good general study of the issues involved in the Bank War. The positions of probank and antibank forces are carefully analyzed.

Remini, Robert V. *Andrew Jackson and the Bank War*. New York: W. W. Norton and Co., 1968. A good, short introduction to the Bank War. Remini is partial to Jackson, but his account is generally a fair, succinct exposition of the issues.

Temin, Peter. *The Jacksonian Economy*. New York: W. W. Norton and Co., 1969. Temin presents a provocative, revisionary interpretation of the sources of the Panic of 1837. While his analysis is not entirely convincing, he adds a new dimension to the study of the Bank War.

Wilburn, Jean Alexander. *Biddle's Bank: The Crucial Years*. New York: Columbia University Press, 1967. Wilburn refutes the Jacksonian allegation of the unpopularity of the bank. She shows the support for the bank's services from the people, their congressional representatives, and many local bankers.

C. Edward Skeen

ALBERT BIERSTADT

Born: January 7, 1830; Solingen, Germany
Died: February 18, 1902; New York, New York
Area of Achievement: Art
Contribution: Using an exaggerated, romantic style, Bierstadt painted giant landscapes of spectacular Western vistas that helped to shape the myth of the American West, establish the Rocky Mountain School of art, and interest Easterners in preservation of Western scenic areas as national parks.

Early Life

Albert Bierstadt was born in 1830 at Solingen, Germany, near the city of Düsseldorf, which was a mecca for émigré American artists. He migrated to the United States with his parents at the age of two and was reared amid the maritime atmosphere in the whaling town of New Bedford, Massachusetts. He exhibited his first painting in Boston at the age of twenty-one but returned to Europe for further training at Düsseldorf and in Rome. On the Continent, he was attracted to pastoral scenes, sketching castles along the Rhine and taking hiking expeditions among the Alps. Bierstadt returned to the United States in 1857 and painted in New England. The following year the bearded, sharp-featured artist seized the opportunity to see the trans-Mississippi regions for the first time, when he joined Colonel Frederick W. Lander on a survey party that set out for the West from St. Louis. This expedition literally opened new vistas for Bierstadt and shaped the rest of his artistic career, establishing his place in the history of both the American West and American art.

The explorer, scientist, and artist traveled hand in hand and contributed jointly to the opening of the trans-Mississippi West and in the shaping of its image in the national consciousness. Prior to the exploration of the region, most American painters had slavishly imitated the themes and styles of their European counterparts and mentors. It was almost inevitable, however, that the rising tide of nationalism would find artistic expression, as the United States sought to establish its own and unique cultural identity. Two traditions, the scientific and the artistic, were eventually conjoined in that search.

The artistic tradition established its roots in the eastern part of the country during the 1820's and 1830's as several artists, including Thomas Cole and Asher B. Durand, honed the vision and produced the work that established the Hudson River School. They grappled with the balance between civilization and wilderness and focused upon the vistas of the Hudson River, the White Mountains, Niagara Falls, and other northeastern features as expressions of truth, beauty, and eternal laws and values. Their appreciation of and emphasis upon landscape and nature would shape the perceptions of later artists, including Bierstadt, who spent time at the emerging artists' colony at

North Conway, New Hampshire, on the Saco River in the White Mountain region.

In the meantime, following the historic expedition of Meriwether Lewis and William Clark, explorers and scientists were beginning to penetrate the great unknown of the trans-Mississippi West. Their expeditions often enlisted artists who traveled along and sketched the plants, animals, people, and lands they encountered both for artistic purposes and to document visually the information acquired. They traveled and worked under primitive conditions foreign to the overwhelming majority of their artistic colleagues past and present, and they were virtually to a man overwhelmed and deeply impressed by what they saw and recorded.

First were two Philadelphians, Samuel Seymour and Titian Ramsay Peale, who accompanied the Stephen Long expedition to the Rockies in 1820. They were soon followed by George Catlin, who made several trips up the Missouri River in the 1830's and produced pictorial records of the Plains Indians prior to extensive contact with white civilization. Later came the Swiss artist Karl Bodmer, who produced extremely accurate depictions of the Indians and painted landscapes of the American interior as well. In the late 1830's, Baltimore artist Alfred Jacob Miller traveled the Oregon Trail and depicted the world of the mountain man, and within a few more years John James Audubon was at work painting the animals along the Missouri River. These and other artists created the scientific-artistic tradition which was part of Albert Bierstadt's milieu.

Life's Work

After his return from Europe, Bierstadt learned of Colonel Frederick W. Lander's proposed expedition to prepare a survey for a railroad route from the Mississippi River, across the north fork of the Platte, through Nebraska Territory, across South Pass, and connecting with San Francisco and Puget Sound. Bierstadt and photographer F. S. Frost joined the party and in 1858-1859 journeyed as far as the Wasatch range on the western slope of the Rockies. They then returned on their own, traveling through the Wind River range and the land of the Shoshone, producing sketches and photographic images of the scenery and people they encountered. Bierstadt was thus the first artist to utilize photography to supplement his own sketches and watercolors while on a journey of Western exploration. Bierstadt and Frost paid their own way and none of their work from this expedition survives, but the artist had been captivated by what he had seen.

Upon returning to the East, Bierstadt relocated his studio from New Bedford to New York City, where in 1860 the first of his paintings went on public display. Among them was *The Base of the Rocky Mountains, Laramie Peak*, which measured some four and a half by nine feet. This canvas was prototypical of the Bierstadt style, which the public enthusiastically applauded. It was characterized by a seeming realism, which in fact presented a romanticized and even falsified depiction of a Western scene on a grandiose scale. It reflected both the romanticization of nature and the cultural nationalism which were to be representative of the Rocky Mountain School.

Bierstadt was soon getting higher prices in Europe for his paintings than any other American artist had ever received, and with his new wealth he built a large house on the Hudson River at Irvington and a second studio in San Francisco, which served as a base for further excursions into the Western regions. He traveled through the Colorado Rockies, the Great Salt Lake region, the Pacific Northwest, and in 1863 into California's Yosemite and Hetch Hetchy valleys, sketching the vistas which became the subjects for some of his most commercially successful paintings. A series of paintings of grandiose dimension, produced in the mid-1860's, sold for the highest sums ever earned by an American artist. Featuring towering mountains, shimmering waters, and dark forests, these canvases carried the romantic concepts of nature to their apex of grandeur. While some critics scoffed, the public loved the huge size and detail of the Bierstadt canvases.

The giant paintings were done in Bierstadt's studio, based on his field sketches, photographs, stereoscopic views, and watercolors. The artist rearranged the features, gave names to nonexistent locales, and generally falsified his portrayals, even as the public praised his "realism." It is not accidental that the growing interest of the American people in the spectacular land features of the West and their preservation coincided chronologically with the popularity of Bierstadt and Thomas Moran, whose paintings of Yellowstone would contribute to the creation of the national park in 1872.

Ironically, at the height of Bierstadt's popularity two trends were developing which would relegate his large canvases to relative obscurity and general critical disdain by the turn of the century. First, with the rise of the Impressionist style in Europe, realistic painters of the Romantic school fell out of fashion. Second, those who were interested in literal depictions of the West could now examine the striking photographs of William Henry Jackson and others who were elevating photography to the status of an art form.

Bierstadt continued to paint, and his elevated reputation secured large commissions, as in the late 1870's, when he received fifteen thousand dollars from the Earl of Dunraven to paint a large landscape of Estes Park, Colorado, and Long's Peak. Bierstadt's sales and commissions steadily diminished, however, even as his critical reputation continued to decline. By the time he died in 1902, fashion and popularity had passed him by.

Summary

Although not considered a great artist by most critics, Albert Bierstadt remains a major figure in the history of both American art and the trans-Mississippi West. A founder of the Rocky Mountain School, Bierstadt's giant landscapes of the American West—its mountains, forests, waterfalls, and spectacular landforms—brought romantic appreciation of nature to a new artistic peak in nineteenth century America. Although he took numerous liberties with fact in his larger works, the general public regarded Bierstadt's paintings as quite realistic, and he thus helped to generate the mythic perception of the American West and its landscapes that contributed to the movement for preservation of spectacular landforms in national parks. Ironically, although not as well-known as his large canvases, Bierstadt's smaller pieces and sketches, done during or immediately following journeys in the field, have retained a much higher critical standing. Bierstadt's works are found in major collections across the United States and have enjoyed constant popularity among those interested in the West and its history.

Bibliography

Hassrick, Peter. *The Way West: Art of Frontier America*. New York: Harry N. Abrams, 1977. A profusely illustrated introduction to the work of major artists of the nineteenth century West, including Bierstadt.

Hendricks, Gordon. *Albert Bierstadt: Painter of the American West*. New York: Harry N. Abrams, 1974. The standard biography. Makes extensive use of Bierstadt's letters. Of the 428 illustrations, sixty-three are in color. Includes a catalog of Bierstadt's paintings and a bibliography.

Hine, Robert V. *The American West: An Interpretive History*. Boston: Little, Brown and Co., 1973. An excellent survey of Western history, with a first-rate chapter, "The Image of the West in Art."

Huth, Hans. *Nature and the American: Three Centuries of Changing Attitudes*. Berkeley: University of California Press, 1957. Evaluates the developments and factors which shaped the conservation movement in the United States. The contributions of artists, including Bierstadt, are an important part of the story.

McCracken, Harold. *Portrait of the Old West*. New York: McGraw-Hill Book Co., 1952. A scholarly account with material on Bierstadt's early career.

Nash, Roderick. *Wilderness and the American Mind*. 3d ed. New Haven, Conn.: Yale University Press, 1982. While Bierstadt is mentioned only in passing, this is the standard work on the evolution of American attitudes toward wilderness.

Runte, Alfred. *National Parks: The American Experience*. Lincoln: University of Nebraska Press, 1979. Assesses Bierstadt's importance as part of a discussion of cultural nationalism as a significant factor in the establishment of the national parks.

James E. Fickle

GEORGE CALEB BINGHAM

Born: March 20, 1811; Augusta County, Virginia
Died: July 7, 1879; Kansas City, Missouri
Area of Achievement: Art
Contribution: Bingham was the first American artist to record life on the mid-nineteenth century frontier in paintings of sensitive social commentary and high aesthetic quality.

Early Life

Known throughout his career as "the Missouri Artist," Bingham was, in fact, born into a long-established Southern family. Henry Vest Bingham, his father, whose ancestors probably came from England in the latter half of the seventeenth century, married Mary Amend, of German and French Huguenot descent, and they started their married life farming tobacco in Virginia. George, born on the farm, which was just west of Charlottesville, Virginia, was one of eight children. In 1819, Bingham's father got into financial difficulties, lost his business, and went west with his family to Franklin, Missouri. In 1820, he opened an inn and dealt in tobacco as a sideline. On his death in 1823, the family moved to a farm outside town, where Mrs. Bingham ran a small school.

There is some biographical evidence that Bingham was interested in drawing, but there is no proof that he ever had any formal training. Apprenticed to a cabinetmaker at sixteen, he may have worked as such, and perhaps as a sign painter, and there is some suggestion that he planned to study law. In 1833, he was a professional portrait painter. His early work is awkward and somewhat primitive, and seems to indicate that he was self-taught. Nevertheless, he was able to make a living at it, moving around the Columbia, Missouri, area, and in 1836, he was sufficiently confident to offer his services in St. Louis. In that year, he married Sarah Elizabeth Hutchinson of Boonville.

In the late spring of 1838, he went to Philadelphia, evidently to study. There is no record of him entering any art school, but he did buy a collection of old master engravings and some antique sculpture casts, both of which were commonly used for art instruction at the time. The city itself was rich in examples of international art, and Bingham must have seen some of it. He may have gone on to New York also, since a painting of his, one of his first genre pieces, *Western Boatmen Ashore*, was shown at the Apollo Gallery in New York in the autumn.

In 1840, he exhibited six paintings at the National Academy of Design in New York. By that time he was technically much more accomplished; already evident in these works is the flair for genre subjects, simple incidents of everyday life, which was to become his distinctive mark as an artist. He also decided to move to Washington, D.C., ambitious to try his skills painting federal politicians. He spent four years, off and on, in the capital, during which he painted portraits of important figures including John Quincy Adams and Daniel Webster. By this time, he was a painter of some modest reputation, but he had not produced any works of serious moment. Looking at his *Self-Portrait of the Artist*, which he had painted a few years earlier, it would be hard to guess that this square-jawed young man with the wide brow and the slight curl in his forelock, rather tentatively painted, would suddenly in the mid-1840's produce paintings of considerable importance.

Life's Work

It is, in the main, the painting which Bingham did roughly in the ten years between 1845 and 1855 that has given him his reputation as one of America's foremost artists. After that time, for several reasons, the quality of his art fell back into competent professionalism, with occasional paintings reminding the art world of his heights in what is called his "great genre period." During this period, he continued to paint portraits, but his best work was in studies of simple life in Missouri, with special emphasis placed upon the world of the flatboatmen plying their hard trade on the Missouri River. He had antici-pated the theme in his *Western Boatmen Ashore* in the late 1830's, and in the 1840's he found a market for the theme, rather surprisingly in New York.

The celebration of the simple life of the American plainsman, trapper, and boatman had already been prepared for in literature in the writing of Wash-ington Irving, James Fenimore Cooper, John Greenleaf Whittier, and Henry Wadsworth Longfellow. Bingham, in a sense, was following the Eastern painter William Sidney Mount in putting that growing admiration for the muscle and sweat of American frontier life into pictorial terms, but in his own way.

The American Art-Union in New York City was dedicated to supporting American artists through purchase, sale, and reproduction of their paintings, and in a seven-year period it purchased twenty paintings by Bingham, all of them examples of his genre themes.

Fur Traders Descending the Missouri was one of the first paintings so pur-chased, and it stunningly reveals the power of Bingham as a painter, which had never been revealed in his portrait work. It is, at one and the same time, his most powerful painting and the most representative of his studies of those singular men who, in working the river, seem to exemplify an admirable truth about American life. Variations on the theme were to occupy Bingham through the next ten years, and occasionally the theme was to catch the popular imagination in ways which Bingham could hardly have imagined.

If *Fur Traders Descending the Missouri* has a focused intensity that re-minds viewers of Le Nain and slightly awes on sight, Bingham also had the ability to use the theme charmingly. *The Jolly Flatboatmen*, showing its sim-ple subjects in a moment of dance and song, was engraved by the Art-Union and eighteen thousand copies were sent out to American homes. Part of the secret lay, undoubtedly, in Bingham's fastidious choice of how he saw the humble boatmen. He eschewed the real vulgarity of their lives, the hard toil, the danger, for gentle, often humorous scenes of cardplaying or quiet moments of rest. He did not patronize them, but he did not tell all the story. The paintings of lively, unsentimental masculinity framed by the beauty of the western riverscapes brought out the best in Bingham, both as an artist and as a recorder of an aspect of American frontier life.

In the early 1850's, he carried the taste for paintings of Missouri life a step further in his "Election" series. These were quite as popular as his studies of the working Westerners, and he spent considerable time not only in painting them but also in promoting the sales of the originals and of engravings of the same. As in his first series, he avoided adverse comment. William Hogarth's famous election works may be seen as an influence, but while Hogarth was intent on satire, Bingham never was. Although the characters in these technically complicated paintings of speech-making, polling, and post-voting celebration may sometimes be less than proper, they are never savaged. A cheerful, sensitive appreciation of the democratic process in action, however makeshift it might be in the rural fastness of Missouri, was the dominant tone in these works, which brought Bingham praise for his appreciation of the American way of choosing their legislators.

However modest the topics of this period were, Bingham's use of them was not unsophisticated. He displayed a strong sense of composition, a considerable talent for marshaling large groups of people, and a use of light and shadow which complemented the mood succinctly. His drawing was confident, and his settings appropriate and sometimes charming. He was no longer merely a journeyman painter.

Despite the support of the Art-Union, he was never as popular in the East as he was out West. There was constant sniping at his rude subjects and at his use of color. He quarreled with the Art-Union administrators over criticism of his work printed in their house journal and became dissatisfied with the prices they paid him for his paintings.

By the mid-1850's, Bingham, dissatisfied with his career, was determined to move on to more important work. He had painted a Daniel Boone subject a few years earlier, and he saw the historical painting as the kind of theme that he wanted to pursue. He hoped to convince Washington of the appropriateness of having a Boone painting, of major proportions, commissioned for the Capitol. A step in that direction came in the form of a commission from the state of Missouri to provide paintings of George Washington and Thomas Jefferson, and in 1856, Bingham went to Europe to work on those paintings. He visited Paris but settled in Düsseldorf, then a center for painters and sculptors, and he completed his Washington and Jefferson there. Unfortunately, in the eyes of some critics, Düsseldorf, with its emphasis on high technical polish in painting, influenced Bingham adversely, and there is some informed opinion which sees a decline in the quality of his work dating from the Düsseldorf experience.

Bingham returned to Missouri with his commissions and was asked to provide two further paintings, one of Henry Clay and one of Andrew Jackson. Yet the hoped-for major commission from Washington did not come, and he kept busy doing portraits until the Civil War broke out. Always interested and sometimes involved in politics as a Whig (Republican) supporter, he served from 1862 until 1865 as the state treasurer, painting as time permitted. Although an active supporter of the war against the South, he split with the party after the war over the excessive zeal with which Republicans conducted themselves; his painting *Order 11*, not a particularly good example of his talents, got him into a continuing battle, since it illustrated the arrogance of the military during the war. It was one of the few occasions on which he used his talent to make political comment, and it did him little good.

He continued to paint portraits, landscapes (which had always been least interesting to him), and genre topics, and to take a hand in Missouri politics. There was some desultory talk at one time of standing for governor, and he served as adjutant general in the 1870's. In 1877, the University of Missouri made him its first professor of art, a post which seems to have been largely honorary; he had a studio on the campus but spent little time there. When he died in 1879, he was almost totally forgotten in the East but honored in Missouri as the state's own painter, the "Missouri Artist."

Summary

Despite the length of his career, the amount of work produced, the constant comings and goings between Missouri and the East, and the sales of his engravings and paintings, Bingham's reputation in the main was confined principally to the Midwest, and he was patronized as a competent portraitist and a sometime regional genre artist.

After his death he remained relatively unknown until 1917, when an article in *Art World* suggested that he was more than a simple hack. The first important confirmation of that idea came in 1933, when the Metropolitan Museum of Art purchased *Fur Traders Descending the Missouri*. In 1934, the City Art Museum in St. Louis mounted the first major show of his works, and in 1935, the Museum of Modern Art in New York exhibited his work.

Since then his reputation has been secure, but it is based, in the main, not upon his entire life's work as a painter but on the output of that ten-year period between 1845 and 1855 when he was principally concerned with recording the working, social, and political lives of the native Missourians. He is recognized as the first master painter of the American West, and his political paintings are a vivid record of the brash, lively vitality of a world which he knew so well—not only as an artist but also as a participant.

His reputation as a painter of serious quality, however, is centered on those brilliantly evocative paintings of trappers, flatboatmen, river people, and other simple citizens of the West, whom he sees with a stunningly poetic clarity that transcends the particularity of detail which he was so determined to record. Some critics have seen in this aesthetic aura touches of an American "luminism," that quality which gives great paintings a universal ideality and connection with the "oneness" of all things. In those paintings, the truth of Bingham's record of simple life goes beyond its factuality.

Bibliography
Baigell, Matthew. *A History of American Painting*. New York: Praeger Publishers, 1971. This book is theoretically less adventurous than the Novak work, but it does, in a genial way, put Bingham into the American tradition, and that is where it is easiest to understand and appreciate him.
Bingham, George Caleb. *An Address to the Public, Vindicating a Work of Art Illustrative of the Federal Military Policy in Missouri During the Late Civil War*. Kansas City, Mo., 1871. Expresses Bingham's conviction that it is the duty of the artist to make political use of his gift.
_____. "Art, the Ideal of Art and the Utility of Art." In *Public Lectures Delivered in the Chapel of the University of the State of Missouri, Columbia, Missouri, by Members of the Faculty, 1878-79*, course 2, vol. 1, 311-324. Columbia, Mo.: Statesman Book and Job Print, 1879. One of Bingham's rare statements about art and the role of the artist.
Bloch, E. Maurice. *George Caleb Bingham*. 2 vols. Berkeley: University of California Press, 1967. The major study of Bingham's work. Excellent illustration. Very careful discussion of his major paintings.
Larkin, Lew. *Bingham, Fighting Artist: The Story of Missouri's Immortal Painter, Patriot, Soldier and Statesman*. St. Louis: State Publishing Co., 1955. The title of the book may seem a bit fulsome, but Bingham was much more than simply a painter, and something less than a statesman. This book tries to bring the multiple lives of the man into context.
McDermott, John Francis. *George Caleb Bingham: River Portraitist*. Norman: University of Oklahoma Press, 1959. The title of this full-scale critical biography is misleading. It does, in fact, cover Bingham's entire career, using specific paintings or groups of paintings as a critical focus in the chapters but filling out his career and life around them. Good illustrations.
Novak, Barbara. *American Painting of the Nineteenth Century: Realism, Idealism, and the American Experience*. New York: Praeger Publishers, 1969. This book is helpful in putting Bingham in the tradition of American painting in interesting ways. He has a chapter to himself, and his connections, implicit and explicit, to other painters are explored with much grace.

Charles H. Pullen

HUGO L. BLACK

Born: February 27, 1886; Harlan, Alabama
Died: September 25, 1971; Bethesda, Maryland
Area of Achievement: Law
Contribution: As a Justice of the Supreme Court, Black sought to define and
in some areas extend constitutional protection of civil liberties, while
delineating the prerogatives of government; for more than one-third of a
century, he propounded the absolute inviolability of the Constitution as the
basis of the nation's jurisprudence.

Early Life

The youngest of eight children, Hugo La Fayette Black was born in Harlan, Alabama, on February 27, 1886. His father, William L. Black, was a
country storekeeper who surrendered periodically to bouts of secret drinking; his mother, Martha Toland Black, from a well-bred family, was the village postmistress. From the age of six, the young Hugo attended trials at the
Clay County courthouse in Ashland. He was educated for a while at Ashland
Academy. He attended Birmingham Medical College for one year and, at the
age of eighteen, enrolled at the University of Alabama. By virtue of his
excellent academic record, Black was granted early admission to the law
school and was graduated with the university's LL.B. degree in 1906.

Black began his practice in Birmingham, where he pleaded labor cases and
damage suits. He served briefly as a judge on the city's police court; in 1914,
he was elected the county solicitor, or prosecutor. Increasingly, he came to
oppose, and sometimes took action against, the summary and forcible extrac-
tion of confessions from suspects. During World War I, Black enlisted in the
army and, although he was not called for combat duty, he was discharged as
a captain in the field artillery. Upon his return to civilian life, he resumed his
law practice in Alabama; in 1921, he married Josephine Foster, the daughter
of a Presbyterian minister, whose lovely dark features had attracted him.
During the next twelve years, they became the parents of two sons and one
daughter.

Black gave the impression of formidable tenacity and reserve. He was five
feet eight inches tall and wiry; his features were distinguished by his sharp,
hooked nose and piercing blue eyes. He spoke in a gentle, melodious drawl
that could be sharpened by interrogatory tones or softened with personal
warmth. He had a brisk, energetic gait and, for recreation, played a vigorous
game of tennis.

Life's Work

During his private practice, Black occasionally had taken cases of white clients against blacks; as his political ambitions grew, he joined a number of

civic organizations. In 1923, he made a decision that later seemed fraught with fateful implications: He became a member of the Ku Klux Klan. It may have been that for a time he was attracted by the Klan's populist appeal, or that he recognized its political strength; he spoke to several meetings of the Klan and then, less than two years later, withdrew abruptly and unceremoniously. Black emerged first into national political prominence in 1926, with a spirited campaign that won for him a seat in the United States Senate. During the early years of the Depression, Black sponsored legislation to promote public works programs and called for a national thirty-hour workweek. In 1932, he won reelection on a platform of broad support for the national Democratic Party and its presidential candidate, Franklin D. Roosevelt. Although he would not risk public disfavor on issues on which his home state was sensitive, such as a proposed antilynching law or the sensational Scottsboro rape cases, Black became nationally known for his chairmanship of major Senate investigations of public utilities and airmail contracts. Moreover, though he differed with the Roosevelt Administration on some economic proposals, he roundly condemned the Supreme Court's rulings against New Deal legislation. Black became an early and staunch proponent of the Administration's proposal that would allow the president to appoint additional justices to sit alongside those on the Court who had passed the age of seventy. Much as this measure divided even the Democratic Party, Black's standing in the Senate, and his broad agreement with the Administration on economic and judicial matters, were vital considerations when Roosevelt nominated him, in 1937, to succeed retiring Supreme Court Justice Willis Van Devanter. While Black was confirmed easily enough, questions about his Klan affiliation persisted and grew. In response to allegations in newspaper stories, the new justice delivered a brief and compelling statement, which reached millions of radio listeners, disavowing any connection with that organization since his resignation twelve years before.

Expectations that Black would be intellectually unsuited for the Court, or that he would act merely at the Administration's behest, were gradually shown to be unfounded. In spite of an education that was limited and exiguous when compared with those of other justices, Black was a fervent autodidact, and even during his years in Washington he had read widely in constitutional law, philosophy, American, British, and ancient history, and the social sciences. During his early years on the Court, Black evinced a basic support for the government on questions of antitrust and held with the Administration on controversial economic issues. Questions of civil liberties were enlivened when he wrote the Court's opinion in *Chambers v. Florida* (1940), which invalidated a criminal confession obtained during incommunicado confinement. In *Betts v. Brady* (1942), writing for himself and two colleagues, he contended that indigent defendants should not be convicted without the benefit of counsel. On the other hand, in *Korematsu v. United*

States (1944), he held for the Court that wartime circumstances justified the forcible resettlement of Japanese Americans.

Black frequently found with a minority in cases that heralded the onset of the Cold War. In several notable dissents he maintained that Communists and other radicals were entitled to the constitutional protection of free speech. In *Dennis v. United States* (1951), he argued in dissent that mere speech, albeit of an admitted Communist, could not be proscribed as inciteful or tending to overthrow the government. Elsewhere, Black opposed loyalty oaths or other limitations on the civil liberties of avowed Communists. In another celebrated dissent, *Beauharnais v. Illinois* (1952), he contended that the states could not abridge the freedom of speech by attempting to suppress white supremacist literature. On another front, in 1952, Black wrote the Court's opinion in ruling against President Harry S Truman's use of government force to curtail strikes in the steel industry. Trying times on the bench were made more difficult by the early and unexpected death of Black's wife in 1951. His outlook undoubtedly improved with his remarriage, to Elizabeth De Meritte, six years later.

After Earl Warren became Chief Justice, in 1953, the Court as a whole took a more expansive view of the civil liberties which Black had defended; other troubled issues also came before it. Justice Black held with the Court in *Brown v. Board of Education of Topeka* (1954), the landmark decision that struck down racial segregation in public schools. Black's own concern for freedom of expression was further stated in *Konigsberg v. State Bar of California* (1957), in which he held for the majority that political affiliations, such as possible membership in the Communist Party, did not constitute grounds for an applicant's exclusion from the practice of law. Black's objections to other limitations on the freedom of speech were reflected in his opinions in cases of alleged obscenity, such as a New York case of 1959, involving the film version of D. H. Lawrence's novel *Lady Chatterley's Lover* (1928). Black believed that the First Amendment afforded extensive protection against claims of libel, and he found with the majority in the celebrated case of *New York Times v. Sullivan* (1964); he also did not consider massive adverse publicity grounds for retrial in criminal cases, and thus he dissented when such a case, involving Dr. Sam Sheppard of Ohio, was brought before the Court in 1966.

Black was often regarded as a moving spirit in many of the Court's libertarian decisions, and, to nearly the same extent as Chief Justice Warren, his guidance was provided in controversial decisions. Black wrote for a majority on the Court when he found the sponsorship of prayer in public schools unconstitutional, in *Engel v. Vitale* (1962); in a matter of recurrent concern to him, the right of poor defendants to legal representation, he wrote the Court's opinion in *Gideon v. Wainwright* (1963). Nevertheless, though there and elsewhere Black upheld the rights of criminal defendants, he dissociated himself from other decisions thought to be part of a liberal trend on the Court. He did not believe that public demonstrations or sit-ins, whether to promote racial equality or for other purposes, were speech in the strict sense, and thus he differed from his colleagues in holding that they were not protected by the Constitution. In *Griswold v. Connecticut* (1965), he dissented from the Court's view that a right of privacy extended to married couples using contraceptives. Claims of increasing conservatism, or discomfiture with modern times, were bruited about, but Black persistently maintained that his constitutional faith was unchanged. His last official act on the Court was a separate opinion in the *New York Times v. United States*—or Pentagon Papers—case of 1971, in which he contended that the public had a right to know about the origins of a controversial war; the First Amendment precluded any exercise of prior restraint on the part of the government. For some time failing health had taken its toll, and at the age of eighty-five, Black suffered a sharp decline. On August 27, 1971, he was admitted to Bethesda Naval Hospital; on September 17, his resignation from the Court was formally tendered; on the next day, he suffered a stroke, from which he died on September 25, 1971.

Summary

Justice Black served under five chief justices; during his tenure on the bench, vital questions of the New Deal, the Cold War, and the Civil Rights movement came before the Court. Throughout this period, Black formulated and repeatedly maintained his adherence to a specific and distinct view of constitutional law. In his many opinions, presented for the most part in a clear, direct, unvarnished style, Black held that a literal reading of the Constitution bound the nation's highest court to uphold civil liberties even, as arose with claims of libel and obscenity, in unusual and improbable contexts. On the other hand, Black increasingly objected to any legislative function on the part of the Court and rejected any implied doctrines that were not clearly stated in the Constitution itself. From this standpoint, it is useful to note Black's long-standing debate with Justice Felix Frankfurter, who referred to other criteria, such as the balancing of rights and obligations, or the nation's conscience, in deciding difficult cases. Black's libertarian strain led him often to side with Justices Frank Murphy and, particularly, with William O. Douglas; yet he maintained that beyond those rights clearly granted in the Constitution there were limitations, and toward the end of his term Black found the views of Chief Justice Warren Burger congenial.

It is a measure of Black's importance in American jurisprudence that, though many of the cases and concerns with which he dealt have receded from public attention, the views he espoused still command respect. There will continue to be some dispute as to whether the resolution of modern dilemmas actually is implicitly stated in the Constitution. Some of Black's opinions decidedly would find more present-day adherents than others; yet his simple but forthright reading of the Constitution must still be reckoned an important force in modern legal thought.

Bibliography
Ball, Howard. *The Vision and the Dream of Justice Hugo L. Black: An Examination of a Judicial Philosophy*. University: University of Alabama Press, 1975. Topical examination of Black's opinions by an admiring scholar; social relations and the economy are dealt with as well as the justice's better-known positions on civil liberties. Argues that there is a broad consistency to Black's opinions, both in various areas of the law and over the thirty-four years he was on the Court.
Black, Hugo, Jr. *My Father: A Remembrance*. New York: Random House, 1975. Breezy, offhand account of Justice Black's life by his son. The most useful parts of this work concern the elder Black's personal and professional relations with others on the Court, notably Felix Frankfurter and William O. Douglas. The younger Black also depicts vividly the hostility and bitterness with which the Court's decisions on racial issues were received in his father's native state.
Black, Hugo L. *A Constitutional Faith*. New York: Alfred A. Knopf, 1969. Succinct statement of Black's judicial philosophy, taken from lectures at Columbia University. His views on the states' obligations under the Bill of Rights and the Fourteenth Amendment, and his determination to uphold the First Amendment in applicable cases, are set forth in a clear, trenchant fashion.
Black, Hugo L., and Elizabeth S. Black. *Mr. Justice and Mrs. Black*. New York: Random House, 1986. This book comprises the fragmentary memoirs of Justice Black, which discuss his life and career until 1921, an interstitial explanatory passage, and the diaries of Elizabeth Black from 1964 until Hugo's death in 1971. Mrs. Black's remarks show much about the justice's vitality and commitment to his work on the Court; personal asides indicate his devotion as husband. There is also a touching portrayal of his final illness and last months.
Dunne, Gerald T. *Hugo Black and the Judicial Revolution*. New York: Simon and Schuster, 1977. Thorough and panoramic biography which strikes a judicious balance between the legal and the personal elements in Black's career on the Court. The political and historical context of his most notable opinions is set forth; relations with other justices reveal the extent to which Black shaped, or was affected by, the Court's positions on controversial issues.
Hamilton, Virginia Van Der Veer. *Hugo Black: The Alabama Years*. Baton Rouge: Louisiana State University Press, 1972. Lively, colorful account which traces the offsetting influences of principle and expediency in

Black's early legal work and political career. This work provides the most substantial examination of his brief membership in the Ku Klux Klan and provides extensive coverage of his service in the United States Senate. Collections of documents and newspapers that are important for the history of Alabama have been used to advantage here.

Magee, James J. *Mr. Justice Black: Absolutist on the Court*. Charlottesville: University Press of Virginia, 1980. A critical assessment of Black's opinions, notably his interpretation of the Bill of Rights, and particularly the First Amendment. This study points out the difficulties of settling intricate modern cases by a literal construction of the Constitution; nevertheless, Black's efforts in this direction have enriched the nation's legal culture.

Silverstein, Mark. *Constitutional Faiths: Felix Frankfurter, Hugo Black, and the Process of Judicial Decision Making*. Ithaca, N.Y.: Cornell University Press, 1984. A fairly abstruse study of conflicting legal philosophies, this work outlines points of contention between the two justices on the First and Fourteenth Amendments. Even when they agreed, it was difficult to reconcile Black's absolutism with Frankfurter's conception of a broader Anglo-American legal tradition that enveloped the Constitution.

Strickland, Stephen Parks, ed. *Hugo Black and the Supreme Court: A Symposium*. Indianapolis: Bobbs-Merrill Co., 1967. Studies by nine legal scholars, examining Black's positions on civil liberties, the New Deal, federal taxation, antitrust, and federal civil procedures. The editor concludes that Black may not easily be characterized as liberal or conservative; his extraordinary contribution has been to demonstrate the vitality of the Constitution during the modern age.

J. R. Broadus

BLACK HAWK
Ma-ka-tai-me-she-kia-kiak

Born: 1767; Rock River, Illinois
Died: October 3, 1838; near the Des Moines River, Iowa
Areas of Achievement: Indian leadership and literature
Contribution: Black Hawk was a leader in the last Indian war of the old
   Northwest; he also dictated one of the most interesting Indian autobiog-
   raphies, *Life of Ma-ka-tai-me-she-kia-kiak, or Black Hawk* (1834).

Early Life

Black Hawk (or Ma-ka-tai-me-she-kia-kiak) was the adopted brother of a
chief of the Foxes and was brought up by the Sauk (Sacs)—"Sac" was the
original French spelling. The Sauk and Foxes were small tribes which formed
an alliance, sometimes including the Potawatomi and Winnebago, to defend
themselves against larger neighboring nations. Black Hawk was already a
warrior and a leader among his people at the age of fifteen. In his autobiography he described how he became chief at the death of his father when they
were fighting together against the Cherokee near the Meramec River, a short
distance below modern St. Louis. Black Hawk fell heir to the chieftainship
but was obliged to mourn, pray, and fast for five years in what he called a
"civil capacity," hunting and fishing. When he was twenty-one he became
head chief of the Sauk and Foxes. The two tribes were united and lived
together as a single group.

Black Hawk's early years were spent in warfare against neighbors, primarily the Osage, Kaskaskia (a member of the Illinois Confederacy), and Chip-
pewa. According to Black Hawk, there were two major reasons for warfare
among the Indians: the preservation of hunting grounds and revenge for the
deaths of relatives. Despite Black Hawk's renown as a warrior, there was a
highly developed ethical and spiritual side of his character, and he tried to do
what the Supreme Spirit directed.

Life's Work

Black Hawk's personality was complex, and it would be a mistake to over-
simplify the main events in his life. Probably he should not be considered a
great leader. He was highly individualistic, often impulsive, colorful, and
emotional. His policies did not significantly help his nation, and other Indian
leaders such as Pontiac and Crazy Horse were greater than he. It could be
argued that his leadership was shortsighted and brought disaster on his people. The Black Hawk War could have been avoided.

Black Hawk never liked the American settlers, and for this he may be
easily forgiven—during his lifetime the Sauk continually suffered from white
armies, white officials, white traders, and white settlers. His adopted son

was murdered by white American settlers. He liked the British. He was on good terms with a British trader and with Robert Dixon, British agent in the War of 1812, during which Black Hawk took an active role against the Americans. Most of Black Hawk's life prior to his capture in 1832 was marked by his dislike of Americans. The experience that contributed to this attitude more than any other was the St. Louis treaty of 1804, which Black Hawk rejected. In his own words, "It has been the origin of all our difficulties."

Napoleon sold Louisiana to the United States in 1803; soon after, United States officials arrived in St. Louis to claim control and sign treaties with Indian tribes in the area. According to Black Hawk, the treaty with the Sauk was fraudulent. The Sauk had sent four representatives to St. Louis to obtain the release of a Sauk imprisoned there for killing an American—these were negotiators with a specific mission, not diplomats or chiefs. Much later they returned dressed in fine coats and wearing medals, and they could not remember much of what had happened. They were drunk most of the time they were in St. Louis. They also signed a treaty ceding all the Sauk lands east of the Mississippi to the United States. Black Hawk and the rest of the Sauk were indignant. Not long after, a United States Army detachment came to erect Fort Madison near the Sauk villages. Black Hawk was scandalized by the treaty, asserting that the Sauk and Fox signers of the treaty had no authority from their nations. Twentieth century historian Milo Quaife, however, claims that "no more than the usual cajolery of the Indians was indulged in by the white representatives in securing the cession." The rejection of this treaty by the Indians, and the acceptance of its legality by the United States, says much about the quality of American law during this period.

The second major event in Black Hawk's life prior to his battles in the 1830's against the Illinois militia and the United States Army was his rivalry with another Sauk chief, Keokuk. Although not a chief by birth, Keokuk rose by the exercise of political talents to a position of leadership in his tribe. He was more of a realist than Black Hawk, and although he may not have liked the Americans any more than Black Hawk did, he tried not to antagonize them. As a nation the Sauk were divided, some favoring Black Hawk and others, Keokuk. In 1819, Keokuk and other members of the nation were persuaded by American authorities to leave the Sauk home on Rock Island and go to the western side of the Mississippi. Keokuk ultimately triumphed over Black Hawk after the war of 1832, which placed Black Hawk under the governance of Keokuk.

The rivalry between Black Hawk and Keokuk had a long history. Throughout the 1820's, Black Hawk resisted the encroachments of white settlers, and he tried to hold on to the Sauk's ancestral home on Rock Island. At first Black Hawk favored negotiation with the white Americans no less than Keokuk. Eventually, however, having exhausted all means of peaceful resistance,

Black Hawk took up arms and tried to recruit allies among the Potawatomi. He led his entire nation—warriors, women, and children—on a long anabasis from Rock Island to Bad Axe River, winning some battles and losing others, culminating in the final attempt to reach the safety of the western bank of the Mississippi. The most pitiful aspect of the tragedy was the fate of the Sauk women and children. In the words of one historian, Reuben Thwaites,

> Some of the fugitives succeeded in swimming to the west bank of the Mississippi, but many were drowned on the way, or cooly picked off by sharpshooters, who exercised no more mercy towards squaws and children than they did towards braves—treating them all as though they were rats instead of human beings.

Black Hawk led the last great war between Indians and whites on the eastern side of the Mississippi; if it terrified numerous white settlers in the frontier regions of the old Northwest—what is now Illinois and Wisconsin—it should be stressed that the Indian civilian populations living on ancestral lands had been terrorized by whites for a far longer period of time. Although Black Hawk initiated the battle, the final tragedy was not his doing. The deliberate killing of noncombatants was an act of the United States, not an Indian act. A few Sauk managed to reach the western bank only to be attacked by a war party of Sioux Indians under the orders of General Atkinson. Black Hawk would have been the first to condemn these military practices, and he fully expressed his indignation in his autobiography. These massacres went far beyond his conception of the conduct of war. Some historians have been hasty to blame him, failing to consider the requirements of defensive warfare at the time. Although the Indians received few favorable settlements in their negotiations with the whites, those who suffered the most were perhaps the most pacific—those who, because they never fought the whites, never signed treaties with them either, and consequently never received rights or privileges. Most of these nations have completely disappeared, leaving no survivors. One of Black Hawk's most telling critiques of Keokuk is the following: "I conceived that the *peaceable disposition* of Keokuk and his people had been, in a great measure, the cause of our having been driven from our village."

Black Hawk had a quixotic, romantic temperament. He could be impulsively emotional and also ethical, courageous, even idealistic and chivalrous in battle. Some of these traits might surprise a modern reader accustomed to clichés about Indians. Repeatedly Black Hawk complimented the braver of his adversaries, whether enemy Indians or whites. If he encountered an enemy group that had less than half his number, he declined to do battle. He admired both determination and heroism in war, and the traits he came to admire in his white conquerors after 1832 were largely military virtues. It was probably not a coincidence that he struck up a spontaneous friendship with

Lieutenant Jefferson Davis in 1832; these two leaders of rebellion had traits in common. Jefferson Davis was to repeat Black Hawk's act of defiance against superior military forces twenty-five years later as president of the Confederate States, and the results would be comparable.

Black Hawk's autobiography was dictated and translated on the spot in 1833; there is no extant text in the Sauk language. The book has a seemingly childish quality that is probably more attributable to the interpreter and editor than to Black Hawk himself. There are many exclamation points, underlinings, and expressions of delight, and much reveling in the good fight. Nevertheless, the document gives an ample, three-dimensional portrait of a man spontaneously describing his thoughts and feelings, trying to account for what he has done and what has happened to him.

Black Hawk died a broken man on an Indian reservation in Iowa in 1838. A decade later, his rival Keokuk died a wealthy man in Kansas, where he had moved after selling the Sauk and Fox lands in Iowa.

Summary
After the Black Hawk War, the combined population of the Sauk and Foxes was greatly diminished. They were finally resettled in an area west of the Mississippi in a segment of what was known as "the Permanent Indian Frontier of 1840." It adjoined the Potawatomi to the west, the Sioux to the north, and the Winnebago to the northeast. The Sauk and Foxes would still need military virtues as well as diplomacy when they jostled with these Indians and, later, with whites in their new habitat. Military abilities did not immediately become obsolete—far from it. Soon, however, the Indians' greatest adversaries were to become alcoholism, diseases such as cholera, and starvation.

Black Hawk's major weakness was probably diplomacy. In his war against the whites he did not secure the adherence of a significant number of other Indian nations, nor did he spend much time or effort in attempting it. Seventy years earlier, Pontiac had been more successful in forging an antiwhite alliance. Whether Black Hawk could have been more successful if he had put more effort into negotiations, especially with other Indian nations, is a matter of speculation. Black Hawk thought in broad ethical categories. He believed the Great Spirit would reward him if he fought for justice. Patient diplomacy, with its concomitant drudgery and uncertainty, was not for him.

Bibliography
Black Hawk. *Life of Ma-ka-tai-me-she-kia-kiak, or Black Hawk*. Boston: Russell, Odiorne, and Metcalf, 1834. Black Hawk's autobiography is a fascinating document; at the same time, it has many inaccuracies and biases, and should be read with critical skepticism. His account of the British is naïve, as well as his description of the "prophet" White Cloud. Black

Hawk grossly understates his own losses in the battles of 1832. Still, a vivid picture of an admirable human being emerges from the pages of his autobiography.

Drake, Benjamin. *The Life and Adventures of Black Hawk*. Cincinnati: G. Conclin, 1844. Half history and half fiction, written shortly after the events described.

Eby, Cecil. *"That Disgraceful Affair," the Black Hawk War*. New York: W. W. Norton and Co., 1973. Perhaps the best book about the Black Hawk War. Very thoroughly documented and at the same time a readable narrative; also an incisive critique of the major actors in the war.

Quaife, Milo Milton. *Chicago and the Old Northwest, 1673-1833*. Chicago: University of Chicago Press, 1913. Well-documented and thorough general history that draws somewhat specious conclusions.

Slotkin, Richard. *Regeneration Through Violence: The Mythology of the American Frontier, 1600-1860*. Middletown, Conn.: Wesleyan University Press, 1973. A critical or "revisionist" account of the frontier; a welcome antidote to earlier sentimental accounts of the frontier wars, but obsessively overstated.

Stevens, Frank E. *The Black Hawk War*. Chicago: F. E. Stevens, 1903. A thorough account, still useful.

Thwaites, Reuben G. *Story of the Black Hawk War*. Madison: Wisconsin State Historical Society, 1892. A narrative by one of the best American historians of the period; Thwaites combined great erudition with a keen critical spirit.

Whitney, Ellen M., ed. *The Black Hawk War, 1831-1832*. Springfield: Illinois Historical Collections, 1970-1973. Documents and lists.

John Carpenter

ELIZABETH BLACKWELL

Born: February 3, 1821; Counterslip, England
Died: May 31, 1910; Hastings, Scotland
Area of Achievement: Medicine
Contribution: While Elizabeth Blackwell endeavored to open medical educa-
tion to women, her major effort was concentrated in the field of preventive
medicine.

Early Life

Elizabeth Blackwell, the first American woman to receive a degree in
medicine, was the third daughter of the twelve children born to Samuel
Blackwell and Hannah (Lane) Blackwell and one of two girls in the family to
become physicians. Two of her brothers and their wives were well-known reformers and leaders in the women's rights movement. Samuel Blackwell, a
prosperous sugar refiner, was an active Dissenter and lay preacher in the
Independent church. Reformers were always welcome in his home; he was a
champion of social reform, women's rights, temperance, and the abolition of
slavery. Her mother provided a tempering influence through music and
books. The task of disciplining the children was given to Samuel's four
unmarried sisters who lived with the family.

Because Dissenters' children were barred from school in England, Samuel
engaged private tutors, who were instructed to ignore tradition and custom
and teach the girls the same subjects as the boys. In this atmosphere, the
children were encouraged to develop individuality, social consciousness, and
character. Elizabeth, a voracious reader, studied German and French, became proficient in music, and dabbled in art. As a child, she practiced self-
discipline by occasionally sleeping on the bare floor.

After suffering severe financial losses in 1832, Samuel Blackwell moved the
family to New York City when Elizabeth was eleven. His efforts to introduce
more modern methods for refining beet sugar met with little financial success. His abolitionist activities and his friendship with William Lloyd Garrison caused him difficulty with business associates. Three years later, the
Blackwells moved to larger quarters in Jersey City, New Jersey. Samuel suffered new losses in the depression of 1837. In May, 1838, the family moved to
Cincinnati, for what was to be a fresh start. Within three months, Samuel
Blackwell died, leaving the family almost penniless.

The next few years were difficult. The older children worked to earn a living and provide an education for the younger members of the family. Blackwell, a blonde with blue-gray eyes, was smaller (five feet, one inch) than her
sisters. Yet she had great strength and courage. Along with her mother and
two older sisters, she established a small private school. After four years, the
school closed, and money was still difficult to obtain. She went to Hender-

son, Kentucky, for a year of teaching. In her autobiography, *Pioneer Work in Opening the Medical Profession to Women* (1895), she admitted that neither teaching nor the prospect of marriage intrigued her. In fact, the thought of marriage made her ill.

One day, she visited a friend, Mary Donaldson, who was dying of cancer. Because her emotional encounters with male physicians had been very disquieting, Donaldson urged Blackwell to study medicine. At first, she was strongly opposed because she disliked everything connected with the body. Then the idea began to intrigue her. Finally, it became an obsession.

She decided to seek a career in medicine and use it as a barrier against marriage. She began to seek the opinions of various physicians about her plans. All discouraged her. Some suggested that she disguise herself as a man and go to Paris to pursue medical training. Blackwell, however, wanted to be accepted as a woman. To raise money for medical school, she spent the next two years, 1845-1847, combining teaching with an intensive study of medicine, first with physician-clergyman John Dickson of Asheville, North Carolina, and then with his brother, Samuel Dickson, a distinguished physician of Charleston, South Carolina.

Blackwell went to Philadelphia in the spring of 1847. Joseph Warrington and William Elder, two Quaker physicians, tried to help her to gain admission to one of the city's medical schools, then considered among the nation's best. She made a personal appeal to faculty members. Although she impressed them with her poise and preparation, she was eventually turned down by some twenty schools in the eastern United States. The nation's doctors were already squabbling over the few patients available. Thus, they were convinced that there was no need for women physicians to add to their difficulties. More determined than ever, she studied anatomy in the private school of Dr. Joseph M. Allen and began to apply to rural medical schools. Finally, Geneva College in west central New York accepted her. Long afterward, she learned that the faculty had denied her application. Reluctant to take a stand, they turned the matter over to the students, insisting upon a unanimous vote for acceptance. The students, thinking this to be a joke and also hoping for some high-spirited recreation, approved the application.

Blackwell began her studies on November 6, 1847, and quickly experienced isolation and loneliness. The townspeople considered her immoral. At first, she was barred from classroom demonstrations. With quiet firmness, however, she soon gained the respect of both faculty and students. At the end of the term, Blackwell applied to several hospitals, seeking practical experience. All refused her. After much political lobbying, she was admitted to the staff of Blockley Almshouse in Philadelphia. While some patients rejected her, the worst hostility came from the young resident physicians who chose to ignore her. Still, she persisted in her training. A typhoid epidemic among the patients provided the subject for her thesis. Published in the *Buf-*

falo Medical Journal and Monthly Review (1849), it emphasized the importance of sanitation and personal hygiene in combating disease and stressed the impact of negative psychological factors on disease. Much of this would become the core of her medical philosophy.

Blackwell returned to Geneva, completed her studies, and on January 23, 1849, was graduated first in her class. In April, shortly after becoming a naturalized American citizen, she went to Europe in search of additional education. Medical education in Paris, her ultimate objective, proved disappointing. Only by enrolling as a student midwife at the large state hospital, La Maternité, could she secure practical experience. When she contracted purulent ophthalmia after treating a child suffering from the disease, her training came to a halt. During the next year, she lost the sight in one eye and was left with only limited vision in the other. Her dream of becoming a surgeon was abandoned. In October, 1850, she returned to England, and through the efforts of her sponsor, Dr. James Paget, was able to continue her training on the wards of St. Bartholomew's Hospital.

Life's Work

In August, 1851, Blackwell returned to New York, eager to begin her medical career. Yet over the next seven years, she experienced every possible discouragement. She was barred from practice in city dispensaries and hospitals and told to establish her own dispensary. She was ignored by medical colleagues and attacked in anonymous letters. Unable to rent decent office facilities, she was forced to buy a house she could not afford. In the hope of attracting patients, Blackwell placed an advertisement with the *New York Tribune*. Meanwhile, refusing to admit defeat, she began a series of lectures outlining the principles of good hygiene, later published as *The Laws of Life in Reference to the Physical Education of Girls* (1852). Her practical message appealed to a number of Quaker women who attended the lectures. With their encouragement and help, she gained patients and the friendship of a number of influential people.

In 1853, Blackwell opened a one-room dispensary in the tenement district of New York. Fours years later, she expanded this to a hospital, the New York Infirmary for Indigent Women and Children, staffed entirely by women and dedicated to teaching hygiene and the prevention of disease. Sufficient funds had been raised, including a small sum granted by the New York state legislature and another small sum from the New York City Council. When it opened, she had two capable coworkers: her sister Dr. Emily Blackwell, just returned from postgraduate surgical training in Europe, and Dr. Marie E. Zakrzewska, newly graduated from Western Reserve, who became the resident physician. A number of male physicians, along with Horace Greeley, founder of the *New York Tribune*, and Henry J. Raymond, founder of *The New York Times*, endorsed the venture. In the midst of her work to establish the infirmary, Blackwell, in 1854, adopted Katharine Barry, a seven-year-old orphan. Kitty remained daughter, friend, secretary, and companion to the doctor all of her life.

In the late summer of 1858, Blackwell went to England to help advance professional opportunities for women in medicine. She practiced medicine in her native land before the Medical Act of 1858 was passed. Consequently, she was legally qualified for, and became the first woman to have her name entered on, the Medical Register of the United Kingdom. The following August, Blackwell returned to New York. Soon, she was deep in plans for a medical college for women, a nursing school, and a chair of hygiene.

The Civil War postponed this project. In the early days of the war, Blackwell called a meeting of the women managers of the infirmary. The result was the formation of the Women's Central Association of Relief, which ultimately led to the creation of the National Sanitary Aid Association and the Ladies' Sanitary Commission. Throughout the war, both Blackwell and her sister Emily were involved in the selection and training of nurses.

On April 13, 1864, the New York state legislature passed an enabling act for a women's medical college. This act was necessary because the existing reputable schools in New York did not admit women. Four years later, her plan was realized, the college opened, and she was appointed to the first chair of hygiene. Because women would be carefully observed by the medical profession, Blackwell set higher standards than existed at other schools for women, including entrance examinations, a three-year graded course with longer terms, and an independent examining board. At last, women could obtain a good education, including the necessary clinical training and experience. The school continued to function until 1899, when Cornell University Medical School began to admit women.

Once the infirmary and college were operating successfully, Blackwell left them under her sister's control. In 1869, at age forty-eight, she returned to England, where she remained for the remainder of her life. Throughout the decade, she worked to gain the acceptance of women in medicine, which took longer than in the United States. She established a successful practice in London and in 1871 formed the National Health Society, whose motto was "Prevention is better than cure." In the early 1870's, Blackwell presented a series of lectures, "How to Keep a Household in Health." She suggested in this series that young people be taught about sex at an early age. In another series, "The Religion of Health" (1871), she attacked doctors and drugs and strongly preached prevention.

Blackwell accepted the chair of gynecology at the New Hospital and London School of Medicine for Women in 1875. After one year of lecturing, however, she suffered from biliary colic and realized that her health would not permit her to continue. Reluctantly, she retired to Hastings, Scotland. In a house by the sea, she and her daughter spent the next thirty years.

During this period, Blackwell remained active, speaking out on issues of concern to her. She shocked England by writing about taboo subjects. In *Counsel to Parents on the Moral Education of Their Children* (1878), *The Human Element in Sex* (1880), and a number of essays, articles, and lectures, she became a crusader against the double standard of morality and urged an end to prostitution. In other writings, she advocated higher standards of hygiene and sanitation. Blackwell was also critical of what she believed to be the excessive use of surgery in medical practice. She voiced strong opposition to vaccination, and her hostility to animal experimentation was expressed in *Scientific Method in Biology* (1898).

In these later years, she was influenced by Charles Kingsley, the Christian Socialist. He directed her attention to social problems she had never seriously considered. Her pamphlet *Christian Socialism* (1882), a reflection of this new thinking, called for the application of Christian principles to contemporary problems, specifically a more just distribution of income and workers' insurance.

Blackwell made only one more trip to the United States, in 1906, to say farewell to her family. Since 1902, she had spent every summer at Kilmun on Holy Loch in Argyllshire, the Scottish Highlands. In 1907, she fell headlong downstairs at Kilmun. Although her injuries were considered slight, she never fully recovered and remained bedridden for the last three years of her life. She died at Hastings in 1910 but at her own request was buried at Kilmun.

Summary

In the early nineteenth century, woman's place was in the home as wife and mother. Any other work was acknowledged to be only a temporary position in a profession closely related to her maternal role—for example, teaching. Medicine was unheard of as a female career.

The professional woman was a contradiction in terms, since professions were developed to exclude the irregular practitioner, the poorly or inadequately trained, that is, the female. By 1820, medical schools, open only to men, had been established in every state in the Union. Graduation from a qualified medical school was necessary to practice medicine.

Since female seminaries were still in their infancy, most women had very little formal education in this period. Blackwell was the exception, well prepared and a good student. Her deep emotional frustration and the influence of a family strongly committed to the concept of women's rights inspired her. She insisted on her right to enter medicine on an equal footing with men: In no other profession was male reaction so strong.

She believed that women, because of their role as mothers, could play a special part in improving human health and welfare. Consequently, women could and should become doctors. She worked to break the barrier that prohibited women from pursuing a professional life by challenging the concept of sex-linked roles.

Blackwell had always viewed her medical training as a stepping-stone to work for moral reform. She became an advocate of sex education for young women and battled the double standard. She was the first American woman to be graduated from a medical school and serve as an intern, the first to have her name listed on the Medical Register of the United Kingdom. She founded hospitals for women, staffed by women, in both the United States and Great Britain and established the first school of nursing in the United States. In demanding strict standards of hygiene in hospitals and rigorous curricula in medical schools, she was far ahead of her time, as she was also in her emphasis on preventive medicine.

Perhaps her most important legacy, however, was her impact on the way women were treated, both within the profession and as patients.

Bibliography
Baker, Rachel. *The First Woman Doctor: The Story of Elizabeth Blackwell, M.D.* New York: Julian Messner, 1944. Specifically designed for teenage readers. A good general biography.
Flexner, Eleanor. *Century of Struggle: The Woman's Rights Movement in the United States*. Cambridge, Mass.: The Belknap Press of Harvard University Press, 1959. Covers the women's rights movement from the time of the *Mayflower* to 1920, when women won the vote. Flexner provides significant information about many smaller movements within the larger one. Of particular interest is chapter 8, which provides background information on the intellectual pursuits of women.
Hays, Elinor Rice. *Those Extraordinary Blackwells: The Story of a Journey to a Better World*. New York: Harcourt Brace and World, 1967. Presents both the personal and the public lives of the various members of the Blackwell family and interweaves their story with social and cultural developments in America during this period. Well documented.
Lerner, Gerda, ed. *The Female Experience: An American Documentary*. Indianapolis: Bobbs-Merrill Co., 1977. Drawn entirely from primary sources, this volume covers various women's experiences from the Colonial days to the mid-1970's. Includes two brief excerpts from Blackwell's autobiography and the *First Annual Report of the New York Dispensary for Poor Women and Children* (1855).
Lovejoy, Esther Pohl. *Women Doctors of the World*. New York: Macmillan Publishing Co., 1957. Emphasizes the history of women's medical role in the United States from Colonial days to the mid-1970's. The first nine chapters are extremely well documented and concentrate on women's attempts to gain admission to the male profession.
Smith, Dean. "A Persistent Rebel." *American History Illustrated* 15 (Janu-

ary, 1981): 28-35. A brief popular account of Blackwell's life.

Thomson, Elizabeth. "Elizabeth Blackwell." In *Notable American Women, 1607-1950: A Biographical Dictionary*, edited by Edward T. James, Janet W. James, and Paul S. Boyer, 161-165. Cambridge, Mass.: The Belknap Press of Harvard University Press, 1971. A good biographical sketch. Draws material from a variety of sources, including Blackwell's autobiography.

Wilson, Dorothy Clarke. *Lone Woman: The Story of Elizabeth Blackwell, the First Woman Doctor*. Boston: Little, Brown and Co., 1970. Presents a sympathetic profile of Blackwell but does not fully cover the last thirty years of her life in England. Includes an excellent bibliography.

Rita E. Loos

JAMES G. BLAINE

Born: January 31, 1830; West Brownsville, Pennsylvania
Died: January 27, 1893; Washington, D.C.
Area of Achievement: Politics
Contribution: Blaine was the most popular Republican politician of the late
  nineteenth century. Through his personal appeal and his advocacy of the
  protective tariff, he laid the basis for the emergence of the Republican
  Party as the majority party in the 1890's.

Early Life
    James Gillespie Blaine was born January 31, 1830, in West Brownsville,
Pennsylvania. His father, Ephraim Lyon Blaine, came from a Scotch-Irish
and Scotch-Presbyterian background. Blaine's mother, Maria Louise Gillespie, was an Irish Catholic. Blaine was reared a Presbyterian, as were his
brothers, while his sisters followed their mother's faith. In later life, Blaine
became a Congregationalist but was tolerant of all creeds and avoided the
religious issue in politics. Blaine's maternal background gave him an electoral
appeal to Irish-Catholic voters.
    Ephraim Blaine was a lawyer who was elected to a county clerk position in
Washington County, Pennsylvania, in 1842. His son entered Washington and
Jefferson College, a small school in the area, and was graduated in 1847.
Blaine then taught at the Western Military Institute in Georgetown, Kentucky, from 1848 to 1851. He admired the policies of Henry Clay, the Whig
leader, during his stay in the state. He also found time to court and then
marry a teacher at a woman's seminary, Harriet Stanwood, on June 30, 1850.
Leaving Kentucky in late 1851, Blaine taught at the Pennsylvania Institute
for the Blind from 1852 to 1854. He also pursued legal studies while in
Philadelphia.
    Mrs. Blaine's family had connections in Maine. When a vacancy occurred
for editor of the *Kennebec Journal* in 1853, her husband was asked to take
over the management of this Whig newspaper. Money from his brothers-in-
law helped this arrangement succeed. By November, 1854, Blaine was at
work in Augusta, Maine, as a newspaperman, not a lawyer. His growing family eventually reached seven children, four of whom outlived their father.
From this point onward, he became known as Blaine of Maine.
    Over the next decade, Blaine became identified with the young Repub-
lican Party in his adopted state. He was elected to the Maine legislature in
1858, was reelected three times, and became Speaker of the House of Representatives during his last two terms. He was named chairman of the Republican State Committee in 1859, a post he held for two decades. Blaine
attended the Republican National Convention in 1860 as a delegate. In 1862,
he was elected to the United States Congress and took his seat in the House

of Representatives in 1863.

As he entered the national scene at the age of thirty-three, Blaine had already shown himself to be a gifted politician. He had a charismatic quality that caused some who knew him to be loyal to him for life, becoming "Blainiacs." His speeches were received enthusiastically in an age that admired oratory. Blaine knew American politics intimately and could remember faces and election results with uncanny accuracy. Yet there was another side to him. His health and temperament were uncertain, and his illnesses often came at moments of crisis. In his private affairs, Blaine gained wealth without having a secure income, and he would not reveal information about his finances to the public. Enemies said that he was corrupt. That went too far, but he lacked, as did many of his contemporaries, a clear sense of what constituted a conflict of interest. In fact, James G. Blaine was a diverse blend of good and bad qualities—a truth reflected in the Gilded Age quip that men went insane about him in pairs, one for, and one against.

Life's Work

Blaine spent thirteen years in the House of Representatives, serving as its Speaker between 1869 and 1875. He was a moderate on the issues of the Civil War and Reconstruction, endorsing black suffrage and a strong policy toward the South without being labeled as a "radical." He became known as a "Half-Breed" in contrast to such "Stalwarts" as New York's Roscoe Conkling. Blaine and Conkling clashed on the House floor in April, 1866. His description of Conkling as having a "majestic, supereminent turkeygobbler strut" opened a personal and political wound that never healed for the egotistic Conkling. His opposition proved disastrous to Blaine's presidential chances in 1876 and 1880.

By 1876, Blaine had left the House of Representatives to serve in the Senate. He was a leading candidate for the Republican presidential nomination in that year. Then a public controversy arose over whether Blaine had acted corruptly in helping to save a land grant for an Arkansas railroad in 1869. The facts about favors done and favors repaid were allegedly contained in a packet of documents known as the Mulligan Letters, named for the man who possessed them. The letters came into Blaine's hands, he read from them to the House, and his friends said that he had vindicated himself. Enemies charged that the papers proved his guilt, and the reform element of the time never forgave him.

Shortly before the Republican convention, Blaine fell ill. Nevertheless, his name was placed in nomination as Robert G. Ingersoll called him the "Plumed Knight" of American politics. The Republican delegates decided that Blaine was too controversial to win, and they turned instead to Rutherford B. Hayes of Ohio. Four years later, after Hayes's single term, Blaine led the opposition to a third term for Ulysses S. Grant and again was seen as a contender for the nomination. Blaine was more interested in his party's success than in his own advancement in 1880, and he was pleased when James A. Garfield of Ohio became the compromise nominee. In the fall campaign, Blaine stumped widely for the national ticket and developed the arguments for the protective tariff that he would advance in the 1880's.

After Garfield's narrow victory, he asked Blaine to be his secretary of state. In his first brief tenure at the State Department, Blaine pursued his concern for a canal across Central America, the fostering of Pan-American sentiment, and greater trade for the nation. Garfield's assassination in the summer of 1881 ended his presidency and led to Blaine's resignation at the end of the year. The administration of Chester A. Arthur that followed did not cut into Blaine's popularity with the Republican rank and file. He received the Republican nomination on the first ballot in 1884. John A. Logan of Illinois was his running mate.

Blaine wanted to make the protective tariff the central theme of his race against the nominee of the Democrats, Grover Cleveland, the governor of New York. Instead the campaign turned on the personal character of the two candidates. Republicans stressed Cleveland's admission that he had had an affair with a woman who had given birth to an illegitimate son. Democrats attacked the legal validity of Blaine's marriage and revived the charges of the Mulligan Letters. These sensational aspects overshadowed Blaine's campaign tour, one of the first by a presidential aspirant. The election was close as the voting neared. All accounts of the election of 1884 note that on October 29, Blaine heard the Reverend Samuel Burchard say in New York that the Democrats were the party of "rum, Romanism, and rebellion." These words supposedly alienated Catholic voters, swung New York to the Democrats, and thus cost Blaine the victory. This episode, however, has been given too much importance. In fact, Blaine improved on Garfield's vote in the state and ran stronger than his party. The significance of 1884 was not that Blaine lost in a Democratic year but that he revived the Republicans and laid the groundwork for the party's victory in 1888.

Over the next four years, Blaine continued to speak out for the tariff. He set the keynote for the 1888 campaign when he responded publicly to Cleveland's attacks on tariff protection in his 1887 annual message to Congress. "The Democratic Party in power is a standing menace to the prosperity of the country," he told an interviewer. Blaine stayed out of the presidential race and supported strongly the party's nominee, Benjamin Harrison of Indiana. After Harrison defeated Cleveland, it was logical that Blaine should again serve as secretary of state.

Blaine faced a variety of diplomatic issues, including Canadian fisheries and a running argument with Great Britain over fur seals in Alaska. He summoned the initial Pan-American Conference to Washington in October, 1889, sought to achieve the annexation of Hawaii, and was instrumental in obtaining reciprocal trade authority in the McKinley Tariff of 1890. In many ways Blaine foreshadowed the overseas expansion of the United States that occurred later in the decade. His working relationship with President Harrison deteriorated as the Administration progressed and Blaine's own health faltered. The death of two children in 1890 added to his personal troubles. Shortly before the Republican convention, on June 4, 1892, Blaine resigned as secretary of state. It is not clear whether Blaine was actually a candidate for the presidency this last time. He received some support when the Republican delegates met, but the incumbent Harrison easily controlled the convention and was renominated on the first ballot. Blaine made one speech for the Republicans in the 1892 race as Harrison lost to Grover Cleveland. In the last months of his life, Blaine gradually wasted away. He died of Bright's disease and a weakened heart on January 27, 1893.

Summary

When Blaine died, a fellow Republican said, "His is a fame that will grow with time." In fact, he is now largely a forgotten historical figure who is remembered only for a vague connection with "rum, Romanism, and rebellion." That impression does an injustice to one of the most popular and charismatic political leaders of the Gilded Age. Blaine embodied the diverse tendencies of the Republican Party in the formative stages of its development. In his advocacy of economic nationalism and growth, he spoke for a generation that wanted both to preserve the achievements of the Civil War and to move on to the fresh issues of industrial development. He was an important participant in the affairs of the House of Representatives in the early 1870's, and his tenure as Speaker contributed to the growing professionalism of that branch of government.

Blaine also symbolized the popular unease about the ethical standards that public servants should observe. In the Mulligan Letters episode and in his own affairs, he raised issues about conflict of interest and propriety that clouded his historical reputation. He became the epitome of the "spoilsman" who lived on patronage and influence. Blaine correctly understood these attacks as being to some degree partisan, but he failed to recognize the legitimacy of the questions that they posed.

Despite these failings, Blaine was a central figure in the evolution of the Republican Party during the 1870's and 1880's. His conviction that tariff protection offered both the hope of party success and an answer to the issue of economic growth laid the foundation for the emergence of the Republican Party as the majority party in the 1890's. In the 1884 presidential race, he improved the Republican performance and prepared the party for later success. As secretary of state, he was a constructive spokesman for the national interest. He educated his party on the tariff issue and, in so doing, fulfilled the essential function of a national political leader. For a generation of

Republican leaders and voters, James G. Blaine came to stand for inspiration and commitment in politics. Although he failed to reach the presidency, Blaine was the most significant American politician of his era.

Bibliography

Blaine, James G. *Twenty Years of Congress: From Lincoln to Garfield*. 2 vols. Norwich, Conn.: Henry Bill Publishing Co., 1884-1886. Blaine's memoir of his service in Congress does not contain any striking personal revelations.

Dodge, Mary Abigail. *The Biography of James G. Blaine*. Norwich, Conn.: Henry Bill Publishing Co., 1895. A family biography which is most useful for the many private letters of Blaine that it contains.

Morgan, H. Wayne. *From Hayes to McKinley: National Party Politics, 1877-1896*. Syracuse, N.Y.: Syracuse University Press, 1969. The best analytic treatment of American politics during the heyday of Blaine's career. Morgan is sympathetic and perceptive about Blaine's role as a Republican leader.

Muzzey, David S. *James G. Blaine: A Political Idol of Other Days*. New York: Dodd, Mead and Co., 1934. The best and most objective biography of Blaine. Argues that he was not consumed with the desire to be president.

Stanwood, Edward. *James Gillespie Blaine*. Boston: Houghton Mifflin Co., 1905. A short biography by a scholar who was related to Blaine.

Thompson, Margaret Susan. *The "Spider Web": Congress and Lobbying in the Age of Grant*. Ithaca, N.Y.: Cornell University Press, 1985. An innovative and interesting treatment of the House of Representatives and the Senate in the years when Blaine was Speaker. Reveals much about the political system in which he operated.

Tyler, Alice Felt. *The Foreign Policy of James G. Blaine*. Minneapolis: University of Minnesota Press, 1927. An older but still helpful examination of Blaine as a diplomat and shaper of American foreign policy.

Lewis L. Gould

FRANZ BOAS

Born: July 9, 1858; Minden, Westphalia
Died: December 21, 1942; New York, New York
Area of Achievement: Anthropology
Contribution: Boas made anthropology a vital discipline in the history of twentieth century social science, and his scholarship, in time, had a significant impact on public policy in the United States.

Early Life

Franz Boas was born July 9, 1858, in Minden, Westphalia (in modern West Germany). He was the only son of six children (three of whom survived childhood) of Meier and Sophie Meyer Boas, who were Jews. His father was a successful businessman, while his mother was extremely active in political and civic affairs. A spirit of liberalism and freethinking prevailed in the Boas household. It was a family legacy of the ideals of the German Revolution of 1848.

Although a sickly child, Boas had a lively interest in the natural world around him—an interest much encouraged by his mother. His enjoyment of nature, music, and school shaped his early life. After attending primary school and the gymnasium in Minden, Boas began his university studies. For the next four years, he studied at Heidelberg, Bonn, and Kiel. In 1881, at the age of twenty-three, he took his doctorate in physics at Kiel; his dissertation was entitled *Contributions to the Understanding of the Color of Water*. Later, his academic interests moved from physics and mathematics to physical, and later, cultural, geography.

In 1883, after a year in a reserve officer-training program and another year in further study, Boas made his anthropological trip to Baffinland, a territory inhabited by Eskimos. The experience changed his life, for he determined that he would study human phenomena in nature. Following a year in New York City, he became an assistant at the Museum for Volkerbunde in Berlin. As docent in geography at the University of Berlin, he made a field trip to British Columbia to study the Bella Coola Indians.

Life's Work

The year of 1887 was a critical one in Boas' career. He decided to become an American citizen; he married Marie Krackowizer, who, over the years, was an active supporter of his varied projects; he became assistant editor at the magazine *Science*. In the summer of 1888, he returned to British Columbia to continue his studies of the Northwestern Native American tribes. Eventually, during his lifetime, he published more than ten thousand pages of material from this area of research.

From 1888 to 1892, he taught at Clark University. He then served as chief assistant in the Department of Anthropology at the World Columbian Exposition. He was also the curator of anthropology at the Field Museum in Chicago and worked for the American Museum of Natural History as curator of ethnology and somatology. From 1899 to 1937, he served as professor of anthropology at Columbia University, where he shaped the disciplinary future of the "science of man" by teaching the leading members of the next generation of anthropologists.

His varied activities continued. Boas took part in the Jesup North Pacific Expedition. As honorary philologist at the Bureau of American Ethnology, he published a three-volume work, *Handbook of American Indian Languages* (1911). Boas founded the International School of American Archaeology and Ethnology in Mexico (1910) and the *International Journal of American Linguistics* (1917). He served from 1908 to 1925 as editor of the *Journal of American Folk-Lore*, which was matched by chairmanship of a committee on Native American languages for the American Council of Learned Societies.

During all these institutional and educational activities, Boas constantly wrote scholarly and popular books and articles. In 1911, he published *The Mind of Primitive Man* (revised edition in 1938), "the Magna Carta of race equality." His book destroyed a claim current among intellectuals that physical type bore an inherent relationship to cultural traits. Other books followed: *Primitive Art* (1927), *Anthropology and Modern Life* (1928), *General Anthropology* (1938), and *Race, Language, and Culture* (1940), a collection of his most important papers. During his lifetime, Boas published more than six hundred articles in both the scholarly and popular press.

Boas' writings, museum work, and teaching contributed to the modern concept of cultural pluralism (or relativism). He moved anthropology away from its nineteenth century origin in armchair theory and speculation and toward its twentieth century development as a science, a careful recording of fact and scholarly monographs grounded in empirical history. Thus, Boas contributed to the development of functionalism. Boas discredited the theory of unilinear evolutionism, with its easy assumption of the innate superiority of Western society. He successfully argued that historical differences were significant because environmental opportunity worked diversely on a basically similar human nature.

During his long and productive career, Boas did not neglect his family. He was a strong and loving father; his letters reveal a man committed to his family's welfare and happiness. Unfortunately, two of his six children died suddenly, and his wife was killed in an automobile accident in 1929. Despite these tragic events and a heart attack at seventy-three, Boas continued his scholarly effort. At a Columbia University Faculty Club luncheon, he died suddenly, on December 21, 1942.

Summary

In his own antiauthoritarian style, Boas created modern anthropology. He disliked authority in all of its cultural forms, which included his own scholarship. Highly critical, he was never satisfied with his work; he never accepted as permanent any single anthropological concept. His scholarly style created a "school," but his personality did not. His life, thought, and significance in American history are of a piece.

Influenced by his freethinking family, Boas never hid his views, such as his dislike of racism and anti-Semitism, from public knowledge. While he was not prepared to accept Germany as the sole villain in World War I, Boas was one of the first of his generation of intellectuals to see the terror behind Adolf Hitler's rise to power. Boas acted accordingly. He publicly denounced Nazism early in its reign. His scholarship, in addition to adding to human knowledge, contributed to human liberation from fear and unreasonable authority.

The spirit of liberalism and the scientific method shaped his work and personality. His belief in cultural relativism was evident not only in his scholarship but also in his kindness to others, whom he met in the academy and in the field. As a result of this attitude, Boas accepted, without judgment, people as he met them—in all of their varied ways.

Boas' work linked him with every major methodological and theoretical doctrine in modern anthropology. Rejecting conventional wisdom, he held a theory only as long as it challenged the current dogma. In that way, he remained in the forefront of anthropological theory.

Boas was not a remote scientist, but a citizen-scholar. His study of the children of the Hebrew Orphan Asylum in New York City, for example, stressed the developmental importance of home environment and resulted in a change in the institution's administration. *The Mind of Primitive Man* was a prime weapon against the intellectual assumptions of racism. With this topic, he was concerned with practical humanitarian consequences for public policy.

In brief, with his personal integrity and varied scientific accomplishments, Boas shaped the course of anthropology in the United States. His precision and scholarly certainty in anthropology were extended to his commitment to the policy consequence of the discipline. In both his life and his thought, Franz Boas made vital contributions to the development and ideals of cultural pluralism in America.

Bibliography

Boas, Franz. *The Shaping of American Anthropology, 1883-1911: A Franz Boas Reader*. Edited by George W. Stocking, Jr. New York: Basic Books, 1974. A brilliant introduction, it places Boas in the intellectual context of his time. Organized chronologically, these selections allow the student to follow the evolution of Boas' scholarship.

Helm, June, ed. *Pioneers of American Anthropology: The Uses of Biography*. Seattle: University of Washington Press, 1966. Particularly good on Boas' fieldwork among the Native Americans of the Pacific Northwest, this is a splendid work on how he moved anthropology from an "armchair" or speculative enterprise to a science based on empirical data.

Hinsley, Curtis M., Jr. *Savages and Scientists: The Smithsonian Institution and the Development of American Anthropology, 1846-1900*. Washington, D.C.: Smithsonian Institution Press, 1981. This book illustrates the changing intellectual and institutional context for the study of man during Boas' early career. In his later career, Boas came to dominate the discipline.

Kardiner, Abram, and Edward Preble. *The Studied Man*. Cleveland: World Publishing Co., 1961. Delightfully written, this book is possibly the best introduction to modern anthropology available for the person just starting to explore the field.

Langness, L. L. *The Study of Culture*. San Francisco: Chandler and Sharp, Publishers, 1974. Brief and clearly written, this book is another excellent introduction. It provides a basic orientation.

Leaf, Murray J. *Man, Mind, and Science: A History of Anthropology*. New York: Columbia University Press, 1979. A solid academic history, this study has many merits, but it should be read after consulting some other works.

Penniman, Thomas K. *A Hundred Years of Anthropology*. 3d rev. ed. London: G. Duckworth, 1965. This book is a standard history, particularly strong on the British contributions to the creation of the discipline. The scope includes the related topics of imperialism and colonialism and how they shaped the early concerns of gentlemen-anthropologists—a legacy that Boas rejected.

Silverman, Sydel, ed. *Totems and Teachers: Perspectives on the History of Anthropology*. New York: Columbia University Press, 1981. Former students of famous anthropologists tell about their mentors. The essay on Boas is particularly thoughtful and informative because it reveals him as a private person whose ideas about citizenship and contemporary issues influenced his scholarly concerns.

Spencer, Frank, ed. *A History of American Physical Anthropology: 1930-1980*. New York: Academic Press, 1982. A good source for understanding how Boas changed the emphasis in anthropology from racist assumptions to a cultural focus.

Stocking, George W., Jr. *Race, Culture, and Evolution: Essays in the History of Anthropology*. New York: Free Press, 1968. Stocking is the leading historian of American anthropology. His collection of essays is the best intellectual history of anthropology and its place in American thought. The book is richly informative.

Donald K. Pickens

DANIEL BOONE

Born: November 2, 1734; Berks County, Pennsylvania
Died: September 26, 1820; near St. Charles, Missouri
Areas of Achievement: Exploring and pioneering
Contribution: In addition to opening the trans-Appalachian frontier, Boone became a legendary symbol of the early American frontier.

Early Life

Daniel Boone was born on a Berks County, Pennsylvania, farm on November 2, 1734, the sixth of eleven children. His father, Squire Boone, was the son of an English Quaker who came to Philadelphia in 1717; his mother, Sarah Morgan, was of Welsh ancestry. Young Boone received little, if any, formal schooling, but he learned to read and to write, although his spelling was erratic. His real interest was in the forest, and as a boy he developed into an excellent shot and superb woodsman.

Squire Boone left Pennsylvania in 1750, and by 1751 or 1752, the family was settled on Dutchman's Creek in North Carolina's Yadkin Valley. Daniel hunted and farmed, and he was a wagoner in General Edward Braddock's ill-fated 1755 expedition against Fort Duquesne. He may have been a wagon master three years later, when General John Forbes took the fort. During the 1750's, Boone met John Finley, who captivated him with tales of the lovely land called Kentucky. In young manhood, Boone was five feet eight or nine inches tall, with broad shoulders and chest. Strong and quick, he possessed marvelous endurance and calm nerves. He had blue eyes, a Roman nose, a wide mouth with thin lips, and dark hair that he wore plaited and clubbed. Boone detested coonskin caps and always wore a hat. Mischievous and fun-loving, he was a popular companion, but Boone was happiest when alone in the wilderness. Honest, courageous, quiet, and unpretentious, he inspired confidence, and he accepted the leadership roles thrust upon him.

On August 14, 1756, Daniel married Rebecca Bryan, four years his junior. Between 1757 and 1781, they had ten children, and Rebecca carried much of the burden of rearing them during Daniel's long absences. One child died in infancy, and sons James and Israel were killed in Kentucky by Indians. Rebecca ended Daniel's interest in Florida by refusing to move there in 1766. Boone, sometimes accompanied by brother Squire and brother-in-law John Stuart, explored westward, always tantalized by stories of the fine lands and bountiful game to be found in Kentucky.

Life's Work

On May 1, 1769, Boone, Finley, Stuart, and three hired hands left Boone's cabin for his first extended visit into Kentucky. A successful hunt was spoiled by a band of Shawnee, who took their catch and most of their equipment.

Stuart was later killed, and when the rest of the party went back for supplies in 1770, Boone remained behind to hunt and explore westward. In 1771, some other hunters investigated a strange sound and found Boone, flat on his back, singing at full volume for sheer joy. The seizure of another catch by Indians was a small price to pay for such delights.

In September, 1773, Boone attempted to take his family and some other settlers into Kentucky, but they turned back after an Indian attack in which Boone's son James was among those killed. On the eve of Lord Dunmore's War in 1774, Boone and Michael Stoner were sent to warn hunters and surveyors in Kentucky of the impending danger. In sixty-one days, they covered more than eight hundred wilderness miles, although Boone paused at the incipient settlement at Harrodsburg long enough to claim a lot and throw up a cabin. During the short Indian war, Boone's role as a militia officer was to defend some of Virginia's frontier forts.

During these years, Boone became associated with Judge Richard Henderson, who dreamed of establishing a new colony (Transylvania) in the western lands claimed by the North Carolina and Virginia colonies. Boone helped persuade the Cherokees to sell their claim to Kentucky, and agreement was reached at Sycamore Shoals on March 17, 1775. Anticipating that result, Boone and thirty axmen had already started work on the famed Wilderness Road that brought countless thousands of settlers into Kentucky and helped destroy the wildnerness solitude that Boone loved.

Boonesborough was soon established on the south bank of the Kentucky River, and crops were planted in hastily cleared fields. When Henderson arrived with a larger party, a government was set up with representatives from the tiny, scattered stations. Boone introduced measures for protecting game and improving the breed of horses. Indian raids frightened many of the settlers into fleeing eastward, but during the summer of 1775, Boone brought his family to Boonesborough. Had he joined the exodus, the settlements would probably have been abandoned. Even the capture of a daughter and two other girls by Indians did not shake his determination to hang on. Henderson's grandiose scheme failed when Virginia extended her jurisdiction over the region by creating a vast Kentucky County in December, 1776.

The American Revolution was fought largely along the seaboard, but the British used Indians to attack the Kentucky settlements; the war in the West was fought for survival. Boone accepted the new nation created in 1776, but he was later charged with Toryism and treasonable association with the enemy. A court-martial cleared him of all charges, and he received a militia promotion.

During a raid led by Shawnee chief Blackfish, Boone's life was saved by young Simon Kenton, one of his few peers as a woodsman. The Indian incursions brought the settlers near starvation, as both hunting and farming were dangerous. When Boone was captured near Blue Licks by a large Shawnee raiding party on February 7, 1778, he persuaded his twenty-six salt-makers to surrender to save their lives. Boone then convinced Blackfish to return home, that Boonesborough would capitulate in the spring. Boone was adopted by Chief Blackfish, who refused to sell him to the British in Detroit. "Big Turtle," as Boone was called by the Shawnee, enjoyed Indian life, but he escaped in June, 1778, to warn Kentuckians of an impending attack. By horse until it failed, and then on foot, Boone covered 160 miles in four days with only one meal, and upon his arrival Boonesborough's defenses were hastily improved. In any event, the attacking party of four hundred Indians and a dozen French Canadians did not arrive until September 7. The settlers prolonged negotiations, hoping that help would arrive, and the nine-day siege was one of the longest in Indian warfare. All hostile stratagems failed, and Boonesborough survived.

George Rogers Clark's 1778-1779 campaign in the Illinois country and later expeditions against the Indian towns eased some of the danger. Indeed, Boonesborough was becoming too crowded for Boone, and in October, 1779, he moved to Boone's Station, a few miles from the fort. Boone had acquired some wealth, but he and a companion were robbed of between forty and fifty thousand dollars when they went east in 1780 to purchase land warrants. Boone felt honor-bound to repay the persons who had entrusted money to him.

Boone's hunting exploits, escapes from Indians, and other feats of skill and endurance made him a legend in his own time. Kentucky was divided into three counties in November, 1780, and Boone's importance was recognized by appointments as Fayette's sheriff, county-lieutenant, lieutenant-colonel of militia, and deputy surveyor, and election to the Virginia legislature. Captured by the British in Charlottesville in 1781, Boone soon escaped or was paroled.

In August, 1782, after an Indian attack on Bryan's Station failed, Boone's warnings went unheeded, and the rash pursuers were ambushed near Blue Licks; Boone's son Israel was among the sixty-four white casualties. Boone participated in expeditions across the Ohio River to curb the Indians, but he criticized Clark for not moving his headquarters to the eastern settlements for better protection. This criticism failed to take into account Clark's responsibilities for the Illinois country as well as for Kentucky: Louisville was a central location from which Clark could move quickly in either direction.

About 1783, Boone moved to Livestone (Maysville) on the Ohio River, where he opened a store, surveyed, hunted, and worked on prisoner exchanges with the Indians. His fame spread throughout the nation and to Europe after 1784, when John Filson added a thirty-four-page Boone "autobiography" to *The Discovery, Settlement and Present State of Kentucke* (1784). In 1789 or 1790, Boone moved to Point Pleasant, in what became West Virginia, but he was in the Blue Licks area by 1795. By then, defective land titles had cost him most of his good lands, and Boone ceased to contest any claims brought against him. Disappointed by his treatment and convinced that Kentucky, a state since 1792, was becoming too crowded, Boone decided to move to Missouri, where Spanish officials welcomed him. In 1799, just before he was sixty-five, Boone led a party across the Mississippi River and settled on land some sixty miles west of St. Louis.

The next few years were happy ones. Despite rheumatism, Boone could still hunt, and the wilderness lured him into long journeys westward, perhaps as far as the Yellowstone. He received large land grants, and as a magistrate he held court under a "Justice Tree." The old pioneer was incensed in 1812, when he was rejected as a volunteer for the War of 1812; he was only seventy-eight and ready to fight. Rebecca died in 1813, and Boone probably made his last long hunt in 1817. He had a handsome coffin made and stored for future use. After the Louisiana Purchase, through carelessness and a series of misunderstandings, he lost most of his Missouri land, just as he had earlier lost his holdings in Kentucky.

Boone probably made his last visit to Kentucky in 1817; he was reputed to have only fifty cents left in his pocket after he paid the last of his creditors. Two years later, Chester Harding painted Boone's only life portrait. Boone died at a son's home near St. Charles on September 26, 1820, after a brief illness. In 1845, his and Rebecca's remains were reinterred on a hill above Frankfort, Kentucky.

Summary

Despite his preference for the wilderness, Boone contributed mightily to the end of the Kentucky frontier—by opening roads, building settlements, surveying land, and fighting Indians. Without his leadership, Kentucky's settlement would have been delayed, for he inspired trust that kept settlers from fleeing to safety. This clash between the wilderness paradise and the restrictions of civilization has been a common theme in the history of the American frontier; it remains an issue still.

In addition to his notable accomplishments, Daniel Boone became the symbol of the American frontier during the first half-century of nationhood. James Fenimore Cooper and Lord Byron were only two of many authors who depicted Boone in their works. Both his character and his exploits made Boone a natural hero; men saw in his career the virtues of a way of life that was rapidly vanishing.

Bibliography

Bakeless, John Edwin. *Daniel Boone: Master of the Wilderness*. New York: William Morrow and Co., 1939. Based on the mass of Boone papers in the Draper manuscript collection, this was the best Boone biography until the appearance of Michael A. Lofaro's study.

Chaffee, Allen. *The Wilderness Trail: The Story of Daniel Boone*. New York: T. Nelson and Sons, 1936. A readable account that tells much more about Boone than his connection with the Wilderness Trail, one of the major routes for pioneers who entered Kentucky.

Eckert, Allan W. *The Court Martial of Daniel Boone*. Boston: Little, Brown and Co., 1973. This well-researched and well-written historical novel reconstructs the charges brought against Boone and his successful defense. The trial record disappeared, but this version sounds plausible.

Filson, John. *The Discovery, Settlement and Present State of Kentucke: . . . To Which Is Added . . . the Adventures of Col. Daniel Boon*. Wilmington, Del.: James Adams, 1784. This rare book has been reprinted many times. Although the "autobiography" was written by Filson and contains many errors, he did interview Boone and a number of other Kentuckians for information.

Lofaro, Michael A. *The Life and Adventures of Daniel Boone*. Lexington: University Press of Kentucky, 1979. Despite the size constraints of the Bicentennial Bookshelf series, this is the best of the Boone biographies. It is a concise, highly readable book, and the author succeeds in separating fact from myth.

Thwaites, Reuben Gold. *Daniel Boone*. New York: D. Appleton and Co., 1902. Despite its years, this book remains a well-written and generally accurate biography. The author was one of the first Boone biographers to make use of the Draper manuscripts.

White, Stewart Edward. *Daniel Boone: Wilderness Scout*. New York: Doubleday, Doran and Co., 1926. Frequently reprinted, this flowing narrative was aimed at younger readers. Most of the exciting Boone stories are here.

Lowell H. Harrison

EDWIN BOOTH

Born: November 13, 1833; near Bel Air, Maryland
Died: June 7, 1893; New York, New York
Area of Achievement: Acting
Contribution: The most talented member of a family of actors, Edwin Booth suffered greatly from identity with his younger brother, the assassin John Wilkes Booth, but came to be admired for his art and his role in advancing the profession of acting in the United States.

Early Life

Edwin Thomas Booth was born November 13, 1833, on the family farm near Bel Air, Harford County, Maryland. His mother and father immigrated from London, England. She was the former Mary Ann Holmes, and he was the celebrated but temperamental actor Junius Brutus Booth. Ten children were born to the Booths, but only six of these survived early childhood. Edwin's older brother was Junius Brutus, Jr., and his older sister was Rosalie; his younger sister was Asia, and his younger brothers were John Wilkes and Joseph Adrian. Most of them, like Edwin, were short, slim, dark, and sensitive.

Edwin's formal education was cursory, but he was highly intelligent and a quick learner. Traveling with his alcoholic and unstable father as a boy, he determined to become an actor. He made his formal debut in Boston in a minor role in William Shakespeare's *Richard III* (1592-1593); two years later, in 1851, he played the lead for the first time in the same play in New York when his father refused to go on. In 1852, Edwin played the California gold camps. Junius Brutus Booth died later that year, and "Booth the Younger" was heralded in San Francisco as a worthy successor; still, it took several more years before Edwin equaled, and then exceeded, the reputation of his father.

In 1854, Booth joined a troupe headed for Australia, headlined by the distinguished actress Laura Keene; they performed in Sydney and Melbourne. Booth parted company with the troupe in Hawaii, following an argument, but while in Honolulu he was able to perform *Richard III* before King Kamehameha IV, using the king's throne for a prop. Then, in Sacramento, California, Booth proved that he could play romantic as well as tragic roles with remarkable skill when he played Raphael in a new melodrama by Charles Selby, *The Marble Heart: Or, The Sculptor's Dream* (1854). By the time he returned to his family at last in 1856, he had the wide experience of a versatile actor.

Life's Work

Between 1857 and 1859, Booth triumphed upon the stage in Boston and

New York, and became so celebrated in these and other cities for his portrayal of Richard III that both his father's version and that of his namesake, Edwin Forrest, were almost forgotten. Booth's voice was resonant and beautiful, and his gestures and looks were expressive and penetrating. No Shakespearean character was beyond him, but his Richard, Iago, Mark Anthony, Macbeth, and Hamlet were especially well received.

Admired by many, the young Edwin Booth had few close friends, among them journalist Adam Badeau and actor David Anderson. They knew better than most of his independent nature and penchant for drinking, and were surprised when he married an actress on July 7, 1860. This was the charming young Mary Devlin, daughter of a bankrupt Troy Devlin, a New York merchant. The Reverend Mr. Samuel Osgood, an Episcopalian clergyman, officiated at the ceremony in his home in New York City. On December 9, 1861, Mary gave birth to their only child, Edwina, but the mother grew ill and died on February 21, 1863. In 1869, Booth married Mary McVicker, stepdaughter of the proprietor of McVicker's Theater in Chicago; the only child of his second marriage, Edgar, died shortly after birth, and his second Mary became insane before her death in 1881.

Making his home in New York in the 1860's, Edwin played opposite Charlotte Cushman in a Philadelphia run of *Macbeth* (1606) and starred in *The Merchant of Venice* (1596-1597) and several other plays in London. In England, however, he was not as satisfied with his performances and their reception as he was in New York. The outbreak of the Civil War in the spring of 1861 also convinced him to stay close to home. Edwin, like most of the Booths, but certainly unlike John Wilkes, was supportive of the Union.

After becoming comanager of New York's Winter Garden Theatre, Edwin was able to produce his favorite Shakespearean plays and star in them as well. Obviously one of these favorites was singularly popular, as his production of *Hamlet, Prince of Denmark* (c. 1600-1601) ran for one hundred consecutive performances. Then, too, his production of *Julius Caesar* (c. 1599-1600) with Edwin as Brutus and his brothers Junius as Cassius and John Wilkes as Mark Anthony, was very well received. The assassination of President Lincoln, however, by the latter brother five months later, in April 1865, disgraced the family and forced Edwin to suffer an almost nine-month retirement from the public view.

Having been performing in Boston, Edwin returned to New York for his self-confinement. There he received several death threats, and the *New York Herald* treated him savagely. At first he expected never to perform again, but debts mounted and the *New York Tribune* appealed to him in print that he not waste his considerable talent. At last, on January 3, 1866, a nervous Booth appeared at New York's Winter Garden as Hamlet. The theater was packed, and the audience rose as one to applaud him at the opening curtain.

On January 22, 1867, Booth received a much-delayed gold medal for his unparalleled achievement two years before in the first hundred-night run of *Hamlet*. His popularity was such now that theatergoers in almost every major city in North America asked to see him. A renewed *Hamlet* was followed by a production of Lord Lytton's *Richelieu: Or, The Conspiracy* (1839), then *The Merchant of Venice*, and then *Brutus: Or, The Fall of Tarquin*, by John Howard Payne. All were well received, but in *Brutus* fire was used to portray the burning of Rome, and it burned out of control one day in March to engulf the theater. With the destruction of the Winter Garden, Booth lost his finest costumes and was compelled to play benefit performances in Chicago and Baltimore.

Upon the advice of friends such as William Bispham, Booth built his own, superior, theater at the corner of Twenty-third Street and Sixth Avenue. Richard A. Robertson, a Boston businessman, was taken in as a partner. The Booth Theatre opened February 3, 1869, with a lackluster performance of *Romeo and Juliet* (c. 1595-1596). The critics felt that Booth and Mary McVicker were unconvincing in their romantic, title roles, yet they were married soon thereafter.

The excellent building, new costumes, props, and actors made the Booth Theatre the outstanding showplace for Shakespearean drama in America. Charlotte Cushman and others were coaxed out of retirement when given the opportunity to perform there. The great Edwin Forrest, however, refused to play in Booth's theater.

Booth's productions followed the Shakespearean texts rather than later adaptations, and historians were consulted to gain authenticity for the sets. Still, Booth was a poor businessman, and when he quarreled with Robertson the latter sold out to Booth, leaving the actor-manager heavily in debt. Booth's brother Junius tried to straighten out his affairs, but the Panic of 1873 destroyed their hopes. Early in 1874, Edwin Booth filed for bankruptcy, owing almost $200,000.

Repayment came, however, after Booth made a comeback in New York in October, 1875, when he played his unassailable Hamlet at Augustin Daly's Fifth Avenue Theater. A budding star in his own right also in the cast then was Maurice Barrymore, father of Ethel, Lionel, and John. In desperation, Booth now dared even to play Richard II and King Lear, although the former was new to him and the latter role had long been thought the special property of Edwin Forrest. These performances too won him much credit. He also played to packed houses in the South, although he had formerly refused to go there. In 1876, Booth performed with distinction at the California Theater in San Francisco.

Although his debts were paid off within two years of his bankruptcy and he was becoming more popular than ever, he still received threats on his life. On April 23, 1879, a madman named Mark Gray shot at him, twice, from the audience while Booth was acting the role of Richard II at McVicker's Theater in Chicago. Both shots went wild, and a composed Booth strode to the footlights so that he might point out the culprit to the police.

In the 1880's, Booth performed in Europe: in London (with Henry Irving) and elsewhere in the British Isles, in Berlin and other German cities, and in Vienna. Everywhere, but especially in Berlin, he was lauded for his Shakespearean roles, and invitations were extended from France, Spain, Italy, and Russia. Booth declined these offers; his dream was semiretirement in New England, and he returned to build a cottage called "Boothden" on the Rhode Island coast near Newport. He also acquired a larger house in Boston.

In 1888, Booth founded and served as first president of New York's club, The Players. When he performed in his later years, he liked to costar with accomplished younger actors such as Tommaso Salvini, Helena Modjeska, and Otis Skinner, and especially with another "old trouper," Lawrence Barrett. After Barrett's death in 1891, Booth, in ill health, gave fewer and less inspired performances. His last effort was as Hamlet on April 4, 1891, at the Brooklyn Academy of Music. He weakened, suffered a brain hemorrhage, and died in New York on June 7, 1893, at the age of fifty-nine.

Summary

Booth, in his prime, was probably the world's preeminent tragedian. His performance as Hamlet moved even Germans unfamiliar with English to tears. His apt movements and the quiet but perfect modulation of his voice, its timbre and clarity, seemed to late nineteenth century audiences much more natural and refined than the loud, forced theatrics of a previous generation. Like Forrest's, Booth's King Lear was considered exquisite, but almost all the other tragic characters in Shakespeare's plays were also his meat.

Unfortunately, Booth's private life echoed the tragedy he played out upon the stage. His actor-brother's assassination of Lincoln, his father's and his own bouts with alcoholism, the failure of the Booth Theatre, the early deaths of his two Marys, and his own rapid aging were truly components of a tragic life. At last he lost heart and almost seemed to will his own death.

While the solid structure of the Booth Theatre was torn down in his lifetime, the subtle delicacy of his acting technique remains in the better theatrical performances of today. In his lifetime, he was forever compared, usually unfavorably, to his father, but Edwin Booth is universally recognized today as the greater actor of the two, and by far superior to Junius, Jr., and John Wilkes. Yet it is the continuing tragedy of the Booths that the best known of their number is the one who killed Abraham Lincoln.

Bibliography
Goodale, Katherine. *Behind the Scenes with Edwin Booth*. Boston:

Houghton Mifflin Co., 1931. This is a charming and lively account of Booth's professional life during the years when the author knew him (after 1870). Goodale, who performed under the stage name Kitty Molony, makes excellent observations relating to Booth's mastery of his craft and is one of several authors to suggest that, despite his personal tragedies, he led a "charmed life."

Grossman, Edwina Booth. *Edwin Booth: Recollections by His Daughter*. New York: Century Co., 1894. Booth's sole surviving child was especially close to him during the years of his greatest success. His letters to her and some of his letters to friends such as David Anderson and William Bispham give this eulogy added strength and research value.

Kimmel, Stanley. *The Mad Booths of Maryland*. Indianapolis: Bobbs-Merrill Co., 1940. One of the best and most readable books ever written about the Booth family, this one does much to explain the strained relationship between Edwin Booth and his brother, John Wilkes. All the Booth family members are dealt with here and treated with balance and fairness.

Lockridge, Richard. *Darling of Misfortune*. New York: Century Co., 1932. This is a sound enough biography, but one that was superseded by Ruggles' work (see below). It is, perhaps, most valuable on the brief life span of the Booth Theatre.

Ruggles, Eleanor. *Prince of Players: Edwin Booth*. New York: W. W. Norton, 1953. At this writing still the definitive biography of Booth, the book reflects the author's exhaustive research. While sympathetic toward her tragic subject, Ruggles does not hesitate to reveal the extent of his early struggle with alcoholism, which she believes to have been quieted only by the shock of his first wife's death.

Skinner, Otis. *The Last Tragedian*. New York: Dodd, Mead and Co., 1939. Skinner, the father of the renowned actress Cornelia Otis Skinner, based this insider's account of Booth on their performances together, also making effective use of selected Booth letters.

Winter, William. *Life and Art of Edwin Booth*. New York: Macmillan, 1893. The celebrated drama critic of the *New York Tribune* was a longtime friend and confidant of Booth; he was also a prolific author, many of whose other works refer to the celebrated actor. This book contains much of value on the ups and downs of a remarkable career.

Joseph E. Suppiger

WILLIAM E. BORAH

Born: June 29, 1865; Jasper, Illinois
Died: January 19, 1940; Washington, D.C.
Area of Achievement: Politics
Contribution: For more than three decades in the United States Senate, Borah was a leading nationalist who spoke and voted courageously for his idealistic view of American democracy.

Early Life

William Edgar Borah was born on June 29, 1865, in Wayne County in southern Illinois. The seventh child in a family of ten, he grew up in a household where hard work and religious devotion were stressed. His father, William Nathan Borah, was a strict disciplinarian and lay preacher at the local Presbyterian church. His mother, Elizabeth, moderated her husband's sternness. Grammar school, reading at home, and the tedium of farm chores marked the early life of young Borah. He attended the Cumberland Presbyterian Academy at nearby Enfield but left after only one year, largely because of insufficient family finances.

At the invitation of his sister, Sue Lasley, Borah moved to Kansas to continue his education, entering the University of Kansas in the fall of 1885. He left in 1887, after contracting tuberculosis, but not before developing an interest in the history and economics courses of Professor James H. Canfield and demonstrating proficiency at debate. He studied law in the office of his brother-in-law, Ansel Lasley, passed the bar examination in September, 1887, and entered practice with Lasley in Lyons, Kansas. Both men found the legal profession less profitable as poverty spread throughout Kansas in the late 1880's; when the Lasleys moved to Chicago in 1890, Borah set out for the developing West to make his mark.

Although associated with Idaho for his entire political career, he landed in the state almost by accident. He allegedly traveled to the Northwest until his money ran out, near Boise, which he saw as a fertile area for a young lawyer. He quickly built a solid reputation there. At the age of twenty-five, Borah was powerfully built, with a thick neck, a broad face, and a deeply cleft chin which denoted honesty and forthrightness; these physical attributes, combined with his oratorical abilities and a capacity for hard work, made him a forceful figure in the courtroom. He built a large practice and a statewide reputation as a criminal lawyer before 1900; thereafter, he mainly practiced corporate law, which earned for him an annual income of thirty thousand dollars.

Borah entered Boise politics in 1891 and was chairman of the Republican State Central Committee the next year. In 1895, Borah married Mary McConnell, the daughter of the state's Republican Governor, William J.

McConnell, for whom Borah worked as secretary. Following his bolt from the Republican Party for William Jennings Bryan and "free silver" in 1896, Borah returned to lead Idaho's Progressive Republicans to statewide victories in 1901-1902. He campaigned for the United States Senate in 1906, as a vigorous supporter of President Theodore Roosevelt, and was selected by the state legislature early in 1907.

Before taking his seat in the Senate later that year, Borah was involved in two significant trials in Idaho; the first helped establish him as a national figure of importance, while the second threatened to end his public career as it was beginning. In the earlier case, Borah was appointed special prosecutor against William D. Haywood and two other leaders of the Western Federation of Miners, who were charged with conspiracy in the bombing death of former Governor Frank Steunenberg. While the jury voted to acquit the three, Borah was nevertheless outstanding in the fairness and clarity of his nine-hour summation for the prosecution. Borah was himself the defendant in the second case, in which he was charged with timber fraud while serving as attorney for the Barber Lumber Company. Although the incident was an ordeal for Borah, the evidence presented against him at the trial was flimsy, substantiating his charge that the affair was devised by his enemies to kill his political future. The jury acquitted him after less than fifteen minutes of deliberation. He was now free to assume the office in Washington which he would hold through five more elections, until he died.

Life's Work

Borah entered the Senate at a favorable time. The Progressive viewpoint was ascendant in national political affairs, and Borah was closely aligned with the Senate Progressive bloc on a number of issues. Furthermore, he was especially fortunate in being in a position to act, since Senate leader Nelson W. Aldrich assumed that Borah's former position as a corporate attorney meant that he shared Aldrich's pro-business, anti-labor outlook; consequently, Aldrich assigned Borah to choice committee appointments, including the chairmanship of the Committee on Education and Labor.

It was mainly during his first term that Borah earned his reputation for Progressive leadership. He sponsored bills for the creation of the Department of Labor and a Children's Bureau, and pushed for an eight-hour day for government-contracted labor. In addition, he was a mainstay in the fight for the direct election of United States Senators (which became the Seventeenth Amendment in 1913) and for the income tax (the Sixteenth Amendment, 1913). In the latter struggle, his major early contribution was his effective argument for the constitutionality of the income tax, contrary to the Supreme Court's finding in an 1895 case.

Borah also proved to be an effective representative of Idaho and other Western states on several key issues. He favored President William Howard

Taft's proposal for a reciprocal trade agreement between the United States and Canada, involving free trade in some raw materials and agricultural products, an agreement favored by Western farmers. (The agreement passed in Congress but failed in the Canadian legislature.) He successfully promoted a plan for government-issued reclamation bonds, mainly used to finance irrigation projects in the Western states. He was the cosponsor of the Borah-Jones Act (1912), which reduced, from five years to three years, the period required for residence before homesteaders could acquire patents to the land they claimed. Finally, he managed to free, for private development, some Western land which the federal government had set aside for conservation.

Borah was not included in the roll call of other Progressives on all these issues, especially in regard to conservation matters. He was critical of the federal government's administration of conservation policy, believing that the individual states should play a greater role. In the *cause célèbre* over Interior Secretary Richard Ballinger's removal of Chief Forester Gifford Pinchot, Borah broke with the Progressives in supporting Ballinger and the Taft Administration; he also supported the Administration on the controversial Payne-Aldrich Tariff. In the election of 1912, Borah led the Theodore Roosevelt forces in the National Republican Convention but refused to bolt from the Republican Party when Roosevelt's followers formed the Progressive Party. During Woodrow Wilson's first term, Borah continued to be a selective Progressive, as he voted against legislation such as the Federal Trade Commission Act, the Clayton Antitrust Act, and the creation of the Federal Reserve system. Although opposition to some of these bills was based on partisan political considerations, Borah generally opposed federal centralization and often referred to states' rights in explaining his votes against measures supported by other Progressives.

Borah began to change the focus of his interests to international affairs with the onset of World War I; in the decades following the war, he became the acknowledged Senate spokesman on foreign policy for his party. He supported preparation for war in 1916, backed Wilson's breaking of diplomatic relations with Germany in February, 1917, and voted for the declaration of war in April. Like other Progressives, however, he became disillusioned with the war effort, which severely limited reform achievements, and stated that, if it were possible, he would change the vote he had cast in favor of war. At the end of World War I, he led the Senate irreconcilables in the fight against the Treaty of Versailles and the League of Nations, stating that it was not in the best interests of the United States to become entangled in the affairs of Europe.

As a nationalist in foreign affairs, Borah opposed any international agreements that would restrict the country's freedom of choice to act in world affairs. While he opposed American membership in the World Court as well as in the League of Nations, he was a strong proponent of disarmament plans.

He was instrumental in organizing the Washington conference on disarmament in 1921 and, as Chairman of the Senate Committee on Foreign Relations after 1924, he supported plans for the international outlawry of war, which culminated in the Kellogg-Briand Pact of 1928. In the face of the international crises of the 1930's, Borah became increasingly isolationist, favoring the restriction of American trade and diplomatic involvement abroad.

Borah differed with the Republican Party on major political issues during the 1920's, but he refused to leave the party in 1924 to support his longtime political ally, Robert M. LaFollette, the Progressive Party candidate for president. He was a leading campaigner for Herbert Hoover in 1928, although he became a consistent critic of Hoover policies after the election. He supported most of the major legislation of the New Deal, with the exception of the National Industrial Recovery Act, which he criticized for its suspension of antitrust laws. Following his sixth consecutive election to the Senate, in 1936, he concentrated most of his energy on opposing the foreign policies of Franklin D. Roosevelt's administration. In January, 1940, he suffered a cerebral hemorrhage and died three days later. Following a funeral in the Senate chamber, he was buried in Boise.

Summary

In 1936, journalist Walter Lippmann wrote a trenchant description of Senator Borah as "an individualist who opposes all concentration of power, who is against private privilege and private monopoly, against political bureaucracy and centralized government." Lippmann was describing Borah the Jeffersonian Democrat, who believed in an ideal vision of the United States, with a relatively uncomplicated political system based on direct democracy, with guarantees for the freewheeling expression of rights by the individual, and without favoritism for special interests. These were the essential beliefs of Borah's political life, formed in his youth by family guidance and by reading authors such as Ralph Waldo Emerson, reinforced by his rural environment in Illinois, Kansas, and Idaho, and forged by his contacts with the Populists in the 1890's. Such beliefs formed the underpinnings of Borah's Progressive leadership.

Borah attempted to apply these principles throughout his public career. In his speeches and actions, he made it clear that his conscience and convictions served as his guide on major national issues, rather than considerations of party loyalty or personal popularity. In writing to a constituent about his religious ideals in opposition to the Ku Klux Klan, Borah averred, "If the time ever comes when I shall have to sacrifice my office for these principles, I shall unhesitatingly do so."

Borah's idealistic conception of the United States, while not always based on a realistic appraisal of modern conditions, influenced the nation during his career in the Senate because of his brilliance as an orator. He shared the belief of many other Progressives in the power of public opinion as a moral force and sought to mobilize that force through scores of well-researched and well-rehearsed addresses in Congress and the nation. His oratorical abilities, as well as the courageous pursuit of his convictions, placed him in the front rank of public men of his time.

Bibliography

Ashby, LeRoy. *The Spearless Leader: Senator Borah and the Progressive Movement in the 1920's.* Urbana: University of Illinois Press, 1972. Treats Borah's involvement in domestic affairs from 1920 to 1928, while most other accounts concentrate only on his foreign policy views as chairman of the Senate Committee on Foreign Relations. Valuable not only for Borah's viewpoints but also as a consideration of the fate of Progressivism in the 1920's.

Borah, William Edgar. *Bedrock: Views on Basic National Problems.* Washington, D.C.: National Home Library Foundation, 1936. Includes speeches and a few articles from 1909 to 1936, organized by topic. Introduces the reader to the flavor of Borah's speeches on a wide range of topics and presents Borah's viewpoints on what he considered to be paramount issues.

Cooper, John M., Jr. "William E. Borah, Political Thespian." *Pacific Northwest Quarterly* 56 (October, 1965): 145-153. A stimulating discussion of Borah's career, in which the author maintains that Borah's decision to deliver moral exhortations on issues, rather than to take bolder actions in the Senate, limited his effectiveness in public life. The article is followed with comments by two other Borah scholars and a reply by Cooper.

Johnson, Claudius O. *Borah of Idaho.* New York: Longmans, Green and Co., 1936. Reprint. Seattle: University of Washington Press, 1967. The reprint edition includes a section on Borah's last years and the author's reevaluation of his career. Based largely on interviews with Borah, as well as the Borah papers, the book is thorough (to 1936) but often partial in its advocacy of Borah's views.

McKenna, Marian C. *Borah.* Ann Arbor: University of Michigan Press, 1961. The most complete and balanced biography of Borah. A well-written book, it is based, in part, on papers relating to Borah's early career, which the Idaho State Historical Society received in 1956.

Maddox, Robert James. *William E. Borah and American Foreign Policy.* Baton Rouge: Louisiana State University Press, 1969. Evaluates Borah's positions on major foreign policy issues from World War I until the eve of World War II. Maddox asserts that Borah's seemingly paradoxical (for an isolationist) interest in international conferences and treaties was actually a smoke screen for obstructing meaningful United States involvement in international organizations.

Vinson, John Chalmers. *William E. Borah and the Outlawry of War*. Athens: University of Georgia Press, 1957. Treats Borah's growing interest, from 1917, in the movement to "outlaw" war, which resulted in the 1928 Kellogg-Briand Pact. A thoroughly documented account based primarily on Borah's papers in the Library of Congress.

Richard G. Frederick

WILLIAM BRADFORD

Born: March, 1590; Austerfield, England
Died: May 19, 1657; Plymouth, Massachusetts
Areas of Achievement: Government and historiography
Contribution: Bradford was the leader of the Pilgrims once they settled in America, and he was the author of a history of Plymouth colony, one of the great works of early American literature.

Early Life

William Bradford was born in March, 1590 (baptized on March 29), at Austerfield, Yorkshire, England, one of three children and the only son of William Bradford, a yeoman farmer, and Alice Hanson. His father died when he was sixteen months old. Upon his mother's remarriage when Bradford was four, he was put into the custody of his grandfather, after whose death in 1596 he went to live with his uncles, Robert and Thomas Bradford. "Like his ancestors," William Bradford pursued "the affairs of husbandry." At age twelve, Bradford started attending religious services conducted by Richard Clyfton, at Babworth, eight miles from Austerfield. The group was made up of Separatists, who believed in the sovercign authority of the Scriptures and the autonomy of each church. The Separatists had spun off from the Puritan movement, which sought reform toward greater simplicity in the worship and practices of the Church of England. When Clyfton's own congregation split, he took part of the original group to hold services at the bishop's manor house in Scrooby. William Brewster, who became a mentor and tutor for Bradford, was the local bailiff and postmaster and resided at the bishop's decaying mansion. John Robinson, who later would be the leader of the group when they went to Holland, was teacher of the congregation. Bradford had only to walk three miles to attend services at Scrooby, which was in Nottinghamshire, 150 miles north of London.

The Scrooby Separatists, completely at odds with the national church and fearing further persecution after King James I ascended the throne, sought refuge in the Netherlands. Failing in their first attempt to leave England in 1607, having been betrayed by the ship's captain, the following year via a Dutch vessel they went to Amsterdam, where they stayed briefly, and then moved to the university town of Leyden. The Netherlands offered the refugees full freedom of conscience. Their new home proved a relief, as Bradford said, from the situation which the Pilgrims (as they were to be called) had faced in England, where they were "hunted and persecuted on every side, so that their former afflictions were but as flea-bitings in comparison of those which now came upon them."

At Leyden the Pilgrims worked as artisans, with Bradford becoming a maker of fustian (a twilled cloth of cotton and linen). While in Leyden,

Bradford learned some Latin and Hebrew. Coming of age in 1611, he gained an inheritance from his uncles, which he applied to buying a house; he also became a Dutch citizen. In December, 1613, Bradford married Dorothy May. The Pilgrims were unhappy in their new home for a variety of reasons, but chiefly for that of being an alien people in a strange land. In 1617, Bradford was one of a committee to make arrangements to take the congregation to America.

With the expedition financed by a joint stock company formed by English merchants and a patent from the Virginia Company (which was invalid because of where the Pilgrims had settled and was replaced a year later with one from the Council of New England), the Pilgrims set out for America. Shares in the company were ten pounds each, with an actual settler receiving one free. Bradford was among the 102 persons who crossed the Atlantic in the *Mayflower*, and was a signer of the Mayflower Compact in November of 1620 as the ship anchored off the tip of Cape Cod. This document, as John Quincy Adams observed, was "the first example in modern times of a social compact or system of government instituted by voluntary agreement conformably to the laws of nature, by men of equal rights and about to establish their community in a new country." Bradford led exploring parties, and the colonists chose a site at what is now Plymouth, Massachusetts. On December 17, 1620 (N.S.), Bradford's wife fell overboard and drowned, possibly a suicide. In August, 1623, he married Alice Carpenter, widow of Edward Southworth.

Life's Work

Upon the death of John Carver in 1621, William Bradford was elected governor of the colony, remaining in that office until his death in 1657, with the exception of the years 1633 to 1634, 1636, 1638, and 1644. He received no salary until 1639, when he was paid twenty pounds annually. Bradford virtually dominated the colony's government, which had no standing under English law and had no charter from the king. Bradford, however, shared executive, legislative, and judicial powers with a court of assistants, which by the 1640's numbered eight people. The governor and assistants were elected annually by the freemen at large. Beginning in 1638, legislative powers were divided with a lower house of two representatives from each town, starting with those from Plymouth town, Duxbury, and Scituate. Bradford assisted in the codification of the Plymouth laws in 1636, significant as the first such embodiment of statutes in the Colonies, also noteworthy for setting forth basic rights.

Bradford and his colony faced many hardships. The people who emigrated to the settlement were poor, and for the most part the land was of poor quality. Lacking means for capital investment, the Pilgrims made little progress in establishing shipping and fishing industries. For a while they enjoyed success in the fur trade, but had to compete with the Dutch, the French, and the English in that pursuit. The colony struggled to pay off its indebtedness. Bradford, realizing that the communal system discouraged initiative, had it abandoned in 1623. In 1627, he and seven other colonists and four Londoners associated as "Undertakers" to pay off the eighteen-hundred-pound debt to the English members of the joint stock company, which was now dissolved. Bradford and the other "Undertakers" were given a monopoly of the fur trade and offshore fishing. Still, it was not until the 1640's that the debt was paid. Also at the time of dissolving the connection with the English merchants, all property in the colony, real and personal, was divided equally among heads of families and free single men.

Bradford and the Pilgrims fortunately had scant troubles with the Indians. The Patuxet Indians, who had lived in the vicinity of Plymouth town, had died off from the white man's diseases, principally the plague (typhus) brought over by English fishermen. Two Indians, Samoset and Squanto, who had themselves been to Great Britain and spoke the English language, served at the outset as a vital liaison with other Indians. Bradford was successful in keeping the friendship of Massasoit, chief of the Wampanoags, the only strong tribe in close proximity to the colony.

Indeed, though troops were mustered on several occasions to be sent against the Indians (for example, during the Pequot War of 1637), the colony under Bradford's administration contended with no large Indian hostility. Miles Standish's butchery of several Massachusetts Indians at Wessagusett can, however, be charged to Bradford's blame.

Amazingly, the latitude of freedom at Plymouth was great, in contrast to the Puritan colonies. At first seeking to oust dissenters, Bradford came to favor a policy of tolerance, allowing persons of other faiths to settle in the colony. Yet Bradford was thin-skinned with those who put the Pilgrims in a bad light in England, and once, upon intercepting the letters of two such individuals, forced them to return to England. A major blotch on Bradford's career was his overreaction to the "wickedness" of the times, namely during the alleged sex-crime wave of 1642. During this brief hysteria, induced largely by anxiety over an Indian crisis, a teenager was hanged for buggery. Otherwise, to the Pilgrims' credit, there were only executions for murder. In addition to serving as governor, Bradford was a commissioner of the Puritan defensive confederation, the United Colonies of New England, in the years 1647 to 1649, 1652, and 1656.

Of Plimmoth Plantation is Bradford's masterpiece. Probably intended only for the enlightenment of his family, it was not published in its entirety until 1856. For a long time, the manuscript was lost, probably taken out of the country by a British soldier during the Revolution; it surfaced at the Bishop of London's Library at Fulham Palace. In the late nineteenth century, as a goodwill gesture, it was returned to the United States. Bradford worked on it at various times, from 1630 to 1650, writing from notes, correspondence, and memory. The history traces the whole Pilgrim story from their English exile to 1646. Other writings of Bradford include admonitory poems and two dialogues between "some Younge-men borne in New-England" and "Ancient men which came out of Holand and Old England." Bradford was also the coauthor of the promotional tract, *Mourt's Relation* (published in London, 1622), and letters, printed as *Governor Bradford's Letter Book*, in the *Collections of the Massachusetts Historical Society*, first series, volume 3 (1794; reprinted in 1968).

Besides his home in Plymouth, Bradford had a three-hundred-acre farm on the tidal Jones River and scattered real estate elsewhere, which made him the largest landowner in the colony. Bradford, during the evening of the day in which he dictated his will, died, on May 19, 1657 (N.S.). He was buried on the hills overlooking Plymouth. He left four children: John (by his first wife), William, Mercy, and Joseph.

Summary

William Bradford's life epitomized the plain and simple virtues of a people longing to be free. From yeoman farmer in England to artisan in Leyden to immigrant in a primitive land, he displayed the courage and faith of one who believed that there was a better way. With skill, a sense of fair play, and an open-mindedness, he guided his people to founding a successful community, which would eventually grow into some twenty towns. Bradford's colony was unable to secure a charter, largely because of the lack of resources needed to support a lobbying effort in England. Plymouth colony would later be incorporated into the royal colony of Massachusetts Bay, an event that Bradford probably would not have been too happy about, considering the differences between the Puritans and the Pilgrims. While Bradford discouraged people from hiving off and forming new settlements, he himself became a suburbanite, tending his farm outside of Plymouth.

Bradford's administration brought peace and stability to Plymouth, and the Pilgrim experience in founding government served as a model for the establishment of other colonies. In Plymouth colony, under Bradford, there was a rigid separation of church and state, as to officeholding, though between them there was a mutuality of action.

Bradford's history of Plymouth exemplifies highest standards of clarity and straightforward prose; at the same time, it is enlivened by an understated humor that belies the popular image of the Pilgrims. It is regarded as one of the major works of Colonial American literature.

Bibliography

Bartlett, Robert M. *The Pilgrim Way*. Philadelphia: United Church Press, 1971. Sponsored by the Pilgrim Society, Plymouth, Massachusetts. Discusses the Pilgrims only through the early years in America. Though emphasizing the role of John Robinson and religious issues, it probes the thinking and actions of the Pilgrim leaders, including Bradford.

Bradford, William. *Of Plimmoth Plantation*. Edited by Charles P. Deane. Boston: Massachusetts Historical Society, 1856. Reprint. New York: Random House, 1952. This work has undergone a number of editions since it was first published. Samuel E. Morison's 1952 reprint with the modernized title *Of Plymouth Plantation* is the most readable of the various editions. Morison lists all the previously published editions.

Dillon, Francis. *The Pilgrims*. Garden City, N.Y.: Doubleday and Co., 1973. Popularly written but well researched, this narrative traces the Pilgrim story to the time of the death of Bradford. Views the Pilgrim experience through Bradford's eyes.

Langdon, George D., Jr. *Pilgrim Colony: A History of New Plymouth, 1620-1691*. New Haven, Conn.: Yale University Press, 1966. A scholarly and perceptive examination of the Plymouth colony until its union with Massachusetts Bay colony. Emphasis is on the government and institutions.

Runyan, Michael G., ed. *William Bradford: The Collected Verse*. St. Paul, Minn.: John Colet Press, 1974. Contains the seven items of verse attributed to Bradford. Places the poems in their historical context and in the context of Bradford's life as well as discussing their literary qualities.

Shurtleff, Nathaniel B., and David Pulsifer, eds. *Records of the Colony of New Plymouth in New England*. Boston: Press of W. White, 1861. Reprint. 11 vols. New York: AMS Press, 1968. All of Bradford's service as governor can be discerned from this collection, which contains the records of the General Court (governor, assistants, and deputies). Volume 11 is a compilation of the colony's laws.

Smith, Bradford. *Bradford of Plymouth*. Philadelphia: J. B. Lippincott Co., 1951. The only full-scale biography of Bradford. It is well researched but glosses over many topics.

Westbrook, Perry D. *William Bradford*. Boston: Twayne Publishers, 1978. Examines all of Bradford's writings from the point of view of literary criticism. Contains a chronology of Bradford's life.

Willison, George F. *Saints and Strangers*. New York: Reynal and Hitchcock, 1945. This is a lively and thorough narrative of the Pilgrim experience to 1691, stressing the early years. On small points the reliability and interpretations of the author are questionable. An appendix identifies all members of the "Pilgrim Company" who arrived in the colony during the formative period.

Harry M. Ward

OMAR N. BRADLEY

Born: February 12, 1893; Clark, Missouri
Died: April 8, 1981; New York, New York
Area of Achievement: The military
Contribution: Bradley provided stability and continuity within the American
  military establishment during the critical period following the end of World
  War II and the onset of the Cold War.

Early Life

Omar Nelson Bradley was born on February 12, 1893, just outside the small town of Clark, Missouri. His father, John Smith Bradley, was a schoolteacher, and his mother, Sarah Elizabeth Hubbard Bradley, was a homemaker. Though "desperately poor," to use Bradley's words, his family took in the two daughters of his mother's sister when the latter died and they became his "sisters." A second son was born to the Bradleys, but died of scarlet fever before his second birthday.

Bradley's father, who supplemented the modest income he received from his teaching with what odd jobs he could find, contracted pneumonia and died in January, 1908. The family moved to Moberly, where Bradley attended high school and became interested in Mary Quayle, the daughter of his Sunday school teacher and his future wife. Having been graduated in 1910 with good grades, "but not the highest," Bradley planned to become a lawyer, though he was uncertain as to how he would fund his education. His Sunday school superintendent suggested that he consider the United States Military Academy at West Point in New York.

Bradley took the advice, competed for and won an appointment to West Point, and entered the academy in 1911. In later life, he would remark that the four years spent at West Point were "among the most rewarding of my life." Considering the subsequent career which sprang from those four years, one might say that the country as a whole was handsomely rewarded as a result of Bradley's decision.

When he was graduated from West Point in 1915, Bradley stood forty-fourth in a class of 164. He later confessed that his affinity for sports—Bradley played on the varsity football and baseball teams—might have detracted from his academic performance. Bradley's class would gain fame as the one that "the stars fell on." Bradley, who would ultimately wear five of those stars, was always proud of a complimentary entry in his senior yearbook, which described "his most promising characteristic" as "getting there. . . ." The words of praise came from fellow classmate Dwight D. Eisenhower, who was himself destined to wear five stars and be twice elected president of the United States.

Life's Work

Following graduation, Bradley was assigned to duty with the Fourteenth Infantry Regiment at Fort Laughton near Seattle, Washington. He was later transferred to Douglas, Arizona, but did not join the Pershing expedition into Mexico. On December 28, 1916, Bradley, by then a first lieutenant, married his high school sweetheart, Mary Quayle. Four months later, the United States entered World War I. Convinced that his career would suffer irreparable harm if he did not see duty in France, Bradley desperately tried to secure assignment to a combat unit. He never succeeded; instead he spent the war guarding copper mines in Montana. When he was finally ordered to report for overseas duty, his destination was not France but Siberia. Fortunately, those orders were canceled, and Montana suddenly looked much better than it had before.

Like most career officers, Bradley found duty in the peacetime army to be rather routine and advancement quite slow. He spent five years teaching in one capacity or another, one year as an instructor in the ROTC program at South Dakota State University, and four years in the math department at West Point. He became a father during his tour at West Point, when Mary gave birth to a daughter, Elizabeth. An earlier stillborn birth and complications arising during the second pregnancy convinced the Bradleys that they should have no more children.

After completing his tour at West Point in 1923, Bradley attended infantry school at Fort Benning, Georgia, for one year and was then assigned to duty in Hawaii for three years. While there he met George S. Patton, then serving as chief intelligence officer of the Hawaiian Division and described by Bradley as "one of the most extraordinary men— military or civilian—I ever met."

Returning to the United States in 1928, Bradley attended the Command and General Staff School at Fort Leavenworth, Kansas, after which he had a choice of assignments between Fort Benning and West Point. He chose the former, later recalling that it was "the most important decision of my life." While at Benning he attracted the attention of George C. Marshall, who would later, as Chief of Staff of the Army, prove to be instrumental in Bradley's rapid rise to high command during World War II. In fact, after attending the Army War College and serving another four years at West Point, Bradley served under Marshall following the latter's appointment as Chief of Staff in April, 1939. When, in late 1940, Marshall offered Bradley command of the Eighty-second Division, he became the second in his class to get two stars and the first to command a division.

Like so many of his colleagues, Bradley first attracted widespread public attention during World War II. Though he never reached the pinnacle of command achieved by Eisenhower or assumed the almost legendary proportions of the flamboyant George Patton, he carved his own special place in

United States military history as the "G.I. General." Newsman Ernie Pyle, whose cartoons and reports made household names of many wartime personalities, confessed that it was a challenge to write about Bradley because he was so "damn normal." Rather tall and solidly built, Bradley was never described as handsome. In his late forties, when the United States entered the war, he was balding and bespectacled, conveying a congeniality not usually associated with a combat general.

Bradley was not assigned to overseas duty until February, 1943, when he joined Eisenhower in North Africa. For a brief time he served as deputy commander of the United States II Corps under George Patton and later assumed command of that unit when Patton was called to head Seventh Army operations in the Sicilian campaign. Bradley again served under Patton in Sicily, where he became disillusioned with his superior's methods both on and off the battlefield. Patton's involvement in the infamous slapping incidents in Sicily, in which he struck two enlisted men who were suffering from battle fatigue, cost him any chance he might have had for immediate advancement. Consequently, when Sicily was safely in Allied hands, it was Bradley who was chosen to command American forces in the next major operation of the war—Normandy—while Patton remained behind.

Bradley played a key role in operation "Overlord," first as commander of the American First Army and later as head of the Twelfth Army Group, on an equal footing with Britain's Field Marshal Bernard Law Montgomery. In an ironic twist, Patton, who assumed command of the newly activated Third Army on August 1, 1944, was now subordinate to Bradley. This proved to be a workable combination when Bradley the strategist and Patton the tactician combined to parlay operation "Cobra" into a theater-wide breakout, leading to the eventual liberation of most of northern France. Bradley proved to be an asset to Eisenhower in more ways than one. He not only demonstrated great competence as a strategist and battlefield manager, but also held a tight rein on Patton and frequently served as a buffer between him and the equally irascible Montgomery.

As the war in Europe drew to a close, Bradley did not have to worry about a new assignment. Marshall, Eisenhower, and President Harry S Truman were unanimous in the opinion that he should be made head of the Veterans Administration. In August, 1945, Bradley assumed the new duties of his office and all the headaches that went with it—chief among them being administration of the G.I. Bill and upgrading the quality of medical care for veterans. He found his job to be challenging and rewarding, deriving the greatest satisfaction from the improvements made in the quality of medical care which veterans received.

In February, 1948, Bradley left the Veterans Administration to become Chief of Staff of the Army, a post he held for about eighteen months before becoming chairman of the Joint Chiefs of Staff in August, 1949. This was the position he held when the so-called Cold War turned hot in Korea in June, 1950. Bradley's view that the United States was right to intervene in Korea while not seeking to expand the war in Asia represented a consensus within the military; his often quoted statement that a wider war in Asia would be "the wrong war, at the wrong place, at the wrong time, and with the wrong enemy," succinctly summarized the military's position. This conviction put him at odds with General Douglas MacArthur, then commander of United Nations forces in Korea, but ultimately it was Bradley's viewpoint which prevailed.

The Korean War ended in 1953 during Bradley's tour as chairman of the Joint Chiefs of Staff, and shortly thereafter he resigned from full-time active service. Ceremonial duties as one of the nation's senior military statesmen took some of his time, but most of it was devoted to his business interests. He served for a while as chairman of the board of the Bulova Watch Company and was a director on several other corporate boards. In 1965, Bradley's wife died, and for several months he suffered from severe depression. In September, 1966, he married Kitty Buhler, a gregarious Hollywood screenwriter, who, despite being thirty years his junior, remained devoted to him until his death in April, 1981.

Summary

Omar Bradley was the product of rural, Midwestern America— the values of which were always reflected in his career. Cognizant of his own modest beginnings, he identified and sympathized with the plight of the common soldier. He successfully made the transition from combat general to administrator and from total war, as required by World War II, to the concept of limited war, as imposed by the constraints of the Cold War. His career spanned two world wars and the Korean conflict. During World War II, his professional military talents had carried him to the position of Army Group command. He ultimately wore five stars as General of the Army, served as head of the Veterans Administration, Chief of Staff of the Army, and chairman of the Joint Chiefs of Staff. Who could doubt, to paraphrase Dwight D. Eisenhower, that the farm boy from Missouri had truly "gotten there."

Bibliography

Blumenson, Martin. *Patton: The Man Behind the Legend, 1885-1945*. New York: William Morrow and Co., 1985. This book offers insights into Patton's candid assessment of Bradley, first as a subordinate and later as a superior. Patton displays great respect for Bradley while objecting strenuously to some of his military decisions.

Bradley, Omar N. *A Soldier's Story*. New York: Henry Holt, 1951. Published during Bradley's tenure as chairman of the Joint Chiefs of Staff, these wartime memoirs, though informative, reflect the restrictions imposed on

Bradley by his official position and government classification of many World War II documents.

Bradley, Omar N., and Clay Blair. *A General's Life*. New York: Simon and Schuster, 1983. Begun as an autobiography and subsequently completed by Blair after the general's death, this is the only work which entirely covers Bradley's life and career.

Chandler, Alfred D., Jr., and Louis Galambos, eds. *The Papers of Dwight David Eisenhower*. 11 vols. Baltimore: Johns Hopkins University Press, 1970-1979. Bradley and Eisenhower confronted many common problems from different perspectives both during and after World War II. These volumes are useful and illuminating for both periods.

Eisenhower, Dwight D. *Crusade in Europe*. Garden City, N.Y.: Doubleday and Co., 1948. Eisenhower's wartime memoirs contain much information on Bradley and the major compaigns in which he participated. Eisenhower's appreciation of Bradley's talents is apparent.

Pogue, Forrest C. *Ordeal and Hope, 1939-1943*; *Organizer of Victory, 1943-1945*. Vols. 2-3 of *George C. Marshall*, 3 vols. New York: Viking Press, 1963-1966. Perhaps more than any other man, Marshall was instrumental in Bradley's rapid climb to Army Group command in 1944. The works cited here cover only the war years; volume 4 and a possible fifth volume, however, will undoubtedly shed some light on Bradley's career beyond 1945.

Weigley, Russell F. *Eisenhower's Lieutenants: The Campaigns of France and Germany, 1944-1945*. Bloomington: Indiana University Press, 1981. A brilliant work describing the last major military campaigns of the European war. This book evaluates Bradley's skills as a strategist while inviting comparisons with his colleagues, British and American.

Kirk Ford, Jr.

MATHEW B. BRADY

Born: c. 1823; Warren County, New York
Died: January 15, 1896; New York, New York
Area of Achievement: Photography
Contribution: Brady brought to the American public a panorama of personalities and scenes through the photographic medium, and he was instrumental in creating a pictorial record of the Civil War.

Early Life

Mathew B. Brady's birth date is not known other than that he was born about 1823 near Lake George in Warren County, New York. The year is that given by Brady. Little is known about his parents, though his father was probably an Irish immigrant. The death certificate for Brady, which was completed in 1896, lists his father's name as Andrew and his mother's name as Julia. Brady's wife had preceded him in death, and he was therefore listed as a widower, with no name given for his spouse. This contributes to a problem surrounding Brady, because his wife, Juliet Elizabeth Handy, was apparently called "Julia," too. The literature about Brady does not deal with this matter of his parents' names, perhaps because there are so many unknowns about the man. Even the odd spelling of his given name, with a single "t," has no explanation, and as for the middle initial, Brady said it meant nothing. What is known of him comes from the sparest materials. There are no letters, notebooks, diaries, or other written matter. Despite his large enterprise, there are no wills, real estate transactions with his personal signature, or anything that is written by him. He was probably illiterate, though it has been suggested that he could read if not write. Yet this is improbable, as there is no evidence to support the claim; indeed, some historians even doubt that the signatures on his photographs are by his hand.

There is no record or account of Brady's education. Considering that all of his life seemed to be spent promoting himself in society and cultivating the prominent and the wealthy, he may have chosen to be mysterious about his humble background. His basic education was practical, beginning when he spent time in Saratoga, New York, where he met a William Page, who was a painter. Saratoga, located just south of Lake George, has a long history as a popular resort and vacation area for prominent Americans. Because of its natural hot springs and attractive setting, as well as its location close to Albany and New York City, it was already an important health spa when Brady arrived. Page became his first mentor, encouraging the young man from the lake country to sketch and draw. The life-styles of the wealthy on their summer vacations and perhaps the work ethic of the artist Page, who, like most artists, placed himself in close proximity to potential clients, must have affected Brady. He moved with Page to New York City, where he did odd jobs and came in contact with Samuel F. B. Morse, a professor at the University of New York, which later became New York University. Morse, who later became famous for the invention of the telegraph, was experimenting with the daguerreotype reproduction process. He and a colleague, John William Draper, taught some young men the process; Brady was among them. Brady also learned the rudiments of photography from Morse and Draper.

As early as 1843, Brady was listed in the New York *Doggett's* directory as a manufacturer of jewelry cases specializing in making miniature boxes with embossed tops. He also made cases for surgical instruments and storage and presentation boxes for daguerreotypes. It was shortly thereafter that Brady combined case-making with the production of daguerreotypes, setting up a gallery in a building just off Fulton Street and Broadway, directly across from P. T. Barnum's popular American Museum and a block from the famed Astor House. This location was in the center of potential commercial traffic and in close proximity to the people of power who frequented the Astor House. Brady was quite successful, charging between three and five dollars for a sitting, with posing hours from ten o'clock to three o'clock. During those early years, he maintained his association with Page, Draper, Morse, and other men who were experimenting with new technology.

Brady had adopted the costume and style of his artistic and academic associates. A quick, nervous man of five feet, seven inches in height, he allowed his hair to grow long and frame his face. He later grew a mustache and goatee and took a fancy to bright scarves and a flat-topped, broad-brimmed hat. Sometimes he wore a cape and a cavalier-type hat graced with a feather. By 1855, his eyes were failing him, and he wore increasingly thick-lensed wire-framed glasses. In the prime of life, he was virtually blind.

The United States of the 1840's rewarded technology and industry more than anything else, and Brady quickly prospered, expanded his operations, gave up his case-making business, and increasingly concentrated on a grand project: to photograph and publish pictures of every distinguished American. The newly formed American Institute of Photography held contests, and Brady won medals each year from 1844 to 1850. "Brady of Broadway" was what he was called, and in 1849 he received the first gold medal awarded for a picture taken using the daguerreotype process. He worked with reproductions on porcelain and ivory, with tinting and various exposures and light diffusion. Competition in the business was intense, all shops offering something unique to gain customers' attention. Brady pursued the great and the wealthy to complete his grand plan. It was not unusual for him to pick up the work of others and simply attach his name to it. He began to take on and quickly train a number of "operators" to take the pictures, as he could no longer focus the camera himself. He also branched out, establishing an office in Washington, D.C. There the Anthonys, Edward and Henry, had already set up a gallery and were attracting public officials and foreign dignitaries as subjects. They also set up a prosperous photography supply business on Broadway, which became the foundation for the Ansco company. Many of their pictures were sent to be put on display in their Broadway studio. It is believed that Brady, when frustrated in attempts to attract subjects for his great project, simply purchased the photographs he wanted from men such as the Anthonys.

Life's Work

Brady's ambitious project was designed to meet the growing competition from studios which stood side by side along Broadway. Camera operators rushed to open their own shops once they learned the rudiments of the craft. Physically unable to operate the equipment alone, Brady sought the grand idea that would sustain him. His master volume, *Gallery of Illustrious Americans* (1850), was a critical success but a financial failure at thirty dollars a copy. Undaunted, Brady hoped to bring out another volume and purchased the lithographic stones at one hundred dollars each. The project had caused him to neglect the paying part of his business. Brady also contributed to his own losses by mimicking the life-style of the rich in his choice of colognes, brandy, clothes, hats and scarves, and restaurants. Many of his prestigious clients he photographed free, ignoring the ordinary public which had sustained him. At twenty-eight, he was already well-known, but still not financially secure.

During this period, Brady married Juliet Elizabeth Handy, a woman from Maryland whom he seems to have met when he was in Washington soliciting sittings. Though there is considerable speculation about her family's status and wealth as well as her ostensible beauty, there is no support for the former, and Brady's pictures of his wife do not flatter her. The date of the wedding is not known, but it had to be prior to his planning for a trip to London in 1851. Brady's new idea was to enter a collection of forty-eight pictures in the London exposition that was being sponsored by Prince Albert. He won a prize for his entry, traveled through parts of Europe, again attaching himself to influential people, and supposedly took their pictures and purchased others for sale in his New York studio.

Returning home, he immediately embarked on the revitalization of his business. He won a prize in the New York World's Fair competition in 1853, but he was never accepted into the community of craftsmen who were moving ahead in technology. He planned a bold move at this time—establishing a permanent Washington studio and hiring Alexander Gardner to manage it. Located on Pennsylvania Avenue between Sixth and Seventh streets, the studio was ideally situated to attract important people. Brady had also moved his New York studio farther uptown, to 359 Broadway. He experimented with skylights to bring greater illumination to his work, as well as blue glass.

The future really lay with the collodion wet plate method of photography, but Brady was still infatuated with the primitive daguerreotype. Photography had come of age and Brady rushed to catch up, but the technical skills that would make him famous in history belonged to others.

Stock companies to promote various new techniques and products—Crystalotype, Ambrotype, Melaintype, and tintype—were formed with the most creative inventors as principals. Brady was not among them. A development of which Brady took advantage to his profit, however, was the creation of life-size portraits which, when touched up and tinted with colors, rivaled oil paintings and commanded a high price. They consumed great amounts of time for exposure, however, and tied up studio facilities that were needed for other works. In 1857, the new rage, *cartes de visite*, captivated the nation and the world. The small portrait-bearing calling cards, printed on thin cardboard, were cheaply produced and very profitable. Brady and others saw the demand increase as immigrants wanted pictures to send abroad, Easterners wanted pictures for relatives moving to the West, and the newly married wanted pictures for family and friends. The collecting of cards was another demand that had to be satisfied, and Brady leaped into the competition, offering fees to actors, statesmen, outlaws, and others to sit for the cards, which were then peddled throughout the country. Despite a lull in sales after a few years, the Civil War revived the market for the cards as servicemen rushed to the studios.

Brady was never close to those who were on the cutting edge of photographic innovation. He was more a promoter than an operator-photographer, and the fact that he was known to appropriate the work of others and attach his own name to it did not sit well with his competitors. He picked competitive shows very selectively, such as the 1854 New York Crystal Palace show, in which he drew top honors for his daguerreotypes.

He was concentrating on his new gallery and studio, the most ornate in New York. In Washington, he placed Alexander Gardner in charge. Gardner was exactly what he needed, as the man had mastered the Archer wet-glass process in England before coming to the United States in 1856. Gardner later was to break from Brady and go on to film the history of the American West, but his experience as Brady's photographer of the Civil War projected them both to early prominence. Business was booming, and Brady again moved his New York studio further uptown in 1860, a location where his name became indelibly linked with that of Abraham Lincoln, who had come to give his celebrated Cooper Institute address.

The election of Lincoln and the advent of the Civil War encouraged all serious photographers to plan the filming of the dramatic times. Brady's early mentor, John W. Draper, formed a committee to approach the secretary of war with a project to photograph events. They were put off, however, and it was now Brady who seized the initiative. Lincoln again sat for a formal picture, this time with beard (he had previously been photographed clean-shaven), and Brady's Washington contingent also took pictures of both the inauguration and the Tyler Peace Commission. Two more photographers were sent to Washington to join Gardner as Brady gained presidential clearance to underwrite privately the photographing of the impending crisis.

More than three hundred photographers were involved in covering the Union during the Civil War, many in the direct employ of the War Department, who were not commercial people such as Brady's men. Countless others, most unknown, filmed Confederate exploits as well. Few, however, had the elaborate laboratories on wheels that Brady put in the field. His black wagons, called "what's its" by the troops, were at Bull Run to catch the first disaster of the long war.

After that debacle, Brady had seen enough of the war to realize that New York was the place for him. Keeping eighteen people in the field demanded money, and the studio in New York had to cover expenses that included his own high-toned life-style. The burdens of salaries, rent, transport, chemicals, and the like soon overwhelmed him, precipitating his collapse. His practice of filming dignitaries at no charge eroded his resources, and after Appomattox he drifted into virtual seclusion. He closed down his field operations and missed such events as the huge fire at P. T. Barnum's American Museum, in the same neighborhood as his studio. It was Gardner who persevered in capturing dramatic events in Washington.

Brady soon found that the market was saturated with war pictures. He stored thousands of plates and turned others over to satisfy debts that caused him to go bankrupt in 1873. America was exhausted by war and the bloody-shirt politics which followed it. The new excitement lay in the promise of the West, but Brady stayed home while a new army of photographers followed the sun. He sought to interest the government in his collections, to no avail. Ironically, the government was a successful bidder for thousands of wartime plates when he could not pay a storage bill of $2,840. Brady got nothing, and many pictures were destroyed in moving. A petition on his behalf was drawn up by General Benjamin Butler and James A. Garfield in 1875 to reward Brady with twenty-five thousand dollars for full title to his collection. The money was appropriated too late; the collection passed to the Anthony supply firm in lieu of payment on his debts. Although Brady had fallen on hard times, he won a bronze medal for his entry in a competition of photographs at the Centennial Exposition in Philadelphia. Still, he desperately needed money.

Sporadic interest continued in the 1880's, as aging veterans' groups made inquiries about his pictures. The government called in Albert Bierstadt, the famous painter and photographer, to make an assessment of their holdings. The pieces held by the Anthony firm changed hands several times until some seven thousand glass negatives were recovered and turned over to the government by John C. Taylor of Connecticut. The prohibitive cost of making prints meant that the negatives would remain in storage. Brady nevertheless persevered in the Washington gallery at 627 Pennsylvania Avenue, working with his wife's nephew, Levin Handy. His wife, Juliet, had died of a heart condition on May 20, 1887, leaving him childless. In 1891, a newspaperman was startled to find Brady alive, wiry, and vigorous, with white hair and white mustache and goatee and wearing blue-tinted spectacles. In a revealing comment at that time, Brady suggested that he might have better spent his time becoming a craftsman instead of seeking out personalities to photograph.

He continued to struggle to keep his studio going. On April 16, 1895, however, he was struck by a carriage and suffered a broken leg. This came when he was planning a new exhibition of his personal war slides: 128 pieces to be shown in New York on January 30, 1896. Still ailing, Brady went to the city alone to confirm details with officials of the Seventh Regiment organization. He stayed in a rooming house on East Tenth Street but soon took ill with a kidney ailment. A friend took him to Presbyterian Hospital, where he died in the indigent ward on January 15, 1896. His remains were shipped to Washington, where he was buried, most probably at Congressional Cemetery.

Summary

Matthew Brady was a man possessed of vision and a passion for greatness. He was an indefatigable worker and promoter, as well as a believer in the dream of success. He believed in himself and committed his resources to photographing history. The horror and carnage of the war recorded by Brady's men will forever haunt American history. Brady was not a historian with a camera; he was the entrepreneur who put cameramen in the field to make as much of a record as they could. His pictures do not interpret events as history does; rather, they present scenes, many of which would be indescribable in words.

As with many great figures in history, there is much that was not admirable in Mathew Brady. He might have been more humble and less self-serving. He might have better stayed abreast of technology. He might have been less enamoured of great men and women and more conscious of that large constituency which he ignored to the detriment of history. He might have been kinder to those who did the photography, which is the only durable vestige of his glory. He might have been a better businessman. Nevertheless, Brady's initiative in the use of the craft of photography has provided an irreplaceable record of critical times in the history of the United States.

Bibliography

Hood, Robert E. *Twelve at War: Great Photographers Under Fire*. New York: G.P. Putnam's Sons, 1967. This volume has a short essay which establishes Brady as the first of the leading war photographers.

Horan, James D. *Mathew Brady: Historian with a Camera*. New York: Crown Publishers, 1955. This is a confounding but necessary book, which must be read very carefully as the author plays loose with dates and historical evidence and often passes off conjecture as reality. With regard to Brady, it is adulatory to a fault.

Kunhardt, Dorothy Meserve, and Philip B. Kunhardt, Jr. *Mathew Brady and His World*. New York: Time-Life Books, 1977. This work grew from the collections of Frederick Meserve and, though published as a picture book for popular consumption, is clear, well-developed, and more historically correct than most works on Brady. The book also provides what has been a universal weakness in books dealing with Brady: a critique of the photographs and real effort into determining who actually took the picture.

Kunhardt, Philip B., Jr. "Mathew Brady," Parts 1, 2. *Smithsonian* 8 (July, August, 1977): 24-35, 58-67. Some of this material can be found in the book by Dorothy and Philip Kunhardt, which developed from the research done for these articles.

Meredith, Roy. *Mathew Brady's Portrait of an Era*. New York: W. W. Norton and Co., 1982.

_____. *Mr. Lincoln's Camera Man*. New York: Charles Scribner's Sons, 1946. These are large-format picture books much like that of James Horan, though they weave a narrative around the illustrations. *Mathew Brady's Portrait of an Era* has considerable information concerning the activities of Brady at various times in his career, although much of the book seems to cry out for reexamination, especially since the object of the work is to tell a good story.

Townsend, G. A. "Still Taking Pictures." *World* (New York). April 12, 1891: 23. This is a newspaper reporter's interview with the elderly Brady which, because of the dearth of material directly relating to the man, is exploited in many accounts of his life.

Jack J. Cardoso

LOUIS D. BRANDEIS

Born: November 13, 1856; Louisville, Kentucky
Died: October 5, 1941; Washington, D.C.
Areas of Achievement: Social reform and law
Contribution: Brandeis was a leading social reformer from 1897 to 1916, gaining the unofficial title of the "people's attorney"; he was the leader of the American Zionist movement from 1914 until 1939 and served as Associate Justice of the United States Supreme Court from 1916 until his retirement in 1939.

Early Life

The son of Adolph and Frederika (Dembitz) Brandeis, refugees from Prague, Czechoslovakia, Louis Dembitz Brandeis was born on November 13, 1856, in Louisville, Kentucky. His parents and relatives had fled the failed liberal revolutions of 1848, and he grew up in an atmosphere that was intellectual, open-minded, progressive, and dedicated to freedom. This heritage was evident throughout his career.

At fifteen, Brandeis was graduated from Louisville public schools and then lived and studied in Europe for three years. In 1875, he entered Harvard Law School. Although lacking a college degree, he completed the three-year program in only two years, being graduated in 1877 with the highest grades in the law school's history.

Life's Work

Brandeis' career centered on the law and public service. His law practice was enormously successful, and his early clients included major railroads and manufacturing companies. In 1889, Brandeis argued, and won, his first case before the United States Supreme Court, on behalf of the Wisconsin Central Railroad. In 1890, Brandeis and his former partner Samuel Warren jointly published a path-breaking article in the *Harvard Law Review*, "The Right to Privacy." The article helped create a new concept in law, one which Brandeis later supported from the bench.

By the mid-1890's, Brandeis was earning more than seventy thousand dollars a year—a large sum in those days. Through frugal living and careful investments, he became a millionaire by 1900. As his wealth grew, so did his generosity; between 1905 and 1939, he gave away approximately one and a half million dollars. Brandeis also used his wealth to free himself from the necessity of taking on paying clients. In 1891, when he married his second cousin Alice Goldmark, the two decided to dedicate their lives to public service. By 1895, he had begun to devote most of his energies to public interest work. Brandeis not only worked without a fee but also paid money to his law firm so that his partners would not suffer from his *pro bono* activities. Brandeis brought his expertise as a corporate lawyer to social causes.

In 1892, Brandeis was profoundly affected when plant owners used armed guards against workers in the Homestead Steel Strike. Brandeis later wrote, "I think it was the affair at Homestead which first set me to thinking seriously about the labor problem. It took the shock of that battle, where organized capital hired a private army to shoot at organized labor for resisting an arbitrary cut in wages, to turn my mind definitely toward a searching study of the relations of labor to industry."

After 1892, Brandeis became known as the "people's attorney" for his willingness to take public interest cases for free or for a very small fee. In 1904, as the unpaid counsel, Brandeis convinced Boston officials and the gas company to adopt a sliding scale for gas prices that guaranteed the company a minimum of seven percent profit on its assets while lowering rates to consumers from a dollar to ninety cents per thousand cubic feet of gas. The sliding scale formula allowed the company to raise its dividends by one percent for every five cents it reduced the price of gas. This built-in incentive for increased efficiency and lower prices brought the cost of gas to eighty cents within a year, while return on the gas company's investment rose to nine percent.

In 1906, Brandeis resigned from the board of directors of the United Shoe Manufacturing Company when the company tried to monopolize the industry and used illegal methods to stop competition. Years later, Brandeis testified against United Shoe at public hearings and served as counsel for competitors seeking to prevent a monopoly of the industry. Eventually, the shoe monopoly was broken and fair competition restored. Brandeis also investigated corruption in the life insurance industry. Brandeis helped create savings-bank life insurance in Massachusetts, which provided low-cost life insurance through state-regulated banks. As with gas prices, Brandeis showed that enlightened and regulated capitalism could work for the benefit of all. The banks made money from selling the insurance, the customers gained safe insurance at reasonable prices, and in order to compete, the major insurance companies lowered their premiums. Other states adopted the program, and by 1914 Brandeis estimated that the various reforms saved Americans twenty million dollars a year.

Starting in 1905, Brandeis led a coalition of businessmen, civil leaders, and reformers in fighting the New Haven Railroad's attempt to monopolize all rail traffic in New England by acquiring its main competition, the Boston and Maine Railroad. Brandeis opposed monopolies because he believed they were inefficient and harmful to consumers. The struggle against the New Haven monopoly lasted until 1914, when the Wilson Administration forced the New Haven Railroad to give up the Boston and Maine. During this struggle, public attacks on Brandeis became personal. Newspapers controlled by those with financial interests in the New Haven Railroad pictured him as "King Louis of New England." Anti-Semitic caricatures of Brandeis falsely accused him of corruption.

In 1914, Brandeis published *Other People's Money and How the Bankers Use It*. This extremely influential book stimulated the passage of some banking regulations. Brandeis' major recommendations were ignored, however, until after the failure of thousands of banks in the 1930's. Only at that point did Congress adopt the kind of legislation for which Brandeis argued in 1914.

The *pro bono* cases profoundly affected Brandeis' life. *Muller v. Oregon* (1908) involved an Oregon statute that limited the working day to ten hours for women employees. This statute reflected a national movement to limit hours for all workers, prohibit child labor, and create minimum wages. In 1905, the Supreme Court, in *Lochner v. New York*, had struck down a similar statute regulating working hours for men.

In arguing the Muller case, Brandeis had few legal precedents with which to work. *Lochner v. New York*, the most obvious precedent, was something Brandeis had to overcome. Brandeis brilliantly met the challenge. His brief was more than one hundred pages long. Only two of those pages, however, were devoted to legal precedents and principles. The rest of the brief discussed the social facts of industrial employment. Using statistics from numerous American and foreign sources, Brandeis demonstrated the physical costs of the industrial employment of women. The brief was a masterful combination of economics, sociology, and public health data. Without overruling *Lochner v. New York*, a unanimous Supreme Court upheld the Oregon statute as a reasonable exercise of the state's police powers. The Court took the unusual step of noting the importance of "the brief filed by Mr. Louis D. Brandeis." The "Brandeis brief," as it was called, revolutionized legal argument by legitimizing a court's use of social science data. The Court's decision was a personal triumph for Brandeis and a major victory for the Progressive movement in America.

In 1910, Brandeis successfully mediated a New York garment industry strike. During these negotiations, Brandeis came in contact with large numbers of immigrant Eastern European Jews. This led Brandeis to rediscover his own Jewish roots and the Zionist movement. Although born and reared Jewish, Brandeis had never been actively involved in his faith. Of his relatives, only his uncle Louis Dembitz had been a practicing Jew. Dembitz had also been an ardent Zionist even before Theodor Herzl organized the World Zionist Congress. Brandeis had obviously been influenced by his uncle, because as a young man he had changed his middle name from David to Dembitz, in honor of his uncle. In 1912, Brandeis met with representatives of the World Zionist Congress.

As a democratic movement striving to provide liberty and opportunity for an oppressed minority, Zionism was consistent with Brandeis' own social goals. From 1914 until 1921, Brandeis was the leader of the Zionist Organization of America. Zionism was Brandeis' only extrajudicial activity after he joined the Supreme Court in 1916. As the Holocaust loomed on the horizon, Brandeis increased his donations to the cause, giving more than a quarter of a million dollars between 1933 and 1939.

Brandeis was gradually drawn into politics. He never sought elective office and was never a regular party man. In 1912, he campaigned for Woodrow Wilson and served as an adviser to the candidate. After Wilson's victory, Brandeis worked with the Administration on antitrust matters and drafted legislation creating the Federal Reserve System (1913) and the Federal Trade Commission (1914).

In 1916, President Wilson nominated Brandeis to the Supreme Court. As the "people's attorney," Brandeis had offended moneyed interests throughout the country. The American Bar Association and some elite reformers opposed Brandeis because he was not "one of the boys." Former president William H. Taft opposed Brandeis because Taft himself wanted to be on the Court and foolishly believed that Wilson might appoint him. The Boston establishment adamantly opposed the man who had exposed the greed of the insurance and banking industries and had successfully prevented monopolies in the shoe manufacturing and railroad industries. Executives from United States Steel, the United Shoe Manufacturing Company, the New Haven Railroad, various Wall Street law firms and Boston banks, the president of Harvard University, and *The Wall Street Journal* opposed Brandeis. Those who had financial interests in these industries hated him because he had so often defeated them in court. They also disliked him because Brandeis was not "one of them." Throughout the confirmation hearings, there were undertones of anti-Semitism. Brandeis was the first Jew appointed to the Supreme Court. For many Americans, particularly the elite in Boston, this alone disqualified Brandeis.

Brandeis was supported by Progressives from around the nation. While the incumbent president of Harvard, A. Lawrence Lowell, the son of a Massachusetts industrialist, opposed the institution's alumnus, the university's president emeritus, Charles Eliot, a renowned scholar, supported Brandeis. Many of the Republican supporters of Theodore Roosevelt rallied to Brandeis. The four-month confirmation struggle was the longest in American history. In the end, Brandeis received support from all but one Senate Democrat as well as five Progressive Republicans.

Brandeis was sixty years old when he joined the Court. He remained until he was eighty-two. Except for his last few years on the bench, Brandeis was almost always in the minority—a Progressive voice on the conservative, or even reactionary, Court. Thus, for much of his career Brandeis was a dissenter. As a lawyer Brandeis had defended legislative regulation of the economy; as a justice he usually deferred to the will of the people, as reflected in legislation. Two exceptions to Brandeis' deference to legislatures involved early New Deal legislation and all civil liberties cases.

Brandeis supported President Franklin D. Roosevelt but, in 1935, he joined a unanimous Court in striking down the National Industrial Recovery Act because he found that Congress had exceeded its constitutional authority. This did not signal that Brandeis had become an economic conservative. Rather, he thought the act poorly drafted and overbroad. After 1936, Brandeis consistently supported Roosevelt.

When it came to the protection of individual liberty and rights, Brandeis never deferred to a legislature. In protecting intellectual and personal freedom, Brandeis thought it was the duty of the Court to protect minority views from a tyranny of the majority. It was in this area of law that Brandeis made his mark as one of the Court's greatest justices and as one of America's most important legal philosophers.

Brandeis' career was marked by his desire to protect human liberty and dignity. In *Whitney v. California* (1927), Brandeis argued that free speech allowed a society to find truth. He declared,

> Those who won our independence by revolution were not cowards. They did not fear political change. They did not exalt order at the cost of liberty. To courageous, self-reliant men, with confidence in the power of free and fearless reasoning applied through the processes of popular government, no danger flowing from speech can be deemed clear and present, unless the incidence of that evil apprehended is so imminent that it may befall before there is opportunity for full discussion. If there be time to expose through discussion the falsehood and fallacies, to avert the evil by the processes of education, the remedy to be applied is more speech not enforced silence.

In *Olmstead v. United States*, Brandeis wrote a powerful and prophetic dissent, arguing that wiretapping without a warrant constituted a "search" in violation of the Fourth Amendment. Brandeis brilliantly refuted Chief Justice Taft's majority opinion that a wiretap did not constitute a search because there was no physical invasion of the property. Brandeis argued that the framers "knew that only a part of the pain, pleasure and satisfactions of life are to be found in material things." Thus, the framers "sought to protect Americans in their beliefs, their thoughts, their emotions and their sensations. They conferred, as against the government, the right to be left alone— the most comprehensive of rights and the right most valued by civilized men." Brandeis declared that "men born to freedom are naturally alert to repel invasion of their liberty by evil-minded rulers. The greatest dangers to liberty lurk in insidious encroachment by men of zeal, well-meaning, but without understanding." Brandeis further asserted that "to declare that in the administration of the criminal law the end justifies the means—to declare that the government may commit crimes in order to secure the conviction of a private criminal—would bring terrible retribution." Not four years following his retirement from the Court, Brandeis died, in 1941.

Summary

By his own example, Brandeis set a modern standard for high-priced lawyers taking *pro bono* cases. In the "Brandeis brief," he gave lawyers a new tool and helped liberate the legal profession from a dependence on stale and dry precedents to deal with the realities of the world. He worked to make the legal profession a servant of the people and the public good and not simply the servant of the rich and powerful. As an adviser to state and federal officials, Brandeis helped shape progressive reforms. Insurance regulation, antimonopoly statutes, and banking reform all benefited from his wisdom and ideas.

On the Court, Brandeis left an unsurpassed legacy of support of civil liberties and social justice. His confirmation in the face of a widespread anti-Semitic opposition helped break down barriers for minorities in the United States. His dissents on freedom of speech and criminal law later became precedents for a more enlightened Court. People meeting Brandeis for the first time often noticed his eyes, penetrating and deep, like his mind. While of only average height, Brandeis resembled a beardless Lincoln in his sharp features. As an aging justice, he looked the part of a philosopher and prophet. President Franklin D. Roosevelt referred to him as "old Isaiah," and like the biblical prophet, Brandeis was a foe of injustice and a friend of liberty.

Bibliography

Freund, Paul A. "Mr. Justice Brandeis." In *Mr. Justice*, edited by Allison Dunham and Philip B. Kurland. 2d ed. Chicago: University of Chicago Press, 1964. Essay on Brandeis by a former law clerk who later became a distinguished law professor at Harvard Law School.

Konefsky, Samuel J. *The Legacy of Holmes and Brandeis: A Study of the Influence of Ideas*. New York: Macmillan Publishing Co., 1956. Traces the influence of the two great dissenters on the Court.

Mason, Alpheas Thomas. *Brandeis: A Free Man's Life*. New York: Viking Press, 1946. A classic biography of Brandeis by a leading scholar in constitutional history. This is the best introduction to Brandeis.

Todd, Alden L. *Justice on Trial: The Case of Louis D. Brandeis*. Chicago: University of Chicago Press, 1964. A prizewinning study of the struggle to confirm Brandeis as a justice of the Supreme Court. Excellent for its details and descriptions.

Urofsky, Melvin I. *American Zionism from Herzl to the Holocaust*. Garden City, N.Y.: Anchor Press, 1975. This book details the importance of Brandeis to the Zionist movement in America.

_____. *Louis D. Brandeis and the Progressive Tradition*. Boston: Little, Brown and Co., 1980. Places Brandeis in the context of the Progressive movement. Useful biography.

_____. *A Mind of One Piece: Brandeis and American Reform*. New York: Charles Scribner's Sons, 1971. Excellent study of the role of Brandeis in twentieth century reform.

Paul Finkelman

JOSEPH BRANT
Thayendanegea

Born: 1742; the Ohio country
Died: November 24, 1807; near Brantford, Ontario, Canada
Area of Achievement: Indian tribal leadership
Contribution: Brant demonstrated the impact which an educated Native American leader could have on his people's destiny.

Early Life

Known to his Mohawk kin as Thayendanegea, Joseph Brant was the son of Argoghyiadecker (also known as Nickus Brant), a prominent leader on the New York Indian frontier during the mid-eighteenth century. He had an older sister known as Molly who became an extremely influential tribeswoman. She combined her own political acumen with her role as consort to the British Indian superintendent, William Johnson, to build a powerful network within the tribe; some observers believed her capable of influencing tribal decisions in a major way. Major Tench Tilghman, an American observer in the Iroquois country in 1776, observing Molly Brant and the other Iroquois women, reflected that "women govern the Politics of Savages as well as the refined part of the world."

Brant grew up in the Mohawk village of Canojoharie, where he enjoyed the traditional teachings of the tribal elders as well as the efforts of Anglican missionaries who came to convert the Indians to Christianity and to teach them basic educational skills. So bright was the young Brant, however, that this village education was insufficient. Accordingly, when David Fowler and Samson Occum visited the Mohawk country as representatives of the Reverend Mr. Eleazar Wheelock's school in Lebanon, Connecticut, Brant was one of three young Mohawks designated to return eastward for additional education.

Upon their arrival in Lebanon, Brant and his Mohawk companions were so frightened by their surroundings that they kept their horses ready at a moment's notice for flight back to their village. Of the three new students, the schoolmaster had the highest praise for Joseph Brant: "The other being of a family of distinction among them, was considerably cloathed, Indian-fashion, and could speak a few words of English."

Within three months, Brant's two companions returned to the safety of their home country, but Brant remained to study and to help teach the Mohawk language to a young missionary named Samuel Kirkland. When Kirkland went west in November on a recruiting mission, Brant went along to interpret and help persuade two more Mohawks to attend school. During his sessions in Lebanon, Brant improved his written Mohawk and his English skills, which would serve him well as both interpreter and then spokesman for his people. As early as March of 1768, he assisted Ralph Wheelock in conferring with an Onondaga chief, to the visitor's obvious approval: "By Joseph Brant's help I was able to discourse with him, and delivered to him my discourse to this nation."

Brant's stay at school was curtailed by the outbreak of war in the West. When Pontiac and his followers attempted to drive the British out of the Ohio country, Brant's sister, Molly, urged her brother to come home, lest some revenge-seeking colonist murder him.

Although he never returned to Wheelock's school, Brant retained not only his literary skills but also his belief that education was the key to success and survival for his people. In time he was regarded as the most able interpreter in the British northern Indian department. He had the advantage of being a respected Mohawk who could attend such important meetings as the tribal council at Onondaga, where he could take notes on the proceedings and then report them accurately to the British officials.

In the years before the American Revolution, Brant married Margaret, daughter of the Oneida chief Skenandon. At her death, he married her sister Susanna, who cared for Brant and his young children until her death. His third wife was Catherine Croghan, the Mohawk daughter of George Croghan, a member of the British Indian department and a confidant of William Johnson.

Life's Work

The coming of the American Revolution turned the world of Brant and the Mohawks upside down. He would emerge from his position as an official in the British Indian department to become the most feared Mohawk warrior of the time. In time, indeed, some historians described him as the most ferocious Indian leader of the colonial period. Such accusations, however, were largely frontier hyperbole.

What Brant did during the American Revolution was accompany Guy Johnson, who had succeeded to the office of Indian superintendent at the death of his uncle in 1774, to London in 1775-1776. Feted by the royal court, Brant dined with the famous and had his portrait painted, both alone and as a figure in the background when Benjamin West painted Colonel Guy Johnson. In both cases, the depiction of a powerful and dignified young man suggests the sagacity which Brant would use to lead the Mohawks through the difficult war years.

When Brant finally made his way back to America, he had to slip through the countryside in disguise to avoid capture. To his dismay he found the Mohawk country in an uproar over the war, with many Mohawks already planning to emigrate to the British post at Niagara. Brant first went to Niagara to secure the safety of his family and then recruited warriors to return with him to the Mohawk country, where they might attempt to drive out American invaders and aid British expeditions coming through the Indian country. Despite the accusations of frontiersmen in later years, there is no evidence to support the contention that Brant was a bloodthirsty killer. For most of 1777 and 1778, Brant was active in the Mohawk country with his band of warriors. In 1779, however, they had to withdraw toward Niagara in the face of the major expedition launched through the Iroquois country by the Americans under General John Sullivan.

When he had a disagreement with his old friend Guy Johnson in 1780, he withdrew to the Ohio country in an attempt to rally the Indians of that territory. In 1781 he joined in an attack on an American flotilla on the Ohio River, destroying supplies destined for George Rogers Clark in the Illinois country. This success, however, did not change the plight of the Ohio Indians, for as Brant heard at Detroit late in 1781, many of the western tribal leaders believed the British would walk away from them when the end of the war came. As Brant soon came to know, the fear was well-founded, for the rumors of peace first heard in late 1781 were confirmed in early 1782.

Immediately, Brant wrote to General Frederick Haldimand in Canada, seeking to hold the British officer to his promise of sanctuary in Canada for the Mohawks. A man of his word, General Haldimand agreed that Brant and his people had sacrificed too much. By March, 1783, Joseph Brant and General Haldimand agreed on a Mohawk homeland along the Grand River in present-day Ontario. As a reward for his faithful service, Joseph Brant was commissioned by General Haldimand as "Captain of the Northern Confederate Indians."

With this commission in hand and with the general's help in clearing title to the land, Joseph Brant began leading the Mohawks and others to Canada. By virtue of his newfound rank, Brant assumed the role of spokesman for all the pro-British Iroquois, especially those migrating to Canada. In his role as tribal leader and frontier entrepreneur, Brant would have his critics. Some accused him of profiting from the establishment of the Mohawks in Canada, and his opponents were especially bitter when he opened up unused Mohawk lands for settlement by whites, from whom he collected a kind of real estate commission. Others may have resented the baronial style which he had copied from William Johnson:

> Captain Brant . . . received us with much politeness and hospitality. . . . Tea was on the table when we came in, served up in the hansomest China plate and every other furniture in proportion. After tea was over, we were entertained with the music of an elegant hand organ on which a young Indian gentleman and Mr. Clinch played alternately. Supper was served up in the same gentel stile. Our beverage, rum, brandy, Port and Maderia wines . . . our beds, sheets, and English blankets, equally fine and comfortable. . . . Dinner was just going on the table in the same elegant stile as the preceding night, when I returned to Captain Brant's house, the servants dressed in their best apparel. Two slaves

attended the table, the one in scarlet, the other in coloured clothes, with silver buckles in their shoes, and ruffles, and every other part of their apparel in proportion.

In the face of criticism, Brant often countered by using his support system within the traditional Iroquois matriarchy, the so-called mothers and aunts who dominated village politics, nominated the sachems, and influenced the councils. With their assistance, he silenced opposition. Since his sister was the brilliant and powerful Molly Brant and his wife, Catherine, was from a prominent Iroquois family, he well understood the most effective means of playing politics within the Iroquois council.

One of Brant's long-term goals was advancing the cause of Christianity and education among the Iroquois. Within a few years after his relocation in Canada, he was joined by his longtime friend and supporter, Daniel Claus, in editing the Prayer Book of the Anglican Church in Mohawk. This new volume, published in 1786, contained not only the Mohawk version of the Book of Common Prayer but also the Gospel of Mark.

In the 1780's, funds were obtained to erect a church in the Grand River settlement. Then, in 1788, the former Anglican missionary at Canojohare, the Reverend Mr. John Stuart, came to visit, bringing with him some of the silver communions plates that once had been in the Mohawk church at Fort Hunter in New York. According to Stuart, the church which Brant had seen constructed "in the Mohawk village is pleasantly situated on a small but deep River—the Church about 60 feet in length and 45 in breadth,—built with squared logs and boarded on the outside and painted—with a handsome steeple & bell, a pulpit, reading-desk, & Communion-table, with convenient pews." Stuart had no great love for Brant; he was convinced that Brant would accept no clergyman for the Mohawk church whom he could not dominate. Indeed, believed Stuart, the Mohawks "were afraid of the restraint which the continued residence of a Clergyman would necessarily lay them under." Evidently there was some substance to this belief, since the number of white missionaries at Grand River remained quite low as long as Brant was in a position of influence there.

Brant remained the active frontier speculator until the last years of his life. Constantly involved in land transactions, travel, and farming, he never lacked for activity, yet his home was always the place of choice for visitors. As many callers pointed out, he lived in a grand style, and when he decided to build a new home early in the nineteenth century, it closely resembled Johnson Hall, the home of Sir William Johnson in New York where Brant had spent so much time as a child and as a young adult. From youth to death, Joseph Brant lived in two worlds.

Summary

Joseph Brant's life was a success story, judged by most standards. He grew up among the elite of the Iroquois. His father was a prominent leader and his sister Molly a respected woman among the Mohawks. Because of his intellectual ability, he was offered a chance for an education which few of his contemporaries enjoyed. Once he had acquired that education, he chose to walk the extremely narrow path between the two worlds of his own people and the neighboring Europeans. One of the most powerful role models in his life was Sir William Johnson, whose splendid home was the center of conviviality, diplomacy, and trade in the Mohawk Valley. Watching the success with which Johnson played patron to the Iroquois, military leader, land speculator, colonial politician, and wilderness baron had to have an impact on Brant. During the course of his travels, Brant was always careful to cultivate his patrons and the right politicians. Such adroitness served him well in maintaining his leadership position in the face of all opposition.

While Brant had his enemies and his detractors, he succeeded in surviving and in guaranteeing the survival of the Mohawks who followed him. While a strictly traditionalist tribal leader might not have approved of Brant's feet being in two worlds, others might agree that he found the only way for Native American peoples to survive in a world of rapid change.

Bibliography

Chalmers, Harvey, and E. B. Monture. *Joseph Brant, Mohawk*. East Lansing: Michigan State University Press, 1955. An attempt at a modern biography, lacking the ethnographic detail and psychological insights which it should have.

Graymont, Barbara. *The Iroquois in the American Revolution*. Syracuse, N.Y.: Syracuse University Press, 1972. An overview of the Iroquois in the American Revolution by the leading student of Six Nations affairs. While a bit naïve about the motives of the missionaries, it is extremely useful for its accounts of the battles in which the Iroquois took part.

Hagan, William T. *Longhouse Diplomacy and Frontier Warfare: The Iroquois Confederacy in the American Revolution*. Albany: New York State American Revolution Bicentennial Commission, 1976. While only a brief overview of the Iroquois in the American Revolution, this study is a testament to Hagan's superb insight into Native American culture. Recommended for the general reader.

Johnson, Charles. *The Valley of the Six Nations*. Toronto: Champlain Society, 1964. An indispensable source for understanding Brant and the Mohawks in Canada. Reprints a number of sources that reveal the tensions with which Brant had to contend.

Kelsay, Isabel Thompson. *Joseph Brant, 1743-1807: Man of Two Worlds*. Syracuse, N.Y.: Syracuse University Press, 1984. While it is the latest study of Brant, and contains much useful information, this lengthy book tends to be awkwardly ethnocentric and offers little genuine insight into its subject; it is also marred at times by an irritatingly familiar tone.

O'Donnell, James H., III. "Joseph Brant." In *American Indian Leaders: Studies in Diversity*, edited by R. David Edmunds. Lincoln: University of Nebraska Press, 1980. This essay provides a readily understandable analysis of Brant, his role models, and his career. Less ethnocentric than the biography by Kelsay.

Stone, William L. *The Life of Joseph Brant—Thayendanegea*. New York: G. Dearborn and Co., 1838. The classic nineteenth century account; the author tries to unearth every story and scrap of evidence, both real and imagined, about Brant. It is still the place to start for anyone doing serious research on Brant.

Wood, L. A. *The War Chief of the Six Nations*. Toronto: Glascow, Brook and Co., 1914. An older work which tends to follow the lead of Stone, without adding much insight.

James H. O'Donnell III

WERNHER VON BRAUN

Born: March 23, 1912; Wirsitz, Germany
Died: June 16, 1977; Alexandria, Virginia
Area of Achievement: Astronautics
Contribution: A pioneer in German rocketry and a visionary of space flight, von Braun dominated the early American space program by directing construction of the Saturn rocket which propelled the first astronauts to the Moon.

Early Life

Wernher von Braun was born into the landowning aristocracy of Prussian Silesia on the eve of World War I, in Wirsitz, Germany (modern Wyrzysk, Poland). His father was Baron Magnus von Braun, his mother Baroness Emmy (von Quistorp) von Braun. Because his father rose to be minister of food and agriculture in the Weimar Republic, the family—including one older brother and one younger—often moved between cities. Though the father expected his son to succeed him as a Prussian landholder, the baroness unwittingly sabotaged this goal by giving Wernher a telescope for his confirmation into the Lutheran church, thus whetting his interest in the universe. In 1925, an article by the Rumanian Hermann Oberth on interplanetary space flight by rocket convinced von Braun to devote his life to space flight. Thus motivated, he overcame a weakness in mathematics to excel, and in 1930 he undertook a course in engineering at the technical institute of Berlin.

Life's Work

That year, at the age of eighteen, von Braun and a group of friends organized a club (*Verein für Raumschiffahrt*, society for space travel) to build and fire small crude rockets outside Berlin. Inspired also by the writings of the American rocket theorist Robert H. Goddard, von Braun that very summer assisted Oberth in early liquid-fuel rocket experiments. He also learned to fly gliders and other aircraft. In 1932, the year he took his degree in mechanical engineering and entered the University of Berlin, the German army was sufficiently impressed with von Braun not only to underwrite his experiments but also, that autumn, to appoint him to its rocket experiment station at Kummersdorf, near Berlin. Already his rockets were attaining an altitude of one mile, and with the welcome military funding, von Braun gradually refined and improved the army's projectiles. In June, 1934, the twenty-two-year-old "boy wonder" of German rocketry received the Ph.D. in physics from the university.

The Nazi dictator Adolph Hitler began actively supporting the rocket program in 1936; the next year, it shifted to Peenemünde on the Baltic Sea—an isolated site recommended by von Braun's mother, whose father had hunted ducks there. The result was a sprawling development center, equipped to produce, among lesser devices, a large, long-range ballistic military rocket. By 1938, von Braun had the first model of it ready, the A-4, capable of hitting a target eleven miles away. With the outbreak of war the next year, Hitler downgraded the rocket program, but von Braun pressed ahead until able to lift a rocket to an altitude of sixty miles, in October, 1942. In 1940, he had become a nominal member of the Nazi Party.

Anxious for miracle weapons, Hitler resumed his plans for von Braun's A-4 missile in 1943, when it reached as far downrange as 190 miles, carrying a one-ton warhead. It was now renamed the V-2, a "vengeance weapon," and Hitler gave von Braun the high distinction of full professor, charging him to mass-produce the V-2 for use against England. Allied intelligence enabled a massive night bombing raid on Peenemünde in August, 1943, to kill many engineers and set back production by perhaps four months. The following February, Gestapo chief Heinrich Himmler tried to take over the program, and when von Braun refused to agree, Himmler arrested and imprisoned him. Soon released as indispensable to the project, von Braun initiated the V-2 barrage on London in September—the first of some 3,255 to be successfully fired at England, the occupied port of Antwerp, and other selected targets on the Continent. Though they killed or seriously wounded more than 9,200 people, inflicted much damage, and affected Allied morale, the V-2's could not prevent the final Allied victory.

In February and March, 1945, von Braun personally directed the movement of about four hundred personnel, with V-2 components and plans, from Peenemünde and the advancing Soviet army to Bavaria in order to surrender to the Americans. They did so in May, and three months later, von Braun and 118 of his rocket engineers signed contracts with the United States Army to help produce improved V-2's for the Americans. As a result of this highly secret "Operation Paperclip," in September, 1945, the team—which included von Braun's Peenemünde military counterpart General Walter Dornberger and younger brother Magnus von Braun—was flown to Fort Bliss, Texas, where von Braun became technical director for the tests, conducted at the White Sands Proving Ground, New Mexico. Early in 1947, the thirty-five-year-old von Braun married his second cousin Maria Louise von Quistorp, seventeen years his junior; they had two daughters and a son. In 1950, the Army Ordnance Guided Missile Center was relocated at the Redstone Arsenal near Huntsville, Alabama, with von Braun as civilian director and eventually chief of missile research and development. He became an American citizen in 1955.

Already an exuberant, charismatic, and dynamic visionary (and an accomplished cellist and pianist), the tall, blond-haired, handsome von Braun now returned to his main interest—the notion of space flight. Beginning in 1948, he wrote and coauthored numerous papers and books projecting interplanetary travel, beginning with a small Earth satellite but eventually including space stations and trips to the Moon and Mars. His work during the 1950's centered on a nuclear-armed, long-range missile, the second-generation V-2 called Redstone, improved to the Jupiter-C in 1956. When the Soviets put Sputnik 1 into orbit the next year, however, von Braun was ready to use the Jupiter-C to place America's first scientific satellite, the Explorer 1, into orbit, a feat accomplished early in 1958. The tiny spacecraft promptly discovered the Van Allen radiation belts girdling the earth.

Von Braun and his team were transferred to the National Aeronautics and Space Administration (NASA) upon its establishment later that year, with von Braun being appointed director of NASA's George C. Marshall Space Flight Center at Huntsville. In the 1960's, his greatest rocket, the huge, three-stage Saturn V, was used to deliver the Apollo spacecraft to the Moon. Its success, in thirteen perfect launches, was largely a result of his effective leadership. One of his associates since 1928 ascribed the team's achievements primarily to von Braun's "technical ability, passionate optimism, immense experiences and uncanny organizing ability." His reward was appointment in 1970 to be NASA's deputy associate administrator for planning, charged with long-range American programs in space.

When the space effort was reduced, however, von Braun resigned from NASA in 1972 to join the aerospace firm of Fairchild Industries as vice president for engineering and development. In this capacity, he participated in the company's development of an applied technology satellite. Three years later, he helped found and lead as president the private National Space Institute for promoting public support of space flight, continuing always to advocate his original interplanetary ideas. Cancer, however, forced him into complete retirement at the end of 1976. Mankind's first giant step toward the stars had been accomplished largely through the technical and promotional leadership of Wernher von Braun.

Summary

The name and person of Wernher von Braun absolutely dominated the first generation of space flight; the very mention of his name evokes images of the early efforts aimed at the conquest of outer space. He was not only a singular proponent and visionary of interplanetary explorations from the days of his youth but a practitioner as well. Before he was twenty-five, the skills and achievements of his team had already surpassed the pioneering work of the earliest trio of theoretician-experimenters in rocketry, Goddard, Oberth, and the Russian Konstantin Tsiolkovsky. Indeed, no one missile engineer-administrator-prophet had begun even to equal him by the time of his death. Von Braun was the first and only great captain of missile technology in an era of institutionalized science.

308					Great Lives from History

A genius in his calling, von Braun was also an articulate spokesman in scientific and technological circles and in addressing the public. Repeatedly he was called upon to account for his role in producing the V-2 strategic missile and lesser weapons of war for the infamous Nazi regime. Understandably, it was a question Americans were prone to ask of a former enemy, just as they did of the developers of their own atom bomb, but not of the Wright brothers or other inventors who depended upon military contracts to develop and market similar major inventions. Von Braun's answer was that of many thoughtful scientists: namely, that science needs no justification, that the use—or misuse—of scientific knowledge, and thus the moral responsibility for it, lies in the hands of political leaders. For, in the industrialized world, virtually every tool has a potential military application.

In order to attain his ambitions in space, von Braun welcomed the much-needed funds that government could provide in pre-Hitlerian Germany as well as under the Third Reich. At the start, he found a kindred champion in young Captain Dornberger, who accompanied him to Peenemünde and White Sands. It was Dornberger, a major general, who rescued him from Himmler's jail by direct intercession with Hitler. Neither man, nor many in their closely knit team, had any love for the rigid controls of the Fascist state over their work.

They tried to defend their homeland in spite of these internal obstacles, hindrances which in the final analysis prevented them from using the V-2 early enough to thwart the Allied assault at Normandy and the ensuing liberation of Western Europe. Also, being isolated in one place under stringent Gestapo security, Peenemünde could be pinpointed by the Allies and bombed. By contrast, the Allied democracies generally subcontracted weapons research to private or university laboratories, thus stimulating the free exchange of scientific ideas and data which produced the weapons of victory (the Manhattan atom bomb project was one of the few exceptions).

No friend of dictatorships, von Braun and his colleagues opted to cast their lot with the postwar United States rather than the Soviet Union. In Huntsville, von Braun vigorously renewed his Lutheran faith and became a pillar of the community. There and in Washington, he epitomized the space program, utilizing his extraordinary managerial talents to mastermind many of the nation's accomplishments in the first golden age of space flight. Though public enthusiasm waned, he carried on his crusade in the private sector as a beacon for future generations to follow. Wernher von Braun had matured from boy wonder of earliest rocketry into universal spokesman for the future.

Bibliography
Bergaust, Erik. *Reaching for the Stars*. Garden City, N.Y.: Doubleday and Co., 1960. The only full biography, based on ten years of interviews with

von Braun but complete only to the date of publication. It is the nearest work to an autobiography.

Bilstein, Roger E. *Stages to Saturn*. Washington, D.C.: NASA, 1980. A "technological history of the Apollo/Saturn launch vehicles," this superb, official, highly annotated history —one of many produced by NASA on the United States' early space programs—places von Braun's style of management in the context of the total Saturn program. The book is dedicated to von Braun.

Braun, Wernher von. "Prelude to Space Travel." In *Across the Space Frontier*. Edited by Cornelius Ryan. New York: Viking Press, 1953. A major publication of its day, in which von Braun forecasted the first earth satellites, three-stage rockets, a space station, a moonship, and a space telescope. The essay is illustrated by the most eminent "space artist" of von Braun's generation, Chesley Bonestell.

Dornberger, Walter. *V-2*. New York: Viking Press, 1954. A valuable prewar and wartime memoir of the A-4/V-2 program by its military commander, who continued his work in the postwar American aerospace industry.

Ley, Willy. *Rockets, Missiles, and Men in Space*. New York: Viking Press, 1968. A major, comprehensive account of rocketry from antiquity to the early Apollo moonproject. A member of the German space club, Ley was a contemporary of von Braun and he gives many autobiographical insights into rocketry of the 1930's and 1940's and includes many long passages written by von Braun.

Ordway, Frederick I., III, and Mitchell R. Sharpe. *The Rocket Team*. Cambridge, Mass.: MIT Press, 1982. The definitive book on von Braun's team, focusing on the years 1931 to 1945 but with a useful though brief overview of the development of the Saturn V "moon rocket." Von Braun himself wrote the introduction less than a year before his death.

Clark G. Reynolds

PERCY WILLIAMS BRIDGMAN

Born: April 21, 1882; Cambridge, Massachusetts
Died: August 20, 1961; Randolph, New Hampshire
Areas of Achievement: Physics and philosophy of science
Contribution: Through his invention and investigations, Bridgman vastly extended the range of high pressure physics. Through his development of the philosophical notion of operational analysis, he greatly aided his colleagues in coping with the new ideas of twentieth century physics. His work contributed significantly to the coming of age of physics in America.

Early Life

Percy Williams Bridgman was born April 21, 1882, in Cambridge, Massachusetts, the only son of Ann Maria (Williams) Bridgman and Raymond Landon Bridgman, a professional journalist who wrote on social and political matters. During his school years, the family lived in a suburb of Boston—Newton, Massachusetts—where young Percy attended public schools. He was a good student, rather shy but interested in sports and games. He was an excellent chess player.

Bridgman entered Harvard College in 1900 and was graduated summa cum laude in physics in 1904. He continued at Harvard as a graduate student, receiving his A.M. in 1905, his Ph.D. in 1908. By that time he was already drawn to studying the behavior of materials when subjected to high pressure. His doctoral dissertation was titled "Mercury Resistance as a Pressure Gauge."

Upon completion of his doctoral studies, Bridgman was first named research fellow, then instructor in physics at Harvard. He subsequently rose through the professorial ranks, never leaving Harvard for more than brief periods of military research or sabbatical leaves.

A man of small stature with an obviously intelligent face, wearing steel-rimmed glasses, he seemed a rather austere figure in public, but he exhibited a warm, kindly personality in his association with family and friends. Nicknamed "Perce" as a boy, he was usually called Peter in his adult years.

Life's Work

In his professional research, Bridgman devoted himself single-mindedly to exploring high pressure physics. Others had worked in this area before him, but he was able to attain much higher pressures than had any previous investigator. Starting, in 1910, with pressures of about sixty-five hundred atmospheres, he was able, over the years, to reach pressures of nearly 400,000 atmospheres. (One "atmosphere" corresponds to about fifteen pounds per square inch.) He was able to accomplish this feat in part because of the improved strength of materials that became available in the twentieth century. His success can also be attributed to his own early invention of a leak-proof pressure seal for the vessel in which his samples were placed. Bridgman said that his discovery of this seal was partly accidental but gave no further details.

The improvements in Bridgman's laboratory setup allowed him to measure the effect of increasingly high pressures on the physical properties of virtually every substance he could lay his hands on. He studied, for example, variations in melting points, electrical resistivity, compression, viscosity, fracture strength, and polymorphism. The results that he published proved of great value to theoreticians in solid-state physics. His findings also aided geophysicists interested in regions beneath the Earth's surface that are subjected to very high pressure caused by the weight of the material above. His results had important industrial application as well.

Bridgman possessed great mechanical ability, which he enjoyed using in designing, building, and manipulating his equipment. At no time did he have more than two laboratory assistants. He never collaborated with others in research. All of his papers were published under his sole authorship and often used the first-person singular, unlike most scientific papers, which are written very impersonally. He put in long hours in his laboratory, arriving on his bicycle about 8:00 A.M. even on Saturdays during the academic year. During the summer months he retreated with his wife and two children to Randolph, New Hampshire, to garden, mountain climb, photograph, organize his philosophical thinking and writing, and only occasionally to experiment. His success has been ascribed to a rare combination of ingenuity, drive, and efficiency. In 1946 he was awarded the Nobel Prize for Physics.

Bridgman's experience as a physics teacher transformed him into a critic of physical theory and a philosopher of science. When charged with the responsibility of teaching thermodynamics and electricity and magnetism to students, he came to view critically the way in which basic concepts in those fields were defined and used. He said that this caused him considerable "disquietude." This discomfort impelled Bridgman to undertake a study of dimensional analysis of the basic equations of physics and caused him to inculcate in his students a deeply critical, searching attitude in all of their subsequent study. Bridgman believed that, unfortunately, the thinking of his predecessors and contemporaries was marred by metaphysics.

Spurred by the introduction into physics of new ideas from relativity and quantum theory and by the widespread dilemmas facing the physics community in the early twentieth century, Bridgman began composing *The Logic of Modern Physics* (1927). He said that he wrote this book primarily for himself, to organize and clarify his own thinking.

Basically, Bridgman's thinking was in the tradition of Ernst Mach and Albert Einstein. Meaningful concepts, he believed, were those that can be defined as a set of operations, either physical or mental—hence the term "operationalism," which became uniquely associated with the name of Bridgman. (He himself preferred "operational analysis," since he thought "operationalism" sounded too dogmatic.) In brief, he believed that a concept is defined by its corresponding set of operations.

Bridgman's operationalism received wide attention not only from physicists and other scientists but also from psychologists, sociologists, and philosophers. It continued to permeate his later writings in physics as well as other fields. In all, he published some sixty papers and six books on the philosophy of science and its implications for other areas of human endeavor and thought.

In addition to his primary efforts in physics and philosophy, Bridgman was an active, concerned member of society. During World War I he worked on the development of sound detection systems for antisubmarine warfare. During World War II he investigated the plastic flow of steel under high pressure and studied the compressibility of uranium and plutonium for the Manhattan Project, which was responsible for developing the atom bomb.

With the rise of totalitarianism in Germany, Italy, Russia, and Japan during the 1930's, Bridgman became increasingly concerned for the cause of individual freedom. As a personal statement, in 1939 he issued a "manifesto" denying access to his laboratory (where he usually welcomed visitors) and refusing to engage in discussion with citizens from any totalitarian state. He believed that cessation of scientific intercourse with totalitarian states would make more difficult the misuse of scientific information by these states and would give individuals (such as himself) the opportunity to express their abhorrence of totalitarian practices. This document, posted on his laboratory door, was published in the press and widely commented upon. Many, including some fellow scientists, disagreed with the wisdom of Bridgman's course of action, but none doubted Bridgman's sincerity and depth of concern. It was also about this time that his book *The Intelligent Individual and Society* (1939) was published.

Bridgman continued as an active member of the Harvard physics department and attempted, with little or no success, to promote operational thinking in the social sciences. He believed that many of the difficulties experienced by individuals and societies arose from a lack of clear thinking.

Bridgman remained physically active until shortly before his death, by his own hand, on August 20, 1961, at the age of seventy-nine, victim of a crippling form of bone cancer.

Summary

When Bridgman entered the world of physics at the beginning of the twentieth century, physics in Europe was about to move into its "modern" phase. America had few practicing physicists, almost all of them experimentalists far removed from the mainstream of physics both intellectually and geographically. Bridgman's outstanding high pressure investigations attracted worldwide attention, resulting in invitations to international conferences and culminating in his being awarded the Nobel Prize in 1946. Highly respected at home and abroad, Bridgman contributed significantly to the maturing of the American physics profession.

His own research was entirely experimental, but he carefully followed the theoretical developments in relativity and quantum physics that were taking place. His operational approach to all physics was espoused by many colleagues. Generations of physics students at Harvard were influenced by his philosophical outlook, many going on to incorporate it into their own subsequent teaching. Thus Bridgman's influence on physics in America extended far beyond the confines of Harvard University. Through his articles, lectures, and books on social and philosophical topics, he reached a wide audience outside physical science.

Bibliography

Bridgman, Percy W. *Reflections of a Physicist*. New York: Philosophical Library, 1950. A collection of Bridgman's short, nontechnical essays addressing scientific and social questions. His "Manifesto," referred to above, is reproduced here.

——————. *The Intelligent Individual and Society*. New York: Macmillan Co., 1938. Bridgman's attempt to bring clear thinking into the social domain.

——————. *The Logic of Modern Physics*. New York: Macmillan Co., 1927. Bridgman's first full-length book dealing with the philosophical question of meaning in physics and setting forth his "operational analysis." Highly influential, especially among fellow scientists, it was subsequently translated into German, Italian, and Russian.

——————. "P. W. Bridgman's 'The Logic of Modern Physics' After Thirty Years." *Daedalus* 88 (Summer, 1959): 518-526. A retrospective view which discusses the ways the author might change the original text in the light of subsequent developments in physics and responses from some of his readers.

——————. *A Sophisticate's Primer of Relativity*. Middletown, Conn.: Wesleyan University Press, 1962. Bridgman's final work, published posthumously, analyzing his comprehension of relativity as developed over his lifetime.

Kemble, Edwin C., and Francis Birch. "Percy Williams Bridgman." In *National Academy of Sciences Biographical Memoirs*, vol. 41, 22-67. New York: Columbia University Press, 1970. The most complete biographical study available. Written by two of Bridgman's former colleagues, it summarizes his work in high pressure physics and his philosophical outlook as well as presenting a personal picture of his character and style. A complete bibliography of Bridgman's publications is appended.

Nobelstiftelsen, Stockholm. "Physics 1946." In *Physics*, 7-72. New York: Elsevier Publishing Co., 1964. Includes the citation and presentation speech made on the occasion of the awarding of the Nobel Prize in Physics to Bridgman and his responding lecture "General Survey of Certain Results in the Field of High Pressure Physics."

Katherine R. Sopka

JOHN BROWN

Born: May 9, 1800; Torrington, Connecticut
Died: December 2, 1859; Charlestown, West Virginia
Area of Achievement: Abolitionism
Contribution: Brown has come to symbolize the struggle over the abolition of
slavery in the United States. He was the catalyst for change from polite
debate and parliamentary maneuvering aimed at modification of the institution to physical violence and a direct onslaught on Southern territory and
the supporters of slavery.

Early Life

John Brown was born in a state that, like many others in New England in
1800, was agriculturally exhausted and in religious turmoil. His parents,
Owen and Ruth (Mills) Brown, were affected by both problems at his birth.
Economically, the Brown family was barely at the subsistence level. John's
father moved from job to job: farmer, carpenter, handyman. Though the
family descended from the early Mayflower settlers, they were never able to
capitalize on their ancestry. Religiously, Owen Brown was a harsh practitioner of the piety of his Puritan forebears, and he instilled in his son a lifelong fear and adoration of a militant and volatile God.

The elder Brown had been married twice and fathered sixteen children.
His first wife, John's mother, suffered from mental disease as did others in
her family. According to some accounts, John did not take well to his stepmother, but there is little evidence to support this conjecture. The peripatetic
life of the family was probably more disturbing to him. When John was five,
his father moved to Hudson, Ohio, following the line of the moving frontier.
Again, the family was without the necessary capital to take advantage of the
opportunities available in the rich Ohio Valley. His father became a herds-
man and then a tanner, a vocation that the son quickly mastered. His father
had some plans for his son which included sending him to Plainsfield, Massachusetts, to study for the ministry. John did not stay long, however, either
because of poor preparation or because of his poor eyesight.

John Brown returned to Hudson to help his father with the cattle and the
tanning shop. At the age of twenty, he married Dianthe Lusk, who bore him
seven children in twelve years of married life. She, like his mother, had mental problems. Dianthe Brown died in 1831, and within a year of her passing,
Brown married Mary Anne Day, then sixteen, who bore him thirteen more
children in twenty-one years. Brown, possessing a modicum of education in a
frontier region, became a surveyor as well as a tanner like his father. Also
like his father, Brown was a mover. In 1825, he moved to Pennsylvania,
cleared land, and set up what was to become a successful farm and tannery.
He also became a postmaster, but still he was unsatisfied. Quick fortunes

were being made in land and business speculation, and Brown sold off his holdings and moved back to Ohio. There he hoped to take advantage of land speculation and canal building contracts. He lost heavily and began pyramiding debt while turning to cattle and sheep selling. His creditors moved in on him and he was compelled to declare bankruptcy.

Life's Work

Brown's work in the woolen business brought him a partnership with another man, Simon Perkins, to establish a wool brokerage in Springfield, Massachusetts. Fluctuating prices and market instability, however, confounded his efforts to make a success of the business. He was also accused of "weighting" the packs of hides, which were sold by weight to English markets. The collapse of this last business venture was followed by numerous lawsuits, one involving sixty thousand dollars for breach of contract. Brown settled his affairs as best he could. He was fifty years old and virtually penniless, with a large family to support.

Even as a young man, Brown had learned from his father the biblical precept that it was sinful to earn one's living from the sweat of others and that slavery was wrong. In Ohio both he and his father had lent their resources to aiding the underground movement of runaway slaves. John Brown's barn at his farm in Pennsylvania was a station in that movement, and he formed a League of Gileadites among blacks in Springfield to encourage them to defend both themselves and fugitive slaves. Brown's activity in New England brought him in touch with men whose lives would never be the same after meeting him. Gerrit Smith, a New York benefactor of abolitionism who owned much of the Adirondack Mountains, was attracted to Brown. He had given land for use by runaway slaves in a small community known as North Elba. He gave Brown a farm from which he could train and educate the former slaves. Given the severe climate, short growing season, and lack of arable land in the region, not to mention Brown's spotty record as a farmer, problems developed. Brown himself declared that he felt "omnipotent" in his new role as guide and exemplar to the blacks in his charge.

Within two years, however, he was in Akron, Ohio. His mind was turned to developing a grand plan for an attack on slavery. As early as 1847, he had talked about gathering a band of men from the free states to make forays into slave territory to rescue blacks from bondage. He talked of setting up a mountain stronghold as a base of terrorist activity, but the ideas did not take coherent form until the Fugitive Slave Act, part of the Compromise of 1850, was passed. The Kansas-Nebraska Act, four years later, further agitated him and his sons, five of whom moved to the territory to help make Kansas a free state. In May, 1855, John Brown, Jr., wrote a mournful letter to his father explaining the conditions and imploring him to send arms to battle proslavery forces. Brown dispatched his family to North Elba again and set out for Kansas with a wagonload of guns and ammunition.

He found his sons impoverished and ill when he arrived at Osawatomie. Though he was to join the colony as a surveyor, he quickly assumed leadership of the local militia and made Free Soil a vengeance-wreaking crusade. His group fought in the ineffectual Wakarusa War and then, after the sacking of Lawrence by proslavery forces, he and his party, which included four sons and two others, ritually slaughtered five settlers at Pottawatomie. He had reached a personal turning point, viewing himself as an instrument in the hands of an angry god. His own colony was overrun and burned and one of his boys killed in retaliation. Brown now was gray in hair and features, with a bent back and glittering gray-blue eyes; he had grown a full beard that was streaked with gray, which made him appear older than his fifty-six years. His fervent attitude toward slavery fired his listeners, many of whom, such as Franklin Sanborn, Thomas W. Higginson, Theodore Parker, Gerrit Smith, G. L. Stearns, and Samuel Gridley Howe, were ripe for the leadership which Brown promised. He met with these members of the Massachusetts State Kansas Committee, and they responded with some arms and ammunition and money to take with him to Kansas again.

Kansas had no stomach for bloodshed in 1857 as it moved closer to voting the issue of free or slave, and Brown now thought of a daring plan to liberate slaves in the South itself. In the spring of 1858, he visited the colony of runaway slaves in Catham, Canada, to gain volunteers. His money gone, he turned again to Smith and the Massachusetts group. They argued for a delay, gave him some money and supplies, and Brown again headed for Kansas, this time under the name of Shubel Morgan. There he led a raid on some plantations in Missouri in which one planter was killed and some slaves liberated. Brown was now a wanted man with a bounty on his head. He headed for Canada with the slaves in tow and then proceeded east, making speeches in Cleveland and Rochester to solicit funds. Again the old group came through with thirty-eight hundred dollars, knowing full well that Brown was bent on violence.

It was Harpers Ferry that became fixed in Brown's mind; to the commander in chief of a provisional army for liberation it was an ideal objective. The federal arsenal in the town was noted for the quality of arms and its technology since its creation in 1798. The complex of forges, shops, tool and die works, and assembly areas turned out rifles and handguns in an assembly line process that foretold mass production. John Hall of Maine had gained a contract in 1819 to turn out breech-loading rifles using his idea of interchangeable parts, and his contract was renewed yearly until 1844, when a totally new rifle plant was built to produce the Standard United States Model military rifle. The skilled workers were mostly transplanted Northerners who were regarded as "foreigners" by local Southerners. A canal and a railroad as well as a macadam road led to the town of three thousand, which included

1,250 freed blacks and some eighty-eight slaves.

The Brown contingent of fourteen whites and five blacks established themselves in a farm five miles from the Ferry to lay plans for their attack. On Sunday, October 16, 1859, they marched by night down the dirt road leading to the town. By mid-morning, the men had taken both the town and its leading citizens.

Brown did not know what to do with his victory. He had control of the engine house, the federal armory, the railroad, and the town of Harpers Ferry, and the very magnitude of his success overwhelmed and confused him. He let a train continue, certainly with the knowledge that the passengers would alarm state and federal officials. He did nothing about searching out possible followers from the town population or the countryside. He had guns, powder and shells, and a well-situated natural fortress, as well as a small though very devout band of followers. Brown lost his revolutionary compass at this critical moment. His willingness to fight was not in question. Shots were fired and lives were taken until Lee's troops stormed the engine house and cut Brown down. Though he was not severely wounded, there was little recourse for his men but to surrender. The military quickly restored order and moved Brown to prison while dispatching squads to investigate the farm which had been the band's headquarters. There they found letters and documentation which implicated Brown's Northern associates in the Harpers Ferry venture. Why Brown had kept, let alone brought with him, these damning materials is uncertain. He certainly treasured his association with successful and influential men, and given his life on the margin of society, this connection was important enough to be sustained with physical evidence. Furthermore, Brown was concerned about the shifting commitment of antislavery reformers and therefore by keeping documentation he could hold them to the course. The discovery of these materials, however, proved the conspiracy case against Brown and his men and threw fear into those who had aided them.

Of the twenty-one men who had followed him to Harpers Ferry on October 16, only eleven remained alive. Brown had seen two of his sons killed in the melee that followed the arrival of the militia from Charlestown (modern Charles Town, West Virginia) and Lee's marines. On October 18, he was jailed in Charlestown to await indictment, which came a week later.

Brown, Aaron Stevens, Edwin Coppoc, Shields Green (the black who had chosen to go with Brown despite the admonition and concerns of Frederick Douglass), and John Copeland were all indicted on October 25 for treason against Virginia, for conspiring with slaves to rebel, and for murder. All of them pleaded not guilty and requested separate trials. The court agreed and determined that Brown would be tried first. The prosecution was headed by Charles Harding, state attorney for Jefferson County, and Andrew Hunter, a seasoned Charlestown attorney. The court was presided over by Judge Richard Parker, who had just begun the semiannual term of his circuit court and already had a grand jury seated. Turner had just gaveled the court to order when Brown's defense attorney read a telegram from one A. H. Lewis of Akron, Ohio, declaring that Brown's family was suffering from hereditary insanity. It proceeded to list the people on his mother's side who were known to have severe mental problems. The inference was that Brown himself was insane and therefore not fit for trial. His attorney had shown Brown the telegram and Brown admitted to his mother's death by insanity and the fact that his first wife and two of his sons were afflicted. Brown, however, rejected the plea of insanity on his behalf, though he apparently gave his attorney permission to use the document. The judge ruled out the plea on the basis that the evidence was in unreliable form. He also rejected a delay to enable Brown to get a new attorney.

Brown's trial began on October 27, 1859, and lasted for less than four days. He was carried to the court each day in a litter, and with each day, he became more irritated with his court-appointed attorneys. They had been joined by a twenty-one-year-old Boston attorney, George Hoyt, who had been retained by some Brown supporters who hoped to learn more about the case on behalf of the group of backers who were facing possible indictment as coconspirators. Botts and Green gratefully withdrew from the defense team, leaving the inexperienced Hoyt alone. Legal help soon came in the form of Samuel Chilton of Washington and Hiram Griswold of Cleveland, who were persuaded to take up what Brown himself realized was a lost cause.

The prosecution's case was devastating. Brown's request that he be tried as commander in chief of a provisional army, according to the laws governing warfare, was rejected. Brown's vision of himself as a messianic leader of a noble crusade against slavery was ignored. On October 31, at 1:45 P.M., the case went to the jury, which, after only forty-five minutes, declared Brown guilty on all counts. The verdict cast a pall on the audience, which days before had been vociferous in its rage against Brown. Brown himself said nothing as he lay quietly on his cot. The sentence of death by hanging was passed on November 2, with the date for execution set for December 2. The coconspirators captured with Brown were tried as well and all sentenced to the same fate. Brown had visited with them in jail, calling on them to be firm and resolute and to implicate no one. Friends of Brown had sought to bring his wife from North Elba, but Brown insisted that she remain at home. Only on the afternoon before his execution did she visit with him and then stand by to claim his body.

Governor Henry Wise was besieged with demands for clemency, threats, and warnings of plots to free Brown. Martial law was proclaimed in Charlestown, and fifteen hundred soldiers, including a company of cadets from Virginia Military Institute commanded by Thomas "Stonewall" Jackson, ringed the gallows.

John Brown's death on a rope in Charlestown was but the end of a beginning. The larger crisis that Brown had foreshadowed soon came with a character of violence and death that would have perhaps given even Osawatomie pause. The South, by insisting on dealing with Brown's case, had arrogated to itself police authority over what was a crime against federal property. It thereby threw down a gauntlet of defiant sectionalism and states' rights.

None of this was lost on Brown's supporters in the North, who, after suffering gag rules in Congress blocking their petitions against slavery, after almost thirty years of relentless electioneering, pamphleteering, lecturing, haranguing, debating, and propagandizing against slavery, and after suffering dismaying defeats at the hands of every branch of government and in virtually every attempt to work within the system, were ready to exploit John Brown's fateful end. Antislavery reformers took charge of the body, and by wagon, train, and steamer they took it to the hills where Brown had felt "omnipotent." It was a cortege that would be duplicated six years later on the death of Abraham Lincoln—a slow, somber taking of martyred remains home. Through Lake Placid and on to the little village of North Elba they took Brown, and near his little home they buried him. Gerrit Smith, the man who had given him the land, was not with him at the burial. Smith had become mentally deranged after Brown's capture and was institutionalized. Others who were closely involved with Brown, such as Frederick Douglass, found it convenient to flee to Canada or travel abroad. Brown, the guerrilla fighter and terrorist who had taken the struggle against slavery beyond rhetoric, had made clear that the approaching confrontation would be violent.

Summary

John Brown was a tragic figure central to the great tragedy of Civil War America. Whether he was a hero in that era is, at best, controversial. There seems little doubt that had his earlier ventures been successful, he would have melded with other entrepreneurs of the moving frontier and probably been lost as another subject representing an enterprising nation. A failure as a businessman, he turned all of his energies to what became for him a holy mission: rooting out the evil of slavery. Social, economic, and political displacement encouraged many in his region to seek redress. Brown, however, personalized these conflicts to an extreme degree and placed himself at a point from which there was no turning back.

Bibliography
Boyer, Richard O. *The Legend of John Brown: A Biography and a History*. New York: Alfred A. Knopf, 1972. This is a fine piece of biography that takes the story of Brown up to his arrival in Kansas in 1855. Boyer died before he could complete the second volume.
Malin, James C. *John Brown and the Legend of Fifty-six*. Philadelphia:

American Philosophical Society, 1942. Malin's work is highly critical of Brown's activities in Kansas and of Brown personally. It is useful, however, for its detail of that period of Brown's life.

National Park Service. *John Brown's Raid*. Washington, D.C.: Superintendent of Documents, 1974. Here is an outstanding piece of work based on reports by William C. Everhart and Arthur L. Sullivan that gives sweep and substance to Brown and his men at Harper's Ferry in the space of sixty-eight pages.

Oates, Stephen B. *To Purge This Land with Blood: A Biography of John Brown*. New York: Harper and Row Publishers, 1970. Oates's book is the most modern full biography of Brown and establishes the point of view that Brown's puritanical heritage was at the base of his thought and action. He also has something to say in a bibliographical essay. See also his article: "John Brown and His Judges: A Critique of the Historical Literature." In *Civil War History* vol. 17, 1971, pp. 5-24.

Sanborn, Franklin B., ed. *The Life and Letters of John Brown*. New York: Negro Universities Press, 1891. This is a book to be used carefully as it is biased toward Brown; the gathering of Brown's letters makes this a valuable resource.

Villard, Oswald Garrison. *John Brown, 1800-1859: A Biography Fifty Years After*. Gloucester, Mass.: Peter Smith, 1910. Villard's biography is still a standard work on Brown and his time. It cannot be ignored in any study.

Jack J. Cardoso

WILLIAM JENNINGS BRYAN

Born: March 19, 1860; Salem, Illinois
Died: July 26, 1925; Dayton, Tennessee
Areas of Achievement: Politics and oratory
Contribution: With his crusader's zeal for righteousness and a determination to champion the cause of the common man, Bryan used his dramatic oratorical skills to gain the leadership of the Democratic Party from 1896 to 1912. Three times he won the Democratic nomination for president, but he lost all three elections.

Early Life
William Jennings Bryan was born March 19, 1860, in Salem, Illinois. His mother, née Mariah Elizabeth Jennings, was reared as a Methodist; his father, Silas Lillard Bryan, of Scotch-Irish descent, was a devout Baptist and became a frontier lawyer, judge, and politician in south central Illinois. As a trial lawyer, Silas was known for his habit of quoting Scripture to the jury. William Jennings Bryan grew up on a large farm which his father had purchased. The nearby town of Salem had an economy based primarily on agriculture, and Bryan's roots were in an agrarian environment that valued hard work, individualism, and religious faith. Especially influential in the Salem area were those churches stressing the necessity of a conversion experience. The revivalistic emphasis of the evangelicals in southern Illinois had a profound effect on young Bryan. Indeed, in later years, he would become what one historian has described as a "political evangelist," a politician whose oratory resembled that of a revival preacher and whose political faith contained a strong moralistic tone. Bryan the politician saw himself as God's warrior sent to destroy the Philistines, and he tended to see his own political concepts as baptized in light while those of his opponents as covered with darkness.

Bryan's father sent him to Whipple Academy for two years and then to Illinois College in Jacksonville for four years, where he was graduated in 1881. During his college days, Bryan showed little interest in physical exercise or athletics, but he did demonstrate at least modest ability as a debater. For two years, he studied law in Chicago, graduating from the Union College of Law in 1883. He then returned to Jacksonville, where he practiced law from 1883 to 1887. While still a struggling young lawyer, Bryan married Mary Baird on October 1, 1884. During the first month of marriage, he gave a major share of his time to the campaign to elect Grover Cleveland as president. Mary Baird Bryan defied the conventions of her time by studying law and gaining admission to the bar in 1888.

In his early years, Bryan had an excellent physique and a handsome appearance. He was six feet tall, with a strong muscular frame. His clear baritone voice was resonant and pleasing. Age, lack of exercise, and gluttonous eating habits would in later life create a more corpulent figure.

In 1887, Bryan moved to Lincoln, Nebraska, and sought to establish a law practice there, but he quickly became involved in politics. Lincoln was a rapidly growing town that could afford opportunities for a young lawyer. The staunch Republican district that included Lincoln had recently sent a Democrat to Congress. Perhaps Bryan's decision to move to Nebraska was motivated in part by hopes of getting in on the ground floor of the growing Democratic structure in Nebraska.

Life's Work

In 1890, although he lived in a normally Republican district, Bryan won election to Congress as a Democrat. His district reelected him in 1892, but in 1894, when he sought a United States Senate seat, the Nebraska legislature chose his opponent. During his congressional years, Bryan gradually espoused the Free Silver movement. Those who favored the gold standard, he believed, would force debtors to pay back their debts with a dollar more valuable than the one they borrowed. The Populist Party, silver-mining interests, farmers, and silver state Republican senators were forming a coalition to fight for a bimetallic standard. In Congress, Bryan voted against repeal of the Sherman Silver Purchase Act, and he began vociferously condemning his own Democratic president, Cleveland, who sided with the "goldbugs." After his congressional career's sudden end, Bryan intensified his prosilver lecture campaign and became the most popular orator for the cause. The silver advocates were gaining control of the Democratic Party and were turning out Cleveland's supporters.

In 1896, Bryan managed to secure an opportunity to speak before the Democratic National Convention in Chicago. In his deeply moving and moralistic "Cross of Gold" speech, he mesmerized the delegates. Speaking to the "sound money men," he laid down the challenge, "You shall not press upon the brow of labor this crown of thorns, you shall not crucify mankind upon a cross of gold." When Bryan used this closing metaphor, he dramatized the crucifixion scene by holding his fingers to his head so that his hearers actually visualized the thorns piercing the brow of the working man. When he spoke of the cross, he held his arms extended horizontally for a full five seconds as the audience sat in a transfixed and reverent silence. The hush continued until he walked off the platform: Then came a wild outburst of enthusiasm as state banners were carried to the Nebraska delegation. The next day, the convention nominated him for the presidency. The more radical agrarian People's Party (the Populists) also took him up as their presidential candidate: For them to reject Bryan would have split up the prosilver advocates in the nation and possibly ensured defeat.

During the 1896 campaign, Bryan's opponent William McKinley conducted a quiet, dignified campaign, staying at his home in Canton, Ohio. While Mc-Kinley seemed a safe, sane candidate who would not upset business conditions in the country, Bryan seemed to many a dangerous demagogue whose radical views on the currency system would destabilize the economy. Bryan traveled eighteen thousand miles by train during his campaign, speaking up to nineteen times a day and sleeping only a few hours each night. In 1896, it was not yet considered tasteful for a presidential candidate to solicit votes in such a frenetic manner. McKinley's well-organized campaign won for him the presidency.

Bryan supported McKinley's decision to go to war against Spain in 1898 in support of Cuban independence. The governor of Nebraska appointed Bryan a colonel, and the "Great Commoner" recruited a regiment, but he never succeeded in leaving his base in Florida to take a hand in the fighting. After the conflict, Bryan stood with the anti-imperialists in opposing the acquisition of the Philippine Islands. Yet surprisingly, he encouraged Democratic senators to vote for ratification of the Treaty of Paris of 1898, which gave the Philippines to the United States. Bryan believed the matter could be settled later. The next election could become a referendum on both "free silver" and "free Cuba."

In 1900, Bryan gained his party's nomination a second time. Yet the depression that had plagued Cleveland's second term (1893-1897) gave way to prosperity in McKinley's administration (1897-1901). Farm prices rose, unemployment decreased, and the amount of gold being mined increased, causing a needed moderate inflation of the currency. Since Bryan's early popularity had been based on an appeal to those who were enduring hard times, he failed to compete successfully against McKinley's "A Full Dinner Pail" slogan. Bryan received fewer votes in 1900 than he had received in 1896.

In January, 1901, Bryan began editing a weekly newspaper, the *Commoner*, and was actively involved in its publication until he became secretary of state in 1913. He also spent his years lecturing on the Chatauqua circuit. He did not seek the 1904 Democratic nomination, but in 1908 he did become the nominee and lost again, this time to William Howard Taft. Bryan's choice as the nominee demonstrated that he was once again the acknowledged leader of the Democratic Party. This leadership continued until the election of a Democratic president in 1912, Woodrow Wilson.

Wilson chose Bryan to be secretary of state primarily because of the latter's political influence within the party. As secretary of state, Bryan turned his energies toward peacemaking. He secured "conciliation treaties" between many nations, treaties which included the promise to submit differences to arbitral commissions rather than seek military solutions. When war did come to Europe in 1914, Bryan diligently sought to prevent American entry. When Wilson sent a remonstrance to Germany for sinking a passenger liner (the Second Lusitania note), Bryan resigned in protest rather than approve what he thought an overly provocative message.

In his final years (1920's), Bryan spoke on college campuses against the theory of evolution. He defended the right of taxpayers to determine what should be taught in the public schools. In Tennessee, he supported Baptists in their drive to establish an antievolution law. When John Scopes, a Tennessee high school teacher, tested the constitutionality of the law, Bryan came to Dayton, Tennessee, to argue for the prosecution. The so-called Monkey Trial was held in an almost carnival-like atmosphere and received media attention across the nation. Clarence Darrow, attorney for the defense, subjected Bryan's defense of creationism to a withering barrage of ridicule and criticism. The ordeal of the trial, the heat of summer, Bryan's unfortunate habit of overeating, along with diabetes, all hastened his death, which came only five days after the trial.

Summary

Bryan's greatest achievement was his leadership of the Democratic Party during the years 1896 to 1912. During this time, he moved the Democrats toward progressive reformism. He failed to win the presidency because he did not succeed in uniting the farmer's protest crusade and the laborer's interests into a single movement. The Democratic Party was too diverse to be controlled by a single ideology in Bryan's time. Yet Bryan did press for reforms (many inherited from the Populists and others) which became legislative and constitutional realities in the twentieth century. These include the graduated income tax, popular election of United States senators, woman's suffrage, stricter railroad regulations, currency reform, and, at the state level, adoption of the initiative and referendum.

Bryan is also remembered as a peace activist. He was almost, though not quite, a pacifist. He opposed Wilson's neutrality policy before the United States' entry into World War I as too pro-British. In 1915, he supported Henry Ford's effort to settle the European troubles by sending a peace ship to Europe with leading peace advocates aboard. He frequently gave lectures on the "Prince of Peace." He crusaded also against imperialism and the liquor traffic.

His role as an influential voice for conservative Christianity is well-known. He helped the Fundamentalists win a temporary victory when they took leadership positions in the Presbyterian Church in 1924; Bryan himself became vice-moderator of the denomination. Although lacking biblical scholarship, he willingly took part in the Scopes trial, casting himself in the role of a defender of the Genesis creation story.

Bibliography
Cherny, Robert W. *A Righteous Cause: The Life of William Jennings Bryan.*

Boston: Little, Brown and Co., 1985. A readable, brief biography that covers not only the life of the man but also the social and political context. A final chapter offers an evaluation of Bryan's contribution.

Clements, Kendrick A. *William Jennings Bryan: Missionary Isolationist.* Knoxville: University of Tennessee Press, 1982. Clements views Bryan as a microcosm of the average man and his foreign policy views, creating a sample of how the typical American would approach foreign affairs. He thought Bryan sought a balance between the escapism of traditional isolationism, on the one hand, and a missionary impulse to give aid, on the other.

Coletta, Paolo E. *William Jennings Bryan.* 3 vols. Lincoln: University of Nebraska Press, 1964-1969. Because of its thorough research and detailed coverage, this is the most important biography of Bryan. The title of volume 1, *Political Evangelist*, suggests Coletta's interpretation of Bryan. He sees him as more of a moralist than a statesman, as a humanitarian who tried to encourage others to be guided by righteousness and ethics in their conduct of economic and political affairs.

Glad, Paul W. *The Trumpet Soundeth.* Lincoln: University of Nebraska Press, 1960. This volume concentrates on the era of Bryan's Democratic Party leadership (1896-1912). It attempts to understand Bryan in the context of Midwestern society. Glad views Bryan's later years (1920-1925) as a tragic era when the "Great Commoner's" views no longer suited the intellectual climate of the United States. Yet Glad sees him, during the earlier era, as a constructive leader of the political opposition.

Koenig, Louis W. *Bryan: A Political Biography of William Jennings Bryan.* New York: G. P. Putnam's Sons, 1971. This is the most complete one-volume biography. To Koenig, Bryan's career is extremely significant because he was a champion of causes that were far advanced for his day. He fought for economic and social justice in the same manner that mid-century Democratic liberals would do later. Although Koenig views Bryan as intellectually shallow, he portrays him as a brilliant politician.

Levine, Lawrence W. *Defender of the Faith.* New York: Oxford University Press, 1965. Levine concentrates on the last decade of Bryan's career (1915-1925). The book represents an attempt to understand the "change" in Bryan from his early to later career, how he was transformed from a crusader for economic justice and social reform into an ultraconservative champion of lost causes. Levine's answer: No such change ever took place. Bryan continued to be what he had always been, a paradoxical figure, one who could champion reform and reaction at the same time.

Stone, Irving. *They Also Ran.* Garden City, N.Y.: Doubleday and Co., 1943. Stone's chapter on Bryan, in a book about defeated presidential candidates, is a good example of the more negative approach to Bryan. Liberals have found it difficult to forgive Bryan for his defense of Fundamentalist Christianity. Stone's colorful chapter portrays Bryan as a psychopath, a religious fanatic, and an intellectual dolt.

Richard L. Niswonger

WILLIAM CULLEN BRYANT

Born: November 3, 1794; Cummington, Massachusetts
Died: June 12, 1878; New York, New York
Areas of Achievement: Poetry and journalism
Contribution: As a poet, Bryant is often described as a transitional figure because of his fluency in exploiting Romantic themes drawn from nature in conventional neoclassical verse forms. In his half-century as an editor for the New York *Evening Post*, he was a vigorous spokesman for American liberal thought.

Early Life
  William Cullen Bryant was born November 3, 1794, in Cummington, Massachusetts. His father, Dr. Peter Bryant, was a physician who left Cummington to escape his debts soon after Bryant was born. When he returned two years later, the precocious child had already begun to read the Bible under the tutelage of his mother, née Sarah Snell, and her father, who was a noted deacon in the Congregationalist church. The child was reared in an atmosphere of Calvinist piety and sober devotion to literature.
  Bryant wrote his first notable poem when he was ten years old, a fifty-four-line celebration of American education composed for the commencement exercises at his school. In 1808, when the Embargo Act was creating a violent national controversy, he wrote a twelve-page poem, "The Embargo," attacking Thomas Jefferson—a piece of youthful invective that the mature Bryant, a Jeffersonian Democrat, came to regret. Bryant continued to write verses and to study under tutors, and, in 1810, he entered Williams College. By then, Bryant was already known as a poet, a reputation romantically enhanced by his tall, slender physique crowned with a shock of brown hair. He left Williams after two years, disappointed by the instruction and in the hope of attending Yale.
  Family finances, however, prohibited study at Yale, and, in 1811, Bryant went to Worthington to study law under Samuel Howe; in 1814, he moved again to Bridgewater to undertake his office training. In 1815, he was admitted to law practice. He continued to write verse, and, in 1817, five of his poems, including the first version of "Thanatopsis," appeared in the *North American Review*, to which they had been submitted by his father. Over the next few years, Bryant published more poems and essays in the *North American Review*. In 1821, firmly established in his legal practice in Great Barrington, Massachusetts, Bryant married Frances Fairchild, read "The Ages" as the Phi Beta Kappa poem at Harvard College's commencement ceremony, and published his first book of poetry. *Poems* was published through the efforts of three friends—Edward T. Channing, Richard Henry Dana, and Willard Phillips—and included such well-known works as "To a

Waterfowl," "Inscription for the Entrance to a Wood," and the final version of "Thanatopsis." This successful year marked the beginning of his adult career as a stable husband and father and as a national man of letters.

Life's Work

The ambitious Bryant was not to be confined for long to the drudgery of practicing law in a small town, and, in 1825, he moved to New York City and assumed editorship of the *New York Review*. The new journal had circulation problems right from the beginning, however, and, in 1829, Bryant abandoned efforts to give it life and became part owner and editor-in-chief of the New York *Evening Post*. This crucial change shaped the remainder of his life, for he was able to turn the *Evening Post* into both a personal and a commercial success. Under his direction and often through his own editorials, the *Evening Post* became a major organ of democratic principles in American journalism.

The political quarrels in which Bryant involved the *Evening Post* became acrimonious at times. In one contretemps with the *Commercial Advertiser*, Bryant ended up beating William Stone, one of its editors, with a cowhide whip on Broadway. Although he was suspicious of William Lloyd Garrison and the abolitionists, fearing that they would cause terrible harm to the Union, he defended eloquently the rights of antislavery writers. His outrage at the murder in Alton, Illinois, of the Reverend Elijah Lovejoy for his anti-slavery editorials produced a splendid defense of free speech:

> The right to discuss freely and openly, by speech, by the pen, by the press, all political questions, and to examine and animadvert upon all political institutions, is a right so clear and certain, so interwoven with our other liberties, so necessary, in fact to their existence, that without it we must fall at once into despotism or anarchy. To say that he who holds unpopular opinions must hold them at the peril of his life, and that, if he expresses them in public, he has only himself to blame if they who disagree with him should rise and put him to death, is to strike at all rights, all liberties, all protection of the laws, and to justify or extenuate all crimes.

Bryant expressed his humanitarianism in many ways. In 1857, he attacked the Dred Scott decision, fearing that it would make slavery a national institution. He was a fervent supporter of reform in the country's prisons and printed several editorials denouncing flogging and capital punishment. He was especially critical of the policy of imprisoning young people with veteran criminals, lamenting the corruption to which the practice led.

Bryant frequently wrote in the interest of civic reforms in New York City. He scrutinized both police and fire departments, urging that the police be given uniforms and that a paid fire department be organized. He editorialized in 1860 about the city's deplorable slum housing, demanding government regulation of tenement construction and rental. He conducted a long campaign to create a park in Manhattan, and when Central Park was planned, he fought the entrepreneurs who wanted to build apartments in the park. He was an enthusiastic friend of American dramatists and artists, lauding their efforts to produce truly American art. Aware of the lack of satisfactory copyright laws, Bryant sought the establishment of an international copyright law.

Over the years, Bryant had read such eighteenth century economists as Adam Smith, and their influence probably stood behind his swing from Federalism to Jacksonian democracy. Yet Bryant was never a completely faithful adherent of party politics and could be independent when he believed that individual liberties were being threatened. Thus, in one editorial, he attacked the practice of burning abolitionist propaganda by Southern justices of the peace. In 1839, he assailed the Democratic Administration for ruling that a group of slaves who mutinied on the *Amistad* should be returned to their owners. Bryant described the mutineers as "heroes not malefactors."

As a result of the respect he commanded for his forthrightness, Bryant achieved some influence in politics. When the Civil War broke out, Bryant urged that the slaves be quickly freed and that the war be brought to an end. He supported Abraham Lincoln, apparently influenced him in his cabinet choices, and wrote to him concerning political issues.

The man of practical affairs continued to write poetry. A devoted traveler, Bryant visited Illinois in 1832 and wrote one of his most famous poems, "The Prairies," as a result. His later volumes of verse included *The Fountain and Other Poems* (1842), *The White-Footed Deer* (1844), and *Thirty Poems* (1864). In 1870-1872, Bryant published his translations of Homer's *Iliad* (c. 800 B.C.) and *Odyssey* (c. 800 B.C.).

Bryant's poems of nature celebrate the opening up of the new nation: its topography and its flora and fauna. Famous poems such as "A Forest Hymn" and "Inscription for the Entrance to a Wood" are infused with a religious feeling that makes them confessions of personal faith. Although he did not embrace the Transcendentalism of Walt Whitman and Ralph Waldo Emerson, his poems often express a deep piety toward nature, an attitude that is essentially spiritual. Thus, in "A Forest Hymn" he sees in a "delicate forest flower,"

> An emanation of the indwelling Life,
> A visible token of the upholding Love,
> That are the soul of this great universe.

Summary

Bryant was certainly one of the giants of nineteenth century journalism. He has been praised for introducing culture to American newspapers, as well as for his important championing of free trade, civic consciousness, and the virtues of a rational liberalism. He was respected by his contemporaries as a man of high moral standards and varied literary accomplishments, and he proved to be a hardheaded businessman who made a substantial success of the New York *Evening Post*. He was tireless in his role as a public figure, and his brief final illness was precipitated by his delivery, in Central Park, of an address honoring the Italian patriot Giuseppe Mazzini.

Although his poetry was extremely popular in his own day and was praised by Edgar Allan Poe and Emerson, he has not been accorded the highest honors by posterity. Such memorable poems as "Thanatopsis" and "To a Waterfowl" are moving dramatizations of universal emotions couched in simple language, but most of his works lack the complexity and richness associated with great poetry. Scholars have judged Bryant an able student of prosody, who influenced other poets both in his theory and in his practice, and he has been praised as the first American poet to respond sensitively to the literature of Latin America.

Bryant earned an honorable place in American history for his journalistic eloquence as an advocate of democratic principles, and he has given pleasure to many readers by his lyrical power in stating a true piety and idealism in smooth verse and assuring sentiments. He will be remembered for these accomplishments.

Bibliography
Bigelow, John. *William Cullen Bryant*. Boston: Houghton Mifflin Co., 1890. Bigelow was a close friend and business partner of Bryant. His book lacks critical depth but is important for its firsthand account of Bryant's life and character.
Brown, Charles, H. *William Cullen Bryant*. New York: Charles Scribner's Sons, 1971. A well-written, comprehensive, and reliable account of Bryant's life. The study of Bryant's long career at the New York *Evening Post* is excellent. Little literary analysis.
Bryant, William Cullen, II. "Painting and Poetry: A Love Affair of Long Ago." *American Quarterly* 22 (Winter, 1970): 859-882. Traces Bryant's involvement with painters such as Thomas Cole and his help in establishing the National Academy of the Arts.
Donovan, Alan B. "William Cullen Bryant: Father of American Song." *New England Quarterly* 41 (December, 1968): 505-520. Identifies the importance of Calvinism and neoclassicism in shaping Bryant's Romantic verses. Finds in Bryant's work "the first native articulation of the art of poetry."
McLean, Albert F., Jr. *William Cullen Bryant*. New York: Twayne Publishers, 1964. A thorough and sensitive study of Bryant's poetry, divided into three main sections: "The Poems of Nature," "The Poems of Death," and "The Poems of Progress." Sees Bryant as a poet who "could never make the basic decision which Emerson was to formulate as the choice between

self-reliance and conformity."

Nevins, Allan. *The Evening Post: A Century of Journalism*. New York: Russell and Russell, 1922. Includes a long account of Bryant's accomplishments as an editor, praising his business judgment, his cultural influence, and his liberal stance on social issues.

Parrington, Vernon, L. "William Cullen Bryant: Puritan Liberal." In *Main Currents in American Thought*, vol. 2, 238-246. New York: Harcourt Brace and Co., 1930. Explicates Bryant's liberal politics and describes him as "the father of nineteenth-century journalism."

Phair, Judith Turner. *A Bibliography of William Cullen Bryant and His Critics: 1808-1972*. Troy, N.Y.: Whitston Publishing Co., 1975. An extremely useful annotated bibliography of critical commentary on Bryant.

Ringe, Donald A. "Kindred Spirits: Bryant and Cole." *American Quarterly* 6 (Fall, 1954): 233-244. Compares Bryant's aesthetics with those of the painter Thomas Cole, finding that Bryant had much in common with Cole and the other artists of the Hudson River School.

Frank Day

JAMES BUCHANAN

Born: April 23, 1791; Mercerburg, Pennsylvania
Died: June 1, 1868; Lancaster, Pennsylvania
Area of Achievement: Government
Contribution: Buchanan worked hard to preserve the Union. His presidency was devoted to trying to maintain the Democratic Party's North-South coalition.

Early Life

James Buchanan was the second child of James and Mary Buchanan, both of whom were from strong Northern Irish-Scottish Presbyterian families. The year James was born, his elder sister died, so, understandably, James received an unusual amount of attention and affection. After James, the Buchanans had nine more children: five girls followed by four boys. One of the girls and one of the boys did not live to be one year old. The arrival of so many brothers and sisters, however, did not diminish the special place James held in the Buchanan household.

James's formal education began at the Old Stone Academy in Mercerburg. In the autumn of 1807, he entered the junior class at Dickinson College. Although he was expelled once for disorderly conduct, he still managed to be graduated in 1809. James's personality was the source of most of his difficulties in college: He had a high opinion of himself and was quite obnoxious at times.

Buchanan's self-confidence was at least partially justified. He was an able student who became an extremely successful lawyer. Along with his intellectual ability, Buchanan was distinguished in appearance. He was tall with broad shoulders, had wavy blond hair, blue eyes, and fine features. He walked in a distinctive manner, with his head tilted slightly forward. His size, appearance, and mannerisms made him stand out, even in large crowds. After college, Buchanan studied law in the office of James Hopkins of Lancaster and was admitted to the Pennsylvania Bar in 1812. He quickly established a successful law practice. The two main ingredients of his success were his knowledge of the law and his talent for oral presentation.

Life's Work

The political career of James Buchanan began with his election to the Pennsylvania House of Representatives in 1813. As a Federalist, he opposed the war with England, but once war was declared, he became a volunteer in a company of dragoons. In 1815, he was reelected. During this period, he spent considerable time and energy trying to delay the return of specie payment to protect the United States Bank.

Buchanan emerged on the national political scene in 1820, as a member of the United States House of Representatives. In 1824, with the demise of the Federalist Party, he found himself increasingly at odds with President John Quincy Adams. By 1826, Buchanan was working on a new Amalgamation Party in Pennsylvania, a mixture of Federalist Congressmen and old-line Democrats. What held the group together was its desire for a new political party and its support of Andrew Jackson. The main result of the creation of this new, vaguely defined party was that Buchanan became the primary dispenser of patronage in Pennsylvania.

After ten successful years in the House of Representatives, Buchanan was offered and accepted the ministry to Russia. Before taking this post, he had been giving serious thought to leaving public life and returning to private law practice.

Buchanan stayed in St. Petersburg (now Leningrad) until August of 1833, returning home to run for the United States Senate. By that time, Buchanan was clearly identified with the Democratic Party, and he realized that this meant supporting President Jackson, which included following Vice President Martin Van Buren's lead in the Senate.

Buchanan was quickly recognized as a loyal and principled partisan. Although the United States Bank was located in his home state, Buchanan remained true to the Jackson Administration's commitment to getting the federal government out of the banking business. Everyone knew that destroying the bank would move the United States' financial center from Philadelphia to New York; still, Buchanan believed that the interests of the nation should come before the interests of his home state. Buchanan's ability to place the nation's interests above those of his state or region were motivated, at least in part, by his political ambitions. In 1838, many of his friends encouraged him to run for the office of governor of Pennsylvania; he chose instead to remain in the Senate and focus his attention on national issues.

President James K. Polk appointed Buchanan to serve as his secretary of state in 1844. Buchanan shared Polk's desire to expand the territory of the United States, but negotiating treaties for the rigid Polk was difficult at times. Buchanan's skills at settling disputes and striking compromises were perfected during his tour of duty at the State Department.

Buchanan's friends were surprised to learn that he was considering retirement as the 1848 presidential race approached. Whether it was the bitter division in the Democratic Party or the heightened concern over sectional rivalry, Buchanan sensed that 1848 would not be a good year for the Democratic Party. His instincts were correct. Buchanan's retirement from the State Department left him time to take care of some private affairs. He purchased his country estate, Wheatland, and began the groundwork for the 1852 presidential race. Buchanan's four years of retirement were some of the happiest he had known: He pursued the life of a gentleman farmer and spent time with the niece and nephew he was rearing. Unfortunately, his presidential ambitions were not well served by his temporary retirement.

The 1852 Democratic Convention was greatly divided. After some political maneuvering, much heated debate, and many caucuses, Franklin Pierce received the party's nomination. Pierce defeated Winfield Scott in the general election and then persuaded Buchanan to end his political retirement and serve as minister to Great Britain. Though Buchanan accepted this assignment reluctantly, it proved to be a good decision for him politically.

The Kansas-Nebraska Act was passed in 1854, repealing the Missouri Compromise and leaving both the nation and the Democratic Party bitterly divided. Buchanan's chief rivals for the 1856 Democratic presidential nomination were damaged by the sectional strife. When Buchanan returned home from London, many believed that he was the only candidate who could mend the Democratic Party's wounds and save the Union.

The 1856 party nomination did not come easily. Only after Stephen A. Douglas withdrew from the race was Buchanan able to acquire the sixty percent of the vote needed for the nomination. Fortunately for Buchanan, it was a transitional year for those who opposed the Democratic Party. Buchanan did not get a majority of the popular votes but was able to secure enough electoral college votes to win the presidency.

Buchanan's long journey to the White House was over. His quest for the presidency had been difficult, and so were his years in the White House. Buchanan's administration was haunted by the question of slavery in the United States territories. He hoped that the Supreme Court's Dred Scott decision would settle the issue once and for all, but his hopes were in vain. In many respects the Court's decision complicated the issue. Stephen Douglas found the Court's ruling to be a thorn in his side throughout the Lincoln-Douglas debates of 1858. The battle raging within the Democratic Party was over the same issue. Douglas believed that "popular sovereignty" was the solution to the slavery controversy. Buchanan, like Abraham Lincoln, did not accept Douglas' solution. Unlike Lincoln, Buchanan believed that the Dred Scott decision denied the federal government authority over the institution of slavery in the territories and that only states had the authority to prohibit slavery within their boundaries. The end result was that Buchanan, the great compromiser and diplomat, could not settle the controversy.

Buchanan believed that the Democratic Party had held the Union together for the past decade; as president, he believed that it was his job to unite the party before 1860. Yet Buchanan was unable to unify his party, and the Democrats lost the 1860 presidential campaign; then, as he expected, the Union came to face its greatest threat ever: civil war.

Summary

Buchanan realized that the nation's strength was its ability to strike a compromise among conflicting interests. The Constitutional Convention of 1787 succeeded because it was able to forge a consensus among the different groups represented at the Convention. The Democratic Party's success had been built upon its ability to rise above sectional disputes and focus on national issues. The United States, according to Buchanan, was a compromise republic that had succeeded in bending when necessary so that it would not break. Buchanan's unswerving commitment to the Union kept him from seeing that many Americans were tired of compromises. The old North-South coalition had been pushed to the breaking point, and the westward expansion had given the North a decided advantage. Those in the North knew this; those in the South knew this; but Buchanan seemed not to know.

What are often interpreted as Buchanan's Southern sympathies were really little more than his sense of fair play coupled with his sincere desire to preserve the Union. One of the nation's great compromisers had the misfortune of being president at a time when compromise was no longer possible. Unfortunately, James Buchanan is remembered not for his thirty-eight successful years in politics but for his four unsuccessful years. Buchanan, like most other politicians in the United States, is remembered for what he did last.

Bibliography

Auchampaugh, Philip G. *James Buchanan and His Cabinet: On the Eve of Secession*. Lancaster, Pa.: Author, 1926. As the title indicates, this work deals with the Buchanan Administration. Special emphasis is placed on Buchanan's handling of the slavery issue.

Curtis, George Ticknor. *The Life of James Buchanan*. 2 vols. New York: Harper and Brothers, 1883. By far the most comprehensive work on the life of James Buchanan.

Jaffa, Harry. *Crisis of the House Divided*. New York: Doubleday and Co., 1959. The best work on the theoretical issues involved in the Lincoln-Douglas Debates of 1858. Provides a good perspective for the issues that dominated American politics at that time.

Klein, Philip. *President James Buchanan: A Biography*. University Park: Pennsylvania State University Press, 1962. A comprehensive study that covers some secondary literature that was not available to Curtis.

Moore, John Bassett, ed. *The Works of James Buchanan*. 12 vols. Philadelphia: J. B. Lippincott Co., 1908. A complete collection of Buchanan's public addresses and selected private papers. Includes a fine biographical essay by Moore.

Nichols, Roy F. *The Disruption of American Democracy*. New York: Macmillan, 1948. A careful examination of the Democratic Party from 1856 to 1861. Deals extensively with the differences between Douglas and Buchanan.

Smith, Elbert B. *The Presidency of James Buchanan*. Lawrence: University Press of Kansas, 1975. This work argues that Buchanan's actions were motivated by strong Southern sympathies.

Donald V. Weatherman

CHARLES BULFINCH

Born: August 8, 1763; Boston, Massachusetts
Died: April 4, 1844; Boston, Massachusetts
Areas of Achievement: Architecture and government
Contribution: One of the first American architects to have used drawings extensively for the construction of buildings, Bulfinch exercised a wide influence on the architecture of the early national period of American history, especially in his native New England.

Early Life

The son of Thomas and Susan Apthorp Bulfinch, well-to-do and socially prominent Bostonians, Charles Bulfinch was born at the family home on Bowdoin Street on August 8, 1763. One of the first American architects to complete a college education, he was graduated from Harvard in 1781, though not in architecture. Bulfinch's interest in architecture appears to have been awakened in 1785-1787, during a leisurely tour of England and the Continent. In Paris, where Bulfinch lingered for a time, Thomas Jefferson, the American ambassador to the French court, took a friendly interest in the young man. It was at Jefferson's suggestion that Bulfinch continued his travels through southern France and Italy. After spending three weeks in Rome studying the city's ancient monuments, Bulfinch revisited Paris and London on his homeward journey. Upon his return to Boston, he took a position in the accounting office of a local merchant. In his spare time, he studied architectural works and, as did other gentleman-architects of the day, dabbled in design and construction.

Soon after his return from Europe, Bulfinch pointed toward his future dedication to architecture as a profession by submitting plans for a new Massachusetts statehouse, a project which eluded him until 1795, when he was chosen to design the building. Though he designed other important buildings during these early years, he continued to be only casually involved with architecture until he went bankrupt in 1796. On November 20, 1788, he married his cousin Hannah Apthorp, by whom he would have eleven children, including the author Thomas Bulfinch. In the spring of 1789, he visited Philadelphia and New York; his observations on this tour proved to be as influential in forming his style as those he had made while abroad.

Like most other early American architects, Bulfinch was self-taught. Nevertheless, he did not wish to design buildings simply by adapting various elements of architecture chosen from books. As did later architects, he tried to understand buildings, their materials and functions, and the methods by which they were built. He was concerned about how buildings related to their surroundings, about the connections between buildings and streets, walks, parks, other structures in the vicinity, and the city as a whole.

It has been said that between about 1790 and 1825, Bulfinch practically rebuilt Boston, transforming it from a provincial town with few buildings and meandering streets into a tasteful city of well-designed buildings set amid trees, plantings, and parks. One reason for his success was the excellence of his buildings. Another was his involvement in the affairs of Boston through his civic work. He would come to understand thoroughly the city and its needs by serving as a member, and chairman, of the board of selectmen.

Life's Work

Though his later buildings are of the classical revival style, which came to be preferred by such architects as Benjamin Latrobe and Jefferson, Bulfinch's early work was Georgian in character, by way of the brothers Adam (Robert, John, James, and William) in England. In 1788, the Hollis Street Church in Boston was constructed from his plans. Representing Bulfinch's initial attempt at church design, it was followed by plans for churches in Taunton and Pittsfield, Massachusetts, and during a later period, others in Boston. His classical interests were exhibited in his triumphal arch, built in 1789 in Boston for George Washington's reception, and in his Beacon Hill Memorial Column, of Doric order, constructed in 1790-1791. More ambitious in scale than anything previously attempted in New England, the statehouse in Hartford, Connecticut, was begun from Bulfinch's plans in 1793. The same year, he provided the plans for the Boston Theatre. Erected at the corner of Franklin and Federal streets, it burned in 1798 and was rebuilt by Bulfinch in the same year.

Bulfinch was elected to Boston's board of selectmen in 1791; he would serve on the board, with only one break, for twenty-six years. He was active on the board committees which lighted Boston's streets for the first time in 1792 and admitted both male and female children to the city's public schools. For the last eighteen of these years, he chaired the board, a position similar to that of a mayor.

During the early 1790's, Bulfinch began a reformation of New England's architecture as he introduced the delicate detail of the Adam style. Many of his designs were built on or around Beacon Hill in Boston. It has been argued that their impact on the city was even stronger than that of his churches and public buildings because the houses and their settings established an atmosphere of beauty and charm long preserved in the Beacon Hill area. His first houses were for Joseph Coolidge, Sr. (1791-1792), and Joseph Barrell (1792-1793), both of which contained the first circular staircases in New England. The Barrell house in Somerville, Massachusetts, had an oval parlor projecting from the garden side beneath a semicircular portico with tall columns. Its layout was soon used in the Elias Hasket Derby mansion (1795-1799) in Salem, which was designed by Bulfinch, then modified and executed by Samuel McIntire.

Bulfinch joined with others in the mid-1790's in planning a block of sixteen houses in Boston known as the Tontine Crescent. Work on this project was partially completed when trouble with England brought unsettled business conditions to Boston. During the ensuing financial crisis, Bulfinch's partners withdrew, leaving him to assume the cost of completing the work. Losing both his own fortune and that of his wife, he was adjudged bankrupt in January of 1796. About the time of his bankruptcy, he resigned from the board of selectmen. Previously regarded as a scholar and gentleman of fortune but an amateur in architecture, Bulfinch was now faced with earning a livelihood. He turned his talent and full attention to the practice of architecture, with most successful results. In 1796, Bulfinch designed a house for the prominent and powerful Boston politician Harrison Gray Otis. He followed it with two others for Otis: the second in 1800, usually considered the finest of the three, and the third in 1805.

The Massachusetts statehouse (1795-1797) on Boston's Beacon Hill represents the crowning achievement of Bulfinch's early work. Though by the twentieth century it became only a part of a much larger complex—having been added on to a number of times—it has survived in good condition. A simple rectangular structure in plan and exterior, it is two stories high with a basement and a portico in front. The whole is crowned by a dome made of wooden planks, matched to fit tightly against one another. With its elegant proportions, the relationship of the dome to other elements, and its richly ornamented and spacious interiors, Bulfinch's Massachusetts statehouse was immediately hailed as a masterpiece.

In 1799, Bulfinch was returned to the Boston board of selectmen, serving as its chairman until his departure for Washington in 1817. He soon found himself deeply involved in all the financial, commercial, and governmental affairs of the city. The time of his chairmanship marked the years of the great development of old Boston. Its form would be attributable largely to Bulfinch in his dual capacity as city official and architect. During this period, his architecture and civic work complemented each other. In addition to designing theaters, hospitals, churches, schools, government buildings, markets, prisons, wharves, warehouses, multifamily houses, and numerous single-family dwellings, he planned several portions of Boston. The neglected Common was turned into a park; three sides were fronted with fine buildings of uniform character: Park Street, in 1803-1804; Colonade Row on Tremont Street, in 1810-1812; and Beacon Street, from about 1800. Bulfinch laid out plans for the lands on Boston Neck, in South Boston, and on the site of the Mill Pond. He also inaugurated the development of Franklin Street and certain changes in the city's street system.

Of Bulfinch's five churches in Boston, four were built after 1800. It is said that he followed the schemes of Christopher Wren's churches in London, paying great attention to the varieties of the type. Bulfinch designed the first

Roman Catholic church in Boston, the Church (later Cathedral) of the Holy Cross (1800-1803) at the corner of Franklin and Federal streets. Contemporary sources describe it as in the Italian Renaissance style. Completed in 1804, the New North Church (later St. Stephen's Catholic Church) is the only surviving example of Bulfinch's Boston churches. It has been much modified and is not considered one of his best designs. The Federal Street Church of 1809 represents Bulfinch's first and only Gothic work. The New South Church was completed in 1814. Generally considered Bulfinch's most beautiful church, it was the first stone church erected in Boston since Bulfinch's grandfather, Charles Apthorp, got Peter Harrison to design King's Chapel. The distinctive features of the New South Church were an octagonal ground plan and a Doric portico of freestanding columns. One of the two surviving Bulfinch churches is the Church of Christ in Lancaster, Massachusetts, which was built in 1816. Its most prominent feature, the triple coeval arches in the portico, is an unexplained "improvement" by the master builder sent out from Boston to supervise the work.

Bulfinch's public buildings in Boston completed after 1800 include the almshouse (1799-1801); the admirable warehouses of India Wharf (1803-1807); the Boylston Hall and Market (1809), later occupied as the city's first public library; the Suffolk County Court House (1810-1812); and the first and central unit of the Massachusetts General Hospital (1818-1823). Among the public buildings built outside Boston from Bulfinch's plans, the best known are the state prison at Charlestown, Massachusetts (1804-1805), University Hall at Harvard (1813-1814), and the statehouse in Augusta, Maine (1829-1832). The private houses Bulfinch designed after 1800 were built mainly in Boston, typical examples being those at 85 Mount Vernon Street, 45 Beacon Street, and numbers 13, 15, and 17 on Chestnut Street.

In 1817, President James Monroe appointed Bulfinch to succeed Latrobe as architect in charge of rebuilding the United States Capitol, which had been burned by the British in 1814. Moving his family to Washington, Bulfinch remained in this position until 1830. Essentially, he was called upon to complete the wings and construct the central part along lines established by the Capitol's earlier architects. Bulfinch joined the two wings with a central dome. His principal contribution was the detailed form of the western front, a portico with steps and terrace forming an approach to it. Though his dome was later replaced by a larger and grander one, the west front remains. In addition to completing the Capitol, Bulfinch designed a church in Washington and acted as a consultant for several other government buildings. Returning to Boston at the age of sixty-seven, he lived in retirement, with occasional visits elsewhere, until his death in 1844.

Summary
During and before Bulfinch's day, American architects generally fell into

one of two groups: amateur gentleman-architects who pursued some other career while designing buildings as an avocation, or architect-builders who were more concerned with construction than design. Though he began as one of the former, Bulfinch soon became totally involved with architecture. Unlike the architect-builders who actually worked on their buildings, Bulfinch saw his role—much in the same vein as later professionals—as that of supervising construction to ensure the proper implementation of designs and quality of workmanship.

Bulfinch's American practice of architecture combined his New England background with his European tastes. Appropriately, the site of his remains in Cambridge's Mount Auburn Cemetery is marked by the Franklin Urn, which Bulfinch placed in front of the Tontine Crescent in 1795 as a symbol of his plans to remake Boston in the image of neoclassical London. Early in his career, Bulfinch's city honored him for his architecture and his civic work, showing an appreciation which continued to grow. Over the years, his architecture came to belong not only to Boston and New England but also to the country as a whole.

Bibliography
Brown, Glenn. *History of the United States Capitol*. 2 vols. Washington, D.C.: Government Printing Office, 1901-1904. Relates the story of Bulfinch's long and sometimes frustrating assignment in Washington.
Bulfinch, Ellen Susan. *The Life and Letters of Charles Bulfinch*. Boston: Houghton Mifflin Co., 1896. The major source for biographical information. Bulfinch's granddaughter provides a good treatment of the forces which shaped his ultimate professional commitment.
Kimball, Fiske. *Mr. Samuel McIntire, Carver: The Architect of Salem*. Salem, Mass.: Essex Institute, 1940. Details Bulfinch's work for the Derby family of Salem.
Kirker, Harold. *The Architecture of Charles Bulfinch*. Cambridge, Mass.: Harvard University Press, 1969. Concentrates on the works themselves. Bulfinch's commissions are arranged chronologically; each is treated separately. One of the appendices deals with "minor commissions and attributions." Well illustrated.
Kirker, Harold, and James Kirker. *Bulfinch's Boston, 1787-1817*. New York: Oxford University Press, 1964. Deals largely with the social and cultural history of Boston during the period. Bulfinch's architectural work is subordinated to his public career.
Morison, Samuel Eliot. *The Maritime History of Massachusetts, 1783-1860*. Boston: Houghton Mifflin Co., 1921. Provides a good summary treatment of Bulfinch's architecture as well as a picture of the Boston merchants who were his chief clients.
Place, Charles A. *Charles Bulfinch: Architect and Citizen*. Boston: Hough-

ton Mifflin Co., 1925. A biographical treatment which focuses on Bulfinch as a citizen and Christian gentleman.

L. Moody Simms, Jr.

RALPH BUNCHE

Born: August 7, 1904; Detroit, Michigan
Died: December 9, 1971; New York, New York
Areas of Achievement: Education and diplomacy
Contribution: Bunche played a major role in making Americans conscious of the contradictions between their racial policies and their democratic aspirations. He helped bring better understanding between nations, participating in the drafting of the United Nations Charter, and through diplomatic negotiations helped to maintain peace in the Middle East and Africa, winning the Nobel Peace Prize for his efforts.

Early Life

Ralph Johnson Bunche was born in Detroit, Michigan, on August 7, 1904. His father, Fred Bunche, was a barber. His mother, Olive Agnes Johnson Bunche, named him for his grandfather, Ralph Johnson, who was born a slave. The family moved frequently during Ralph's early life, and he remembered that in each community a different ethnic group was singled out for contempt: the Italians in Detroit; the blacks in Knoxville, Tennessee, where he spent a winter when he was six; the Mexicans in New Mexico, where the family moved because of his mother's poor health; and the Chinese and the Japanese in California, where he and his younger sister, Grace, lived with their grandmother after their mother's death. These early memories of the different faces of prejudice clearly influenced his later interests and outlook on life.

In the fall of 1916, Bunche's father left home, never to be heard from again. The following February, his mother, who suffered from rheumatic fever, died. His maternal grandmother, Lucy Johnson, kept the family together, but within a few months, his favorite uncle, who suffered from tuberculosis, committed suicide. In less than a year, Bunche had lost three of the most significant adults in his life. His grandmother, widowed early in life, had reared her children alone and now became his anchor. A light-skinned woman who could have passed for white, she was a dominant influence in her family. Her husband, Ralph's grandfather, had been a schoolteacher, and education was a value she continued to uphold for her grandchildren.

Even as a child, Bunche was accustomed to hard work. By the age of seven he was selling newspapers, and before his mother died he worked in a bakery after school until nearly midnight every day. In Los Angeles, where he went to live with his grandmother, he was graduated as valedictorian from Jefferson High School. He attended the University of California at Los Angeles (UCLA) on an athletic scholarship, where he was also a teaching assistant in the political science department, and was graduated magna cum laude in 1927. He received an M.A. degree from Harvard in 1928 and in June, 1930, married Ruth Ethel Harris, one of his students, with whom he had three children: two daughters, Jean and Jane, and a son, Ralph.

A handsome man of medium height and build, Bunche was destined to attract favorable attention for his accomplishments and pleasing personality. On a Rosenwald field fellowship, he toured Europe, England, and North and West Africa in 1931-1932 and in 1934 received a Ph.D. from Harvard, winning the Tappen Prize for the best doctoral dissertation in the social sciences for that year. His dissertation was a study of colonial administration in French West Africa; the transition of the former African colonies to independent statehood was one of his abiding concerns through the remainder of his life. His Harvard years were followed by postdoctoral work in anthropology and colonial policy at Northwestern University, the London School of Economics, and the University of Capetown, South Africa, in 1936-1937. A Social Science Research Council postdoctoral fellowship allowed him to visit Europe, South and East Africa, Malaya, and the Netherlands East Indies between 1936 and 1938.

During these years, Bunche was also teaching. He began teaching political science at Howard University in 1928 and served as chairman of the department from 1929 to 1950, when he left Howard to teach government at Harvard. He codirected the Institute of Race Relations at Swarthmore in 1936 while on leave from Howard. By his early thirties, his brilliance, hard work, and breadth of interests made him one of the most highly educated, well-informed men in the United States.

Life's Work

In 1939, Bunche became a member of the staff of the Carnegie Corporation Survey of the Negro in America. This project was headed by a Swedish economist, Gunnar Myrdal, and resulted in a two-volume work, *An American Dilemma: The Negro Problem and Modern Democracy* (1944). Bunche was one of a half dozen staff men who helped Myrdal with this massive project, based primarily on hundreds of interviews and personal observations of the participating scholars. He toured the South by automobile in 1939 with Myrdal, and most of the interviews were conducted by his assistants in 1939 and 1940.

Bunche's part of the study dealt mainly with black organizational life, leadership, and ideology. He emphasized the extent to which disfranchisement of black voters had corrupted politics in the South, cutting off reform possibilities at the grass roots. He castigated the use of the poll tax and the white primary and pointed out the lack of secrecy in voting, which made political independence unlikely for poor people of either race in the South. Bunche emphasized the glaring inconsistencies between democracy and discrimination, stating,

If democracy is to survive the severe trials and buffetings to which it is being subjected in the modern world, it will do so only because it can demonstrate that it is a practical, living philosophy under which all people can live the good life most abundantly. It must prove itself in practice or be discredited as a theory.

His work on race relations in the United States was followed by work for the United States government, in which he dealt with race relations on a global scale. In 1941, he was asked to work as a senior social science analyst on Africa and the Far East areas of the British Empire section of the Office of Strategic Services. He became chief of the African section in 1943 and then became a territorial specialist in the Division of Territorial Studies of the United States State Department in 1944-1945. In 1945, he was the first black division head in the State Department. He also helped draft the United Nations Charter.

Bunche was made director of the Division of Trusteeship of the United Nations from 1946 to 1948, then principal director of the Department of Trusteeship from 1948 to 1954. In 1947, he became special assistant to representatives of the secretary general of the United Nations Special Committee on Palestine. Tensions were very high in Jerusalem as the question of the partition of Palestine was being considered. The Arab high command forbade Arabs to testify before the special United Nations commission, so Bunche and others met with them secretly in Syria and Lebanon. After meeting separately with both sides, Bunche composed both the majority and minority reports to the satisfaction of both parties. His ability to grasp the problems involved and his empathy for the opposing factions made him a unique diplomat, trusted and acceptable to both Jews and Arabs.

When the Arabs declared war in Israel in 1948, Bunche was sent as the chief representative of the secretary general of the United Nations to help mediate the dispute, along with Count Folke Bernadotte, the head of the Swedish Red Cross. Bernadotte was shot and killed just before the two were to leave the Middle East to meet in Paris, and Bunche became the acting mediator through 1948 and 1949, finally achieving a peaceful settlement. In 1950, he received the Nobel Peace Prize for his peacemaking success in the Middle East. In 1957 he again successfully negotiated a peaceful settlement between Egypt and Israel.

In 1960, Bunche was a special representative of the secretary general of the United Nations in peacemaking efforts in the Congo. Dag Hammarskjöld had planned to take Bunche back to the Congo with him on the last trip he made, which ended in a fatal plane crash, but had decided against it at the last minute. The new secretary general of the United Nations, U Thant, appointed Bunche deputy secretary general, making him the highest-ranking American to serve under three secretary generals of the United Nations. He resolved the dispute between Prime Minister Cyrille Adoula of the Congo Republic and President Moise-Kapenda Tshombe of the Katanga province. He was sent to Yemen in 1963 to help contain another civil war. In 1964, he was sent to Cyprus to mediate Greek-Turkish hostilities, and, partially as a result of his efforts, peace was preserved there for another ten years until a Turkish invasion in 1974.

In 1965, Bunche turned his attention once again to racial problems at home. In the 1930's and 1940's, he had been much involved in efforts to improve the racial situation in the United States. He served on the national executive board of the National Association for the Advancement of Colored People (NAACP), helped organize a National Committee Against Discrimination in Housing, helped organize the National Negro Congress in 1935, and served as a member of President Franklin D. Roosevelt's "Black Cabinet" of advisers. When he joined the Security Council of the United Nations, he had taken an oath, as an international civil servant, to refrain from activity in domestic problems. Nevertheless, he joined the march led by Martin Luther King in Selma, Alabama, in 1965 and addressed the crowd of thirty-five thousand Americans gathered there, remarking that his wife's father had made civil rights speeches in that same city at the turn of the century and apologizing to the crowd for having to speak from the capitol steps, where Dixie's flag still waved.

By that time, his health was beginning to fail. In 1951, he discovered that he suffered from diabetes. When he returned home from Selma, he had hepatitis, but he continued to work until he developed heart failure in 1970. He recovered from a heart attack and pneumonia, only to suffer a fall at home and die the following year on December 9, 1971. He was buried in Woodlawn Cemetery, Bronx, New York, next to his daughter Jane, who had preceded him in death.

During his lifetime, he received thirty-nine honorary degrees, the Nobel Peace Prize in 1950, the Presidential Medal of Freedom in 1963, and other honors too numerous to mention. He remained a modest man, finding more pleasure in work than in fame and firm in his commitment to build a more truly democratic society.

Summary

Ralph Bunche presents both a model and a challenge to all Americans. Facing poverty, discrimination, and a family broken through death in his early life, he became one of the most highly educated men in the United States. He used that education to serve his people and his nation, to sound the alarm about the state of democracy in America, forcing others to deal with the contradiction between racial discrimination and democracy. He demonstrated the potential for peace in the world when intelligence and perseverance are applied to achieve it. Through his work with the United

Nations, he helped to contain several disputes, any one of which could have escalated into a third world war.

Bibliography

Bunche, Ralph J. *The Political Status of the Negro in the Age of FDR*. Edited by Dewey W. Grantham. Chicago: University of Chicago Press, 1973. Consists of the notes Bunche made for the Carnegie-Myrdal report. Gives a good sketch of Bunche's life and career.

Cornell, Jean Gay. *Ralph Bunche: Champion of Peace*. Champaign, Ill.: Garrard Publishing Co., 1976. One of a series, Americans All Biographies, written especially for young people. Balanced but brief.

Franklin, John Hope. *From Slavery to Freedom: A History of American Negroes*. 3d ed. New York: Alfred A. Knopf, 1967. An overview of American black history with scattered references to Bunche, placing him in the context of major events.

Franklin, John Hope, and August Meier, eds. *Black Leaders of the Twentieth Century*. Urbana: University of Illinois Press, 1982. Contains a brief sketch of Bunche.

Haskins, James. *Ralph Bunche: A Most Reluctant Hero*. New York: Hawthorn Books, 1974. Small, compact biography written by a young freelance black scholar. Includes information on Los Angeles black community support for Bunche in his youth.

Johnson, Ann Donegan. *The Value of Responsibility: The Story of Ralph Bunche*. San Diego, Calif.: Value Communications, 1978. A good biography for young children. Emphasis is on character building.

Kugelmass, Joseph Alvin. *Ralph J. Bunche: Fighter for Peace*. New York: Julian Messner, 1952. The first biography of Bunche, written for older children and teenagers. Well-balanced coverage of his life.

Mann, Peggy. *Ralph Bunche: UN Peacemaker*. New York: Coward, McCann and Geoghegan, 1975. Best, most accurate biography available. The Bunche family, Roy Wilkins, and United Nations coworkers assisted the author. Major emphasis is on Bunche's work at the United Nations.

Betty Balanoff

LUTHER BURBANK

Born: March 7, 1849; Lancaster, Massachusetts
Died: April 11, 1926; Santa Rosa, California
Area of Achievement: Horticulture
Contribution: As a plant breeder, Burbank introduced more than eight hundred new plants and gave the world a lesson in the value of horticultural science: Make plants work for the benefit of man.

Early Life

Luther Burbank was the thirteenth child of Samuel Walton Burbank, a farmer and brickmaker and a descendant of seventeenth century English stock. Luther's mother, Olive Ross, a strong-featured and strong-willed woman of Scottish and French descent, was Samuel's third wife. Luther Burbank was born on March 7, 1849, in Lancaster, Massachusetts, thirty miles from Boston.

Burbank was a shy youngster seldom disciplined by his parents. His siblings included a brother and sister as well as three half-brothers and two half-sisters. He received an elementary school education near his home but was never comfortable with oral recitation. At the age of fifteen, he entered Lancaster Academy, a preparatory school for Harvard and Yale, and studied the basic curriculum of Latin, Greek, French, geometry, algebra, arithmetic, philosophy, drawing, and English. Burbank was apparently a good student, ranking eighth out of the top ten students in his class in 1867. He was an avid reader, as is evidenced by his early familiarity with the works of Charles Darwin, Alexander von Humboldt, and Henry David Thoreau. The writings of these naturalists were to have a lasting impact on young Burbank, but the most important influence in developing his scientific curiosity was his cousin Levi Sumner Burbank, the curator of geology at the Boston Society of Natural History.

As a young man, Burbank was five feet, eight inches tall, about 125 pounds, with sparkling blue eyes. After his school experience, he attempted two nonacademic careers. The first was a job in the Worcester branch factory of the Ames Plow Works. Burbank had gone to the factory for three or four summers to learn the trade of a mechanic. After high school, he worked at the Ames Plow Works turning plow rounds on a lathe at a wage of three dollars a week. He soon designed an improvement in his machine that increased productivity, and his piecework wages rose significantly. He was not able to keep this job very long, however, since his health suffered because of the sawdust in the air.

Burbank next studied medicine under a local doctor for several months. He gave this up when his father died, in 1868. Burbank was not interested in farming at this time, although as a young boy he had shown some interest in gardening. (To the dismay of his father, Burbank transplanted weeds into the family garden plot to see if they would grow.)

In 1870, the young Burbank, always afflicted with a frail constitution, decided to take a sea voyage to improve his health. The schooner was wrecked, and he almost lost his life.

Life's Work

In 1871, Burbank made a decision that would change his life dramatically: He resolved to try his hand at truck-gardening. At the age of twenty-one, he bought seventeen acres of land adjoining his mother's home in Lunenburg, Massachusetts. He pursued this profession for about five years, but he was more interested in experimenting with plants than in growing them for market. In 1872, Luther found a seed ball on the plant of a potato containing twenty-three seeds, a rare occurrence. He planted the seeds and discovered one good potato (later named the "Burbank") of attractive shape with a white skin. The tuber was destined later to become a huge commercial success. Burbank sold sixty bushels of the potatoes to James J. H. Gregory, a seedsman of Marblehead, Massachusetts, for $150. With this money, Burbank left for California in October, 1875, as the climate there was better suited for the horticultural work that he had decided to pursue. (His mother packed him a nine-day box lunch for the long train trip.) He arrived in San Francisco on October 29, 1875. Burbank was shocked at the amount of liquor consumed in the city and he vowed never to drink it. On October 31, 1875, Burbank reached Santa Rosa, a frontier town blessed with a temperate climate. The plants he saw there grew larger than any he had ever seen, since the area had no frost.

Burbank lived for a short time with his brother Alfred and another bachelor in an eight-foot by ten-foot cabin. To earn money, Burbank did carpentry work and odd jobs in the area. In the winter of 1876, Burbank went to work in Petaluma, California, at the large nursery of W. H. Pepper. He saved his money and soon returned to Santa Rosa.

In the summer of 1877, Burbank's mother and sister Emma came to Santa Rosa and bought a house with four acres of adjacent land. Burbank rented the land and started his own nursery. Within ten years, the quality of his fruit and shade trees was famous, and he was making sixteen thousand dollars annually with his plants. His skill in plant-breeding was to assure his commercial success. In the spring of 1881, he received an order for twenty thousand prune trees for delivery in the fall. According to other nurserymen, it would take eighteen months to fill such a large order, but Burbank used the technique of "force budding" to deliver the trees on schedule.

Burbank was interested in cross-breeding domestic plant stock with foreign material, so in 1885, he imported plum seedlings from Yokohama, Japan. One of these seedlings became the famous "Burbank plum" that is still popular today. That same year, Luther bought eighteen acres at Sebastopol near Santa Rosa to use for experimental growing. By 1888, he was committed to the development of new varieties of plants, so he sold part of his retail nursery business (the fruit and shade tree segment) to his partner, R. W. Bell. Burbank could now concentrate on the creation of new or unusual plant materials to sell at wholesale to other nurserymen.

On September 23, 1890, the forty-one-year-old horticulturist married a domineering young widow, Helen A. Coleman, from Denver, Colorado. Almost immediately, conflicts developed between Helen and Burbank's mother and sister. The marriage, which lasted six years, caused Burbank much mental and physical aggravation, partly because of Helen's violent temper.

By 1893, Burbank had developed enough different varieties of walnuts, berries, plums, prunes, roses, lilies, potatoes, and quinces to list them in his nursery catalog, *New Creations in Fruits and Flowers* (1893). Stark Brothers' Nurseries of Missouri and several large Eastern retail nurseries made significant purchases from this catalog, thereby assuring Burbank's future financial success. As the years passed, Burbank attracted a large clientele of professional nurserymen both in the United States and abroad. By 1900, Burbank's products were being grown throughout the world, and his reputation as the "wizard of horticulture" was well established. There was no magical formula, however, to the Burbank success story, only hard work, perseverance, and a keen intuition as to what plants would prove a commercial success. At this time, Burbank developed the Shasta daisy, a perennial favorite of home gardeners. His breeding method consisted of choosing American wild daisies as breeding stock, introducing pollen from European daisies, and crossing the resultant hybrids with a Japanese species. Any plant in any part of the world was fair game in Burbank's search for marketable products.

Burbank was to come increasingly under the criticism of other horticulturists, particularly those attached to university experiment stations. (Burbank did not have the formal college education in the plant sciences that some university-trained experts thought necessary, although he did receive an honorary doctor of science degree from Tufts College in 1905.) It was true that he did not keep proper records of his experimental crossings or always guard against self-pollination in his work, but he was more interested in the results of experimentation, not the theory. He gave the impression at times of being a consummate egotist; he was the most famous plant breeder in America, and none too modest about this reputation. He allowed others to exaggerate the merits of his products, and because of the sheer volume of the materials he was turning out, he did not take as much time to prove the reliability of those creations as he had been able to earlier in his career.

The Carnegie Institute became interested in Burbank's techniques and plants and, between 1905 and 1909, awarded him a grant of ten thousand dollars annually with the stipulation that a representative from the Institute would observe Burbank's methods and write a report on them. (The report on the observations was never compiled by the Institute, in part because of the difficulty of interpreting Burbank's experimental notes.)

Burbank had been working on the development of a spineless cactus for use as cattle food, and in 1906, he introduced this cactus to the nursery trade. It proved to be a disappointment since it was not completely spineless, and the resultant unfavorable publicity damaged Burbank's reputation. Other products that did not live up to the claims of his catalog included the "Winter rhubarb" and a hybrid berry which Burbank called the "Sunberry." These failures called into question his credibility, particularly among those horticulturists and breeders who may have felt resentful of his fame.

In 1912, the Luther Burbank Society and the Luther Burbank Press were formed for the purpose of promoting and selling a multivolume work on the man and his accomplishments, *Luther Burbank: His Methods and Discoveries and Their Practical Applications* (1915). Unfortunately, the promotional tactics and "hype" associated with marketing the twelve-volume set cast a further shadow upon his reputation, although the color photographs and illustrations in them were quite unusual for that time.

That same year, 1912, saw the organization of the Luther Burbank Company, another vehicle used by exploiters, with Burbank's unwitting consent, to promote his name in association with the marketing of his horticultural creations. Rollo J. Hough and W. Garner Smith received the exclusive rights to sell Burbank's products. These financiers, however, knew very little about the nursery business. Soon quality control grew lax, and Burbank's reputation suffered accordingly. By 1916, the Luther Burbank Press went out of business, and many investors lost their money in the enterprise. That same year the Luther Burbank Company declared bankruptcy and Burbank resumed control of his nursery and seed business. These failures suggest that Burbank was not a very good businessman in his later years, but in spite of these failures, he still prospered financially.

In 1916, at the age of sixty-seven, Burbank married his young secretary, Elizabeth Jane Waters. International affairs were to involve the United States in World War I by the next year, and although Burbank was a pacifist, he was to support the American war effort. During the war he introduced a wheat, "Quality," which turned out to be a previously bred Australian variety. His credibility as a cereal breeder was called into question, although he initially believed that he had developed a new hybrid.

For all the criticisms arising from the professional horticultural ranks, Burbank's popular image remained intact. His health, however, never robust, grew worse. During the first few years of the 1920's, a series of illnesses beset him that were to undermine further his already failing constitution. On March 24, 1926, Burbank suffered a heart attack; on April 11, he died. He was buried in the yard of his old home in Santa Rosa, under a cedar of Lebanon that he had grown from a seed years before.

Summary
In order to evaluate the work of Luther Burbank it is necessary to evaluate the man. Born into a strict New England Puritanical background, he changed his religion to that of the Baptist faith, then to Unitarianism. He believed that he had psychic powers, a conviction which may have contributed to his high-strung, nervous personality. Something of a hypochondriac and diet faddist, he ascribed in his latter years to the practice of Yoga.

Burbank the man was always different from those around him, as is so often the case with those who might be labeled "creative." He saw things differently from the way most of his peers did, and because of his outspoken opinions, he often became the center of controversy, both in his professional and personal life. The maverick in Burbank dictated his unique approaches to horticulture. He dared to experiment, to attempt the new and untried, and sometimes to fail. These failures were difficult for a man who needed the approval and praise of his colleagues and adoring supporters.

It was among the general gardening public that Burbank was to have the greatest appeal. He popularized horticulture as a science among those amateur gardeners who wanted something new, something different, something unique. It is for this spirit of seeking the unknown that Burbank should best be remembered: He was a pioneer unafraid to reach for the unreachable. Burbank epitomized that spirit of discovery coupled with the hope of success that so characterized early twentieth century America.

Bibliography
Burbank, Luther, with Wilbur Hall. *The Harvest of the Years*. Boston: Houghton Mifflin Co., 1927. This alleged autobiography was ghostwritten by Wilbur Hall and published the year after Burbank's death. An introductory biography gives no real background to his life. The volume in general is a laudatory account of Burbank's work. Not documented, but Burbank does attempt to dispel the aura of mystery surrounding his plant developments.

_____. *Partner of Nature*. Edited by Wilbur Hall. New York: D. Appleton-Century Co., 1939. This book, ghostwritten and published after Burbank's death, is a single-volume condensation of the twelve-volume work by Burbank *Luther Burbank: His Methods and Discoveries and Their Practical Application*, which was edited by John Whitson, Robert John, and Henry Smith Williams and published in New York by the Luther Burbank Press between 1914 and 1915. The condensed volume is aimed at a general audience interested in gardening rather than in the technical aspects of plant breeding.

Dreyer, Peter. *A Gardener Touched with Genius: The Life of Luther Burbank*. New York: Coward, McCann and Geoghegan, 1975. Rev. ed.
Berkeley: University of California Press, 1985. This revised edition of the
original 1975 work is still the definitive biography of Luther Burbank.
Incorporating the correspondence of his friend Edward J. Wickson and the
papers of the plant scientist George H. Shull, this book expands and re-
fines the previous 1945 biography of Burbank by Walter L. Howard and
the unpublished critical work of the plant geneticist Donald Jones. Well
documented, but no separate bibliography is included.

Harwood, W. S. *New Creations in Plant Life: An Authoritative Account of
the Life and Work of Luther Burbank*. New York: Macmillan, 1905. An
exaggerated account of Burbank's achievements. Misleading statements
abound in this work, giving Burbank the status of a miracle worker with
almost supernatural powers. This was, however, the first complete account
of Burbank's plant breeding techniques.

Howard, Walter L. "Luther Burbank: A Victim of Hero Worship." *Chronica
Botanica* 9 (Winter, 1945): 299-506. Written by an emeritus professor of
pomology at the University of California, this book-length article is a successful effort at portraying the real Burbank beneath the exaggerated fa-
cade that the general public knew. Points out the controversial episodes in
Burbank's life and brings him "down to earth." Supplies the honest facts
about Burbank's work without prejudice or judgmental rhetoric.

Kraft, Ken, and Pat Kraft. *Luther Burbank: The Wizard and the Man*. New
York: Meredith Press, 1967. The first of the modern biographies of Burbank that dared to point out some of his faults and omissions. This well-
written, readable work contains one particularly interesting chapter on
Burbank's attitudes on diet and health. Generally informative, balanced
account of the "plant wizard."

Charles A. Dranguet, Jr.

DANIEL HUDSON BURNHAM

Born: September 4, 1846; near Henderson, New York
Died: June 1, 1912; Heidelberg, Germany
Areas of Achievement: Architecture and urban planning
Contribution: Energetic and practical, Burnham was master of the utilitarian, technical, and financial aspects of architecture. He made important contributions to the development of the American skyscraper form, the organization of the modern architectural office, and the encouragement of comprehensive urban and regional planning.

Early Life

The son of Edwin Burnham, later a wholesale merchant of drugs, and Elizabeth Weeks Burnham, the daughter of a Swedenborgian minister, Daniel Hudson Burnham was born on September 4, 1846, near Henderson, New York. He moved to Chicago with his family when he was nine years old. An indifferent student, he received his education in the city schools, excelling only in freehand drawing. Burnham was then sent to Bridgewater, Massachusetts, to study with a private tutor. There, his interest in architecture and his talent for drawing became increasingly apparent.

After failing the entrance examinations of both Harvard and Yale, Burnham returned to Chicago in 1868. For short periods, he tried one thing after another—clerking in a Chicago retail store, mining for gold in Nevada, and running unsuccessfully for a seat in the Illinois senate. Burnham's dissatisfactions with these undertakings led his father to seek advice from William Le Baron Jenney (1832-1907), one of Chicago's leading architects. Shortly thereafter, Burnham became an apprentice in Jenney's architectural office. He gained further experience by working with John Val Osdel and Gustav Laureau.

In 1872, at the age of twenty-six, Burnham joined the firm of Carter, Drake and Wight. Working as a draftsman under Peter Bonnett Wight, he acquired a deeper appreciation of architectural scholarship and broadened the scope of his training. Among his fellow draftsmen was a young Georgian, John Wellborn Root (1850-1891). Their friendship led to a new partnership in an architectural office of their own in 1873. Root was inventive, romantic, and versatile; Burnham was businesslike and practical, bringing to the partnership a keen understanding of the points that make an office building a profitable enterprise. One of the firm's first draftsmen was William Holabird (1854-1923), who later established his own reputation as an architect. After a slow start, the partnership's practice grew rapidly; between 1873 and 1891, the firm designed 165 private homes and seventy-five buildings of various types.

Life's Work

In 1874, Burnham and Root completed a large and fashionable house for their first important client, John B. Sherman, a wealthy Chicago stockyard executive. Two years later, Burnham married Sherman's daughter, Margaret. Three sons and two daughters were born to Daniel and Margaret Burnham during the first decade of their marriage. Two of the sons—Hubert and Daniel, Jr.—eventually became architects and joined their father's firm.

Burnham and Root concentrated on house design during the partnership's first few years. Their first big commission was the Montauk Building (1882, since demolished), followed by the Calumet Building (1884). Both in Chicago, they were composed of masonry with cast-iron columns. The term "skyscraper" is said to have been applied first to the Montauk Building, which, at ten stories in height, was the first distinctly tall building in Chicago. Its commercial success made it the forerunner of tall, fireproof buildings throughout the country.

Other masonry buildings in Chicago followed, the most notable being the Rookery (1886) and the Monadnock Building (1891). Austere and subtlely proportioned, the latter structure was sixteen stories high, with brick bearing walls. It demonstrated Burnham's belief that architecture should express the uses intended for a building. In 1890 came the Rand-McNally Building (since demolished), the first all-steel, skeleton-framed building. The firm did several other metal, skeleton-framed buildings which were designed before and constructed after Root's death. Among these were the Masonic Temple (1892, since demolished), with a steel frame, and the Great Northern Hotel (1892, since demolished), with a wrought-iron and steel skeleton. Twenty stories in height, the Masonic Temple was, at the time, the tallest building in the world.

The Reliance Building is considered by many to represent the partnership's finest design. Planning for the structure had begun before Root's death and was finished by the head of the firm's design department, Charles B. Atwood (1849-1895). The design of the Chicago skyscraper is said to have reached its logical conclusion in the Reliance Building, with its steel skeleton, its glass and terra-cotta walls (revealing the structure underneath), and its skillfully balanced proportions and details.

With Root and landscape architect Frederick Law Olmsted, Burnham worked out the master plan for the World's Columbian Exposition in Chicago. Jackson Park, then a sandy waste, was selected as the location; improvements were designed to fit the area ultimately for use as a city park. Five outside and five local firms of architects were selected to design the principal buildings. Root died during the first meeting of the architects in January, 1891. Burnham, as chief of construction and then chief consulting architect, assumed the responsibility of maintaining the teamwork necessary to accomplish an opening date for the exposition in 1893.

The eastern architects had already determined that the buildings surrounding the exposition's Court of Honor should be classical in design. Although no building of classical design had been erected previously in Chicago, their plan was adopted. It is commonly argued that things would have been different had Root lived. Supposedly, his authority and predilection for the romantic would have given the exposition an altogether different appearance. It should be noted, however, that the classical design of the Court of Honor had been decided upon before Root's death, with both his and Burnham's assent. Moreover, the minds of both men were already attuned to the classical notes struck in the East, especially those of the firm of McKim, Mead and White. In addition, Burnham found attractive the sense of orderliness and the largeness of conception in a series of related public buildings.

To Burnham, the World's Columbian Exposition not only represented an opportunity to express American prowess in invention, manufactures, and production, but also gave Americans a vehicle for demonstrating the capacity of the country in such areas as architecture, painting, and sculpture. Burnham found great satisfaction in the associations created and cultivated during the two years of the exposition's construction period. His management and leadership style allowed for an opportunity for individual creative activity, and his generous nature led him to give full credit to those who worked under him.

Immediate results of the exposition's success were honorary degrees bestowed on Burnham by Harvard and Yale, election to the presidency of the American Institute of Architects, and membership in New York's Century Club. Burnham was now the best-known architect in the United States. Yet the exposition's conclusion also left him with an architectural practice broken by the death of Root and two years of interrupted work. In 1896, he took on three new partners, Ernest R. Graham, Edward C. Shankland, and Charles B. Atwood, all associates at the exposition.

As early as 1897, Burnham had begun thinking about a plan for the development of the Chicago lakefront. Later, working with Jens Jensen (1860-1951) as the landscape architect, he would see this planning result in the construction of Grant Park and other Chicago parks, beginning in 1904. It would also lead to his widely acclaimed Chicago Plan of 1909.

Burnham was called to Washington, D.C., in 1901, to become chairman of a commission to plan the enlargement and extension of the L'Enfant plan for the District of Columbia. To assist him, Burnham chose Charles McKim, a leading New York architect, and Olmsted. He insisted that studies be made of those European capitols which had furnished precedents for L'Enfant's plan. The unity of the Mall was to be restored. Burnham obtained the consent of the Pennsylvania Railroad to remove its tracks from the Mall. The Union Station and the adjoining Post Office Building were planned to be subordinate to the Capitol. In this subordination and in the monumental nature of these buildings, Burnham secured results which marked his desire for teamwork and his sense of proportion.

Among Burnham's more notable later buildings are the Fisher Building (1896), the Field Museum of Natural History (1900), and the Railway Exchange Building (1904)—all in Chicago. In 1902, his Flatiron Building, New York's first skyscraper, became the tallest building in the world. Nevertheless, with the Washington project, Burnham embarked on a new phase of his career, city planning, which occupied much of his time and thought for the remainder of his life. A number of large city governments—San Francisco, Cleveland, Detroit, and Chicago—sought his aid in developing comprehensive city plans. He used these plans for civic development to express his own ideas of dignity, orderliness, and beauty. In 1904, at the request of William Howard Taft, the secretary of war, Burnham served as head of a commission to undertake the rebuilding and modernization of Manila in the Philippine Islands. There, the French idea of turning outgrown fortifications into boulevards was carried out successfully.

In 1910, President Taft appointed Burnham to head a newly organized National Commission of Fine Arts. One of the first important pieces of business for the commission was the location of the proposed Lincoln Memorial and the selection of an architect and sculptor. Early in 1912, Burnham's health began to fail. To the very end a keen student, he died during a trip to Europe in Heidelberg, Germany, on June 1, 1912.

After Burnham's death, Ernest Robert Graham (1868-1936), who had administered the company since 1900, continued the firm in partnership with Burnham's sons, Hubert and Daniel, Jr. The firm continued later as Graham, Anderson, Probst, and White.

Summary

By the late 1920's and early 1930's, as Louis Sullivan's critical writings became more widely known and as European modernist architects spread their message, the derivative neoclassicism of Burnham's day came increasingly under attack in the architectural community. Recent historians and critics have tried to redress the fashionable practice of attacking the Burnham school—a revisionist movement long overdue.

Burnham was as important as his contemporaries believed, and as great as he knew himself to be. Above all others, Burnham made distinguished and original contributions in four areas: first, in the creation of the large, modern architectural office, a hierarchical system of specialists working together in various departments; second, in the development of the skyscraper form, in the perfection of the internal arrangement and layout of tall office-building systems; third, in his early call for comprehensive planning, which included entire urban and geographical regions; and, fourth, in his work as an architectural philanthropist and cultural entrepreneur who organized and encouraged the cultivation of both the public and the private arts in the United States.

Bibliography

Condit, Carl W. *The Chicago School of Architecture: A History of Commercial and Public Building in the Chicago Area, 1875-1925*. Chicago: University of Chicago Press, 1964. The definitive treatment of the Chicago School and its influence. Any recent work on Chicago architecture during the latter part of the nineteenth century and the early part of the twentieth century is in debt to Condit's study.

Hines, Thomas S. *Burnham of Chicago: Architect and Planner*. New York: Oxford University Press, 1974. The standard biography of Burnham. Solid on architectural criticism. "On Sources" is a particularly valuable section.

Hitchcock, Henry Russell. *Architecture: Nineteenth and Twentieth Centuries*. 4th ed. New York: Penguin Books, 1977. The classic one-volume history of modern architecture which deals with Burnham and his contemporaries judiciously and intelligently, if sometimes briefly.

Hoffmann, Donald. *The Architecture of John Wellborn Root*. Baltimore: Johns Hopkins University Press, 1973. The standard study of Root's work. Good on Root's relations with Burnham.

Moore, Charles. *Daniel H. Burnham, Architect, Planner of Cities*. 2 vols. Boston: Houghton Mifflin Co., 1921. A valuable source of an almost primary nature. Moore knew Burnham well and had access to friends, relatives, and associates.

Reps, John W. *The Making of Urban America: A History of City Planning in the United States*. Princeton, N.J.: Princeton University Press, 1965. A helpful overview of American urban planning. Brief text but extensive illustrations.

Schuyler, Montgomery. *American Architecture and Other Writings*. Edited by William Jordy and Ralph Coe. Cambridge, Mass.: Belknap Press of Harvard University Press, 1961. Writings of the best contemporary architectural critic, who wrote extensively about Burnham and the Chicago School.

L. Moody Simms, Jr.

AARON BURR

Born: February 6, 1756; Newark, New Jersey
Died: September 14, 1836; Port Richmond, Staten Island, New York
Areas of Achievement: Politics and law
Contribution: Burr developed the political organization which assured the presidential victory of Thomas Jefferson, and was the force behind the liberalization of New York's penal codes and political process.

Early Life

Aaron Burr was born February 6, 1756, in Newark, New Jersey. His mother, Esther Edwards Burr, was the daughter of the Reverend Mr. Jonathan and Sarah Edwards; his father, the Reverend Mr. Aaron Burr, was pastor of the Newark Presbyterian Congregation and president of the College of New Jersey, which, within the year, moved to Princeton. When Burr was nineteen months old, his father died. Within the year, his mother and grandparents died as well, leaving Burr and his older sister Sarah wards of their twenty-year-old uncle, Timothy Edwards.

After graduation from Princeton at age seventeen, Burr completed his study for the ministry but decided to become a lawyer. His preparations were interrupted by the Revolution. After serving with distinction at the battles of Quebec, New York, and Monmouth and commanding American forces in Westchester, Colonel Burr's health forced him to resign (he was about five feet, two inches in height, thin, and always looked frail), and he returned to the study of law.

In 1782, he was admitted to the New York Bar and then was married to Theodosia Bartow Prevost, ten years his senior and the widow of a British army officer. The Burrs moved to New York City as soon as the British evacuated it. Four children were born: two sons, who died at birth; a daughter, who died in 1789; and Theodosia, the firstborn, who disappeared at sea in 1812.

Burr became noted as a superior attorney; he won many cases "by default." The city's other lawyers, including Alexander Hamilton, sought Burr as co-counsel in arduous litigations. People reported other traits: Burr seldom ventured opinions on public issues, he had difficulty in expressing his wishes or seeking favors, and he seldom joined groups—though groups joined him. Observers noted his unusual interest in the well-being of children. Mental health professionals indicate that the trauma of early parental death can lead to such behavior.

Life's Work

As a military hero and the heir of the Reverend Mr. Edwards and the Reverend Mr. Burr, Colonel Burr would be an asset to any of the political groups forming in New York, but he refused to join the factions led by Senator

Philip Schuyler, Governor George Clinton, or Chancellor Robert Livingston. In 1784, a radical group convinced him to allow his name to be placed in nomination for the state assembly; he agreed and was elected. In February, 1785, he sponsored a bill to emancipate all those of "Negro, Mulatto, Indian and Mustee blood born in New York." The measure failed, but Burr continued to seek legislative means to end slavery, Burr was reelected but seems not to have served; he declined further nomination. Refusing to join any faction, Burr nevertheless developed friendly relations with Schuyler's son-in-law, Hamilton, and Livingston's brother, Edward. The Schuyler and Livingston factions supported the new Constitution, while Clinton opposed ratification. In 1789, after New York joined the Union, Clinton attempted to placate Burr by appointing him attorney general. Burr was an efficient official and before resigning prepared a series of recommendations to liberalize the state's laws.

In 1791, the Livingstons, angered by Hamilton's use of his friendship with President George Washington to secure favors for the Schuyler group, combined with the Clintons to prevent the reelection of Senator Schuyler. Burr was elected in his place. Outwardly, Burr and Hamilton remained friends, but Hamilton was determined to "destroy" Burr.

As senator, Burr became identified with the Thomas Jefferson group led by James Monroe in the Senate and James Madison in the House. Burr supported measures to make Senate sessions public and liberalize laws. Because of his stand on slavery, however, he was not fully trusted by the Jeffersonians. He praised the French Republic and objected to the presence of British forts on American soil; he favored funds to the military to protect Americans from Indian raids. After Monroe left the Senate, Burr was acknowledged as Jeffersonian spokesman in the Senate, and his name was unsuccessfully put forward for vice president in the 1796 campaign.

Following the death of his wife, Burr did not seek reelection. Returning to New York, he entered the legislature, where he was instrumental in passing a manumission law, securing the construction of public and private roads and canals and in creating the Manhattan Company with its "notorious" bank. The Bank of the Manhattan Company, by providing venture capital, enabled New York City to replace Philadelphia and Boston as the preeminent American financial center. The bank also provided an alternative source of capital to the Bank of the United States, dominated by the Schuyler faction (or Federalists), which had used the bank to deny loans to Anti-Federalists.

As an attorney, Burr represented individuals being prosecuted under the Federalist-sponsored Alien and Sedition laws. Although never a member, he helped restructure the Tammany Society into a political organization. Despite his leadership role in the Anti-Federalist, or Democratic Republican, Party, Hamilton, in 1798, convinced Federalist governor John Jay to appoint Burr overseer of the state's defenses to prepare for war with France.

Burr blueprinted a plan which would have prevented a foreign fleet from entering New York Harbor. The legislature rejected most of the plan as too costly. Burr, however, was able to convince many Federalists, most of whom had considered the Anti-Federalists as too pro-French, to switch parties. He gathered a slate of candidates which would ensure that pro-Jeffersonians would be selected as presidential electors for the election of 1801. When, for the first time, the state elected an Anti-Federalist slate, the Jeffersonians agreed that Burr would be their vice presidential candidate.

Unfortunately, Burr and Jefferson received an equal vote for president; the House of Representatives would have to elect the president. The balloting started February 11, 1801. Burr received a majority of the votes, but, for him to be elected, nine states had to concur; Jefferson had a majority in eight states, Burr a majority in six, and two states split evenly. By February 16, the Federalists, having reached an understanding with Jefferson's spokesman, Samuel Smith, abandoned their opposition to Jefferson, who was elected president while Burr became vice president.

With the Senate evenly split between Federalists and Republicans, Burr's role as president of the Senate became crucial in securing passage of Jeffersonian legislation. Only when the Administration attempted to impose an embargo on trade with the black revolutionists of Haiti did Burr act in opposition. By 1804, however, Burr, realizing that Jefferson was grooming Madison as his successor, decided to seek the governorship of New York. Much to Hamilton's annoyance, the Federalists decided to support Burr. Tammany also endorsed Burr, but the Livingston and Clinton groups combined to nominate their own candidate. Burr carried New York City, Albany, and a few urban centers but was overwhelmed in rural areas.

After the defeat, Burr's supporters persuaded him to question Hamilton about some comments he allegedly had made. Despite the efforts of Hamilton's friends, Hamilton exacerbated the issue. He was fatally wounded in the resulting duel. Burr's enemies in New York and New Jersey (where the duel took place), attempted to arrest Burr, who fled to Philadelphia.

Burr returned to Washington, where as president of the Senate he frustrated another Administration attempt to place an embargo on trade with Haiti and presided over the unsuccessful attempt to impeach Judge Samuel Chase. Following an emotional farewell speech, Burr left the Senate.

Unable to return to New York or New Jersey because of the illegal murder indictments—dueling was legal in New Jersey, and New York had no jurisdiction in the matter—Burr, having secured the temporary presidential appointment of several of his friends to important posts in Louisiana Territory, took a trip down the Ohio and Mississippi rivers to New Orleans. He returned to Washington in the fall of 1805 and held a series of meetings with Jefferson, who, in January, 1806, sought and received Senate confirmation of the appointment of Burr's friends. Amid talk of war with Spain, Burr embarked on a second voyage down the rivers. Soon rumors began to circulate that Burr planned either to separate the Mississippi Valley from the rest of the country or to invade Spanish territory. All Burr would say was that he had purchased land along the Washita River and that he intended to populate the region with individuals capable of organizing a strike force in the event of war with Spain.

Burr's ally, General James Wilkinson, the highest-ranking officer in the army, governor of Louisiana, and a paid Spanish agent, suddenly declared that Burr was a traitor. After a series of trials along the Mississippi in which he was found innocent, Burr was captured by troops and dragged to Richmond, Virginia, to stand trial for treason. Burr acted as his own attorney, although he was assisted by some of the best legal minds in the country. Chief Justice John Marshall acted as circuit judge. The trial became a landmark, because it defined the constitutional meaning of treason, clarified who had the right to declare martial law, and established the right of a defendant to subpoena the president. Burr was found not guilty. The government then charged him with committing a misdemeanor. He was found not guilty. When the government ordered that he stand trial on the same charges in Ohio, he fled to Europe.

In England he was welcomed by Jeremy Bentham and William Godwin, the widower of Mary Wollstonecraft, whose feminist views Burr shared. Burr attempted to convince the British government to help liberate Latin America. He also tried to persuade those Spaniards who were resisting the French occupation of their country to adopt the liberal constitution developed by Bentham. He failed in both attempts. He left England for Germany, Sweden, and France. In Paris he sought the aid of Napoleon in removing all European colonies from the Western Hemisphere. Again he failed.

He returned to New York in 1812; he learned that his only grandchild had died and that his daughter's ship had disappeared at sea. Burr remained in New York—the murder indictments had been quashed, but the treason charges would not be dropped until 1816. He resumed his legal practice and maintained a low profile. His private and legal papers, however, indicate that he was still active in politics. He corresponded with South American revolutionists and was offered a post in their army. He maintained his friendship with Andrew Jackson and Martin Van Buren, the latter serving as co-counsel on several cases. Toward the end of his life, he became interested in bringing German settlers to Texas and attempted to establish contact with Texan revolutionists.

Burr suffered a minor stroke in June, 1830, but that did not prevent him from either continuing his work or, on July 1, 1833, marrying Eliza Jumel, a wealthy widow twenty years his junior. A year later, Mrs. Burr sued for divorce, charging that Burr had taken some of her money for the Texas project. After a sordid trial—the legal grounds for divorce being adultery—

the divorce was granted July 14, 1836, to become effective September 14. Since Burr died on that day, Mrs. Burr decided that she did not want the divorce.

Summary

In some ways, Burr represented the America that was to be rather than the America that was. He opposed slavery and favored the education of blacks; he was a feminist who believed that women should be educated to the same degree as males and that women should be able to divorce men who abused them; he opposed property qualifications for voting and did everything possible to void or circumvent the laws. He encouraged government support for commerce and industry; to protect American commerce and independence, he favored the military and naval establishment. He advocated the annexation of Florida and Texas and the United States' support for the liberation of Latin America. In his legal work, he insisted that the burden of proof rested with the prosecution and challenged the validity of circumstantial evidence; he demanded that courts follow the rules of evidence.

The contested election of 1801, the killing of Hamilton, and the treason trials made Burr a political pariah. Many of his friends would publicly shun him but privately seek his advice. Most of the legislation he proposed as attorney general became law; Tammany Hall became a model for democratic urban political machines; the Bank of the Manhattan Company blueprinted a policy that was to become normal in the 1980's and Martin Van Buren secretly called upon his expertise during the War of 1812. People would follow Burr's ideas as long as they could omit his name.

Bibliography

Burr, Aaron. *The Papers of Aaron Burr*. Edited by Mary-Jo Kline. 27 reels. New York: Microfilm Corporation of America, 1978. The basis for all current scholarly research. All known and available documents to and from Burr are included, as are all his existing legal papers. Where the original document has disappeared, printed versions are included. At times a typed transcription of the manuscript is appended. Includes not only all archival documents but also documents from private collectors and family collections which have never been used.

_____. *Political Correspondence and Public Papers of Aaron Burr*. Edited by Mary-Jo Kline. 2 vols. Princeton: Princeton University Press, 1983. Using selections from the microfilm edition of Burr's papers, the editor has grouped well-edited and well-annotated papers into topical sections which are introduced by superb long historical essays. While recognizing Burr's personality faults, it presents a positive view of his role.

Daniels, Jonathan. *Ordeal of Ambition: Jefferson, Hamilton, Burr*. Garden

City, N.Y.: Doubleday and Co., 1970. An excellent popular political biography of Burr, Jefferson, and Hamilton, in which the author is rather impartial.

Davis, Matthew Livingston, ed. *Memoirs of Aaron Burr*. 2 vols. New York: Harper and Brothers, 1836-1837. Reprint. New York: Da Capo Press, 1971. A political ally of Burr, Davis used Burr's papers to write a defense of his actions prior to 1809. Liberties were taken with the documents.

_____. *The Private Journal of Aaron Burr*. 2 vols. New York: Harper and Brothers, 1838. Reprint. Upper Saddle River, N.J.: Literature House, 1970. A continuation of the memoirs, covering the period 1809-1836. The basis of the work is the journal kept by Burr while in Europe, letters written to his daughter and son-in-law, and letters from various individuals interested in Latin American affairs. The journal, written in abbreviated English, French, German, Swedish, and Latin, is quite salacious and shocked Davis, who sanitized it for publication. The original manuscript was sold to William K. Bixby, who decoded and translated it as *The Private Journal* (published by The Genesse Press in 1903).

Geissler, Suzanne. *Jonathan Edwards to Aaron Burr, Jr.: From the Great Awakening to Democratic Politics*. New York: Edwin Mellin Press, 1981. Using unpublished documents, the author traces the development of a democratic ideology. An excellent defense of Burr's position.

Hammond, Jabez D. *The History of Political Parties in the State of New York*. 2 vols. Cooperstown, N.Y.: H. and E. Phinney, 1845. Well written, this is still the best work describing the conflict among the supporters of Burr, Hamilton, Clinton, and Livingston.

Lomask, Milton. *Aaron Burr: The Years from Princeton to Vice President, 1756-1805*. New York: Farrar, Straus and Giroux, 1979.

_____. *Aaron Burr: The Conspiracy and Years of Exile, 1804-1836*. New York: Farrar, Straus and Giroux, 1983. A popular biography. The first volume repeats much that had been previously written. The second volume, however, benefited from the publication of the microfilm edition of the Burr papers and presents some positive new insights.

Parmet, Herbert S., and Marie B. Hecht. *Aaron Burr: Portrait of an Ambitious Man*. New York: Macmillan Publishing Co., 1967. Making extensive use of documents in various archives, the authors have presented a well-written, scholarly, but unflattering biography.

Syrett, Harold C., and Jean G. Cooke, eds. *Interview in Weehawken: The Burr-Hamilton Duel as Told in Original Documents*. Middletown, Conn.: Wesleyan University Press, 1960. A complete collection of all the letters, memoranda, editorials, and testimony leading up to and following the Burr-Hamilton duel.

J. Lee Shneidman

NICHOLAS MURRAY BUTLER

Born: April 2, 1862; Elizabeth, New Jersey
Died: December 7, 1947; New York, New York
Area of Achievement: Education
Contribution: Butler was a leading figure in the creation of the modern American university.

Early Life

Nicholas Murray Butler was born April 2, 1862, in Elizabeth, New Jersey, to Henry Leny and Mary Jones (Murray) Butler. When coming to the United States from England in 1835, his grandfather had changed the family name from Buchanan to Butler. His father was a financially comfortable textile importer and manufacturer in Paterson, New Jersey. The youth attended local schools, and was graduated from Paterson High School at the age of thirteen. After private study to make up deficiencies in his preparation, he entered Columbia College in 1878. Although reared as a Presbyterian, he became while at Columbia an Episcopalian. He was graduated in 1882 after compiling an impressive record and stayed on with a fellowship for graduate study in philosophy. He received his master of arts degree in 1883 with a thesis entitled "The Permanent Influence of Immanuel Kant." His Ph.D. dissertation was "An Outline of the History of Logical Doctrine." After receiving his Ph.D. in 1884, he did a year's further study in philosophy and educational theory in Europe.

Butler returned to Columbia in 1885 as an assistant professor of philosophy and rose rapidly through the ranks to become full professor in 1890. His major areas of teaching were the history of philosophy, the history and principles of education, and modern British and German philosophy. His own personal allegiance was to a neo-Kantian idealism that assumed the universal validity of such principles as private property, individual liberty, and limited government. During those years, the Columbia faculty and trustees were sharply divided over the institution's future direction; whether Columbia should remain primarily a liberal-arts undergraduate college or become a university emphasizing graduate study, professional training, and advanced research. The so-called university party had won a significant victory in 1880 when John W. Burgess gained approval by the trustees of his plan for a graduate-level Faculty of Political Science. Although not himself a scholar of importance, Butler became a leader of the group pushing for the organization of parallel faculties in philosophy and the natural sciences. The selection of Seth Low as Columbia president in 1889 marked the triumph of the pro-university faction. When the Faculty of Philosophy was formally established the following year, Butler's colleagues elected him dean. After Low resigned as president in 1901 to run for mayor of New York City, the trustees named

Butler acting president and, in 1902, made the appointment permanent. He would continue in that position for more than forty years.

Life's Work
Before he ascended to Columbia's presidency, Butler's major interest lay in the improvement of public education through professionalization of teacher training and nonpartisan administration of the schools. He was instrumental in the founding in 1889 of the New York College for the Training of Teachers (renamed Teachers College after 1892) and its later affiliation with Columbia. He served on the New Jersey State Board of Education from 1887 to 1895 and was president of the Paterson Board of Education from 1892 to 1893. After moving his residence to New York in 1894, he was a leader of the successful battle to abolish the existing decentralized system of ward school boards and concentrate control over the city's schools in the hands of an appointed professional superintendent. He was similarly active in the fight for establishment of a powerful state commission of education for tighter centralized control at that level. As president of the National Education Association from 1894 to 1895, Butler was the moving spirit behind the work of the association's Committee of Ten and Committee on College Entrance Requirements in laying down guidelines for the high school curriculum. He was one of the organizers of the College Entrance Examination Board in 1900, acted as its first secretary, and served as its chairman from 1901 to 1914. He was founder—and from 1892 to 1919 editor—of the *Educational Review*.

Following in his father's footsteps, Butler took an active part in Republican Party affairs. He viewed himself at a Tory reformer who stood for an enlightened gradualist approach that avoided the extremes of standpattism and radicalism. In practice, however, Butler was more Tory than reformer. The major exception was his interest in administrative reorganization aimed at improving governmental efficiency. An elitist by temperament with a Hamilton-like fear of demagogues, Butler opposed such measures for direct democracy as the direct primary, popular election of United States senators, and the initiative, referendum, and recall. Reflecting the links that he had forged as president of Columbia with New York's business and legal elite, he was hostile to the income tax, trustbusting, and labor legislation. For a time, he had close ties with Theodore Roosevelt, but their relationship cooled because of Roosevelt's support for stricter federal regulation of business. Becoming a confidant of President William Howard Taft, Butler allied himself with the party's Old Guard in thwarting Roosevelt's bid for the 1912 GOP presidential nomination. When the GOP vice presidential nominee died during the campaign, Butler received the votes of the Republican electors for that place.

There was talk of Butler himself as possible Republican candidate in 1920 with the slogan "Pick Nick for a Pic-Nic in November." Although he was receptive, even hopeful, his support at the convention remained limited to the New York delegation. He was on friendly terms with President Warren G. Harding, but he grew increasingly unhappy over the Republican Party's continued support for Prohibition. He opposed Prohibition not only as involving the expansion of governmental power beyond its proper sphere but also as a source of hypocrisy and lawlessness. In 1928, he became a publicly declared candidate for the GOP presidential nomination as the champion of repeal. Butler was no admirer of the successful Republican aspirant, Herbert Hoover. He was strongly hostile to Hoover's Democratic successor. In his eyes, Franklin D. Roosevelt was a reckless spender and dangerous leveler; Butler regarded the New Deal program as undermining individual initiative and responsibility.

Next to running Columbia, Butler's major commitment was the promotion of international peace. He was a leader of the "conservative"—or to be more accurate, "legalist"—wing of the American peace movement. In 1907, he organized the American Association for International Conciliation to promote better international understanding through cultural exchanges. His larger ambition was the elimination of war through the development of a clearly defined body of international law enforced by an independent judiciary. He played a key role in persuading Andrew Carnegie to set up in 1910 the Carnegie Endowment for International Peace with a ten-million-dollar gift. Butler's access to the Carnegie funds in turn gave his views on international questions added weight. He had especially close ties with German official circles, including Kaiser Wilhelm II. For a time, he had visions of himself as a moderator who could bring about an Anglo-German rapprochement. At the time of the outbreak of World War I, he blamed militarists on both sides for the conflict. By 1916, however, he had become a vocal champion of the Allied side. He supported United States membership in the League of Nations with no more than "mild" reservations, and whether from sincere belief or Republican Party loyalty, he joined other Republican mild reservationists in issuing a public statement that the election of Harding was the best way of assuring United States membership in the League.

Even though disappointed on this score, Butler continued his efforts on behalf of peace during the 1920's. In 1925, he took over the presidency of the Carnegie Endowment—a position he would retain until late 1945. He supported United States membership in the World Court. He was the person probably most responsible for drumming up popular support in this country for the proposal made in 1927 by French foreign minister Aristide Briand for a pact renouncing war. Asked by the State Department to draft the treaty, Butler turned the job over to two of his Columbia members—Joseph B. Chamberlain and James T. Shotwell—and he led the campaign that succeeded in winning Senate ratification of the resulting Kellogg-Briand treaty outlawing war. He was joint recipient with Jane Addams of the Nobel Peace

Prize for 1931. By that time, he had come to see the economic nationalism stimulated by the Depression as the gravest threat to world peace and thus made his top priority encouragement of international cooperation to deal with world economic difficulties. He opposed the isolationist-inspired neutrality legislation of the 1930's, and after the outbreak of war in Europe in 1939, he joined—as he had during the previous conflict—the ranks of those calling for United States support for the Allies.

Butler's major importance was as one of the group of energetic and imperious academic empire-builders who in the late nineteenth century and early twentieth century reshaped American higher education. The years from his becoming president to 1917 constituted Columbia's golden age: the time when Columbia was generally recognized as the nation's leading university. The basis for that preeminence had been laid under Butler's predecessor, Seth Low, but he made major contributions of his own. A tireless fundraiser, he built Columbia's endowment by 1914 into the largest of any American university. He kept a watchful eye upon all aspects of the institution— from undergraduate athletics to the hiring and promotion of faculty. He was by the standards of the time a liberal on higher education for women. With a keen eye for spotting talent, he was instrumental in hiring established names from outside such as philosopher John Dewey from the University of Chicago and promoting from within such promising younger men as the historian Charles A. Beard. He brought in future United States Supreme Court Chief Justice Harlan Fiske Stone as dean of the Law School. Thanks to his support, Teachers College became the nation's leading center of pedagogical innovation—although Butler personally had no sympathy with the child-centered approach that became its hallmark. He was largely responsible for making the School of Journalism, established with a gift from publisher Joseph Pulitzer, into the country's most prestigious training ground for aspiring journalists.

There were, however, accompanying costs. Extremely conscious of public relations, Butler was excessively sensitive about anything that he feared might reflect unfavorably upon the institution. His emphasis upon strengthening graduate and professional education led him to downgrade the undergraduate program. To the extent that he was interested in undergraduate instruction, he was a traditionalist favoring the old general-education ideal and dubious about the elective system. His centralization of authority in his own hands—after 1905, for example, the deans of the different faculties were appointed by him rather than elected by their colleagues—rankled many on the faculty. Even more damaging was a series of faculty dismissals and resignations raising charges of the violation of academic freedom. Although paying lip service to scholarship for its own sake, Butler's major goal was to make the university a training center for an enlightened elite dedicated to upholding sound values. He took the position that what the

Germans called *Lehrfreiheit* was limited to the work of a scholar in his field of academic specialization and did not apply to violations of accepted moral and social standards. The beneath-the-surface frictions came to a head in October, 1917, with the firing of three antiwar faculty members. The affair attracted nationwide attention because of the dramatic resignation by Charles A. Beard in protest. In one sense, the crisis had a salutary effect. During the remaining years of Butler's presidency, there would be no further significant problems of academic freedom at Columbia. Despite his own personal hostility to the New Deal, Butler took pride in the role played by Columbia faculty in the Roosevelt Administration as exemplifying his ideal of the university as a center for public service. Yet the institution—and his own reputation—never fully overcame the stigma growing out of the 1917 affair.

Most serious in the long run was Columbia's worsening financial status compared to that of rival institutions. At least part of the difficulty lay in the overexpansion of the graduate and professional programs relative to the undergraduate program. The situation was aggravated by the changing socio-economic and ethnic composition of the undergraduate student body as the number of commuters attending Columbia College grew. In his latter years, Butler was widely suspected of anti-Semitism. The charge was unfair. Columbia was more open to Jewish faculty and students than most Ivy League schools of the time. Butler personally virtually ordered a reluctant English Department to retain the distinguished literary critic Lionel Trilling. Butler was without question, however, a socially pretentious snob—and this snobbery, combined with his personal and political identification with the old-line New York establishment, impeded his ability to tap the city's newer money. In the 1930's, faculty salaries were low and promotions slow. Columbia's success in retaining as distinguished a faculty as the institution continued to have owed much to the larger attractions of New York City. As those attractions increasingly faded in the post–World War II years, so did Columbia's position among American universities.

With a "nobly domed forehead, a cool, piercing gaze, and an aggressive beak," "Nicholas Miraculous" (as he became nicknamed) exuded a commanding presence that made him appear larger than his medium height. He could be charming, but he was an overweening egoist whose conversations all too often became monologues about the famous personages he had known. Such name-dropping similarly ran through his two-volume autobiography, *Across the Busy Years: Recollections and Reflections* (1939-1940). A lover of pomp and ceremony, he was what an irreverent observer called "the champion international visitor and retriever of foreign orders and degrees." He had married on February 8, 1887, Susanna Edwards Schuyler; they had one daughter, Sarah Schuyler Butler. After his first wife's death in 1903, he married Kate La Montagne on March 5, 1907; this union had no offspring. Afflicted by near-blindness and worsening deafness, Butler retired as president of Columbia effective October 1, 1945. Before his death on December 7, 1947, of bronchopneumonia, he gave his blessing to the selection of General Dwight D. Eisenhower as his successor.

Summary

Butler never produced any major work of scholarship. Although he had to his name an imposing bibliography of published books and articles, those were mostly expositions of his views on current issues. He was not a deep or penetrating thinker; rather, he excelled as a publicist for other men's ideas. As an educational reformer, he was more interested in improving the efficiency of the system's administrative machinery than in questions about education's larger purpose. Although not without influence within the Republican Party, he was at odds with the dominant currents of American political life during much of his life. He had a deep and sincere commitment to the promotion of international peace, but his effectiveness was limited by his narrowly—and naïvely—legalist approach. He impressed foreigners—who exaggerated his influence—more than he impressed most of his fellow countrymen. There is no question that he was an extraordinarily able academic empire-builder, but even here he appears to have been moved more by ambitions of institutional aggrandizement than by any intellectual vision of what a university should be. Sadly, he lived to see his beloved Columbia slip from its former preeminence.

Bibliography

Burgess, John W. *Reminiscences of an American Scholar: The Beginnings of Columbia University.* New York: Columbia University Press, 1934. The autobiography of Butler's most important ally in the transformation of Columbia from a liberal-arts undergraduate college into a major university.

Butler, Nicholas Murray. *Across the Busy Years: Recollections and Reflections.* 2 vols. New York: Charles Scribner's Sons, 1939-1940. Butler's own autobiography is anecdotal rather than analytical, self-congratulatory rather than introspective, and makes all too evident his egoism and snobbery. The work nevertheless remains the fullest available account of his multifarious activities.

Coon, Horace. *Columbia: Colossus on the Hudson.* New York: E. P. Hutton and Co., 1947. Provides a breezy—and at times irreverent—survey of Columbia during the years of Butler's presidency.

Herman, Sondra R. *Eleven Against War: Studies in American Internationalist Thought, 1898-1921.* Stanford, Calif.: Hoover Institution Press, 1969. Provides an insightful analysis of Butler's "legalist" approach to international relations.

Johnston, Alva. "Cosmos." In *Profiles from the New Yorker*, edited by Clifton Fadiman, 219-238. New York: Alfred A. Knopf, 1938. A skillfully done, if overly eulogistic, profile of Butler that first appeared in the November 8 and 15, 1930, issues of *The New Yorker*.

Kuehl, Warren F. *Seeking World Order: The United States and International Organization to 1920*. Nashville, Tenn.: Vanderbilt University Press, 1969. Contains the fullest information about Butler's efforts to promote international peace during the years covered.

Summerscales, William. *Affirmation and Dissent: Columbia's Response to the Crisis of World War I*. New York: Teachers College Press, 1970. A detailed account of the World War I academic freedom crisis at Columbia that is sympathetic to—though not uncritical of—Butler.

Veysey, Laurence R. *The Emergence of the American University*. Chicago: University of Chicago Press, 1965. A provocative and penetrating analysis of the restructuring and reshaping of American higher education that, on balance, gives a negative appraisal of Butler's role as university-builder.

Whittemore, Richard. *Nicholas Murray Butler and Public Education, 1862-1911*. New York: Teachers College Press, 1970. A generally admiring examination of Butler's contributions to the professionalization of teacher training and the administrative reorganization of public education, although the author acknowledges Butler's preoccupation with the organizational aspect and his lack of philosophical depth.

John Braeman

RICHARD E. BYRD

Born: October 25, 1888; Winchester, Virginia
Died: March 11, 1957; Boston, Massachusetts
Areas of Achievement: Aviation and exploration
Contribution: Byrd played a central role in the development of naval aviation and was a major figure in Arctic and Antarctic exploration.

Early Life

Richard Byrd was the son of Richard Evelyn Byrd, a lawyer, and Eleanor Bolling Flood. The families of both his parents were active in Virginia politics, and Richard's brother, Harry, became an influential United States senator. Small and slender, Richard was nevertheless strong and athletic. Playing war games with his brothers Harry and Tom and exploring the woods and hills near Winchester increased Richard's desire for adventure. When he was twelve, he was invited to visit a family friend who was serving as United States circuit court judge in the Philippines. Richard had his parents' permission to go to Manila by himself. He remained a year, writing about his experiences for a Winchester newspaper. He then completed his journey around the world alone. It was about this time that he wrote in his diary that he wanted to be the first person to reach the North Pole.

Three years at the Shenandoah Valley Military Academy prepared him for admission to Virginia Military Institute, where he studied from 1904 to 1907, before transferring to the University of Virginia for a year. In 1908, he was appointed to the United States Naval Academy at Annapolis, from which he was graduated in 1912, sixty-second in a class of 155. As a midshipman, he played tennis and football, wrestled in the 135-pound class, and specialized in the rings in gymnastics. While engaging in these sports, he suffered injuries that would later cause him to terminate his active duty with the Navy. He broke bones in his ankle playing football and broke them again in a fall during a gymnastics routine. Shortly after receiving his commission, he fell down a hatchway on the USS *Wyoming*, reinjuring his right foot and causing him to walk with a slight limp. Despite this setback, he served with distinction in the Caribbean, twice saving men from drowning. It was at this time, in the summer of 1914, that he took his first airplane ride.

In 1915, Byrd married his childhood sweetheart, Marie D. Ames. Secretary of the Navy Josephus Daniels asked Byrd to serve as his aide on the USS *Dolphin*, but after a few months Byrd asked to be retired on a medical disability because his injured foot prevented him from performing regular naval duties. The political influence of his family enabled him to be promoted to Lieutenant J.G. and assigned as administrator of the naval militia of the state of Rhode Island upon his retirement. As a retired officer on active duty, he served in various posts for the next forty years.

Life's Work

During World War I, Byrd persuaded the Navy to allow him to enter flight training at the naval air station in Pensacola, Florida. He received his pilot's wings on April 7, 1917, and began making plans to be the first person to fly across the Atlantic. Wartime duties took him to Nova Scotia, where he helped to establish naval air stations. When the Navy was slow in supporting his plan for a transatlantic flight, he turned to his friend Walter Camp, the popular football coach at Yale University. With Camp's help, Byrd convinced the Navy to create the Transatlantic Flight Section of the Bureau of Aeronautics. Navy regulations prohibited Byrd from accompanying the flight he had organized, so he failed to share the glory of the crew of the NC-4 flying boat when it reached Lisbon, Portugal, on May 27, 1919. Undaunted, Byrd began planning a solo flight across the Atlantic. Navy orders again thwarted his dream when he was sent to England to assist in navigating a British-built dirigible to the United States. He was fortunate, however, when he missed a trial flight that ended in a fatal crash.

Byrd spent the next three years on aviation duty with the Bureau of Navigation. In 1925, he commanded a naval unit on an expedition to northern Greenland. Encouraged by his success in using airplanes in the Arctic, Byrd decided to enter the aerial race for the North Pole. The Norwegian explorer Roald Amundsen and the American aviator Lincoln Ellsworth flew to within a few hundred miles of the pole during the summer in which Byrd was in Greenland. Knowing that Amundsen, Ellsworth, and the Italian adventurer Umberto Nobile all had plans to fly to the pole, Byrd moved quickly. After being released from active duty with the Navy, he secured financial backing from Edsel Ford, organized a team of pilots and mechanics, and sailed for Spitzbergen Island. On May 9, 1926, he and Floyd Bennett flew north in a Fokker monoplane named *Josephine Ford* in honor of Edsel's daughter. Fifteen hours later, they returned with the news that they had flown over the pole. Although their claim would later be disputed, Byrd and Bennett returned to the United States as heroes. Both were awarded the Congressional Medal of Honor. In his book *Skyward* (1928), Byrd explains that they were considered heroes because "in us youth saw ambition realized."

In June, 1927, less than a month after Charles Lindbergh, Byrd finally flew across the Atlantic. Flying with Bert Acosta, Bernt Balchen, and George Noville in a Fokker trimotor, Byrd demonstrated that regular commercial transatlantic flights were practical, despite the fact that his plane was forced to crash-land on the French coast because of heavy fog in Paris. The energetic and ambitious Byrd now turned his attention to the South Pole. Receiving financial support from Ford, the Rockefellers, the Guggenheims, and others, Byrd sailed with forty-one men, ninety-four dogs, a Ford snowmobile, and three airplanes on two ships, the *City of New York* and the *Eleanor Bolling*.

On January 1, 1929, the party began building a base camp, Little America, on the ice shelf at the Bay of Whales. Eleven months later, on November 28 and 29, Byrd, Balchen, Harold June, and Ashley McKinley flew their Ford trimotor to the South Pole and back. In addition to the historic flight, the expedition mapped and photographed a large section of the unexplored continent; made geological, meteorological, and zoological observations; and proved the feasibility of a permanent base in Antarctica. Byrd again returned home to a hero's welcome, and Congress promoted him to the rank of rear admiral.

Three years later, in the depths of the Depression, Byrd organized a second Antarctic expedition, this time with fifty-five men, three airplanes, an autogyro (a forerunner of the helicopter), and several snowmobiles. After reestablishing Little America, Byrd sent a small party to build an advance base more than one hundred miles south, where he planned to station three men to make weather observations through the winter (April through August) of 1934. When storms prevented the planes and sledges from transporting enough supplies, Byrd decided to remain at Bolling Advance Base alone. Although he nearly died from inhaling carbon monoxide leaking from his stove, Byrd made most of his daily observations. The scientific achievements of the second expedition surpassed the first in many ways. The thickness of the ice was measured in several places, the outline of the continent was mapped more accurately, new astronomical and meteorological observations were made, and oceanographic data were collected.

The four-and-a-half-month struggle for survival at Advance Base left Byrd exhausted mentally and physically, and his career after 1935 was less spectacular than it had been. On the eve of World War II, President Franklin D. Roosevelt recalled Byrd to active duty and put him in command of the first government-sponsored Antarctic expedition since the voyage of Charles Wilkes in 1838-1842. During the war, Byrd helped find new air routes in the Pacific. In 1946, he returned to Antarctica with Operation Highjump, a naval exercise involving four thousand men, the largest expedition ever sent to that area. In 1955, he visited Antarctica for the fifth and last time during the International Geophysical Year (IGY) activities involving thirteen nations. He died two years later secure in the knowledge that he had contributed significantly to America's awareness of the importance of Antarctica and the need for international cooperation in scientific exploration.

Summary

Richard Byrd was a complex and controversial person. His drive and success aroused strong feelings, and he was never without his critics. In a sense, Edwin Hoyt is correct in calling him "the last explorer" of the generation of Amundsen, Robert Scott, and Robert Peary, a man driven by the desire to be the first to stand on uncharted ground and to survive incredible hardships.

Certainly his failure to be the first to fly the Atlantic and the little accidents that plagued his early naval career drove him to seek recognition in Antarctic exploration, but there is also a mystical side to Byrd's character. He confesses in *Alone* (1938) that he chose to remain at Bolling Advance Base by himself less for science than "for the sake of experience." He compares himself to Henry David Thoreau at Walden and to Robinson Crusoe. Ultimately he found a harmony with the universe in the freezing Antarctic night.

Byrd's plans for the first two Antarctic expeditions were as much an experiment in social organization as in natural science. There was a traditional American utopianism in the "constitution" he drew up for the government of Little America. "We have no class distinctions as in civilization," he wrote in *Alone*. "He who may have failed back there has his chance to make good here; and he will not be judged by the position he holds so much as by the way he plays the game and does his job, however humble it may be. . . ." Byrd played the game of life in the context of the social and economic upheavals of World War I and the Depression. The failures of the old world made the exploration of a new one all the more urgent. Utilizing the advances in airplane technology, aerial photography, and meteorological instruments, Byrd may also be called the "first explorer of the modern age."

Bibliography
Bertrand, Kenneth J. *Americans in Antarctica, 1775-1948.* New York: American Geographical Society, 1971. A scholarly history that places Byrd's expeditions in a larger context. Excellent bibliography.
Byrd, Richard E. *Alone.* New York: G. P. Putnam's Sons, 1938. Reprint. Los Angeles: Jeremy P. Tarcher, 1986. The most interesting of Byrd's books because it is the most personal. Byrd describes his struggle to survive alone for four and a half months in Antarctica. More than a diary, this book is a discussion of the reasons for seeking extreme hardships. Obviously written to establish the author's reputation as a literary adventurer, it bears comparison to Charles Lindbergh's *We* (1927) and Joshua Slocum's *Sailing Alone Around the World* (1900).
_____. *Discovery: The Story of the Second Byrd Antarctic Expedition.* New York: G. P. Putnam's Sons, 1935. Reprint. Detroit: Tower Books, 1971. Detailed history of the expedition of 1933-1935, omitting discussion of the solitary four and a half months at Advance Base. Good on equipment-testing and life in Little America.
_____. *Little America: Aerial Exploration in the Antarctic, the Flight to the South Pole.* New York: G. P. Putnam's Sons, 1930. Details of the first Byrd expedition, 1828-1930, and the building of Little America.
_____. *Skyward: Man's Mastery of the Air as Shown by the Brilliant Flights of America's Leading Air Explorer: His Life, His Thrilling Adventures, His North Pole and Trans-Atlantic Flights, Together with His Plans*

for Conquering the Antarctic by Air. New York: G. P. Putnam's Sons, 1928. Reprint. Chicago: Lakeside Books, 1981. Hastily written first book; the subtitle shows how Putnam promoted Byrd. Portions of this book had already appeared in magazines such as *Collier's, The Ladies Home Journal, The Saturday Evening Post*, and *National Geographic*.

Hoyt, Edwin P. *The Last Explorer*. New York: John Day Co., 1968. Written without access to Byrd's private papers, this will remain the most complete account of the great explorer's life until the publication of Peter J. Anderson's work, in progress.

Jackson, Donald Dale. *The Explorers*. Alexandria, Va.: Time-Life Books, 1983. Chapters on the flights by Byrd and others over both poles. Well illustrated with photographs, maps, and other material.

Parfit, Michael. *South Light: A Journey to the Last Continent*. New York: Macmillan, 1985. Updates Bertrand and describes conditions in Antarctica in the late twentieth century. Good discussion of the 1959 treaty under which fourteen nations maintain fifty-two year-round scientific stations without relying on territorial claims.

Rose, Lisle A. *Assault on Eternity: Richard E. Byrd and the Exploration of Antarctica, 1946-47*. Annapolis, Md.: Naval Institute Press, 1980. Detailed account of Operation Highjump, a naval training and scientific mission in which Byrd was marginally involved.

Bernard Mergen

JOHN CABOT

Born: c. 1450; Genoa?, Italy
Died: c. 1498; place unknown
Area of Achievement: Exploration
Contribution: Cabot persuaded Englishmen to explore new lands beyond the western horizon and laid the foundations of England's claim to and eventual control of the North American continent.

Early Life

Juan Caboto (John Cabot) was probably born in Genoa around 1450. By the early 1460's, he had moved to Venice, and in the late 1470's he became a citizen and married a Venetian named Mattea. Venice was then the center for Asian goods, especially spices, entering the European market. Thus Caboto became a merchant in the spice trade. He learned what he could about the trade by reading Marco Polo. A desire for direct knowledge and a willingness to venture his life prompted the young merchant to disguise himself as a Moslem and make the pilgrimage to Mecca. Whether the knowledge he gained through reading or travel helped him is doubtful. He was only one man in a city of wealthy merchants engaged in a trade that was already beginning to diminish, thanks to the Turkish control of the eastern Mediterranean.

Seeking broader economic opportunity, Caboto and his family settled in Valencia in 1490. Juan Caboto, the Venetian, as he became known, developed a reputation as a cartographer and navigator. In 1492, Caboto presented local officials with a proposal for harbor improvements. The project material was forwarded to King Ferdinand, then residing in Barcelona—two hundred miles along the coast above Valencia. Caboto had several audiences with the ruler to discuss the harbor proposal. That royal approval followed suggests how persuasive the arguments and the plans of the foreign expert could be. Unfortunately, the project was later abandoned. What is important about this incident is that it brought Juan Caboto to Barcelona at the time when Christopher Columbus entered to announce that he had reached the land of the Great Khan.

Caboto was skeptical. There was no evidence that Columbus had reached the densely populated and highly cultivated lands described by Marco Polo. Caboto tried to persuade potential backers in Seville that Columbus had reached only an island partway to his destination. Thus the wealth of the Indies could yet be attained by organizing an expedition under Caboto. While some Spaniards shared the doubts of Caboto, King Ferdinand and Queen Isabella did not. Besides, given the choice between two men from Genoa, it made sense to support the one who had already crossed the Atlantic Ocean and had returned with gold. Like Columbus, Caboto decided to move to where support for his project might be found.

In the late fifteenth century, Bristol was, after London, England's most active port, and its venturesome spirit was unmatched anywhere. Its ships carried local wool to Iceland and returned with dried codfish. Bristol merchants dominated the wine trade with Spain and Portugal. Always ready to try new trades, the merchants had sent ships to the eastern Mediterranean and to the islands of the Atlantic—especially Madeira. From the 1480's, Bristol ships made voyages of discovery seeking the legendary Isle of Brasil in the western Atlantic. The men of Bristol, both merchants and mariners, had more experience in the waters of the Atlantic than any men in any country. Naturally, John Cabot, as he was known thenceforth, selected Bristol as his new home and base of exploration.

Life's Work

Soon after his arrival in 1495, Cabot persuaded several Bristol merchants to try the westward route to Asia. A westward course in the high latitudes would bring a ship to the northeast part of Asia, which, Cabot argued, was much closer to Europe than the tropical region reached by Columbus. Cabot constructed a globe to demonstrate the advantages of his route. Like Columbus, Cabot reduced the size of the earth and increased the eastward limits of Asia to shorten the western route. The Cabot proposal was sent to King Henry VII.

Henry Tudor of England was famous for persuading reluctant subjects to make large contributions to the royal treasury. To such a ruler, Cabot's proposal was quite attractive. It was a second chance for the ruler who had rejected, in 1489, a similar scheme by Bartholomeo Columbus on behalf of his brother Christopher. Still, Henry VII was not about to risk his own money in a doubtful venture. He granted a patent to Cabot in March, 1496, to discover islands in the world unknown to Christians. Cabot would govern and receive the revenue (minus one-fifth for Henry VII) of the towns and islands he could "conquer, occupy and possess."

With the royal patent and the financial backing of some Bristol merchants, Cabot put to sea, only to return a short time later. Officially he returned because of a shortage of provisions. Unofficially, the crew probably lacked confidence in the foreign expert and decided to end the voyage. Masters of ships at this time had limited powers and generally acceded to the wishes of their crew. On his next voyage, for example, Cabot followed the wrong course and made his landfall on the French coast because his crew did not trust the more northerly (and correct) heading proposed by Cabot.

In May, 1497, Cabot tried again. His small ship was named *Matthew*—probably an Anglicized version of his wife's name, Mattea. Cabot and his crew of eighteen men sailed toward the southwest tip of Ireland and then headed directly west. The passage was swift, thanks to smooth seas and fair winds. Land was sighted on June 24, only thirty-three days after leaving Ireland. As late as the eighteenth century, ships might take three or four months to make the same passage. Some scholars believe that Cabot's speed is attributable to the fact that he timed his departure and course to coincide with favorable weather patterns learned by earlier voyagers from Bristol. Cabot probably made landfall at the northern tip of Newfoundland. That particular site had been settled briefly by Vikings nearly five hundred years earlier. The crew of the *Matthew* went ashore and raised the standards of Henry VII, the Pope, and Venice. Cabot claimed possession of the land but wisely kept his men near the water's edge; they had found evidence of local inhabitants. This brief ceremony was the only time that the men ventured ashore.

For the next month Cabot coasted along the foreign shore. Circumstances suggest that the *Matthew* sailed along the eastern coast of Newfoundland and then headed southwest past Nova Scotia to Maine. The southwest heading of the land mass matched the one Cabot had predicted for the easternmost area of Asia. The ship then turned home, crossed the Atlantic in fifteen days, and arrived at Bristol on August 6, 1497.

Cabot wasted no time. He left Bristol within hours of his arrival bound for London and Henry VII. Four days later the king received Cabot and presented him with honors and a pension (the latter to be paid by the Bristol Customs House). There was general agreement that Cabot had reached the northwest corner of Asia and that the next voyage would reach the Indies and the much-desired spice trade. Bristol merchants were also excited over the vast quantities of fish reported off the "new found land." Whatever became of the western passage, Bristol now possessed a new source of fish to replace the declining trade with Iceland. Thus Cabot's brief voyage of 1497 promised rich returns to merchants prepared to risk the trade with Asia and fish to men of more modest means and ambitions.

There was no shortage of backers for the follow-up voyage. Henry VII outfitted a large ship, and London and Bristol furnished four more vessels. This was not a voyage of exploration. Cabot expected to establish an island base to service British ships making the long passage to the Indies. If Cabot failed to build and hold such a base, then he possessed nothing and lacked a claim to any revenue from the Asian trade. Discovery entailed more than simply finding a site: One had to inhabit the site. (Columbus met this requirement when his flagship was wrecked and its crew built a camp ashore to await their leader's return from Spain.) Cabot's fleet departed in May, 1498. A storm struck the fleet, and one damaged ship entered an Irish port. There was no further news of the fleet.

There have been many guesses about the fate of Cabot's fleet. The discovery by Portuguese explorers in 1501 of Newfoundland Indians with several items of Italian origin provides a possible clue. Perhaps Cabot did establish his base during the mild Newfoundland summer. If so, then no one would have been prepared for the Arctic winter conditions common to the northern part of the island.

Summary

John Cabot, whose activities gave Great Britain its claim to North America, remains almost unknown to this day. There are few references to him. Unlike Columbus, Cabot left no journals to detail his work. Whereas Columbus had sons who preserved and enlarged their father's claim to fame, Cabot had Sebastian, a scoundrel who claimed his father's work as his own.

Cabot was not the first European to set upon the North American continent. The Vikings certainly came earlier, and in turn they may have been preceded by Romans and Greeks a thousand years before. Cabot's arrival, however, was different. He was the first of a constant stream of European explorers. Cabot ended the ancient isolation of the North American continent. The charts he made during the voyage of 1497 have long since disappeared. His contemporaries, however, made use of the charts. Juan de La Cosa's famous world map of 1500 shows a series of Tudor banners along the coast visited by Cabot.

It is customary to note the similarities in the lives and careers of Cabot and Columbus. Both were born in the same Italian city at about the same time (although in Cabot's case, place of birth is not certain); both convinced foreign monarchs to back a search for a westward route to Asia. While Columbus achieved greater fame and fortune, he lived long enough to suffer greater disgrace. Cabot the explorer simply disappeared and left all controversy behind. He died an explorer's death.

Bibliography

Beazley, Sir Charles Raymond. *John and Sebastian Cabot: The Discovery of North America*. London: T. Fisher Unwin, 1898. With the people of the United States and Italy engaged in many celebrations over the four hundredth anniversary of Columbus' voyage to America, there was an attempt by English historians to commemorate John Cabot and strengthen his claim as the discoverer of North America. This biography was part of that effort. Although many of the author's conclusions are now questioned, the work does contain useful details about John Cabot.

Davis, Ralph. *The Rise of the Atlantic Economies*. Ithaca, N.Y.: Cornell University Press, 1973. Although only the first chapter of this book deals with fifteenth century exploration, the author's description and analysis of the maritime trades that used the Atlantic Ocean is unequaled.

Harrisse, Henry. *John Cabot, the Discoverer of North America, and Sebastian, His Son*. London: B. F. Stevens, 1896. Like the Beazley biography, this volume is best viewed as part of the late nineteenth century effort to make Americans aware of the role of England in the discovery and exploration of North America.

Morison, Samuel Elliot. *The European Discovery of America: The Northern Voyages, A.D. 500-1600.* New York: Oxford University Press, 1971. The most famous maritime scholar and the leading authority on Columbus presents detailed chapters on all known explorers. The book is distinguished by excellent charts and photographs of the possible landfalls of the various explorers.

Parry, J. H. *Discovery of the Sea.* New York: Dial Press, 1974. The preeminent maritime historian discusses the development of skills and technologies that opened up maritime exploration in the fifteenth and sixteenth centuries.

Penrose, Boles. *Travel and Discovery in the Renaissance.* Cambridge, Mass.: Harvard University Press, 1952. A fascinating study of how scholars and navigators, from the time of ancient Greece to fifteenth century Europe, viewed the world.

Quinn, David Beers. *England and the Discovery of America: 1481-1620.* New York: Alfred A. Knopf, 1974. Though working with very limited sources, the author presents a strong case for the discovery of North America by English seamen before Columbus.

Skelton, R. A. *Explorers' Maps: Chapters in the Cartographic Record of Geographical Discovery.* London: Routledge and Kegan Paul, 1958. An outstanding description of how the discoveries of explorers were incorporated into the rapidly changing world maps of sixteenth century cartographers.

Williamson, James A. *The Cabot Voyages and Bristol Discovery Under Henry VII.* Cambridge, Mass.: Harvard University Press, 1962. In addition to presenting the best balanced account of Cabot's work, the author has assembled all known documents about the explorer so that the reader may draw his own conclusions.

Joseph A. Goldenberg

JOHN C. CALHOUN

Born: March 18, 1782; Abbeville District, South Carolina
Died: March 31, 1850; Washington, D.C.
Areas of Achievement: Politics and political theory
Contribution: In addition to wielding great influence in national politics for
   four decades, Calhoun wrote incisively on the problem of protecting
   minority rights against majority rule in a democracy.

Early Life

John C. Calhoun was born on March 18, 1782. His birthplace was a settlement on the Savannah River in South Carolina, near the modern Abbeville. Of Scotch-Irish ancestry, Calhoun's forebears had made their way from
Pennsylvania to Bath County, Virginia, then had been forced to migrate to
South Carolina by the turmoil of the French and Indian War (1754-1760).
The Up Country—as the western part of South Carolina is called—was a
wild, untamed region, as evidenced by the murder of Calhoun's grandmother
by marauding Cherokees in 1760. Calhoun's father, Patrick, was the youngest
of four brothers who tenaciously carved out lives in the wilderness surrounding "Calhoun's Settlement." Patrick's first wife having died, he married Martha Caldwell, with whom he produced a daughter and four sons; the next-to-
youngest child was named John Caldwell, after one of Martha's brothers.

Calhoun spent his youth on the family farm working in the fields with his
father's slaves. Patrick's death in 1796 left John with a future seemingly
bound by the needs of the farm and responsibilities to his family. Yet upon
the urging of an older brother, he enrolled in Yale College in 1802 and was
graduated with honors in 1804.

After Yale, Calhoun studied law at Tapping Reeve's Litchfield (Connecticut) Academy. During the two-year regimen at Litchfield, he developed habits in logic and discipline that would be his trademark in later years. Yet he
also discovered that the prospect of being an attorney bored him. A stint in
Henry De Saussure's Charleston law office and, shortly thereafter, his opening a successful practice of his own near Abbeville did not enliven his interest. He soon left the profession to become a prosperous planter and to follow
his consuming interest in politics.

This career change was made possible by his marriage, in 1811, to his second cousin, Floride Bonneau Calhoun. The marriage brought Calhoun property which, when added to his, allowed him financial independence. Although Floride was ten years his junior, they were quite happy, and the
marriage produced nine children. Calhoun would eventually establish residence at a plantation he built near his birthplace. He named it "Fort Hill"
because the site once had been a garrison against Indian attack.

By the time of his marriage, Calhoun had developed those traits that would distinguish him for the remainder of his life. Physically imposing, standing over six feet tall, lanky, and with a rather hawklike face, he was craggily handsome. As the years wore away at him, ceaseless labor and care combined with checkered health to render the stern countenance fixed in the minds of students by the photograph taken by Matthew Brady around 1848. In it, Calhoun, nearing sixty, sits with a face that is lined, hollow, and unsmiling, yet lit by an arresting and wild stare. Perhaps this face was merely a mirror of his lifelong personality. Even as a boy, he was overly serious, and he seems to have always conducted relationships outside his family with the same cold logic he applied to his political theories. Anything but outgoing, Calhoun commanded respect but seldom inspired affection. Associates sometimes referred to him as the "cast iron man," describing a man who, while not unfriendly, nevertheless remained ever aloof and hence, on a personal level, essentially alone and friendless.

Life's Work

Calhoun entered state politics in 1807 and, after one term in the South Carolina legislature, won election to the United States House of Representatives in 1810. There he joined the ranks of the War Hawks, that group of influential congressmen (Speaker of the House Henry Clay was the most conspicuous of their number) who were intent upon war with Great Britain to protect American maritime rights.

During the War of 1812, Calhoun steadfastly supported all measures to bolster the nation's failing defenses. When the Treaty of Ghent ended the war in 1814, he remained convinced that it was only a truce before the renewal of the conflict. Beginning in 1816, he urged the adoption of a national program to prepare for another wave of British aggression. He supported a protective tariff, a national bank, an improved transportation system through federally financed internal improvements, and a large standing army. His nationalism won for him both praise and a place in James Monroe's cabinet as secretary of war in 1817. Seeking to correct the many flaws made apparent by the poor showing of American forces in the recent war with Britain, Calhoun initiated numerous improvements for the army. These included the establishment of new departments, especially those of commissary, quartermaster, and surgeon general. Well suited to the administrative demands of the War Department, he filled the post during Monroe's two terms with a flair for innovative management.

Calhoun adroitly remained aloof from the angry political turmoil that marked the end of the Era of Good Feelings and the beginning of the formation of a new national party system. Elected to the vice presidency in 1824 and 1828, he thus served in the administrations of both John Quincy Adams and Andrew Jackson, despite the bitter feud between the two. At the end of the 1820's, it appeared that he would succeed Andrew Jackson as president with Jackson's blessing, but the nullification controversy in South Carolina irrevocably estranged them and nearly ruined Calhoun's political career.

In spite of his earlier advocacy of the protective tariff, he became convinced that steadily increasing its duties financially victimized Southern agriculturalists for the benefit of Northern industrialists. When he wrote "South Carolina Exposition and Protest" in 1828, which stated his theory of Nullification, it marked a significant turning point in his political career. Because he still hoped to attain the presidency, he kept secret his authorship of the doctrine. By turns, however, he rapidly transformed from an American nationalist into a Southern sectionalist. Elaborating upon Thomas Jefferson's ideas in the Kentucky Resolutions of 1798, Calhoun declared that a state could nullify a federal law it deemed unconstitutional or harmful to its interests by refusing to enforce the statute within its borders. Essentially then, Nullification was a device whereby a minority could protect itself against the harmful will of the majority.

When South Carolina attempted to apply his theory by nullifying the Tariff of 1832, it brought the nation to the brink of civil war. Dismissing Nullification as illegal, Jackson threatened to invade South Carolina to enforce federal law, and when it was revealed that Calhoun was the doctrine's father, Jackson branded him a subversive. In disgrace with the Administration, Calhoun resigned the vice presidency, his national reputation in shambles. Yet the governor of South Carolina promptly appointed him to the Senate, and there he worked feverishly with Henry Clay to draft a compromise tariff that helped to diminish the immediate crisis.

After the Nullification controversy, Calhoun dropped all vestiges of his earlier nationalism and became the champion of Southern planter interests in particular and Southern rights in general. In the process, he earned the admiration of many Southerners, and in South Carolina he came to exert virtually total control over a political system which only occasionally was not a reflection of his will. His towering reputation and talent made him a fixture in the Senate, wherein he increasingly focused his intellectual and political energies on combatting what he perceived as Northern assaults upon the Southern way of life. Even his brief absence from the Senate—to serve as John Tyler's secretary of state from 1844 to 1845—was marked by his sectionalism: He successfully managed the annexation of Texas into the Union as a slave state.

As a strident antislavery movement grew in the North, Calhoun countered that slavery was a positive good. He opposed the Mexican War (which most of his Southern colleagues supported) because he feared that Northerners would try to exclude slavery from Western territories gained in the conflict. When his fears proved true, he was ultimately persuaded that Northern restriction of slavery in the territories was a preliminary step toward the thorough abolition of the institution in the South as well. The result, he thought, would be economic and social chaos, avoidable only by the South's secession from the Union.

His apprehension over both abolitionism and secession compelled him in his final months to attempt the unification of the South into an implacable front threatening secession. By so menacing the Union he hoped to frighten the North into concessions on the slavery question. Therein lay the safety of the South and the Union as well. His plan was unsuccessful, and as the nation reeled ominously toward disruption under the compounded sectional crises of 1850, he appeared before the Senate on March 4, 1850, almost for the last time. So ill that a colleague had to read his speech, Calhoun sat glowering from his chair as the chamber and crowded galleries heard his dire prediction that Northern agitation over the slavery issue would inevitably destroy the Union. His warning, unhappily prophetic, went unheeded. As the nation strained toward yet another compromise, his shattered health forced him to his deathbed. He died on March 31, 1850, in his Washington quarters. His last words were "The South . . . the poor South."

Summary

John C. Calhoun ranks as one of the most innovative political theorists in American history. Beginning with his complex arguments to justify Nullification, he ever afterward sought legal and logical means whereby to protect minority rights against the overriding and insensible will of the majority. His fears over the diminishing influence of the South in national councils drove him, in 1843, to begin drafting proposals for significant innovations in American constitutional government. The notion of the concurrent majority became central to his thesis in both *A Disquisition on Government* (1851) and *A Discourse on the Constitution of the United States* (1851).

In these works, Calhoun declared that the nation was composed of not only sections and states but also communities, each of these last possessing a unique character and interests different from the rest. The problem lay in the fact that any one community might be significantly smaller in relation to the others. The great danger in a democracy thoroughly wedded to majority rule, he insisted, was that a combination of larger communities could unjustly impose its will on any such minority through sheer force of numbers, ignoring the rights and privileges of the injured community. The resulting tyranny of the majority would be the very antithesis of the American ideal of government.

In order to avoid this result, he proposed that each unique community, regardless of its size, be given an equal voice in matters affecting the whole nation. A majority obtained under this arrangement would not reflect merely numerical strength, but would assure a general concurrence from all sectors of the society. In short, a concurrent majority would protect the rights of any minority. To reinforce the method further, he proposed instituting a dual presidency, one executive from each major section, each to have a veto on national measures.

Neither *A Discourse on the Constitution of the United States* nor *A Disquisition on Government* was completed when he died—indeed, his involvement in the sectional controversy of 1850 and his labors on these manuscripts combined to destroy his health—but they were published posthumously in 1851. They were lauded at the time by many Southerners and scorned by many Northerners, but Calhoun's theories were complicated and the occasionally obscure prose of the former work, and the latter work was often misunderstood. As the nation stumbled toward the disruption he had predicted, and after it had suffered the terrible Civil War, he was dismissed as both an ugly prophet of secession and a major cause of the catastrophe that followed.

Undoubtedly, before the Civil War he influenced in some degree the thinking of virtually every Southerner and, it might be argued, a significant number of Northerners. Yet subsequent scholarship has been unable to reach a consensus about Calhoun and the real meaning of the theories he produced. Cited as a major contributor to the outbreak of the Civil War, he also has been praised for tirelessly searching for ways to avoid it. Branded as little more than a sophisticated opportunist, always seeking his own advancement, he also has been eulogized as a careful statesman, aloof from the ordinary concerns of office and election. Labeled a stultifying obstructionist of the majority will, he also has been hailed as an innovative protector of minority rights.

In spite of the diversity of interpretation, one certainty emerges. For all of his imagination and mental agility, Calhoun never escaped the boundaries of his time and place. He bent his considerable talents to protecting and even extending the institution of slavery, a mockery of the ideals of liberty and, even in his time, disgraced by the considered judgment of mankind. Possessed of boundless vision, he yet remained blind to the fundamental evil of slavery and thus was at once a great man and a tragic figure.

Bibliography
Calhoun, John C. *The Papers of John C. Calhoun*. Edited by Frank M. Merriwether, Edwin W. Hemphill, and Clyde N. Wilson. 16 vols. Columbia: University of South Carolina Press, 1959-1985. An ambitious project consisting of Calhoun's papers from 1801 to 1843, with skillful editorial comment integrated throughout.
Capers, Gerald M. *John C. Calhoun, Opportunist: A Reappraisal*. Gainesville: University of Florida Press, 1960. A revisionist biography which argues that self-interest was the primary motive for all of Calhoun's actions. Marred by a polemical tone, but valuable as a counterweight to uncritical biographers.
Coit, Margaret L. *John C. Calhoun: An American Portrait*. Boston:

Houghton Mifflin Co., 1950. Pulitzer Prize–winning biography that offers an extraordinarily favorable view of its subject. Coit lauds the agrarian ideal and praises Calhoun as its defender who resisted the evils of an industrial society. The most humanized depiction of Calhoun, but frequently overly sympathetic.

_____, ed. *John C. Calhoun*. Englewood Cliffs, N.J.: Prentice-Hall, 1970. A brief compilation consisting of selections from Calhoun's writings, contemporary observations about him, and scholarly interpretations regarding his political theories. A good introductory survey of the diversity of modern scholarly opinion concerning those theories.

Freehling, William. *Prelude to Civil War: The Nullification Controversy in South Carolina, 1816-1836*. New York: Harper and Row, Publishers, 1965. An excellent work on the great crisis which marked Calhoun's shift from nationalism to sectionalism. Includes a good description of his reluctant participation in the event and provides a penetrating analysis of the real significance of Nullification.

Hamilton, Holman. *Prologue to Conflict: The Crisis and Compromise of 1850*. Lexington: University Press of Kentucky, 1964. An indispensable study of the complex problems afflicting the nation at the time of Calhoun's death. His significant part in the drama is competently portrayed and explained.

Lindsey, David. *Andrew Jackson and John C. Calhoun*. Woodbury, N.Y.: Barron's Educational Series, 1973. Dual biography of these major figures that is surprisingly thorough, given its brevity. Offers a good introduction to Jackson and Calhoun and is marked by measured judgments supported by broad research.

Spain, August O. *The Political Theory of John C. Calhoun*. New York: Bookman's Associates, 1951. A learned and well-researched exposition of the origin, development, and maturation of Calhoun's theories on government, but flawed by Spain's defense of Calhoun's racial attitudes.

Wiltse, Charles M. *John C. Calhoun, Nationalist, 1782-1828*. Indianapolis: Bobbs-Merrill Co., 1944.

_____. *John C. Calhoun, Nullifier, 1829-1839*. Indianapolis: Bobbs-Merrill Co., 1949.

_____. *John C. Calhoun, Sectionalist, 1839-1850*. Indianapolis: Bobbs-Merrill Co., 1951. Grounded in decades of research and loaded with a wealth of detail, these three works (this and the two previous entries) comprise an almost definitive biography. Especially good in placing Calhoun in perspective with the social, economic, and political forces of the early nineteenth century, but somewhat imbalanced by an overly sympathetic view of Calhoun and his ideas while hypercritical of his adversaries.

David S. Heidler

BENJAMIN NATHAN CARDOZO

Born: May 24, 1870; New York, New York
Died: July 9, 1938; Port Chester, New York
Area of Achievement: Law
Contribution: Cardozo's twenty-five-year career on the New York Court of Appeals and the United States Supreme Court made him one of the most admired and respected judges in American history. As a scholar, he illuminated the nature of the judicial process; as a judge, he helped transform American law to meet the needs of a changing, modern society.

Early Life

Benjamin Nathan Cardozo was born in New York City on May 24, 1870, to one of the most prominent Sephardic Jewish families in the United States. Ancestors on both sides could be traced back to the seventeenth century and included distinguished rabbis, educators, businessmen, lawyers, and writers, including the poet Emily Lazarus, whose words grace the Statue of Liberty. His mother, Rebecca Nathan Cardozo, was noted for her beauty and culture. She was descended from a family that had made important contributions to the American Revolutionary cause in the eighteenth century. His father, Albert, was one of the most brilliant judges on the New York State Supreme Court.

Yet Benjamin's youth was marked by a number of tragedies which profoundly influenced the course of his life. Shortly after his birth, an uncle for whom he had been named, Benjamin Nathan, was murdered in his New York City town house under mysterious circumstances. When he was three years old, his father was forced to resign from the court amid charges of corrupt involvement with the infamous Boss Tweed and the notorious financier Jay Gould. Six years later, Cardozo's beloved mother died, leaving the eldest daughter, Ellen, to care for Benjamin, his twin sister, Emily, an older brother, Albert, and two other daughters.

The resulting publicity left an already private family more determined to isolate itself from the outside world. Thus, Benjamin received his early education through private tutors at home. One of these was the famous writer Horatio Alger. He easily passed the entrance exams for Columbia University, graduating in 1889, at the top of his class. He then entered Columbia Law School but left after two years to begin legal practice (at that time a law school degree was not a universal requirement for admission to the bar).

Cardozo's father died in 1885. Benjamin never married and continued to live with his older sister, Ellen, until her death in 1929. Sheltered and in frail health as a child, he grew to be reserved and almost painfully shy as an adult. At the same time, his charm, humility, and gentleness were almost legendary. He was of medium stature, his face characterized by an almost feminine softness, with pale blue eyes beneath bushy eyebrows and a shock of pale, fine hair.

Life's Work

Cardozo began his career in law working in his brother Albert's New York City law firm. His deceptively gentle personality hid an advocate of remarkable persuasiveness, and he soon established a reputation as an outstanding corporate and commercial attorney. Although he stayed out of politics and bar activities, his name was put forth as a judicial candidate in 1913 by reformers anxious to wrest control of New York government from the Tammany Hall political machine. Cardozo narrowly won election to the state supreme court (the intermediate appellate court in New York). Shortly after he assumed his position on this court, the governor appointed him to a temporary vacancy on the state's highest court, the court of appeals. In 1917, he was made a regular member of that tribunal and was elected with bipartisan support to a fourteen-year term.

Within a few years, Cardozo became the dominant intellectual force on the court of appeals, and in 1926 became its chief judge as well. He also helped solidify that court's reputation as one of the preeminent state high courts in the nation. The primary work of such courts involved issues of private law, such as contract liability, commercial relations, wills and estates, property, and torts (private wrongs). It was in these areas that Cardozo made many of his most important contributions, primarily by reformulating many of the formal doctrines and precedents of the nineteenth century common law to fit the changing realities of an urban, industrial, and increasingly complex society.

Several examples from among Cardozo's many opinions illustrate this process. Perhaps the classic example of Cardozo jurisprudence was his 1916 opinion in the case *MacPherson v. Buick Motor Company*. Mr. MacPherson was driving his motor car when one of the wheels, later proved to be made of defective wood, crumbled, causing MacPherson to be thrown from the car and injured. Under traditional legal doctrine, MacPherson should have sued the dealer who had sold him the defective car, not the manufacturer, with whom he had had no dealings. Through clever reasoning and eloquent language, however, Cardozo gave the plaintiff a cause of action against the third-party manufacturer. This decision marked a whole new direction in product liability law, for now manufacturers of products, increasingly important in a society that was rapidly becoming consumer oriented, were now on notice that they must exercise care in the production of their goods or suffer the consequences.

Another of Cardozo's famous court of appeals decisions involved a rather remarkable set of factual circumstances. A railroad conductor on a commuter train inadvertently jostled a passenger who was attempting to board the train at the last moment. The passenger dropped a package which happened to contain fireworks. The resulting explosion caused a set of scales at the other end of the station platform to fall, injuring a nearby passenger and her child, who were waiting for another train. In *Palsgraf v. Long Island R.R.*, Cardozo ruled that the railroad company was not liable for the harm done to Mrs. Palsgraf and her baby, thereby setting off in new directions previously accepted nineteenth century doctrines of strict liability and causation of wrongful acts.

Cardozo's intellect and style reached a wider audience in 1921, with the publication of a series of lectures he delivered at Yale University entitled *The Nature of the Judicial Process*. This and subsequent short works, *The Growth of the Law* (1924) and *The Paradoxes of Legal Science* (1928), firmly established him as one of the finest legal minds in the country. As the titles suggest, Cardozo was less interested in what the law should be than in how judges go about deciding what the law is. While recognizing traditional reliance on formal logic and past decisions on the judicial process, he argued that other factors were and should be taken into account by judges in reaching their decisions. Larger economic and social ends are and should be part of judicial decision making, enabling judges, if necessary, to "bend symmetry, ignore history, and sacrifice custom" in pursuit of these larger ends.

By 1930, Cardozo had become one of the most celebrated jurists in the country. When, in 1932, Justice Oliver Wendell Holmes, Jr., resigned from the United States Supreme Court, there was near-unanimous approval when President Herbert Hoover appointed Cardozo to the seat left vacant by the man Cardozo himself always referred to as "the Master." Although he made much of his unworthiness to replace his friend and mentor and complained about having to leave the congenial atmosphere of the court of appeals in Albany for the uncertainties of the more public and demanding life in Washington, Cardozo readily accepted his nomination (it has been suggested that Cardozo's famed humility and reserve masked a compelling ambition to eradicate the stain on the family name resulting from his father's disgrace).

At the time Cardozo took his seat on the Supreme Court, the United States was in the midst of confronting the Great Depression. Worsening economic conditions helped produce the landslide victory of Franklin D. Roosevelt in 1932 and the subsequent passage of a barrage of New Deal federal economic reforms and regulations. The great uncertainty was how the Supreme Court would view the constitutionality of these programs. Throughout the 1920's, the Court had consistently struck down federal and state economic and social legislation. This practice was generally followed despite the dissents of the three "liberals" on the Court, Oliver Wendell Holmes, Louis D. Brandeis, and Harlan Fiske Stone.

During the first years of the New Deal, the Court continued this trend, striking down many of the most important attempts to deal with the plight of

American workers and farmers. In most of these cases, Cardozo found himself in the minority, dissenting along with Brandeis and Stone. Then, in 1937, Roosevelt unveiled his plan to pack the Court with new appointees. The Supreme Court in turn made what was called "the switch in time that saved nine" (whether there was a direct cause-and-effect relationship between the plan and the switch is a matter of debate). The Court began upholding New Deal legislation: Cardozo, for example, authored the Court's decision in *Helvering v. Davis* (1937), which upheld the constitutionality of the Social Security Act.

During these years, the Court had also begun slowly to deal with more cases and issues involving civil liberties and the Bill of Rights. In the 1920's, the Court had extended for the first time the protections of the First Amendment to the states, using as its justification the "due process" clause of the Fourteenth Amendment. In *Palko v. Connecticut* (1937), Cardozo, speaking for the majority, greatly expanded this doctrine. He held that while the entire Bill of Rights was not applicable, or incorporated, to the states, those provisions that partook "of the very essence of a scheme of ordered liberty" were. This doctrine became the guiding force in the Court's expansion of civil liberties protections involving state action over the next quarter century.

During the latter months of 1937, Cardozo experienced a series of heart problems, and on January 8, 1938, he suffered a stroke that left him partially paralyzed. Although he refused to resign from the Court, his continuing poor health forced him to move to the home of his longtime friend, Judge Irving Lehman, in Port Chester, New York. There he died on July 9, 1938.

Summary

Although he served for only a brief time on the Supreme Court, Cardozo is generally conceded to be among the great chief justices, in part because he came to the Court already a legend. His work on the court of appeals alone had an enormous impact on the development of American law in the twentieth century, and his opinions in private and commercial law cases became required study for law students everywhere—not only for the legal principles involved but also as models of legal reasoning and linguistic elegance.

Moreover, Cardozo does not easily fit into the simple categories of "liberal" or "conservative" often used to characterize Supreme Court justices. In his belief in the evolutionary and progressive nature of the law and his willingness to use the law for economic and social reform, he reflected the basic tenets of American liberal thought in the twentieth century. Similarly, his tolerance and commitment to human rights and his extension of Bill of Rights protections would place him in the liberal camp. Yet his consistent warnings and urgings to judges to exercise restraint, to defer to the wishes of the people as expressed in their legislative bodies, were reflective of conservative doctrine in the United States, especially after the 1950's.

Bibliography

Abraham, Henry J. *Justices and Presidents*. New York: Oxford University Press, 1974. A fascinating and highly readable history of Supreme Court appointments, including a small section on Cardozo's nomination by Hoover. Also includes the 1970 survey in which law professors and historians ranked Cardozo among the twelve great Supreme Court justices.

Cardozo, Benjamin N. *The Nature of the Judicial Process*. New Haven, Conn.: Yale University Press, 1921. Cardozo's best-known work, a short book, but one filled with insights on the role and function of judges and the impact of history, tradition, and sociology on the judicial process.

_____. *Selected Writings of Benjamin Nathan Cardozo*. Edited by Margaret E. Hall. New York: Fallon Publications, 1947. A collection of Cardozo's writings and speeches outside the courtroom. They display the broad range of his intellect and his interests.

Harvard Law Review 52 (1939). The entire issue is dedicated to memorial tributes to and essays on Cardozo's contributions to public law, the law of contracts, and the law of torts. It was published simultaneously with the *Columbia Law Review* (39, 1939) and the *Yale Law Journal* (volume 48, 1939).

Hellman, George S. *Benjamin N. Cardozo: American Judge*. New York: McGraw-Hill Book Co., 1940. Written by a family friend, this is the most detailed account of Cardozo's personal life. Very good on his family and friendships, but almost worshipful.

Levy, Beryl H. *Cardozo and the Frontiers of Legal Thinking*. New York: Oxford University Press, 1938. A selection of some of Cardozo's opinions. With the exception of his decision in *Helvering v. Davis*, all are from his years on the New York Court of Appeals. There is also a readable introductory essay by Levy with a biographical sketch and an outline of Cardozo's thought.

White, G. Edward. "Cardozo, Learned Hand, and Frank: The Dialectic of Freedom and Constraint." In *The American Judicial Tradition*, 251-291. New York: Oxford University Press, 1976. In this perceptive analysis of important American judges, White places Cardozo in the context of American legal development. Cardozo, Learned Hand, and Jerome Frank were not only friends and colleagues but also shared the philosophy of "judicial restraint."

Robert M. Goldman

ANDREW CARNEGIE

Born: November 25, 1835; Dunfermline, Scotland
Died: August 11, 1919; Lenox, Massachusetts
Areas of Achievement: Steel manufacturing and philanthropy
Contribution: One of the wealthiest men in the world at the time of his
retirement from business in 1901, Carnegie achieved great fame for his
business success and for his many benefactions, which became the chief
interest of his later years.

Early Life

Andrew Carnegie was born November 25, 1835, in Dunfermline, Scotland.
His father, William Carnegie, a prosperous handloom weaver at the time of
Andrew's birth, was unable to compete with the new technology of steam
looms and fell into poverty as Andrew grew older. Andrew's mother, Margaret Morrison Carnegie, proved under these circumstances to be the bulwark of the family. Ambitious for her two sons, Andrew and younger brother
Thomas, she organized a move to the United States in 1848.

They settled in Allegheny, Pennsylvania, where they had relatives and
attempted to rebuild the family's fortunes. Although William Carnegie was
never again a success, the family got by through hard work and timely assistance from the Pittsburgh area's close-knit Scottish community. Working
long, hard hours in factories, Andrew improved his skills, learning double-
entry bookkeeping in night school, and in barely a year left factory work to
become a telegraph messenger in 1849, an operator in 1851, and in 1853, secretary and personal telegrapher to Tom Scott, superintendent of the Pennsylvania Railroad's western division.

Life's Work

Carnegie remained with the Pennsylvania Railroad for a dozen years,
acquiring managerial skills and a sharp insight into the economic principles
of the capitalist economy, and forming close personal relationships with several entrepreneurs who were to prove instrumental in his own success. Scott,
who delegated increasing responsibility to the resourceful Carnegie, became
vice president in 1859; he then named Carnegie superintendent of the western division, perhaps the most challenging position of its kind with any
railroad in the United States. The demands of the Civil War would vastly
increase his responsibilities, but Carnegie proved equal to them. At Scott's
behest, he organized the movement of Union troops into beleaguered Washington in April, 1861, restored regular rail service between Washington and
the north, and stayed in the capital for some months as Scott's assistant in
charge of railroads and telegraph services (Scott had been appointed assistant secretary of war with special responsibility for railroads). Carnegie then

returned to Pittsburgh to resume his duties with the Pennsylvania Railroad.

Carnegie was already losing interest in a salaried position. On a tip from Scott, he had purchased six hundred dollars' worth of stock in the Adams Express Company in 1856. The first dividend check he received was a revelation, and legend has it that Carnegie, thrilled to realize that he could earn money without physical toil, exclaimed, "Here's the goose that lays the golden eggs." More investments followed: in the Woodruff Sleeping Car Company, the Columbia Oil Company, and the Keystone Bridge Company, in which Carnegie held a one-fifth interest, enough to make him the dominant shareholder.

By 1863, Carnegie was earning more than forty thousand dollars annually from his investments, several times his salary, and left the Pennsylvania Railroad at the end of the Civil War to devote more of his time to the management of Keystone and to the Union Iron Mills, which was a principal supplier of Keystone. Carnegie left the operating decisions to experts in bridge construction, while concentrating on sales and finances. With Keystone, he secured contracts to sell materials to such projects as the Eads Bridge at St. Louis, the Ohio River bridges at Cincinnati and Point Pleasant, West Virginia, and the Brooklyn Bridge.

Carnegie's involvement in finance required that he travel often to Europe, and his life-style changed. Always interested in the world of ideas, he never allowed his lack of formal education to keep him from broadening his knowledge. He read extensively and cultivated friendships in Europe and in New York City, to which he moved with his mother in 1867. A bachelor throughout these years, Carnegie enjoyed the companionship of women and led an active social life. He also actively sought the company of intellectuals and eventually would count among his friends the British statesman William Gladstone and literary figures such as Matthew Arnold, Richard Watson Gilder, John Morley, Herbert Spencer, and Mark Twain. A man of much personal charm, the small-statured Carnegie—he stood but five feet, three inches tall—was equally at ease discussing ideas with the learned and business with financiers or potential customers.

Carnegie was still not content with his lot in life, for he believed that he had become too involved in financial speculation and wished instead to turn to manufacturing, which he considered a more constructive and respectable pursuit. His familiarity with the needs of railroads made him believe that there were large profits to be made in steel, for improved rails would be needed in immense quantities. In 1872, he organized a partnership, drawing on Pittsburgh business acquaintances of long duration to establish Carnegie, McCandless and Company to manufacture steel by the Bessemer process. After several reorganizations involving many different combinations of partners over the years, this firm would become known as Carnegie Steel Company, Limited, in 1892. By 1874, the gigantic new Edgar Thomson Works was under construction, its development supervised by Alexander Holley, the foremost American expert on the Bessemer process, and its operations turned over to Bill Jones, who brought in top-notch department heads from other companies. Characteristically, Carnegie turned over the day-to-day operations to experts such as Jones, while he concentrated on sales and finances, employing the efficient cost-based management techniques learned in the railroad business.

Always alert to technological improvements that would lower the cost of production and lead to increased sales and profits, within a decade, Carnegie introduced to his plants the open-hearth steel production process. Carnegie's business philosophy led him to expand and diversify. In the mid-1880's, his organization acquired the massive Homestead Works and developed a major new market by selling steel structural members to the elevated railways and skyscrapers which were beginning to appear in major American cities.

In 1880, Carnegie met Louise Whitfield, the twenty-three-year-old daughter of a prominent New York merchant. Louise endured the tribulations of a relationship troubled by Carnegie's frequent and extended business travel. Moreover, he initially refused to marry, out of deference to his mother's wishes. The two were finally married in 1887, less than a year after the death of Carnegie's mother. The couple had one daughter.

At the time of his marriage, Carnegie was a millionaire several times over. The 1890's brought more prosperity, as well as some of Carnegie's greatest disappointments. The prosperity came in substantial measure from Carnegie's faith in the continued growth of the American economy and the business acumen of Henry Clay Frick. Chairman of the company since 1889, Frick conducted an aggressive campaign of expansion and cost-cutting which led to one of the bitterest episodes in American labor history, the Homestead Strike of 1892. During this period, Carnegie remained in virtual seclusion in Scotland, giving Frick authority to handle negotiations with the Amalgamated Association of Iron and Steel Workers. The labor-management strife led to intense press criticism of Carnegie in both England and the United States and, along with other issues, precipitated a split between Carnegie and Frick.

Carnegie, who held an interest of more than fifty percent in the firm, resumed a more active role in company affairs, forcing Frick out as chief operating executive at the end of 1894 and leading the business to its most profitable years. The key was Carnegie's success in increasing the firm's share of the market during the depression of the 1890's, acquiring ownership of more of its basic raw materials, its own railroads and its fleet of ore-carrying ships, and its modernizing facilities. Carnegie Steel's annual profits grew eight hundred percent between 1895 and 1900. In Charles Schwab, a brilliant executive totally loyal to Carnegie, the company at last had a worthy successor to Frick.

At the end of the 1890's, new troubles arose from competitors. On the one hand, Carnegie relished a fight; on the other hand, he was willing to sell out, provided the price was right. It was—nearly $500,000,000, of which Carnegie's share was $300,000,000 in five percent first-mortgage bonds in the successor company, United States Steel. The investment banker J. P. Morgan, who had handled the transaction, said that Carnegie was "the richest man in the world." While a similar claim has been made for Carnegie's contemporary, John D. Rockefeller, there is no doubt that Carnegie had built one of the most formidable business enterprises of the nineteenth century; Carnegie Steel produced more than the combined output of the entire steel industry of Great Britain.

Carnegie devoted his remaining years to philanthropy. It was, however, philanthropy with a difference. In Carnegie's hands, philanthropy, a term which he disliked, itself became big business. In two articles published in 1886, Carnegie, a widely published author, had called for an understanding of the needs of the working man and for the acceptance of unions. The bitterness of the Homestead Strike had inevitably made Carnegie appear a hypocrite, and Carnegie was determined to demonstrate to the world that he was not insensitive to the needs of the less privileged. In an essay entitled "Wealth," first published in 1889 and often reprinted as "The Gospel of Wealth," he had set forth the essentials of his views on charitable giving. He held that the man of means should spend his fortune during his own lifetime in ways that would advance society. The millionaire, he argued, was but a trustee who should approach philanthropy scientifically and endow institutions such as universities, public libraries, and recreational areas for the masses.

On a relatively small scale, he had begun to dispense grants at the end of the 1880's, increasing the number and size of his benefactions as the years passed. In retirement, Carnegie had the time to systematize his giving. While he did provide some money for medical facilities, his usual response to a request for support from a hospital or medical school was to say "That is Mr. Rockefeller's specialty." The great bulk of Carnegie's support went to libraries and the support of education. He ultimately provided more than fifty million dollars to establish twenty-eight hundred public libraries, the vast majority in the United States and Great Britain. Carnegie ordinarily provided funds for the building only, for he expected the communities concerned to provide the revenues needed for books and maintenance. Fond of the limelight, Carnegie often appeared at the dedication of his libraries.

He also gave large amounts of money to Edinburgh University and three other universities in Scotland, and he established the Carnegie Institute of Technology in Pittsburgh (later the Carnegie-Mellon University) and the Carnegie Institution in Washington, D.C., which subsidized basic research in several disciplines. Another substantial sum went to the Carnegie Foundation for the Advancement of Teaching. Ostensibly a pension plan for college faculty, in practice the foundation did much to set standards that raised the quality of higher education in the United States. The largest sum of all, $125,000,000, was used in 1911 to endow the Carnegie Corporation of New York, which had the mission of advancing knowledge through the promotion of schools, libraries, research, and publication. Carnegie dispensed still more money to causes designed to promote international peace, while he spent various amounts on such diverse items as church organs; the Hero Fund, which recognizes valorous needs performed in everyday life; New York City's Carnegie Hall; and pensions for the widows of United States presidents and for tenant farmers on his Scottish estate, Skibo Castle.

During his lifetime, he had succeeded in giving away slightly more than $350,000,000, utilizing the Carnegie Corporation as his principal means of organizing the distribution of his fortune. Its establishment indicated Carnegie's recognition that it was impossible for a single individual as wealthy as he to supervise personally the administration and meaningful use of his own fortune, the tenet he had advocated in "The Gospel of Wealth." After his death at his summer home in Lenox, Massachusetts, in 1919, his will revealed that there were but thirty million dollars left to distribute; he had already made provisions for his wife and daughter. Praise for his generosity in the press was widespread.

Summary

Andrew Carnegie was a man of contradictions. Despite having little formal education himself, he had a great respect for knowledge, writing books and essays on several topics, reading widely, and making it possible for countless others to read through the thousands of libraries he established. A ruthless businessman, he made platitudinous statements about the dignity of labor but denied many workers that dignity through the practices of his company, a denial which culminated in the Homestead Strike. Yet, as a businessman, he must be remembered as an outstanding success, for, in three separate fields, he showed mastery. His first triumph was with the Pennsylvania Railroad, in whose employ he rose from secretary to one of its most responsible executives at a time when railroads were at the forefront of establishing patterns of modern business management. His next and greatest triumph was in building the giant Carnegie Steel Company. Finally, the practices that had served him so well in the business world enabled him to organize philanthropy on an almost unprecedented scale, as he spent his fortune generously and, on the whole, wisely. To many, he symbolized widely shared values in American culture: generosity combined with the success ethic.

Bibliography

Bridge, James Howard. *The Inside History of the Carnegie Steel Company.*

New York: Aldine Book Co., 1903. Written by a man who assisted Carnegie in some of his writing endeavors. The author knew not only Carnegie but also most of his key associates. Tends to see the management controversies of the 1890's from Frick's perspective.

Carnegie, Andrew. *The Autobiography of Andrew Carnegie*. Boston: Houghton Mifflin Co., 1920. Published the year after Carnegie's death, this book contains a wealth of interesting information but tends to be self-serving.

_____. *Triumphant Democracy: Or, Fifty Years' March of the Republic*. New York: Charles Scribner's Sons, 1886. Carnegie wrote several books, even more essays, and still more letters which appeared in newspapers under his name. This book and "The Gospel of Wealth" are perhaps his best-known works. Makes clear his ardent faith in capitalism, democracy, and opportunity.

Hendrick, Burton J. *The Life of Andrew Carnegie*. 2 vols. Garden City, N.Y.: Doubleday and Co., 1932. Written in a vigorous style by a man who had a chance to talk with Carnegie's widow and many of his business associates.

Hendrick, Burton J., and Daniel Henderson. *Louise Whitfield Carnegie*. New York: Hastings House, 1950. Begun by Carnegie's first major biographer and completed by Henderson. Sympathetic but only marginally concerned with Carnegie the businessman

Hessen, Robert. *Steel Titan: The Life of Charles M. Schwab*. New York: Oxford University Press, 1975. The best study of any of the hard-driving executives who did so much to put Carnegie Steel at the top of American industry. The first half of this biography deals with Schwab's early life and his years with Carnegie. The latter part discusses Schwab's own considerable success after he left United States Steel.

Hogan, William T. *Economic History of the Iron and Steel Industry in the United States*. 5 vols. Lexington, Mass.: D. C. Heath and Co., 1971. The first two volumes of this five-volume work provide invaluable work on the steel industry during the years in which Carnegie was its dominant personality.

Livesay, Harold C. *Andrew Carnegie and the Rise of Big Business*. Edited by Oscar Handlin. Boston: Little, Brown and Co., 1975. Brief but invaluable biography that places Carnegie's business accomplishments in the context of developments in nineteenth century business management.

McHugh, Jeanne. *Alexander Holley and the Makers of Steel*. Baltimore: Johns Hopkins University Press, 1980. Biography of the man generally considered to be the foremost American expert in the Bessemer process. Attempts to place its subject in the context of the late nineteenth century technological revolution in steelmaking.

Swetnam, George. *Andrew Carnegie*. Boston: Twayne Publishers, 1980.

While Carnegie will always be remembered as an industrialist and philanthropist, he became an author even earlier. This valuable, brief book examines his interest in writing and his best-known works.

Wall, Joseph Frazier. *Andrew Carnegie*. New York: Oxford University Press, 1970. More than a thousand pages in length, this is the definitive biography of Carnegie and is likely to remain so for many years.

Lloyd J. Graybar

KIT CARSON

Born: December 24, 1809; Madison County, Kentucky
Died: May 23, 1868; Fort Lyon, Colorado
Areas of Achievement: Western exploration, Indian relations, and the
  military
Contribution: As trapper, guide, Indian agent, and soldier, Carson helped
  open the American West to settlement. His frontier adventures continue
  to impress those fascinated by the West's romantic era.

Early Life
Christopher "Kit" Carson was born into a large Kentucky family on the
day before Christmas, 1809. Of Scotch-Irish heritage, Lindsey Carson fought
in the American Revolution and fathered five children before his first wife
died in 1793. Three years later, he married Kit's mother, Rebecca Robinson.
The second marriage yielded ten more children, Christopher being the sixth.
Before he was two years old, the family moved to Missouri, settling in Howard County. A falling tree limb killed his father when Kit was only nine years
old. At fourteen, he was apprenticed to a saddler in Franklin. Kit received
little formal schooling and remained illiterate most of his life (many years
later, he did learn to write his name). Instead, he earned an education in the
American wilderness from men tutored in frontier ways.
Before long, the young apprentice found the saddle trade "distasteful" and
vowed to flee his fate at the first chance. Longing to visit new lands, he
decided to join the first party headed for the Rocky Mountains. With his
master's apparent connivance, Carson thus ran away in August, 1826, following a wagon train bound for Santa Fe. Taos, New Mexico, then became
Carson's adopted home, where he always returned after his long journeys.
From 1827 to 1829, Carson served as a cook, drove a wagon to El Paso,
interpreted Spanish, and worked for a copper mine near the Gila River. In
August, 1829, he joined Ewing Young's trapping party bound for California.
Although not the first trapping venture to cross the continent, the Young expedition provided Carson with invaluable experience and helped shape his
life. After trapping beaver along several Arizona streams, the party moved
on to California, trapped in the San Joaquin and Sacramento valleys, and
finally returned to Taos in April, 1831. Carson once again joined an experienced trapper's expedition, this time that of Thomas Fitzpatrick, known to
Indians as "Broken Hand." Fitzpatrick's men headed north to trap in the
central Rockies. For the next ten years, Carson roamed the American interior, hunting and trapping in much of present Colorado, Wyoming, Utah,
Idaho, and Montana.
Carson immediately established a reputation as a reliable trapper and a
man useful in a fight. Although later known for his wise counsel, at this point

in his life he craved action and adventure. Experience taught him the value of caution; though excitable, he remained firm and determined in dangerous situations. Carson admitted that his most fearful moment came when two angry grizzly bears forced him up a tree. In 1835, an insufferable French trapper goaded him into a celebrated duel at point-blank range—so close, in fact, that Carson's face received powder burns. Wounded in the arm, the Frenchman gave Carson no more trouble.

Carson and his fellow trappers often fought Indians, particularly the Blackfeet, who struggled with the whites over hunting grounds and supplies of valuable horses. In 1835, a Blackfoot warrior wounded Carson in the shoulder, his most serious injury. Early in life, Carson decided that Indians could not be trusted; subsequent clashes confirmed his view that wayward Indians must be severely chastised. Still, he had no special hatred for Native Americans; he respected and understood them well enough to take two native women as his wives (although the second union ended in divorce).

In the Rockies, Carson traveled with many noted mountain men, including Jim Bridger, "Old Bill" Williams, Richard Owens, and Alexis Godey. Trappers lived a rigorous yet unrestrained life, no sooner trading their beaver pelts than setting off again for the mountains. By 1840, overtrapping brought their days to an end, but not before they began to pacify the frontier. Just over thirty years of age, Carson was left with an uncertain future.

In 1836, Carson acquired an Arapaho wife, Waanibe (or Singing Grass). She bore him two daughters but died sometime in 1840-1841. For a wandering trapper, Carson was considerate of his Indian wife; her death meant that he had to care for two young daughters. In 1842, he decided to leave one daughter with Missouri relatives. Returning westward, he met John C. Frémont on a Missouri River steamer. This chance meeting proved a turning point in Carson's life.

Despite his fame as a mountain man and Indian fighter, Carson was barely average in height and spoke in a soft, nearly feminine voice. He nevertheless immediately impressed army explorer John C. Frémont, who described the frontiersman in his memoirs as "broad-shouldered and deep-chested, with a clear steady blue eye and frank speech and address; quiet and unassuming." Others agreed that Carson was a man of rare character: honest, dependable, fierce under fire, and modest. Younger than many experienced trappers, he became their equal and then won greater fame as Frémont's guide.

Life's Work

In 1842, John C. Frémont was directed by the United States Army to survey the Oregon route as far as South Pass in Wyoming. Known to be reliable, Carson had traveled the mountains extensively, and thus Frémont hired him as guide and hunter at one hundred dollars a month. Eventually, the two men developed great respect for each other, and their friendship proved of lasting benefit to both. Frémont later swore that "Carson and truth are one."

Beginning in June, 1842, Carson guided the main party along the Platte River to Fort Laramie. There rumors of Indian reprisals against white travelers compelled Carson to make an oral last will, a trapper custom. Frémont persisted, and the party safely crossed the Rockies. Carson assisted the explorer in planting the American flag atop one of the Wind River peaks, then accompanied him in a rubber raft down the Platte on the return trip. The party escaped injury in an otherwise costly accident; then Carson took his leave at Fort Laramie. In January, 1843, he returned to Taos to marry his third wife, Josefa Jaramillo, who eventually bore him seven children.

Carson again served as guide (along with Thomas Fitzpatrick) for Frémont's second expedition of 1843-1844 to Oregon and California. Crossing the Rockies, Frémont and Carson examined the Great Salt Lake in a rubber boat, then continued to the British posts in the Oregon country. Frémont next struck southward to explore the Great Basin, finally deciding to enter California across the high Sierra Nevada in the dead of winter. From a Sierra pass, Carson caught a glimpse of the California Coast Range which he had first seen as a member of the Young party fifteen years earlier. After much hardship, he helped guide Frémont to the familiar Sacramento Valley.

The party encountered further trouble returning on the old Spanish Trail. A band of Indians robbed a Mexican family of their horses and then killed most of the family. Carson and Alexis Godey volunteered to pursue the marauders, expecting others to do the same. When none did, the two guides tracked the offenders for fifty miles and alone attacked the camp of thirty braves. The Indians were caught off guard and fled. Carson and Godey returned with two scalps and most of the horses, earning Frémont's everlasting praise. Later, another man was killed by Indians, but the addition of famed trapper and guide Joseph R. Walker helped the party to reach Bent's Fort on the Arkansas River without further injury in July, 1844.

The publication of Frémont's reports of his first two expeditions in 1843 and 1845 brought Carson to the attention of an American nation eager to create heroes of its drive to the West. In his first report, for example, Frémont wrote that "mounted on a fine horse, without a saddle, and scouring bareheaded over the prairies, Kit was one of the finest pictures of a horseman I have ever seen." Such descriptions created a frontier legend that helped Carson earn further fame in the service of his nation.

Along with Richard Owens, Carson started a farm in New Mexico but gladly sold their assets at a loss in August, 1845, to serve on Frémont's third expedition. The party crossed the Rockies and again investigated the Great Salt Lake. Frémont decided to strike straight across the desert to the West, sending Carson and an advance party on a forced march to locate water and grass. Crossing the Great Basin and then the Sierra again in winter, the party arrived in California amid growing turmoil between Mexico and the United

States. In March, 1846, Mexican authorities ordered Frémont's army of American frontiersmen to leave the province. After a show of defiance, Frémont did pass northward into Oregon. On the route, Carson joined much of the party in attacking an Indian village, leaving more than a hundred dead in their wake. He believed this "butchery" justified as a deterrent to attacks on American settlers. The same night, a messenger from Washington arrived; Klamath Indians surprised Frémont's camp, killing three of the party. Carson was angered at the death of his friends, and he led the men in exacting vengeance on a nearby Indian village. In a subsequent encounter with the Klamath, quick action by Frémont and James Sagundai, one of Frémont's Indian auxiliaries, spared Carson's life.

Frémont had received messages that induced him to return to California to lead a revolt of American settlers in June, 1846. Although not authorized by the United States government, Frémont's actions earned for him more national acclaim and raised his guide's renown as well. Carson served in the volunteer California Battalion, assisting in the occupation of San Diego and Los Angeles. Apparently at Frémont's direction, Carson's men executed three Mexican prisoners in retaliation for the killing of two Americans. Carson avoided mentioning this grim episode in his memoirs. With California apparently pacified, Frémont sent Carson east in September, carrying news of the conquest to Washington.

Crossing New Mexico, Carson encountered General Stephen Watts Kearny commanding a force of United States dragoons. With great reluctance, the famous guide agreed to lead the general to California. Arriving in December, 1846, the small American army clashed with determined Californians at San Pasqual. Riding in an advance party, Carson barely escaped death when his horse tumbled and his gun was broken. Many of the soldiers were killed, and Kearny was wounded. The command urgently needed help, so Carson, Navy Lieutenant Edward F. Beale, and a Delaware Indian crept away at night and ran barefoot to San Diego. Despite the hardship and heroism of their actions, a relief force had already been dispatched to rescue Kearny. Carson was again present to see Los Angeles occupied by American forces.

In 1847 and 1848, Carson traveled twice across the continent carrying government dispatches. In the spring of 1848, George Brewerton accompanied Carson from California of New Mexico. The young lieutenant later wrote of his ride with the famous scout. Carson arrived in the East with early news of the California gold strike. At the capital, he and Jessie Benton Frémont urged President James K. Polk to assist her husband in a dispute over authority with General Kearny. Carson had another meeting with the president and was appointed first lieutenant in the United States Army. The Senate, however, refused to confirm the nomination, because of hostility toward the Frémont family. Informed of the rebuff, Carson nevertheless fulfilled his duty in carrying dispatches overland to California. Late in 1848, he returned to private life.

Carson did not accompany Frémont on his ill-fated final expeditions, but he did succor the exhausted explorer in Taos after his fourth expedition had ended in disaster in the San Juan Mountains. For the next several years, Carson engaged in various pursuits, often aiding government parties. In 1849, he guided soldiers seeking to rescue Mrs. James White and her child, who had been taken by Apache. Carson was saddened when the commander hesitated to follow his instructions; the Indians killed the mother and escaped with the child. In 1853, he took part in a great drive of sheep to California. Early in 1854, he began a new career as an Indian agent, primarily for the Ute.

From his office in Taos, Carson distributed government supplies to the Ute and took part in numerous efforts to pacify other tribes. In 1855, he helped government troops defeat hostile bands in battles at Saguache and Ponca Pass in Colorado. Despite the handicap of illiteracy, Carson proved an effective Indian agent. His facility with Spanish and many Indian languages offset his inability to read and write. Moreover, he knew and respected Indian customs. His hope was to see Indians removed from harmful contact with whites, where they could learn to provide their own support. Sometime in 1856, he dictated his memoirs, probably to his secretary. In 1860, a fall from his horse left Carson in declining health.

Until June, 1861, Carson continued in his post as Indian agent. Then the Civil War came to New Mexico Territory, bringing him a new career as military leader. Born a Kentuckian, Carson sided with the Union, helping to erect a United States flag in Taos after secession sympathizers raised the Confederate banner. He was commissioned a colonel in a New Mexico volunteer regiment. In February, 1862, his troops engaged invading Confederates at Valverde, New Mexico. Later action forced the rebels to withdraw.

For the remainder of the war, Carson sought to pacify several Southwestern Indian tribes. Most notable was his 1863-1864 campaign against the Navajo, a large and proud nation. Following the orders of General James H. Carleton, he fought essentially a scorched-earth campaign, destroying crops and seizing livestock. His efforts to force the Navajo to surrender earned for him the name "The Rope Thrower." In January, 1864, his troops drove the Navajo from their Canyon de Chelly stronghold. Relatively few were killed in the conflict; cold and starvation forced the defeated people to move to the Bosque Redondo, a remote reservation. Hundreds of Navajo died on the journey, however, because of inadequate provisions. Carson had not been responsible for the harsh policy and urged that more food be provided. His campaign helped settle the government reservation system, but in 1868 the Navajo were allowed to return to their tribal lands.

Carson's largest battle took place at Adobe Walls along the Canadian River in Texas. In November, 1864, he led more than three hundred troops (and seventy-five Ute and Apache) against a large force of Kiowa and Comanche. His troops destroyed an Indian village before perhaps as many as three thousand Indians forced him to withdraw. Carson was not beaten; his caution and experience prevented a potential disaster similar to General George A. Custer's defeat. Carson's foray inaugurated a long campaign to pacify the Kiowa and Comanche. In March, 1865, he was breveted brigadier general of United States Volunteers for his valuable service in New Mexico.

In 1866, Carson commanded Fort Garland in Colorado. The next year, he resigned his military position and was appointed superintendent of Indian affairs for the Colorado Territory. In poor health, he accompanied several Ute chiefs on a tour of Eastern cities, hoping to negotiate a favorable treaty. He also visited his old friends the Frémonts and sought medical help. On his return to Fort Lyon, Colorado, his wife died after giving birth to another child. A month later, on May 23, 1868, the famous scout succumbed to death from an aortic aneurysm. Buried initially at Boggsville, Colorado, both Carsons were later moved to Taos, New Mexico, their beloved home. A river, a mountain pass, and the capital city of Nevada bear the Carson name.

Summary

Kit Carson was an ideal representative of the American frontiersman. Unlettered but resourceful, he and his fellow mountain men lived a brief, romantic existence before decline of the beaver population brought their way of life to an end. Forced to become guides, traders, or Indian agents, former trappers continued to facilitate the West's settlement, but in roles subordinate to the more powerful agents of American expansion. As Frémont's guide, Carson surpassed all the mountain men and emerged as a legendary figure of the American frontier. At the same time, his judgment and experience contributed to the success of Frémont's ventures. Through such former trappers as Carson, geographical knowledge of the West passed into the hands of army explorers such as Frémont. As an Indian agent, Carson sought to end Indian-white conflict, while his Civil War service helped protect the Southwest from Confederate attack and Indian unrest.

Carson's adventures require little embellishment, yet writers created a fictional Kit Carson, familiar to most Americans as a loyal army scout and Indian slayer. An early example of the Western hero, the Carson figure linked earlier Eastern woodsmen (such as Daniel Boone) to the Indian fighter of the Western mountains and plains. Barely civilized himself in these fictional accounts, the famous scout assisted in the spread of American civilization to barren Western lands. More than most legendary heroes, however, the historical Kit Carson approaches his fictional reputation. Several brutal encounters with Indians and Mexicans mar his otherwise impressive career. Carson was nevertheless a man of simple courage and devotion to duty. He remains an American character deserving regard.

Bibliography

Brewerton, George D. "A Ride with Kit Carson." *Harper's Magazine* 7 (August, 1853): 307-334. This is one of the few accounts of Carson written by a man who knew and rode with the famous guide.

Carter, Harvey Lewis. *"Dear Old Kit": The Historical Christopher Carson.* Norman: University of Oklahoma Press, 1968. This authoritative work provides a richly annotated edition of Carson's memoirs, virtually the only source of information for his life to 1856. Includes a survey of works on Carson and assesses his character and later life.

Estergreen, M. Morgan. *Kit Carson: A Portrait in Courage.* Norman: University of Oklahoma Press, 1962. Inaccurate in some respects, this helpful account is based partly on Carson family memories.

Guild, Thelma S., and Harvey L. Carter. *Kit Carson: A Pattern for Heroes.* Lincoln: University of Nebraska Press, 1984. Readable and generally reliable, this biography is based primarily on Carson's memoirs.

Jackson, Donald, and Mary Lee Spence, eds. *The Expeditions of John Charles Frémont.* 3 vols. Urbana: University of Illinois Press, 1970-1984. The widely read reports of John C. Frémont's first two expeditions (in volume 1) made Carson a national hero.

Kelly, Lawrence C., ed. *Navajo Roundup: Selected Correspondence of Kit Carson's Expedition Against the Navajo, 1863-1865.* Boulder, Colo.: Pruett Publishing Co., 1970. Generally favorable to Carson, this source contains many valuable documents covering his Navajo campaign.

Sabin, Edwin Legrand. *Kit Carson Days.* Chicago: A. C. McClurg and Co., 1914. Rev. ed. New York: Press of the Pioneers, 1935. Dated and flawed in parts, this standard biography is still useful for Carson's later career. Includes his agent and military reports.

Trafzer, Clifford E. *The Kit Carson Campaign: The Last Great Navajo War.* Norman: University of Oklahoma Press, 1982. This work examines Carson's 1863-1864 campaign from the Navajo perspective.

Vernon L. Volpe

RACHEL CARSON

Born: May 27, 1907; Springdale, Pennsylvania
Died: April 14, 1964; Silver Spring, Maryland
Areas of Achievement: Science and literature
Contribution: A gifted writer, Carson used the power of her pen to express her love of nature and to create public concern for environmental and ecological issues.

Early Life

Rachel Louise Carson was born May 27, 1907, in Springdale, Pennsylvania, where her father, Robert Warden Carson, had bought a sixty-five acre farm in 1900. While her father worked as an insurance and real estate agent and her sister Marian and brother Robert were in school, Carson enjoyed the affectionate attention of her mother, Marie McLean Carson, a musician and former schoolteacher. The close mother-daughter relationship, continuing until Maria's death in 1958, was responsible for Carson's early interest in nature. Maria taught her daughter not only to enjoy the outdoors but also to respect its many living creatures.

Carson's mother also encouraged the child's interest in literature. At a very early age, Carson decided that she wanted to become a writer. When she earned ten dollars for "A Battle in the Clouds," published in *St. Nicholas*, a children's magazine, the ten-year-old Carson believed that she had wisely chosen her career.

That early independence and capacity for self-direction stood Carson in good stead. To her classmates in the local high school, the small, slender girl with smooth skin, short, light brown hair, a prominent nose, and pretty blue eyes seemed quiet and shy, perhaps even antisocial. To Carson's few close friends, she was a warm, friendly young woman with a superb sense of humor and an adventurous spirit. To her teachers, Carson was a highly intelligent, exceptionally motivated student who performed well in her classes.

When Carson entered Pennsylvania College for Women (later Chatham College) in 1925, she still hoped to be a writer, so she majored in English. A required biology class taught by Mary Scott Skinker, however, so intrigued her that she changed her major to science and, as she then believed, abandoned a literary career. After graduation, Carson received a fellowship for summer study at the Woods Hole Marine Biological Laboratory in Massachusetts. This first encounter with the ocean was such a powerful one that she sensed her destiny must somehow be linked to the sea.

A fellowship at Johns Hopkins University in the fall of 1929 allowed Carson to continue her studies. Part-time teaching at that institution and at the University of Maryland supported her, even beyond her 1932 graduation with an M.A. in zoology.

The Depression years of the 1930's were difficult ones for most American families. Carson's was no exception. When her father died suddenly in 1935, the situation worsened, and Carson had to find a way to support her mother. Luckily, Elmer Higgins of the United States Bureau of Fisheries in Washington needed a scientist who could write radio broadcasts about ocean life, her specialty. Carson had finally found a way to unite her love of science with her talent for the written word. This part-time job marked the beginning of a unique career.

Life's Work
In 1936, Carson became one of the first professional women to be permanently employed by the Bureau of Fisheries. Her position as junior aquatic biologist was a welcome one financially, since her sister Marian had died recently, leaving two young girls to be reared by her and her mother.

Carson's new position still demanded a certain amount of writing, which she eagerly tackled. When asked to write an introduction to a booklet, she became so engrossed in her subject that she created an extraordinary essay. When it was rejected as inappropriate for the bureau, Higgins suggested that she should send it to the *Atlantic Monthly*. "Undersea" was published in September, 1937, and was praised so highly that Carson was encouraged to write other articles and to expand the original one into a book. The book, *Under the Sea-Wind*, received enthusiastic reviews when it came out in 1941, but the bombing of Pearl Harbor soon drew attention away from the literary field and readership dwindled. When rediscovered years later, however, it became a best-seller.

During the war years, Carson wrote many governmental publications, including conservation bulletins for the bureau, which had become the United States Fish and Wildlife Service. She also gathered much information from several government-sponsored oceanographic expeditions. After the war, she longed to formulate the material into a book, but her free time was curtailed by job promotions which culminated in the position of editor-in-chief in 1949. Nevertheless, that same year she was able to take her first deep-sea voyage and, with the help of a Eugene F. Saxton Fellowship, she took a short leave to work on *The Sea Around Us* (1951).

The Sea Around Us was an immediate best-seller, staying on the list for eighty-six weeks. The success of the book (it won the National Book Award in 1951 and the John Burroughs Medal in 1952) catapulted the shy, reserved Carson into the public arena. While she preferred her privacy, Carson was happy that her book was so well received and that she was awarded a Guggenheim Fellowship (for 1951-1952) to write another.

The Sea Around Us presented Carson's scientific explanations of the sea and its life forms with such beauty, drama, and enthusiasm that many called it a poetic work of art. In response to the praise, the unassuming author simply remarked, "no one could write truthfully about the sea and leave out the poetry."

As the royalties from *The Sea Around Us* came pouring in, Carson realized that she could return her fellowship money, retire from her government job, and devote the rest of her life to her writing—the fulfillment of a dream. The next year, another dream became reality when she was able to buy land on which to build a summer cottage overlooking Sheepscot Bay in West Southport, Maine. This would be the setting for her next book.

Edge of the Sea (1955) is in many ways the culmination of Carson's work, for it reveals her delicate mastery of prose as well as her underlying philosophy of nature. At the shoreline—whether rocky coast, sandy beach, or coral reef—she discovers the interdependence of all living things: "Each living thing is bound to its world by many threads, weaving the intricate design of the fabric of life." Combining scientific evidence and personal experience, she once again captured the majesty of life.

Unfolding the mysteries of life to young, receptive minds was the central purpose of Carson's next article, "Help Your Child to Wonder," published in *Woman's Home Companion* (July, 1956) and posthumously in book form as *The Sense of Wonder* (1965). The article was inspired by Carson's grandnephew Roger. When Roger's mother died in 1957, Carson gladly adopted the son of her favorite niece and tried to share with him her sense of awe in the presence of nature. They spent many pleasant hours together, observing the living creatures of the sea and shore.

While Carson always enjoyed her role as the sea's biographer, as the years went by she discovered that its life and, indeed, all life was being threatened by man's insatiable desire to conquer and control the environment. As scientific evidence became available on the destructive power of man, especially in the use of pesticides and herbicides developed during World War II, Carson became convinced that she must speak out for the future of the universe. The result of extensive, meticulous research, *Silent Spring* (1962) was Carson's indictment of the cruelty and irresponsibility of man's use of non-selective pesticides which kill beneficial as well as undesirable forms of life.

Carson hoped that this book, so unlike her others, would awaken the public to the problems of the environment. While she anticipated opposition to her ideas, she never expected the furor with which she was attacked by the chemical industry and the United States Department of Agriculture. The tremendous public outcry created by this immediate best-seller forced the government to investigate Carson's charges. President John F. Kennedy's Science Advisory Committee examined the information available on pesticides and submitted a report in 1963 which was considered an official endorsement of Carson's position. Subsequent investigations revealed that Carson was correct in demanding that more research was needed prior to the release of a new chemical and that its use should be subject to strict control. The polemical book indeed served a useful purpose, thus giving Carson some satisfaction in her final days. She died of cancer and heart disease on April 14, 1964.

Summary

The impact of Rachel Carson's *Silent Spring* has been compared to that of Harriet Beecher Stowe's *Uncle Tom's Cabin* (1852) and Upton Sinclair's *The Jungle* (1906). These works related information about a contemporary societal problem in such a provocative manner that Americans were forced to come to terms with the flaws in their world. The authors were motivated by intense personal feelings, by a concern for future generations, and by a fear of man's irresponsible use of power.

In writing *Silent Spring*, Carson's devotion to the living world, so beautifully evoked in her earlier works, became an indignant plea for respect, for the reverence for life that she had learned from Albert Schweitzer's philosophy. Like Schweitzer, she believed in an ethical system that placed value on all life—whether plant, animal, or man. In 1963, Carson was honored with the Schweitzer Medal of the Animal Welfare Institute, an appropriate award for a life dedicated to arousing a love of nature in the hearts and minds of mankind. Rachel Carson's legacy was aptly phrased by President Jimmy Carter in posthumously presenting her the Presidential Medal of Freedom in 1980: "Always concerned, always eloquent, she created a tide of environmental consciousness that has not ebbed."

Bibliography
Brooks, Paul. *The House of Life: Rachel Carson at Work.* Boston: Houghton Mifflin Co., 1972. A sympathetic, indispensable biography by Carson's editor which provides excerpts from her books and a complete bibliography of her work. Used by all subsequent biographers.
Downs, Robert B. "Upsetting the Balance of Nature." In *Books That Changed America*, 260-268. New York: Macmillan, 1970. Notes the public impact of Carson's *Silent Spring* and places it in historical context alongside other influential works. Inaccurate in a few details.
Gartner, Carol B. *Rachel Carson.* New York: Frederick Ungar Publishing Co., 1983. By a thorough examination of her works, presents a strong case for Carson's place in literary history. Provides a helpful chronology of Carson's life and limited biographical information.
Graham, Frank, Jr. *Since "Silent Spring."* Boston: Houghton Mifflin Co., 1970. Gives history of the controversy over *Silent Spring* and additional supporting evidence for Carson's position. Scientific data and government information simplified for the nontechnical reader. Some information outdated.
Mattill, John. "Looking Anew at *Silent Spring.*" *Technology Review* 87 (November, December, 1984): 72-73. Suggests that man's use of pesticides

to control nature continues to be a vital issue. While the chlorinated insecticides are no longer in use, others have been developed which need further testing.

Sterling, Philip. *Sea and Earth: The Life of Rachel Carson*. New York: Thomas Y. Crowell, 1970. An excellent biography for a young audience. Conveys Carson's chief concerns and delves into her private as well as public life. Bibliography provided.

Whorton, James. *Before "Silent Spring": Pesticides in Pre-DDT America*. Princeton, N.J.: Princeton University Press, 1975. Chronicles the effects of insecticides on humans from the Civil War to post–World War II. Balanced, readable, yet scholarly account which supports Carson's warnings concerning the irresponsible use of chemicals.

Alice Taylor

JIMMY CARTER

Born: October 1, 1924; Plains, Georgia

Area of Achievement: Politics

Contribution: President Carter was a conservative in some policies and a liberal in others. On the one hand, he attacked government bureaucracy, moved away from détente with the Soviet Union, and increased military spending; on the other, he supported racial equality, took seriously the problems of underdeveloped countries, and pressured repressive regimes to respect human rights.

Early Life

James Earl Carter, Jr., thirty-ninth President of the United States, was born on October 1, 1924, in Plains, Georgia, a town of 550 in Sumter County. Jimmy, as he liked to be called, was the first child of James Earl Carter, Sr., an up-and-coming farmer and rural businessman, and Lillian Gordy Carter, a registered nurse. Along with his sisters Gloria and Ruth and his brother William (Billy), he grew up on the family farm three miles from Plains. After being graduated from Plains High School in 1941, he briefly attended Georgia Southwestern College and Georgia Institute of Technology. Carter was appointed to the United States Naval Academy in 1943 and was graduated three years later, standing fifty-ninth in a class of 820. On the seventh of July, 1946, he married Rosalynn Smith, a friend of his sister Gloria. They had four children: John William (Jack), James Earl III (Chip), Jeffrey (Jeff), and Amy.

After two years' work on battleships, Carter transferred to the Navy submarine service in 1948 and then to the nuclear submarine program in 1951. Subsequently he served on the precommission crew of the nuclear submarine *Seawolf* and rose to the rank of lieutenant commander. Following his father's death in 1953, Carter returned to Plains, took charge of the family businesses, and quickly became a local leader. Between 1955 and 1962, he chaired the Sumter County Board of Education. In 1962, he was elected to the Georgia Senate. During two terms, he advocated governmental efficiency, regional planning, and better schools. In 1966, Carter lost the Democratic nomination for governor but ran a strong third in a field of six.

Carter's defeat produced a mild depression that led in turn to an important though undramatic religious experience. He had been reared a Baptist, conducted Bible classes in the Navy, and taught Sunday school at the Plains Baptist Church. Following his primary loss, however, Carter began to feel insufficiently devout. Guided by his sister, evangelist Ruth Carter Stapleton, he was "born again" and vowed to live a more godly life.

This religious conversion caused no basic change in his personality. On the contrary, Carter's determination to be a better Christian fitted into his long-

standing habit of placing high demands on himself. He worked systemati-
cally, sometimes taking special courses to improve his memory, reading
speed, and knowledge of art, music, and Spanish. He disciplined his body as
well as his mind. A cross-country runner at Annapolis, he jogged in middle
age to keep fit. In his late forties, Carter stood five feet, ten inches tall and
weighed a trim 160 pounds. His stern commander in the nuclear submarine
program, Admiral Hyman Rickover, reinforced his perfectionism. Carter set
high standards for his family and subordinates. Anyone who fell short risked
"the look," as Carter's staff called a piercing stare from his hazel eyes.

Nor did spiritual rebirth dampen Carter's political ambition. Between 1967
and 1970, he both visited Northern cities as a missionary and prepared for his
next gubernatorial campaign. In 1970, he defeated former Governor Carl
Sanders in the Democratic primary and easily won the governorship.

Life's Work

Governor Carter's inaugural address in January, 1971, attracted national
attention when he declared that the "time for racial discrimination is over."
Although Carter sometimes courted segregationist voters, he had remained
personally moderate on civil rights issues. Now moving in a more liberal
direction, he appointed blacks to state office and displayed a portrait of Martin Luther King, Jr., in the executive mansion. As governor, Carter worked
hardest to streamline state agencies, but discrediting prejudice as a political
issue was his greatest accomplishment. In 1972, he was mentioned as a dark-
horse contender for the Democratic vice-presidential nomination. Yet, ineli-
gible for reelection and more conservative than leading Democrats, he was
not a major figure in party or national affairs.

Four years later, Carter used his image as an outsider to win the presidency
of a nation unsettled by the Vietnam War, the Watergate scandal, the cultural upheaval of the late 1960's, and the energy crisis of the early 1970's.
Carter's book, *Why Not the Best?* (1975), announced the central theme of his
campaign: government with effective leadership could be open, compas-
sionate, and competent. Furthermore, claiming a governor's managerial skill,
a nuclear engineer's technological expertise, and a born-again farmer's sound
morality, Carter presented himself as uniquely qualified to lead. In addition,
he blamed President Gerald R. Ford for high unemployment and Machiavel-
lian foreign policy. Despite the wide appeal of these themes, Carter probably
would have lost the Democratic nomination if liberal rivals had coalesced
against him, and might have lost the general election if the economy had not
been afflicted with rising unemployment and inflation. Carter beat Ford by
1.7 million votes.

Although Carter won a narrow victory, the country greeted the start of his
term with enthusiasm. By the end of 1977, however, his legislative program
had bogged down in Congress and, according to polls, fewer than half of all

Americans approved of his leadership. With some justification, Carter attributed these problems to prejudice against a rural Southerner in the White House, but other factors were more significant. While continuing to think of himself as an outsider, the president presented a legislative agenda that would have taxed the skill of an old Washington hand. Moreover, impatient with loose ends, Carter offered what he liked to call "comprehensive" programs. In 1977, he backed bills to reorganize the civil service, restructure the welfare system, lift regulations on major industries, create two new cabinet departments, and end price controls on natural gas. Furthermore, Carter and his aides initially underestimated the need to cultivate powerful senators and House representatives. More important than these considerations of style, temperament, and tactics, was Carter's ideological position to the right of most congressional Democrats. Unmoved by his rhetoric of efficiency, they resented his disinclination to promote national health insurance, full employment, and comparable liberal measures.

Conflicting aspirations, great expectations, and tactical errors also marked Carter's first efforts in international affairs. The president's chief foreign policy advisers symbolized his (as well as the country's) ambivalence about the Soviet Union. Secretary of State Cyrus Vance wanted to continue détente while National Security Council Chairman Zbigniew Brzezinski took a tough anti-Communist line. Giving mixed signals himself in 1977, Carter both decided against building a new intercontinental bomber and reneged on campaign promises to reduce military spending, while both repudiating the "inordinate fear of Communism" and condemning Soviet suppression of freedom. This criticism of the Soviets may have hindered progress on a strategic arms limitation treaty to succeed the limited accord (SALT I) signed by President Richard M. Nixon. A more decisive factor was Carter's presentation of a typically comprehensive disarmament plan. Suspicious Soviet officials rejected it, accusing the United States of reopening issues seemingly settled with President Ford.

From the outset, President Carter showed unprecedented concern about human rights abroad. Regimes sanctioning harassment, imprisonment, or murder of dissenters risked White House censure and loss of American aid. *Realpolitik*, congressional pressure, and bureaucratic maneuvering rendered Carter's human rights policy less "absolute" than he had promised in his inaugural address. Nevertheless, there were notable successes. Carter's intervention saved lives in Argentina, Brazil, Chile, and other nations ruled by military juntas. His ambassador to the United Nations, Andrew Young, a black, cultivated Third World delegates, and, in April, 1978, Carter became the first president to visit Africa. Also in April, 1978, he secured Senate ratification of treaties that would end American control of the Panama Canal in 1999. Carter's human rights campaign and empathy for the Third World, however, were less popular at home than abroad. By late 1977, Republican and Democratic cold warriors charged that his soft and self-righteous policies damaged American interests.

Despite growing criticism from both the Left and the Right, Carter secured impressive victories between mid-1978 and mid-1979. Congress revised the civil service system, eased regulations on airlines, and enacted decontrol of natural gas prices. After grueling negotiations at Camp David, Maryland, Carter persuaded Egyptian President Anwar Sadat and Israeli Prime Minister Menachem Begin to accept a "Framework for Peace in the Middle East." In December, 1978, he established full diplomatic relations with the People's Republic of China. At the Vienna summit conference in June, 1979, Carter and Soviet President Leonid Brezhnev finally signed a strategic arms limitation treaty (SALT II). Yet none of Carter's successes was unmixed. Liberals complained that decontrol of natural gas prices enriched big business. Conservatives condemned the recognition of China and viewed SALT II as a needless concession to the Soviets. Perhaps most disappointing to Carter, though he brokered an Egyptian-Israeli peace treaty in March, 1979, the Camp David accords inspired no other Middle East settlements.

During the summer of 1979, Carter faced a faltering economy, oil shortages, and an angry nation. "Stagflation," the combination of rising unemployment and inflation, reappeared after two years in remission. Furthermore, when a revolution that deposed the Shah of Iran in January, 1978, also disrupted Iranian oil exports, the Organization of Petroleum Exporting Countries (OPEC) limited production and doubled prices. As American motorists clamored for scarce gasoline, Carter's bills promoting energy conservation and synthetic fuels stalled in Congress. On July 15, 1979, Carter attempted to rally the country against what he called a "crisis of the American spirit." This speech temporarily improved his standing in the polls and on Capitol Hill. Carter's subsequent decision, however, to remove several cabinet secretaries and fight inflation instead of unemployment cut short this resurgence. By the early fall, Senator Edward M. Kennedy had decided to contest the president's renomination.

In October, 1979, Carter made the most important decision of his presidency, allowing the exiled Shah of Iran to enter the United States for medical treatment. On November 4, Iranian revolutionaries seized the United States embassy in Tehran; fifty-two of the original sixty-six Americans stationed there (fourteen were released after a few weeks) remained captive for 444 days. The Middle East situation deteriorated further when Soviet forces invaded Afghanistan in December. Carter responded by withdrawing SALT II from Senate consideration, halting grain sales to the Soviet Union, urging a boycott of the Olympic Games in Moscow, and asking a large increase in military spending. According to the Carter Doctrine announced in January, 1980, attempts by outside forces to control the Persian Gulf would be "repelled by any means necessary, including military force." The president's rhetoric masked relative American weakness in the region. Indeed, a military mission to rescue the hostages failed in April when American helicopters collided far from Tehran.

Although Carter turned back Kennedy's challenge to win renomination, his inability to free the hostages combined with the faltering economy cost him the presidency. On November 4, 1980, Republican nominee Ronald Reagan defeated Carter by 8.4 million votes. During his last months in office, Carter, now a convinced cold warrior, stopped aid to the leftist Sandinista government in Nicaragua. Negotiations to free the hostages remained his chief concern. They were released minutes after Ronald Reagan took office on January 20, 1981, and former President Carter flew to greet them at an American base in Germany.

Carter resettled in Plains but secular and religious interests often pulled him away from home. He represented the United States at Anwar Sadat's funeral in Cairo, received accolades in Latin America for his human rights efforts, and joined a church group repairing slum housing in New York City. Although his memoir *Keeping Faith* (1982) dealt primarily with foreign affairs, Carter also criticized Washington insiders who had opposed his domestic program. *The Blood of Abraham* (1985), his well-informed study of the Arab-Israeli conflict, rebuked President Reagan for failing to pursue the peace process begun at Camp David. By and large, however, Carter avoided public attacks on his successor.

Summary

Jimmy Carter was a more significant—and much better—president than his overwhelming defeat in 1980 suggests. Ironically, part of his significance lay in legitimating themes, such as the need to shrink the federal government, that Ronald Reagan used against him during the campaign. Similarly, by lifting regulations on major industries, moving away from détente, and increasing military spending, Carter initiated policies later continued by Reagan. Notwithstanding these unintended contributions to American conservativism, Carter's most important accomplishments derived from his liberal side. In the White House as in the Georgia state house, Carter, a white Southern supporter of racial equality, discredited race prejudice as a political issue. His presidential appointments included many women and Hispanics as well as blacks. In foreign policy, Carter encouraged Egyptian-Israeli peace by accepting an evenhanded approach to the Middle East, paid respectful attention to underdeveloped countries, and placed human rights on the international agenda.

Bibliography

Califano, Joseph A., Jr. *Governing America: An Insider's Report from the White House and the Cabinet.* New York: Simon and Schuster, 1981. A

critical retrospective by the liberal secretary of health, education, and welfare whom Carter fired in 1979. Califano presents the president as an
incompetent conservative but credits him with a good record on minority
recruitment.

Carroll, Peter. *It Seemed Like Nothing Happened: The Tragedy and Promise
of America in the 1970's*. New York: Holt, Rinehart and Winston, 1982. A
lively history of the decade, especially perceptive on cultural trends and the
social development of minorities. Places Carter in context and views him
as a conservative Democrat.

Carter, Jimmy. *The Blood of Abraham*. Boston: Houghton Mifflin Co., 1985.
Carter brings together a detailed knowledge of the Bible, recent Middle
Eastern politics, and his own experiences in the region. Cautiously hopeful
about the possibilities of peace, he offers sensible policy recommendations.

_____. *Keeping Faith: Memoirs of a President*. New York: Bantam
Books, 1982. This defensive memoir shows Carter and liberal Democrats
talking past each other. Contains comprehensive accounts of the Camp
David negotiations and the Iran hostage crisis.

_____. *Why Not the Best?* New York: Bantam Books, 1976. This
combination memoir and campaign tract contains Carter's fullest account
of his childhood, naval service, and governorship. Especially useful for
understanding his evolving position on Civil Rights.

Carter, Rosalynn. *First Lady from Plains*. Boston: Houghton Mifflin Co.,
1984. A much more candid book than either of Jimmy Carter's memoirs.
Although Mrs. Carter discusses her own experiences as a mental health reformer, the book is most valuable for the portrait of her husband.

Glad, Betty. *Jimmy Carter: In Search of the Great White House*. New York:
W. W. Norton and Co., 1980. One of the best biographies of a sitting president. Glad presents the most detailed scholarly interpretation of Carter's
youth, early career, religious beliefs, and 1976 campaign strategy. Relatively little on the presidency.

Lynn, Laurence E., Jr., and David deF. Whitman. *The President as Policymaker: Jimmy Carter and Welfare Reform*. Philadelphia: Temple University Press, 1981. This thorough account of Carter's unsuccessful attempt to
restructure the welfare system effectively uses interviews with cabinet
members, senators, representatives, and civil servants. Reveals Carter's
strengths and weaknesses as a policymaker along with the institutional constraints he encountered.

Mazlish, Bruce, and Edwin Diamond. *Jimmy Carter: A Character Portrait*.
New York: Simon and Schuster, 1979. A subtle psychobiography by an
intellectual historian and media critic. Especially good on Carter's religious
beliefs, family relationships, and rhetorical exaggerations.

Smith, Gaddis. *Morality, Reason, and Power: American Diplomacy*

During the Carter Years. New York: Hill and Wang, 1985. The best analysis of Carter's foreign policy. Smith places the Administration in broad historical context, applauds his human rights record, and regrets his abandonment of détente.

Leo P. Ribuffo

GEORGE WASHINGTON CARVER

Born: c. 1865; near Diamond Grove, Missouri
Died: January 5, 1943; Tuskegee, Alabama
Areas of Achievement: Science and education
Contribution: Through his work with plant diseases, soil analysis, and crop
   management, Carver enabled many Southern farmers to have greater crop
   yield and profits. In his role as educator and friend, he motivated hundreds
   of blacks to improve their lives and inspired white friends to work toward
   racial equality.

Early Life

George Washington Carver was born a slave near Diamond Grove, Missouri, sometime around 1865. According to an unconfirmed but plausible story, George and his mother, Mary, were kidnaped by slave raiders shortly after his birth. Mary's owner, Moses Carver, hired a neighbor to search for them. Unable to find Mary, the man returned with George and received a racehorse as payment. George was reared by Moses Carver and his wife, Susan. Slaves were given only first names, so George took the Carver name as his own. Later he added the initial *W* to distinguish himself from another George Carver. The *W* came to stand for Washington.

A sickly child, George became Susan's helper in the house. He proved adept at household tasks, and he displayed keen interest and ability in growing plants. Intelligent and curious, Carver was frustrated that he could not attend the white school in Diamond Grove. About 1877, Carver moved to neighboring Neosho so that he could go to school there. He lived with a black couple and did household chores for his room and board, a situation that was repeated often in his quest for education.

After attending schools throughout Kansas, Carver applied to a small Presbyterian college in Highland, Kansas, in 1884. He was accepted by mail, but when the school learned that he was black, he was denied admission. After homesteading in Beeler, Kansas, Carver moved to Winterset, Iowa. In 1890, he entered Simpson College in Indianola, Iowa. The only black on campus, he soon won the respect and affection of the other students. He supported himself by doing laundry, but students anonymously gave him concert tickets and extra money.

Carver enrolled in Simpson to study art, but he doubted that he could make a living as a black artist. When his art teacher learned of his skill with plants, she suggested that he attend Iowa State, the agricultural college at Ames, Iowa. Believing that he could help his people as a trained agriculturist, he enrolled at Iowa State in 1891. While at Ames, Carver met three future United States secretaries of agriculture: James Wilson, Henry C. Wallace, and Henry A. Wallace. The latter influenced his training in agriculture and helped him later in his work at Tuskegee.

In 1894, Carver received his bachelor of science degree and began graduate work. He was appointed to the faculty as an assistant in botany and was given charge of the greenhouse. Doing graduate work with L. H. Pammel, a noted authority on mycology, Carver developed his expertise in the study of fungi and plant diseases. Before Carver finished his graduate work, Booker T. Washington asked him to head a new agricultural school at Tuskegee Institute in Alabama. Carver accepted the position, believing that it was the mission which God had prepared him to undertake.

Life's Work

In the fall of 1896, Carver completed requirements for his master's of agriculture degree and arrived at Tuskegee to head the agricultural department and direct a new experiment station. In addition to teaching, conducting research, and working with the Tuskegee extension program, Carver was assigned administrative and caretaking duties.

Small in build and high-pitched in voice, Carver already was unorthodox in appearance and habits. He wore the same clothes for years, simply adding more patches, but he always had a fresh flower in his lapel. Somewhat of a loner, he made few close friends on campus, although he welcomed visitors who were interested in his work. Most of his close friends were white, and he sustained many friendships through correspondence.

Because Carver wanted to assist the poorest farmers, he conducted soil-building experiments and research on crop diversification. He also studied plant diseases and how to prevent or control them. For the homemaker, he investigated methods of food dehydration and preservation. He also developed color washes from the clay soil which the farmers could use to beautify their homes. In laymen's language, his findings were printed in bulletins and distributed freely.

Before Carver arrived at Tuskegee, Washington was holding yearly Farmers' Conferences which were attended by farmers and interested whites. The two-day conference gave information and motivated farmers to work for economic independence. Carver expanded conference activities and gave tours of the station grounds, during which he explained the institute's experiments. Carver obtained free garden seed from the United States Department of Agriculture (USDA) to distribute to the farmers. Although conferences helped, Carver wanted to educate the farmers on how to improve their land. As a result, in 1897 he organized monthly Farmers' Institutes. Members received specific advice on what fertilizers to use, how to improve soil, and when and what crops to plant.

The next step was to inaugurate farm demonstration work and a "movable school." Carver designed the Jesup Wagon, which carried supplies and opened up for displays. The movable school began operations in 1906 and reached more than six thousand people that summer. All farm extension work was limited by a lack of funds, but the program succeeded in helping farmers improve their farms and living conditions.

As Carver became more aware of the nutritional deficiencies of the Southern diet, he looked for a source of protein that could easily be grown and would enrich the soil. The three main crops that met these requirements were cowpeas, sweet potatoes, and peanuts. He developed recipes using them and eventually displayed over one hundred products from the sweet potato and about 325 products made from the peanut. In 1923, he was given the coveted Spingarn Medal of the National Association for the Advancement of Colored People (NAACP) for his achievements in agricultural chemistry.

His first experiments with the peanut were simply intended to help Southerners improve their diets. Eventually, though, he sought to establish industries to manufacture his products and improve the economic outlook for the South. His plans for commercialization never materialized.

In 1921, his testimony, showmanship, and exhibit of peanut products before the House Ways and Means Committee caused Congress to write the highest tariff peanuts had ever had. His success brought him immediate fame. From 1924 to 1938 he served as an industry consultant, speaker, and writer for publications.

In the early 1930's, peanut growers had a problem with peanuts rotting and failing to mature. United States Department of Agriculture officials concluded that the problem was not disease and refused to help. Two employees from the Tom Huston Company processing plant disagreed and turned to Carver. After he visited infected fields, Carver agreed that fungi were the cause. His report on peanut diseases and their prevention was circulated, and USDA officials were aroused to conduct further research.

Paul Miller, a mycologist with the USDA, was assigned to investigate the problem. Impressed with Carver's ability to locate and identify fungi, Miller persuaded the USDA to make Carver a collaborator who would collect specimens for them. This work brought him appreciation and recognition from specialists. Carver continued to provide technical advice to the Tom Huston Company, and his publicity for the peanut benefited the entire industry. His peanut and sweet potato exhibit won the award for best exhibit at the Southern Exposition at New York in May, 1925. This success established Carver as an influence in the New South movement and the peanut industry.

In the 1920's and 1930's Carver spoke to various groups all over the country, including diverse black and white civic clubs, churches, colleges, and camps. In these speeches he urged racial harmony and shared his vision for a better world. His life and talks inspired people to respect all races, work toward brotherhood, and strive to improve the world they shared.

Before his death, on January 5, 1943, Carver established the George Washington Carver Foundation and Museum and donated his life savings to it. He personally directed the museum displays of his work and paintings. The foundation provided laboratory facilities for the school and set up a fund for research fellowships.

Summary

Carver's farm institutes, movable school, and readable bulletins were an important contribution to agricultural education. His research and teaching on soil conservation, crop diversification, and nutrition helped raise the standard of living for the families he reached.

The peanut industry greatly benefited from Carver's publicity and research. His work helped peanuts become a leading crop of the South. Carver's primary research was undertaken to find ways of improving life for poor farmers. He also interpreted his own and others' research to laymen. Farmers could benefit from science because Carver showed them how to apply it in their own lives.

George Carver was a symbol of personal triumph over poverty and racial discrimination. At the University of Iowa he displayed great talent and skill in science, but he sacrificed a career in research to serve his people in the South. His religious faith gave him a missionary zeal to improve the lives of the oppressed. One of Carver's greatest achievements was the impact he had on individuals. He gave youth, especially, a vision of what the world could be, and he encouraged them to work toward love and understanding of all races.

The publicity attending Carver's achievements prompted contributions to the Carver Foundation, and its establishment may be Carver's greatest legacy. Foundation grants continue to encourage students to study and use their education to benefit mankind.

Bibliography

Coulter, Ellis Merton. *The South During Reconstruction: 1865-1877*. Baton Rouge: Louisiana State University Press, 1947. Portrays the South and its people—black and white—during the Reconstruction years. Discusses the Freedmen's Bureau, postslavery labor, Southern economics, and agricultural changes.

Harlan, Lois R. *Booker T. Washington: The Making of a Black Leader*. New York: Oxford University Press, 1972. As head of Tuskegee Institute, Washington recruited Carver to teach there and was Carver's supervisor until the former's death in 1915. This biography gives another perspective on the policies and happenings at Tuskegee.

Holt, Rackham. *George Washington Carver: An American Biography*. Garden City, N.Y.: Doubleday, Doran and Co., 1943. Laudatory and somewhat inaccurate, this interesting story of Carver's life includes many anecdotes not found in other biographies. It pictures Carver as humble and misunderstood, a brilliant scientist, an able educator, and an inspiration to all who knew him.

Kluger, Richard. *Simple Justice*. New York: Alfred A. Knopf, 1975. Traces the practice of segregation in America from its beginnings in slavery to the 1954 Supreme Court decision to end legal segregation in public schools. Detailed and scholarly history of the people and organizations involved in the struggle for human dignity and equality.

Logan, Rayford W. *The Negro in the United States*. New York: Van Nostrand Reinhold Co., 1970. A history of the black people in America from 1619 to 1945, with emphasis on politics. It examines civil rights laws, court decisions, economic conditions, and the availability of education. Includes documents and speeches.

McMurry, Linda O. *George Washington Carver: Scientist and Symbol*. New York: Oxford University Press, 1981. Well-documented biography; disproves the myths surrounding Carver and describes his most significant accomplishments. Examines his contributions to agriculture, science, race relations, and education.

Weinstein, Allen, and Frank Otto Gatell, eds. *The Segregation Era, 1863-1954: A Modern Reader*. New York: Oxford University Press, 1970. In nineteen varied essays, leading historians consider blacks' fight for freedom, beginning with their role in the Civil War. Describes the failures of Reconstruction, the economic oppression of blacks, and the events leading up to the 1954 school desegregation ruling.

Woodward, C. Vann. *Origins of the New South, 1877-1913*. Baton Rouge: Louisiana State University Press, 1951. Details the history of the South after Reconstruction and examines the effects of industrial changes, populism, and Progressivism. Woodward's description of Southern economics provides insight into the plight of blacks after slavery.

Elaine Mathiasen

MARY CASSATT

Born: May 22, 1844; Allegheny City, Pennsylvania
Died: June 14, 1926; Château de Beaufresne, France
Area of Achievement: Art
Contribution: Using Impressionist techniques to create vivid, unsentimental portraits, Cassatt became America's foremost woman painter at a time when the art world was regarded as an exclusively male domain.

Early Life

Mary Stevenson Cassatt was the second daughter and fourth child of Robert and Katherine Johnson Cassatt. Robert Cassatt earned a comfortable income from stock trading and real estate. In 1849, the family moved to Philadelphia, but in 1851, they left for an extended stay in Europe.

The Cassatts first lived in Paris, but in 1853 they moved to Germany, where the eldest son, Alexander, could study engineering, and another son, Robert, could receive medical attention. In 1855, Robert died and was buried in Darmstadt; many years later, Mary Cassatt would have his body moved to be interred with others of the family at her French château.

The family returned to the United States in 1855, settling first in the Pennsylvania countryside and then back in Philadelphia, where Mary enrolled, in 1861, at the Pennsylvania Academy of Fine Arts. During her four years at the academy she received a solid, if uninspiring, education in artistic fundamentals. Students began with drawings from casts of statues, progressed to live models, and completed their training by making oil copies of paintings. The faults of this process were that the instructors were competent but undistinguished, and the paintings available for students were mediocre. At this time there were no major collections of art in the United States. Cassatt realized that to become an artist she needed exposure to the best in art, so she decided she must go to Europe.

In 1865, it was unheard of for a young woman to become a professional artist, and shocking for her to leave family and embark alone on a tour of Europe. Yet these were precisely the goals which Cassatt determined to achieve. There was considerable opposition from her family, to both her desire for an artistic career and the European visit, but she convinced them to accept her plans. This determination was characteristic of Cassatt, and its lifelong nature could be seen in her appearance. She was tall, thin, with fine but strong features and blue-gray eyes. Direct and forceful, she expressed her beliefs and opinions without reserve or regard for the sensibilities of others. Extremely energetic, she could work from dawn until the light faded but was able to put her paintings aside to care for her family; she herself never married. Such was the young woman who sailed for Europe in 1866, anticipating the first steps in her real artistic apprenticeship.

Life's Work

In Paris, Cassatt enrolled in the École des Beaux Arts and studied briefly with a fashionable society painter. Soon she left to study independently, mainly visiting museums and galleries and copying their paintings.

In 1867, the Paris World's Fair was held. Outside the official exhibitions, the painters Gustave Courbet and Édouard Manet held a private show. Unlike conventional painters, Courbet and Manet chose subjects which were contemporary rather than classical and portrayed them with vivid, unsparing realism, precise in observation and presentation. Cassatt was deeply influenced; Manet had the most important impact on her work prior to her association with Edgar Degas.

During the Franco-Prussian War of 1870, Cassatt returned to Philadelphia, but in 1871 she was back in Europe, spending eight months in Parma, Italy, where she made an extensive study of the painter Antonio Allegri da Correggio. The result can be seen in her work, chiefly in her depictions of children, which owed much to Correggio's paintings of Madonna and Child. She visited Spain, where she was particularly impressed by Diego Rodriguez de Silva Velázquez and El Greco. She also visited the Netherlands, where the paintings of Peter Paul Rubens, with his outstanding flesh tints and mastery of the human form, made a profound contribution to her style.

In 1873, Cassatt decided to settle permanently in Paris. Given the artistic ferment of the French capital and its central role in art, at the time it was the only natural place for a serious artist. In 1872, a painting of hers, signed "Mary Stevenson," had been accepted by the Paris Salon. She continued to submit work to the Salon for several years but grew increasingly disenchanted with the Salon's arbitrary and restrictive standards. One of her paintings was rejected because the background was too light; with a darkened background the painting was resubmitted and accepted.

Decisions such as this were one reason Cassatt ceased exhibiting in the Salon after 1877. The most important reason, however, was her discovery of the Impressionist movement and her association with Edgar Degas. The first Impressionist show was held in 1874, with works by such artists as Degas and Manet. The exhibition was fiercely attacked by traditional critics, but Cassatt perceived immediately the breakthrough which had been made. The Impressionist group contained widely diverse artists, who shared a common preoccupation with light—how to capture it, how to set it down on canvas. Their use of light and color was the key element in the movement, and after Cassatt viewed their work, light and color became essential in her work as well.

Degas had seen her work and admired it, and in 1877, they met. At forty-three, he was ten years older, an established artist known for his paintings and his sharp, often cutting remarks. The two had a stormy but productive relationship that lasted forty years. Although some have speculated on a romantic liaison between the two, it appears likely that their friendship, while close, was mainly professional. They had bitter arguments, over painting, politics, or personalities, but they always reconciled, usually at Cassatt's initiative. Degas was certainly the most important influence on Cassatt's artistic career.

Degas asked her to join the 1877 exhibition of the Impressionists. "I accepted with joy," she later said. "Now I could work with absolute independence without considering the opinion of a jury. I had already recognized who were my true masters. I admired Manet, Courbet, and Degas. I took leave of conventional art. I began to live."

Cassatt's relationship with Degas reinforced her natural strengths. They both chose contemporary subjects, preferring the human figure rather than landscapes, and both insisted on the importance of drawing and line. It was through Degas that Cassatt came to know the Japanese prints which had been introduced to France in the 1850's. From these she developed a simple, strong style that emphasized unusual angles of vision (from above, from the side, with the main figure only partially in view), a flattening of perspective, and the use of contrasting areas of pattern. Some of her best pieces were aquatints inspired by the Japanese prints.

By 1880, Cassatt was an acknowledged member of the Impressionist movement and exhibited regularly in their shows; she was the only American painter ever to do so. Urged on by Degas, she branched into pastels and prints, showing great promise in both.

Her father, mother, and sister Lydia joined her in Paris in 1877; nursing them through a series of illnesses often deprived her of painting time. In 1880, her brother Alexander and his family came to live with the Cassatts. Inspired by her nieces and nephews, Mary began her paintings of mother and child, the theme with which she is most popularly associated.

The 1890's were Mary Cassatt's most creative and productive period. In addition to her paintings and pastels, it was then that she produced the series of aquatints inspired by Japanese wood prints, which she exhibited in her first one-woman show of 1891.

Back in the United States, her fame grew slowly. An exhibit of the Impressionists in 1886 included three of her works, and her paintings were shown in Philadelphia, Boston, New York, and other cities. By 1891, she was well-known enough to receive a commission for a mural on the theme of "modern woman" at the Chicago World's Fair. She painted the canvas, her largest work, at the Château de Beaufresne, which she had recently purchased. Still, full recognition in her homeland lagged; her first one-woman show in New York (1895) had a lackluster reception, and she was not fully appreciated until after her death. In France, however, Cassatt was well-known. Her second one-woman show, held in Paris in 1893, was a large one: ninety-eight works, consisting of oils, pastels, and graphics. Her exhibition was well received by the public and the critics. Other shows were equally acclaimed, and she was quickly recognized as a major artist. In 1904, she was awarded the Legion of Honor.

In addition to being a creative artist, Cassatt was extremely important in bringing artwork to the United States. In 1873, she met Louisine Elder, who shared her interest in art. In 1901, Cassatt went on an extended European purchasing tour with Elder and Elder's husband, the wealthy banker H. O. Havemeyer. Over the next decade Cassatt advised them on a large number of purchases. Thanks to her perceptive eye and knowledgeable advice, the Havemeyers bought many Impressionist works and many important earlier paintings, such as El Greco's *View of Toledo* and his *Assumption of the Virgin*—the two most notable works of that artist to be found outside Spain. In 1929, the Havemeyer Collection went to the New York Metropolitan Museum of Art, forming the foundation of a national treasure.

After 1900, Mary Cassatt's work declined in quantity and, to some extent, in quality. Partly this was a result of her extensive work in collecting, but primarily her artistic decline was caused by family problems and failing eyesight. Her sister Lydia had died at an early age; in 1895, her mother died after a long illness, during which Cassatt was occupied as her nurse. The death of her favorite brother, Alexander, in 1906 was another severe blow, and five years later, after a tour of Egypt, her brother Gardner fell seriously ill and died in Paris. For a time, Mary Cassatt suffered from what she, and others, termed a "breakdown." It was not until 1912 that she began to work again.

When she did, it was in pastels, mainly because her failing eyesight did not allow the precision of prints or oils. Bothered by cataracts, she submitted to treatments and operations, none of which restored her sight; by 1913 her work was ended. She spent World War I removed from her beloved Château de Beaufresne because it was close to the battle lines.

In 1917, her friend and fellow professional, Degas, died. He had been the last link with the work and success of earlier years. She returned to her château in 1920 and remained there for the rest of her life. Nearly blind, she could not work but entertained young artists, mostly Americans, with her fiercely held, forcefully delivered views on art. She died at the Château de Beaufresne on June 14, 1926.

Summary

"I am not willing to admit that a woman can draw that well," Degas said upon viewing a work by Cassatt. This remark of an exceptional artist, who was Cassatt's closest friend and influence, reveals the obstacles facing a woman artist in the latter half of the nineteenth century. It is proof of Cassatt's determination and talent that she was accepted during her lifetime as one of the premier artists of the day; significantly, Degas purchased the very picture which inspired his comment.

Cassatt's contributions to art came in two phases: her own creations and her work in collecting. As an adviser to wealthy Americans such as H. O. Havemeyer and the banker James Stillman, Cassatt helped build some of the truly outstanding art collections of this century and brought priceless treasures to American museums. Cassatt made certain that no American art student would again face her early dilemma of living in a country which possessed no great artistic works. Such collections were important to Cassatt, because she firmly believed that the only way of learning to paint was to see, and copy, great paintings.

The energy that went into building collections was energy lost to her own work. She was also burdened with caring for her family, and she was increasingly troubled with eye problems. Cassatt, therefore, had a relatively limited production as an artist: about 225 prints and 617 oils and pastels, many of them studies rather than finished works.

It is the excellence of her work, rather than its quantity, which assures her undeniable achievement. In her chosen subjects, mothers and children, and the female form, she achieved a powerful, accurate, and original vision that rejected traditional sentiment and convention. She brought together the emphasis on light stressed by the Impressionists, the new angles of vision revealed by photography and Japanese prints, and the clarity and directness demanded by all great painters. Mary Cassatt blended these qualities together through her own honesty, efforts, and genius, producing a body of work that is among the most important in modern art.

Bibliography

Breeskin, Adelyn. *Mary Cassatt: A Catalogue Raisonné of the Oils, Pastels, Watercolors and Drawings*. Washington, D.C.: Smithsonian Institution Press, 1970. Contains a short but highly informative biography of Cassatt's life and career. The notes which accompany the illustrations are excellent and provide the reader with a solid guide to Cassatt's development as an artist.

Bullard, E. John. *Mary Cassatt: Oils and Pastels*. New York: Watson-Guptill Publications, 1976. The introductory sketch of Cassatt's life is excellent, and the commentary on the pictures is first-rate. Cassatt believed that the only way to learn painting was to copy great works; the best way to study her is to look at her works.

Carson, Julia. *Mary Cassatt*. New York: David McKay Co., 1966. A fine introductory biography, geared toward the younger reader.

Cassatt, Mary. *Cassatt and Her Circle: Selected Letters*. Edited by Nancy Mowll Mathews. New York: Abbeville Press, 1984. A generous collection of letters by Cassatt and her associates. More of interest to the specialist than the general student.

Hale, Nancy. *Mary Cassatt*. Garden City, N.Y.: Doubleday and Co., 1975. This biography is generally good on facts and relationships, but occasionally strays into confusing speculation about Cassatt's thoughts and motives.

McKown, Robin. *The World of Mary Cassatt*. New York: Thomas Y. Crowell, 1972. A wide-ranging view of Cassatt's development as an artist; the work assumes that the reader already has a fair understanding of the period under discussion. Contains an excellent bibliography.

Sweet, Frederick. *Miss Mary Cassatt: Impressionist from Pennsylvania*. Norman: University of Oklahoma Press, 1966. This biography has good sources—Sweet was one of the first authors with wide access to letters of Cassatt and her associates—and excellent documentation. The approach, however, is uncritical and nonanalytical.

Michael Witkoski

WILLA CATHER

Born: December 7, 1873; Gore, Virginia
Died: April 24, 1947; New York, New York
Areas of Achievement: Literature and journalism
Contribution: At a time when such careers were nearly unheard of for women, Cather became a celebrated theater and music critic, crusading magazine editor, and accomplished novelist-poet in the tradition of American naturalism.

Early Life

The life of Willela Sibert Cather is filled with small surprises. Though she became identified in the minds of her readers with Nebraska, the setting for much of her fiction, she was actually born and lived the first nine years of her life at Willowshade, her family's home in rural western Virginia. Then too, although many biographies report the year of her birth as 1874 and her tombstone reads 1876, her actual year of birth was 1873. S. S. McClure, founder of *McClure's* magazine, suggested the first alteration when he hired Cather as one of his editors in 1906, while she herself chose 1876 upon publication of *Youth and the Bright Medusa* in 1920. Though almost every picture ever taken of Cather shows a round-faced, kindly-looking Midwestern farm woman in middy-blouse and tie, she actually lived half of her life in New York, first in Greenwich Village and later on Park Avenue. Her plain, almost mannish appearance served her well, both in the male world of journalism and later as adjunct to her distinctively American fiction. In later life, she would wear bright, sometimes almost garish colors and prints.

Cather liked to say that she had been named after both her grandfathers, William Cather and William Lee Boak, and for her mother's brother Willie Sibert Boak, who fell fighting for the Confederacy. The family Bible, however, lists her name at birth as "Willela," the same name as that of her father's deceased sister. This small list of minor alterations and harmless deceptions tells much about Cather's ability to recognize the importance of romantic characterization. It also implies, correctly as it appears, that many of Cather's most appealing fictional protagonists reflect aspects both of their creator and of people she knew and often admired.

Cather was the eldest of seven children born to Charles Fectigue and Mary Virginia Boak Cather. Rachel Boak, Cather's maternal grandmother, owned the house in which Cather was born. It was located in Back Creek Valley near the town of Winchester. Boak was a widow with five children, the youngest of whom was Cather's mother. Even in her youth, Cather was attracted to the strength and self-sufficiency of both her mother and her grandmother. In contrast, Cather's father remained boyish and impractical even to his last days. These, too, seemed attractive qualities to Cather, and she would later immortalize all three in her fiction.

The isolated life of Back Creek Valley as well as the divided North-South loyalties of Cather's family gave her a more immediate insight into post–Civil War America than her date of birth alone would have allowed. Opportunities for homesteading in the Midwest, very real in the 1870's, also tempted Cather's father, and he decided in 1877 to settle his growing family in Nebraska. In 1883, the entire family made the difficult journey on the thirteen-year-old transcontinental railroad. Thus, the association of Cather and Red Cloud, Nebraska, began amid the child's longings for the Virginia of her birth.

Though Red Cloud, with approximately twenty-five hundred residents, was considerably more populous than Back Creek Valley, it was still isolated. Furthermore, because it had become a railroad hub, the population was increasing and housing was scarce. The house which the Cathers rented (which still stands) is identical to Thea Kronborg's home in *The Song of the Lark* (1915). Cather was as delighted as Thea to have been given her own room; like Thea's it had roses on its wallpaper, and it became a sanctuary for the sensitive ten-year-old with six younger brothers and sisters.

College at the University of Nebraska in Lincoln was a period of happiness and great awakening for Cather. Jim Burden, in *My Ántonia* (1918), described the university as it must have appeared to Cather in 1890, a campus filled with new paths and young trees, a school located where there had been only prairie a few years before. It was in Lincoln that Cather met Dr. Julius Tynsdale, drama critic for the Lincoln *Evening News*, and his sister Emma Tynsdale Westermann, wife of the newspaper's owner and the mother of six boys who would be fictionalized as the Erlichs in *One of Ours* (1922). Cather was impressed by the intelligence and unaffected intellectuality of the family. Before her graduation in 1895, she would be writing drama criticism for the Lincoln *Journal* and would become known for pithy and sometimes savage reviews of local drama and music events. Her earliest works, mostly criticism and poetry, were published in *Hesperian*, the university's literary magazine.

Life's Work

It was only natural, given her considerable experience in newspaper work, that Cather would begin her career in journalism, though it was an unusual field for a woman in the 1880's. For a time she continued at the *Journal*, but by late summer of her graduation year had moved her column, now called "The Passing Show," to the Lincoln *Courier*. In these early years, she tried to balance journalism against creative writing, doing the latter evenings in her room. The year after graduation, she also applied for a teaching position in Nebraska's English Department when a former professor of hers retired. The appointment was denied, however, possibly as much because Cather lacked a master's degree as because of her sex.

At the age of twenty-two, Cather was offered the post of editor of a women's magazine published in Pittsburgh, Pennsylvania, the *Home Monthly*. Cather saw this as an important opportunity, not only because she would be living a mere 350 miles from New York but also because the magazine could provide an outlet for her fiction. Indeed, her short story "Tommy the Unsentimental," which appeared in *Home Monthly*'s first issue, is a portrait of the young Cather, who left Nebraska at this early stage of her life and would never again reside in that state.

Pittsburgh's cultural life was surprisingly rich in the mid-1890's, and Cather was struck by its contrasting wealth and grinding poverty. She would write her famous short story "Paul's Case" while there and use the city as its background. Cather became so well-known locally that in 1897 she was offered the position of full-time drama critic of the Pittsburgh *Daily Leader*. This led to her serving as guest critic for the New York *Sun*. All the while she was sending pieces back to Nebraska for publication in the *Courier*. By the turn of the century, Cather was a solidly established and respected Eastern-based journalist and critic.

In 1900, Cather worked for a brief time as editor of a Pittsburgh literary magazine known as *The Library*. Charles (Chuck) Clark intended it to be an American version of London's *The Spectator*, and while it lasted *The Library* also provided an outlet for Cather's fiction. Cather was also contributing to national publications at this time. The April, 1900, issue of *Cosmopolitan* contained her short story "Eric Hermannson's Soul." The November *Ladies' Home Journal* carried her tribute to a friend, composer Ethelbert Nevin, who would die suddenly the following February. Nevin had lived the kind of restless questing life typical of many characters in Cather's novels.

By 1901, *The Library* had ceased publication. Rather than seek another job in editing, Cather believed, wrongly as it appears, that teaching would allow her more time to pursue her writing career. Therefore, she taught the spring term at Pittsburgh's Central High School. Though she found the work tedious and considerably more time-consuming than she had expected, Cather still managed to publish several pieces: a poem in *Lippincott's*, a short story in *New England Magazine*, assorted reviews and articles for the Lincoln *Courier*. She occasionally used a pseudonym, "Henry Nicklemann," for these early works, especially if she had doubts about their content or quality.

Cather was fortunate during her Pittsburgh years to have the friendship and moral support of Isabelle McClung and her father, Judge Samuel McClung. The McClungs came to regard Cather almost as a second daughter. She resided in their comfortable home, even accompanied their daughter on a European tour in 1902, and continued her high school teaching, writing important short stories such as "Paul's Case" (based on one of her students), "The Sculptor's Funeral," and "A Wagner Matinee" during this period. The last two works appeared in a collection entitled *The Troll Garden*, handsomely published in 1905 by McClure and reviewed in *The New York Times*. This, added to *April Twilights*, a book of poems which had appeared in 1903, meant that Cather was now making solid progress in her career as a writer.

Cather's sudden celebrity spurred the always impulsive McClure personally to come to the McClungs' Pittsburgh home and offer her an editorial post on *McClure's*, his famous magazine. To accept meant a bright future, residence in New York's Greenwich Village, and most important, a nationally published outlet for her writing. Though the McClungs were reluctant to see Cather leave Pittsburgh for the uncertainties of New York, and though Cather herself had doubts about reentering the world of journalism, she did accept the offer and began a spectacularly successful period at *McClure's*.

There was real irony in the fact that the essentially conservative Cather found herself, in 1906, the managing editor of America's foremost magazine of social protest, famous for its "muckraking" exposés by Lincoln Steffens, Ida Tarbell, John Phillips, and Ray Stannard Baker. She also found herself living among writers such as Theodore Dreiser in the bohemian atmosphere south of Washington Square. Still, Cather met the challenge, successfully editing a controversial serialized profile of Mary Baker Eddy, founder of the Christian Science Church, which made *McClure's* circulation soar. She continued to write and began her novel *Alexander's Bridge* (1912). It first appeared serialized in *McClure's* under the title *Alexander's Masquerade*.

All this work took its toll, and Cather began a holiday in the spring of 1912 in New Mexico and Arizona. She loved the Southwest, and it would provide inspiration for her *The Song of the Lark*, which appeared in 1915, immediately following *O Pioneers!* (1913), her poignant evocation of the Midwest. Cather recognized after the success of these works that her great strength lay in her ability to portray the yearnings of apparently simple people and to realize strikingly the settings in which they lived. She would refine, though never essentially change, her method throughout a long series of novels.

Upon returning to New York in 1913, Cather moved into a Bank Street, Greenwich Village apartment with Edith Lewis, a woman with whom she would share the remainder of her life and who would become her literary executrix. Bank Street provided the retreat Cather needed to write after frantically busy days at *McClure's*. On Friday afternoons, she and Lewis would hold open house in their apartment; their guest list would read like a "who's who" of the literary world. The onset of the war in 1914 prohibited Cather from traveling outside the United States; she came to know the Southwest even better during the war years. Even so, World War I would figure importantly in the concluding portions of *One of Ours*, in which she fused familiar themes of hopeless ambition and the menacing force of the war to produce an affectingly tragic novel.

In 1917, Cather received an honorary doctor of letters degree from her alma mater, the University of Nebraska. She and Edith Abbott, the assistant of social worker Jane Addams, were the first women ever awarded honorary degrees by that institution. The honor meant much to Cather, for it implied recognition by the state she had always considered her own. Cather spent the balance of that summer in Jaffrey, New Hampshire, visiting her friend Isabelle McClung, who had recently married; she wrote much of *My Ántonia* while there. Despite generally mixed reviews when it appeared in 1918, *My Ántonia* has come to be considered by many Cather's masterpiece, perhaps the most typically American novel of the twentieth century. It is based on Cather's Nebraska childhood, and many of its characters resemble people she had known in Red Cloud.

Cather was disappointed by the initial sales of *My Ántonia*. Her dissatisfaction with Houghton Mifflin caused her to seek out Alfred A. Knopf, then new in the field, a man who, like Cather, believed that books should have both durability and a pleasing appearance. Knopf also had a reputation for treating his authors as artists and consulting them in matters of format and publicity. All this was congenial to the by now established author, who during her lifetime refused to allow her works to appear in paperback editions; Cather remained with Knopf for the balance of her career. Their business relationship deepened into warm friendship, which endured until Cather's death twenty-seven years later.

Despite that fact that *My Ántonia* had appeared in 1922 in French serialization, the year was a difficult one for Cather. *One of Ours*, which had been published that year, was criticized severely for its melodramatic war passages. Heywood Broun, writing in the New York *World*, believed Cather had sentimentalized the war, while L. M. Field of the *Literary Digest* believed that the book's message was that the world was no place for an idealist. These critics failed to see that Cather's real purpose was to show the universal human need to devote one's life to some cause greater than oneself. That Claude Wheeler, the hero of the novel, was able to find his cause only on the battlefields of France is the essence of human tragedy. *One of Ours*, nevertheless, became a popular success, and received the Pulitzer Prize in 1923. Still, Cather had been deeply hurt by what she considered unfair criticism, and thought that her world had been shaken to its foundations. She sought consolation in religion, and at the end of 1922 was confirmed a member of the Episcopal Church.

The mid-1920's brought lectures at the Breadloaf Writers Conference, Middlebury, Vermont, and the University of Chicago, as well as an invitation to the MacDowell Colony, Peterborough, New Hampshire. Cather also published *The Professor's House* (1925), her most personal novel since *The Song of the Lark*. In 1925, she returned to New Mexico, having by now been discovered by D. H. Lawrence and his circle. Her conversations with Lawrence, a writer she admired, were uneasy but cordial. This visit to New Mexico inspired her novel *Death Comes for the Archbishop* (1927), based on her reading of William Joseph Howlett's *The Life of the Right Reverend Joseph P. Machebeuf* (1908). In 1927, she moved to the Grosvenor, the Fifth Avenue apartment hotel she would make her home for the last twenty years of her life.

In the last third of her life, Cather received numerous honors: doctorates from Yale University (1929), the University of California, and Princeton; a profile in *The New Yorker*, which was written by Louise Bogan and subtitled "American-Classic," and a *Time* magazine cover story (all in 1931); the Gold Medal of the National Institute of Arts and Letters (1944). Though she wrote several more novels, *Shadows on the Rock* (1931), *Obscure Destinies* (1932), *Lucy Gayheart* (1935), and *Sapphira and the Slave Girl* (1940), she turned increasingly to short stories and personal memoirs. World War II publication restrictions and her own failing health curtailed her output considerably during the 1940's. Her short-story anthology *The Old Beauty and Others* appeared posthumously in 1948.

Summary

On April 17, 1947, Cather wrote to her longtime friend Dorothy Canfield asking for her recollections of a meeting they had had forty-five years earlier with the distinguished English poet A. E. Housman. Cather was preparing a memoir on that meeting, unfortunately one she would not live to write. She no doubt was looking back on an incredibly productive and distinguished career of her own. She would die quietly in her New York apartment on April 24 and be buried in her beloved Jaffrey, New Hampshire, a place where she had spent many happy summers.

Cather's works provide an unmatched legacy of American life. Though she was always an admirer of Henry James and though critics have deduced Jamesian influences in Cather's fiction, her spare, lean style and bold characterizations made her unlike any author before her or since. Though she believed that setting should serve characterization, it is certainly true that the America in which she lived provided inspiration for her most memorable works.

Bibliography

Bennett, Mildred R. *The World of Willa Cather*. Lincoln: University of Nebraska Press, 1961. A biography, particularly good in recalling Cather's Nebraska girlhood. It is filled with vivid descriptions of Red Cloud and the Midwest of the last quarter of the nineteenth century.

Brown, Edward K., and Leon Edel. *Willa Cather: A Critical Biography*. New York: Alfred A. Knopf, 1953. The standard scholarly biography, completed by Edel, the well-known biographer of Henry James. This volume concentrates on biographical information which can be deduced from Cather's works.

Daiches, David. *Willa Cather: A Critical Introduction*. Ithaca, N.Y.: Cornell University Press, 1951. An appropriate book for readers new to Cather's works. It is scholarly, well indexed, and a classic reference text.

Lathrop, JoAnna, ed. *Willa Cather: A Checklist of Her Published Writing*. Lincoln: University of Nebraska Press, 1975. An annotated list of all of Cather's works including the lesser known posthumously published essays on writing as well as her travel essays, reviews, and student works.

Lewis, Edith. *Willa Cather Living: A Personal Record*. New York: Alfred A. Knopf, 1953. A famous memoir written by Cather's longtime friend, companion, and literary executrix.

Robinson, Phyllis C. *Willa: The Life of Willa Cather*. Garden City, N.Y.: Doubleday and Co., 1983. A popular biography, with good material on Cather's family and friends. It contains some biographical analyses of Cather's major works.

Sergeant, Elizabeth Shepley. *Willa Cather: A Memoir*. Philadelphia: J. B. Lippincott Co., 1953. A recollection written by a longtime friend. Sergeant provides interesting information on Cather's life in Pittsburgh and New York as well as Cather's several meetings with American writer Sarah Orne Jewett and her friendship with Annie Anderson Fields, widow of James T. Fields, the publisher of Nathaniel Hawthorne and Herman Melville.

Robert J. Forman

GEORGE CATLIN

Born: July 26, 1796; Wilkes-Barre, Pennsylvania
Died: December 23, 1872; Jersey City, New Jersey
Areas of Achievement: American Indian art and ethnology
Contribution: Catlin provided some of the earliest paintings showing the culture of the upper Missouri River Valley Indians, and his books include much significant ethnological material about tribal ceremonies.

Early Life

George Catlin was born July 26, 1796, in Wilkes-Barre, Pennsylvania. The fifth of fourteen children born to Polly Sutton and Putnam Catlin, he achieved the most fame. Polly, his mother, had been born on the Pennsylvania frontier and as a child had been captured by the Indians during the 1778 "Wyoming Massacre." His Connecticut-born father, Putnam Catlin, served as a fife major during the American Revolution. After the war, Putnam studied law, moved to Wilkes-Barre, and married Polly Sutton. The Catlins hoped that young George would become a lawyer also, and in 1817, they sent the twenty-one-year-old back to Connecticut to study.

His training completed, in less than two years he returned home with reasonable skills but little enthusiasm for the law. Rather, he wanted to become a portrait painter, and even during court proceedings he sketched scenes and people in the room. Sometime between 1821 and 1823, he quit his law practice and moved to Philadelphia, where he set out on his life's work. A handsome young man of no more than five feet nine inches, he had a deep scar on his left cheek, black hair, blue eyes, and a medium complexion. He was a friendly, outgoing person, who made friends easily and usually kept them for life. These attributes enabled him to penetrate the artistic society in Philadelphia, and by early 1824, he became a member of the Pennsylvania Academy, the literary and artistic group in that city.

Soon he had enough commissions for miniatures and portraits, and financial security seemed at hand, yet Catlin was restless and dissatisfied. A visiting group of Indian leaders who were in the East to negotiate with the government caught his attention. They seemed natural and dignified compared to his city acquaintances, and Catlin decided to paint them and record their customs. Before he could do so, he continued to do portraits and to make friends with wealthy and prominent people to finance his later western travels. While in Albany, New York, working on a portrait of Governor De Witt Clinton, Catlin met Clara Bartless Gregory, and on May 20, 1828, the two were married. Between portrait assignments, Catlin traveled to nearby reservations to paint Indian leaders, and he did several portraits of the noted Seneca leader Red Jacket. Despite his marriage, his continuing restlessness overcame him, and in early 1830, Catlin set out for St. Louis to begin what was to be his life's work: painting, observing, and describing the western Indians.

Life's Work

In St. Louis, Catlin met the famous explorer William Clark, who was then superintendent for Indian affairs for the tribes beyond the Mississippi. Clark knew the western tribes as well as anyone and proved to be very helpful. He answered Catlin's questions and invited him to paint portraits of the Indians who came to the city to confer with him. During the summer of 1830, Catlin accompanied Clark to Prairie du Chien, Wisconsin, to observe a treaty council meeting there, and later that same year, they visited Indians encamped along the Kansas River. In late 1830, Catlin traveled to Fort Leavenworth to observe and paint tribes there, while the next spring, he accompanied an Indian agent up the Missouri River to what is now Omaha, to visit other villages. By the end of 1831, the artist had observed, met, and painted Indians from perhaps fifteen distinct tribes, and he had acquired artifacts from many of them in addition to his sketches and portraits.

Still, Catlin wanted to observe villages and tribes that were farther removed from white society. His chance came in March, 1832, when he set off up the Missouri River on the American Fur Company steamboat *Yellowstone*, traveling upstream to Fort Union, at the mouth of the Yellowstone River in western North Dakota. Catlin worked as rapidly as possible, painting as many as five or six pictures a day. From Fort Union, Catlin and two trappers went back down the Missouri in a small skiff. Along the way, they halted at the Mandan villages in central North Dakota, where Catlin drew detailed pictures of the Mandan Okeepa Ceremony. Five years later, a smallpox epidemic virtually destroyed this tribe; his data, as a result, constitute almost the only information about the ceremony that survived.

Two years later, Catlin accompanied an army expedition west onto the southern plains. Catlin also traveled north to Fort Snelling at what is now Minneapolis-St. Paul to paint villagers there. In 1836, he decided to visit the famous Pipe Stone Quarry in southwestern Minnesota, the site from which the Sioux obtained the red stone which they used for their pipes. Despite the Indians' efforts to discourage them, Catlin and several companions traveled to the quarry, where he made sketches and gathered samples of the stone. A geologist later named the mineral Catlinite in his honor. By this time, Catlin had executed approximately six hundred paintings and sketches of Indians, as well as collecting artifacts that varied from a Crow tepee to beads and feather headdresses. He had taken copious notes which he would later transcribe and publish along with his drawings.

By 1837, he had moved this collection east, and late that year, he began exhibiting his paintings and artifacts, or Indian Gallery, as he called the collection. The exhibit drew large crowds, and he soon took it to Washington, Philadelphia, and Boston. Catlin, however, proved to be an inept businessman. He hoped to sell his material to the United States government and worked for some years to interest Congress in buying it. When it became apparent that the government had little serious interest in Indian materials, a disappointed Catlin set sail for England. He arrived there in 1839, and again exhibited before large and enthusiastic crowds. In 1841, he published the first of his several books about the Indians. Always short of money, by 1845 he moved to Paris, where he was asked to exhibit the paintings at the Louvre.

Catlin's years in France were among the most unhappy of his life. On the edge of bankruptcy, and with little chance of getting back to the United States, he became discouraged at the news that Congress voted repeatedly not to buy his paintings. Then, in July, 1845, his wife, Clara, died of pneumonia, and a year later his three-year-old son George died as well. His wife's family arranged for his three daughters to return to the United States, but Catlin remained mired in debt and unable to leave Paris. In 1852, Joseph Harrison, a wealthy American, bought Catlin's paintings and took them back to Philadelphia, leaving the artist more or less free from debt. With little more than determination, he began to paint new copies of his original Indian Gallery during the 1850's. He also made several trips to South America and to the west coast of North America. In 1870, he returned to the United States and was reunited with his daughters. Catlin died in 1872, believing that his country had spurned his life's work and that the Indian Gallery had been lost.

Ironically, had Congress bought the paintings in the 1840's, they would not have survived the Smithsonian fire. As it was, when Catlin's exhibit of his cartoon collection failed in New York in 1870, Joseph Henry of the Smithsonian invited the artist to display them in Washington.

Summary

George Catlin stands out as a man with single-minded purpose: to preserve knowledge of the western Indians, their dress and customs, for all Americans. This goal took him west, where he painted Indians from dozens of tribes. As art, his work does not rank as great. He was largely self-taught, and he often painted hurriedly and under crude conditions. When he had time, he used a style similar to that which he had employed as a Philadelphia portrait painter. Often he sketched quickly, focusing on a person's face and barely sketching in the remainder of the body. Regardless of the style, Catlin's work is considered among the most accurate and unadorned in depicting Native Americans. Hundreds of his paintings have survived, and he did succeed in preserving knowledge of Indian life.

In addition to his paintings, Catlin kept knowledge of the Indians alive in other ways. As a showman and exhibitor, he exposed thousands of Americans to Indian scenes and artifacts during the mid-nineteenth century. Of more significance, his writings provide valuable ethnological data for knowledge of the tribal societies that he visited. His more significant books include *Letters and Notes on the Manners, Customs and Conditions of the North American Indians* (1841), *Catlin's North American Indian Portfolio* (1844), *Life Amongst the Indians* (1861), and *Last Rambles Amongst the Indians of the Rocky Mountains and the Andes* (1867). In addition to these, Catlin published catalogs of his exhibits and many articles for newspapers in the United States. Throughout his career, he labored to bring knowledge of the Indians to white society. For artists and ethnologists, his legacy is rich.

Bibliography

Catlin, George. *Episodes from Life Among the Indians and Last Rambles*. Edited by Marvin C. Ross. Norman: University of Oklahoma Press, 1959. Includes selections from Catlin's first and last books about his experiences with Indians. This well-edited collection includes more than 150 photographs of Catlin's paintings.

——————. *Letters and Notes on the Manners, Customs and Conditions of the North American Indians*. 2 vols. London: D. Bogue, 1841. Reprint. Mineola, N.Y.: Dover Publications, 1973. This is a clearly reprinted edition of Catlin's most significant ethnological writing, done only a few years after he left the West.

Ewers, John C. *Artists of the Old West*. New York: Doubleday and Co., 1965. Ewers is probably the most knowledgeable student of Catlin's contributions to ethnology, and he discusses those in his chapter on Catlin.

Haberly, Loyd. *Pursuit of the Horizon: A Life of George Catlin, Painter and Recorder of the American Indian*. New York: Macmillan, 1948. A full length popular biography of Catlin which gives a balanced treatment of his long life, including his years in Europe. It has neither notes nor bibliography but is based on solid research.

Hassrick, Royal B. *The George Catlin Book of American Indians*. New York: Watson-Guptill Publications, 1977. This volume, featuring both color and black-and-white plates, reproduces a generous selection of Catlin's paintings. It briefly discusses his life, art, and writings, but its value lies chiefly in the illustrations.

Haverstock, Mary Sayre. *Indian Gallery: The Story of George Catlin*. New York: Four Winds Press, 1973. This popular biography focuses primarily on Catlin's pre-1839 activities. The last four decades of his life are compressed into a mere fifty pages.

McCracken, Harold. *George Catlin and the Old Frontier*. New York: Dial Press, 1959. The result of thorough research, this well-written biography focuses almost entirely on Catlin's life to 1839; it devotes only two of twenty-two chapters to his career between 1839 and 1872.

Roehm, Marjorie Catlin. *The Letters of George Catlin and His Family: A*

Chronicle of the American West. Berkeley: University of California Press, 1966. Based on several hundred Catlin family letters used for the first time, this book combines the author's narrative with extensive selections from family correspondence. Half of the book considers Catlin's activities after he left the country. The use of family papers gives an immediacy to the story.

Roger L. Nichols

SAMUEL DE CHAMPLAIN

Born: c. 1567; Brouage, France
Died: December 25, 1635; Quebec, Canada
Areas of Achievement: Exploration and settlement
Contribution: Widely respected as the Father of New France, Champlain
represented the French attempt to acquire and settle North America, one
of the great might-have-beens of American history.

Early Life

Little is known of Samuel de Champlain's early life, not even his date of
birth. Scattered evidence and informed speculation have placed it as early as
1564 and as late as 1573; authorities seem to be divided fairly equally
between 1567 and 1570. He was born and reared on the Atlantic coast of
France in the town of Brouage, a small seaport important for the salt trade.
During the years of his youth, Brouage was a minor prize in the bitter religious wars between the Catholics and the Calvinist Huguenots. He may well
have come from a Huguenot family, though as an adult he was a staunch
Catholic. As he climbed the social ladder, he officially described his father as
a captain in the merchant marine, attributing to him the "de" before Champlain, implying nobility. As a young man, however, the explorer was simply
Samuel Champlain, and there is no record of a patent of nobility for the family. He had little formal education, but he learned the practical skills of seamanship and navigation from an early age and developed a straightforward
and effective writing style, unembellished by Latinisms.

Like many of the other pioneers of the New World, therefore, he was a
self-made man. He was strongly religious, justifying his projects by a desire
to save heathen souls for Christ as well as by arguments for the economic and
political benefits to the kingdom of France. Personally he was ascetic and
self-denying, enduring the hardships of ocean voyages and frigid winters
without complaint and ignoring the feminine companionship offered by Native Americans to the Europeans. He was a courageous soldier and an honest administrator. He married late in life and had no children. No authentic
contemporary portrait of him survives; he was described as being modest in
stature with substantial toughness of both mind and body.

Life's Work

Champlain made his first voyage to the Americas in 1599, signing on with a
Spanish fleet to the Caribbean. His skill as an observer, author, cartographer,
and sketch artist has left an admirable record of this voyage into the Spanish
Americas. He described the Spanish empire, speculated on the possibility of
building a canal in Panama, and noted the injustices of the heavy-handed
Spanish rule over the native peoples. His handwritten and illustrated account

brought him to the attention of Henry IV, King of France, under whom he had served as a soldier, and he received an appointment as what has been described as a "royal geographer." In 1603, he accompanied François Pont-Gravé, a sea captain, to North America with the royal commission to establish a French colony. The St. Lawrence river valley had been visited and claimed for France by Jacques Cartier in 1534-1536, but the forbidding winters and the lack of either precious metals or an obvious passage to the Pacific Ocean had discouraged French settlement. Each year, nevertheless, French, Basque, and assorted other European fishermen had braved the North Atlantic to fish in the teeming waters and engage in some offhand trade with the Indians. After a stormy voyage of ten weeks, Champlain first set foot on North American soil. In the course of his sixty-odd years of life, he crossed the Atlantic no less than twenty-five times, tirelessly working to establish his dream of New France in America.

In 1604-1605, Champlain spent his first winter in America, at St. Croix Island, which eventually became a United States National Monument along the border of Maine and New Brunswick, Canada. It was a disastrously cold winter and thirty-five of the seventy-nine men died. The settlement was abandoned the following spring. The next year Champlain and his men, reinforced by newcomers and supplies from France, tried an alternate site, Port Royal, on the protected inner coast of present-day Nova Scotia, which the French called Acadia. From this base, Champlain led exploratory expeditions down the American coast as far south as Cape Cod. He wrote descriptions and sketched navigational maps and charts of the New England coast which are remarkable for their accuracy. A decade and a half later, the English pilgrims landed at Plymouth Rock, believing that they were actually several hundred miles farther south, along the coast of Virginia.

The Port Royal colony proved unsatisfactory because of its high cost and modest return to the investors of the French colonial company. The French monarchy itself was disinclined to bear its costs, and there were no precious metals and few furs to be acquired. Champlain returned to France and laid a plan before Henry IV for a new colonial venture. The vast watershed of the St. Lawrence offered two attractive possibilities. It funneled the trade in Canadian furs to a single point, the natural fortress of Quebec, and it held the promise of a passage to the Orient, because Indian tales spoke of vast seas which could be reached by following river routes to the west and north. The king approved, and in 1608 three ships sailed from Honfleur, France, to establish a permanent settlement at Quebec. (Only a year earlier, the English had founded Jamestown in Virginia.) Had Champlain but pressed his New England exploration south of Cape Code, charted the natural harbor to be known later as New York and the lower Hudson River, and petitioned the French monarch to establish his settlement there, the history of North America might have been very different indeed. New France, however, remained centered at Quebec to the north.

Champlain and his men built a snug settlement on what is today the lower town of Quebec City. For himself he constructed an elaborate "habitation," part fortress and part château. His sketch of this three-story building, complete with a moat and a tower, bears an extraordinary resemblance to the "lieutenance," the royal headquarters building at Honfleur, from which he sailed. The first winter at Quebec was a very rough one; of the twenty-four Frenchmen who stayed on when the ships sailed for home, only Champlain and seven others survived. The settlement was reinforced from the mother country in the spring. He constantly tried to encourage families to settle and establish farms, but with little success. He brought his young wife, Hélène, with him in 1620; she disliked the isolation of Quebec and went back to Paris in 1624, never to return. By the time Champlain had died at Quebec in 1635, the number of European settlers in the colony had still not surpassed two hundred.

Recalling his skirmishes with local Indians along the New England coast and the repressive Spanish rule he had seen, Champlain strove to establish and maintain good relations with the Indians of the St. Lawrence basin, the Montagnais, the Algonquians, and the Hurons. He respected their way of life and nurtured the hope that they could be converted to Christianity gently rather than by force. Their goodwill was essential to the colony, because they controlled the sources of the beaver pelts upon which Quebec's economy was based. Champlain cemented relations with them by promising military aid in their warfare against their traditional rivals, the Iroquois. In 1609, he accompanied a war party of Montagnais and their allies against the Mohawk Iroquois. They traveled south from the St. Lawrence to Lake Champlain, in modern New York State, and met their enemy near the site of Fort Ticonderoga. Champlain and two other Frenchmen, protected by armor and firing harquebuses, quickly scattered the Iroquois. The victory was by no means decisive, however, and traditional enmity remained. In 1615, Champlain led another war party west to Lakes Huron and Ontario and then southward, where he fought a battle near modern-day Syracuse, New York. The Iroquois were now better informed about the limitations of the harquebus and turned back the invaders. Champlain was wounded and the myth of European invincibility was broken. Throughout the history of Quebec, the French maintained their alliance with the local tribes, but paid for it with the hostility of the Iroquois in the British-American Colonies to the south.

From time to time, Champlain would return to France to lobby for governmental and commercial support for the struggling colony. The situation in Europe was volatile, a residual effect of the wars of religion. King Henry IV was assassinated in 1610 and followed to the throne by Louis XIII, a mere boy. During the 1620's, Cardinal Richelieu stabilized the government of France by becoming the young king's first minister. In 1627, he founded a company called the "Hundred Associates," a royally chartered monopoly to develop the Canadian colony. Champlain was confirmed the company's and the king's lieutenant in Canada, strengthening his authority. Nevertheless, direct government aid to New France was meager, and without the profits from the fur trade, the whole enterprise would have collapsed. In 1628 and 1629, France and Britain were briefly at war, and Champlain was besieged at Quebec by British privateers and forced to surrender the colony to them. Canada was returned to France by the Treaty of Saint-Germain-en-Laye in 1632, and Champlain sailed from France for the last time to reestablish the colony and govern it in 1633. He died on Christmas day, 1635, and was buried beneath the little Catholic church he had founded, Notre Dame de la Recouvrance, much lamented by Europeans and Indians alike.

Summary

Like the hardy explorers and early settlers from Great Britain, the Netherlands, and Spain, who also established the European presence on the North American continent during the sixteenth and seventeenth centuries, Champlain combined the virtues of fortitude for the hardships of the time and vision for the possibilities of the future. Like many, though by no means all, of them, he also was a man of strong Christian convictions, which he sought to bring to the Indians even as he used them to discipline fellow Europeans who were given to brutal and exploitive behavior. He sought honest alliances with the Native Americans, using his superior military technology to aid them in their traditional battles. He sought to turn a fair profit for French merchants through the fur trade, but he constantly argued that what America needed most was families of settlers who would clear and work the land. He realized that a purely commercial, missionary, and military colony could never create a permanent New France in the Americas.

The British colonies in New England and Virginia grew into thriving settlements, based upon agriculture and artisan manufacturing, as well as trade. By the 1750's, Champlain's New France had extended its net of military and trading posts over thousands of miles from the St. Lawrence to the lower Mississippi, laying the foundations of Detroit, Chicago, St. Louis, and New Orleans, yet the thinly settled French were outmanned and outgunned by the British and their American settlers. By 1763, New France was no more. Nevertheless, a Francophone culture continues to thrive at Champlain's Quebec, and it directly influences the northeastern United States.

Champlain, like Christopher Columbus, reminds Anglo-Americans that their ancestors were not the only ones whose daring and foresight served to bring Western civilization to this continent. Champlain is justly recognized as the Father of New France and ranks also as one of the great American discoverers.

Bibliography

Bishop, Morris. *Champlain: The Life of Fortitude*. New York: Alfred A. Knopf, 1948. A solidly written biography organized around Champlain's many voyages to the New World. There are lengthy quotations from Champlain's own colorful descriptions of the country and people he found and several of his own sketches, as well as excellent modern maps and several appendices on some of the more controversial aspects of his life and times.

Eccles, William J. *France in America*. New York: Harper and Row, Publishers, 1972. A volume in Henry Steele Commager's New American Nation Series, this standard history covers French colonization in North America and the Caribbean from the earliest contact until the American Revolution. In his first chapters, Eccles puts the contributions of Champlain into a broader context.

Garrod, Stan. *Samuel de Champlain*. Don Mills, Ontario: Fitzhenry and Whiteside, 1981. A brief paperback, lucidly and attractively setting forth the major phases and accomplishments of Champlain's life. Based largely upon Bishop's book, it would be appropriate for the younger or more casual reader.

Morison, Samuel Eliot. *Samuel de Champlain: Father of New France*. Boston: Little, Brown and Co., 1972. This prolific and esteemed naval historian has combined in this biography both scholarship and graceful prose. Morison was himself a sailor and navigated many of the waters along the New England and Canadian coasts with Champlain's descriptions and charts at hand. In the appendix is a translation of Champlain's "Treatise on Seamanship" of 1632.

Parkman, Francis. *Pioneers of France in the New World*. Boston: Little, Brown and Co., 1865. Reprint. *France and England in North America*. Vol. 1. New York: The Library of America, 1983. This classic of nineteenth-century historiography established Parkman's popular reputation. His bias in favor of the British and the Protestants is clear, but he nevertheless gives a vivid and not unfavorable picture of Champlain. For those with the patience to savor the style of Victorian prose, this well-known book can still pay substantial dividends.

Gordon R. Mork

WILLIAM ELLERY CHANNING

Born: April 7, 1780; Newport, Rhode Island
Died: October 2, 1842; Bennington, Vermont
Area of Achievement: Religion
Contribution: Channing led the attack by Unitarian clergy on New England
 Congregationalism and helped establish the basis for modern liberal
 Christianity.

Early Life

William Ellery Channing was born in British-occupied Newport toward the end of the Revolutionary War, one of ten children of William and Lucy (née Ellery) Channing. Young Channing was the grandson of a signer of the Declaration of Independence on the paternal side, and of perhaps the richest merchant in Newport on the maternal side. The boy attended school in Newport until the age of twelve, at which point he was sent to New London, Connecticut, to prepare for Harvard. He began his collegiate studies at Harvard in 1794 and spent four happy years there. During his Harvard years, young Channing had an adolescent religious experience, and the event convinced him to seek a career in the clergy. He was a popular student, and at the end of his stay at Harvard, the class of 1798 elected him as their graduating speaker.

Upon graduation, Channing went south to Richmond, Virginia, to take a post as a tutor to the socially prominent Randolph family. The young New Englander felt ill at ease in Richmond's heady atmosphere of dancing, drinking, and Deism, and for the most part he shunned society and read books. Alone in his study, Channing again had a conversion experience, and his letters of 1800 demonstrate the intensity of his encounter and his belief that faith alone provided the basis of Christian belief. He returned to Newport in 1800 and struck up a friendship with the local minister, Samuel Hopkins, who had once been a follower of the great Jonathan Edwards. Hopkins had shed some of his earlier adherence to the rigid Calvinist notions of predestination, and in turn his thinking influenced Channing. In December, 1801, Channing returned to Harvard as a divinity student, and upon his ordination in 1803, he was called to the ministry of the well-to-do Federal Street Church in Boston, a post he held until his death four decades later.

Channing postponed marriage until 1814, when he wed his cousin Ruth Gibbs. The couple had four children over the next six years, but only two survived infancy. Channing himself suffered from ill health throughout his adult life. He was a small man, only five feet tall, and weighed little more than a hundred pounds. Portraits painted of him each decade after his coming to Federal Street show a once handsome man with a face growing ever thinner and more pinched. Yet if his frame was unprepossessing, his voice more than made up for any deficiency in stature. By all accounts, Channing was one of the finest religious speakers in nineteenth century America.

Life's Work

William Ellery Channing's name has come down in history in connection with the famous "Unitarian Controversy" in early nineteenth century New England. Few of his contemporaries at divinity school might have predicted that the quiet, intense Channing would someday lead a revolt of rationalist Christians against the remnants of the Congregational church established by the Puritans in the 1630's. The controversy first became public in 1805 when Harvard appointed a known Unitarian, Henry Ware, to a chair in theology. The name "Unitarian" implied a host of beliefs at the time, not simply the contention that the deity was single and unfragmented, as opposed to the more traditional "Trinitarian" concept of God as Father, Son, and Holy Ghost. Many clergymen opposed to Ware publicly protested the appointment, and after failing to get Ware dismissed, the recalcitrants in 1809 established their own rival school of theology at Andover.

The years between 1805 and 1820 saw bitter intellectual and personal struggles between the Harvard and Andover wings of New England Congregationalism. The vituperation of the controversy seems out of proportion to the actual differences between the two camps, but it is worth remembering that the split came at a time of general religious fervor in the nation, a period known as the Second Great Awakening, and a time when toleration was difficult to practice. Beyond the nominal difference between Unitarianism and Trinitarianism over the nature of God, Unitarians differed from traditional New England Calvinists in disputing the total depravity of man. Men such as Channing believed that human beings were a mixture of good and bad and that part of the clergy's job was to encourage the former and discourage the latter. Unitarians also had doubts about the Calvinist doctrine of predestination, or the notion that God had already determined the fate of all human beings and that mortal actions on earth could have no influence on the divine. Moreover, Channing and other Unitarians refused to believe the old Congregationalist doctrine that mankind on earth could be divided into the "elect" (those who knew their salvation) and all the rest. Unitarians, under Channing's leadership, came to believe that salvation was within all men's power but that people needed careful religious instruction in order to avoid the many falsehoods and errors inherent in the various denominations of Christianity.

Channing kept a low profile during the most heated years of the Unitarian Controversy, between 1809 and 1815. He emerged as a Unitarian leader only in 1819 with a deliberately crafted public address that served as a counterblast to the Andover wing. Indeed, his address was so compelling and succinct that the split in Congregationalism became permanent. After Channing's 1819

"Baltimore Sermon," Unitarianism and Trinitarian Congregationalism went their separate ways.

The location for his grand theological pronouncement was a bit unusual. Instead of Boston, Channing chose the Southern city of Baltimore and as the setting, the ordination of a Harvard-trained minister named Jared Sparks as the occasion. Sparks had been called to the pulpit of the newly established First Independent Church of Baltimore, an outpost as far south as any that Unitarianism had established.

Channing took as his text for his Baltimore Sermon a verse from 1 Thessalonians: "Prove all things; hold fast to that which is good." The audience was filled with a host of Unitarian ministers, and Channing sought to summarize for them his belief that rationalism should be the core of Unitarian religious practice. He told the ordination assembly that as Christians they needed to affirm that the Bible was, in part, God's revelation to mankind but also, in part, man's imperfect attempt to understand God. Channing emphasized that the Old Testament was full of errors and superstitions and that Christians should concentrate on the teachings of Jesus. The job of the Unitarian minister, he went on, was to separate the divine in the Bible from the mundane by use of reason and scholarship, all for the benefit of the congregation. This required a sound education in many fields for the would-be clergyman, from knowledge of the ancient languages to a familiarity with modern science. More than any other Unitarian leader, Channing sought to push the clergy into seeing its role as primarily one of scholar-teacher.

Channing also used the occasion of Sparks's ordination in Baltimore to pull together the separately articulated but as yet uncollected strands of Unitarian doctrine. He insisted that the notion of a Trinity was a logical absurdity and maintained as well that the doctrine of Original Sin mocked God by ascribing base motives to Him such as jealousy and rage. From these two assumptions, Channing went on to reason that the purpose of Christ was to perform an errand for the superior God by sending a message that mankind was forgiven its sins. Moreover, Channing proposed that Christ had only partly completed his mission, which, fully understood, involved transforming mankind into a species marked by complete love and goodness.

The Baltimore Sermon of 1819 circulated widely in print and made its author famous on both sides of the Atlantic. In the early 1820's, Channing and his family journeyed to England and the Continent, where he was received by many leading intellectuals, including William Wordsworth and Samuel Taylor Coleridge. He continued to speak out forcefully against the Trinitarian Congregationalists (many of whom called him an infidel), and in 1825, he helped establish the American Unitarian Association, thereby officially ratifying the schism in the Church that John Winthrop and John Cotton had created in 1630.

Though honored as a leader while still a comparatively young man, Channing had a less than happy tenure at Federal Street Church in the years after 1819, particularly in his last decade. He faced two great challenges, one moral and one intellectual, that troubled him until his death. The first was the problem of slavery in America. Channing knew of Southern slavery from his Richmond days, but a visit to the West Indian island of St. Croix in 1831 upset him deeply. He saw directly the hard lot of black slaves on the sugar plantations, and he returned to Boston just as the abolitionist movement began organizing in that city. American abolitionism in the 1830's was highly unpopular, in large part because its backers were thought to favor interracial marriage. Boston and other cities were wracked by antiabolitionist mob violence, and while Channing condemned the mob, he also earned the scorn of the abolitionists for not wholeheartedly endorsing their cause. Only in his "Duty of the Free States," written in 1842 just before his death, did he come to see slavery as a manifestation of evil so great that forceful means would be required to overcome it. Until that time, Channing had hoped that Christian appeals to the conscience of the Southern slaveholder would work to end the institution without violence.

The other great challenge to Channing and the new Unitarian Association was from within: the intellectual challenge of the Transcendentalists. The sources of Transcendentalism are complex, found partly in European Romanticism, partly in the reflected enthusiasm of Jacksonian America, but in any event, its notions of the primacy of sensation, intuition, and nature posed a direct challenge to the rationalist approach to Christianity. Channing died before his former student Ralph Waldo Emerson would call Boston Unitarianism "corpse-cold," but even by 1842, Channing could see that Unitarianism was not satisfying the spiritual needs of many its adherents.

Summary

By devising a rational Christianity still reliant on faith, Channing reached an optimistic end similar to that proposed by a contemporary New England "Universalist" preacher named Hosea Ballou, who interpreted the Crucifixion as the sign that all sinners everywhere and forever had been pardoned in advance and that salvation would be "universal." In their own ways, the rationalist Channing and the Universalist Ballou built the basis for an American liberal Christianity that offered hope without resorting to threats of hellfire and brimstone. Indeed, after the Civil War, Unitarians and Universalists saw their common interests and, after many fits and starts, eventually effected a merger in the twentieth century.

Channing also took liberal Christianity in the direction of social reform. His stress on the goodness of man and the possibility of moral instruction got him involved in many of the reform movements of Jacksonian America. He was an active temperance enthusiast, supported the emerging antiwar movement, and advocated an extensive system of public education. Channing communicated many of these concerns to the public, first in sermons at Federal Street and then in pamphlets written for a wider audience. At the same time, Channing served as mentor to many of the young writers and thinkers in Boston, men such as Ralph Waldo Emerson, Henry Wadsworth Longfellow, and Robert Lowell. Channing's 1830 pamphlet *Remarks on American Literature* was a direct call for American writers to create a new, national and republican literature that was divorced from the monarchical and antidemocratic British literature then in fashion. The call was taken up in the great flowering of New England culture in the last decades before the Civil War. Like any good teacher, then, Channing should be remembered as much for the students he helped tutor as for the ideas he advanced himself.

Bibliography

Channing, William Ellery. *The Works of William E. Channing*. 6 vols. Boston: J. Munroe, 1848. The chief virtue of Channing's papers is that they allow one to gauge the breadth of his interests. Here is a clergyman involved in an extraordinary range of religious and secular matters.

Delbanco, Andrew. *William Ellery Channing: An Essay on the Liberal Spirit in America*. Cambridge, Mass.: Harvard University Press, 1981. This work is concerned mostly with placing Channing in the context of American thought in the early nineteenth century. Especially good at discussing the intellectual origins of Unitarianism as a reaction against Calvinism.

Edgell, David D. *William Ellery Channing: An Intellectual Portrait*. Boston: Beacon Press, 1955. The first modern biography of Channing. Seeks to understand him as the synthesizer of rational Christianity.

Mendelsohn, Jack. *Channing the Reluctant Radical: A Biography*. Boston: Little, Brown and Co., 1971. Mendelsohn gives considerable detail about Channing's personal and family life. A sympathetic account of liberal Christianity then and now.

Robinson, David. *The Unitarians and the Universalists*. Westport, Conn.: Greenwood Press, 1985. Strong on the Unitarian Controversy and its aftermath, this work also considers Channing's response to the Transcendentalist challenge.

Wright, Conrad, ed. *A Stream of Light*. Boston: Unitarian Universalist Association, 1975. A series of essays commemorating the establishment of an official Unitarian church. The chapter by Charles Forman is helpful in giving Channing's place in the Unitarian Controversy.

_____. *Three Prophets of Religious Liberalism: Channing, Emerson, Parker*. Boston: Beacon Press, 1961. This handy volume contains Channing's Baltimore Sermon, as well as a helpful introduction to American Unitarianism.

James W. Oberly

CHARLES CHAPLIN

Born: April 16, 1889; London, England
Died: December 25, 1977; Vevey, Switzerland
Area of Achievement: Film
Contribution: Through his screen persona of the Tramp, Chaplin represented the American "forgotten man" and presented the image of indomitable courage in the face of overwhelming social and political obstacles.

Early Life

Charles Spencer Chaplin was born April 16, 1889, in London, England, into a theatrical family. His father, Charles Chaplin, Sr., was an alcoholic music-hall performer who soon abandoned his family; his mother, née Hannah Hill, was an unsuccessful music-hall performer who suffered from mental illness most of her adult life. As a result of the unstable family life, Charles, Jr., and his older brother Sydney spent much of their youth in charity institutions, though Hannah, whom Chaplin revered, did what she could for her sons. In fact, Chaplin remained devoted to his mother, one of the most influential people in his life, until her death in 1928.

Chaplin's career as a professional entertainer began in 1898, when he began touring with Eight Lancashire Lads, who worked in the English music halls. For the next seven or eight years Chaplin served a kind of apprenticeship in that he acquired in England those comedic talents which were to lead to his unprecedented success in the United States. From his music-hall sketches he learned about character development; from pantomime, also popular with English audiences, he learned clowning; from the circus he learned acrobatics. His success finally brought him to the attention of Fred Karno, who had several acting troupes in his employ. While working for Karno, Chaplin appeared in *Jimmy the Fearless*, an important act because "Jimmy" in many ways served as a forerunner of the later "Tramp." During his employment with Karno, Chaplin also traveled to the United States, where he attracted the attention of Mack Sennett, who produced the famous Keystone comedies.

In 1913, Chaplin joined Keystone and began what was to become the most illustrious film career in history. The Tramp was not long in making his debut: He first appeared in *Mabel's Strange Predicament* (1914), Chaplin's third Keystone comedy. The costume, complete with ill-fitting clothes, small hat, cane, and mustache, had its roots—as did the distinctly Chaplinesque walk—in the English music-hall tradition. Despite his meteoric rise as an actor, Chaplin was not content until he directed his own films and achieved a measure of independence; while there is disagreement about which is his first directorial effort, he began directing his films in early 1914, probably with *Twenty Minutes of Love*. After making almost forty films in his two-year association with Sennett, Chaplin signed with Essanay and, after working briefly in their Chicago studios, moved to new studios in California.

The early California years prior to his full participation in United Artists, the company he formed with Douglas Fairbanks, Mary Pickford, and D. W. Griffith, were important ones in terms of Chaplin's cinematic development. During the years (roughly 1915 to 1923) in which he worked with Essanay, Mutual, and Associated First National, Chaplin followed an impressive production schedule: In only eight years, he made some seventy films. Despite the quantity of films, the quality was also high, primarily because he was a "workaholic" who made severe demands on himself as well as on the "stock company" he created. Although he relied heavily on improvisation, his extensive use of rehearsals and his frequent retakes suggest that he was also a perfectionist.

While Chaplin's screen image as the Tramp was beloved by Americans, it was also during this period that his public image became a bit tarnished. The political problems which followed him throughout his American career and which culminated in his eventual self-imposed exile began in World War I, when his failure to serve in Great Britain's armed forces (he did make quite a war effort in the Allied cause) resulted in adverse publicity. His "image" problems were, unfortunately, compounded by his marital difficulties. Chaplin, who seemed almost obsessed with his young leading ladies, married Mildred Harris when she was sixteen years old, but the marriage ended in divorce two years later in 1920. (Ironically, the death of their son in 1919 seems tied to Chaplin's *The Kid*, 1921, which starred Jackie Coogan and which is perhaps the best of his Associated First National films.)

Life's Work

In many ways, *A Woman of Paris* (1922), Chaplin's first film for United Artists, signaled a significant change in his filmmaking career: The actor-director also became a producer with control of all phases of production. He was truly an *auteur* filmmaker, the veritable "author" of his films, one of the few filmmakers who wrote, acted in, directed, and produced his films—in fact, after the advent of sound, he wrote musical scores for some of his re-issued silent films. In the post–Associated First National films, he also altered his filmmaking methods to give greater attention to shooting scripts while he made less use of on-set improvisation. In general, his emphasis seems to have shifted from quantity to quality, and he considerably slowed his production schedule.

After *A Woman of Paris*, a disappointment because he did not appear in his own film and because the film simply was not funny, Chaplin made the critically acclaimed and financially successful *The Gold Rush* (1925), the high point of his career. After *The Circus* (1928), his films became less comic and more political as they became "reflexive," more related to his problems and concerns. While *Modern Times* (1936) attacks modern technology and its dehumanizing effect on people, it dramatizes Chaplin's emerging economic philosophy. *The Great Dictator* (1940), in which Chaplin exploits his startling physical resemblance to Adolf Hitler, is also overtly political, but the excellence of the film is tainted, for many, by the lengthy final speech appealing for world peace.

The Great Dictator was the culmination of a blending of life and art in its espousal of unpopular pacifist sentiments associated with the political Left. It also indicated the extent to which Chaplin's domestic and political problems replaced his artistic achievements in the eyes of the American public. Chaplin's disastrous romantic affairs continued. After a widely publicized affair with actress Pola Negri, he had two more unsuccessful marriages: The first, to leading lady Lita Grey, lasted from 1924 to 1926; the second, to actress Paulette Goddard, lasted from 1936 to 1942. In addition, his tax problems with the Internal Revenue Service, which were to plague him throughout his American career, first surfaced in 1927. It was Chaplin's political activity, however, notably his continuing flirtation with "socialist" causes and the Soviet Union, that brought him to the unwelcome attention of the American government, particularly the Federal Bureau of Investigation. Its interest in Chaplin, which began as early as 1922, eventually resulted in his coming under scrutiny by the House Committee on Un-American Activities during the McCarthy era.

The 1940's and early 1950's were particularly turbulent years for Chaplin, who made only two films, *Monsieur Verdoux* (1947) and *Limelight* (1952), before he left the United States in 1952. Both films are far removed from the comic image of *The Tramp* (1915), which is the Chaplin trademark. Verdoux, for example, is a capitalistic "Bluebeard" who defends himself against murder charges by claiming that murder is only a logical extension of business; Calvaro, the protagonist of *Limelight*, who has a career which parallels Chaplin's, maintains that the artist must be selfish because art is happiness. Calvaro's insistence on selfishness seems to be Chaplin's defense of his own ego-centered life. Chaplin's lack of productivity was partly the result of becoming out of step with an America that revered the simple virtues of the Tramp while it preferred to ignore the political issues of the day.

Not only did Chaplin become less popular, but he also became embroiled in political and domestic issues that consumed much of his time and energy. His unpopular leftist political views, regarded as communistic by many, were attacked by conservative and reactionary groups, who urged his deportation. Chaplin himself did little to appease his detractors; indeed, his comments only seemed to incense the opposition. Adding to his political problems, which led to the American government rescinding his reentry pass when he left the United States in 1952, was a sordid paternity suit initiated by Joan Barry and an indictment against him for violating the Mann Act. Although blood tests proved that he was not the father of Joan Berry's child, he lost the paternity suit. While he was found innocent of Mann Act charges, the notoriety associated with both cases doubtless contributed to the government's continued harassment of Chaplin.

Chaplin and Oona O'Neill, his fourth wife (although she was in the mold of his other young wives, their marriage lasted), moved to England and then to Switzerland, but his last two films were neither commercially nor critically successful. *A King in New York* (1957) was quite autobiographical, dealing with an exiled king who arrives in New York full of optimistic hopes for peace. In the film, Chaplin bitterly attacked the Cold War witchhunt mentality which had been responsible for his own fate. During his last years he turned inward: He published *My Autobiography* in 1964, and he spent much time reissuing his old films and writing musical scores for his old silent films. Ironically, the public which deserted him when he abandoned comedy for political philosophy returned to offer him the recognition he so richly deserved. In the 1970's he was knighted by Queen Elizabeth and received several film awards, including an honorary Academy Award and the Golden Lion at the Venice Film Festival. Vindicated and fittingly honored, he died in his sleep on December 25, 1977.

Summary

Though he never became an American citizen, Chaplin captured the American spirit as few other performers have. In his Tramp persona he dramatized humanity's tragicomic struggle with fate as he portrayed the forgotten American, the underdog who overcame outsize adversaries, upperclass exploiters, and stubborn "machines" with an irreverence that was more American than British. The most popular performer of his time, he earned $670,000 when he was but twenty-five years old.

That success, however, was not achieved without an incredible dedication to his craft, an ego that brooked no opposition, and a consuming desire to create his own film kingdom over which he would have complete control. Though he was at home before live audiences, for he had appeared as a child in English music halls, film was his medium because it allowed for "perfect" performances and did not depend on interaction between performer and audience. Film mistakes do not live; they are cut and are replaced by successful retakes. So great was his authority that he was "the great dictator" on the set, where he forced actors to duplicate his performances in their parts. Perhaps his desire to exercise total control explained his preference for young performers who might be more malleable than older, more established actresses. Indeed, control seemed to be an obsession for Chaplin, who was a dictator at home as well as on the set and who for years dreamed of making a film about Napoleon—a film that never became a reality.

As long as his Tramp persona represented the American underdog who could aspire to make the American dream come true (one of his most beloved films was *The Immigrant*, 1917), Chaplin caught the American spirit and rode the crest of popularity. He failed, however, to adapt to change—he resisted the coming of sound films—and to recognize a shift in American thought and values. When the Tramp discarded his costume and assumed the robes of preacher, his was a message at odds with a conservative America which expected laughs, not philosophy, from its comic genius. When he left the United States, his alienation from American values and culture became even more pronounced, and his last two films seem at their best old fashioned and at their worst simply irrelevant. Today it is Chaplin's silent films featuring the Tramp that endure, and it is the image of the Tramp that advertisers exploit. Chaplin was the Tramp, and his public was unwilling to accept him in any other role.

Bibliography

Chaplin, Charlie. *My Autobiography*. New York: Simon and Schuster, 1964. Chaplin's account of his life is quite accurate, considering that the work was written primarily from memory. As might be expected, the focus is on Chaplin, and many of his close associates were omitted from the book.

Jacobs, Lewis. *The Rise of the American Film*. New York: Harcourt, Brace and Co., 1939. Chapter 13 (pages 226-247) is devoted to Chaplin as individualist. Jacobs lauds Chaplin as a "contemporary Don Quixote" whose social awareness was not outdated in 1939.

Kerr, Walter. *The Silent Clowns*. New York: Alfred A. Knopf, 1975. Kerr devotes three chapters to Chaplin's development in the silent film. The book is valuable for putting Chaplin in context with other great silent comedians.

Lyons, Timothy J. *Charles Chaplin: A Guide to References and Resources*. Boston: G. K. Hall, 1979. The standard bibliographical guide for Chaplin students; includes an annotated bibliography and a filmography. The book is indispensable.

McCaffrey, Donald W. *Great Comedians: Chaplin, Lloyd, Keaton, Langdon*. New York: A. S. Barnes and Co., 1968. A serious comparative study of the great silent comedians, this book also discusses their ability to adjust to the advent of the sound film.

Robinson, David. *Chaplin: His Life and Art*. New York: McGraw-Hill Book Co., 1985. The only authorized biography of Chaplin, Robinson's book is exhaustive in its treatment of the London influence, the political problems, and Chaplin's work habits. Contains invaluable appendices.

Thomas L. Erskine

SALMON P. CHASE

Born: January 13, 1808; Cornish, New Hampshire
Died: May 7, 1873; New York, New York
Areas of Achievement: Civil rights, politics, and law
Contribution: As an attorney, politician, and constitutional theorist, Chase
 contributed to the abolition of slavery. During the 1850's, he served as a
 United States senator and as governor of Ohio, and he participated in the
 formation of the Republican Party. He was later appointed secretary of the
 treasury and was Chief Justice of the Supreme Court.

Early Life
 Salmon P. Chase was born in Cornish, New Hampshire, in 1808. His
father, Ithamar Chase, whose family had come to America during the 1640's,
was a farmer who held minor local offices and occasionally served in the state
legislature. His mother, Janette Ralston, was the daughter of Scottish immigrants who became prominent landowners in Keene, New Hampshire.
Ithamar died when the younger Chase was eight, so the boy spent his youth
living with various friends and relatives, including his uncle, Philander
Chase, the bishop of the Episcopal Church in Ohio. In 1821, Chase entered
Cincinnati College, where his uncle Philander was president. Philander's
influence on his nephew was profound. For the rest of his life, Chase would
be extremely pious. His later commitment to the abolition of slavery would
be as much religious as political. By 1823, Chase had returned to New Hampshire, where he briefly taught school before entering Dartmouth College. In
1826 he was graduated eighth in his class, a member of Phi Beta Kappa.
Chase then moved to Washington, D.C., where he taught school before
beginning law studies under William Wirt in 1827. In December, 1829, he
was admitted to the bar.
 In 1830, the athletic, tall, vigorous, and ambitious Chase settled in Cincinnati, where he practiced law and took an active role in civic affairs.
Between 1831 and 1833, he published historical essays in *The North American Review*, anonymous editorials in Ohio newspapers, and a three-volume,
comprehensive compilation of Ohio's laws, *The Statutes of Ohio* (1833-1835).
Chase was neither brilliant nor eloquent in court, but he was hardworking,
careful, and scholarly. These traits brought him a comfortable and growing
commercial practice which, by 1835, included such clients as the Bank of the
United States and the Lafayette Bank of Ohio. By 1845, his firm of Chase
and Ball earned an estimated ten thousand dollars a year—an extraordinarily large sum for the era. In 1834, Chase married his first wife, who died in
1835. Two other marriages (in 1839 and 1846) would also end with the death
of his wives. Of his six daughters only two, Katherine Chase Sprauge and
Jeanette Chase Hoyt, survived to adulthood.

Life's Work

Chase's national career had four phases: abolitionist lawyer; United States senator and governor of Ohio; secretary of the treasury; and Chief Justice of the United States.

From 1830 to 1849, Chase lived in Cincinnati, where his law firm flourished. In addition to this profitable practice, Chase offered free legal services to abolitionists, fugitive slaves, and free blacks. In 1836, mobs destroyed the office of Cincinnati's antislavery newspaper, the *Philanthropist*, and threatened the life of its editor, James G. Birney. Also threatened was Chase's brother-in-law, Dr. Isaac Colby. Through this incident, Chase became an attorney for the antislavery cause. Chase was initially attracted to the abolitionist movement because he abhorred the mob violence and disrespect for law directed against it. He evolved into a passionate and articulate supporter of the cause. In 1836, he won a damage suit against members of the mob, recovering some money for Birney to rebuild the office of the *Philanthropist*. A year later, Chase unsuccessfully defended the freedom of a fugitive slave, Matilda, who had been harbored by Birney. Birney was then convicted for helping Matilda, but Chase won a reversal on appeal

By 1841, Chase was a leading antislavery attorney in Ohio. Chase rejected the anticonstitutionalism of William Lloyd Garrison and instead developed a constitutional theory consistent with opposition to slavery. In 1843 and 1848, he was the chief author of the platform of the national Free Soil Party. Besides his Free Soil political activities, Chase defended numerous fugitive slaves and their white and black allies. In the 1840's, Chase corresponded with antislavery lawyers throughout the Midwest, convincing them to take cases that he had no time to handle and advising them on legal strategies. Chase lost his most famous fugitive slave case, *Jones v. Van Zandt* (1847), but his printed Supreme Court brief, titled "Reclamation of Fugitives from Service," added to his growing national reputation as the "attorney general for fugitive slaves."

In 1849, a small group of Free Soilers held the balance of power in the Ohio legislature. Guided in part by Chase, these political abolitionists secured two victories: They negotiated the repeal of most of Ohio's racially restrictive "black code," and they secured the election of Chase to the United States Senate.

In the Senate, Chase failed in his attempt to create a "Free Democracy" made up of antislavery Democrats such as himself. Effectively separated from all parties, he remained one of the most uncompromising Senate opponents of slavery, constantly challenging Southerners and their Northern allies. As a politician, Chase was somewhat ponderous, pompous, and self-righteous. While he was not a great debater, his carefully written speeches read well on the stump and in the Senate. In 1850, Chase was one of the leading opponents of the Fugitive Slave Law and other proslavery aspects of the Compromise of that year. While in the Senate, Chase continued to develop his antislavery constitutional analysis, arguing that the Fifth Amendment made slavery unconstitutional wherever the federal government had jurisdiction. This led to his concept of "freedom national, slavery sectional," which became a rallying cry for the Republican Party, especially after the Dred Scott decision (1857). Chase also laid out the theoretical basis for the Republican Party's slogan of 1856: Free Soil, Free Labor, Free Speech, Free Men. In 1854, Chase emerged as a leader of the opposition to the Kansas-Nebraska Act and in the process once again tried to organize a party of "Independent Democrats." No "Independent Democracy" emerged in 1854, but by 1855 a broader coalition of Free Soilers, Northern Democrats, and Whigs had united into an "Anti-Nebraska Party," which soon became the Republican Party. Chase was instrumental in the founding of this new political organization in Ohio. In 1855, he became one of the first Republican governors in the nation by defeating candidates from both the Whig and Democratic parties. In 1857, he was reelected governor of Ohio.

As governor, Chase helped create the Republican Party in Ohio and the nation. In part because of his cold personality, however, he was unable to unify the state party behind his own presidential ambitions; in both 1856 and 1860, he was unsuccessful in gaining the Republican nomination for that office. While governor, Chase opposed the extradition of fugitive slaves but was unable to prevent the removal of the slave Margaret Garner, who killed her own daughter to prevent the child's return to slavery. After the rescue of an alleged fugitive slave near Oberlin, however, Chase gave support to the rescuers and appeared willing to confront federal authorities. In another case, Chase prevented the extradition of a free black accused of helping slaves to escape from Kentucky. This ultimately led to the Supreme Court decision in *Kentucky v. Dennison* (1861), in which Chief Justice Roger B. Taney chastised Ohio for its antislavery activities but refused actually to order the return of the accused fugitive. Throughout his governorship, Chase tried to walk a fine line between actual defiance of federal law and the Constitution, and his thoroughgoing opposition to slavery and the Fugitive Slave Law. When not sparring with the federal government, Governor Chase directed his energies to reorganizing the Ohio militia, which would ultimately be a major asset to the Union during the Civil War.

In 1860, Governor Chase failed to obtain the Republican presidential nomination. He was, however, elected to the United States Senate in the fall of that year. During the secession crisis, he served as a "peace commissioner" from Ohio, where he opposed any extension of slavery into the territories but also disclaimed any intention of interfering with slavery where it already existed. In March, he had barely taken his seat in the Senate when President Lincoln appointed him secretary of the treasury.

In his new office, Chase faced the formidable task of financing the Civil

War. With the aid of financier Jay Cooke, Chase was able to market government bonds, thus providing a constant flow of capital into the national treasury. Chase's initiatives led to the establishment of a national banking system in 1863 with a system of currency backed by federal bonds and securities. Because the Treasury Department was also responsible for confiscated and abandoned property from the Confederacy, Chase was able to take an active role in the dismantling of slavery.

Chase, the most radical abolitionist in Lincoln's original cabinet, used his office to chip away at slavery in the period before the Emancipation Proclamation (1862). He supported generals who used their power to undermine or destroy the institution, as long as they did not overtly go beyond administration policy. Under Chase's protégé, Edward L. Pierce, the first steps toward educating ex-slaves for life as free men and women took place in 1862 on the sea islands of South Carolina. Chase encouraged dedicated abolitionists to run this "rehearsal for reconstruction." In the Cabinet, Chase argued for an early end to slavery itself. Chase strongly supported the Emancipation Proclamation, even though he believed that it did not go far enough. Chase's personal piety led him to convince Lincoln to ask for the "gracious favor of Almighty God" at the end of the proclamation.

Throughout his tenure of secretary of the treasury, Chase's relationship with Lincoln was strained. He had serious policy disagreements with Lincoln, especially on such issues as emancipation and black rights. Chase was far ahead of his president on these matters. In addition, Chase wanted Lincoln's job: Chase had his eye on the White House in 1856 and 1860. He thought that after a single term Lincoln would step aside, and he could step forward. Chase's feuding with Secretary of State William H. Seward and his persistent campaigning for the Republican presidential nomination in 1864 made it increasingly difficult for him to remain in the Cabinet. In June, 1864, a conflict over the appointment of a subordinate led Chase to offer his resignation. This was the fourth or fifth time he had done so. Much to his surprise, Lincoln accepted the resignation and Chase was out of the Cabinet.

In spite of his disagreements with Lincoln, Chase ultimately campaigned actively for the Republican ticket throughout the fall of 1864. After his reelection, Lincoln appointed Chase to replace the late Roger B. Taney as Chief Justice of the United States. Chase was a logical choice. He had been an eminent attorney and had developed the most coherent antislavery legal-constitutional arguments of the antebellum period. He was sympathetic to emancipation and the other war policies of the Lincoln Administration.

Rather than marking a fitting end to his lifetime of public service, however, Chase's years in the Supreme Court were an anticlimax if not an embarrassment. Chase joined a court that was deeply divided between antislavery Lincoln appointees and proslavery holdovers from the prewar years. During Reconstruction, the court was asked to decide on questions which were at the heart of the political crisis of the period. The court's answer, and Chase's leadership, were mixed.

Chase presided over the impeachment of Andrew Johnson with fairness and skill. He earned the respect of most of the Senate, and of much of the nation. This might have been the capstone of his career. Chase still had his eye on the presidency, however, and he used his newfound prestige to campaign for the office. Chase's hunger for the White House led him to repudiate his previous support for black suffrage, in hopes of getting the Democratic nomination. He failed in this effort and in the process lost support from moderates as well as former abolitionists.

When he appointed Chase, Lincoln told a friend "we wish for a Chief Justice who will sustain what has been done in regard to emancipation and the legal tenders." Had Lincoln lived, he would have been disappointed by Chase on the latter issue. In *Hepburn v. Griswold* (1870) and in the Legal Tender cases (1871), Chase voted to void the financial system that he had set up as the secretary of the treasury. The chief justice was severely criticized for this.

On black rights, Chase's record was more consistent. Despite his willingness to oppose black suffrage in order to gain the presidential nomination in 1868, Chase was a genuine supporter of black rights. In the Slaughter-house cases (1873), Chase vigorously dissented, arguing that the majority opinion undermined the rights of the freedmen. In other Reconstruction decisions, Chase generally supported Congress over the president or the states. The one major exception was the loyalty oaths, which Chase opposed from the bench. In his most important Reconstruction decision, *Texas v. White* (1868), Chase upheld the basic theory of Congressional Reconstruction in an opinion that was sensitive to the political realities of the era. Chase also upheld the power of Congress to limit Supreme Court jurisdiction in the postwar South in *Ex parte McCardle* (1868). In *Ex parte Milligan* (1866), however, he denied the right of the executive branch to abolish civilian courts in those states which remained within the Union.

Summary

Few men in American history have held so many important governmental positions. Chase's contributions to the antislavery movement and the Republican Party were critical. His defense of fugitive slaves and abolitionists was unmatched by other lawyers of his age; his development of a coherent antislavery constitutional theory helped pave the way for Lincoln's victory in 1860 and the ultimate abolition of slavery. As secretary of the treasury, Chase was a valuable and hardworking member of Lincoln's cabinet. Besides organizing the financing of the war effort, Chase helped develop Reconstruction policy. In the early years of the war, he also helped Lincoln manage the War Department, which was being incompetently and corruptly run by Secretary of War Simon Cameron.

As chief justice, Chase was a disappointment. He was unable to assert the authority and leadership that he had displayed in his other public positions. His opinions were never as sharp as his prewar speeches had been. Moreover, his positions, so clear and consistent in the antebellum period, were sometimes vague on the bench. His grasping for the presidency reflected poorly on him and on the office he held. Nevertheless, Chase guided the Supreme Court through the impeachment crisis with dignity. He also avoided running afoul of Congress at a time when that branch might have seriously damaged the Supreme Court, had Chase and his brethren opposed Congressional Reconstruction. Similarly, Chase left the bench on a high note, vigorously asserting the rights of the freedmen in the Slaughter-house cases, at a time when a majority of the Supreme Court and the nation were rejecting any commitment to racial equality.

Bibliography

Chase, Salmon Portland. *Inside Lincoln's Cabinet: The Civil War Diaries of Salmon P. Chase.* Edited by David H. Donald. New York: Longmans, Green and Co., 1954. Chase kept a detailed diary while in the cabinet. This carefully edited edition offers great insight into Chase and his role in the cabinet. Part of the diary is also available, along with many Chase letters, in volume 2 of the *Annual Report of the American Historical Association for the Year 1902*, published by the United States Government Printing Office in 1903.

Foner, Eric. *Free Soil, Free Labor, Free Men: The Ideology of the Republican Party Before the Civil War.* New York: Oxford University Press, 1970. Contains an important chapter on Chase's constitutional theory and its relationship to Republican ideology. Throughout this book, Chase is a major figure.

Hart, Albert Bushnell. *Salmon Portland Chase.* Boston: Houghton Mifflin Co., 1899. Although dated, this volume remains the best available biography of Chase. The book is relatively weak on his judicial career, but it is an excellent introduction to his abolitionist efforts and political career.

Hyman, Harold M., and William M. Wiecek. *Equal Justice Under Law: Constitutional Development, 1835-1875.* New York: Harper and Row, 1982. Covers the developments in constitutional and legal thought during Chase's career.

Kutler, Stanley I. *Judicial Power and Reconstruction Politics.* Chicago: University of Chicago Press, 1968. Best short introduction to the problems of the Supreme Court under Chase.

Schuckers, Jacob W. *The Life and Public Services of Salmon Portland Chase.* New York: Da Capo Press, 1970. Written by one of Chase's protégés (and originally published in 1874), this book presents an overly heroic portrait of its subject but is nevertheless useful, particularly for the many Chase letters and speeches that it reprints.

Warden, Robert. *An Account of the Private Life and Public Services of Salmon Portland Chase*. Cincinnati, Ohio: Wilstach, Baldwin, and Co., 1874. Much like the Schuckers biography, this volume is useful but uncritical.

Wiecek, William M. *The Sources of Antislavery Constitutionalism in America, 1760-1848*. Ithaca, N.Y.: Cornell University Press, 1977. Places Chase's antislavery theories and legal arguments in the context of other abolitionist constitutional theorists.

Paul Finkelman

LYDIA MARIA CHILD

Born: February 11, 1802; Medford, Massachusetts
Died: October 20, 1880; Wayland, Massachusetts
Areas of Achievement: Literature, abolitionism, and social reform
Contribution: Child was one of America's first successful women writers and
  editors, combining popular writing with a lifetime's dedication to the
  causes of racial equality and general public enlightenment.

Early Life

Lydia Maria Child, born Lydia Maria Francis in Medford, Massachusetts,
on February 11, 1802, wished when young that her father had paid as much
attention to her as he did to her older brother, Convers. Maria, as she preferred to be called, envied her brother's inquisitive spirit and her father's
willingness to encourage it. Throughout her life, her choices would reflect
the strength of mind and heart that she so early learned from having to act
on her own.

Maria's father, David Convers Francis, a prosperous baker, had little time
for his strong-minded daughter. When his wife, Susannah (Rand) Francis,
died, he sent twelve-year-old Maria to live with a married sister in Norridge-
wock, Maine. By age fifteen, Maria was already reading the works of John
Milton, Homer, and Sir Walter Scott and was beginning to show the literary
interests that were soon to make her famous. At eighteen, she opened a private academy, which had become well established when next she decided to
join her brother Convers, now a Unitarian minister, and his wife in
Watertown, Massachusetts, just outside Boston. There, her literary career
began to flower.

Francis' first novel, *Hobomok* (1824), was an instant success. This romance, involving an Indian male and a white female, reflected her childhood
talks in Maine with local Abamake Indians and foreshadowed her lifelong
opposition to the United States government's Indian policies. *Hobomok* also
hinted at Maria's radical social views, since the plot featured an interracial
marriage. A second work, *The Rebels: Or, Boston Before the Revolution*
(1825), also sold well, and in 1826 she began publishing the *Juvenile Miscel-
lany*, America's first periodical created exclusively for children. All the while,
Francis continued to teach in the private academy which she had founded in
Watertown. Her childhood dream of being as independent as her brother
was rapidly becoming a reality.

Her popular writing soon brought her notice in Boston's aristocratic literary circles, where she became known for her charm and intelligence,
though she was not regarded as a natural "beauty." By 1827, she had been
successfully courted by David Lee Child, a dashing figure eight years her
senior, who had diplomatic experience in Europe and who aspired to become

a politician. They were married on October 19, 1828, and settled in Boston, where David, for a meager salary, edited a political newspaper. To augment family income, Child published yet another successful book, *The Frugal Housewife* (1829), which passed on to readers the methods she was learning for running a household at low cost. (One cake recipe, however, did call for twenty-eight eggs and three pounds of butter.) The volume, which sold widely in both Europe and the United States, brought the Childs much-needed income, for from the start David Child did poorly in his career. His newspaper attacks on Andrew Jackson for forcibly removing the Cherokee Indians from their land in Georgia after the discovery of gold there made him unpopular, as did his sudden decision to become a vigorous opponent of slavery.

Child, however, agreed with her husband's radical views. While he editorialized, she wrote a history of the Indians in her own region, *The First Settlers of New England* (1829); she soon became an abolitionist as well. In 1831, she encountered William Lloyd Garrison, the most militant of New England's antislavery leaders, and was immediately converted to his cause. Yet once she had embraced this controversial new reform, her popularity as a writer vanished. Patrons snubbed her, and publishers refused her work. Her lucrative career was at an end. "Hardly ever was there a costlier sacrifice," remarked Wendell Phillips, a close friend of Child and another leading Bostonian abolitionist. "Fame and social position [were] in her grasp. But confronted suddenly by the alternatives—gagged life or total wreck—she never hesitated." In 1832, Child had irrevocably committed herself to emancipating the slaves and to seeking social justice. From then on, her brief enjoyment of fame was transformed into a lifetime of struggle against the formidable challenges of poverty and unpopularity.

Life's Work

In 1833, Child published her views on slavery, *An Appeal in Favor of That Class of Americans Called Africans*, a highly influential work which guaranteed her banishment from Boston's literary circles and sealed her public commitment to a career as a social reformer. The work persuaded Charles Sumner, Wendell Phillips, Thomas Wentworth Higgins, and others to examine the slavery question, particularly because Child presented her case in such a logical fashion. (In all of her radical publications, Child seldom made use of overemotional rhetoric.) In calm tones, she denounced racial prejudice, called for equal education and employment opportunities for blacks, demanded an immediate abolition of slavery, and called for the repeal of all segregation laws, including those prohibiting racial intermarriage. Several other abolitionist publications soon followed, and the sales of her other books dwindled in proportion. Even another romantic novel, *Philothea* (1836), set in ancient Greece, failed to sell.

In the place of popularity came mobs of enraged citizens, anxious to purge the North of dangerous radicals such as Child. The famous Boston mob of 1835 specifically aimed at suppressing the Boston Female Anti-Slavery Society of which Child had become a leading member. By 1840, she had secured prominence in antislavery circles, becoming a close associate of Henry B. Chapman and Maria Weston Chapman and of Ellis Gilman Loring and Louise Gilman Loring, as well as of Phillips, Garrison, and other Bostonians who provided leadership for the American Anti-Slavery Society. In 1840, she was named to the executive committee of that society, and in 1841, Child moved to New York City to edit its official weekly newspaper, *The National Anti-Slavery Standard*.

When Child left for New York, David Lee Child remained behind in Massachusetts, nearly destitute but committed to the goal of producing sugar from beets, hoping to develop free-labor alternatives to slave-grown cane sugar from the South. In 1837, he and Child purchased a ramshackle farm in Northampton, Massachusetts, where for three years they had struggled to eke out a living. The need for additional income explained much of Child's reason for assuming the editorship of *The National Anti-Slavery Standard* and for temporarily leaving her husband. While the paper's readership grew substantially under her direction, she found the day-to-day work demoralizing and the endless controversies with her abolitionist colleagues distracting. When she resigned in 1843, her husband (now disengaged from the sugar beet business), briefly replaced her before moving on to Washington, D.C., to lobby at an uncertain salary for antislavery causes. In the meanwhile, Child remained in New York. The patterns of extended separation between her and her husband that would be repeated over the years had now become established. Though each would always profess and show deep love for the other, David's inability to secure a rewarding career had caused their marriage to fracture partially. The couple would always remain childless.

Alone in New York City, Child succeeded somewhat in reestablishing her literary career. Her popular *Letters from New York* (1843) gave readers vivid pictures of all aspects of life in the nation's major metropolis. Some of her scenes depicted the grinding poverty of New York's slums, the injustices endured by the black community, and the degradation suffered by its unskilled workers. She also investigated prison conditions and the bistros and bawdy houses of the notorious Five Points District. She passed no smug judgments on the social outcasts she encountered, writing, "They excite in me more of compassion than dislike." God alone knew, in her opinion, "whether I should not have been as they are, with the same neglected childhood, the same vicious examples, the same overpowering temptation of want and misery." Such insights soon led her to publish *Fact and Fiction: A Collection of Stories* (1846), a book describing the plight of New York's prostitutes.

Though *Letters from New York* proved a popular success, and though

Child contributed frequently to other literary periodicals, by 1849 she and her husband continued to face destitution. Still lacking a stable income, David returned to his spouse, and in 1850 both moved to Weymouth, Massachusetts, to take up farming on land furnished at no cost by their Boston friends, the Lorings. By 1852, however, penniless and exhausted, they moved again, this time into a house in Wayland, Massachusetts, owned by Child's father (now in his eighties). There, Child tended to both her husband's and her father's needs, until the latter died, in 1856. During this arduous period of domestic labor, she somehow continued to write a history of Western religion, *The Progress of Religious Ideas* (1855), in three volumes, which few purchased. Her next work, *Autumnal Leaves* (1857), a set of inspirational selections for those facing old age, suggested that, at age fifty-five, Child, too, believed her career to be ending. Indeed, she had written little about social questions since leaving New York City, though she participated in anti-slavery gatherings in Boston in the 1850's.

John Brown's 1859 raid on Harper's Ferry changed this state of affairs. "Before this affair," she wrote, "I thought I was growing old and drowsy, but now I am as strong as an eagle." She defended Brown's effort at violent emancipation in numerous pamphlets and letters that circulated all over New England. Her offer to nurse the injured Brown as he awaited execution provoked a widely read exchange of letters between Child and the wife of Virginia Senator James M. Mason. By mid-1863, as the Civil War raged, Child had moved fully into the forefront of the struggle against slavery, a struggle she continued by demanding full black equality once the war ended. In 1865, she published *The Freedmen's Book* at her own expense, a compilation of writings of successful blacks for the instruction of newly emancipated slaves. In the immediate postwar period, she pressed the Republican Party to legislate racial equality through the Fourteenth and Fifteenth amendments and supported the impeachment of President Andrew Johnson.

By 1868, however, Child was clearly feeling her age. She rarely traveled from Wayland, where she and her husband, now crippled from arthritis, began living in near seclusion. In that year, she published her last important reform statement, *An Appeal for the Indians*, recalling her first humanitarian efforts nearly forty years earlier. In 1874, when David Lee Child died, Child felt even less reason to engage the outside world. She became intensely reclusive, developing an interest in spiritualism. Few noticed when her last set of essays, *Aspirations of the World*, was published in 1878. When she died in Wayland at age seventy-eight, the few surviving abolitionist crusaders attended; John Greenleaf Whittier rendered a poem, "Within the Gate," and Wendell Phillips delivered the oration.

Summary

Lydia Maria Child embodied the idealism and reform spirit that lay behind the great crusade against slavery. Her most enduring work, *An Appeal in Favor of That Class of Americans Called Africans*, is recognized as a classic expression of the abolitionist's version of a racially just and egalitarian society. Her many-sided interests, her noteworthy sense of humor, her suspicion of self-righteous rhetoric, moreover, disproved the stereotype of the abolitionists as a collection of narrow-minded fanatics and eccentrics. Further, her long association with the cause of black equality illustrated the depth and sincerity of the abolitionist's commitment.

Child's literary career and her long struggle for self-sufficiency also suggest the limits and possibilities of female emancipation in the pre–Civil War years. Clearly, her novels and other writings mark her as a pathfinder in the area of women's literature. Yet she wrote often about the virtues of housework and cheerful obedience to the demands of husband and children. Her lifelong struggle to maintain not only herself but also her husband testifies to the tremendous burdens faced in the nineteenth century by "independent-minded" women who still believed in the primary importance of these domestic roles.

Bibliography

Baer, Helen G. *The Heart Is Like Heaven: The Life of Lydia Maria Child*. Philadelphia: University of Pennsylvania Press, 1964. A good modern biography of Child, based on primary research and a grasp of the scholarly literature then available on the antislavery movement.

Child, Lydia Maria. *An Appeal in Favor of That Class of Americans Called Africans*. Boston: Allen and Ticknor, 1833. Her classic abolitionist exposition of doctrines and arguments. Conveys the full range of Child's opinions on slavery, race equality, and racial prejudice, while standing as a fine example of her expository style as a reformer.

_____. *Letters from New-York*. New York: C. S. Francis and Co., 1843.

_____. *Letters from New York: Second Series*. New York: C. S. Francis and Co., 1845. Child's reports on poverty and luxury in America's largest city give vivid glimpses of her social convictions. Other parts show her facility as an art critic, theatergoer, and fashion commentator. The best introduction to Child's "popular" writings.

_____. *Philothea: A Romance*. Boston: Otis Broaders, 1836. Typifies Child's literary romanticism. Set in ancient Greece, the plot features proslavery and antislavery themes but also incorporates a dramatic love story and much melodrama. Since it tried to appeal to both reformers and the general reading public, this romance reveals in one work most of Child's intentions as a fiction writer.

Meltzer, Milton. *Tongues of Flame: The Life of Lydia Maria Child*. New York: Thomas Y. Crowell, 1965. The best popular biography of Child, written by an experienced historian and based on primary research. Presents Child's personality in especially vivid terms while giving a compact, readable summary of her public and private lives.

Stewart, James Brewer. *Holy Warriors: The Abolitionists and American Slavery*. New York: Hill and Wang, 1976. This brief synthesis of the history of the abolitionist crusade gives attention to principal figures and events that bore on Child's career. This work traces the development of antislavery from its origins in the eighteenth century until the end of Reconstruction.

Thomas, John L. *The Liberator, William Lloyd Garrison: A Biography*. Boston: Little, Brown and Co., 1965. This major biography of Boston's leading abolitionist conveys an excellent sense of the culture, people, and movements with which Child was intimately associated. A major scholarly study of the person who most permanently influenced Child's views on social reform.

James Brewer Stewart

GEORGE ROGERS CLARK

Born: November 19, 1752; near Charlottesville, Virginia
Died: February 13, 1818; Louisville, Kentucky
Areas of Achievement: Military leadership and urban development
Contribution: Clark's successful attack against the British forts at Kaskaskia, Cahokia, and Vincennes in 1778-1779 served as the basis for the American claim to the Northwest Territory during negotiation of the Treaty of Paris of 1783. His leadership of the Northwest campaign led in turn to the founding of Louisville, Kentucky, and Clarksville, Indiana.

Early Life

George Rogers Clark was born November 19, 1752, near Charlottesville, Virginia. He was the second of ten children born to John and Ann Rogers Clark. Both parents were of British stock whose roots went deep into Virginia's past. In 1757, the family moved to an inherited plantation in Caroline County. There young George attended a school conducted by a Scottish schoolmaster named Donald Robertson. Clark studied mathematics and surveying and showed a strong interest in history and geography. The Clark family was moderately prosperous, but John Clark believed in instilling in his children a sense of discipline and responsibility. Thus, when George was fifteen, his father gave him his own tobacco crop and then charged the youth's clothing and other personal expenses against it.

The most important element of Clark's education was his early frontier experience. In 1772, after receiving training in surveying from his grandfather, John Rogers, Clark made his first trip west with a party that descended the Ohio River and explored and surveyed land in the vicinity of the Kanawha River. Over the next two years, he spent much time surveying wilderness land, acquiring in the process a substantial knowledge of natural history and an understanding of Indian ways.

No early portraits of Clark exist, but contemporary descriptions suggest that he was a tall, powerfully built man with reddish or sandy-colored hair. His strong physical appearance complemented a winning personality which inspired confidence in others and quickly marked him as a leader.

Life's Work

Clark's military career began in 1774 when he was commissioned a captain in the Virginia colony during Lord Dunmore's War, a conflict between the Shawnee and settlers on the Kanawha River frontier. Clark missed the critical battle of Point Pleasant and saw little or no fighting otherwise, but he displayed a gift for command and acquired a knowledge of Indian fighting tactics and military organization.

With the end of Lord Dunmore's War in early 1775, Clark joined the Ohio Company and spent several months surveying in central Kentucky and aiding in the organization of Kentucky County. Meanwhile, fighting had erupted between American colonists and British troops in Massachusetts. As the rebellion intensified, Clark joined the Kentucky County militia. By 1777, he was a major and temporary ranking officer in Kentucky. He spent several months trying to defend scattered settlements against Indian raids instigated by the British north of the Ohio. As the attacks increased, however, Clark sought ways to take the war to the enemy. In June, 1777, he sent spies to obtain the intelligence necessary to plan a long-distance strike. Using their information, Clark formulated his strategy and presented it to Virginia governor Patrick Henry in December. Impressed with the boldness of Clark's scheme, Henry persuaded the legislature to appropriate funds for the campaign, without revealing the purpose of the expenditure. The governor then promoted Clark to lieutenant colonel and gave him secret orders to raise the troops necessary to attack the British fort at Kaskaskia, located on the Kaskaskia River near the Mississippi.

On May 12, Clark and his regiment of 150 men, along with about a dozen civilian families, sailed for the Falls of the Ohio, located about four hundred miles downriver from Pittsburgh. After picking up a few more recruits along the way, the flotilla landed at Corn Island near the Falls on May 27. A month later, Clark and his regiment departed for the Illinois country, leaving behind the civilians.

By July 4, Clark was poised at the outskirts of Kaskaskia. During the night his troops broke into the fort and captured its garrison without firing a shot. The following day, one of Clark's companies captured Cahokia, about forty miles away, in a similar manner. In August, the British-controlled French garrison at Vincennes, 240 miles east on the Wabash River, surrendered to Clark after learning of the Franco-American Alliance of 1778. Now Clark turned his attention to Detroit, headquarters of Lieutenant Governor Henry Hamilton, the chief British official in the Northwest. Before he could march, however, Clark had to deal with the expiring enlistments of many of his troops and to provide for the administration of the posts under his command. The funds appropriated by the Virginia legislature long since having been exhausted, he used his personal resources and borrowed heavily from friends to continue the campaign. Meanwhile, Hamilton counterattacked, recapturing the inadequately defended post at Vincennes in mid-December. With winter setting in, Hamilton decided to wait until spring to retake Kaskaskia and Cahokia. It was a fatal decision.

While Hamilton waited, Clark plotted a surprise attack against Vincennes. In early February, 1779, he crossed the Kaskaskia river with about 170 men. The troops marched for two weeks through rain-swollen swamps and rivers. On February 23, they arrived at Vincennes, and Clark delivered a surrender ultimatum. Hamilton proposed a truce, but Clark, having deployed his forces in a manner which made their number appear much larger, rejected the proposal and returned surrender conditions which he demanded that Hamilton accept. Realizing that Clark would not be moved, Hamilton capitulated.

Clark began planning immediately to attack Detroit. His plans collapsed, however, because of a lack of troops, and he returned to the Falls of the Ohio in August, 1779. His destination was not Corn Island but the tiny village of Louisville, which had been established a few months earlier when the settlers on the island heeded Clark's message to move to the Kentucky shore. Using Louisville as his base, Clark spent most of the remainder of the war conducting defensive operations along the Ohio. In 1779-1780, he supervised construction of Fort Jefferson on the Mississippi near the mouth of the Ohio. During mid-1780, he coordinated the defense of the Ohio Valley against a British counterattack from Detroit. Later that year Clark began anew planning a campaign against Detroit, but the effort was thwarted again when he became temporarily involved in defending the James River valley in Virginia and when Virginia and Continental officials refused the necessary financial assistance. The objective of taking Detroit was achieved finally through the Treaty of Paris in 1783, during whose negotiations American diplomats used Clark's capture of the Northwest forts as the basis for claiming the entire territory.

Many of Clark's postwar activities were an extension of his wartime service. A skilled Indian negotiator, he worked out the Treaty of Fort McIntosh in 1785 and the Treaty of Fort Finney in early 1786. Later in 1786, he joined Benjamin Logan in an expedition against the Wabash Confederacy in southwestern Indiana. Victimized by inadequate supplies and poor discipline, the campaign was a fiasco. Nevertheless, the pressure prompted the tribes to ask for a council, and peace was arranged in the spring of 1787.

Meanwhile, Clark had become involved in a second venture in town development. In 1783, the Virginia legislature awarded Clark and his regiment a grant of 150,000 acres on the Indiana shore at the Falls of the Ohio. One thousand acres was designated as Clarksville, which ranks as the oldest Anglo-American municipality in the old Northwest. A board of trustees was appointed to govern the town, and a board of commissioners was created to survey the land. Clark chaired both bodies for more than two decades.

Despite his accomplishments, Clark's star sank quickly after 1787. Pressured by creditors for repayment of loans he had obtained for the Illinois campaign, Clark sought assistance from the Virginia legislature. Rebuffed again and again, he became increasingly addicted to alcohol. His intense bitterness and dire financial straits led to participation in schemes which caused many to question his loyalty. In 1789, Clark became involved in an abortive plot to establish American colonies on Spanish soil west of the Mississippi. In 1793, he accepted a commission to command a French revolutionary legion that would descend the Mississippi and seize Spanish possessions. The United States government, however, thwarted the operation before it began.

Clark spent the remainder of the century on his parents' Louisville estate, supervising farm work and attempting to untangle his finances. In 1803, he built a cabin on his Clarksville land overlooking the Falls of the Ohio. There he received numerous visitors and accomplished some competent studies in natural history, but his heavy drinking steadily eroded his health. In February, 1809, he suffered a stroke and fell into his fireplace, causing burns which necessitated the amputation of his right leg. Now an invalid, Clark moved to Locust Grove, the Louisville home of his sister and brother-in-law, Lucy and William Croghan. In 1812, the Virginia legislature awarded him a sword and an annual pension of four hundred dollars in recognition of his wartime service. He died at Locust Grove on February 13, 1818.

Summary

George Rogers Clark's achievements were among the most remarkable and least understood of the American Revolution. Barely thirty years old when the war ended, he had captured a major portion of the Northwest region and commanded the successful defense of the Ohio Valley. These accomplishments resulted from a unique combination of strategic vision, personal courage, and persuasive ability. Yet he was not, as some have claimed, the "Conqueror of the Northwest," nor did his victories alone guarantee American control of that area through the peace negotiations. Because Clark was unable to capture Detroit, the British maintained a foothold in the Northwest. Moreover, the American peace commissioners—John Jay, Benjamin Franklin, and John Adams—were under instructions from Congress to follow the lead of the French, who had no desire to see the American domain expand to the Mississippi. When Jay and Adams learned that their ally was negotiating secretly with the British, they convinced Franklin that the Americans should deal directly with the British, in violation of their congressional orders. The British, wanting to reestablish trade and avert future conflict with the Americans, agreed to provisions in the Treaty of Paris which extended the western boundary of the United States to the Mississippi.

It does not diminish the significance of Clark's accomplishments, however, to place them in their proper perspective. Without his victories the American diplomats would have had difficulty mustering the bargaining power to secure the Northwest. By the middle of the nineteenth century, this territory had been carved into the states of Ohio, Indiana, Illinois, Michigan, Wisconsin, and Minnesota. Clark's exploits also contributed to the creation of a bistate urban region which by 1980 numbered nearly one million people. Louisville, Kentucky, is the state's largest city. Clarksville, Indiana, grew slowly during the nineteenth century, overshadowed by neighboring Jeffersonville and New Albany, both of which are within Clark's Grant. Clarksville mushroomed after World War II, though, and became the second largest incorporated town in Indiana and a major commercial center. Certainly the long-term consequences of Clark's achievements outweigh the tragic circumstances of his postwar years.

Bibliography

Bakeless, John. *Background to Glory: The Life of George Rogers Clark.* Philadelphia: J. B. Lippincott Co., 1957. This detailed biography provides an accurate account of Clark's Northwest campaign and a sympathetic, traditional treatment of his love affair with Teresa de Leyba. Unfortunately, portions dealing with other aspects of Clark's life are riddled with factual errors concerning names, military titles, dates, time sequences, and geographic localities.

English, William Hayden. *Conquest of the Country Northwest of the River Ohio, 1778-1783.* Indianapolis: Bowen-Merrill Co., 1896. This two-volume work is the classic heroic account depicting Clark as the "Conqueror of the Northwest." Although dated in interpretation, it is useful for its abundant illustrations, biographical sketches, lengthy quotations from original documents, and detailed roster of Clark's regiment.

Harrison, Lowell H. *George Rogers Clark and the War in the West.* Lexington: University Press of Kentucky, 1976. This brief, synthetic essay pictures Clark as one of the few revolutionary figures who understood the strategic significance of the frontier and as the person most responsible for saving Kentucky from the British.

James, James Alton. *Life of George Rogers Clark.* Chicago: University of Chicago Press, 1928. Based upon extensive research in primary sources, this is still the most accurate and most complete biography of Clark. Very readable and sympathetic to Clark, it includes a detailed discussion of his financial problems and participation in the Spanish and French conspiracies.

Quaife, Milo M., ed. *The Capture of Old Vincennes.* Indianapolis: Bobbs-Merrill Co., 1927. Essentially a firsthand account of the capture of Vincennes based upon Clark's and Hamilton's memoirs of the event. Clark's peculiar syntax and spelling have been recast for easy reading.

Sosin, Jack M. *The Revolutionary Frontier, 1763-1783.* New York: Holt, Rinehart and Winston, 1967. Providing context for understanding Clark's exploits, this volume explores the roles of land speculation, settlement patterns, Anglo-American politics, development of local government, and Indian affairs on the frontier during the revolutionary period.

Waller, George Macgregor. *The American Revolution in the West.* Chicago: Nelson-Hall, 1976. Based upon secondary sources, this brief narrative is especially useful in establishing the relationship between Clark's victories in the Northwest and the decision of the American peace commissioners to seek a separate peace with the British.

Carl E. Kramer

HENRY CLAY

Born: April 12, 1777; Hanover County, Virginia
Died: June 29, 1852; Washington, D.C.
Area of Achievement: Politics
Contribution: Clay was a dominant figure in American politics during the first half of the nineteenth century. His American System and his efforts to bring compromise in the controversy over slavery helped ease the growing tensions within the Union.

Early Life

Henry Clay was born April 12, 1777, on a farm near Richmond. His parents, the Reverend John Clay, a Baptist minister, and Elizabeth Hudson Clay, were of English descent and reasonably prosperous, though certainly not wealthy. His father died when Henry was four, but his mother was remarried within a year to Captain Henry Watkins, who maintained the family's financial status. Henry received a few years of schooling and developed remarkable penmanship, a skill which served him well when his stepfather moved the family in 1792. Only fifteen, Clay stayed in Richmond to work for the Clerk of the High Court of Chancery. In 1793, Clay was hired by the famous lawyer George Wythe as a part-time secretary. Almost seventy, Wythe was a leader of Virginia's bar and had enjoyed a distinguished career as teacher of law and classics. Under Wythe's tutelage, Clay studied the law and, a few years later, left his clerk's position to study under Robert Brooke, former governor and later attorney general of Virginia. In November, 1797, Clay passed his bar examination.

Like other ambitious Virginians, the young attorney moved to Kentucky, where confusion over land claims created a lawyer's paradise. At twenty, Clay was over six feet tall, thin, and walked with a shambling gait. His face, capable of creating considerable impact with a change of expression, was capped by hair so light as to be almost prematurely white. His eyes were small, gray, and piercing, his nose prominent, and from his large mouth issued his most valuable asset: his voice. Coupled with an emotional temperament, this voice, suited for an actor, made him a formidable opponent in frontier courts, where persuasion was frequently more important than legal knowledge.

The stage for Clay's legal theatrics was Lexington, Kentucky, a village on its way to becoming the "Athens of the West." Though appearing in frail health, Clay demonstrated his skill in local debates and was admitted to the Kentucky bar on March 20, 1798. Before a successful legal career made him a local legend, the budding jurist married Lucretia Hart, daughter of the influential merchant Thomas Hart. The marriage not only connected Clay with an important local family but also provided him with a patient, loving wife, who bore him eleven children. By 1800, Henry Clay was a member of Lexington's establishment.

Life's Work

Clay's debut as a radical Jeffersonian came when he spoke for a liberalization of the state's constitution and made speeches attacking the Alien and Sedition acts. He supported Jefferson in 1800 and, in 1803, won election to the Kentucky legislature. There he demonstrated his talent as a parliamentary tactician and also flirted with disaster by becoming counsel for Aaron Burr, who was charged with an alleged conspiracy to invade Mexico. Unaware of the extent of Burr's activities, Clay successfully defended Burr in Kentucky's courts, but later, as the import of Burr's schemes became apparent, Clay repudiated his dangerous client.

While acting as counsel for Burr, Clay was selected to fill an unexpired term in the United States Senate. Apparently no one paid any attention to the fact that he was a few months short of the required age. This brief performance in Washington, D.C., began a lifelong crusade for a national program based on internal improvements at federal expense and a protective tariff. Such measures were joined by an expansionistic, anti-British foreign policy. Clay's jingoism increased when he moved to the House of Representatives and became its Speaker. There, along with other "war hawks," Clay helped push the nation into the War of 1812. When the struggle did not bring victory, Clay found himself a member of the American delegation sent to Ghent, Belgium, to negotiate an end to the war he had helped to create. In spite of the negative reaction of John Quincy Adams, head of the delegation, who objected to Clay's Western habits of drinking, swearing, and gambling, the Kentuckian proved an able diplomat.

In the postwar years, Clay became a chief proponent of American nationalism and envisioned a truly united country tied together by bonds of economic interest as well as a common ideology. The government's role in his American System was to promote harmony through economic development. Key to his system was a new national bank. Suspicious of the first Bank of the United States, Clay had helped to block its recharter in 1811, but financial confusion during the war convinced him that a centralized financial system was imperative. From this time until the end of of his career, Clay's name would be associated with the idea of a national bank.

His legislative success made it seem that Clay's elevation to the White House was only a matter of time. His successful solution to the slavery controversy further encouraged his supporters. In 1819, Missouri applied for admission as a slave state. Hostility on both sides of the question threatened to divide the Union. Though a slave owner himself, Clay had moral reservations about slavery and supported gradual emancipation coupled with colonization. In fact, Clay had been a founder of the American Colonization

Society in 1816. In his mind, however, the abolition of slavery was of less importance than the preservation of the Union. In the House, he helped frame the famous Missouri Compromise, which brought in Maine as a free state to balance Missouri and divided the rest of the Louisiana Territory. Though many politicians were involved, the compromise was seen as Clay's handiwork.

Clay's popularity did not immediately convert into political success. Clay was unhappy with the Monroe Administration. The president selected a New Englander, John Quincy Adams, as secretary of state, a post that Clay had expected. Sectional harmony had been purchased at the cost of alienating Kentucky's "Hotspur." Clay frequently criticized the Administration's lack of support for the Latin American revolutions, a stand which made him popular in South America. His persistence was rewarded with Monroe's famous declaration in 1823, but from Clay's perspective it was too little, too late. Most important, however, his quibbling with the Monroe Administration obscured a serious threat to his political future: Jacksonian democracy.

Since 1800, the nation had been dominated by Jefferson's party, but, in 1824, four prominent leaders, Clay, Andrew Jackson, William H. Crawford, and John Quincy Adams, entered the contest for president. Almost everyone underestimated the military hero, Jackson. When the final votes were in, no candidate had a majority, but Jackson won a plurality. Shocked and disappointed, Clay came in fourth and was thus eliminated from consideration by the House. When Clay announced his support for Adams, which in effect made Adams president, Jackson was furious. Suspicions of underhanded dealing seemed confirmed when Clay was appointed secretary of state. This supposedly "corrupt bargain" provided a rallying cry for Jacksonians in the next election. While there is no evidence of prior arrangement, Jackson's complaint reveals an important difference between him and his rivals. Adams, Crawford, and Clay were all part of the leadership in Washington. Jackson, while a national military hero, had never been part of the Washington establishment. There was simply not enough room at the top, and Jackson became a lightning rod attracting those in politics and society who felt left out. Moreover, Democrats, taking advantage of extended suffrage, directed their appeal toward the common man even though Jackson and his allies were hardly common men.

Clay's new role in foreign affairs turned out be of little political value. The real drama was taking place internally, where followers of Jackson made a wreck of Adams' administration. The president was no match for the new kind of politician. Adams' style of leadership suited an earlier age; politics now stressed personality. Cold, aloof, and even arrogant, the president introduced a program designed to raise the level of his constituents. Jacksonians were content to direct their appeal to the lowest common denominator. In 1828, Jackson's presidential victory changed American politics forever.

With Jackson and his minions ensconced in the White House, the anti-Jacksonian opposition began to fall apart. By mid-1829, however, Clay's Kentucky estate had become the center of another presidential campaign, and, in late 1831, its master once again returned to the Senate and was quickly nominated for president by a national Republican convention. The ensuing struggle revolved around the second Bank of the United States. Motivated by partisan concerns, the bank's supporters pushed for recharter before it was necessary. Clay believed that the effort would place Jackson in an untenable position. He was wrong. Jackson reacted quickly by vetoing the recharter bill and destroying the bank by removing government deposits. Jackson's policies did cause defections among his supporters, but his enemies miscalculated the impact on the electorate. As ignorant of banking practices as their president, voters sympathized with Jackson's struggle, and the result was a smashing defeat of Clay's presidential aspirations.

There was no time for recriminations. As dust from the election settled, a South Carolina convention passed an Ordinance of Nullification against the tariffs of 1828 and 1832. The power to act rested with the president. Supposedly in favor of states' rights and less than enthusiastic about a tariff, Jackson, as usual, surprised everyone. Standing firmly for national supremacy, he asked Congress to pass the so-called Force Bill, granting the executive special authority in the crisis. Congress began to scramble for a compromise that would avert a military confrontation between South Carolina and the federal government. At center stage was Henry Clay. His compromise tariff gave South Carolina an excuse to back down without losing face. Once again, Clay had been instrumental in saving the Union.

In Jackson's second term, a new opposition party was created by a single idea: hatred of Andrew Jackson. It reached into British history for a name signifying resistance to tyranny: Whig. Its program was dominated by Clay's American System coupled with a bias against executive power, but it also adopted attitudes toward political opportunism pioneered by Jacksonians. To Clay's disappointment, the new party was too fragmented to unite around a single candidate in 1836. Hoping to throw the election into the House, the Whigs selected three sectional candidates to face Jackson's successor, Martin Van Buren. The strategy failed; Van Buren won. Whig frustration vanished when, a few months into the new administration, the country was rocked by an economic depression. Clay, secure in the Senate, was in an excellent position for the election of 1840, but his fellow Whigs were unsure. With his legions of enemies, Clay's name could unite Jacksonians as nothing else could. As a result, the party's convention turned away from its real leader and chose William Henry Harrison. Inwardly furious, Clay publicly supported the Harrison ticket.

The Whigs won, at last, by turning the tables on their enemies. Harrison was a military hero, and the campaign which elected him avoided serious political discussion. Still, most Whigs viewed the victory as a chance to reverse the tide in favor of Clay's American System. They soon realized that they were mistaken. Harrison's death a few months after inauguration brought to the White House a man who did not share Whig ideals. John Tyler had been nominated for vice president to ensure the loyalty of Southern Whigs. When Congress passed the Whig legislative agenda, Tyler promptly vetoed the most significant measure, a bill creating a national bank. The result was chaos. Most of the Cabinet resigned, and Tyler governed without party backing.

Tyler's defection left Clay the unchallenged leader of his party, and the presidency, in 1844, seemed his. Once again, however, fate intervened. Pressure for annexation of Texas had been growing. Clay, like other established leaders, feared Texas would rekindle the slavery controversy. Though generally an expansionist, he came out against annexation, expecting that a similar stand by the likely Democratic nominee, Van Buren, would remove the touchy question. After Clay's nomination, the Democrats repudiated Van Buren and nominated the ardent annexationist James K. Polk of Tennessee. As the campaign progressed, Texas captured the public imagination, and Polk's narrow victory was probably the bitterest defeat of Clay's career.

In such circumstances most men would have welcomed retirement, but Clay's unquenchable love of political combat made it impossible. Moreover, the country needed him. As feared, Texas brought with it the Mexican War and reopened debate over slavery. Clay hoped for the Whig presidential nomination in 1848, but for the last time his party betrayed him. Concerned about his age and poor health, the Whigs nominated another military hero, Zachary Taylor.

Bitter but unbowed, Clay played one last role on the American political stage. Unsophisticated in politics, newly elected President Taylor only exacerbated the conflict over slavery. When California applied for admission as a free state with the Administration's blessing, the country once again faced disunion. As always, the Senator from Kentucky stood in the way of a complete rupture within the Union. In spite of frail health, he framed a series of measures that became the famous Compromise of 1850. Working in the brutally hot Washington, D.C., summer until his health broke, Clay turned over the leadership of the compromisers to a younger colleague, Stephen Douglas of Illinois, and watched from the sidelines as Douglas pushed through the final legislation. This desperate attempt at sectional peace had only a brief life, but Henry Clay did not live to see it collapse. He died in Washington, D.C., the scene of so many of his triumphs, on June 29, 1852, two years before his last compromise unraveled.

Summary

Throughout his long career, Clay's programs and personality were always controversial. To supporters, he was the best that American politics had to offer, and they often regarded him with near adulation. To enemies, he represented America at its worst, and they hated him with unbridled passion. Like most politicians, some of his positions changed with time and circumstance, but one element remained consistent—his vision of national purpose. Clay saw his country as the hope of mankind. He genuinely believed the republican system to be superior and looked forward to its spread. In a sense, his American System was designed to further this aim by making America stronger. The Union could continue to exist, Clay believed, only if the states would work for mutual benefit. The cement which would glue the nation together was a cooperative economic system managed by the common government.

Clay's vision was a short-run failure. During his own time, the American System was submerged under the rising tide of Jacksonian democracy and the new style of politics it spawned. Only eight years after Clay's death the country he loved was embroiled in the civil war that his many compromises had sought to avert. Like so many of his generation, Clay had been unable to face the moral dilemma created by slavery, which could not be compromised away. In the long run, however, Clay's vision was a success. The country that emerged from the Civil War was much closer to Clay's America than to Jackson's.

Bibliography
Eaton, Clement. *Henry Clay and the Art of American Politics*. Boston: Little, Brown and Co., 1957. A concise biographical treatment in "The Library of American Biography," edited by Oscar Handlin. Concentrating on Clay's political career, it follows the evolution of Clay from an advocate of Western interests to a true nationalist.
Howe, Daniel Walker. *The Political Culture of American Whigs*. Chicago: University of Chicago Press, 1979. A thoughtful analysis of Whig ideology. Clay is a central figure, and the book contains valuable insights into the source of Whiggery.
Mayo, Benard. *Henry Clay: Spokesman of the New West*. Boston: Houghton Mifflin Co., 1937. The classic, scholarly biography of Clay. A colorful, well-written account which deals with Clay's private as well as public life. The treatment of Clay's early life in Kentucky is particularly valuable.
Poage, George Rawlings. *Henry Clay and the Whig Party*. Chapel Hill: University of North Carolina Press, 1936. A biographical treatment which concentrates on Clay's role in the founding and development of the Whig Party. The work is well documented but somewhat dated.
Sargent, Epes. *The Life and Public Services of Henry Clay down to 1848*. Buffalo, N.Y.: Derby, Orton, and Mulligan, 1853. Completed soon after Clay's death as a memorial to the leader of American Whiggery. Biased

and dated, but still an excellent example of the pro-Clay biographies written during his era.

Van Deusen, Glyndon G. *The Life of Henry Clay*. Boston: Little, Brown
and Co., 1937. A somewhat critical biography of Clay. Well researched and
written, the study provides balance when compared with the usual attitude
of Clay's biographers.

David Warren Bowen

GROVER CLEVELAND

Born: March 18, 1837; Caldwell, New Jersey
Died: June 24, 1908; Princeton, New Jersey
Areas of Achievement: Politics and government
Contribution: Cleveland, who was both the twenty-second and the twenty-fourth president of the United States, brought great strength of character and inestimable political courage to the United States during years of political turmoil and economic crisis.

Early Life
Steven Grover Cleveland was the fifth of nine children born to Richard Falley and Ann Neal Cleveland. His father, a graduate of Yale University, was a minister who moved his growing family from Caldwell, New Jersey, to Fayetteville, New York (where Grover spent most of his youth), Clinton, New York, and thence to Holland Patent, New York. The Cleveland family, staunchly middle-class, was influenced by their Puritan heritage, their Presbyterian faith, and their belief in hard work. Young Grover had few intellectual, cultural, or academic interests, preferring instead the outdoor life and fishing. When his father died in 1853, Grover found it necessary to work and help support his family. After teaching for one year as an assistant at the New York Institute for the Blind, he decided that his fortune and future lay to the West.

Cleveland followed the westward path, however, no further than the booming town of Buffalo, New York. There, Cleveland worked for and lived with his uncle, Lewis P. Allen, a wealthy cattle farmer, helping to keep the record books for the farm. After a year, he decided to read law and joined the office of Henry W. Rogers, Dennis Bowen, and Sherman Rogers as a clerk. By 1856, young Cleveland was completely self-supporting. In that year, also, he determined to join the Democratic Party—not a typical choice but one which reflected the party affiliation of the law office in which he worked and his own opinion that the Republican presidential nominee, John C. Frémont, was too radical. Cleveland began to work for the Democratic Party, attending meetings and working in the wards. At the age of twenty-five, he was elected ward supervisor and the same year served a brief appointment as assistant district attorney.

Cleveland's years in Buffalo served as preparation for his meteoric rise to national fame. There he astounded his colleagues with his capacity for long hours, attention to tedious detail, powers of concentration, and phenomenal physical energy. He showed little flair or imagination or awareness of either a cultural world or a world much beyond the boundaries of Buffalo. Cleveland, a bachelor, associated in his spare time with the other young men of the town, hunting, fishing, and enjoying an occasional beer in the local saloons.

He was a large, round-faced man, with sandy hair and brilliant blue eyes. His girth led his nieces and nephews to call him "Uncle Jumbo"; his size represented considerable strength, however, rather than excess fat.

Cleveland was a staunch Unionist, a war Democratic, but when the Civil War broke out, he felt no particular inclination to fight. He provided the major support for his mother and two sisters, and, when drafted in 1863, he hired a substitute soldier, as permitted by law. In 1870, Cleveland was elected sheriff of Erie County, a position attractive in part because of the regular income it provided. While sheriff, Cleveland himself pulled the lever to hang two convicts, believing that it was wrong to require of others that which he was not willing to do himself. This incident provided further evidence of the absolute integrity which was an integral part of Cleveland's character. After one term as sheriff, Cleveland resumed his practice of law.

For the next ten years, Cleveland was a diligent and respected member of the bar in the expanding city of Buffalo (its population grew from forty-two thousand in 1850 to 155,000 in 1880). He was a contented plodder, satisfied with his place in the world and admired for his common sense. With its larger size, however, Buffalo government and politics became more corrupt, and when the Republicans nominated a "ring" candidate for mayor in 1881, the Democrats looked for an honest alternative. Attracted to Cleveland by his integrity (though, as a political novice, he was not the party's first choice), the Democrats persuaded him to run. At the age of forty-four, Cleveland was sworn in as mayor of Buffalo in 1882. His attacks on corruption and his courage in defying political bosses quickly gained for him a statewide reputation.

Life's Work

Luck played a part in Cleveland's career. The New York Democratic Party was badly divided over the power of Tammany Hall. The same moral outrage of the people who had elected Cleveland mayor of Buffalo made him an attractive candidate for governor of New York. Once again, the Republicans nominated a machine politician and the Democrats looked for a reformer. The big, bluff man from Buffalo caught the party's attention, was nominated, and in 1882 was elected governor of New York. Cleveland's administration was notable for its honesty, openness, strong values, good appointments, and courage in quarreling with John Kelly, the leader of Tammany Hall.

Once again, luck played a role in Cleveland's career, for the national Democratic Party was seeking a reformer, especially after the Republicans nominated James G. Blaine, a politician tainted with corruption since the Ulysses S. Grant Administration, for President of the United States. The opposition of Tammany Hall to Cleveland's nomination merely endeared his candidacy to other Democrats across the country, and in 1884 he received the Democratic nomination for president. As in his races for mayor and for governor, the major issue was corruption, and Cleveland's strength was his un-questioned honesty and integrity.

The campaign of 1884, however, soon collapsed into mudslinging. Blaine was increasingly identified with corruption in government, while the Republicans countercharged that Cleveland had fathered an illegitimate child. In reaction to the rhyme "Ma! Ma! Where's my pa? Gone to the White House, Ha! Ha! Ha!" Cleveland responded only, "Tell the truth." The truth appeared to be that Cleveland had acted honorably in a relationship with Mrs. Maria Halprin, and his courage and honesty once again impressed itself upon his countrymen. Cleveland made only four speeches during the campaign, while Blaine traveled more widely. A turning point came in the closing days of the campaign, when the Reverend Mr. Samuel D. Burchard, who accompanied Blaine, charged that the Democrats were the party of "Rum, Romanism, and Rebellion." This influenced a heavy turnout among the Irish Catholic voters of New York City, and by a narrow margin Cleveland became America's first Democratic president since 1856.

Cleveland was admirably suited to the needs of the United States in 1885. He headed a government which endeavored to correct the abuses of the past and establish honesty and efficiency in the administration of government. Cleveland appointed an excellent cabinet, including the Southern wing of the party once again. The major issues of his first administration were civil service reform, the role of silver currency, and a reduction of the tariff. He successfully expanded the Civil Service Act and moved toward a more professional government bureaucracy. In connection with the many patronage bills which flowed through Congress, Cleveland vetoed more than three hundred measures in his first administration (compared to 132 vetoes by the previous twenty-one presidents). He opposed the free-silver faction in the party, supporting instead a sound money policy based on gold. He was forced to retreat on the tariff issue in the face of Congressional opposition.

His administration was also noteworthy for the passage of the Dawes Act, which encouraged the Americanization of the Indians. Additionally, the Interstate Commerce Act was adopted under and signed by Cleveland. There was a greater awareness of labor unrest as well, provoked by the Haymarket Square Riot in Chicago in 1886, which left several persons dead and reawakened a fear of organized labor. For the public, however, the most memorable part of Cleveland's first administration was his marriage in 1886 to Miss Frances Folsom, the twenty-two-year-old daughter of his former law partner (Cleveland was the first president to be married in a White House ceremony). The public was delighted with the romance, and, indeed, the marriage was a remarkably happy one.

As the election of 1888 approached, the Republicans began to gather funds and support to regain control of the national government. To oppose Cleveland, they nominated Benjamin Harrison, who vigorously campaigned against Cleveland and especially against tariff reform. Cleveland once again won a majority of the popular vote, but this time he narrowly lost the electoral vote to Harrison. Cleveland took his family to New York City, where he resumed the practice of law and where his first child (known to the country as "Baby Ruth") was born.

As discontent with the extravagant policies of Harrison grew, the Democrats turned once again to Cleveland in 1892. Again opposed by the New York Tammany Hall machine, Cleveland nevertheless was nominated on the first ballot. With his usual courage, he endorsed the gold standard in the face of strong party support for free silver. He was reelected president and returned to Washington (where his daughter Esther became the first child born in the White House) on the eve of the great Panic of 1893. Once again, the country needed a man of courage and honesty and was fortunate to have the leadership of Cleveland—who possessed these qualities in great abundance, along with a certain stubbornness and a lack of vision.

Before attending to the economic problems of the nation, Cleveland had to attend to a problem of his own—a malignant growth was discovered in the roof of his mouth. Fearing that public knowledge of his illness would fuel the panic, Cleveland chose to undergo a secret operation on board a borrowed yacht. The operation was successful, and not for twenty-five years did the full truth of that cruise emerge. Meanwhile, the debate over free silver was spurred on by the economic crisis. Cleveland continued to stand firm for a solid currency. He called a successful special session of Congress to repeal the Sherman Silver Purchase Act, which Cleveland believed contributed to the continuing economic decline. Unable to obtain adequate tariff reform, Cleveland continued nevertheless to protest the high tariff as also contributing to the Panic.

In an effort to avert the constant drain of gold from the United States Treasury, Cleveland agreed to a sale of government bonds handled by J. P. Morgan. Although a financial success, this apparent "sell-out" to the interests of big business hurt Cleveland and his party, already badly divided over the question of free silver. Similarly, his action in sending federal troops to help put down the Pullman worker's strike (1894) and his hostility to the unemployed workers who marched to Washington, D.C., as Coxey's Army convinced the working-class supporters of the Democratic Party that Cleveland had abandoned them in favor of the rich.

In the area of foreign policy, Cleveland opposed imperialism, refusing to bring the treaty for Hawaiian annexation before the Senate. He maintained strict neutrality in the Cuban revolt, though encouraging Spain to moderate her treatment of the Cuban people. In the border dispute between British Guiana and Venezuela, Cleveland encourage arbitration. He supported the Monroe Doctrine and appeared ready to risk war with Great Britain if a peaceful settlement were not reached. Once again, Cleveland acted strongly and courageously and won both the respect of and stronger ties with Great Britain as a result.

Silver continued to be the simplistic, single answer for those in and out of the Democratic Party who sought relief from the Panic. As the election of 1896 approached, it was clear that Cleveland had lost much of his party's support. Once again, Cleveland stood with courage for his principles and against free silver; this time, courage without compromise proved fatal. Although he had no desire for a third term, the Democratic convention repudiated him thoroughly in their platform. With William Jennings Bryan as their candidate and free silver as their issue, the Democrats' repudiation was silently returned by Cleveland, who found his private sympathy with the Republicans in the election. He was satisfied with the election of William McKinley, though it must have hurt to notice that Bryan, in losing, received almost a million votes more than Cleveland had received in his 1892 victory.

After the inauguration of McKinley, Cleveland and his family planned to retire to private life. Because of the children, Cleveland and his wife preferred a less crowded area than New York City and chose to settle in Princeton, New Jersey. There, Cleveland mellowed and enjoyed to the fullest his children and his community. He became deeply involved in the life of Princeton University, where he received an honorary degree and in 1901 was named a trustee. There, the eldest of his five children (his daughter Ruth) died in 1904, leaving a great void in her father's life. There also Cleveland knew, liked, and quarreled with the next Democrat to be elected president, Woodrow Wilson. There, also, Cleveland died, in June, 1908.

Summary

Grover Cleveland was admirably suited to his time. His disciplined life made him more comfortable as a supporter of the status quo rather than reform, and his courage and conscience made him strong in actions he believed best for the interest of the United States. It was Cleveland's misfortune sometimes to be wrong in his judgment of what was best; the rigid strength of character which held him firm before the winds of pressure from special interests held him equally firm against compromise when it would, perhaps, have been wise. Nevertheless, Cleveland brought conscience, courage, and honesty to the White House at a time when those qualities had often been lacking. He provided an image—backed up by reality—of the integrity and leadership which America needed. He worked long hours, bringing his legal intellect to the consideration of all sides of a problem before making a rational decision about the wisest course to follow. Once that decision was made, he did not depart from it.

Though Cleveland was wildly unpopular in 1896, especially among the Bryan faction of Democrats, it was always his position and never his character which came under attack. In later years, he emerged with much greater popularity, and Americans, Democrats and Republicans alike, honored him for his courage and his honesty. The nation had come to realize the value of his leadership and to believe that the economic stability which had eventually prevailed would not have been possible without his strong opposition to free silver. Cleveland was a good man in an age in which goodness was not often cherished. The verse of James Russell Lowell perhaps best memorializes his contribution to America:

> We, who look on with critic eyes
> Exempt from action's crucial test,
> Human ourselves, at least are wise
> In honoring one who did his best.

Bibliography

Cleveland, Grover. *Letters of Grover Cleveland: 1850-1908*. Edited by Allan Nevins. Boston: Houghton Mifflin Co., 1933. Reprint. New York: De Capo Press, 1970. Useful for insight into Cleveland's mind and the reasons for his decisions. Includes some delightful letters of a more personal nature as well.

—————. *Presidential Problems*. New York: Century Co., 1904. Writings of the president after leaving office. Clear and comprehensive but not particularly insightful, which is generally true of the many books and articles Cleveland wrote in his retirement.

Ford, Henry Jones. *The Cleveland Era: A Chronicle of the New Order in Politics*. New Haven, Conn.: Yale University Press, 1919. One of a series of books on American history. Concise, without much interpretation.

Hollingsworth, Joseph Rogers. *The Whirligig of Politics: The Democracy of Cleveland and Bryan*. Chicago: University of Chicago Press, 1963. Excellent coverage of political events from 1892 to 1904. A readable account, especially helpful on the antagonisms within the Democratic Party and the silver issue. Strong analysis of the election of 1896.

Merrill, Horace Samuel. *Bourbon Leader*. Boston: Little, Brown and Co., 1957. Excellent analysis, again largely political, of Cleveland and the Democratic Party both nationally and in New York.

Nevins, Allan: *Grover Cleveland: A Study in Courage*. New York: Dodd, Mead and Co., 1966. Indispensable Pulitzer Prize–winning biography. The definitive study of Cleveland and his political career, covering all the details as well as offering a broad analysis of Cleveland's career. Wonderfully readable style.

Carlanna L. Hendrick

DeWITT CLINTON

Born: March 2, 1769; Little Britain, New York
Died: February 11, 1828; Albany, New York
Area of Achievement: Politics
Contribution: Clinton controlled New York State for his faction of the Republican Party, advocating both social stability and an active role for government. He was an unsuccessful presidential candidate and fought the emerging power of Martin Van Buren. His best-known project is the Erie Canal, concrete and practical, like his approach to politics, and exemplifying a proper resolution of several types of problems in a growing nation.

Early Life

DeWitt Clinton was born in Little Britain, Ulster (later Orange) County, New York colony, on March 2, 1769. His ancestors, Englishmen who were transplanted to Ireland, had immigrated to America in 1729, settling in New York in 1731, where DeWitt's father, James, was born. James, married to Mary DeWitt, of Dutch ancestry, had been a major general in the Revolution; his brigade had received the British colors at Yorktown. DeWitt was educated at the grammar school of the Reverend Mr. John Moffat and then studied for two years at the Kingston Academy, the best in the state. Two years later, in 1786, having emphasized courses in natural philosophy and mathematics, he was graduated from Columbia College at the head of his class. After studying law with Samuel Jones, Jr., he was admitted to the bar in 1790 but did not often practice; his legal training aided him in land transactions and in his growing involvement in politics.

Clinton's uncle, George Clinton, was the first governor of New York and the creator of a powerful political machine; thus, Clinton was accustomed to a political environment. In the *New York Journal* in November, 1787, Clinton published a series of letters from "A Countryman," opposing ratification of the proposed constitution; he attended sessions of the New York ratifying convention at Poughkeepsie and wrote a report from the Anti-Federalist position. He became his uncle's private secretary and shortly thereafter also secretary of the board of regents and of the board of fortification. While early involved in politics, he did not engage in politicking at the lower levels of party workers; this fact may explain his inability to deal with the mechanics and compromises of factional and party maneuvering.

Clinton was an impressive man, six feet tall and often referred to as "Magnus Apollo." His high forehead, large square face and firm features, and dark eyes gave the impression of strength and determination. He married Maria Franklin, daughter of an important Quaker merchant, who brought him four thousand pounds and landed property, on February 13, 1796. They had ten children, of whom four sons and three daughters were still living when Maria Clinton died in 1818. At the time of his marriage, Clinton was not active in politics, as the Republicans had succumbed to the greater political strength of the Hamiltonians (Federalists); Governor George Clinton retired in 1795, and the Federalists elected John Jay to the office. Clinton would undoubtedly have become a scientist of note had not opportunity and environment joined to bring him back into politics. Defeated for the state assembly in 1796, he was elected in 1797, and in 1798 won a four-year term in the state senate.

In 1801, the assembly elected Clinton as one of the four senators who, with the governor, constituted the council of appointment. This body controlled nearly fifteen thousand civil and military appointments and was therefore deeply entwined with the complex politics of both state and nation, still in flux in the early constitutional period, and with a two-party system not yet fully developed. The policy and partisan balances of state and national governments were also still unclear, and the tensions between executives and legislatures stemming from Revolutionary politics were institutionalized in the new constitution and exacerbated when different parties controlled the two branches. With its large number of presidential electors, the state of New York was vital, under the influence of Aaron Burr, in the "Revolution of 1800," which brought the Republicans to national power. State politics, however, were characterized by factions among the Republicans; Burr did not attempt to control the state, and the influential Livingston family, politically neglected by the Federalists, gave its support to the popular Clinton group. Clinton emerged as the state's Republican political leader.

The relative powers of the governor and council had not been completely clarified in the 1777 constitution, and consequently a bitter argument developed, ending in an appointment stalemate. Clinton at this time was young, energetic, and ambitious; his integrity and self-confidence and his ability to attract political loyalty were major advantages, balancing his ineffectiveness in handling people and in developing compromises. He was not a political theorist, always preferring the concrete and the practical, but his ideas were clear concerning the proper approach of the victorious Republicans to the offices of government. Opposing the Federalists' exclusion of Republicans from office, Clinton maintained that Republicans must be appointed in order that appointive positions might correspond to the verdict of the elections. To accomplish this, it was necessary to remove Federalists from most if not all major offices and from a sufficient number of minor ones to equalize the parties. As a dominant council member, Clinton took the lead in removing most of the governor's power over appointments and in implementing the appointment of Republicans. Rather than being the origin of the "spoils system," as many historians have suggested, this policy was simply more active in accommodating the appointive positions rather closely to the elective ones under the new political conditions of a developing national two-party system (rather than the older one of personal and local factions within the state alone).

On February 19, 1802, Clinton was appointed to a vacant seat in the United States Senate. During the next two sessions, he opposed a Federalist proposal to seize New Orleans from Spain over the issue of the right of deposit and supported the proposed Twelfth Amendment. The Senate at this time tended to be overshadowed by the House, however, and Clinton's personal and party interests were in New York. Late in 1803, Clinton resigned from the Senate to accept appointment (from Governor George Clinton and the council) as mayor of New York City. This was an important office, and its fifteen-thousand-dollar annual income was also welcome to Clinton, whose finances were frequently in disorder.

Life's Work

For the remainder of his career, Clinton acted in the state, rather than in the national, political arena. From 1803 to 1815 (except for 1807-1808 and 1810-1811), he was mayor of New York. At the beginning of his political career, in the assembly, he had been concerned with sanitation laws, debt reform, abolition, and the encouragement of steam navigation and agriculture. As mayor, he organized the Public School Society and aided the New York Orphan Asylum and the New York Hospital. In 1806, he supported the removal of political disabilities from Roman Catholics. As required of a mayor, he attended fires, helped to calm mobs, and inspected markets and docks. With a $100,000 defense appropriation, he supervised construction of fortifications on Governor's Island and elsewhere in the city. He took a firm stand against British impressment and blockade attempts off New York City. He supported a plan for city development and presided in the mayor's court. During his tenure as mayor, he served also as state senator (1806-1811) and lieutenant governor (1811-1813).

Dominating New York politics, Clinton assured the nomination of Morgan Lewis as governor in 1804. Thereafter, the Burr wing lost power in the party and Clinton broke with the Livingstonians, succeeding in having his choice, Daniel D. Tompkins, elected governor. Although basically a Republican, Clinton not only often attracted the support of Federalists but also was frequently in opposition to the Virginia Dynasty and to New York's Tammany Society. The Tammany "Martling-Men" or "Bucktails" viewed him as a political heretic and a cunning dealer in political offices and influence.

Federalist leaders in 1812 strongly favored Clinton as a presidential candidate, and the New York Republican legislature nominated him; his position on the War of 1812 was, however, equivocal. Had he received Pennsylvania's twenty-five electoral votes, Clinton, rather than James Madison, would have been president. (Soon afterward, on December 22, 1812, Clinton's father died.) Following his defeat, Clinton turned his energies to the development of "Clintonianism," a political position rather than a party, opposed to party labels and organization, seeking a wide base of support in the state. Clintonian Republicans saw an intellectual and benevolent elite, opposing "Jacobinical" chance, factions, and mobs, urban vice, and crime; yet they considered governmental power as derived from the people as a whole and to be used to meet their needs. An urban politician, hoping to make New York a cultural center to rival Boston and Philadelphia, Clinton was sufficiently Jeffersonian to develop a strong rural bias in his programs; the canal project was designed to stimulate both commercial prosperity and a westward movement, thereby reducing poverty and violence and averting the development of an urban proletariat and demagoguery. Clinton was ambivalent about both urban centers and government itself; appealing to both Federalists and Republicans, operating outside the increasingly delimited national party boundaries, Clinton emphasized the work of private societies to accomplish the necessary expansion of knowledge and the provision of facilities for "the people" in general.

Clinton's involvement in voluntary societies was by no means merely a personal and private activity but was closely associated with his political life. He belonged to several dozen societies, was active in most, and held offices in many. He was a member of several agricultural societies, the New York Bible Society, the American Bible Society, foreign and domestic scientific societies (natural history, geology, biology), the American Antiquarian Society, the Western Museum Society, the American Academy of Arts and Sciences, the American Philosophical Society, the New York Military Society, the New York Historical Society, and the Education Society of the Presbyterian Church. He was a prominent Mason; in 1814, he was cofounder and president of the Literary and Philosophical Society, presenting a book-length paper on American natural history; in 1816, he was able to get one large building to gather all the cultural societies in New York under one roof. His defeat in 1812 reduced his political power; he lost renomination for lieutenant governor and in 1815 lost the mayoralty as well. Yet he was rebuilding his support: His brother-in-law, Ambrose Spencer, was influential in President James Monroe's administration, he continued to attract Federalist as well as Republican voters, and the canal project was very popular.

As early as 1810, Clinton had been one of the commissioners planning a state canal between the Hudson River and the Great Lakes. The War of 1812 delayed the project, but by 1816 Clinton was actively promoting it; he was on the commission responsible for planning the canals between the Hudson, Lake Erie, and Lake Champlain. When Governor Tompkins resigned in 1817 to become vice president, Clinton was nominated (by a state convention including both Federalists and Republicans) and won by a landslide over Tammany's Peter B. Porter. Thereafter, however, President Monroe directed the majority of the federal patronage in New York not to the Clintonians but to their minority opposition, Martin Van Buren's Tammany Bucktail faction.

Monroe's encouragement of intraparty strife was intended to avert a success-ful bid by Clinton in the 1820 presidential election; Monroe also believed that Clinton's associates in Congress were intensifying the Missouri crisis in order to reorganize national parties along sectional lines, a development which he considered a threat to the nation. Although Clinton won the gubernatorial election in 1820, the New York Republican Party schism was permanent: The Bucktails controlled the legislature and therefore the state patronage as well (through the council of appointment). At this point, Clinton attacked Mon-roe for having interfered in the state election process, a states' rights stand which could evoke support from both parties. In order to affect the 1821 state constitutional convention, Clinton had to prove his charges, which he did by submitting bulky documents, in a green cover, to the assembly. His "Green Bag Message" set off a debate over the permissible extent of political activity on the part of federal officials.

The Administration's hostility having prevented him from consolidating his political position, Clinton decided not to seek a third gubernatorial term in 1822. Van Buren was therefore able to develop his control and establish the "Albany Regency," which controlled New York State politics for a long time thereafter. (Tammany Hall was to benefit also from the flood of Irish voters resulting from the constitutional amendment Clinton had supported, elimi-nating the property requirement for voting.) The regency's removal of Clin-ton from the canal commission in 1824 provoked a reaction which helped the "People's" party elect him governor in November of that year. It was there-fore the state's executive that he participated in the 1825 celebrations opening both the Erie and Champlain canals.

Clinton declined the post of minister to England offered to him by Presi-dent John Quincy Adams. In 1827, an Ohio convention nominated him as a presidential candidate, but he would have had little chance: He had a states' rights stand, there was a strong Anti-Masonic movement, and the issues of patronage and party organization continued to alienate support from the Clintonian group. On February 11, 1828, Clinton died suddenly. He was sur-vived by his second wife, Catharine Jones, daughter of a New York physi-cian whom he had married on May 8, 1819; the New York legislature voted to appropriate ten thousand dollars for his minor children, as Clinton had left debts. His chief association in the public mind was with one of his most cherished projects, the great Erie Canal.

Summary

DeWitt Clinton, at the outset of his political career, was associated with the great national political figures of the time, the young postrevolutionary leaders who were to dominate national politics until the Civil War. He was always to be involved in the complex and bitter partisanship of the early nine-teenth century, pitting state, sectional, and national interests against one another, swirling in a confusion of intrastate and intraparty factions. In contrast to his political contemporaries such as James Monroe, John C. Calhoun, John Quincy Adams, Henry Clay, Martin Van Buren, and Andrew Jackson, Clinton's primary political service was to be in his state rather than at the national level. Yet as a dominant politician in New York State, Clinton was necessarily a factor in national politics, and he shared the presidential aspirations of his colleagues: The electoral votes of only one state kept him from the presidency in 1812, and he remained a real political threat to the Virginia Dynasty.

As a politician, Clinton was a figure of ambiguities and contradictons. His preferences and policies placed him from time to time in all th varying political denominations; an elitist with a power base in one state only, he could never have developed a party organization around his own national leadership. He was never able in the mechanics of politics, and his personality, reserved and cold, did not attract supporters. Despite thee shortcomings, he was usually admired and respected for his government abilities and positive programs. He supported states' rights yet viewed govement as the necessary agency for developing programs to ensure general posperity, balance and order in society, economic expansion and opportunitie His version of an earlier "country ideology" led him to numerous local aicultural societies, to the Society for the Promotion of Agriculture, Arts, al Manufactures, and to the canal project. At the same time, he was concoed with urban problems, advocating, for example, the inexpensive Lancastan educational system and supporting the establishment of Emma Willas academy at Troy; from 1805 until his death, he was president of the N York Free School Society. His concept of the role of government frequent ained for him Federalist support, yet he had begun in politics as a Relican. Conflicts with the Virginia Dynasty and Tammany Hall meant that could never control the Democratic Republican Party, despite his support jackson, yet to play a prominent part among the National Republicans, hould have had to cooperate with John Quincy Adams, whom he disliked. atrician elite providing leadership for the independent yeomanry was dea belonging more to the eighteenth century than to the nineteenth, but on was somewhat ahead of his time in his concept of government as a m a tive agency in society.

Closely connected to Clinton's emphasis on learned and benevolen eties was his own work in the sciences. In the undifferentiated field of y nineteenth century science, professionals and amateurs studied and wq over a wide range. Contemporaries (including the eminent scientists L Hosack, Samuel Latham Mitchill, and Constantine S. Rafinesque) co ered Clinton a great naturalist, and he was responsible for the discoverf type of American indigenous wheat and of the archaeological remains oe historic Indian tribes in New York. No theorist, he nevertheless agreeth the intellectual radicals of the day in accepting the concept of biological extinction as opposed to the consensus view of a static "chain of being." He played a major role as a patron and promoter of science, primarily through the voluntary societies and whatever governmental aid he could provide, as in the establishment of the New York Institution for the Promotion of the Arts and Sciences.

Not a Renaissance man, not a scientific theorist, not the founder of a new political alliance, long a state governor but never president, Clinton enjoyed a fruitful career of public service. Less of a national figure in historical perspective than his fellow senators were to be, he has been less well-known than they, to later times. The Eric Canal, one of his favorite projects, has enjoyed greater publicity than the man who helped to develop it in the context of wide programs for public improvement. Although Clinton may have taken a narrower view of public policies than his contemporaries, he nevertheless worked to acquire political support for his programs from a wide range of intrastate interests and areas, a political condition which, if operating at the national level, might have helped avert the increasing political polarization obvious even before the Missouri crisis. Although he died at a relatively young age, he had probably already accomplished nearly all that would have been possible for him in the social and political conditions of his time.

Bibliography

Bobbé, Dorothie De Bear. *De Witt Clinton*. New York: Minton, Balch and Co., 1933. Reprint. Port Washington, N.Y.: I. J. Friedman, 1962. Written in the early 1930's, this is the only full-length biography since James Renwick's in the early 1840's. A rather uncritical admiration.

Fish, Carl Russell. *The Civil Service and the Patronage*. Cambridge, Mass.: Harvard University Press, 1904. Reprint. New York: Russell and Russell, 1963. A general history of the subject. A clear and concise summary, with references to Clinton.

Hanyan, Craig R. "De Witt Clinton and Partisanship: The Development of Clintonianism from 1811 to 1820." *New-York Historical Society Quarterly* 56, no. 2 (1972): 108-131. Clear analysis of the political developments and programs, and intraparty factionalism in the state. Based chiefly on primary sources.

Harris, Jonathan. "De Witt Clinton as Naturalist." *New-York Historical Society Quarterly* 56, no. 4 (1972): 264-284. Examines Clinton as a scientist and concludes that his contributions were more as a promoter of science. Includes 1825 portrait of Clinton by George Catlin.

Hopkins, Vivian C. "The Empire State—DeWitt Clinton's Laboratory." *New-York Historical Society Quarterly* 59, no. 1 (1975): 6-44. Has higher opinion of Clinton as a scientist than in the Harris article. Contains much interesting detail.

McBain, Howard Lee. *De Witt Clinton and the Origin of the Spoils System in New York*. New York: Columbia University Press, 1907. Reprint. New York: AMS Press, 1967. Volume 28, number 1 in "Studies in History, Economics and Public Law," edited by the faculty of political science at Columbia University. This book is based largely on previously unused primary documents. Insightful study of developing party politics in the early national period and Clinton's role.

Nadler, Solomon. "The Green Bag: James Monroe and the Fall of DeWitt Clinton." *New-York Historical Society Quarterly* 59, no. 3 (1975): 202-225. Good examination of national and state politics and issues of the 1810's and 1820's and Clinton's position.

Marsha Kass Marks

TY COBB

Born: December 18, 1886; Narrows, Georgia
Died: July 17, 1961; Atlanta, Georgia
Area of Achievement: Baseball
Contribution: Cobb's aggressive and inventive style of play enabled him to set records in every phase of the game; many believe that he is the greatest player in the history of baseball.

Early Life

Tyrus Raymond Cobb was born in Narrows, Georgia, on December 18, 1886. He was proud of his Southern heritage and his family. His father was a teacher and a landowner, and an ancestor had been a Civil War general who died at the battle of Fredricksburg. Cobb even claimed George Washington as a distant ancestor. As he was born only twenty years after the defeat of the Confederacy, however, Cobb's proud claim to Southern gentility was mocked by the reduced circumstances and opportunities of the area. Cobb's father wanted him to attend college or, perhaps, to win an appointment to West Point, but the young Cobb was determined to be a baseball player. He saw baseball as a career in which he might excel while he could not hope to compete with his father's record in academic studies. Baseball players were not, however, socially accepted at the time; even some of the greatest ballplayers were not admitted to many hotels or restaurants. Yet Cobb had a burning desire to try this career, so his father gave him six fifteen-dollar checks and sent him off to join the minor league team in Augusta.

Cobb played for Augusta for only a few games before he was released because a veteran had returned to the team. Cobb did, however, manage to catch on with the Anniston, Alabama, club, and he performed so well that he was sent back to Augusta. His batting average was only .237 for Augusta that year, but he impressed everyone with his aggressive style of play. He was given a contract for the next year for $125 a month; finally, he was a professional baseball player.

Cobb began to become the Ty Cobb known to history while at Augusta. His new manager, George Leidy, worked with him every day on his hitting, running, and fielding. Cobb was not a natural ballplayer as Babe Ruth and Shoeless Joe Jackson were; he had to learn to hit and to take advantage of the weaknesses of others on the basepaths or in the batter's box. In addition, he was not very tall or heavy; he stood only five feet, ten inches tall and weighed about 155 at the time, but he compensated for his size with desire for excellence and dedication to the game.

Life's Work

Cobb had a mediocre rookie year in the major leagues; he played center-field with the Detroit Tigers for forty-two games and batted a meager .240. In addition, he had a serious conflict with many of the established veterans on the Tigers. Some of those involved later called the treatment Cobb received normal rookie hazing, but Cobb took it personally. He thought there was a clique of players who wanted to drive him off the team. In his typical fashion, Cobb fought back against the veterans—and, in so doing, may have made the problem worse. He challenged any or all of the contentious veterans to a fight and almost got himself traded because of the dissension on the team. Apparently, Cobb never spoke to Wahoo Sam Crawford even though he played next to him for a number of years.

Cobb claimed that he benefited from his trouble with the veterans; since he was isolated, he did not have an opportunity to waste his time at shows or pool halls but could use that time improving his baserunning and hitting skills. He hit .320 and stole twenty-three bases in his second year, 1906.

The season of 1907 was even more successful for Cobb and the Tigers. He hit .350 to lead the league in batting average for the first time, and the Tigers won their first pennant. The Tigers lost the World Series to the Chicago Cubs in four straight games, however, and Cobb only hit .200. On the other hand, the feud between him and the veterans ended, although Cobb was never popular with the players on his team and was hated by the players and fans in other American League cities, especially Philadelphia. The reasons for this conflict and dislike are easy to find. Cobb tried to take advantage of every situation with which he was confronted, whether it was a catcher's arm, a pitcher's attention, an infielder's position, or a sportswriter's influence. This aggressiveness and combativeness carried over to his relationships with his teammates and opponents. He was not a pleasant or sociable man but a loner with an obsession to excel and to take advantage of less dedicated players. Most of Cobb's autobiography is a defense of his side of the many fights and quarrels he got into. He never gave an inch and retaliated when he thought he had been wronged, and it did not take much to make him believe that someone had wronged him.

In 1908, Cobb held out for a salary of five thousand dollars; this was the first of many holdouts for Cobb. He did not trust his owner and tried to get whatever he could out of the recalcitrant boss. Cobb was determined that no one was going to get the best of him on the field or off it. He did win his second straight batting championship that year, although his average was twenty-five points lower; the Tigers also won the pennant again, but they lost the World Series once more to the Chicago Cubs. Cobb had his best series and batted .368.

Cobb won his third straight batting title in 1909 and the Tigers won their third straight pennant. In the World Series with the Pittsburgh Pirates, it was rumored that Cobb had a personal duel with the great shortstop of the Pirates, Honus Wagner. Cobb was quoted as saying "I'll show that Kraut," and some said he threatened to spike Wagner when he came down to steal. Cobb denied making such threats, but the public both expected and believed that Cobb would spike the popular Wagner. Cobb batted only .231, however, and the Tigers lost again. Cobb was never to play on a winning World Series team and would not be on another pennant winner for the rest of his career.

Cobb's performance continued to be superior over the next fifteen years. He won nine straight batting championships from 1907 to 1915 with a personal high of .420 in 1911. He stole a record high of ninety-six bases in 1915. These records remained individual achievements, however, since the Tigers could not win another pennant. Meanwhile, controversy continued to follow Cobb. He was accused of spiking the very popular Frank "Home Run" Baker, thus unleashing the wrath of the Philadelphia fans. He beat up Buck Herzog in a fight in his hotel room and got into a brawl with an umpire, Billy Evans, under the stands. Cobb claimed that he was merely acting in self-defense, but his playing style and attitude seemed to invite trouble. Anyone who played as savagely as he did was bound to spend his life in controversies.

Cobb hit .371 in 1915, but he lost the batting title to Tris Speaker. He did come back to win the next three batting championships for a record total of twelve championships. In 1921, after a dismal finish for the Tigers, Cobb was offered the position of player-manager. Cobb accepted, although he claimed that the job was forced upon him. Cobb certainly was an unlikely candidate for the manager's job since he was baseball's supreme example of a loner who seemed more interested in individual than team records. One reason Cobb was offered the job was the sudden popularity of Babe Ruth as a home-run hitter. Apparently, the Detroit management hoped to increase the fans' interest by making Cobb more visible and more powerful. Cobb spent four years as manager of the Tigers, but under his tenure, the team never won a pennant. In his autobiography, Cobb claimed that the reason the Tigers did not win was that the management refused to buy or trade for the players he believed were needed. Cobb does seem to be very defensive in this book; his problems or failures were always attributable to someone else, while his victories were results of his efforts alone.

In 1926, Cobb was suddenly released by the Tigers because of a betting scandal. The charge was that Cobb and Tris Speaker, who was also released by Cleveland, conspired to fix a game between the Tigers and Indians and then bet on it. Cobb claimed that it was only a rumor started by a player he had released from the team and the charges were never proved, but Cobb was himself released and then joined the Philadelphia A's for his last two years as a baseball player.

Once Cobb ended his career as a ballplayer, he never had another job in organized baseball. He was, by this time, a wealthy man from his investments, especially those he made in Coca-Cola. He was married twice but divorced twice, and he was not very close to his children. The fierce loner on

the field became an angry loner off the field. Cobb's collaborator on his autobiography, Al Stump, has written of Cobb's last years, and Stump's picture of
the once-great ballplayer reduced to near madness is terrifying.

Summary
   There is little doubt that Ty Cobb was one of the greatest baseball players
of all time, a judgment certified by his selection as the first man inducted
into the Baseball Hall of Fame. He set records for base-stealing and batting
that seem unlikely to be broken. Many of them, such as the record for having
made the most hits, and another for having stolen the most bases, in a single
season and in a career, have been broken, but it is doubtful that anyone will
match his nine consecutive batting championships or his lifetime batting average of .367.
   Yet, admittedly, Cobb the man was less successful than Cobb the player. It
has been suggested that Cobb's fearsome, alienating personality was the
result of an intense desire to win, at any cost, the approval of his father, who
had died when Cobb was young. In the course of achieving greatness, however, he did not evoke among fans and colleagues the love that Babe Ruth
inspired or the admiration that Joe DiMaggio received, but only fear and
loathing.

Bibliography
Alexander, Charles C. *Ty Cobb*. New York: Oxford University Press, 1984.
   A highly critical scholarly biography. The author, a historian, drew heavily
   on newspapers and secondary sources for this detailed account of Cobb's
   life and career. Well documented, generally fair-minded, but not engag-
   ingly written. Includes bibliography.
Appel, Martin, and Burt Goldblatt. *Baseball's Best: The Hall of Fame Gal-
   lery*. New York: McGraw-Hill Book Co., 1977. A good, brief summary of
   Cobb's career.
Cobb, Ty, with Al Stump. *My Life in Baseball: The True Record*. Garden
   City, N.Y.: Doubleday and Co., 1961. Cobb's one-sided view of the important events in his career; he is scathing about his enemies and scornful of
   modern baseball.
Grayson, Harry. *They Played the Game*. Freeport, N.Y.: Books for Libraries
   Press, 1972. The chapter on Cobb is very general, cliché-ridden, and not
   informative.
Ritter, Lawrence S. *The Glory of Their Times*. New York: Collier Books,
   1966. Ritter interviewed a number of players from Cobb's era, including
   Wahoo Sam Crawford; they are quite critical of Cobb's ferocity, but none
   disputes his greatness. This is one of the finest books ever written on
   baseball.
Stump, Al. "Ty Cobb's Wild Ten-Month Fight to Live." In *The Baseball*

Reader, edited by Charles Einstein, 282-300. New York: Thomas Y. Crowell, 1980. A revealing portrait of Cobb's demanding and difficult personality by the man who helped Cobb write his autobiography.

James Sullivan

WILLIAM FREDERICK CODY
Buffalo Bill

Born: February 26, 1846; Scott County, Iowa
Died: January 10, 1917; Denver, Colorado
Areas of Achievement: Scouting and showmanship
Contribution: Capitalizing on the legends created about his prowess as a plainsman, Cody popularized the American West through his Wild West show, which brought the sights of the last frontier to eastern America and to Europe.

Early Life

William Cody was born in Iowa but grew up on the Kansas plains. His father, a staunch abolitionist, was pursued and attacked more than once by proslavery fanatics in the Kansas territory, and on several occasions only the young Cody's daring saved his father's life. When his father succumbed to illness in 1857, Cody sought work with what would become the firm of Russell, Majors, and Waddell, who hired him as a cattle driver and later as a Pony Express rider and stagecoach driver. By age twenty, the young man, grown to six feet and sporting shoulder-length, wavy hair and a goatee, had achieved his reputation among plainsmen as a daring scout and buffalo hunter, working for the army and for the railroads. His brief stint in the Union Army during the Civil War brought him no distinction but did provide the opportunity for him to meet and woo Louisa Frederici in St. Louis. They were married in 1866, and Cody took his bride back to Kansas, to share his life on the plains.

Cody's work as a scout and buffalo hunter led to several important encounters that secured his future fame. A dime novelist, traveling the West in search of new material, was introduced to Cody and from that meeting took away ideas for future novels. During the next four decades, more than two hundred novels about "Buffalo Bill" appeared. Eastern America soon was familiar with Cody's exploits as a buffalo hunter (extravagant claims put his total kill for a single day into the thousands) and as an Indian fighter, slayer of chiefs Tall Bull and Yellow Knife.

Cody's skill as a hunter for the railroads, the source of the legends which earned for him the sobriquet "Buffalo Bill," led to other career-enhancing engagements. He was called upon to lead several hunting expeditions for celebrities, including the Grand Duke Alexis of Russia, and a group of wealthy New York businessmen. Some of the latter invited Cody to visit in New York, and from that visit his career as America's premier showman was launched.

Life's Work

When Cody went to New York City in 1872, he was merely accepting the invitation of the East Coast magnates whom he had entertained on a buffalo hunt. Once there, his reputation having preceded him, he found that he was a minor toast of the town. One evening's entertainment included a trip to the theater to see a play, *Buffalo Bill, the King of Border Men* (1871). Cody was captivated by the attention given to him by the audience in the theater, and to his stage character. E. Z. C. Judson, who as novelist Ned Buntline had done much to build Cody's legend, encouraged him to take up the stage part himself. Reluctant at first, Cody finally gave in, and Judson then quickly wrote and produced *The Scouts of the Plains* (1872). While the show was extremely confusing and without dramatic merit, and Cody was stiff in his role, the play was a box-office success, and for several years, Cody appeared in a number of stage dramas. Through this endeavor, he met Nate Salsbury, who was to manage his later efforts with the Wild West show. Salsbury, along with publicist and lifelong friend John Burke, would remain one of Cody's staunchest supporters when that show brought pressures to bear on the flamboyant and somewhat irresponsible Cody.

For several years, Cody alternated his acting career with real-life work as a scout and mediator in the last of the Indian Wars. Then, in 1883, he helped form a traveling troupe which would bring the western plains to the cities and towns of the East and Midwest. Buffalo Bill's Wild West show toured for the next three decades, making stops in virtually every city of significance in the United States.

The troupe for Cody's show consisted of Indians whom Cody recruited from tribes that had been sent to reservations; plainsmen who had driven stagecoaches, herded cattle, or fought some of the same Indians with whom they now toured; and hundreds of horses, cattle, and buffalo. In the early years, Cody was the main attraction, performing feats with his rifle and introducing the cast in their grand parade at each location. He was joined at various times by other legendary figures such as Chief Sitting Bull, the victor of Little Big Horn, and trick-shot artist Annie Oakley. Cody managed to secure for his show the original Deadwood Stage, and the exciting chase that led to its rescue from marauders became a highlight of the performance.

The show played at such diverse locations as the World Cotton Exposition in New Orleans in 1884 and the World's Columbian Exposition in Chicago in 1893. Cody and some of his cast were invited to the Vatican in 1889. Queen Victoria attended a performance in 1887, and the Prince of Wales, later Edward V, saw the show on more than one occasion. New Yorkers saw the show performed in Madison Square Garden; the residents of Paris and Barcelona also witnessed the feats of Cody's performers. Well into the new century, Cody moved with his collection of people, animals, and paraphernalia, collecting huge receipts from people whose appetite for the West seemed insatiable.

Showmanship took its toll on Cody, however, and brought out the worst as well as the best in his character. Always a hard drinker, he was sometimes so drunk while on tour that colleagues feared that he would not be able to perform. A generous man by nature, he often squandered huge sums of money on projects in which unscrupulous entrepreneurs or well-intentioned but ill-fated friends encouraged him to invest.

Cody found himself caught up in the fast life, and his relationship with his wife, never strong, deteriorated. For years, he had been accustomed to leave behind Louisa and his children, first for duty with the army, then for his career onstage and with the Wild West show. Other women pursued him; certainly he pursued some of them. His relationship with Louisa reached its low point in 1904, when Cody sued for divorce, claiming that Louisa had tried to poison him at Christmas in 1900, and that he could no longer live with her. At the divorce trial, Cody's affair with an actress and other improprieties were made public, Louisa was able to generate substantial public sympathy, and the suit was dismissed. After a period of estrangement, the two were reunited, and Cody managed to live amicably with Louisa in his later years.

The Wild West show's prosperity, especially during the first decades of its life, allowed Cody to obtain significant real estate holdings in the West, most notably in the North Platte, Nebraska, area, and in Wyoming. He was also instrumental in founding the town in Wyoming which bears his name. Often, he would retire to one of these places during the off-season, to relax and renew ties with the land which he helped portray to the rest of the world.

Running a business such as the Wild West show entailed certain risks. On one trip down the Mississippi River, a steamboat crash cost Cody half of his livestock. On one of the early tours in Europe, his Indians began to get homesick and to desert the show. Disease took a major portion of his livestock in another year. Competition became fierce at times, and especially after the death of Salsbury in 1902, Cody found himself going more and more in debt to keep the show running. Eventually, he found it necessary to accept offers from outsiders to finance his operation. In 1913, the show was seized by agents to pay creditors.

The last years of Cody's life were not pleasant. He tried his hand at the new motion-picture industry, convincing the aged General Nelson Miles to assist him in producing a documentary of the famous Battle of Wounded Knee. The film was not a commercial success. Other schemes, including a mining venture, were similarly unsuccessful. Meanwhile, Harry Tammen, an unscrupulous editor of the *Denver Post*, managed to loan Cody sufficient capital for his ventures so that Cody soon found himself unable to reach a settlement and break his contract with Tammen. As a result, Tammen was able to force Cody to tour with the Sells-Floto Circus in 1914 and to restrict his activities further by limiting his salary and expense account.

By 1916, Cody was suffering the infirmities of old age. In the winter of

1916, he traveled to Denver to stay with his sister. There, on January 10, 1917, he died in her home. Despite his wishes to be buried in Wyoming, he was laid to rest atop Lookout Mountain, outside Denver.

Summary

As a frontiersman, scout, and hunter, Cody would have achieved a place in American history without the fame that his Wild West show provided him. Even when the exaggerations about his exploits are stripped away, his accomplishments in helping to settle the West were substantial: He helped bring to a successful close several skirmishes and one major uprising in the Indian Wars; he participated as the youngest member of the celebrated Pony Express team; he kept the railroads moving across the country by providing meat for the construction crews.

Cody's Wild West show did more than his real-life exploits on the frontier to bring to the civilized world of the eastern United States and to the countries of Europe a sense of the life of the American West. He was a symbol of that land: handsome, brash, generous, free-living, unafraid of any danger. Carrying on the tradition of the showman established by the legendary Phineas T. Barnum, Cody barnstormed across two continents, sharing the sense of excitement that had characterized the West in its infancy and adolescence. While he toured, the West matured, and the frontier that Cody dramatized in his shows was disappearing. Nevertheless, the thrills Cody and his fellow performers generated in countless youngsters lived on for years after his death. Cody's legacy continues in the games of "Cowboys and Indians" which endure, long after the last buffalo and the last Indian were confined to reservations within a West that has become homogeneous with the rest of the United States.

Bibliography
Burke, John. *Buffalo Bill: The Noblest Whiteskin*. New York: G. P. Putnam's Sons, 1973. A popular biography, providing sufficient details about Cody's early life on the frontier but concentrating on the years Buffalo Bill spent as an actor and showman in the eastern United States and in Europe. Informal style, highly readable.
Cody, William F. *Story of the Wild West and Camp-Fire Chats*. Philadelphia: Historical Publishing Co., 1888. Contains accounts of various plainsmen and one of Cody's several autobiographies. Since many details of Cody's early life are drawn from this autobiography, it is important for scholars; additionally, its informal style and tendency toward exaggeration mark it as typical of popular literature about the West written during the late nineteenth century.
Croft-Cooke, Rupert, and W. S. Meadmore. *Buffalo Bill: The Legend, the Man of Action, the Showman*. London: Sidgwick and Jackson, 1952. A

brief account of Cody's life, relying heavily on Cody's autobiography for details of the early life. Contains an interesting introductory chapter on the impact that the Wild West show had in England.

Havighurst, Walter. *Annie Oakley of the Wild West*. New York: Macmillan, 1954. Life story of one of the star attractions in the Wild West show; provides much information about Cody and others who traveled with him.

Hine, Robert V. *The American West: An Interpretive History*. Boston: Little, Brown and Co., 1973. Provides excellent background about the American West; discusses Cody as the foremost American hero.

Russell, Don F. *The Lives and Legends of Buffalo Bill*. Norman: University of Oklahoma Press, 1960. A well-researched, scholarly biography that goes far in separating the legend from the facts about Cody's life.

Yost, Nellie S. *Buffalo Bill: His Family, Friends, Fame, Failures, and Fortunes*. Chicago: Swallow Press, 1974. A carefully researched biography, relying heavily on records from the nineteenth century and on interviews with people who knew Cody or his family and friends. Debunks many legends and establishes a historical basis for many others.

Laurence W. Mazzeno